DRABEK, Thomas E. Human system responses to disaster: an inventory of sociological findings. Springer, 1986. 509p bibl index 86-15622. 59.00 ISBN 0-387-96323-5. HN 16. CIP

Drabek has done a remarkable job in compiling and presenting a wealth of information. The book is intended to help the reader discern and implement stewardship of the environment and the world's renewable resources. Organized around sequential perspective, preparedness, response, recovery, and mitigation, Drabek's study examines more than 1,250 research findings, 751 major conclusions, and 153 general topics on human response to disaster. On the conceptual side, the author assesses disaster responses at several analytical levels—individual, group, organizational, community, society, and interorganizational. By ably creating a matrix between the disaster sequence and system response, Drabek can analyze the spread of information in each of the levels. He concludes that the behavioral knowledge base is spread across all phases of disasters and system levels, yet there are concentrations in certain specific areas. Drabek concludes by calling the reader's attention to future priorities and new areas of inquiry. Besides providing information on disaster studies, the author provides a model for critical analysis of the literature and for sociological theory building. The master bibliography is one of the strong assets of the book. An effective tool in enlightening readers about the human relationship with the environment. Upper-division undergraduates and above.—R. Varghese, University of Maryland, Baltimore County

Springer Series on Environmental Management

Robert S. DeSanto, Series Editor

Springer Series on Environmental Management
Robert S. DeSanto, Series Editor

Thomas E. Drabek

Human System Responses to Disaster

An Inventory of
Sociological Findings

670394

Springer-Verlag
New York Berlin Heidelberg
London Paris Tokyo

1986

Thomas E. Drabek
Department of Sociology
University of Denver
Denver, Colorado 80208
U.S.A.

On the front cover: Following the 1965 South Platte River flooding in the Denver, Colorado metropolitan area, Public Service Company of Colorado personnel worked around the clock to restore electrical power, including the repair of this flood-wrecked high voltage power tower. Photo courtesy of Public Service Company of Colorado and The Denver Post.

Library of Congress Cataloging in Publication Data
Drabek, Thomas E., 1940–
    Human system responses to disaster.
    (Springer series on environmental management)
    Bibliography: p.
    Includes indexes.
    1. Disasters. 2. Disasters—Planning. 3. Disasters—
Research. 4. Disaster relief. I. Title. II. Series.
HN16.D73 1986   303.4'85   86-15622

Media conversion by David Seham Associates, Metuchen, New Jersey.
Printed and bound by R.R. Donnelley & Sons, Harrisonburg, Virginia.
Printed in the United States of America.

9 8 7 6 5 4 3 2 1

ISBN 0-387-96323-5 Springer-Verlag New York Berlin Heidelberg
ISBN 3-540-96323-5 Springer-Verlag Berlin Heidelberg New York

To Ruth Ann Drabek—
my partner

Series Preface

This series is dedicated to serving the growing community of scholars and practitioners concerned with the principles and applications of environmental management. Each volume is a thorough treatment of a specific topic of importance for proper management practices. A fundamental objective of these books is to help the reader discern and implement man's stewardship of our environment and the world's renewable resources. For we must strive to understand the relationship between man and nature, act to bring harmony to it, and nurture an environment that is both stable and productive.

These objectives have often eluded us because the pursuit of other individual and societal goals has diverted us from a course of living in balance with the environment. At times, therefore, the environmental manager may have to exert restrictive control, which is usually best applied to man, not nature. Attempts to alter or harness nature have often failed or backfired, as exemplified by the results of imprudent use of herbicides, fertilizers, water, and other agents.

Each book in this series will shed light on the fundamental and applied aspects of environmental management. It is hoped that each will help solve a practical and serious environmental problem.

Robert S. DeSanto
East Lyme, Connecticut

Acknowledgments

Compilation of the materials reviewed in this inventory was facilitated greatly by several staff members of the Disaster Research Center, University of Delaware (formerly at The Ohio State University) and the Natural Hazards Research and Applications Information Center, University of Colorado. Two reference librarians—Cindy Dewey and Linda Durfee—at Penrose Library, University of Denver, completed the computer searches required. Word processing and computer programming expertise was supplied by two former University of Denver staff members: Howard Lasus, Computer Services, and Charles Wilson, Computer Laboratory.

I want to thank Fred Grupp who encouraged initiation of this book and arranged for the funds that facilitated partial compilation of this findings inventory. As they were completed, various sections of chapters were critiqued by the following researchers: Ronald Perry, Arizona State University; E. L. Quarantelli, University of Delaware; Gary Kreps, College of William and Mary; Robert Bolin, New Mexico State University; and Dennis Mileti, Colorado State University. Their comments assisted in assuring both validity in interpretation and comprehensiveness in the data base. Of course, neither they, nor any of the other individuals named herein, are responsible for any errors of fact or interpretation that I may have made.

I appreciated the advice and acceptance of Robert S. DeSanto who welcomed this work into the Springer Series on Environmental Management. The administrative and editorial assistance provided by the staff of Springer-Verlag converted our working manuscript into this well-designed book for which I am most appreciative.

To all of the above I express a sincere thanks—for without their varied forms of assistance this project could not have been completed. But a special word of appreciation is due Ruth Ann Drabek who, in the best sense of the term, is my partner in this venture. Without her commitment, concern for detail, and months of effort, this book could never have been. She word processed all of the findings coded from the literature search, maintained inventory control on the acquisition, coding, and word processing efforts, edited the bibliography, and typed the final manuscript and all of its earlier versions. To her I must say—"Thanks for persisting, and doing so with style."

Thomas E. Drabek

Contents

1
The Logic of the Inventory

Through this introductory chapter I want to accomplish six objectives:
(1) describe the intellectual context of this inventory; (2) define its boundaries; (3) explain the literature search processes that produced it; (4) present the conceptual framework into which study findings were grouped;
(5) discuss the major limitations of the inventory and the risks of its use;
and (6) outline briefly the logic and content of the remaining nine chapters.
As with each of these, the last section of this chapter is a selected bibliography listing works of special relevance.

The Legacy of the Past

Several times previously, others have summarized the key findings from
studies focused on human responses to disaster events. The richness, format, and limitations of the inventory I constructed can best be understood
when it is placed within this intellectual context.

Many select Samuel Prince's doctoral dissertation at Columbia University—published in 1920—as one of the earliest empirical studies reflecting a social science orientation. Prince carefully described the organizational responses evoked following a massive explosion that occurred
on December 6, 1917. At 9:06 that morning, a French munitioner (the
Mont Blanc) carrying trinitrotoluene (TNT) collided with a Belgian relief
ship near the docks of Halifax, Nova Scotia. Interspersed within Prince's
descriptive portrait, however, were numerous *hypotheses* —statements
that transcended the detail of this single event. It was Prince's derivation

of relational statements that might be generalized to comparable future events that set his work apart from that of other observers of disaster responses. In short, he used this event as a case record from which to derive primitive elements of social theory. His procedure had many parallels to what Glaser and Strauss (1967) later depicted as the "discovery of grounded theory."

Thirty years passed, however, before a sustained research effort was funded that provided for continuing data collection following major disaster events. In 1954, Fritz and Marks gave a progress report on work completed under a contract with the Army Chemical Center, Department of the Army. "The NORC disaster studies involved the interviewing of nearly 1,000 persons who had recently been involved in over 70 different major or minor disasters—ranging from large-scale tornadoes, explosions, and earthquakes to airplane crashes, industrial fires and accidents, building collapses, train wrecks, and so on" (Fritz and Marks, 1954:27). Key findings had emerged on topics like panic and convergence behavior that had important policy implications for officials responsible for disaster preparedness (Killian, 1954).

Thus, during the 1950s, dozens of specialized topics were dissected in numerous publications prepared by members of the National Opinion Research Center (NORC) research staff and scholars working elsewhere, e.g., Moore, 1958. In a chapter prepared for a "social problems" text edited by Merton and Nisbet, Fritz (1961) reviewed this burgeoning research base and summarized the major highlights. Disasters—be they natural or man-made—were interpreted as being a special type of social problem.

The following year, Baker and Chapman's (1962) *Man and Society in Disaster* appeared. They recruited several top specialists in the discipline to juxtapose disaster research studies with topics like mental health, family, and the aged. Each of these chapters linked observations about human response to disaster events back to more generic aspects of sociological theory. Disasters were viewed by most chapter authors as being episodes of high stress. Thus, they represented natural experiments whereby system dynamics might be explored better.

None of these chapters, however, approximated the theory construction efforts of Barton (1969). He reviewed case study reports with an eye for the general, and carefully constructed several interrelated networks of hypotheses that could direct subsequent field work. Using field reports prepared by others, especially large numbers of unpublished reports prepared by NORC disaster field team members, he derived numerous primitive models of social process. Thus, Barton's codification effort was more of a theory construction exercise than an inventory of findings.

In 1963, the Disaster Research Center (DRC) was established at the Ohio State University. Twenty-one years later it was relocated to the University of Delaware where two of the founders—E. L. Quarantelli and

R. R. Dynes—hold faculty appointments. But one of the first tasks addressed by original DRC staff was a careful review of many of the same studies that had served Barton. This time, however, the focus was on organizational response. Dynes (1970a) synthesized abstracts based on nearly 300 case reports, plus the rapidly growing publication series prepared by DRC staff members who had now resumed the quick response tradition initiated earlier by the NORC field teams. His volume provided a helpful state-of-the-art summary that was enriched greatly by several analytic typologies that highlighted important differences among the range of organizations that respond during disaster events.

In 1972, I was invited to join two colleagues—Dennis S. Mileti and J. Eugene Haas—in a different type of codification effort. Limiting ourselves to 193 works published prior to July 1, 1973, we organized 627 key study findings into a primitive inventory (Mileti, Drabek, and Haas, 1975). Thus, in contrast to the theory construction effort by Barton, or the organizational focus of Dynes, we constructed a general summary of the literature. It had some of the conceptual and propositional qualities of Barton's work, but rested exclusively on published findings. Within each study reviewed, the major findings that had been supported empirically were identified. Each was classified in two ways. First, the social system being studied was noted. That is, did the finding pertain to a group, like a family, or to an entire community or society? Second, reflecting a tradition that dates back at least to an article by Carr (1932), each finding was coded as to disaster phase. That is, at what point in the life cycle of the event did the finding pertain? As will be evident in the next sections of this chapter, the current inventory reflected this approach.

Others, with different objectives and constraints, have approached the disaster studies literature quite differently. Major developments have been summarized in chapters prepared for the *Annual Review of Sociology,* first by Quarantelli and Dynes (1977) and most recently by Kreps (1984b). Space constraints require that these authors be highly selective in the sampling of studies they summarize, topics discussed, and issues raised. As quick updates on major developments, these chapters are exceedingly useful, however. And when fundamental theoretical problems are pinpointed—as Kreps has done with the plea for a taxonomy of disaster events—they may serve as significant catalysts, deflecting subsequent development of the field in a certain way.

So far I have emphasized contributions by sociologists. While a sizable disaster research capability exists within this discipline—one of international bounds—there are other approaches to the study of disaster phenomena. All bring differing emphases. Within the general social-behavioral rubric, the most important among these are: (1) a long tradition of hazard studies by social geographers and (2) risk assessment and risk management studies.

Dating back at least to the earliest work by White (e.g., White, 1945) large numbers of social geographers have examined human responses to many forms of natural hazards (e.g., Kates, 1971; Heathcote and Thom, 1979; Smith and Tobin, 1979). Of special interest has been the exploration of how hazards like flooding are perceived and the modes of adjustment that human communities have adopted. Thus, in contrast to a focus on responses to disaster events as types of "bounded episodes" of collective stress, this tradition has cast the research agenda into a broader perspective. Rather than asking "how do people behave during and after a flood?", they have asked instead, "how do people perceive and try to use lands that are flood-prone?" Of special interest to some has been the exploration of choice processes, both among individuals and collective systems like nation states. The best general synthesis of the social geographic research base is the text prepared by Burton, Kates, and White (1978).

This perspective highlights a fundamental question that one would expect sociologists to ask—that is, "how do societies differ in the ways they seek to cope with and modify their environment, both natural and human-made?" In the last decade, many aspects of this general question have been pursued by researchers using the theoretical orientations developed by geographers, economists, political scientists, anthropologists, and psychologists.

Under White's leadership—and commencing in July, 1984, that of his successor, William E. Riebsame—the Natural Hazards Research and Applications Information Center at the University of Colorado has provided an important forum for interdisciplinary studies and the juxtaposition of analyses from disciplinary specialists who have focused on parallel or complementary research questions. More so than any other setting within the U.S.A., the annual summer workshop sponsored by the Hazards Center has linked researchers from a wide variety of disciplines to practitioners—operations personnel and policy makers from federal, state, and local agencies as well as representatives from powerful networks within the private sector, especially insurance and financial institutions. Together, we seek to extract implications for application and to assess directions for the future. Such activities reflect the implementation of the core recommendations made following an extensive assessment of the potentials for improved hazard management through quicker utilization of scientific research (White and Haas, 1975).

In an insightful critique, Hewitt (1983) questioned the assumptions reflected by most of the work within these traditions. In a penetrating essay he attacked "the dominate view" within hazards research by questioning the very definitions used to delineate its boundaries. Should disasters be viewed as "unmanaged" phenomena? What implications emerge when disasters are viewed as "the unexpected" or "the unprecedented"? Echoing this same theme, Morren put the issue more forcefully. "Indeed, I think that it is a common error to view disasters as events" (Morren,

1983b:285). Thus, both questioned the implications of the assumptions made by most of us—be we sociologists, geographers, or whatever. For by viewing the phenomena of study as "extreme events," a false disjunction may be created.

Yet, most of us have underscored the continuities and linkages to preexisting social values and structures that exert powerful constraint on the range of responses evoked by disaster events (Haas and Drabek, 1970; Quarantelli and Dynes, 1972, 1977). Commonly, we interpret responses to disaster events using a perspective labeled "emergent norm theory" (Dynes, 1970a; Quarantelli, 1978). Until most recently, as evidenced by works like that of Perrow (1984) or Kunreuther and his colleagues (1983), however, the institutional processes that operate to place populations at risk—often for the profit of a few—have received limited attention by the disaster research community. Clearly, some of our effort has been technocratic—rooted in a quest to demonstrate utility, rather than questioning the assumptions and logics of those defined as "the user community." In the coming decade, however, we will witness many seeking to reorient their work so as to be more responsive to the challenges offered by Hewitt who calls for:

> ". . . a revised vision of how and why disaster occurs, giving full credit to the ongoing societal and man–environment relations that prefigure it. This immediately makes the range of phenomena that form the main stream of the social sciences of direct interest. It means that the common concerns and competence of human geography, human ecology and anthropology are of intrinsic interest to the understanding of hazard, rather than fortuitous matters arising only, and in special ways, when there is the impact of natural extremes or their threat" (Hewitt, 1983:27).

In direct contrast to both the sociological and geographic research legacies is the more recent focus on risk assessment and risk management. To a large degree this research direction has emerged through analyses of man-made or technological hazards. During the 1970s the question of "how safe is safe enough?" loomed to the forefront. Researchers sought to examine critically how decisions had been reached regarding the relative safety of nuclear power plants, food additives, and so on. Increasingly, it became clearer that decision processes defined by some as "scientific" were in fact reflective of value choices. Rejecting models of "scientific decision making," a series of scholars pointed out how differing interest groups were more or less effective—albeit temporarily—in stacking the regulatory deck (Kunreuther and Ley, 1982). Thus, going far beyond critiques of various regulatory decisions, these researchers have begun to make cross-national studies of risk estimation processes, risk management strategies, and the role of perception in evaluating risks (e.g., Lowrance, 1976; Rowe, 1977; Whyte and Burton, 1980; Fischhoff *et al.*, 1982; Douglas and Wildavsky, 1983; Kunreuther *et al.*, 1983). Currently, the Center for

Technology, Environment and Development at Clark University serves as a clearinghouse for those attracted to this broad range of questions.

Across these three orientations there is some duplication, some controversy, and even some turf defense from time to time. More recently, however, there has been increased rapprochement with many of us calling for boundary redefinitions among our respective camps (e.g., Drabek, 1983c; Short, 1984). This is not to say that one discipline or another must dictate the "real" research agenda, nor is it to suggest that everyone should ask the same questions in the same way. It is my view, however, that the scope and perspective of the sociological legacy must be broadened—not abandoned, but stretched.

But that is a plea for the future, a topic I will pursue in the last chapter of this book. Within the context of this intellectual legacy, let's now turn to the inventory of findings so as to understand better what it contains— and equally important, what it does not.

What Is a Disaster?

In contrast to other research traditions—those focusing on natural hazards or risk assessments—this inventory presents a codified summary of key sociological findings regarding human response to disaster events. It is thus both broader and narrower than the natural hazard perspective which has influenced heavily many social geographers, just as a disaster event focus has guided most sociologists. Yet, I believe firmly that strategies of mitigation, perceptions of hazards, and attitudes toward adjustment mechanisms like flood insurance should *not* be excluded from the agenda of disaster researchers. Thus, as I encountered findings relevant to these topics I recorded them, but did not initiate an independent search for them.

Like Warheit (1976), I believe that some aspects of responses to man-made and technological disasters can be integrated within the conclusions from natural disaster research. The analytic criteria that should guide such integration remain unclear, however (e.g., see Kreps, 1984b and Perry, 1985). The degree to which human system responses to nuclear accidents, for example—or to take the extreme case, nuclear war—have parallels to those evoked by hurricanes or volcanic eruptions is a matter about which there is disagreement within the social science research community, e.g., see the contrast between Platt's (1984) and Kreps' (1984a) reviews of Perry (1982). But this dimension is only one of several axes of differentiation that a future taxonomy of disaster events must address. Current disagreements will be resolved by future taxonomic work that is rooted in carefully made juxtapositions based on empirical data, not polemics. This problem of taxonomy is the most pressing issue confronting the field at this time.

Following Fritz (1961:655), disasters are accidental or uncontrollable events, actual or threatened, that are "concentrated in time and space, in which a society, or a relatively self-sufficient subdivision of a society, undergoes severe danger, and incurs such losses to its members and physical appurtenances that the social structure is disrupted and the fulfillment of all or some of the essential functions of the society is prevented."

This definition reflects the concept of *Comprehensive Emergency Management* (CEM). An outgrowth of the earlier "dual use" approach to civil defense, CEM—now being implemented as national policy through the Integrated Emergency Management System (IEMS) program—reflects a multihazard approach to emergency planning (McLoughlin, 1985; Perry, 1982). Hence, my focus on disasters was consistent with the definition of "emergencies" specified by the National Governors' Association (1979) Emergency Preparedness Project staff. Disaster events include aspects of: (1) technological and man-made hazards; (2) natural disasters; and (3) internal disturbances, e.g., acts of terrorism. Energy and material shortages, e.g., violence related to labor strikes or price wars, and various forms of hypothetical "attacks," e.g., scenarios regarding nuclear or biological warfare, were excluded, however.

While a *guide*, there were problems. Most of these confront anyone trying to compile a corpus of materials for review. Among the ambiguities were such things as demarcating limits regarding mitigation studies. For example, I included many flood insurance adoption studies, but excluded assessments of industrial plant safety programs. I did not, however, initiate separate search procedures focused on hazard insurance studies. Similarly, I focused on studies of actual or potential life-threatening events. Thus, crop losses due to frost or insect infestation do cause economic disasters for growers at times, but these were not included. War-related events and responses were not searched for independently, and are included minimally. In short, there are a host of ambiguities, but this definition of *disaster events* was my general *guide* in designing a search process.

The Search Process

I focused on identifying *formally published* studies reporting empirical results of analyses of human responses to disaster events. Because of the difficulty in obtaining them within a reasonable time period, and because many result in subsequent publication anyway, Ph.D. dissertations, M.A. theses, technical project reports, and conference/meeting papers were excluded, aside from a few exceptions. Since most of the papers presented at the 1982 World Congress of Sociology, Disaster Research Section, will be published in the next few years, I wrote to all authors requesting copies. This was the single exception, however. Thus, large quantities of empirical studies reported in conference papers, working papers, project reports, and the like were excluded on the assumption that the peer review process commonly associated with more formal versions of publication would serve as a filter—hopefully a valid one. Hence, I chose not to allocate the limited resources available to me into these directions for these reasons.

I reviewed three previously completed inventories that surveyed literature published prior to 1973—Barton, 1969; Dynes, 1970a; Mileti, Drabek, and Haas, 1975. I integrated major conclusions from these three surveys with those reported in studies published between 1972 and 1983. Numerous 1984 and a few 1985 publications were acquired during consecutive revisions of this manuscript. These were included, but did not reflect these search procedures. For the most part, then, the Master Bibliography of nearly 1000 citations was generated through three complementary search strategies.

1. *Computer searches.* Using "disaster" as the keyword, three citation-abstract listings were printed; various other keywords, e.g., events like floods and tornadoes, and other indexes were tried but did not produce relevant materials.

   (a) *Social Scisearch* (1972–1982)
   (b) *Sociological Abstracts* (1972–1982)
   (c) *PsycINFO* (1972–1982)

2. *Journal Review.* Two journals—*Mass Emergencies* (revived in 1983 as *International Journal of Mass Emergencies and Disasters)* and *Disasters*—were reviewed on an article by article basis as were the "Occasional Papers" (Nos. 1–14) issued by the Disaster Research Unit, University of Bradford, England, and "Disaster Studies" (Nos. 1–15) published by the Disaster Study Group, Uppsala University, Sweden.

3. *Selected Bibliographies.* Numerous bibliographies were secured and reviewed item by item.

   (a) Disaster Research Center, University of Delaware (formerly located at the Ohio State University) (*Publications list:* book and monograph list, report series, articles; *Inventory of Disaster Field Studies, 1982; Inventory of the Japanese Disaster Research Literature in the Social and Behavioral Sciences, 1982*).
   (b) Natural Hazards Research and Applications Information Center, University of Colorado (nine selected bibliographies covering natural hazards publications between the years 1975–1984; entire monograph series, Nos. 2–41).
   (c) Academy for Contemporary Problems, Natural Disaster Recovery and Mitigation Resource Referral Service ["A Selected, Annotated Bibliography of Floodplain Management Literature for State and Local Officials" (March, 1982); "A Selected Bibliography of Natural Disaster Recovery Literature for State and Local Officals" (1981); "A Selected, Annotated Bibliography on Evacuation and Crisis Relocation Planning" (January, 1982)].

(d) R. L. Paulsen, *Human Behavior and Fire Emergencies: An Annotated Bibliography*. Washington, D.C.: National Bureau of Standards, U.S. Department of Commerce, 1981.

(e) S. Noel Kiek, "Disaster Research around the World: Study Leave Report." Papua, New Guinea: The Papua New Guinea University of Technology, March, 1982.

(f) Iowa State University, "Sociological Studies in Civil Defense" (23 reports and articles reviewed).

(g) Clark University, "Technological Hazard Management Studies at Clark University: An Annotated List."

(h) Elizabeth Wilson, "A Selected Annotated Bibliography and Guide to Sources of Information on Planning for and Responses to Chemical Emergencies." *Journal of Hazardous Materials* 4 (1981):373–394.

(i) Frederick L. Ahearn, Jr. and Raquel E. Cohen, *Disasters and Mental Health: An Annotated Bibliography*. Washington, D.C.: National Institute of Mental Health, 1984.

In addition, Professor E. L. Quarantelli (Director, Disaster Research Center, University of Delaware) reviewed the DRC holdings of non-English material and selected eighteen items published in French, Italian, and Japanese. These were translated and made available for my review, as were twelve other non-English articles identified through the computer search processes.

While not exhaustive, the codification of the resulting materials is judged to be representative of the sociological knowledge base on human response to disaster existent in 1985. Others, reflecting different interests, might have consulted alternative reference tools, e.g., *Index Medicus* for the medical literature. Thus, while the bibliography, and especially materials included within each substantive chapter, may appear to be uneven and incomplete to specialists in other fields, they should recognize that my focus was sociological.

A Conceptual Taxonomy

Once the books and articles were acquired, I undertook the demanding task of identifying key sociological findings, conclusions, and major insights. The first step was to design some type of general framework that would permit an initial sorting. Using the distinctions that proved helpful in our earlier inventory (Mileti, Drabek, and Haas, 1975), I selected two dimensions, one temporal and the other structural.

The temporal dimension—that is, disaster phases—was modified so as to conform to the nomenclature proposed in the report of the National Governors' Association (1979). Thus, a fourfold division was made initially: (1) Preparedness, (2) Response, (3) Recovery, and (4) Mitigation.

Each of these was split so as to have the eight categories listed in Table 1-1. For example, preparedness was divided into two subtopics—planning and warning.

The structural dimension was the same sixfold category set that had proved useful in the 1975 inventory. Thus, human systems were ordered in terms of increased structural complexity so as to range from individuals and groups to total societies and international response systems. Of course, some ambiguities remained. For example, some data obtained from "households" really pertained to the individuals interviewed, e.g., their age or gender. Conversely, interorganizational data frequently were used to depict community networks or characteristics. While at times perplexing, I tried to examine the variables under study and the referent system to which they pertained given the questions being addressed by the researcher. While not dealing with international systems *per se,* however, I decided to code all cross-national studies into the international system category. Thus, all cross-societal comparisons are located there.

After the key findings in a particular study were identified, I first designated the unit of analysis—was it depicting behavior of an individual, a society, or whatever? Next, I noted the nation state if it was other than the U.S.A. Then the temporal categories were reviewed. In some instances this was more problematic, but generally one classification or another seemed rather clear-cut. Despite internal pressure to do so, I elected *not* to code any findings on a multiple basis.

All findings were maintained in the appropriate computer file (48 categories noted) and then printed on cards. I then took these cards, each of which included a key finding and its citation number, and began the difficult task of synthesis. Only a portion of all findings contained in the original file were reproduced into text for various reasons, e.g., duplication across publications reporting similar analyses, commonalities across studies, and synthesis into text material.

Upon completion, each chapter draft was critiqued by one of the reviewers listed in the Acknowledgments. Their comments aided greatly in rethinking, identifying a few additions covering material missed through our initial search, and substantial redrafting. These procedures, then, are how the chapters which follow were produced.

Limitations and Risks

This inventory has numerous limitations and there are important risks in using it that all readers should keep in mind. Any who simply extract findings from this inventory and rigidly apply them into settings that differ from those in which they were derived will be disappointed. Our present knowledge base simply does not lend itself to routine and uncritical application.

Table 1-1. Typology of system responses to disaster.

Disaster phase	System level					
	Individual	Group	Organizational	Community	Society	International
Preparedness						
Planning	IA	IIA	IIIA	IVA	VA	VIA
Warning	IB	IIB	IIIB	IVB	VB	VIB
Response						
Pre-impact mobilization	IC	IIC	IIIC	IVC	VC	VIC
Post-impact emergency actions	ID	IID	IIID	IVD	VD	VID
Recovery						
Restoration (6 mos. or less)	IE	IIE	IIIE	IVE	VE	VIE
Reconstruction (6 mos. or more)	IF	IIF	IIIF	IVF	VF	VIF
Mitigation						
Hazard perceptions	IG	IIG	IIIG	IVG	VG	VIG
Adjustments	IH	IIH	IIIH	IVH	VH	VIH

If used as a guide, as a source of insight and sensitizing questions, this inventory can be an important tool for both researchers and practitioners. Uncritical acceptance of any finding herein, without regard to its range of generalizability, may bring error of the worst type—mistaken opinion, masked as scientific evidence. Since I have knowledge of a few instances of such acts of pseudoscience that were stimulated by our earlier inventory, this risk of abuse weighed heavily on my conscience when I considered initiating this project. Hopefully, these words of caution and qualification will curtail potential misuses.

Substantively, the most important limitations to be recognized, especially since I did all of the coding myself, are my biases toward the empirical and the conceptual. Repeatedly I reduced several hundred pages of case study detail to a few simple sentences relating three or four variables. Often these sentences were provided by the case study author. At times I wrote them, however. Consistently, I noted whenever I was paraphrasing, rather than quoting directly. I searched for key connectors among variables that I judged to be of theoretical importance, not geographic, historic, nor ethnographic detail.

I did not record every finding reported within any single study. Indeed, I did not even capture a majority. Given the breadth of coverage I was seeking, it was necessary to record *only the major conclusions*—as I saw them—from each study reviewed. My major criterion was whether or not the finding was relevant to the topics and questions addressed by sociologists. Hopefully, the breadth of perspective I brought to the task resulted in a useful sampling and logical integration. But, as Blumer (1939) noted with the portrait of the Polish peasant produced by Thomas and Znaniecki, no other researcher would have confronted this same stack of nearly 1000 books and articles and extracted exactly what I did.

Equally important is the fact that the existent literature base is far richer than this compilation reveals. My cataloguing *only can point readers to key materials* relevant to a topic of interest. There they will find the additional detail necessary for an informed application, be it research or policy. As will be discussed in the last chapter, this experience has convinced me that we must design and implement a series of information retrevial systems that take us to this next level of detail. There is no reason—other than funding neglect—why such systems can't be fully operational in the relatively near future. Indeed, one prototype system has been developed recently by Rogers and Nehnevajsa (1984). While limited, computerization of library holdings has been initiated at the three major U.S.A. centers, i.e., Delaware, Colorado, and Clark Universities.

I identified many findings as hypotheses; these are designated as: (H). Sometimes these were proposed as such by a particular researcher. While not empirically tested in the research reviewed, they struck me as being useful insights that would enrich an overall understanding of a topic or research area. Other times a conclusion had validity for a particular group studied, but I doubted that it would apply to most other settings without major qualification. Unlike Barton (1969), however, I did not try to create a large array of complex theoretical models containing sets of hypothetical propositions. Rather, this is an inventory of empirical findings, not an exercise in theory construction.

Throughout the writing process, I used the following criteria in making this designation:

1. Statement was proposed formally by the author as a hypothesis.
2. Statement was a synthesis derived from several studies or based on several conclusions from one study, but it had not been verified as stated in a separate empirical test.
3. Statement reflected a major reinterpretation of the conclusions offered by the authors cited.
4. Statement was based on data collected through relatively weak research methods and not yet retested.
5. Statement was based solely on a study cited but not conducted by the author. Where secondary sources are not cited in the Master Bibliography, they are listed in the text.
6. Article from which the statement was extracted did not contain sufficient detail regarding research methods to permit any type of evaluation.
7. There were too many conflicting findings from other related studies focused on the topic, e.g., certain types of long-term mental health impacts.

This means that many "findings"—as I have listed them here—will be modified, reformulated, or simply found to be wrong when future research is completed. In part, this is because many "findings" are conclusions based only on one study, of one event, in one setting. At one point in the writing process, I considered labeling as hypotheses all findings that had not been verified by at least one other researcher. This would have resulted in the vast majority of the findings being so labeled and would have blurred greatly the differentiation between these and those ideas that I felt should best be treated strictly as hypotheses, given the above criteria. Relatively few conclusions have been retested, using identical methods and measures in enough settings so as to clearly specify the *range of conditions and cultures* to which they are applicable. In a truly rigorous, scientific sense— at least as I use those terms—our knowledge base about human system responses to disaster events is embryonic at best. Yet, as this inventory demonstrates dramatically, great progress has been made in our understanding of these phenomena. The types of questions being asked today— both in content and precision—simply could not have been formulated a couple of decades ago.

Some readers may be displeased to learn that I designated their interpretation of various types of historical and case study material as a "hy-

pothesis.'' Such a designation is a matter of judgment; a decision of where
to draw the line. It is clearer to me now than ever before that there is
substantial dissensus within the social science research community regarding the criteria that define acceptable rules of scientific evidence. This
point was underscored in one of the many letters that Professor E. L.
Quarantelli and I exchanged during the course of this project. He was
referring to non-English materials, but the same point could be made about
many disciplinary differences, especially with regard to the psychiatric,
historical, and anthropological studies that defined the outer limits of this
sociological review.

> ''. . . I have reached the conclusion that the written material (if it is
> translated) will give you or anyone else only a limited view of the disaster
> research elsewhere. There are a number of reasons for this, but many
> simply have to do with cross-cultural differences in approaching, doing,
> and reporting disaster research. The non-Americans do not slice the sci-
> entific world the same way we do in this country. . . . what we advance
> as the scientific research model might be more accurately called the
> American scientific research model'' (E. L. Quarantelli, personal com-
> munication, December 3, 1982).

Recognizing that cultural differences may alter relationships among
variables, all findings listed herein pertain to studies conducted within the
United States of America, except where noted. That is, whenever the
finding was based on data pertaining to another country, I identified the
nation state at the end of the quotation. But this is far from a total solution,
as no nation state is completely homogeneous. Erikson's (1976a) careful
delineation of the Appalachian subculture provided an important interpretative framework for responses to the devastating flood that struck
Buffalo Creek, West Virginia, for example. Similarly, Geipel (1982) emphasized that responses to earthquakes in Italy (May 6 and September
15, 1976) could be understood only if they were placed within the context
of the Friuli subculture and its economic and political history.

> ''A border population with rather traditional and conservative ways, par-
> ticularly among the more isolated mountain folk, in many countries may
> provide fertile ground for antipathy toward the central regime. Such is
> the case of Scotland with regard to 'London', in Bavaria with respect to
> 'Bonn', and in Friuli regarding 'Rome'. The earthquake catastrophe
> stimulated this emotional feeling of distinctiveness even more'' (Geipel,
> 1982:15).

A cross-national comparative data base is an obvious challenge awaiting
the research community, although a few such studies have now appeared.
Regional and subcultural designations will have to be included. Thus, this
limitation, and my procedure for dealing with it, should be kept in mind.
Also, as certain topics reveal very clearly—for example, long-term
mental health impacts—important methodological differences in study

design and measurement of variables preclude much synthesis at this time. It was far beyond the resources available to me to prepare detailed methodological critiques of every study coded. Hence, some may conclude that this inventory risks misguiding users because methodological differences have been glossed over. This point is exceptionally well developed in a paper by Aguirre (1976). But this matter should not preclude our recognition of the usefulness of broad-brush reviews wherein key observations are summarized.

Given a sociological perspective, the decision to focus on disaster events, and the general criteria and procedures described above, it is obvious that many types of materials were excluded. As indicated above, the most critical impact of my search process—focused as it was on disaster events—was the inadequate coverage of the mitigation phase. Hazard perceptions and attitudes toward adjustments like flood insurance, for example, comprise extensive literatures that would have required search strategies different from the one most relevant to my task. While lacking comprehensiveness, however, I am confident that Chapters 8 and 9 provide a balanced portrait of much larger literature bases.

Without trying to list every category, the following will help readers to understand the range of materials that were not reviewed. I have included one example for each category; these appeared in one or more of the bibliographies above.

1. *Physical science aspects of disasters:* E. D. Attanasi and M. R. Karlinger, "Worth of Geophysical-Data in Natural-Disaster-Insurance Rate Setting." *Journal of Applied Meteorology* 21 (1982):453–460.
2. *Disaster response was peripheral to the central theme or included as a generic term:* Allan Compton, "A Study of the Psychoanalytic Theory of Anxiety:III. A Preliminary Formulation of the Anxiety Response." *Journal of the American Psychoanalytic Association* 28 (1980):739–773.
3. *Disaster training manuals and handbooks:* Roger E. Herman, *Disaster Planning for Local Government.* New York: Universe Books, 1982.
4. *Policy or research needs assessments:* National Science Foundation, *A Report on Flood Hazard Mitigation,* Washington, D.C.: National Science Foundation, 1980.
5. *Disaster response plans:* Miami Federal Executive Board, *Report to the United States Office of Management and Budget: Evacuation of Coastal Residents during Hurricanes: A Pilot Study for Dade County, Florida.* Washington, D.C.: U.S. Government Printing Office, 1973.
6. *Program evaluations:* U.S. General Accounting Office, *Report by the Comptroller General: States Can Be Better Prepared to Respond to Disasters.* Gaithersburg, Maryland: U.S. General Accounting Office, Document Handling and Information Services Facility, 1980.
7. *Federal agency staff reports:* National Oceanic and Atmospheric Administration, *Red River Valley Tornadoes of April 10, 1979.* Natural

Disasters Summary Report 80-1. Rockville, Maryland: United States Department of Commerce, 1980.
8. *General essays:* Gregory S. Kavka, "Deterrence, Utility, and Rational Choice." *Theory and Decision* **12** (March, 1980):41–60.
9. *Methodological studies:* Don G. Friedman, *Computer Simulation in Natural Hazard Assessment.* Boulder, Colorado: Institute of Behavioral Science, University of Colorado, 1975.
10. *Public Attitudes toward Civil Defense:* Ralph Garrett, *Civil Defense and the Public.* Washington, D.C.: Defense Civil Preparedness Agency, 1976.

Finally, as emphasized above, this inventory is sociological in focus. As noted in discussion of the search process, however, I did reach out in a variety of ways so as to capture selected portions of research from other social science disciplines. Torry's (1979a) criticism of the earlier inventory of this type that I coauthored with Mileti and Haas (1975) was well taken. Only six of the nearly 200 bibliographic entries we reviewed then were anthropological. I have not counted the parallel number contained herein, but certainly there are many more. Yet, as before, I did not initiate extensive and separate searches into the anthropological literature. But the same is true for geography, economics, political science, psychology, and several other disciplines that have theory relevant to human responses to disasters.

Bibliographic inclusion is not the total solution, however. I recall coding several anthropological publications this time around *and* the difficulties I encountered because of the case methods used. Too often pages of ethnographic detail did not culminate in a succinct series of propositions at a higher level of abstraction. And so Torry or his counterpart, may once again "express disappointment about the disaster researcher's inattentiveness to anthropological achievements and perspectives" (Torry, 1979a:47). Having offered these words of apology *and* caution, let me describe the logic and sequence of the chapters that follow.

An Overview

Reflecting the conceptual typology discussed above (see Table 1-1), the inventory of findings has been organized into eight substantive chapters. My logic here was to divide the life cycle of a disaster event into eight more-or-less discrete processes and to categorize responses into one of six systemic levels. Starting with the topic of preparedness, Chapters 2 and 3 review findings pertaining to planning and warning. Despite chapter breaks, all major propositions are labeled sequentially. That is, those related to planning are designated with the letter "A"; those for warning, with the letter "B". In contrast, each chapter is divided initially into six major subtopics—one for each system level. Within all chapters and re-

Table 1-2. Numeric summary of topics, major conclusions and specific findings.[a]

	Individual			Group			Organizational			Community			Society			International		
Disaster phase	T	MC	SF	T	MC	SF	T	MC	SF	T	MC	SF	T	MC	SF	T	MC	SF
Preparedness																		
A. Planning	4	10	4	4	5	0	7	25	15	8	39	17	4	6	7	0	6	4
B. Warning	5	20	35	3	12	13	2	5	6	2	3	5	2	4	5	0	1	0
Response																		
C. Evacuation	4	22	27	3	16	8	3	10	0	3	12	5	2	5	1	0	3	0
D. Emergency	3	27	46	2	10	11	6	25	35	6	36	43	0	3	0	2	5	5
Recovery																		
E. Restoration	2	13	12	4	17	3	4	13	13	7	29	25	2	9	0	3	12	9
F. Reconstruction	6	35	47	3	16	18	5	16	11	3	13	13	0	5	7	2	14	11
Mitigation																		
G. Perceptions	3	17	26	0	1	2	3	6	10	2	5	6	0	1	0	2	9	6
H. Adjustment	4	22	11	0	0	0	4	13	3	3	18	12	6	43	21	3	17	20

[a]Grand totals: topics (T) = 146; major conclusions (MC) = 654; specific findings (SF) = 578.

gardless of the substantive topic, findings noted by a "I" refer to individual system responses, a "II" to group system responses, and so on. Thus, proposition "IIA1" pertains to an aspect of a group system response during the planning phase, whereas "IIIB1" designates an organizational response during the warning process.

The second major topic, reflective of the second phase in the life cycle of a disaster event, is response. Thus, Chapter 4 deals with evacuation and other forms of pre-impact mobilization, whereas Chapter 5 chronicles post-impact emergency actions. The recovery phase is divided into the topics of restoration (Chapter 6) and reconstruction (Chapter 7). Findings pertaining to mitigation—a topic that many would start with—is divided into hazard perceptions (Chapter 8) and attitudes toward and the adoption of adjustments (Chapter 9).

The general format of each chapter parallels that described above regarding system level. That is, we begin with the individual system level responses and move to groups, organizations, and other systems of increased structural complexity. Depending upon the number of findings and their diversity, most categories within the 48-cell typology were further divided into two or more subtopics. But there was great unevenness; some topics have been researched in far more depth than others.

Table 1-2 provides a summary of the subtopics and findings. In total, Chapters 2 through 9 contain 146 specific subtopics, 654 major conclusions, and 578 less abstract findings.

The contours in this data base and its growth pattern during the past decade are my initial considerations in the final chapter. There I elaborate what I view as the priorities that should guide disaster research in the coming decade. I also identify several candidate areas that are ripe for either unique application opportunities or theoretical model building. Using the inventory as a guide, I also point out several topics meriting exploration—research questions still awaiting scholarly interest. Finally, I conclude with brief commentary on the payoffs that I see disaster research offering to general sociological theory.

Given the size of the Master Bibliography, I decided that many readers would be aided by some selectivity and subject matter classifications. Thus, I reviewed all works cited within each respective chapter and then identified a small portion to comprise the selected bibliographies that appear at the end of each. Through these, I hope to provide readers with a sense of the range of materials pertaining to each topic.

Selected Bibliography

Baker, George, and Dwight W. Chapman (eds.) [1962] *Man and Society in Disaster.* New York: Basic Books.

Barton, Allen H. [1969] *Communities in Disaster: A Sociological Analysis of Collective Stress Situations.* Garden City, New York: Doubleday and Company, Inc.

Burton, Ian, Robert W. Kates, and Gilbert F. White [1978] *The Environment as Hazard*. New York: Oxford University Press.

Dynes, Russell R. [1970] *Organized Behavior in Disaster*. Lexington, Massachusetts: Heath Lexington Books.

Frazier, Kendrick [1979] *The Violent Face of Nature*. New York: William Morrow and Company, Inc.

Fritz, Charles E. [1961] "Disasters." Pp. 651–694 in *Contemporary Social Problems,* Robert K. Merton and Robert A. Nisbet (eds.). New York: Harcourt.

Fritz, Charles E., and Eli S. Marks [1954] "The NORC Studies of Human Behavior in Disaster." *The Journal of Social Issues* **10** (No. 3):26–41.

Fritz, Charles E., and Harry B. Williams [1957] "The Human Being in Disasters: A Research Perspective." *The Annals of the American Academy of Political and Social Science* **309** (January):42–51.

Haas, J. Eugene, and Thomas E. Drabek [1970] "Community Disaster and System Stress: A Sociological Perspective." Pp. 264–286 in *Social and Psychological Factors in Stress,* Joseph E. McGrath (ed.). New York: Holt, Rinehart and Winston, Inc.

Heathcote, R. L., and B. G. Thom (eds.) [1979] *Natural Hazards in Australia*. Canberra: Australian Academy of Science.

Hewitt, K. (ed.) [1983] *Interpretations of Calamity*. Boston: Allen & Unwin Inc.

Hirose, Hirotada (ed.) [1981] *Socio-Scientific Approach to Disasters* (in Japanese). Tokyo, Japan: Shinyosha.

Kates, Robert W. [1971] "Natural Hazards in Human Ecological Perspective: Hypotheses and Models." *Economic Geography* **47** (July):438–451.

Kreps, Gary A. [1984] "Sociological Inquiry and Disaster Research." *Annual Review of Sociology* **10**:309–330.

Kreps, Gary A. [1981] "The Worth of the NAS–NRC (1952–1963) and DRC (1963–Present) Studies of Individual and Social Responses to Disasters." Pp. 91–121 in *Social Science and Natural Hazards,* James D. Wright and Peter H. Rossi (eds.). Cambridge, Massachusetts: Abt Books.

Kunreuther, Howard, and Eryl Ley (eds.) [1982] *The Risk Analysis Controversy: An Institutional Perspective*. Berlin, Heidelberg, New York: Springer-Verlag.

Mileti, Dennis S., Thomas E. Drabek, and J. Eugene Haas [1975] *Human Systems in Extreme Environments*. Boulder, Colorado: Institute of Behavioral Science, The University of Colorado.

Moore, Harry Estill [1956] "Toward a Theory of Disaster." *American Sociological Review* **21** (December):733–737.

Petak, William J., and Arthur A. Atkisson [1982] *Natural Hazard Risk Assessment and Public Policy: Anticipating the Unexpected*. New York, Heidelberg, Berlin: Springer-Verlag.

Quarantelli, E. L. [1982] *Inventory of Disaster Field Studies in the Social and Behavioral Sciences: 1919–1979*. Columbus, Ohio: Disaster Research Center, The Ohio State University.

Quarantelli, E. L. [1978] *Disasters: Theory and Research*. Beverly Hills, California: Sage.

Quarantelli, E. L., and Russell R. Dynes [1977] "Response to Social Crisis and Disaster." *Annual Review of Sociology* **3**:23–49.

Reid, Joan Innes (ed.) [1979] *Planning for People in Natural Disasters*. Townsville, Queensland, Australia: James Cook University Press.

Smith, Keith, and Graham Tobin [1979] *Human Adjustment to the Flood Hazard*. London and New York: Longman.
White, Gilbert F. (ed.) [1974] *Natural Hazards: Local, National, Global*. New York: Oxford University Press.
White, Gilbert F., and J. Eugene Haas [1975] *Assessment of Research on Natural Hazards*. Cambridge, Massachusetts and London: The MIT Press.

2
Planning

There are many ways to prepare for disaster. Indeed, the list of possible actions is nearly endless. Some activities, however, are best viewed within the concept of mitigation—that is, purposive acts designed toward the elimination of, reduction in probability of, or reduction of the effects of potential disasters. Specific examples include land-use management programs whereby people are restricted from building in flood-prone areas, or the more stringent building code requirements that have been adopted by many communities with histories of seismic activity. These are the focus of Chapters 8 and 9.

In contrast are actions of preparedness. Such activities are predicated on the assumption that disasters of various forms will occur, but that their negative consequences may be reduced—mitigated, if you will, but in this special sense. Thus, various forms of monitoring, warning, planning, and stockpiling are examples of behavioral actions that constitute this phase of disaster response. The line between these actions and those analyzed later is somewhat blurry, however.

From the standpoint of sociological research, disaster preparedness remains a complex black box that few investigators have sought to explore empirically. Indeed, aside from the topic of warning, most of the findings reported in our earlier inventory (i.e., Mileti, Drabek, and Haas, 1975) dealt with some act of mitigation, not preparedness as it is conceptualized today. But in the decade that followed the situation changed. Many empirical studies have been completed and numerous ideas about the behavioral dynamics of planning have been codified.

IA. Individual System Level

Four central themes convey the essence of the information base regarding the individual system and disaster planning: (1) event variation; (2) public acceptance of planning; (3) public preparedness levels; and (4) public belief in disaster myths.

IA1. Event Variation

IA1.1 7 Individual system impacts covary with event qualities.

From a planning standpoint, this fundamental axiom—one we will return to repeatedly—is a logical point of departure. Researchers have long recognized that disasters are not uniform—they vary in many ways. To date, however, we lack a calculus whereby types of event variations, along with implicit social characteristics, can be factored into the human response equation (see Drabek, 1970 and Dynes, 1970a). As will be noted throughout this inventory, the literature of the 1970s contained many instances wherein topics like panic behavior and long-term mental health impacts were recast into frameworks wherein disasters were no longer viewed as uniform.

While this more complex conceptualization of disaster phenomena has gained near universal acceptance within the sociological research community, the comparative design considerations it implies still await implementation. Thus, the conclusions of the 1950s and 1960s still define the limits of precision in our knowledge base. Among the variables that have been suggested as critical characteristics of events are: suddenness (Fritz, 1957; Zurcher, 1968), duration and scope of destruction (Fritz, 1957; Perry, 1985), nighttime occurrence (Lomnitz, 1970), and victim exposure to dead and badly injured persons (Fritz and Marks, 1954).

Beyond these fairly general characteristics (see Section IVA2 for elaboration) Cochrane (1975) has specified death and injury ratios as a function of scope of damage. These ratios may vary widely, however, depending upon warning quality, special characteristics of the population at risk, and event qualities like time of day.

> IA1.2 ". . . a ratio of deaths to total dwellings *destroyed* was calculated for 23 disasters . . . A review . . . shows a fairly consistent relationship— for every 100 houses destroyed one would expect an average of eleven deaths to result. [p. 29] . . . The total number of seriously injured was also found to be related to the number of structures totally destroyed. . . . in tornado disasters an almost one-to-one relationship exists between a house being destroyed and the occurrence of an injury of any type. . . . For water-related disasters, hurricanes and floods, the ratio appears to be one injury for two houses destroyed, with, again, a 20% ratio of serious to total injury [p. 32]" (Cochrane, 1975: 29, 32).

Finally, there is some indication that if all other things are equal, many impacts—including fatalities—disproportionately affect the elderly. In part, this is because of a propensity for more elderly to be located in flood-prone areas and other more hazardous locations.

> IA1.3(H) ". . . those over 64 years of age suffered a proportionately greater level of fatalities" (Cochrane, 1975:37). (See also Hutton, 1976.)

IA2. Public Acceptance of Planning

Although many researchers (e.g., Sood, 1982; Rossi, Wright, and Weber-Burdin, 1982) report that hazard issues rank low in priority for most people—a point we will pursue later—surveys here and in Japan suggest general acceptance of disaster planning efforts (e.g., Turner *et al.*, 1979; Perry and Greene, 1983; Nigg, 1982; Shimada, 1972). For example, Perry and Greene (1983:115) discovered that over three-fourths of those they interviewed following the eruption of Mount St. Helens (May, 1980) indicated a willingness to participate in a community warning plan as "key citizens" responsible to warn others in their area. Similarly, Turner and his associates (1979:57–58) discovered that ". . . 65 to 83 percent of the respondents want *more* coverage of the 'Palmdale bulge and scientific earthquake prediction,' 'what to do when an earthquake strikes,' 'how to prepare for an earthquake,' and 'what government officials are doing to prepare for an earthquake.' "

But these rates may be the extremes given the salience of the threats for those surveyed. Earlier findings from Japan may be closer to a modal response, although the questions asked implied greater levels of activism which may have dampened the positive response rates. "When asked about willingness to participate in disaster defense training . . . 37.7 percent of the respondents answered that they would participate 'actively,' 42 percent 'yes, if told,' 12.9 percent 'don't know,' 5.1 percent 'don't feel like it,' and 2.1 percent would 'not at all.' " [Japan] (Shimada, 1972:215). Be that as it may, disaster planning activities appear to be commonly accepted.

> IA2.1 In general, most citizens accept disaster planning as an appropriate and acceptable function of government. (Based on Turner *et al.*, 1979; Perry and Greene, 1983; see also Akimoto and Ohta, 1980:71–73.)

Furthermore, the California surveys document a clear perception of legitimacy. That is, disaster planning is viewed as a public responsibility.

> IA2.2 "On the basis of the entire battery of questions we must conclude that the theme of public responsibility rather than individual responsibility is dominant. People do see the prospect of an earthquake as requiring collective rather than merely individual and family action. And they see government, especially local government, as the appropriate agency for collective response" (Turner *et al.*, 1979:80).

But as Akimoto and Ohta (1980:73) point out for the Japanese, such acceptance reflects a "rights consciousness" rather than a "duty consciousness." While I did not encounter systematic study of the matter, I suspect that this view is equally applicable to the U.S.A. People have other concerns on their minds—family, work, and leisure. "Disaster planning ought to be taken care of by government; don't bother me with it."

Finally, while awaiting careful testing, it is clear that the acceptance of disaster planning efforts is not distributed randomly. The following *hypothesis* reflects recurrent themes scattered throughout the literature.

> IA2.3(H) The level of acceptance of disaster planning: increases with the frequency of experience with an actual or predicted disaster; is higher among men than women; and varies directly with socioeconomic status. (Based on Shimada, 1972:209; Nigg, 1982:94.)

IA3. Public Preparation

Depending upon the threat reviewed, i.e., tornado vs. earthquake, which undoubtedly reflects aspects of event frequency, public preparation levels have been reported as high *or* rather low. Thus, note how Hodler's (1982) appraisal contrasts sharply to those of Bourque and her associates (1973). "The majority of people (81%) had a prior plan in the event of a dangerous storm. Almost all of those individuals said they intended to go to the basement or other place of shelter. Ninety-three percent (196) ultimately responded according to their pre-arranged plan" (Hodler, 1982:46). "Analysis of survey data collected throughout Los Angeles County following the 1971 earthquake indicates that *few persons had made prior disaster preparations*" (Bourque *et al.,* 1973:ii). Even in the High Impact Zone, the Los Angeles researchers discovered that less than half the population subsequently had made disaster preparations of any type.

> IA3.1 The greater the disaster frequency, the greater the proportion of the population who will have engaged in preparatory actions. (Based on Hodler, 1982:46; Nehnevajsa and Wong, 1977:vi; Bourque *et al.,* 1973:ii, 19; Nigg, 1982:89; Sendai Research Committee of Urban Sciences, 1979.)

Aside from the frequency of disaster events, various socioeconomic indicators appear to be related to preparedness levels. Although these have not been validated on varying populations confronting alternative types of disasters, both earthquake (Bourque *et al.,* 1973) and winter blizzard preparations (Neal, Perry, and Hawkins, 1982) have been found to be associated with such SES indicants as place of residence and occupation.

> IA3.2(H) Married men, especially those evidencing higher socioeconomic characteristics through income, occupation, and place of residence, will make more preparations when warned of disaster than those who are

single and/or of lower SES. (Based on Bourque *et al.,* 1973:18; see also Okabe *et al.,* 1979b; Guard Police Psychology Research Society, 1966; Neal, Perry, and Hawkins, 1982:67.)

Coming at the issue from another vantage point, Okabe *et al.* (1979b) introduced another variable—contact with information. Thus, based on the Japanese experience with earthquake predictions, it appears that this variable impacts preparedness levels.

IA3.3(H) The more often people obtain information: (1) the more they trust an earthquake prediction; (2) the more they prepare against an earthquake; (3) the stronger their anxieties are; (4) the stronger their desires to move are; and (5) the more severe damages they predict. [Japan] (Based on Okabe *et al.,* 1979b; as summarized in Yamamoto and Quarantelli, 1982:A-165–166.)

IA4. Public Belief in Disaster Myths

In an important study—one meriting replication—Wenger and his colleagues (1975) documented that ". . . the myths about disaster are prevalent and widespread, . . . individuals expect looting to occur, panic flight to exist, and disaster shock to be present" (Wenger *et al.,* 1975:45). Further analysis and enlarged data bases permitted a more refined conclusion, i.e., ". . . residents from the disaster communities do not score very highly, averaging about 30 percent correct answers on the scale of disaster knowledge" (Wenger, James, and Faupel, 1980:89). Their data suggest that the following propositions characterize the American mindset today.

IA4.1 Public belief about human responses in disaster reflects aspects of myth, rather than scientifically based knowledge. (Based on Wenger, James, and Faupel, 1980.)

Variations in this mythology of disaster were identified. Most important among these were:

IA4.1a "The residents of the three disaster communities do evidence higher levels of disaster knowledge than the residents from the disaster-free area" (Wenger, James, and Faupel, 1980:89).

IA4.1b "The highest scores are found for those respondents for whom personal experience or public education programs are the most salient source of information" (Wenger, James, and Faupel, 1980:90).

IA4.1c "Within the disaster communities, males score from four to six percent higher than females" (Wenger, James, and Faupel, 1980:90).

IA4.1d "The mass media are the most salient source of information about disasters for all samples of respondents, including those in communities that have experienced disaster. . . . Within the disaster communities those respondents who first cited the media as source of disaster knowledge score lower than others" (Wenger, James, and Faupel, 1980:90).

IIA. Group System Level

Four themes summarize numerous findings regarding group responses to disaster planning, although nearly all pertain to families rather than other forms of groups: (1) life cycles of emergent groups; (2) family disaster planning; (3) family willingness to participate in preparedness activities; and (4) looting fears.

IIA1. Life Cycles of Emergent Groups

Detailed studies of California responses to the earthquake threat suggested a general hypothesis regarding the survival potential of emergent citizen groups involved in disaster planning.

> IIA1.1(H) Most emergent citizen groups seeking to claim disaster pre-paredness for their domain will not survive; those that do will become integrated within a larger ongoing structure and will reflect preexisting interests of their founders.

The following passage from the study by Turner and his colleagues il-lustrates the case materials that are supportive of this hypothesis.

> "Very few new groups were established because of the earthquake threat. The extremely small number of spontaneously created neighborhood groups concerned with family and neighborhood earthquake preparation did not survive beyond single meetings. One group spurred by the en-thusiasm of a student organizer was active during two years at a high school. Other groups were shaped as extensions of the preexisting in-terests of their founders: a hobbyist established an earthquake prediction group using a simple 'tiltmeter' he had constructed; . . ." (Turner et al., 1981:57).

Survivorship potentials were implicit in several of the structural char-acteristics reported by Stallings and Quarantelli (1985) following a survey of 50 non-emergency time emergent citizen groups.

> IIA1.2 "Structurally these non-emergency time groups are also relatively flat and not very complex. Most have a three-tier or circular structure with a handful of active members in the central core supported by our outer core of less active members who can be mobilized for specific tasks with the remainder of members at the periphery who sign petitions, pay dues, receive a newsletter, or attend an occasional meeting or demon-stration" (Stallings and Quarantelli, 1985:96).

Many of these groups, however, had formed after a major disaster— a matter we'll pursue in Chapter 7 (Reconstruction). Others emerged fol-lowing identification of a hazardous dump site or some other potential danger to their neighborhood like a landslide threat. Thus, they differ somewhat from the types of groups that Turner and his associates studied.

Regardless, Stallings and Quarantelli underscored a key systemic feature that few such groups appear to avoid—low turnover among a few core members who do the bulk of the work. Except for a diligent few, most people burn out in a year or two. Thus, failure to routinize the replacement of leadership precludes longer-term group survival.

IIA2. Family Disaster Planning

We do not know how often or how many family groups spend time in activities that might be defined as "disaster planning." Some research indicates that it is rare. Worth and McLuckie (1977:72), for example, reported ". . . that only 3% of the families had developed any emergency plans prior to the flood and they therefore respond to disasters in terms of definitions of the event." This may vary greatly among communities, however.

Furthermore, there may be many actions that families take which they may not define as disaster planning. Hence, when queried by a researcher—"Do you have a disaster plan?"—these actions may be overlooked. Thus, a rather different image of the extent of planning, defined more broadly, is proposed by others. Nehnevajsa and Wong (1977:154) illustrated this point well: "Most residents who thought that they might have to evacuate their homes, as some of them had to do during antecedent floods, made arrangements with friends, relatives and neighbors."

It does appear, however, that the propensity for families to engage in such activities can be impacted by officials. Thus, the very low rate reported by Worth and McLuckie, i.e., 3%, is a sharp contrast to that discovered by Perry and Greene (1983) following the initial Mount St. Helens eruption in May, 1980.

> "The pamphlet distributed by the Cowlitz County Sheriff's Office recommended development of a family emergency plan, so that might explain some of the 81.1 percent in the Toutle/Silverlake area who had either a general or specific plan. In the Woodland area, despite the fact that most people there had not had direct contact with the Sheriff's Office, 84.9 percent had either a general or specific plan" (Perry and Greene, 1983:47).

Of course, in addition to the qualifier regarding event probability, there are a host of other variables that future researchers must examine—matters like the perceived credibility of officials, length of announced time frame, impact of false alarms, and the like. Despite these and other ambiguities, it does appear that the extent and types of family disaster planning can be influenced by governmental officials.

> IIA2.1(H) If encouraged to develop emergency plans for threats that have a high probability of occurring within a fairly short time frame, by authorities who are perceived as credible, a majority of families will do so.

IIA3. Family Willingness to Participate in Preparedness Activities

IIA3.1 Following a community disaster, a majority of families will express general support for and a willingness to participate in emergency procedures designed to unify and protect families and their possessions.

In sharp contrast to an image of pronounced apathy, Perry and his colleagues have documented widespread citizen interest in two potentially important types of preparedness actions. Of course, these data were collected within the context of a recent disaster experience. "Over half the evacuees in Sumner, Fillmore, and Valley indicated they felt a family message center would provide helpful information" (Perry, Lindell, and Greene, 1981:162). (See also Perry, Greene, and Lindell, 1980a:445). Similarly, ". . . more than 75% of the evacuees in all four study sites said that they would participate in some capacity in a citizens' patrol if such a program were organized in their community" (Perry, Greene, and Lindell, 1980a:446). (See also Perry, Lindell and Greene, 1981:162.)

After the Mount St. Helens eruption, parallel results were found. " 'Do you think people would use an "answer line" which outside friends and relatives could call to obtain information on families who had evacuated and arrived at a shelter?' [p. 118] . . . In Toutle/Silverlake 76.7 percent of the respondents found the idea of an answer line useful, and 75.9 percent of the respondents in the Woodland area found such an idea attractive [p. 119]" (Perry and Greene, 1983:118, 119). How lasting the stated commitments might be remains unknown, as does the behavioral dimension. To express a willingness to participate is one thing, to act or commit resources quite another.

IIA4. Looting Fears

The topic of looting will be explored further in several sections of this book—especially in the community system level responses during the restoration phase, Chapter 6 (IVE4). There it will be shown that looting behavior is exceedingly rare following disaster, except under very specific conditions. From a planning vantage point, however, it is important to recognize that mythology may impact behavior. Surveys indicate that many family members do express fears of looting.

IIA4.1(H) When encouraged to evacuate their homes, substantial proportions of families will fear looting, but this is not a relevant behavioral constraint.

Perry, Greene, and Lindell have interpreted their data as supporting the conclusions of Dynes and Quarantelli (1968) regarding looting. "Many evacuees, nearly half in three of the sites, expressed *concern* about looters, but relatively few people said that they did not evacuate because of this concern" (Perry, Greene, and Lindell, 1980a:446).

The message for planners is clear, even though many specifics await future researchers who need to provide more precise estimates of the variation and its correlates. Families that don't evacuate are not motivated primarily by looting fears—there are other factors that are far more important. These will be outlined in the next chapter. Yet, concerns about looting are real and officials should seek to implement a variety of mitigative mechanisms. It is not the prevention of looting behavior that must be the focal point, however. Rather it is the reduction of fear of such in the minds of family members that is needed to facilitate the evacuation process.

IIIA. Organizational System Level

Seven broad categories, largely reflecting differences in organizational mission, emerged when I reviewed findings pertaining to organizational systems: (1) general principles; (2) local emergency management-civil defense agencies; (3) hospital-medical units; (4) first responders; (5) mental health agencies; (6) media organizations; and (7) schools. This categorization is not to imply that planning principles might not have cross-agency relevance. But the limits of generalization remain unspecified at this time thereby precluding integration, except as hypotheticals about how the planning process *ought* to take place.

IIIA1. General Principles

Five general principles can be articulated that appear to have widespread applicability to most organizations.

> IIIA1.1 Organizational planning for disaster responses differs qualitatively from planning for everyday emergencies.

Although various scholars have stated it differently, this message appears throughout the research literature (see also IVA3.1). Why does routine emergency planning differ from organizational disaster planning? That is less clear, but the following themes reflect the essence of numerous disscussions (e.g., Quarantelli, 1984; Drabek, 1985).

> IIIA1.1a ". . . the structural conditions of the emergency period make for uncertainty, diversity, decreased formalization and decentralization. These changes increase communication. The non-routine nature of disaster tasks and the increased complexity of organizations require co-ordination by feedback" (Dynes and Aguirre, 1979:73).

> IIIA1.1b ". . . the dominance of a normative planning model which emphasises co-ordination by plan is, at best, questionable. The crisis event itself creates the conditions where co-ordination by plan is inappropriate. This inappropriateness, however, is not likely to be challenged in post-

disaster critiques of organizational functioning, because the norms used to judge organizational effectiveness are such as to lead to negative evaluations of organizations which utilize co-ordination by feedback. The tremendous increase in communication is taken as a failure of co-ordination, not as a condition necessary for it'' (Dynes and Aguirre, 1979:73–74).

Despite this research base, recently completed studies continued to document a lack of awareness and acceptance of this premise. For example, Quarantelli and other DRC staff (1979) reported that executives in chemical companies viewed planning for plant safety incidents and planning for disasters as being pretty much identical. (See also Gray, 1981:360.)

> IIIA1.2 Role conflict experienced by organizational personnel does not precipitate role abandonment; the tendency is to remain on the job, often for too long. (Based on Quarantelli, 1982b:10.)

Reviewing a variety of studies of the type that I will summarize in the next chapter, Quarantelli concluded that organizational planners should recognize that what many fear rarely occurs. That is, upon learning of a disaster, personnel do not flock to their homes. If they reside in the impact area, however, efforts may be made to ascertain family member safety. Instead of role abandonment, ''. . . there is a strong tendency for staff members to remain on the job too long, or to overuse all personnel concurrently'' (Quarantelli, 1982b:10). Analytic qualities that might define ''outlying'' events wherein role abandonment may occur remain undefined and controversial.

> IIIA1.3(H) The larger the organization, the greater the likelihood that disaster planning will occur.

Through a sample of U.S. chemical firms, Quarantelli et al. (1979) discovered that executives in smaller companies did not see their plant as being a significant threat. Thus, they expressed minimal interest in disaster planning or in getting involved in such planning with other community groups. This is consistent with a Japanese survey among private businesses (Guard Police Psychology Research Society, 1966; as summarized in Yamamoto and Quarantelli, 1982:A-76). However, an earlier study of Japanese transportation companies revealed that organizational size was not related to disaster planning efforts. In part, this inconsistency may stem from the small percentage reporting any type of disaster preparations (in this case earthquake), i.e., 20.4% (Guard Police Psychology Research Society, 1980a; as summarized in Yamamoto and Quarantelli, 1982:A-123). The entire matter of disaster planning within the private sector merits extensive study so as to permit documentation of the range of variation and its determinants.

IIIA1.4 Organizational officials can increase the quality of citizen responses to disasters, if adaptive actions are proposed rather than a sole emphasis on the dangers. (Based on McBride, 1979:126; Bresenhan, 1968:14–15; Perry and Greene, 1982a.)

IIIA1.5 Organizational officials have more insight into human responses to disaster than the public generally.

This principle reflects the surveys completed by Wenger, James, and Faupel (1980). They discovered that while disaster mythology was prevalent within the belief system of local emergency organizational officials, it was less so than among the public at large. That is, more officials (43%) gave correct responses on their disaster knowledge scale than did the public (29.6%). Additionally, they documented numerous other variations such as the following.

IIIA1.5a "The lowest scores were found for local police, fire, military, and medical authorities. . . . The highest levels of insight were evidenced by Directors of local Offices of Emergency Preparedness followed closely by local government and National Weather Service officials" (Wenger, James, and Faupel, 1980:91).

IIIA1.5b "There is a tendency for the officials to overestimate public insight into panic behavior and underestimate public awareness of convergence problems" (Wenger, James, and Faupel, 1980:91).

IIIA2. Local Emergency Management–Civil Defense Agencies

Through studies conducted at Iowa State University and the Disaster Research Center, some headway has been made toward our understanding of local civil defense agencies. Today, in most sections of the U.S.A. these units are referred to as "emergency management offices," signifying a broader conception of domain or responsibility. In a 1969 report, however, Anderson dissected field interview data pertaining to local and state civil defense offices and their relationships with federal level agencies. These data were collected during the course of nearly 70 Disaster Research Center post-event studies. They permitted an extensive mapping of this rather complex multilayered structure. And through links to the then emergent open-system theories of organization, he transformed these descriptive data into a series of important insights. His major conclusion was:

IIIA2.1 ". . . civil defense offices tend to be hampered by undue uncertainty with regard to many of their important organizational dimensions such as their authority relations, task domains, internal structures, and public support. And we will suggest that these sources of uncertainty generate operational difficulties for civil defense offices during disasters" (Anderson, 1969c:1).

Carrying this theme to greater specificity, he offered many additional interpretations, two of which strike me as logical points of departure for future studies, both of the American scene and cross-national comparisons. First, he identified four conditions that are most likely to be associated with successful local civil defense offices (IIIA2.1a). Second, he sensed a highly relevant environmental feature that undoubtedly impacts their functioning—community disaster subcultures (IIIA2.1b).

IIIA2.1a "The conditions which are most likely to be productive of successful involvement are as follows: 1. that local civil defense has developed previous experience in handling community disasters. . . . 2. that municipal government provides a structure which accepts and legitimizes the civil defense function. . . . 3. that the local civil defense director has the ability to generate significant pre-disaster relationships among those organizations which do become involved in emergency activities. . . . 4. that emergency-relevant resources, such as an emergency operations center, be provided and the knowledge of the availability of these resources is widespread through the community" (Anderson, 1969c:60-61).

IIIA2.1b "In disaster subcultural areas, civil defense offices often become one of the key organizations with regard to establishing and implementing emergency plans and procedures. Accordingly, the activity of civil defense offices in such areas is more likely to be defined as essential for the public welfare and they have a greater likelihood of being integrated into their communities. This greater institutionalization of civil defense in disaster subcultural areas often means that some of the uncertainty which characterizes such organizations in other communities is minimized" (Anderson, 1969c:13).

Equally significant has been the documentation of the shift in priorities and concept of mission that occurred during the late sixties and seventies.

IIIA2.2 Within the U.S.A., the concepts of dual use and all hazards—most recently comprehensive emergency management—define the mission of local civil defense–emergency management agencies.

This descriptive proposition reflects a national survey (n = 478) completed in the early seventies by Mulford, Klonglan, and their associates. This data base is unique and to date has not been replicated. Illustrative of the types of conclusions they published are these: ". . . preparedness for nuclear attack is not salient for most coordinators. One clear implication for DCPA is that appeals made to local coordinators on the basis of things a coordinator should do or be able to do in terms of the all-hazards approach are likely to be more readily acted upon than others" (Mulford, Klonglan, and Tweed, 1973:2).

IIIA2.3 Role conceptions and behavioral styles vary among local civil defense directors.

Despite this overall shift in planning emphasis and much intensification of a rhetoric of professionalism (Petak, 1984), diversity in role conception remains. To date, the most thorough documentation of this diversity has been provided by Dynes and Quarantelli (1975). They proposed that the following typology represents the mix found across American communities. Unfortunately, it has not been verified nor have data appeared that might designate the relative distribution across these types.

1. *Maintenance Model:* emphasis on maintaining resources which have been developed over time, such as facilities, supplies, and budget.
2. *Military Model:* emphasis on the necessity for military organization to cope with emergencies.
3. *Disaster Expert Model:* emphasis on a particular type of expert resource within the community.
4. *Administrative Staff Model:* emphasis on organizational skills.
5. *Derived Political Power Model:* emphasis on the necessity for coordination in emergency planning but the motivation for emergency planning is derived from the "imposition" of the mayor's authority.
6. *Interpersonal Broker Model:* emphasis on contacts and informal relationships among personnel in various emergency organizations.
7. *Abstract Planner Model:* emphasis on the development of planning based on a knowledge of various contingencies.
8. *Community Educator Model:* emphasis on overcoming community apathy toward planning.
9. *Disaster Simulation Model:* emphasis on the rehearsal of disaster plans. (Adapted from Dynes and Quarantelli, 1975:57-58.)

> IIIA2.4(H) The greater the degree of centrality of the local CD office within the emergency inter-organizational network, the greater the level of effectiveness.

While empirically untested with designs and measures that permitted my acceptance, several conclusions from both the Dynes and Quarantelli (1975) study and those conducted at Iowa State University point toward this hypothesis. These studies also offer many additional insights regarding the correlates of agency effectiveness and its consequences for directors, e.g., higher job satisfaction.

> IIIA2.4a *Characteristics of local offices which have legitimacy:* 1. Environmental factors, e.g., seasonal threats; 2. structural factors, e.g., location of the civil defense office within local government; 3. relational factors, e.g., the more extensive the relations inside and outside the local government structure, the more legitimacy is provided to the local office; 4. output factors, e.g., EOC's which provide a location for the collection of information about disaster impact. (Adapted from Dynes and Quarantelli, 1975:51–53.)

IIIA2.4b ". . . the most effective coordinators meet on a fairly regular basis with other local coordinators and with state and regional personnel. In addition, effective coordinators have higher levels of *job satisfaction;* i.e., their positions are *salient* for them. . . . the most effective coordinators are in agreement *(at consensus)* with local government officials and state personnel about the goals for the agency and the means to be used to accomplish the goals" (Mulford, Klonglan, and Tweed, 1973:8). (See also Klonglan, Mulford, and Faisal, 1973:5; Griffin, Mulford, and Klonglan, 1972:Summary; Mulford *et al.,* 1972:75; Mulford *et al.,* 1976/77:137.)

The diversity of local civil defense agencies was documented within the U.S.A. by a national survey directed by Hoetmer (1983a, b) under the auspices of the International City Management Association. "Surveys were sent to the chief administrative offices (CAOs) in all counties, to municipalities 10,000 and over in population, and to a regional sample of one out of eight municipalities under 10,000 in population" (Hoetmer, 1983a:11–12). This totaled 6,238 governmental jurisdictions out of the nearly 40,000 local governments in the United States (exclusive of school districts and other special districts). Returns from 1,579 governmental jurisdictions (25.3% return rate) clearly revealed the structural variety that depicts emergency management at the local level. While nearly all (83% of the cities; 93% of the counties) indicated that they had a disaster plan, the structural location of the *function* varied considerably.

"In cities, the city manager (reported by 22.5%), part-time emergency preparedness coordinator (18.8%), or the fire chief (16.2%) was most likely to have this responsibility. On the other hand, in counties, full-time emergency preparedness coordinators (44.3%) or part-time emergency preparedness coordinators (33.3%) were found to have the responsibility for emergency management. Only 32.7% of the cities responding had either a full-time or a part-time emergency preparedness coordinator" (Hoetmer, 1983b:1–2).

Clearly, this survey revealed both the non-standardized quality that characterizes American society and the unevenness regarding the relative priority given to emergency management (Drabek, 1985). Thus, the research team concluded that while some disaster planning was being done by local governments, it was hard to specify how comprehensive the planning was. A compilation of ideas received from the respondents highlight four key policy recommendations.

1. Have a regular comprehensive preparedness program. Keep it updated and know it.
2. Appoint a coordinator who will develop an active program with clearly defined duties and responsibilities.
3. Establish an Emergency Operations Center with full communication capabilities.

4. Place a high priority on public education. (Adapted from Hoetmer, 1983a:11.)

It awaits for future researchers to establish the degree to which local governments may respond to such recommendations, either because of recognized need or because of federal and state initiatives. The link between policies and actions taken at either of these two levels and alterations within local governments remains an important issue that few have explored. (See Mushkatel and Weschler, 1985.)

> IIIA2.5(H) The types of managerial strategies used by local CD office directors covary with environmental, organizational and coordinator characteristics. (Based on Mulford, Klonglan, and Kopachevsky, 1973:6.)

Similar to the preceding proposition, there are numerous clues in the literature that hint at the validity of this idea. To date it has been explored most carefully in the Iowa State University studies. But the conceptualization of such managerial strategies and their measurement remains a complex and important agenda item.

> IIIA2.5a *"The building resource' strategy* . . . is used to get local resources, especially when DCPA monies are not received to the degree desired. . . . DCPA organizations with resources practice constituency to control other organizations in their environment. . . . cooptation is used to establish relationships that will make the local environment more secure. [p. 6] . . . elite representation is used most often by coordinators who lack local support [p. 7]" (Mulford, Klonglan, and Kopachevsky, 1973:6, 7). (See also Hannigan and Kueneman, 1977, for analysis of strategies used by a state-level civil defense organization in Canada.)

Extensive training efforts for local CD coordinators were initiated by the Defense Civil Preparedness Agency (DCPA)—one of the predecessor agencies to the Federal Emergency Management Agency (FEMA). A questionnaire survey ($n = 128$) was completed by the Iowa State research team to ascertain the types of changes these experiences may have produced (four-phase courses).

> IIIA2.6 "The seven behavioral areas in which the LCDCs report having made significant changes were concerned with: (1) the involvement of more private organizations in civil preparedness work; (2) increasing the involvement of local public services in DCPA activities; (3) acquiring an access to the broadcast media; (4) establishing an emergency center for disaster operations; (5) the updating of equipment and procedures used in the EOC; (6) the development and revision of written disaster plans; and (7) coordinating the emergency planning activities of local official and community leaders. The two behavioral areas in which a lesser degree of impact was indicated were related to: (1) designing communication packages for specific audiences and (2) efforts to secure federal and state grants" (Klonglan, Mulford, and Hay, 1973:3).

Today, within the FEMA, the National Emergency Training Center located at Emmitsburg, Maryland, has continued the professionalization process for local and state personnel. Many new curricular designs and instructional formats are being explored. Hopefully, the knowledge base regarding their impacts will be more detailed and precise than that available from the "phase" course curriculum.

IIIA3. Hospital–Medical Units

Among the many components of the emergency social system in a community (Barton, 1962, 1969) are hospitals of various types and other medical units. Within the United States, testing and drills are commonplace, reflecting in part a formal certification requirement of the American Hospital Association. Yet, the knowledge base regarding the impacts of such efforts on behavioral responses during actual disasters remains a near void.

The extent of planning for specialized types of hospitals has been documented and found to be rather lacking. For example, a survey study of 100 Veterans Administration general hospitals secured the cooperation of 46. "Of these 46 hospitals, 22 had no specific plan at all for psychiatric casualties. Fourteen had a rudimentary plan comprising only a general statement to 'provide care' or to 'remain available' on the bed unit to receive casualties from the receiving area. Eight plans specifically called for mental health professionals in the triage area" (Martin, 1980:111).

The few empirical studies on hospital planning efforts that were captured through my search procedures identified inadequacies of various types. Most were rather general while others focused on specific problems (e.g., Star *et al.,* 1980, summarized innovations implemented for the Kennedy airport in New York City).

> IIIA3.1 ". . . most hospital disaster plans do not discuss the special problems associated with the treatment of chemical exposure victims. Moreover, health sector personnel are not aware of a clearinghouse or the equivalent of a poison-control center to contact for information and assistance" (Gray, 1981:364).

In contrast to event qualities or patient demands is the rather unique issue of hospital evacuation. Apparently, this is a matter that has yet to be reviewed carefully by most administrators. And currently, researchers offer little guidance.

> IIIA3.2 ". . . a hospital fire is treated somewhat differently from one in other types of buildings. Given a fire in a normal high rise, the first decision would be to evacuate. Given a fire in a hospital, the first decision is to attempt to avoid an evacuation if at all possible. . . . It is our conclusion— based on what we saw at St. Joseph's— that this approach to fighting fires in hospitals may not be entirely justified" [Canada] (Alldred, Hiscott, and Scanlon, 1982:vii).

IIIA3.3 "Dauphin County, just north of TMI, contained four hospitals ranging in distance from 9.5 to 13.5 miles from the stricken plant. Crash plans put into effect within 48 hours of the initial incident successfully reduced hospital census to below 50 per cent of capacity, but retained bedridden and critically ill patients within the risk-zone. No plans existed for area-wide evacuation of hospitalized patients. Future-oriented disaster planning should include resource files of host institution bed capacity and transportation capabilities for the crash evacuation of hospitalized patients during non-traditional disasters" (Maxwell, 1982:275).

Other types of inadequacies were reflected in such proposed innovations as the use of signs to guide volunteers and relatives during emergency responses. Both are quite likely to be present. Yet, even the extent to which actions as simple as these have been planned and rehearsed so as to be routinely put into place quickly has not been documented using nationally based samples of hospitals.

IIIA3.4 "Much of the portering and similar work in the hospital was done by volunteers, including patients, but these volunteers were hampered by a lack of knowledge of the topography of the hospital. This could have been minimized by better signposting (including portable signs when the function of a room had to be changed, such as the location of the temporary mortuary), and by the issue of simple ground plans of the hospital printed on postcards for the guidance of these workers" [Australia] (Gurd, Bromwich, and Quinn, 1975:642–643).

Finally, the lack of integration of specialized facilities and personnel has been noted. Available studies, like the reports by McIntire and Sadeghi (1977) or Hargreaves and her colleagues (1979), contain tones of criticism but provide few clues as to the extent of this problem.

IIIA4. First Responders

While some studies have been made of the behavioral responses of emergency organizational personnel once they get to the disaster scene—the topic of the next chapter—very little is known about *their use of* the types of information that planners have viewed as critical. For example, a DRC study of chemical emergencies documented that the mere presence of signs denoting hazardous substances was far from the total solution.

IIIA4.1(H) "When responding to transportation incidents, first responders do not always note hazardous materials placards and symbols. Even when they do notice them, they often do not fully understand their meaning" (Gray, 1981:360).

Furthermore, incidents like these and many others may precipitate unique sets of fears or anxieties among some rescue workers (Tokyo Fire Department, 1980). Although a few researchers, such as Mitchell (1982), have begun to explore this issue, the extent of such fears, possible mitigation alternatives, and their relative effectiveness remain unknown.

Py's (1978) laboratory studies of training simulations among fire department recruits in Paris nicely illustrates a research agenda that should include cross-national comparisons. After about one month of instruction that was focused largely on first aid, these recruits were informed of an oral examination. To reach the physician examiner they had to cross a "munitions dump"; they were dispatched in groups of two or three. As they made their way through several poorly lit passageways, one or more explosive sounds were heard. They then entered a simulated munitions workshop in which three actors were located; each had fictionalized but realistic appearing wounds, e.g., a leg severed below the knee with blood gushing out. After two minutes of response time, the course instructor critiqued the spontaneous reactions of the recruits.

Based on observation of 159 groups, each composed of two or three firemen, the responses by the first individual to arrive at the scene were coded as follows: (1) "effective actions"—39%; (2) "sensible" actions—35%, (3) "bizarre or frankly inappropriate" actions—2% and (4) "absence of action"—24% (Py, 1978:70). Thus, Py concluded that in such stressful situations, less than one-half of the recruits were capable of behaving in accordance with what they had been trained to do. Nearly one-fourth can be counted on to do nothing; however, bizarre actions are rare.

As with the studies of police communication under simulated disaster conditions that I (1965) directed while a DRC graduate student, Py's work illustrates a rich set of opportunities that few in the research community have yet to explore. One notable exception is the work of Belardo and his colleagues (1983) who capitalized on a unique circumstance. Less than a week after they had observed a full-scale training simulation, an actual crisis occurred at the Robert E. Ginna nuclear facility in upstate New York. Comparisons of the two responses across such qualities as stress perceptions and both the frequency and structure of communications indicated key similarities. "The qualitative similarity between the structure of communication networks suggests that simulation can serve as a training and research vehicle for the analysis of pairwise communication linkages during a crisis" (Belardo et al., 1983:600).

As microcomputers are used to link both internal and external resource bases for organizational managers—a major trend illustrated by Belardo, Karwan, and Wallace's (1984) study of decision support systems for four different types of disaster management organizations (American Red Cross, U.S. Coast Guard, a regional emergency medical organization, and the New York State Office of Disaster Preparedness)—the role and utility of such simulations can be enhanced greatly for both practitioners and researchers (see also Wallace and De Balogh, 1985). The Congressional Research Service (1984) report on *Information Technology for Emergency Management* documented a wide variety of new managerial aids that are now being implemented. Certainly a major component of the research agenda for the 1990s will be the assessment of the impacts of the adoption of these on both the planning and response phases of disaster.

IIIA5. Mental Health Agencies

During the mid-1970s, the need for expanding community disaster plans to include a mental health dimension was articulated with increased frequency. The literature contains numerous case histories like the school bus accident reviewed by Ciuca, Downie, and Morris (1977), which left 28 dead and 24 critically injured.

> "This event also dramatized the need for integration of a mental health team into the hospital disaster plan and designation of a place where family members can gather and professionals can assist them with their emotional crises. . . . Because of the tragic nature of the accident and the intensity of emotion involved, the staff at the disaster center had to deal with their own reactions as well. These reactions paralleled those of the families, although they were less intense" (Ciuca, Downie, and Morris, 1977:456).

But what specifically are the mental health needs that disaster planners should anticipate? A wide-ranging set of images have been propagated by professionals whose view of disaster was fixated on extreme cases like the horrifying flash flood that struck Buffalo Creek, West Virginia, in 1972. Using case reports from that incident (e.g., Titchner and Kapp, 1976; Erikson, 1976a), some envisioned acute mental health needs as an organizational planning requirement. Others, taking a broader view of the range of cases—wherein both the type and volume of potential mental health needs would vary considerably—have seen the requirement very differently. Presently, the following assessment appears to be a reasonable one for planning purposes. It must be stressed, however, that future empirical validation across a range of events with differing qualities may indicate marked variations.

> IIIA5.1 "Planning for the management of all of these issues at the receiving hospital level requires a disaster plan considerably different from the typical disaster plan of many general hospitals. . . . [1.] The problem, therefore, is not to devise disaster plans for hospitals designed to deal with individuals who have become psychotic or have decompensated into hysterical reactions or panic, since there is not significant incidence of such response in disasters. . . . [2.] individuals who have sustained sudden severe losses and disruptions in their lives are under intense stress and may be suffering from acute grief and/or severe anxiety. [3.] Rescue workers and relief workers may also be subject to high levels of emotional tension, from which some may need to muster psychological defenses to such a degree as to produce maladaptive behaviors and prevent the appropriate psychological integration of their experiences. [p. 111] . . .

[4.] The plan recognizes that mental illness requiring hospitalization is the least important and least significant role for mental health services during disasters. The emphasis should be directed toward providing support and appropriate intervention to all involved in helping them deal with the various psychological stresses encountered during disasters [p. 113]" (Martin, 1980:111, 113).

By the end of the seventies, several individuals had identified elements of an overall "disaster counseling philosophy" that could serve as a general set of guidelines for planners.

IIIA5.2 "Underlying Principles Supporting Guidelines . . . [1.] Crisis counselors should assume that victims are potentially capable of handling their own problems after being helped to recognize barriers to solutions . . . [2.] Counselors should discourage dependence upon them, . . . [3.] Advice should generally be given with caution, . . . [4.] Crisis intervention focuses on current life problems. Victims need help in resolving the present crisis produced by the disaster. They need to talk about the 'here and now' " (Cohen and Ahearn, 1980:75–76). (See also Peter McDonald, 1979:130.)

These planning guidelines have been implemented, although the extent of such remains unknown. So too is the relative degree of their effectiveness. By 1981, however, a few reports were appearing wherein these frameworks were acknowledged as helpful.

"Cohen and Ahearn's (1980) recent monograph offers a generalizable framework to assess delivery of mental health services after disasters. This framework includes the following components: 1) knowledge; 2) sanction and support; 3) information-assessment; 4) action; 5) evaluation. In an effort to move toward greater congruence in the literature on disasters, the Cincinnati Plan, which evolved historically from a clinical base, is analyzed from this community organization perspective" (Lindy and Lindy, 1981:18).

Acknowledging that disaster victims typically do not request services from mental health agencies, Hartsough (1982) formulated five key barriers that mental health planners must recognize. Presumably, failure to overcome these will impair program effectiveness.

IIIA5.3 "Since conducting a mental health response to community disasters is a change for most centers, it is appropriate to examine the barriers likely to impede progress toward the goal. Five barriers can be identified, one of which is external to the system and four of which are internal: (a) lack of sufficient external resources to support a disaster program; (b) lack of information on the mental health needs of disaster victims; (c) lack of an intervention method matched to the needs of victims; (d) lack of linkage with the community network that manages disaster relief; and (e) lack of guidelines for a long-range disaster response plan" (Hartsough, 1982:256).

IIIA6. Media Organizations

Two major studies reported a series of conclusions regarding media organizations and disaster planning. First, using DRC data from 12 U.S. cities, Kueneman and Wright (1975) documented several behavior patterns among 72 media organizations. Three hypotheses summarize these.

IIIA6.1(H) An expectation of public excitability guides broadcast decisions of media personnel. (Based on Kueneman and Wright, 1975:671.)

IIIA6.2(H) Media organizations approach disasters and civil disturbances with different planning assumptions. (Based on Kueneman and Wright, 1975: 674–675.)

IIIA6.3(H) The greater the impact of a disaster on a media organization, the greater the amount of changes made in subsequent disaster planning. (Based on Kueneman and Wright, 1975:676, 677.)

This last hypothesis must be qualified, however. Although most media organizations (i.e., 80%) made changes of some type (48% mechanical; 58% operational; and 28% both), not all forms of disaster (i.e., civil disturbances vs. natural) had comparable impacts. Also, whether or not a disaster subculture existed (e.g., Moore, 1956) constrained the force of impact. So did the degree to which a perception of public excitability was present. Thus, once again the fundamental taxonomic issue outlined in Chapter 1—"types of disasters"—reappears. Specification of the ranges of generalization for these findings, like the others, is precluded until the research community better solves the problem of a disaster taxonomy.

IIIA6.3a "Seventy-eight percent of the stations reporting no perception of public excitability indicated that they had made no changes of any kind, while only 9% of those reporting any excitability indicated no changes" (Kueneman and Wright, 1975:676).

IIIA6.3b "Changes were found to be significantly related to disaster experience but not to civil disturbance experience" (Kueneman and Wright, 1975:677).

IIIA6.3c "Changes were also found to be related to the presence of a disaster subculture. Without one, 66% of the stations reported changes, while with a disaster subculture, 91% indicated that changes were made" (Kueneman and Wright, 1975:677).

IIIA6.3d ". . . going off the air occasions dramatic shifts in the occurrence and nature of changes. Twenty-seven percent report no changes if they have not gone off the air, while only 8% report none if they have gone off the air" (Kueneman and Wright, 1975:677).

The second study—analyses by Turner et al. (1981)—suggested the following hypothesis derived from responses by Los Angeles media to preparedness issues during the mid-seventies (1976–1978).

IIIA6.4(H) The greater the extent to which prepackaged materials are available, the greater the impact of media reports on public preparedness. (Based on Turner *et al.*, 1981:15.)

The following conclusions illustrate the types of variables that may constrain the media's content and its public impact.

IIIA6.4a "Prepackaged materials were available generally when an organization had interests at stake, so published accounts may have overstated the extent of public and private organizational earthquake preparedness" (Turner *et al.*, 1981:15).

IIIA6.4b "Since no organization has a specific stake in individual and household earthquake preparedness, treatments of this topic appeared only after much delay, and they lack the sustained and cumulative nature of some other topics" (Turner *et al.*, 1981:15).

IIIA7. Schools

Two conclusions—one behavioral and one a planning guideline—appeared within the data base. Neither the extent of school disaster planning nor explorations of patterned variation have yet to capture the attention of the behavioral research community.

IIIA7.1 "Except for the scattered responses of individual teachers and officials, the public schools did not initiate programs or intensify vigilance on the basis of the Uplift" (Turner *et al.*, 1981:19).

IIIA7.2 "The following guidelines should be considered when working with students from a disaster stricken community. [1.] *Maintain Focus.* While the entire community may represent a group with which to work, the mental health worker should respond to the demonstrated needs of students in the school. . . . [2.] *Encourage the Victim.* While a disaster may immobilize its victims, school children should be encouraged to participate in the day-to-day learning activities of the classroom. . . . [3.] *Support from Adults.* Research has indicated that children and adolescents respond favorably to open and honest communication from adults. The mental health worker's role is to involve the teaching staff and other adult school workers in providing this much needed emotional support while serving as a stabilizing force. [4.] *Confront the Crisis.* . . . The mental health worker can assist school children to ventilate inner feelings and adjust to the loss. [5.] *Honest Appraisal.* . . . In many instances, the victim's world will never be the same and statements to the contrary instill false hope. . . . [6.] *Develop Support Systems.* . . . [7.] *Consult with Teachers.* The mental health worker should be active in organizing the school's response to the environmental disaster" (Crabbs, 1981:166).

IVA. Community System Level

At the dawn of the 1980s, the community disaster planning scene in the U.S.A. was a mixed picture. At least that was the portrait that emerged from several surveys. There was some good news. For example, Quarantelli and Tierney (1979a) highlighted the following trends in local disaster planning:

> ". . . 1) a broadening of the scope of disaster planning to include more potential community crises; 2) a decreasing willingness on the part of local civil defense personnel to extend nuclear emergency planning to cover all types of community emergencies; 3) an increasing emphasis on the survival of the local community, rather than on national security; 4) an increase in the degree of integration among local disaster planning organizations actively engaged in planning; and 5) an increase in the degree of integration among local disaster planning organizations" (Quarantelli and Tierney, 1979a:272).

In sharp contrast, however, were reports focused on more specific topics—sheltering and emergency medical services, for example. Regarding sheltering, Quarantelli (1982a) offered this assessment.

> "To the extent that temporary sheltering planning is undertaken, it is often fragmented among various emergency organizations, and generally incomplete. There seems to be little consensus on which community organizations should be involved and which should be the lead agency in preparing for temporary sheltering. Congressional mandate and tradition may give the local Red Cross chapter a major responsibility for the problem, but this is not always known or accepted, especially outside of the larger metropolitan areas" (Quarantelli, 1982a:74).

Dynes was even more critical following his extensive review of the EMS planning literature.

> "Exceptions can be found, but the current disaster-relevant EMS literature is almost useless for planning purposes in connection with mass casualty situations; it is generally very limited and selective in coverage, has an administrative focus or bias, ignores many real operational problems, and rests in the main on impressions derived from single case anecdotal accounts" (Dynes, 1979:57).

Basing his conclusions on 21 field studies by DRC, Dynes identified four principal qualities that characterized the inadequacies of the EMS facet of community disaster planning:

> "[1.] Few localities and their health care system have undertaken realistic and overall planning for handling large numbers of casualties; . . . [2.] There is widespread lack of basic knowledge about the overall EMS system in almost all communities . . . [3.] Political considerations enter into all aspects of EMS planning . . . [4.] Few EMS systems have any institutionalized mechanisms for learning from disaster experiences" (Dynes, 1979:57).

Shifting to a specific event, field studies documented the ways that local officials were warned of the increased probability of a destructive eruption by Mount St. Helens (e.g., Perry and Greene, 1983; Drabek et al., 1981). Many forms of community planning took place. Had they not, the loss of life undoubtedly would have been greater. Yet, beyond the scene of the blast itself, few were prepared for the ash-filled cloud and the consequences it brought. Based on extensive interviewing in Ellensburg, Ritzville, and Cheney, Washington, and Missoula, Montana, Warrick *et al.* (1981) rounded out the picture of community planning in America as it existed at the end of the decade.

> "Of all the individuals queried in the study sites, *only a few claimed prior knowledge of ashfall hazard to their community, or of impacts of volcanic ash or the possible adjustments to it.* No one interviewed was aware of the existence of volcanic hazard maps. [p. 102] . . . the lack of response was due, in part, to three deficiencies of the warning message: first, the message was not specific about areas to be affected by ashfall; second, no specific precautionary actions or procedures were prescribed; and third, the warning lacked a sense of urgency [p. 103]" (Warrick *et al.,* 1981:102, 103).

After reviewing the coded findings, trying several organizational typologies, and revising them considerably, I derived eight major themes into which this diverse array of conclusions seemed to cluster: (1) the planning payoff; (2) event variability; (3) planning principles; (4) unique requirements of disaster planning; (5) community mental health planning; (6) major planning weaknesses; (7) variability in extent of planning; (8) community acceptance of planning.

IVA1. The Planning Payoff

Why engage in community disaster planning? What evidence is there that planning done prior to a disaster has any payoff? Based on reviews of several case studies, our earlier inventory proposed:

> IVA1.1 "In communities where particular disaster related functions have been assigned to specific organizations as a result of the planning process, there is less post-impact confusion regarding responsibility and communication channels" (Mileti, Drabek, and Haas, 1975:21).

More recent studies indicate support for this general premise, although the matter has yet to be tied down with much precision.

> IVA1.1a ". . . the stronger and more well defined that interorganizational linkages are prior to an event, the 'smoother' subsequent evacuation related activities will go. For example, in a chlorine barge incident studied by DRC, the local civil defense office had developed a pattern of ongoing interaction with other agencies long before the event. At the time of the incident it easily emerged as the legitimate local coordinating authority, a situation which facilitated the response of other local organizations involved in the evacuation which eventually took place" (Quarantelli, 1980b:50–51). (See also Wolensky, 1977.)

> IVA1.1b "In 1976 the province of Ontario abolished its Emergency Measures Act. This was the act which required all municipalities to have

an emergency plan. . . . The data on both Niagara and Prince Edward County suggest that emergency planning is necessary. Without it unexpected events such as a severe snowstorm are not dealt with in a coordinated, effective way. . . . A point-by-point examination of some of the problems of both regions suggests that Niagara, with planning, functioned better on the whole than did Prince Edward County, without it. . . . in four key areas— roads, police, fire, some social services, and in the use of the militia— Niagara, because of planning, was better off than Prince Edward County, at least in the sense of a controlled and co-ordinated response to an emergency'' [Canada] (Scanlon and Taylor, 1977:1).

IVA1.2 "Once emergency plans are in existence, they have a reasonably high legacy value in that they are usable in the future and, at least in part, against emergencies other than those for which they were more specifically designed'' (Nehnevajsa and Wong, 1977:155).

Planning for a wide variety of potential threats—the basic premise implicit in the concept of ''comprehensive emergency management''—may have generalizable power. Field data and operational experience have led many to agree with this premise, but exceptional cases—recall Veblen's ''trained incapacity''—await specification.

IVA2. Event Variability

As noted at the outset of this chapter, community planners must recognize that disasters vary along several dimensions; these may have important behavioral consequences (Fritz, 1961; Barton, 1969; Drabek, 1970; Mileti, Drabek, and Haas, 1975:4–5).

IVA2.1 ". . . differing types of disaster agents produce contrasting kinds of community responses. . . . attributed to the characteristics of the events, i.e., the amount of warning given, their scope, duration and intensity and, in addition, to the normative context in which the emergency arises'' (Warheit, 1972:138).

Dynes (1970a:52–55) proposed nine features in which disaster agents differ: (1) *frequency,* (2) *predictability,* (3) *controllability,* (4) *cause,* (5) *speed of onset,* (6) *length of possible forewarning,* (7) *duration,* (8) *scope of impact,* and (9) *destructive potential.* More recently numerous other analytic schemes have been proposed, although none have gained widespread acceptance.

Three concepts appear to be especially critical: (1) event magnitude; (2) adaptive capacity of impacted system; and (3) normative context. For example, Foster (1976:241–245) proposed to use the life-event stress scales as an analogy to develop a scale of event magnitude using four criteria: (1) number of fatalities, (2) number of seriously injured, (3) infrastructural stress, (4) total population affected. Similarly, Schulberg (1974) argued effectively for the inclusion of the second variable, i.e., adaptive capacity: ". . . the probability of disaster can be viewed as a function of the degree of danger inherent in a hazardous situation *times* the risk of people being exposed to it *times* the vulnerability, or adaptive capacity, of affected persons" (Schulberg, 1974:86). And finally, Warheit (1972) stressed the normative context. "This varying normative consensus (and dissensus) which provides the operational context for a community's emergency subsystem is perhaps the most important difference between natural disasters and civil disturbances" (Warheit, 1972:134).

To a limited extent, the concept of collective stress (Barton, 1969; Haas and Drabek, 1973) offers conceptual integration—that is, assessing the state of a system as denoted by the discrepancy between disaster-generated demands and capacity. More recently, Rossi *et al.* (1978) have operationalized impact ratios, i.e., ratios of damages to available resources. But as Kreps (1981) noted, this is but one of the dimensions implicit in the stress concept. Furthermore, none of these attributes reflects qualities like the degree of victim horrification (Titchener and Kapp, 1976), potential for future occurrence, or control over future impact (Berren, Beigel, and Ghertner, 1980).

The most precise measurement system I encountered was used by Geipel (1982) in his study of 60 communities following the earthquakes (May 6 and September 15, 1976) that struck the Friuli region in northeastern Italy. To examine the differential patterns in the recovery process among these communities, he constructed an index that aggregated five qualities:

1. percentage of dead out of total population of commune;
2. percentage of homeless on May 6, 1976, within a commune;
3. percentage of homeless on September 15, 1976, within a commune;
4. percentage of commune population that was evacuated by December 18, 1976;
5. percentage of people in the commune living in prefab housing on May 1, 1977. [Italy] (Adapted from Geipel, 1982:30.)

IVA3. Planning Principles

IVA3.1 Everyday measures used for ordinary emergencies can not be extrapolated for use in major disasters. (Based on Quarantelli and Tierney, 1979a, and Quarantelli, 1984.)

As noted above (IIIA1.1), many officials who direct local emergency agencies continue to assume that expansion of the routine will meet the needs generated by disaster. This is not the case, however. Why? Because conditions are changed. That is, disasters differ from more routine emergencies because of at least six qualities: (1) uncertainty; (2) urgency; (3) the development of an emergency consensus; (4) expansion of the citizenship role; (5) convergence; and (6) de-emphasis of contractual and impersonal relationships. (Adapted from Dynes, Quarantelli, and Kreps, 1972:48–49.)

Disaster Research Center studies have produced two other key principles.

IVA3.2 ". . . community . . . disaster planning typically or usually assumes that people should adjust to the planning or the plans. . . . Realistic disaster planning requires that plans be adjusted to people and not that people be forced to adjust to plans" (Quarantelli, 1981d:2-3). (See also Quarantelli, 1984.)

IVA3.3 ". . . it is a mistake to equate disaster planning with the drawing up or the production of written plans. [p. 2-3] . . . Studies show that disaster preparedness planning is most effective when officials view the planning activities as an unending process [p. 2-4]" (Quarantelli, 1981d:2–3, 2–4). (See also Quarantelli, 1981a:2; Perry, 1979c:447.)

Reflecting agreement with the basic conclusions from the American research literature, Hultaker and Trost (1978) have proposed that Swedish disaster planners ought to be aware that they may be basing their efforts on myths about human behavior. "Lack of knowledge about disaster may lead to incorrect preparations: planners will plan for difficulties which will not occur while they will disregard the real difficulties" [Sweden] (Hultaker and Trost, 1978:9).

IVA3.4 The greater the degree that disaster plans reflect myths about social behavioral responses, the greater the likelihood they will be ineffective.

Adding precision to this general proposition, Dynes, Quarantelli, and Kreps (1972) have specified many of the myths that commonly have led to a planner's downfall.

IVA3.4a "Information about dangers should be disseminated and not withheld because of a fear that people will panic" (Dynes, Quarantelli and Kreps, 1972:31).

IVA3.4b "It should be assumed that persons in disaster-impacted areas actively respond to the emergency and will not wait for community officials to tell them what to do" (Dynes, Quarantelli, and Kreps, 1972:32).

What can be said in the way of direct advice? Several types of prescriptions have been offered. Among the best of these are the following eight points:

IVA3.5 *"Planning for Disasters* . . . [1.] Plans must not therefore be made in isolation by any one service. There must, during the planning stage, be frequent discussions between all services and organisations likely to become involved in a joint intervention at a disaster. . . . [2.] Planning can best be achieved by the establishment of a Joint Services Planning Committee on which the fire, police, ambulance, hospital and local authority organisations are represented. . . . [3.] . . . plans must also link in with the plans of surrounding areas especially in the field of casualty documentation and press liaison procedures. . . . [4.] Whilst incidents can cover a vast field it is important that there should be only one overall general plan which must be kept simple, short and concise. . . . [5.] . . . the major incident plan should be based on everyday working methods and procedures . . . [6.] Plans must be kept flexible, thereby permitting a supervisory officer to readily adapt the basic procedures to suit the incident at hand. . . . [7.] Planning is a continuous process. . . . [8.] The personal name of an officer should not be mentioned in the plan, the official appointment, the position involved, should be used instead" [England] (Fisher, 1978:46–47).

In a somewhat similar vein, Tierney identified four qualities that characterize a good disaster plan.

IVA3.6 ". . . a good plan is [1.] based on *realistic expectations*. Similarly, a good plan is [2.] brief and *concise:* . . . [3.] details a response that can be expanded by *stages,* calling up resources as needed and avoiding the potentially disruptive effects of overresponse and convergence at the site. . . . [4.] possesses an *official stamp of authority"* (Tierney, 1980:100– 101).

Finally, Quarantelli (1981a:2) emphasizes that ". . . planning is not management and management is not planning. . . . If we continue our military analogy, the principles of disaster planning refer to the general strategy whereas the principles of emergency management have reference to the tactics which need to be considered in the situation" (Quarantelli, 1981a:2). Pushing this theme he juxtaposed the principles of disaster planning against those he views as comprising emergency management.

IVA3.7 Disaster planning differs from emergency management in both content and implementation. (Based on Quarantelli, 1981a, 1980b, 1984.)

The substance of the proposition is best understood by the juxtaposition of the two following conclusions.

IVA3.7a "Principles of disaster planning: a. A continuous process; b. Reducing the unknowns in a problematical situation; c. Evoking appropriate actions; d. What is likely to happen; e. Based on valid knowledge; f. Focused on general principles; g. An educational activity; h. Overcoming resistances; i. Testing; j. Not management" (Quarantelli, 1981a:Contents). (See also Quarantelli, 1984.)

IVA3.7b "Principles of emergency management: (1) Agent-generated demands; a. Warning; b. Pre-impact preparations; c. Search and rescue; d. Care of injured and dead; e. Welfare needs; f. Restoration of essential community services; g. Protection against continuing threat; h. Community order. (2) Response-generated demands; a. Communication;

b. Continuing assessment of disaster situation; c. Mobilization and utilization of human and material resources; d. Coordination; e. Exercise
of authority'' (Quarantelli, 1981a:Contents).

Arguing that a "command and control" response model is inappropriate,
Dynes (1983) formulated seven "implications" that point toward an alternative—what he labels an "emergent human resources model." "The
basic assumption in the emergent human resources model is that the local
social system is the logical and viable base for emergency action, rather
than that the local system must be held together by strengthened centralized control" (Dynes, 1983:659). Thus, those responsible for planning
should: (1) utilize existing habit patterns as the basis for emergency action;
(2) utilize existing social units, rather than create new *ad hoc* ones; (3) if
outside resources are needed, employ resources that are consistent with
local sociocultural practices; (4) utilize the existing authority structure,
rather than create new ones; (5) utilize existing channels of communication
and increase them, rather than restrict and narrow them to "official messages"; (6) recognize that the aim of any emergency planning is to move
back to "normal" as quickly as possible; and (7) not regard the recovery
stage as the opportunity for massive (and directed) social change. (Adapted
from Dynes, 1983:659.)

Coming at the matter from a somewhat different vantage point, Perry
(1984) identified six requirements that are minimal criteria for assessing
the degree of community preparedness. He offered these to practitioners,
but I suspect that they may be useful to researchers who should construct
better measurement tools for this dimension of disaster response.

IVA3.8 "Six aspects of the process of responding to emergencies have
been selected as evaluative criteria: the problem of notification, damage
assessment, public information, protective strategy, responsibility for
planning and operations, and personnel training" (Perry, 1984:20).

IVA4. Unique Requirements of Disaster Planning

After reviewing the many observations about community level planning,
I was struck by several dimensions that different writers have viewed as
critical. These had to do with such features as evacuation incentives, interorganizational relations, and recognition that the role of local government varies at different phases in the disaster response.

IVA4.1(H) The greater the degree that local communities incorporate
incentives to evacuate in their community disaster planning, the greater
the effectiveness of an actual evacuation effort. (Based on Perry,
1979c:443–46.)

What are some examples of evacuation incentives? Perry has identified
several which seem to square with the *implications* of the literature. Among
these are such ideas as informing citizens of prior evacuation planning so

that they would know about preplanned escape routes and the establishment of message centers so that family members could communicate if they became separated. To date, none of these ideas have been subjected to careful empirical testing, however.

Although family relationships are a core planning constraint, the single most critical variable affecting the quality of community response is interorganizational relations.

> IVA4.2 "Reaction to the disaster thus transforms the social structure of the community. As existing organizations take on new roles, assume heightened importance, or cease operation entirely, and as new organizations appear, the normal system of coordination no longer works. Each organization has to adapt itself to a radically changed environment by negotiating a special domain for the emergency." (Dynes, 1978). (See also Weller, 1972; Dynes, 1978; Drabek et al., 1981; Quarantelli, 1984.)

There are several ways that the planning process can impact the quality of the interorganizational network. Based on her review of emergency medical systems, Neff (1977:187–188) identified three mechanisms whereby coordination might be improved, e.g., establishment of a central communications network.

Without question, communications capabilities play a critical role in constraining the quality of any interorganizational network. Coultrip (1974) highlighted this point in an analysis of the response to the earthquake in Managua (1972). It is verified through numerous case studies, especially those prepared by Scanlon (1981, 1982).

In addition, the degree of domain consensus among organizations comprising the network is critical. But it is clear that not all topics, functions, or responsibilities are equally dealt with in the turf management and domain negotiation processes that the disaster planning process probably reflects.

> IVA4.2a "Within the communities, there seemed to be considerable consensus on the responsibility of organizations to become involved in the range of operational disaster tasks. . . . There is less consensus on: [1.] responsibility for pre-disaster planning and for community coordination. . . . [2.] tasks of great complexity, such as warning and evacuation. . . . [3.] tasks which have little continuity to pre-disaster experience" (Dynes and Quarantelli, 1975:32).

> IVA4.3(H) The effectiveness of community disaster plans varies with the degree that there is recognition that disaster-related tasks vary across the temporal phases of response and alternative mixes of organizational coalitions will have varying degrees of involvement. (Based on Wolensky, 1977.)

This proposition has important planning implications and merits much further empirical exploration along the lines initiated by Wolensky (1977). His data suggested that the role of civil defense agencies varied considerably across the three disaster phases.

IVA4.3a "During the *pre-disaster stage*, the primary concerns with custodial tasks were mainly property-related and the most often mentioned
was 'sandbagging' . . . CD assumed primary leadership responsibilities
for the duration of the immediate predisaster, and did not work in close
cooperation with officials" (Wolensky, 1977:272).

IVA4.3b "During the postdisaster stage custodial tasks were the top
priority and received the largest average number of references. [p. 272]
. . . CD continued in the primary leadership role and one CD executive
commented that many officials were very reluctant to reassume authority
in their communities [p. 273]" (Wolensky, 1977:272, 273).

IVA4.3c "In the *recovery stage*, administrative tasks were the main concern with custodial tasks following close behind. But because administrative matters were largely in the hands of more than two dozen state
and federal agencies, and because most officials were part-time employees
of the city, municipal professionals and semi-professionals carried most
of this responsibility" (Wolensky, 1977:273).

IVA4.4(H) The effectiveness of community disaster plans covaries with
the degree that the authority is positional rather than person specific.

Many case studies of community response document that disasters rarely
happen at convenient times. Hence, as Scanlon (1979:135) documented
in the Darwin Australia response to Cyclone Tracy reflected two problems.
"The first was that before the storm the plan wasn't followed. The second
was that after the storm hit—none of the key people were readily available
to make it work." Recognizing this, Foster (1980:183) has stressed this
point in his advice on how to plan. Curiously, the literature does not contain a rigorous test of the more general hypothesis.

IVA4.5(H) The effectiveness of community disaster plans covaries with
the degree that the planning anticipates volunteer responses and integrates
them into the formal community system. (Based on Quarantelli, 1981b:10.)

As will be detailed in the next chapter, volunteers seem to come out
of the woodwork when disasters strike. Yet, their integration remains
problematic as does specification of the precise mechanisms whereby the
process might be facilitated (for Japanese survey data regarding public
expectations of post-disaster activities, see Shimada, 1972).

IVA5. Community Mental Health Planning

As noted above (organizational level, IIIA5), mental health needs of disaster victims gained increased visibility during the seventies. And as might
be expected, alternative views regarding the extent of these needs emerged.
Indeed, Baisden and Quarantelli (1981:197) concluded that "There are
two competing models in the mental health sector on the organization of
mental health services in disasters. One is essentially a medical treatment

model, the other is a social service delivery model." Thus, recommendations for community disaster planners vary considerably, reflecting alternative definitions of this problem and its solution.

> IVA5.1(H) Community disaster planning effectiveness varies *negatively*
> with the degree that it is ". . . focused on the organization of post-impact
> programs around clinically oriented mental health specialists delivering
> traditional mental health services" (Baisden and Quarantelli, (1981:197).

While much more study is required, there are dimensions of this hypothesis that have been documented. For example, while some victims
will acknowledge emotional problems of some sort, few will seek aid from
mental health professionals (e.g., see Cohen and Poulshock, 1977:266;
Leivesley, 1977b:213; Crabbs and Heffron, 1981:381; Butcher, 1980:1260).

> IVA5.1a "A third of those interviewed indicated that the disaster had
> caused emotional and social changes in members of their family, but
> most felt that such symptoms were natural and would disappear in time.
> Less than 10 per cent of the victims who reported symptoms of emotional
> stress said they would see a mental health professional for those problems.
> Most said they would prefer talking to a relative, a clergyman, or their
> family doctor" (Brownstone *et al.*, 1977:31).

What has been found regarding the types of planning that have been
initiated? After reviewing data from numerous U.S. communities that
Disaster Research Center staff had surveyed, the emergent picture is one
of limited awareness and minimal specificity.

> "Informants in disaster-stricken towns believe that disaster generally in-
> creases stress and adds to community problems. Additionally, informants
> endorse the notion that counseling assistance of some sort should be
> given to disaster victims to mitigate the stress they experience. Beyond
> stating that such counseling should be informal, short-term, and oriented
> to solving problems, few had any specific observations about how a dis-
> aster mental health program should be carried out" (Tierney and Baisden,
> 1979:107).

The situation is in a state of flux, however. It appears clear that the
mental health community has identified disaster responses as a new turf—
an area for domain expansion. The key question for the 1980s is, which
emphases will prevail?

> IVA5.2(H) Community disaster planning effectiveness varies with the
> degree to which mental health programming emphasizes a multipronged
> approach that recognizes variation among victim needs and emphasizes
> pre-existing group support systems.

There are many issues implicit in this hypothesis. But the two premises
from which it begins are ". . . that for the most part, community residents
provided for most of their own psychosocial needs prior to the disaster,
these needs were not met through agency intervention. Second, it is likely

that residents will do so following the disaster if the ecology of intervention efforts, such as in resettlement and temporary shelter programs, permits it" (Harshbarger, 1974:58).

> IVA5.3(H) The effectiveness of community mental health disaster responses will be increased if planning has been developed prior to the event. (Based on Zarle, Hartsough, and Ottinger, 1974:319–320.)

Heffron (1977b) proposed several guidelines for community mental health disaster planning. These still signified the state of the art by the mid-eighties. Each element implies a series of empirical studies, however, before it can be accepted uncritically.

1. Disaster intervention programs should adopt a preventative approach in working with victims. In most circumstances, those who actually develop incapacitating illness will represent a small minority of the disaster-affected population.
2. Community stereotypes relative to the concepts of mental health and mental illness may influence the success of a disaster intervention program. While there is little doubt that victims do experience serious emotional crises, in general they do not look upon themselves as in need of mental health services. In fact, there is a tendency for victims to reject offers of help by mental health personnel.
3. To be most effective, crisis workers should employ an aggressive outreach approach bringing services to the disaster victims. Outreach Counselors would often encounter elderly residents who needed help with a variety of problems. Once plugged into the community recovery programs, they were able to begin the recovery process and needed relatively little further aid.
4. Crisis workers involved directly in disaster intervention programs should be sensitive, not only to the emotional needs and reactions of the victims, but also to the potential stresses on the helpers. (Adapted from Heffron, 1977b:108–110.)

IVA6. Major Planning Weaknesses

What mistakes are most commonly made by disaster planners? Based on a review of 71 plans and in-depth interviews with 50 planning officials, Wenger, James, and Faupel (1980) identified several pitfalls.

> IVA6.1 ". . . there is a tendency on the part of officials to see disaster planning as a product, not a process" (Wenger, James, and Faupel, 1980:156).

> IVA6.2 "Too often, disaster planning is isolated from the day-to-day planning process. It is often assigned to organizations, or units within organizations, that are divorced from traditional, institutionalized sources of social power within the community" (Wenger, James, and Faupel, 1980:156).

IVA6.3 ". . . these plans include almost no expectations for public behavior during a disaster. Furthermore, when attention is given to public
response, it is generally predicated on erroneous conceptions of public
behavior" (Wenger, James, and Faupel, 1980:155).

These insights complement those offered earlier by Dynes, Quarantelli,
and Kreps (1972), although the empirical base they had used was defined
less precisely. Nevertheless, their observations shed much light on the
structural processes of failure. In a few cases, these have been explored
further by other researchers as noted by the references interspersed below.

IVA6.4 "In many communities, disaster plans do not specifically assign
an official or an organization with the responsibility of assessing what
the *overall* emergency is and what it means" (Dynes, Quarantelli, and
Kreps, 1972:77).

IVA6.5 "Arrangements for disseminating emergency information to all
crisis relevant organizations, mass media sources, and the general public
are frequently missing from disaster plans" (Dynes, Quarantelli, and
Kreps, 1972:77).

IVA6.6 "Some disaster plans do not call for the establishment of some
kind of command post at the disaster scene or point of greatest impact"
(Dynes, Quarantelli, and Kreps, 1972:77). (See also Theoret, 1979:213–
216.)

IVA6.7 "Much disaster planning does not adequately deal with the problem of interorganizational coordination at the time of a community emergency" (Dynes, Quarantelli, and Kreps, 1972:78). (See also Dynes and
Quarantelli, 1975:34.)

IVA6.8 "New emergency domains are often either inadequately specified
or not covered at all in some disaster plans" (Dynes, Quarantelli, and
Kreps, 1972:78).

IVA6.9 "Very few disaster plans take into account the transition from
the emergency period to the recovery period and almost none deal with
the inevitable movement to normalcy" (Dynes, Quarantelli, and Kreps,
1972:79).

IVA6.10 "Disaster plans too often remain paper plans and are not rehearsed in whole or in part" (Dynes, Quarantelli, and Kreps, 1972:79).
(See also Worth and McLuckie, 1977:73; Holloway, 1977:138, 145.)

IVA7. Variability in Extent of Planning

Following the 1974 Federal Disaster Act, all 50 states received federal
grants to enhance their disaster planning efforts. Most adopted, if they
had not done so previously, a version of a model act, which included
provisions mandating local governments to meet minimal disaster planning
criteria. The impact of these actions on local communities is an obvious
research agenda item for the 1980s.

But looking backwards in time through the literature I reviewed can provide some insight into the question of variability among American communities regarding their disaster planning efforts—albeit rather limited. A rather general assessment was offered by a former DRC staff member.

> "I have stated a minimal condition for organized preparedness efforts— agreement on the need for preparedness—only exists to a moderate degree in the communities we studied. I have suggested the prevailing social climate does not, on the whole, encourage community sectors to pool their resources and plan together. . . . It should, thus, come as no surprise that disaster preparedness at the community level is not highly developed at the present time" (Tierney, 1981:340).

In equally global terms, Quarantelli offered this view after he completed a rather extensive review of studies conducted on post-disaster sheltering.

> ". . . differential attention is paid in American communities to preparing for the different kinds of sheltering and housing problems. Overall, there is little planning of any kind, but to the extent there is any local com- munity-level planning, it appears aimed at temporary sheltering. The problem of housing disaster victims, whether on a temporary but par- ticularly on a permanent basis, is all but ignored in planning or operational activities. Local officials sometimes address wartime housing matters, especially under the rubric of crisis relocation, but the results from that preparedness planning are seldom extrapolated to the needs of a natural disaster or technological accident situation" (Quarantelli, 1982a:73).

This rather pessimistic tone is not unique to America. As with most other issues involving cross-national comparisons, however, this matter has not been researched. One study does provide a benchmark. Although he was focusing specifically on the earthquake threat, Britton (1978, 1981b) examined the planning efforts within Christchurch, New Zealand: ". . . of twenty-three organizations selected for an examination of the social im- plications of earthquake prediction, only three had specific plans for the mitigation of earthquake hazard" [New Zealand] (Britton, 1981b:387).

It is clear to any who conduct research studies in differing sections of the U.S., however, that there is marked variation in the degree to which a commitment has been made to disaster planning. The variable most fre- quently proposed as the key differentiating factor is prior disaster expe- rience.

IVA7.1(H) The greater the frequency that communities experience dis- asters, the more extensive will be their disaster planning efforts.

Numerous findings have been reported that provide general support for this idea (e.g., see Warheit, 1968:123; Ohta, 1972:179; Nehnevajsa and Wong, 1977:148; Theoret, 1979:213; Britton, 1981a:52). But the evidence is mixed; disaster events do not always precipitate increases in prepar- edness levels (e.g., see Quarantelli, 1980b:139). Thus, the question which emerges is, under what conditions? That is, what are the conditions under

which a disaster experience will precipitate increased planning efforts?
As will be detailed in the reconstruction chapter (Chapter 7), Wolensky's
work (1984) reveals the complexity of this process. There are many interdependencies and mechanisms of neutralization (see Section IVF2).

Aside from disaster frequency, what other factors might influence the
extent of community planning? Based on a survey of 43 communities,
Nehnevajsa and Wong (1977) identified one structural characteristic that
indirectly had been supported earlier; that is, urbanization.

> IVA7.2 ". . . the best planning effort, with the resultant high level of
> preparedness, was characteristic of the larger non-city municipalities.
> . . . The variations in preparedness level were quite consistent across
> the clusters of activities which we specifically took into account: the
> chain-of-command definitions, communications systems, police and fire
> department preparedness, and the planned-for responses of the public
> works departments. Thus communities which were well prepared in any
> one of these key respects were also generally well prepared in the other
> main functional areas" (Nehnevajsa and Wong, 1977:149). (See also
> Stallings, 1971:112; Moore *et al.*, 1963:127.)

The most rigorous study to date, however, is the Disaster Research
Center investigation of chemical hazards (e.g., see Gabor, 1981; Tierney,
1980; and Quarantelli and Tierney, 1981). Based on interviews in 19 communities (typically six organizations each) a theoretical model was constructed to predict the degree of community planning for chemical hazards.
Independent variables included: (1) local community characteristics; (2)
threat; (3) resources; (4) social linkages; (5) social climate; (6) feedback;
and (7) extracommunity setting. By arranging the 19 cities into three
groups—that is, high, medium, and low levels of preparedness—seven
factors were found to be correlated. Generalizing these to all forms of
disaster planning may not be warranted, however.

> IVA7.3 Planning for chemical emergencies will be the most extensive in
> communities that: (1) are larger; (2) are located in the upper Midwest;
> (3) are more frequently victimized by disasters; (4) have objective chem-
> ical vulnerability (e.g., as measured by number of chemical plants per
> square mile); (5) have higher perceived chemical vulnerability (e.g., ratings
> by community and company officials); (6) have greater financial capability
> (e.g., per capita income); and (7) have larger emergency resource avail-
> ability (e.g., number of police personnel per 1,000 population). (Based
> on Gabor, 1981:349.)

Despite these correlations, it is clear that the issue is far from settled,
even for this single band of hazards. While the proposed analytic model
takes us a sizable jump forward, many of the above factors were found
to be multidimensional. Also, there were important interaction effects with
other variables, e.g., community resistance.

> IVA7.4 ". . . belief assumptions [e.g., perceived threat probability] are
> generally supportive of making preparations; value priorities [e.g., in-

tervention into private sector by public for safety reasons] tend to both encourage and discourage preparing for disasters resulting from chemical agents; and norm expectations [e.g., prohibition against public workers being utilized on private property] typically do not lead to preparations. On balance, therefore, we tentatively conclude that while social climate probably affects community disaster planning, at most it is a facilitating rather than determinative factor" (Quarantelli and Tierney, 1979b:458). (See also Tierney, 1980:105.)

IVA8. Community Acceptance of Planning

Reflecting Quarantelli's reasoning, another dimension of "social climate" is the overall acceptance of disaster planning. While minimal headway has been made toward understanding the correlates, determinants, and consequences of this variable, its importance cannot be understated. Indeed, pondering it momentarily places the creative work in England by Barry Turner (1976a) into context. He has asked: "What are the behavioral sequences that characterize the recognition of accident potentials?" Better understanding of these processes appears to be a significant precursor to a full understanding of the variability in the interest and commitment to community disaster planning.

Using 13 large-scale accidents, Turner's sequence model proposed a common "incubation period," i.e., the accumulation of events was either unnoticed or not fully appreciated. Thus, four steps seemed to be common in the cases studied:

1. Events were unnoticed or misunderstood because erroneous assumptions were made.
2. Discrepant events were unnoticed or misunderstood as a result of problems in handling information in complex situations.
3. Some events which offered a warning of approaching danger passed unnoticed, or were misunderstood as a result of a common and well-documented human reluctance to fear the worst, so that danger was frequently belittled even when its onset was noticed.
4. Finally, where formal precautions were not fully up-to-date, violations of formal rules and regulations came to be accepted as normal. [England] (Adapted from Turner, 1976a:759.)

Turner's insightful analysis opens many doors, but really underscores the need for research directed toward general processes operating at the community level. For example, some evidence suggests that general attitudes of fatalism may undercut the efforts of officials to promote disaster planning.

> IVA8.1(H) The more widespread and accepted a fatalist attitude set, the lower the priority community disaster planning will receive.

Case study data from Scanlon's (n.d.) analysis of the tornado response in Woodstock, Ontario, Canada, are illustrative of the types of statements many of us have encountered in field interviews. That is, some people claim that since every disaster is different, planning really can't help. Scanlon also has noted another dimension, however. Some perceive that the emergency response was handled well despite the lack of planning. This may confirm the legitimacy of their neglect. ". . . 'everything went off so darned good, something had to be right.' 'We worked together but there was no official co-ordination. It worked out good' " [Canada] (Scanlon, "The Woodstock Tornado," n.d.:2–3).

> IVA8.2(H) When disaster planning efforts have been developed for threats that fail to materialize, public acceptance of the planning effort is not dampened significantly.

The impacts of near misses are not well understood. I have encountered many local officials, however, who fear that "cry-wolf" experiences will reduce their credibility. Although Nehnevajsa and Wong (1977) have reported evidence supportive of proposition IVA8.2, it is clear, that the matter is a complex one meriting further exploration. Indeed, based on studies of hurricane awareness programs, it is clear that any such assessments must be designed carefully and with an eye toward controlling a wide variety of variables.

> IVA8.3(H) Public acceptance of disaster preparedness efforts is a function of the information content presented and the medium used. (Based on Christensen and Ruch, 1978.)

> IVA8.3a ". . . radio presentations had virtually no effect in producing hurricane awareness or preparedness and may have produced a negative effect. [p. 214] . . . those who had heard the radio spots were significantly more inaccurate in their responses than were subjects who had not heard the radio announcements [p. 211]" (Christensen and Ruch, 1978:211, 214).

> IVA8.3b ". . . the brochure had a positive impact on increasing the accuracy of subjects' information about hurricanes" (Christensen and Ruch, 1978:214).

> IVA8.3c ". . . television spots were beneficial in enhancing subjects' beliefs about the destructiveness of hurricanes" (Christensen and Ruch, 1978:214).

> IVA8.4 Local emergency management organizations lack visibility and their tasks and functions are not well understood. (Adapted from Quarantelli and Tierney, 1979a.)

This general conclusion suggests another causal element in the dynamic. The public perceptions of those organizations promoting planning efforts may be more influential in the acceptance of the ideas than the validity of the ideas as intellectual concepts. While many are quick to challenge the relative credibility of one agency or another, the fact remains that neither the stability nor content of such perceptual sets are well understood. Yet, there is a recurrent theme in the case study literature that

local civil defense agencies are not accorded the highest rankings in prestige or credibility. The degree to which this may be true in other nations
remains unclear as does its consequence for public acceptance of disaster
planning. [For example, see Britton's (1981c) observations regarding New
Zealand.]

Vested interests may be affected by certain aspects of disaster planning.
As we will explore in the mitigation chapter (Chapter 9), those committed
to principles of a free marketplace often remain unimpressed with the
logic of land-use controls and increased government regulation (see
VH4.9). Although exceptions exist, most notably the Southern California
Earthquake Preparedness and Planning Project, only recently has the private sector become more fully involved in most local disaster planning
efforts. Indeed, some private firm interests may conflict directly with
publicity about the risks involved in the manufacture, transportation, or
use of their products.

> IVA8.5(H) Private firms that manufacture or transport hazardous sub-
> stances will resist disaster planning and preparedness efforts more than
> other types of firms.

Reviewing a variety of data on mutual aid systems (MAS), Gabor (1981)
provided limited, but helpful, insights into the American scene and the
complexities of this dimension of the problem. Although the 19 cities
studied were spread across all regions of the U.S.A. and varied in size,
the inferences drawn should be kept within the context of the sampling
limitations.

> IVA8.5a(H) "Companies that transport hazardous materials are rarely
> involved in MAS" (Gabor, 1981:355).
>
> IVA8.5b(H) "Hazard assessment of chemical company facilities, a pre-
> condition to comprehensive planning, is virtually non-existent among
> MAS members" (Gabor, 1981:355).
>
> IVA8.6(H) Scenario techniques can increase the acceptance of disaster
> planning by decision makers.

On a positive note, one particular technique has been identified that
appears to have much promise. While it does not resolve the types of
structured strains that are implicit in the issues related to chemical hazards,
evidence suggests that the scenario technique may have widespread applicability. Purportedly, it creates ". . . images for planning purposes:
images that help portray the consequences of specific actions or the resultant conditions of inaction. That is, the scenario becomes a substitute
for experience so that much should be learnt from the application." (Ericksen, 1975:157).

> IVA8.6a ". . . for three of the characteristics measured, over 75% of the
> respondents [i.e., community decision makers $n = 20$] accorded a fa-
> vorable scale-value of four or five on a five point scale. The measures

were of the scenario's effectiveness in *communicating information* about the flood problem; the extent to which it would be useful in *making decisions* about the flood problem; and whether or not the scenario was found to be *more meaningful* than other forms of information they may have received about the flood problem'' (Ericksen, 1975:87,90).

VA. Society System Level

Within the literature reviewed, few behavioral studies were focused on the societal system—that is, where a total society was the unit of analysis. Indeed, taking a hazard, like flooding, that has persisted for eons, it is disappointing to learn that the annual national losses within the U.S.A. are estimated—and only crudely (National Science Foundation, 1980). By the early 1980s, however, scholars were publishing results based on methodologies whereby a limited range of hazard loss data were aggregated.

> "Based on the estimating procedures used in this analysis the effects produced by natural hazard exposures in the United States in 1970 yielded total annual expected losses of 8.1 billion dollars for 1970, as well as the loss of 113.9 thousand housing units and nearly one thousand lives . . . In addition 1970 natural hazards exposures also resulted in such annual expected impacts as 130 thousand person-years of homelessness and 80 thousand person-years of unemployment. [p. 197] Estimates of national hazard losses and other effects also were developed for the year 2000. These estimates were based on projected increases in building and human populations in the several hazard exposure areas (countries, states, and flood control regions) and generally assumed no change in land-use zoning, building codes, and new construction practices. . . . By the year 2000, the annual per capita loss from natural hazard exposures is expected to nearly double [p. 199]'' (Petak and Atkisson, 1982:197, 199).

VA1. System Variation

Beyond disaster loss projections of this type, it is possible to identify areas wherein planning was found to be lacking following a few events that received intense media coverage. This, in turn, precipitated accelerated planning efforts. Thus, to some extent, societal variation in planning reflects the unevenness of growth spurts stemming from a short-lived consciousness of risk. Within the U.S.A., the most publicized event in recent history was the accident at the Three Mile Island nuclear power plant in March, 1979. Reflecting on a series of conclusions from case studies of this event and others, I formulated the following rather general hypothesis.

> VA1.1(H) In all societies, disaster planning will be uneven and nonuniform across hazard types, reflecting cultural values, assumptions, and power differentials.

VA1.1a "Existing emergency plans were not designed to meet the demands of a protracted crisis. The plans had no mechanisms for establishing reliable communications among the on-site and the several off-site organizations responsible for various aspects of the emergency response" (President's Commission on the Accident at Three Mile Island, 1979:40).

VA1.1b "Training of Met Ed operators and supervisors was inadequate and contributed significantly to the seriousness of the accident. The training program gave insufficient emphasis to principles of reactor safety. . . . The TMI training program conformed to the NRC standard for training. Moreover, TMI operator license candidates had higher scores than the national average . . . the training of the operators proved to be inadequate for responding to the accident" (President's Commission on the Accident at Three Mile Island, 1979:49).

Paralleling the U.S.A. experience, but at the opposite end of the development scale, were the attitudes held in Tonga prior to Tropical Storm Isaac.

VA1.1c ". . . at the time of *Isaac* a formal disaster plan did not exist, although the basic concepts of counter-disaster operations were appreciated in appropriate official circles. [March, 1982] . . . Tonga's Fourth Five Year Development Plan (1980–85) did not consider the potential disturbance that disaster could cause and consequently from the welfare viewpoint did not make disaster preparedness an integral part of development planning. This is a pointer, at the level of concern involved, to the limited perception of the significance of the disaster threat in development terms" [Tonga] (Oliver and Reardon, 1982:66).

Thus, while hints of evidence pointed toward this very general hypothesis, what was most obvious was the void in the empirical data base that this area represents. Reviewing case study observations, and in a few instances more empirically based conclusions, I identified three additional areas: (1) system complexity; (2) system change; and (3) system outputs.

VA2. System Complexity

American society is a highly complex social system and disaster planning is an activity that has been fragmented across both structural levels and functional areas (McLoughlin, 1985; May, 1985). Decisions made by agency staff in one federal level office are not translated directly in a uniform manner across relevant subsystems (Drabek, Mushkatel, and Kilijanek, 1983).

VA2.1(H) The greater the structural complexity of a society, the less the uniformity in disaster planning.

Limited empirical support for this hypothesis is scattered through the literature (e.g., see Quarantelli *et al.*, 1979; Perry, 1982:103–107). But it has not been tested systematically. The most precise specification I found of the variations in local planning that resulted from a federal system initiative was offered by Worth and Stroup (1977) regarding emergency medical systems (EMS).

> VA2.1a [Disaster responses prior to (9 cities) and following (11 cities) federally funded EMS programs revealed:] [1.] "Communications . . . In no case was there an effective, direct communication linkage from the disaster site to the hospital. [p. 160] . . . In the post-EMS communities we still find instances of hospitals informed of a mass casualty situation by the first arriving casualties. . . . [2.] Transportation . . . There was no evidence of a central dispatch to link the transportation and communication processes in the pre-EMS law data. [p. 161] . . . [3.] Treatment . . . Triage at the site was not evident; emphasis seemed to be on moving the patient to the nearest hospital. [p. 162] . . . [4.] Coordination [p. 164] . . . Data indicate the lack of a coordinator or coordinating body still is a problem [p. 166]" (Worth and Stroup, 1977:160–166).

Tierney's (1985) analysis of the implementation barriers that limited the impact of these EMS initiatives is instructive (see also Quarantelli, 1983a). These themes need to be extended to other aspects of the emergency management system if we are ever going to understand the behavioral dynamics that are operative.

> VA2.1b "The federal EMS initiative was complicated by the same factors that make the coordination of any set of diverse organizations problematic: differences in funding bases and organizational goals; professional and organizational status hierarchies; and the tendency of each organization to try to maximize its own autonomy" (Tierney, 1985:82).

VA3. System Changes

Scholars like Mileti (1975a)—and more recently May (1985)—have traced the evolution of federal disaster legislation within the U.S.A. But, to date, the research community offers only the most sketchy ideas as to the dynamics of the change process. As Mushkatel and Weschler (1985:49) propose, however, if we wish ". . . to understand the constraints upon successful implementation of emergency management policy" we cannot divorce the policy process from the intergovernmental system. Clearly, this orientation merits future notice by political sociologists and others interested in the behavioral dynamics of policy formulation and implementation processes (Drabek, 1983c).

> VA3.1 "If impact of whatever type produces broad gauge disaster legislation, the experience may produce increased preparedness for a whole range of hazards. Indeed, Burton and Kates (1964) find that hazard-oriented legislation is usually prompted by a particular disaster rather than evidence of persistent threat" (Mileti, Drabek, and Haas, 1975:19).

Scanlon (1982) has offered some interpretations of the Canadian experience and the factors that have produced changes in the disaster planning emphasis at the federal level. His analysis makes it clear that specific disasters become integrated within the interpretations of political groups who seek to use them to promote reconfigurations in the preparedness apparatus.

> VA3.2(H) Disaster preparedness emphases and priorities within a society will change as there are shifts in political power and disaster events that receive media attention.

> VA3.2a "What was it that sent the government along its path of erratic civil defence planning? Why was there such a boom and bust? . . . Anyone familiar with the pattern of Canadian federal politics can recognize many of the key dates as significant. CD grew in the postwar years under the Liberals but it had its 'hey day' . . . under the Conservatives . . . Civil defence declines steadily . . . and took a nose dive under a Liberal . . . Politics certainly affected its wobbly path" [Canada] (Scanlon, 1982:7).

> VA3.2b "But there were other influences at work . . . The postwar era has seen Canada affected by a series of disasters, some of which were dramatic enough to attract world attention. [p. 8] . . . the blackout led to EMO being given disaster co-ordination responsibilities. The sinking of the Arrow led to courses at Arnprior changing to a peacetime orientation. The crash of Cosmos triggered a flood of applicants for radiation detection courses which had often, before that, had to be cancelled. Mississauga revived the general interest in federal emergency planning [p. 9]" [Canada] (Scanlon, 1982:8, 9).

VA4. System Outputs

As will be explored further in the mitigation chapter (Chapter 9), various researchers have sought to identify the consequences of disaster relief efforts (see Section VH5). To highlight the planning process regarding the distribution of post-disaster relief, however, it is important to note that equity frequently is used as an evaluative criterion.

> VA4.1 ". . . the lower income groups consistently bear a disproportionate share of the losses: they receive, in most instances, the smallest proportion of disaster relief; they are the least likely to be insured (for either health, life or property); and they live in dwellings which are of the poorest construction and most subject to damage" (Cochrane, 1975:110).

Another type of output from recent disaster planning efforts has been related to public information regarding earthquake predictions. When should the public be advised that an earthquake prediction has been made?

> VA4.2 Warning systems for different types of hazards have many parallel functional planning requirements, e.g., timing policy.

A specific policy recommendation that illustrates this proposition is the following, made by Nilson and Nilson (1981) after viewing recent literature on the pros and cons of when an earthquake prediction should be released to the public and various surveys of earthquake preparedness. ". . . a timing policy [is proposed] which alerts the public in *stages* to the increasing likelihood of greater seismic activity, and then reserves the actual prediction announcement until several days before the anticipated event. Specifically, we would recommend that the mass media and the educational system inform the public of an increasing seismic threat with a simple *color code scheme,* similar to those used in the United States to indicate the air quality in urban areas and the fire danger in national forests. To illustrate, *blue* might be used to advise an initial state of anticipation, based on suggestive, long-range, or below 40% to 60% probability signs" (Nilson and Nilson, 1981:395).

VIA. International System Level

The behavioral research literature I reviewed contained few studies directed toward cross-national comparisons or assessment of international planning systems. Only in 1982 was the first comprehensive effort published wherein worldwide environmental trends were identified and measured crudely (Holdgate, Kassas, and White, 1982). Of course, new technologies may enhance future monitoring capabilities—most notably satellites.

> ". . . satellite sensing of both the atmosphere and the Earth's surface can provide valuable and reliable information routinely, very quickly and at relatively low cost, much of which is not available by other techniques. Equally important may be the capability of the satellites to provide information as a check against data from other sources or as a supplement to such data including press releases and *attache* reports of local correspondents" (Howard, Barrett, and Heilkema, 1979:239).

Furthermore, many disasters of tragic consequence demonstrated why nation state interdependencies required disaster planning efforts that were international in scope. Probably none underscored this premise as well as the Sahel drought.

> "Under African direction, the Club des Amis du Sahel has set up and is operating vigorous and supportive relationships among the more than 30 participating states and international organizations. [p. 20] . . . The program, presently being established as the Sahel Development Program (SDP), has set a preliminary budget of $10 billion for expenditure over 10 years. . . . the core problem of the SDP undertaking: that of instituting a very direct management system which adjusts to the political necessities and diplomatic interests of states and international organizations while efficiently and demonstrably allocating resources toward self-sufficiency [p. 16]" (Shear and Clark, 1976:16, 20).

The outcomes of this and numerous other interventions were reviewed in a collection of papers edited by Glantz (1976). We will return to these analyses in the chapter on reconstruction (Chapter 7). But this event and Glantz's analysis illustrate two critical issues. First, there are implications regarding my argument about the importance of the disaster taxonomic problem. While "duration of impact" can be used to differentiate among events, when one like this drought is included in the set, the boundaries among the phases become much more blurred. Recovery and family assistance operations become much more intertwined with all other response functions for an event of multi-year duration.

Second, and far more important, is the way this case highlights the inexorable link between scientific analysis of human responses and fundamental matters of value. Glantz illustrated this problem when he described the controversy that emerged regarding the cause of the drought— a global cooling trend vs. random climatic fluctuations. He concluded: "Whatever the underlying cause (or causes) of the drought in the Sahel, it has been widely acknowledged that the impact of the harmful climatic fluctuations has, at least, been greatly exacerbated by human misuse of the land in this region" (Glantz, 1976:5). As with controversies regarding land-use planning within the U.S.A., any statement about "misuse" reflects a value judgment. This matter merits more attention from the research community.

What can be said about similarities and differences in types and degrees of disaster planning as it is found among nation states with differing structures? Actually, little more than a few general observations can be made.

VIA1.1(H) The greater the degree of similarity in the political and cultural systems among nation states, the less the divergences in disaster responses.

VIA1.1a ". . . Australian communities respond to disaster in much the same way as all those North American communities tested by the field studies of the National Academy of Sciences–National Research Council and more recently of the Disaster Research Center of Ohio State University" [Australia] (Wettenhall, 1979a:242).

VIA1.2(H) Technologically developed nation states tend to share attitudinal orientations toward technological accidents wherein they are defined as unique.

VIA1.2a "One attitude that I have found prevalent among regulators and operators in my research on these two accidents in the oil and nuclear industries has been that of uniqueness. Each accident was viewed as 'impossible' because of the employment of safety technologies in-depth and generally superior safety requirements when compared to the past or to some other industries. In addition, each accident after the fact was viewed as 'unique' or as the result of a particular one-time configuration of weaknesses that in combination led to the accidents" [U.S.A. and Norway] (Fischer, 1980:342).

VIA1.3 Although modal levels of building design requirements will affect
the ratio, the numbers of victims of various types covary.

Comparative data assessed to date preclude more precise statements
of the relationships implied in this proposition, but available findings are
supportive.

VIA1.3a "The number in each class of victims differs approximately by
factors of ten. For a large disaster, such as Managua and San Francisco,
the dead, the injured and their immediate kin may number in the thousands; the unemployed in the hundreds of thousands; the donors and
taxed in the millions" [U.S.A. and Nicaragua] (Kates, 1977:265). (See
also Committee on International Disaster Assistance, 1979:40.)

Akimoto and Ohta (1980:87) pointed to another variable—population
density. Indeed, they described their own surprise at American researchers
who asked at a seminar: "Why does the Japanese team make evacuation
at the time of an earthquake such a big issue?" They replied that because
most American researchers have lived in planned cities that are spread
out over large land areas, it is hard for them to visualize crowds fleeing
toward designated evacuation locations. But, to date, neither population
density nor building design requirements have been factored into injury
or death rate estimation formulas so as to permit reliable damage estimates
in cross-national settings.

VIA1.4(H) Reconstruction following disaster is a patterned sequence and
planners could impact it to a greater extent by prior identification of
major decision areas.

Exploration of the post-disaster recovery dynamic has revealed limited
empirical evidence suggesting important commonalities across nation
states. While still at the most primitive level of precision, it is clear that
those planning for disaster should include the recovery period in their
agenda (Kates, 1977).

VIA1.4a "These do's and don'ts are pithy and perhaps simplistic but
they rest on the detailed findings of the research on reconstruction in
the four cities [p. 68] . . . 1. Don't wait until the restoration period is
nearly over before starting to examine, systematically, the upcoming reconstruction issues. 2. Begin immediately to consider whether new decision-making mechanisms, including the possibility of advisory groups,
are going to be needed. . . . [3.] Don't assume that decision-makers in
the private sector will hold off on their decisions until the most important
public policy decisions have been made. . . . [4.] Remember that despite
the best efforts to shape the character of the reconstructed city, fundamental change is unlikely. Past trends will be accelerated in most cases.
[5.] Don't assume that all temporary housing will be temporary [pp. 67–
68]" [U.S.A. and Nicaragua] (Haas et al., 1977:67–68).

VIA1.5(H) "Developing countries tend to be especially prone to the kind
of disaster which gives rise to serious food shortages. . . . The populations

of developing countries tend to be particularly vulnerable to such catastrophes'' (Fitzpatrick, 1977:218).

Fitzpatrick (1977:218) argues that this ''. . . is because the majority live by subsistence farming. . . . food surpluses are frequently unavailable at national levels to meet severe food shortages.'' At a commonsense level these observations appear valid. But there is a possibility that relief workers, using standards from their own society, will tend to distort disaster impacts. That is, they may fail to differentiate food shortages that routinely exist from those present following a disaster.

Taylor (1979), in particular, has offered observations on the factors that may increase such tendencies.

VIA1.6(H) ''. . . there is a widespread tendency among relief agencies to exaggerate the effects of a disaster and to minimize the ability of local people to cope with it'' (Taylor, 1979:24).

Among the factors that may encourage distorted and exaggerated views of victim needs are: (1) the isolation of donors from victims; (2) local resourcefulness; (3) help from the family and community; (4) incorrect use of statistics; (5) the timing of need; (6) the timing of response; (7) overestimation of damage; (8) exaggeration for political ends; and (9) disaster as an aid magnet. (Adapted from Taylor, 1979:25-28.)

Review of the available data base and the rigor of the propositions that have been validated—or even relationships that have been hypothesized—indicates very clearly that the behavioral dynamics of disaster planning merit the attention of the research community during the 1980s. In contrast to this aspect of preparedness, substantial headway has been made in our understanding of disaster warning responses, especially at the individual system level. These matters are the focus of the next chapter.

Selected Bibliography

Anderson, William A. [1969] *Local Civil Defense in Natural Disaster: From Office to Organization.* Columbus, Ohio: Disaster Research Center, The Ohio State University.

Brown, Barbara J. [1979] *Disaster Preparedness and the United Nations: Advanced Planning for Disaster Relief.* New York: Pergamon Press.

Cohen, Elias S., and S. Walter Poulshock [1977] ''Societal Response to Mass Dislocation of the Elderly: Implications for Area Agencies on Aging.'' *The Gerontologist* **17** (June):262–268.

Cohen, Raquel E., and Frederick L. Ahearn, Jr. [1980] *Handbook for Mental Health Care of Disaster Victims.* Baltimore and London: The Johns Hopkins University Press.

Crabbs, Michael A. [1981] ''School Mental-Health Services Following an Environmental Disaster.'' *Journal of School Health* **51** (No. 3):165–167.

Dynes, Russell R. [1983] ''Problems in Emergency Planning.'' *Energy* **8** (No. 8–9):653–660.

Dynes, Russell R., and E. L. Quarantelli [1975] *The Role of Local Civil Defense in Disaster Planning*. Columbus, Ohio: Disaster Research Center, The Ohio State University.

Dynes, Russell, E. L. Quarantelli, and Gary A. Kreps [1972] *A Perspective on Disaster Planning*. Columbus, Ohio: Disaster Research Center, The Ohio State University.

Fisher, Brian E. [1978] "Mass Emergency Problems and Planning in the United Kingdom from the Perspective of the Police." *Mass Emergencies* 3:41–48.

Foster, Harold D. [1980] *Disaster Planning: The Preservation of Life and Property*. New York, Heidelberg, Berlin: Springer-Verlag.

Gabor, Thomas [1981] "Mutual Aid Systems in the United States for Chemical Emergencies." *Journal of Hazardous Materials* 4:343–356.

Hartsough, Don M. [1982] "Planning for Disaster: A New Community Outreach Program for Mental Health Centers." *Journal of Community Psychology* 10 (July):255–264.

Hoetmer, Gerard J. [1983] "Emergency Management." *Baseline Data Reports* 15 (April). Washington, D.C.: International City Management Association.

Hultaker, Orjan E., and Jan E. Trost [1978] *Katastrofforskning en Lagesbeskrivning* (Disaster Research: A Description of Its Present State) (in Swedish with an English summary). Disaster Studies 6. Uppsala, Sweden: Uppsala University.

Lindy, Jacob D., and Joanne G. Lindy [1981] "Planning and Delivery of Mental-Health Services in Disaster—The Cincinnati Experience." *Urban and Social Change Review* 14 (Summer):16–21.

Maxwell, Christopher [1982] "Hospital Organizational Response to the Nuclear Accident at Three-Mile-Island—Implications for Future-Oriented Disaster Planning." *American Journal of Public Health* 72 (March):275–279.

May, Peter J. [1985] *Recovering from Catastrophes: Federal Disaster Relief Policy and Politics*. Westport, Connecticut: Greenwood Press.

McLoughlin, David [1985] "A Framework for Integrated Emergency Management." *Public Administration Review* 45 (January):165–175.

Perry, Ronald W. [1982] *The Social Psychology of Civil Defense*. Lexington, Massachusetts.: Lexington Books.

Perry, Ronald W., Marjorie R. Greene, and Michael K. Lindell [1980] "Enhancing Evacuation Warning Compliance: Suggestions for Emergency Planning." *Disasters* 4 (No. 4):433–449.

Py, Y. [1978] "Comptements Dans un Cas de Secours D'urgence" (Behavior in Emergency Situations) (in French). *Le Travail Humain* 41 (No. 1):67–80.

Quarantelli, E. L. [1984] *Organizational Behavior In Disasters and Implications for Disaster Planning*. Emmitsburg, Maryland: National Emergency Training Center, Federal Emergency Management Agency.

Tierney, Kathleen J. [1980] *A Primer for Preparedness for Acute Chemical Emergencies*. Columbus, Ohio: Disaster Research Center, The Ohio State University.

Tierney, Kathleen J., and Barbara Baisden [1979] *Crises Intervention Programs for Disaster Victims: A Sourcebook and Manual for Smaller Communities*. Rockville, Maryland: National Institute of Mental Health.

Turner, Ralph H., Joanne M. Nigg, Denise Heller Paz, and Barbara Shaw Young [1979] "Earthquake Threat: The Human Response in Southern California." Los Angeles: Institute for Social Science Research, University of California, Los Angeles.

Wenger, Dennis E., Thomas F. James, and Charles F. Faupel [1980] *Disaster Beliefs and Emergency Planning.* Newark, Delaware: Disaster Research Project, University of Delaware.

Zarle, Thomas H., Don M. Hartsough, and Donald R. Ottinger [1974] "Tornado Recovery: The Development of a Professional–Paraprofessional Response to a Disaster." *Journal of Community Psychology* **2** (October):311–320.

3
Warning

Building upon studies conducted during the 1950s and early 1960s (e.g., Mack and Baker, 1961; Withey, 1962; Moore *et al.*, 1963), researchers have obtained a good understanding of individual responses to disaster warnings. Today, we have numerous analytical propositions; many have been tested repeatedly. While unanswered questions remain, a basic foundation has been constructed to guide future inquiry. Multivariate models, linked with statements specifying appropriate ranges of generalizability, should be produced in the next decade.

Despite the rather successful implementation of hurricane evacuation procedures—the first topic of the next chapter—Americans are still dying in disasters wherein warning systems have failed. Although other examples could be cited, the 1976 flash flood in the Big Thompson Canyon (near Loveland, Colorado) illustrates the point well; there 139 died.

Why? Detailed oral histories (McComb, 1980) and intensive behavioral reconstructions have provided many answers.

> "In the Big Thompson disaster, especially in the canyon where there was little warning, the people and their neighbors saved themselves. There were some police rescues, but not many. . . . residents had no better idea about what to do than tourists. Over half of the 399 people included in the inquiry said that rising water and rain gave them first warning. Older people were less likely to flee. The deadliest situation was to be driving alone. The best action was to climb the mountainside; . . ." (McComb, 1980:43).

Given housing development patterns, general population shifts within the nation, recreational emphases, and a variety of other factors, populations at risk from flash floods and hurricanes are increasing. Precise data to assess the rate of increase, however, are not available. Although hard to separate from warning responses, the topic of evacuation behavior will be dealt with in the next chapter.

IB. Individual System Level

Research findings on warning responses by individuals cluster around five major topics: (1) disaster warnings as a social process; (2) initial responses; (3) message qualities; (4) receiver qualities; and (5) confirmation behavior.

IB1. Disaster Warnings as a Social Process

Dating back at least to the insightful analyses of Harry Williams (1956; 1957; 1964) researchers have argued that disaster warnings must be conceptualized as a social process ". . . involving multiple actors, phases, and feedback" (Quarantelli, 1980b:99). Thus, based on his assessment of the literature and his own analysis of responses in the Rapid City, South Dakota, flood (1972), wherein over 200 lives were lost, Mileti highlighted three important notions about how people respond to warnings: "1. even though several persons may listen to the same warning message, there may be considerable variation in what they hear and believe; 2. people respond to warnings on the basis of how what they hear stimulates them to behave; and 3. people are stimulated differently depending on who they are, who they are with, and who and what they see" (Mileti, 1975b:xvi). (See also Mileti, Drabek, and Haas, 1975:43.)

Various sequential models have been developed that identify the social process that characterizes individual responses. The best of these to date is reflected in the work of Perry (1985) and his colleagues (e.g., Perry and Mushkatel, 1984). They have rooted their work within the empirical literature of the past and have conducted the most rigorous field studies to date.

Also insightful, although presently lacking the empirical testing reflected in Perry's work, is a model proposed by Janis and Mann (1977). Their "conflict model" posits five sequential steps—different coping patterns really. If an individual answers "no" at any one step, presumably they proceed no further until additional information is obtained. The assumption of the model, one we'll examine in the next section, is that individuals exhibit a tendency of *inertia*. That is, no behavioral action will be directed toward a warning response until a sequence of information-processing steps have occurred.

The five psychological conditions that mediate the coping patterns are: (1) *unconflicted inertia* (i.e., Are the risks serious if I don't take protective action? "No" results in unconflicted inertia); (2) *unconflicted change to a new course of action* (i.e., Are the risks serious if I do take the most available protective action? "No" results in unconflicted change); (3) *defensive avoidance* (i.e., Is it realistic to hope to find a better means of escape? "No" results in defensive avoidance); (4) *hypervigilance* (i.e., Is there sufficient time to search and deliberate? "No" results in hypervigilance); and (5) *vigilance* (i.e., "maybe" or "yes" to all other prior questions). (Adapted from Janis and Mann, 1977:36, 39.)

> IB1.1 Disaster warning responses comprise a complex social process. (Based on Williams, 1956, 1957, 1964; Drabek, 1969; Mileti, 1975b; Perry, Lindell, and Greene, 1981; Perry, 1985.)

The elements of the process comprise the remainder of this section of this chapter. While treated spearately, most researchers assume that there are complex feedback loops and interaction effects. Several were summarized nicely by a Swedish researcher who also offered several criticisms of the American data base.

> IB1.1a(H) ". . . the components communicator, communication mode and warning content are interacting, as well as these components are interacting together with the receiver" [Sweden] (Hammarstrom-Tornstam, 1977:16–17).

> IB1.1b(H) "The receiver defines the situation in different ways, depending on these interaction effects. The effects may be evacuation or confirmation. Through the confirmation the receiver may get a renewed definition of the situation, which might be followed by evacuation or not" [Sweden] (Hammarstrom-Tornstam, 1977:16).

> IB1.2(H) "Confirmation may be considered as a renewed warning, that is to say a further warning message. That means that confirmation routines could be elaborated and added to evacuation plans or in the warning message itself" [Sweden] (Hammarstrom-Tornstam, 1977:17).

IB2. Initial Responses

As indicated above, opinion surveys have documented widespread belief in numerous disaster myths (Wenger, James, and Faupel, 1980). Among these is the idea that when warned of an impending disaster, the public will panic. Of course, what might be meant by the term "panic" is subject to question. This term—panic—will be a focal point for discussion in a subsequent chapter (see Chapter 5, ID1.7). Regardless of definitional variations, however, the empirical base refutes the myth. Unfortunately, the mythology persists, despite its inaccuracy, however.

> IB2.1 The initial response to a disaster warning is disbelief. (Based on Drabek, 1969; Moore *et al.,* 1963; Fritz and Mathewson, 1957.)

This proposition—sometimes referred to as a "normalcy bias" (Okabe and Mikami, 1982)—is consistent with the Janis–Mann model discussed above. There are numerous aspects of the process which have been identified.

IB2.1a "Where a disaster is unexpected and the level of emergency preparedness low, most people's immediate reaction to the first warning received is disbelief and a continuation of normal routine, whether the warning comes from an authority or a friend or neighbor" (Perry, Lindell, and Greene, 1981:153).

IB2.1b "The immediate reaction of most people was disbelief, based on a feeling that there had not been sufficient rain in their area, or their own observations of the river height. In consequence, they then sought to confirm the warning received" [Australia] (Irish and Falconer, 1979:323).

IB2.1c ". . . even among the sample who believed the warning message to be authentic, only 23.7 percent expected an imminent earthquake. This suggests the second step of normalcy bias in defining situations. Even though some residents believed that an earthquake warning was actually issued, most of them did not expect the earthquake to strike them immediately" [Japan] (Okabe and Mikami, 1982:13).

IB2.2 After receiving a disaster warning, individuals tend to search for alternative interpretations that will neutralize the threat conveyed by the message. (Based on Drabek, 1969; Quarantelli, 1980b; Ikeda, 1982.)

An initial reaction of *denial* reappears throughout the literature in varying forms and differences in degree. Precise measurement has not been done nor have the patterns of variation been specified, either descriptively or causally.

IB2.2a ". . . human beings under stress initially tend to interpret new data in terms of the known and the familiar. People will generally believe they are not in immediate personal danger until perceptions indicate almost indisputably otherwise" (Quarantelli, 1980b:107).

IB2.2b "The interpretation of such apparently 'uncertain' expert information in a positive vein by the public is consistent with research on other natural hazards which suggests that members of threatened populations will seize upon any 'vagueness' in a warning message which allows them to reinterpret the situation in a nonthreatening fashion (cf. Drabek, 1968; Mileti, Drabek, and Haas, 1975; Perry *et al.*, 1981; Fritz, 1957)" (Greene, Perry, and Lindell, 1981:60).

While seeking to deny that they might be in danger, many will look to others. At the most primitive level, this constitutes a form of message confirmation. What must be stressed is the *diversity* in response. There is no uniform pattern. Today, the contours that shape the varying response patterns await identification.

IB2.3 Behaviorally, initial warning responses are variable ranging from immediate adaptive actions, confirmation efforts, to total denial. (Based on Drabek, 1969; Perry, Lindell, and Greene, 1981; Chandessais, 1980; Hodler, 1982.)

IB2.3a "... misinterpretation of the warning and refusal to consider it, occurs very often. Seventeen examples of this were analysed for both the individual process and the communications net. Concerning the warning behavior, 41% of the subjects withdrew from the warning, 33% conveyed it, 19% sought more information, 19% helped others, 15% were confused, 10% fought the phenomenon (mostly fire fighting), and 6% feed back" [France] (Chandessais, 1980:227).

IB2.3b "The civil defense sirens are tested briefly on the first Saturday of each month. Even so, of those who heard the sirens, 17% (28) did not know the meaning of the warning being sounded. . . . forty-eight per cent (81) of those individuals who heard the warning sirens sought a location of safety, either within their basement or other secure location. Eighteen per cent (31) of the people chose to disregard the warning altogether and did nothing to alter their activities. Twenty-two per cent (37) tried to verify the emergency warning by either looking outside for the tornado or turning on their radio/television to confirm the tornado's existence" (Hodler, 1982:46).

IB3. Message Qualities

Although far from being independent of the characteristics of the receiver, certain message qualities have been identified as evoking generalized response patterns. Three qualities have been found to matter: (1) content; (2) source; and (3) number.

IB3.1 "... more specific messages produce higher levels of warning belief and perceived risk" (Perry, Lindell, and Greene, 1982a:103). (See also Drabek, 1969.)

IB3.1a "... as the warning message increases in its accuracy, and/or information about survival choices, and/or consistency with other warnings, and/or clarity about the nature of the threat, the probability of adaptive response increases (Demerath, 1957; Fritz, 1957; Fritz and Williams, 1957; Williams, 1957; Crane, 1960; Schatzman, 1960; Moore *et al.*, 1963)" (as summarized in Mileti, Drabek, and Haas:1975:48).

All too often, even in disasters that occurred during the late 1970s, researchers encountered victims who described the warning messages they received as being too vague and nonspecific. Their denial processes had rather predictable results.

IB3.1b "... people who receive a vague or location-nonspecific message tend to define risk as low or believe they are outside the risk area altogether" (Perry, Lindell, and Greene, 1981: 153).

In ways yet to be mapped, responses to messages varying in specificity are altered by context. Thus, upon exploring the issue, Perry and Greene (1983, 1982a) discovered that the degree of community preparedness affected responses following the May, 1980, eruption of Mount St. Helens.

IB3.1c ". . . the more specific the message, the more likely warning recipients are to initially undertake a protective activity. . . . when community emergency preparedness is low, nonspecific warning messages
promote social milling—family oriented responses or warning confirmation—with large numbers of people electing to continue a normal routine. . . . due to the history of eruption warnings in Toutle/Silverlake and
Woodland, we are experiencing a kind of ceiling effect: most people rated
warning belief high, no matter how specific the message. . . . The proportion of people defining personal risk as high increases as we move
from a vague warning (20.8 percent), through a severity-specific warning
(36.4 percent), to the most specific warning (53.1 percent)" (Perry and
Greene, 1983:60, 61).

Upon trying to conceptualize a way to dissect behavioral variations,
Perry and his colleagues have proposed that warning belief and perceived
risk must be differentiated. While correlated, these two factors are not
impacted identically when the degree of message specificity has varied.

IB3.1d ". . . more specific messages produce higher levels of warning
belief and perceived risk, and the probability of evacuation (the suggested
adaptive response) is positively related to warning belief and risk" (Lindell, Perry, and Greene, 1980:13).

IB3.1e "1. level of warning belief is positively correlated with level of
perceived personal risk; 2. taken alone, both personal risk and warning
belief are positively correlated with warning response; and 3. personal
risk bears a stronger positive relationship to warning response, because
when the effects of risk are controlled, the magnitude of the relationship
between belief and response declines" (Perry and Greene, 1983:101).

These observations bring us to the edge of the present empirical base.
Thus, while a quantum jump forward, the intricacies of the interaction
effects among these variables, and others, that might be hypothesized as
affecting response, await future study.

IB3.2 "Warnings from official sources (police, state patrol, fire department) are more likely believed" (Mileti, 1975b:21).

Based on several studies, it is clear that different warning sources elicit
different response curves. It is not that one source is totally believed while
another is not. Rather, we are seeing matters of degree in both reported
belief and behavior. In my study of the 1965 flood in Denver, Colorado,
I documented that "persons warned by authorities were more likely to
immediately evacuate or at least attempt to confirm the warning" (Drabek,
1969:341). Contrasts among three types of sources, i.e., officials, primary
groups, and media, appear to be rather consistent.

IB3.2a ". . . warning source has an impact upon warning belief. . . .
People who were first warned by an official were considerably more likely
to believe the message. Warnings from friends, neighbors, or relatives
evoked high warning belief less often than those from authorities, but

more often than warnings conveyed by mass media'' (Perry and Greene, 1983:50). (See also Drabek, 1969.)

Most recently, Perry and Greene (1983) have pursued this dynamic further. Thus, both the levels of prior community involvement and the informational context appear to interact with perceptions of credibility.

> IB3.2b ''. . . where community involvement of emergency officials is low, and channels of official to citizen communication are limited primarily to mass media, the media take on a part of the official function and evoke similarly high levels of warning belief among citizens'' (Perry and Greene, 1983:52).

> IB3.2c ''The higher the credibility of the message sender, the more likely the individual is to believe that he is at risk simply on the word of the authority . . . the warning message itself is an important source of risk relevant information for the individual, particularly regarding where, when, and the probable force of disaster impact . . . the individual's past experience with the disaster agent also forms a basis for assessing risk'' (Perry, 1982:62–63).

> IB3.3 ''Belief in eventual impact increases as the number of warnings received increases'' (Mileti, 1975b:21). (See also Fritz, 1961; Drabek and Boggs, 1968; Drabek, 1969; Perry, Lindell, and Greene, 1981:156; Okabe and Mikami, 1982:10.)

This proposition has been demonstrated repeatedly as the multiple citations indicate. But there is a catch—not all messages received are necessarily consistent. Thus, while the general proposition holds, message inconsistencies may neutralize the emergent perception of risk.

> IB3.3a ''The more accurate and consistent the content across several messages, the greater the belief'' (Mileti, 1975b:21).

Also, as the warning response context is altered in situations where multiple messages are received, it is clear that alternative warning sources are impacted differentially. The precise nature of these impacts across a variety of source points, however, awaits exploration.

> IB3.3b ''. . . the predictive value of several exogenous variables changed over the number of warnings received. Specifically, own-area warnings were a strong predictor of warning belief only after several such warnings were heard. Likewise, mass-communicated warnings did not become a strong predictor of warning confirmation until several warnings had been heard'' (Mileti and Beck, 1975:43).

IB4. Receiver Qualities

Like the analytic features of warning messages, differential responses among categories of persons have been documented. Yet, beyond overall modal trends, precise assessment awaits future research. It is clear that many characteristics of warning message receivers do matter, but the joint consequences of collections of these are unclear, as are their relative impacts in differing warning contexts.

> IB4.1 "The data indicate differing effects of past experience with flooding on warning response, depending on the community [and length of forewarning] . . . while under specific circumstances the probability of evacuation increases with past experience, in virtually every case the probability of undertaking any adaptive behavior is greatly enhanced by the presence of past experience" (Perry, Lindell, and Greene, 1981:153). (See also Quarantelli, 1980b:40; Mileti, Drabek, and Haas, 1975:47.)

Thus, it is clear that past experiences with disasters do impact future interpretations and behavioral responses. Parallel conclusions have been reported regarding responses in Australia and England.

> IB4.1a "A significant difference was noted in the response of people who had experienced the 1974 flood and of those who had not. Although most people initially had difficulty in accepting the warnings, those who had lived in the area in 1974 were quicker to act once they accepted the likelihood of danger" [Australia] (Irish and Falconer, 1979:323).
>
> IB4.1b ". . . the perceived response to a six-hour flood warning is largely determined by social characteristics and the degree of flood experience of the floodplain resident. . . . Probably the most noteworthy trend was that expressed by the non-experienced residents. A relatively high proportion of this group perceived the utilisation of temporary measures to prevent flood water entering their property. It is reasonable to suggest, on the evidence of the 1968 flood, that the majority of these measures would be ineffective in a real flood. It was also found that it was the younger, less experienced residents who perceived unrealistically high financial savings arising from such remedial actions" [England] (Smith and Tobin, 1979:108).

As stated, the proposition (IB4.1) underscores a potential negative effect, at least from the disaster planning standpoint. That is, if warnings are issued and events predicted do not materialize, the consequence of the experience may be to neutralize future warnings. Thus, a "cry wolf" syndrome may emerge.

Extensive laboratory studies by Breznitz (1984) provide much insight into this process, which turns out to be rather complex. In general, however, his results were consistent with the conclusions offered earlier by Janis (1951). That is, false alarms tend to dampen subsequent vigilant tendencies *unless* the warnings provide new information about increased vulnerability. But Breznitz took the matter much further by testing an entire array of additional conditions that may alter the impact of false alarms. Thus, going beyond a "law of initial credibility," he presented 25 summary propositions that specify these conditions. Unfortunately, his laboratory tests did not address various social contexts, such as media organization responses, that Turner (1983) and his colleagues had found to be important in their studies of several earthquake "near predictions" in 1976 that initiated a period of waiting in Los Angeles County.

IB4.1c "The law of initial credibility posits that a warning system that enjoyed high credibility will lose more credibility following a false alarm than one whose credibility was lower in the first place" (Breznitz, 1984:206).

IB4.1d "Tests of seven hypotheses concerning differential susceptibility to false-alarm effects, each with four different dependent variables, were consistently negative. Individual and aggregate changes in earthquake response must be explained by other mechanisms than a false-alarm effect. [p. 69] . . . extent of media attention and extent of informal discussion serve as surrogates for actual events in assessing the credibility of an uncertain threat to the community. The more the threat is talked about, the more credible it seems [p. 70]" (Turner et al., 1981:69, 70).

IB4.1e "Measures of fear, imminent expectation for a damaging earthquake, household preparedness, confidence in scientific earthquake prediction capability, suspicion that information was being withheld, attitude toward releasing uncertain predictions, focus on scientific as compared with unscientific forecasts, and preferred media source of information on forecasts tend to disconfirm the disillusionment, denial, and scapegoating hypotheses, to support reduced urgency and familiarization hypotheses, and to provide weak support for the rehearsal hypothesis" (Turner, 1983:307).

IB4.2(H) "Mack and Baker (1961) have illustrated that a curvilinear relationship exists, in some instances, between socio-economic status and warning belief. There appears to be a tendency for persons of low and high education to disregard the formal meaning of a signal, while persons of middle socio-economic status are more likely to accept the formal meaning" (as summarized in Mileti, Drabek, and Haas, 1975:47).

The lower side of the socioeconomic status curve has been validated in more recent studies within the U.S.A. (see Ralph H. Turner, 1976:182–183) and in Japan (Ohta and Abe, 1977:277). Interestingly, the reluctance of upper classes to attribute credibility to warnings by local officals has not been pursued further. Also, some conflicting evidence has been reported from Japan and Australia that indicates a linear relationship, i.e., the lower the education level, the less the warning belief (Okabe and Mikami, 1982:9; World Meteorological Organization, n.d.:5-4).

IB4.3 "Women are more likely to interpret a signal as valid than men" (as summarized in Mileti, Drabek, and Haas, 1975:47, based on Mack and Baker, 1961, and Drabek, 1969). (See also Okabe and Mikami, 1982:9; World Meteorological Organization, n.d.:5-4; Guard Police Psychology Research Society, 1980b.)

This proposition has been validated in recent Japanese studies. For certain agents like earthquakes, some females may not evidence adaptive behaviors despite acceptance of the warning. Also, there is the distinct possibility that the degree of discrepancy between the sexes will vary among warning sources and socioeconomic status groupings. Thus, the response of college-educated women may be more similar to that of men of comparable educational experience than to that of less educated women. Pinning down these types of variations are among the multitude of issues awaiting future researchers.

> IB4.3a "In December, 1974, the committee for earthquake prediction released information about unusual phenomena observed around Kawasaki city. The information was reported in newspapers, and was regarded as an earthquake prediction. . . . Women rather than men, people who thought that the information was issued by local governments, people who perceived a stronger magnitude and a higher probability than that indicated in the information circulated, and people who had lived at their present residence for a long period, tended to believe the prediction. Women rather than men, people who have lower level of education, and people who had lived at the present residence for a longer period tended to have stronger anxiety. . . . Men are more likely to believe a newspaper report, while women are more likely to believe a T.V. report [Japan] (Abe and Kazama, 1978)" (as summarized in Yamamoto and Quarantelli, 1982:A-44).

> IB4.4 "Older persons are less likely than the young to receive warnings regardless of warning source, and less likely to take protective actions" (Mileti, 1975b:22). (See also Friedsam, 1961, 1962; Mack and Baker, 1961; Ralph H. Turner, 1976.)

Some have argued that the elderly are more reluctant to believe warning messages. To date that remains controversial and not resolvable with the existent data base. What is clear is that elderly persons are less likely to receive warnings in the first place. Hence, what some have interpreted as resistance to act may be spurious, at least in many situations. Thus, the hypotheses below require further testing using comparative designs so that various situational factors can be controlled. My suspicion is that age will turn out to have an important interaction effect, but will not be found to covary consistently by itself regarding either warning belief or response.

> IB4.4a(H) ". . . the older the individual, the less likely he is to interpret the warning as real (Friedsam, 1961 and 1962; Mack and Baker, 1961)" (as summarized in Mileti, Drabek, and Haas, 1975:48).

> IB4.4b(H) "Citizens in the age group 21–30, followed by those aged 31–40 appear to have the keenest understanding of the intent of the warnings" [Australia] (Southern, n.d.:B-1).

> IB4.5 ". . . members of minority groups will assign little credibility to the official sources that disseminate warnings, and consequently will not

be disposed to take appropriate precautionary actions" (Ralph H. Turner, 1976:183).

While I did not encounter any conflicting evidence, it is important to note that the existent empirical base is limited to two groups—Blacks (Perry and Mushkatel, 1984; Moore *et al.*, 1963:125) and Mexican-Americans (Lindell, Perry, and Greene, 1980:13; Perry, Lindell, and Greene, 1982a:97; Perry and Greene, 1982b:327). Thus, while stated in general terms here, and supported empirically for these two groups, there may be exceptions.

In a recently completed study, however, Perry, Greene, and Mushkatel (1983) have taken the initial steps toward making ethnic group contrasts. Appropriately, they linked many of these to alternative message qualities. Their conclusions—which I suggest we treat as hypotheses until replicated—take us to the cutting edge of the field.

IB4.5a(H) ". . . the data showed a positive correlation between warning source credibility and level of perceived risk. In the hazardous materials emergency, both Whites and Mexican-Americans who were warned by a credible source tended to perceive risk as high; conversely, those who reported being warned by a source *not* perceived as credible tended to define risk as lower. This same pattern prevailed for Blacks and Mexican-Americans in connection with the flood disaster" (Perry, Greene, and Mushkatel, 1983:283). (See also Perry and Mushkatel, 1984.)

IB4.5b(H) "When citizens were asked to specify the warning source in which they had greatest confidence, both ethnic differentials and between threat-agent differentials appeared. In connection with the flood threat, most Whites reported having highest confidence in the mass media, with police and fire department officers a distant second choice and personal judgment third. Most Blacks identified police and fire fighters as their source of highest confidence, with neighbors or friends and personal judgment as (again distant) second and third choices, respectively. Mexican-Americans cited neighbors or friends, relatives and mass media as their sources of highest confidence in descending order" (Perry, Greene, and Mushkatel, 1983:283). (See also Perry and Mushkatel, 1984.)

IB4.6 "Small town residents or urban dwellers with small town backgrounds are less likely to interpret a warning as valid than are urbanites (Mack and Baker, 1961)" (as summarized in Mileti, Drabek, and Haas, 1975:48).

IB4.7 ". . . persons belonging to large, complex, and authoritarian organizations are more likely to interpret a warning as valid (Mack and Baker, 1961; Moore *et al.*, 1963)" (as summarized in Mileti, Drabek, and Haas, 1975:47).

IB4.8 The greater the proximity to the threatened area, the greater the likelihood to interpret the message as valid. (Based on Diggory, 1956; see Mileti, Drabek, and Haas, 1975:45–47.)

Since the publication of our previous inventory (1975) no research was encountered wherein these differences in warning responses were assessed. Thus, the propositions stand, but I suspect that future work will reveal that each has important interaction effects with all of the other variables discussed thus far.

In contrast to physical locations are social locations, especially linkage structures that tie people to family members. Primary groups frequently serve as conduits for warning messages. Clearly, many Americans frequently try to contact kin thought to be in threatened areas (Drabek, 1969; Perry and Greene, 1982b). A similar pattern has been documented in Japan (Okabe and Mikami, 1982:19).

> IB4.9 "The greater the frequency of contacts with kin, the greater the number of warnings an individual will receive" (Perry and Greene, 1982b:327).

This proposition brings us to some earlier observations I made (1969) regarding kin linkages and the social processes that comprise warning responses. Data from Perry, Greene, and Mushkatel confirm many of these interpretations.

> ". . . we found that when kin contacts were restricted to only those where warning or threat-relevant information is exchanged, very few respondents reported that most of their warning information came from relatives. These data provide a valuable insight into the nature of kin involvement specifically as it relates to warning response. Namely, while our data show that people (without regard to ethnicity) *interact* with kin during the warning phase, only a minority of these interactions seem to involve exchanges of threat information which enhances the specificity of the warning message. One can therefore infer that contacts with kin not in one's own household possibly focus upon offers of shelter or expressions of concern about safety, rather than principally upon relaying warnings and offering further details about the threat itself. This contention is consistent with a study by Drabek (1969:345) which showed that some flood warning recipients (who contacted or were contacted by relatives) received invitations from relatives to 'come over and spend the evening just in case this thing may be serious.' Hence, these contacts which occurred after a disaster warning, but before impact did not center on providing threatened kinsmen, but instead offered a place of shelter without specific judgment pertinent to the warning message itself" (Perry, Greene, and Mushkatel, 1983:289).

In addition to linkages with kin, which, by the way, may be most critical in unraveling the effects of age on warning responses (Drabek and Boggs, 1968), it is clear that community involvement also impacts disaster response.

> IB4.10 "The greater the level of community involvement, the greater the number of warnings an individual is likely to receive" (Perry and Greene, 1982b:327).

IB4.10a "Membership in an ethnic minority group is inversely correlated with socioeconomic status . . . The lower the individual's socioeconomic status, the lower the level of community involvement" (Perry and Greene, 1982b:327).

As with age, ethnicity and socioeconomic status appear to covary with community involvement. Thus, social linkages may be important mediating variables that partially explain response differences rather than attitudinal predispositions thought to covary with social demographics. But certainly with these ten characteristics of the message receiver codified in this manner, future researchers have a solid platform from which to proceed.

IB5. Confirmation Behavior

The empirical literature is clear—upon receiving a disaster warning, people *do not* panic. In general, disbelief is the pervasive definition. If they do anything at all, the most probable action is to engage in a variety of behaviors that may confirm—or neutralize—the warning. Perry, Lindell, and Greene (1981) summarize the sequence this way.

"The major processes involved in postwarning attempts to restructure the normative environment are: . . . First, there is an intial communication process, milling, which focuses on *confirming* the warning message, gathering further information, and establishing a warning belief. Assuming that a warning belief is established, further milling centers on the problem of assessing personal risk—the determination of one's *proximity* to the impact area and the individual's perception of the *certainty,* and probable *severity* of disaster impact. Finally, if personal risk appears high, necessitating some adaptive response, individuals assess the logistics of making such a response" (Perry, Lindell, and Greene, 1981:28).

IB5.1 ". . . among people who tried to confirm a message, the perception of the threat as real was higher when confirmation was achieved than when the individual failed to get confirmation" (Perry, Lindell, and Greene, 1981:152). (See also Mileti, Drabek and Haas, 1975:46.)

IB5.1a ". . . the proportion of people who try to confirm a preimpact warning is positively related to the amount of lead time prior to impact" (Perry, Lindell, and Greene, 1981:152).

IB5.1b "The more warning messages received by an individual, the fewer the attempts at warning confirmation" (Mileti, 1975b:21).

IB5.1c "If residents are convinced in advance of the warning that their homes are at risk to tornados or hurricanes or flash floods, then a warning is likely to induce attempts to confirm the impending risk. [p. 433] . . . if residents have a prior plan for emergency action, they are much more likely to heed warnings [p. 434]" (Leik *et al.,* 1981:433, 434).

These findings highlight the scarcity of information regarding the determinants of confirmation actions. But none have been linked systematically to the ranges of actions that have been documented as constituting message confirmation.

> IB5.2 "A person is more likely to believe a warning of impending danger to the extent that perceived changes in his physical environment support the threat message" (Mileti, 1975b:21). (See also Williams, 1956; Mack and Baker, 1961.)

Among the environmental elements most commonly observed are the actions of other people.

> IB5.2a(H) "Persons who see others behaving as if they believe a warning to be valid are themselves more likely to believe the warning" (Mileti, 1975b:21). (See also Mack and Baker, 1961:46.)

> IB5.2b(H) ". . . the *context* rather than the *content* of the message is more important in influencing the response. That is, instead of directly responding to the warning message, there is an attempt to assess its validity on the basis again of how known others react to it. . . . If others are leaving there is a tendency to leave; if others are staying there is a tendency to stay" (Dynes and Quarantelli, 1976:234).

There are complexities, however. For example, a series of laboratory studies focused on simulated hurricane warnings indicated that:

> ". . . observing the response of others does not appear to affect the response taken by an individual. However, having an advisory issued by the National Weather Service does produce a more extreme response and telling subjects with prior hurricane experience about surrounding events also produces an increase in the extremity of the response. [p. 207] . . . The failure to find a significant group effect also supports the results of Experiment I in that the hypothesis of a social influence effect is not upheld. . . . The surprising component identified by these two studies is that neither the actions of strangers nor the actions of a friend or spouse had any impact on an individual's response [p. 209]" (Christensen and Ruch, 1980:207, 209).

Thus, while it is clear that confirmation behavior is a critical dimension of warning response, it is equally clear that much remains to be clarified. We will pursue this topic further in the next chapter since it is the behavioral bridge to the first section there, i.e., evacuation. But before turning to that, let's review the insights that have been documented for other system levels.

IIB. Group System Level

Findings regarding group responses to disaster warnings, including the responses of families, remain rather sparse. Three themes offer limited insight: (1) group impacts on warning belief; (2) confirmation and coalescing behavior; and (3) earthquake prediction responses.

IIB1. Group Impacts on Warning Belief

Based on scattered findings from several studies, it appears that warning belief is related to primary group context. What is unclear, however, is the exact nature of the relationship. Available data suggest that families provide contextual impacts that may differ from those provided by other types of groups.

> IIB1.1(H) Primary group context influences warning belief; direction of influence covaries with group type.

> IIB1.1a(H) Individuals in a group of peers are less likely to believe a disaster warning. (Adapted from Mack and Baker, 1961:48.)

> IIB1.1b(H) Informal group interaction is a major source of reinforcement of disbelief in disaster warnings. (Adapted from Clifford, 1956.)

> IIB1.1c(H) Individuals in a family group are more likely to believe a disaster warning. (Adapted from Mack and Baker, 1961:47.)

> IIB1.1d(H) "Persons whose families were separated at the time of the initial warnings evidenced a slight tendency to be less skeptical of the messages when compared to members of intact families" (Drabek and Stephenson, 1971:197).

> IIB1.1e(H) "When warnings were received through the neighborhood association, the rate of evacuation was more than half, whereas through other sources, the rate was only about 36%" [Japan] (Ikeda, 1982:57).

IIB2. Confirmation and Coalescing Behavior

When disaster warnings are defined as credibile enough to alter initial responses of disbelief, persons typically seek more information. Group contexts structure much of this confirmatory behavior. Furthermore, during this time there is a decided movement toward accounting for the whereabouts of group members who are not physically present. Thus, gradually—although depending upon event characteristics and message content the process may quicken—there is a coalescing so that the group can be united prior to impact where possible.

> IIB2.1 ". . . warning recipients tend to be skeptical of the first warning they hear, and attempt to confirm through some additional source the information given in the warning. More than 80 percent of the samples in both Toutle/Silverlake and Woodland tried to confirm the first warning heard with at least one additional source" (Perry and Greene, 1983:66).

> IIB2.1a Families warned in one way seek to confirm through different means. (Based on Drabek, 1969:344.)

> IIB2.2 ". . . unless all members are accounted for, families will be slow to undertake any kind of protective action (Quarantelli, 1960a)" (Perry and Greene, 1983:66).

IIB2.2a "Persons responded to the warning process as members of primary groups and attempted to be together regardless of official interference. . . . extended family relationships were instrumental in message warning, confirmation and offers of shelter" (Worth and McLuckie, 1977:72).

IIB2.2b The intensity and mode of warning confirmation varies with whether or not a family is united at the time a warning is received. (Based on Drabek and Stephenson, 1971; see also Drabek, 1983b.)

I suspect that many families facing an evacuation decision wonder how others will learn of their whereabouts. Thus, based both on my own interviews and Perry's analyses, the acceptance of mechanisms to aid in such information exchanges probably would be rather high if implemented.

IIB2.2c ". . . 90% of the people sampled in each of the four study sites said that they would be willing to use a warning and evacuation information telephone number" (Perry, Greene, and Lindell, 1980a:442).

While evacuation will be the focus of the next chapter, it must be noted that the consequence of coalescing actions results in a pronounced uniformity. That is, from a behavioral vantage point, individuals rarely evacuate—family units do. Furthermore, there are very critical linkages between confirmatory actions and both the routes and locations selected for evacuation.

IIB2.3 ". . . evacuation is a family phenomenon; for the most part, families evacuate as units (Danzig, Thayer and Galanter, 1958; Moore *et al.,* 1963; Drabek and Boggs, 1968; Drabek, 1969; Drabek and Stephenson, 1971)" (as summarized in Mileti, Drabek, and Haas, 1975:49).

IIB2.4 Most people do not telephone emergency agencies to confirm disaster warnings; rather relatives and friends are contacted (Based on Drabek, 1969:343; see also Perry, Lindell, and Greene, 1981).

Some people will try to confirm disaster warnings by contacting emergency agencies. Many will not be successful, however. Thus, dispatchers correctly perceive their telephone lines being overloaded. An abnormally high number of contacts are made during most warning periods. But this load—while overwhelming for the agency—still represents a relatively small portion of the population. My study, for example, of the 1965 flood in Denver, Colorado, documented that nine percent of the families tried to telephone an emergency agency. But nearly one-fifth (19%) received only busy signals (Drabek, 1969:343). Thus, these numbers of attempted communication—while only a fraction of the total population at risk—were sufficient to overload. (See also Okabe and Mikami, 1982:18-20.)

IIB2.5 Disaster warnings are confirmed by families through at least four distinct social processes: (1) appeal to authorities; (2) appeal to peers; (3) observational confirmation; and (4) latent confirmation. (Adapted from Drabek, 1969; see also Okabe and Mikami, 1982:19.)

The last two processes are far more important than the first, i.e., calls to emergency organizations. They are used less frequently than the second, i.e., contacts with relatives, neighbors, and friends. Observational confirmation refers to the fact that many family members will seek to confirm a warning message by direct observation, e.g., going to a river.

> "Another procedure, similar to that of observing the water, was that of observing other persons. For example, some respondents reported that after being warned by a police officer they proceeded to watch the officer as he went to other houses down the street. They made the point very clear that it was not specific information about the flood that acted to confirm the warning, but rather, when I saw him warn all of those other people, I figured it must be true" (Drabek, 1969:343–344).

Similarly, some of the individuals we interviewed described how this warning was confirmed for them unintentionally. Thus, through a wide variety of specific behavioral sequences, warnings were confirmed as latent consequences of other actions. "For example one respondent stated that he had heard initial warnings over his car radio while on his way home from work. He gave these warnings little concern until he reached a police road block near his home. At that instant, he recalled, the flood threat became real" (Drabek, 1969:344).

> IIB2.6 ". . . when given an opportunity to choose, people tend to prefer to evacuate to the homes of friends and relatives rather than to public shelters. Second, the warning message is not necessarily the place where most people hear about the availability of shelter" (Perry, Greene, and Lindell, 1980a:442).

In part through confirmatory actions taken, families are guided in their choices of evacuation locations. Thus, following the 1965 Denver flood, I discovered that many received an invitation when they called a relative. Perry and his colleagues pursued the process and have documented that over one-fourth of the families evacuating participate in this invitational process. Furthermore, they have begun to specify some of the conditions that may alter it.

> IIB2.6a "These findings support Drabek's contention that evacuation by invitation is important in localized disasters and add the qualifiers that this effect is intensified in communities with a history of flooding and that the longer the period of forewarning, the greater is the proportion of evacuations by invitation" (Perry, Greene, and Lindell, 1980a:442).

> IIB2.6b "As the amount of forewarning decreases, people tend to seek shelter in the homes of friends. When forewarning is short *and* community preparedness is low, evacuees often seek only high ground as a means of escaping oncoming waters" (Perry, Greene, and Lindell, 1980a:440).

> IIB2.6c ". . . the use of public shelter increases when community preparedness is high, when the entire community must be evacuated, and when the evacuees anticipate that the necessary period of absence will

be long. Generally though, public shelters seem to attract, even under the conditions described above, approximately one-fourth of the evacuees at a given site" (Perry, Greene, and Lindell, 1980a:440–441).

IIB2.6d ". . . in communities where flooding is recurrent and a disaster subculture (Anderson, 1965) exists, use of public shelter tends to be low, with people primarily seeking shelter in the homes of friends or relatives" (Perry, Greene, and Lindell, 1980a:441).

As we will examine in much more detail later, most families, most of the time, seek refuge in the homes of kin or friends when disaster threatens, rather than in public shelters. As indicated above, Perry and his colleagues have documented several conditionals that affect this process. Hopefully, the research of the next decade will provide a more precise calculus for estimating the scope of this behavior. When validated, such estimation formulas will provide us with a powerful tool for shelter management planning (see Drabek, 1983c).

IIB3. Earthquake Prediction Responses

Since earthquake prediction differs significantly from other forms of disaster warnings in numerous ways, and because so few have tried to examine family responses, I isolated this topic for separate treatment. Also, the methodology used merited such separation in my judgment. Mileti, Hutton, and Sorensen (1981) used a scenario approach, i.e., people were asked how they thought they would respond if a prediction of a certain type was issued. Based on a sample of 246 California families, the research team tried to unravel a complex network of social processes that may be precipitated when predictions of the type they envisioned are issued. Given that this single survey comprises the data base wherein this methodological approach was used, the conclusions are best regarded as insightful hypotheses at this point.

IIB3.1(H) Organizational decision makers—government and business—and family members reported three types of probable coping responses if an earthquake prediction was made that was judged to be credible: (1) relocation; (2) reduction; and (3) reallocation. Their response will reflect six variables: (1) image of damage; (2) exposure to risk (insurance); (3) exposure to risk (others); (4) access to information; (5) commitment to the target area; and (6) resources. (Adapted from Mileti, Hutton and Sorensen, 1981:100.)

IIB3.2(H) [Three variables] ". . . will influence public perception of earthquake prediction credibility: (1) the reputation of the person or organization making the prediction; (2) confirmation of the information given in the prediction from other sources; and (3) certainty of the threat, or how sure the predictor is that the earthquake will occur" (Mileti, Hutton, and Sorensen, 1981: 79).

IIB3.3(H) ". . . Corporations and businesses which are insured against earthquake loss are not apt to take actions or make decisions to further reduce their vulnerability . . . possessing earthquake insurance has no effect on vulnerability reduction or emergency preparedness decisions for citizens (families) or state and federal agencies, bureaucracies and organizations" (Mileti, Hutton, and Sorensen, 1981:105).

IIB3.4(H) "State and federal agencies, as well as local businesses, corporations and families, are more likely to relocate to an area of lesser risk if these units have little commitment or ties to the local community" (Mileti, Hutton, and Sorensen, 1981:112).

IIB3.5(H) "For all decision makers, choosing to reduce vulnerability and increase preparedness is facilitated by the availability of resources, no matter which strategy is used" (Mileti, Hutton, and Sorensen, 1981:115).

Unlike all other forms of disaster warnings, the time window for earthquake prediction may be rather long—quite possibly a decade or more. If you learned that your present house might be damaged in an earthquake a few years from now, would you consider selling before that information became known widely? With this question in mind, and armed with the responses to their prediction scenarios, the research team's initial interpretations received widespread attention. A core conclusion outlined in a report issued by a National Academy of Sciences Committee concerned many policy makers:

". . . if a damaging earthquake were to occur roughly as suggested by their prediction scenarios, both the human toll and the property damage would be less than those expected in an unpredicted earthquake. However, these data also suggest that when the period between the issuance of the initial prediction and the occurrence of the earthquake is extended, the affected community may well experience social disruption and a decline in its economy. They point specifically to such possible economic trends as a prohibition on the sale of new earthquake insurance policies, a sharp reduction in construction, and a decline in the sale of durable goods" (Committee on Socioeconomic Effects of Earthquake Predictions, 1978:18–19).

As the technology of earthquake prediction is improved, it is clear that the behavioral response side must share the research agenda (see Committee on Earthquake Engineering Research, 1982:201–221). But it is equally clear that as with other technologies, applications in the public interest will require important rethinking of public policy and public agency responsibilities and authorities.

IIIB. Organizational System Level

In contrast to group and individual responses to disaster warnings, relatively few behavioral studies of organizational systems were captured through my literature search procedures. The most notable exception was a large-scale study by a team of researchers from the University of Minnesota [e.g., Carter, 1980; see also Leik *et al.*, 1981, and proposition VB1.2]. My review of their work, plus the fragmented set of conclusions available in the few other studies assessed, revealed two broad categories: (1) correlates of organizational response and (2) organization-public interface.

IIIB1. Correlates of Organizational Response

The key dependent variable that most researchers have implicitly—sometimes explicitly—focused on is the speed with which disaster warnings are issued to the public. That is, after some type of information has been received by organizational personnel, what factors have slowed or speeded their processing and decision time?

From a behavioral vantage point there is a prior question, however. That is, which organizations are most likely to even become involved in a typical community warning process? Obviously, the mix will vary by event. The organizational network responding to an approaching flood will not be identical in composition to that elicited by a chemical spill or nuclear power plant accident. Even a gross description of "who is involved" across a wide variety of such events remains empirically undocumented, however, aside from the exploratory work by the University of Minnesota team (see Carter, 1980). And that work was restricted to three types of natural disasters—hurricanes, floods, and tornadoes. Thus, the degree of functional commonality and key points of dissimilarity regarding organizational participation in events of different types remain unknown.

One analytic variable has been proposed; clearly it is only one among many that might determine the likelihood of organizational participation in the community warning process.

> IIIB1.1 "The capacity of an organization for communication is directly related to the probability of that organization's emergent involvement in the warning process in the pre-impact community" (Mileti, Drabek, and Haas, 1975:41).

If involved, what responses are most typical? It is likely that previous disaster history is a key determinant, but as with the public, skepticism is the initial response by most organizational decision makers. Thus, an implicit hypothesis meriting empirical study is:

> IIIB1.2(H) The greater the frequency of disasters of a particular type, the less the degree of initial skepticism among organizational decision makers and the quicker they will recognize a potential danger.

> IIIB1.2a "The area in question has a history which is practically disaster free. It is not surprising then, that one of the first problems which arose was one of getting some skeptical organizational officials to define the situation as an emergency or potential disaster. This difficulty was per-

ceived by respondents to exist at several organizational levels ranging
from local to provincial and included administrators and operatives"
[Canada] (Ponting, 1974:11).

Similarly, as discussed in the previous chapter, official fear of public
panic may cause some to delay. And when they do act they may issue
warnings that lack adequate detail and specificity.

> IIIB1.2b "In our interviews with officials they admitted that they were
> somewhat afraid of causing so-called 'panic', so they had not mentioned
> many specific details about the possible dangers. This seems to have
> created the impression that the situation was not very serious or im-
> minent" [Japan] (Ikeda, 1982:55–56). (See also Ralph H. Turner, 1976:
> 182.)

As with individuals and groups, it appears that certain message characteristics—for example, ambiguity and presence of conflicting information
and perceptions of source credibility—greatly affect responses of organizational personnel. Unfortunately, investigations based on the type of
analytic precision and empirical study exemplified by the work of Perry
and his colleagues on individual and group responses have not been undertaken for organizational systems.

> IIIB1.3(H) The degree of delay in issuing disaster warnings to the public
> by organizational officials varies directly with: (1) the extent of contra-
> dictory information received; (2) ambiguity, clarity and completeness of
> the information; (3) the speed of the interorganizational communication
> flow; and (4) perceived credibility of information source. (Based on Mileti,
> Drabek, and Haas, 1975:42; see also Anderson, 1969a; Mileti, 1975b:17;
> Committee on Socioeconomic Effects of Earthquake Predictions,
> 1978:18.)

> IIIB1.3a(H) "A common problem in predisaster situations is an incon-
> sistency among incoming data. There is a well-established psychological
> principle that, when an individual is faced with conflicting statements,
> he or she is likely to accept as more valid those which are least threatening
> (McDavid J., and H. Harai. 1968. *Social Psychology*. Harper and Row,
> New York.) The same is thought to be true of organizations" (Foster,
> 1980:192).

IIIB2. Organization–Public Interface

Very little has been published regarding the boundary spanning processes
that link the public at large to organizational personnel participating in a
disaster warning event. Certainly many factors could be hypothesized as
impacting this interface. What is clear is the interorganizational quality
of this cross-system interface. A police officer warning of an approaching
flood is a communicator of information that may reflect the input and
evaluations of numerous other agencies. Yet, the homeowner being warned
sees only the police officer. Most commonly, however, the public—at

least in part—is warned through media personnel although this too will vary across events with differing qualities.

IIIB2.1 Most natural disaster warnings initially are received by the public through media organizations.

IIIB2.1a ". . . radio is the most widely used and potentially the most effective and efficient means of communicating warnings. . . . In the Denver flood of 1965, a majority (52%) of people said their first warnings of a possible disaster came from the radio (Drabek and Stephenson, 1971)" (Quarantelli, 1980b:79).

This organizational reality is thought to have its consequences. Carter (1980), in particular, has been most critical of the vagueness of information given and the lack of public response elicited. It is my judgment, however, that the criticism is more or less appropriate depending upon the case selected for study. The next task for the research community is to identify the range of variation and build on Carter's effort to isolate factors that account for the variation. Once that is established, alternative policy options can be formulated that are rooted in empirical fact, not conjecture.

IIIB2.2(H) Most disaster warning information broadcasted by media organizations is general and relatively nonspecific.

IIIB2.2a ". . . the public receives information on threatening weather conditions only from the local weather service office. . . . because this information is invariably unspecific in nature, it is unlikely that this information will prompt large numbers of the public to take immediate defensive actions to protect life and property" (Carter, 1980:228).

IIIB2.2b ". . . very few broadcast stations receive useful information by monitoring the radio transmissions of the emergency service agencies. . . . the percentage of stations with such contact with the local weather service office is greatest for the tornado sites and smallest for the flash flood sites. . . . Across all sites, only about 1 of every 10 broadcast stations has two-way or directed one-way communication systems with any of the five emergency service agencies. . . . [Thus,] the general public is unlikely to receive more than very general information on either the development of hazardous weather or the appropriate actions to take to seek protection" (Carter, 1980:223).

IVB. Community System Level

As with organizational systems, relatively few researchers have sought to assess community level systems and to differentiate among them. Yet, a few insights do appear in the literature that may serve as helpful points of departure for any seeking to penetrate this important, but relatively unexplored area. Two major themes I encountered were: (1) community variation in warning system composition and (2) correlates of community response.

IVB1. Community Variation in Warning System Composition

After extensive study in Hawaii, Sorensen and Gersmehl (1980) have provided the most thorough argument to date that communities can and should
vary in their approach to disaster warnings. Beyond the formal organizations that might participate, the informal system must be recognized
explicitly and integrated into the overall warning effort. Stated less normatively, I would propose the following hypothesis as one meriting empirical study.

> IVB1.1(H) The composition of community warning systems varies along
> a rural–urban dimension.

> IVB1.1a "Communication among many residents of the district is con
> ducted on a very personal basis, often through kinship ties or by citizen's
> band (CB) radio. The role of the media is not paramount, except to the
> newly arrived occupants of subdivision housing, who are not yet fully
> incorporated into the social network of Puna District" (Sorensen and
> Gersmehl, 1980:130).

> IVB1.1b ". . . the efficiency of the entire warning system may owe less
> to the structure of the formal system than to abilities of a few individuals
> operating within an efficient, informal network, a preexistent product of
> the social fabric of an essentially rural district of sharply limited size and
> diversity" (Sorensen and Gersmehl, 1980:133).

Additionally, it is clear that the use of various types of technologies—
be they sirens, or what have you—will vary across communities. Typically,
researchers have argued that sirens alone are relatively ineffectual. Quarantelli (1980b) has suggested, however, that in some communities where
a particular type of event, like tornadoes, has a high frequency, a subculture may develop so as to enhance the effectiveness of siren systems.
As will be addressed later, it is clear that immediate disaster response is
affected by the presence of such disaster subcultures. What has not been
explored in comparative community studies, however, is the variation
that might be reflected in community warning system composition.

> IVB1.1c ". . . the use of warning sirens alone is totally inadequate to
> stimulate people to take immediate protective action. The sirens may not
> even be noticed; if noticed, they may be ignored, assigned everyday
> meaning, or as is most often the case, initiate the seeking of additional
> information. [p. 78] . . . At best, except where they have been a traditional
> part of a disaster subculture . . . sirens may indicate that something might
> be wrong (Mack and Baker, 1961) [p. 79]" (Quarantelli, 1980b:78, 79).

Many planners focus on hardware aspects of warning systems. Equipment failure or lack of availability, however, does not appear to be the
major source of problems. Yet, precise assessment of this matter through
comparative community analyses awaits the attention of the research
community.

IVB1.1d ". . . it is the extremely rare disaster situation where there is complete loss of necessary mechanical communication capabilities . . . Even in the catastrophe at Darwin, despite initial accounts of lack of such facilities (Haas *et al.,* 1976) a systematic study discovered that at all times there were substantial communication capabilities of all kinds available in the area, albeit unknown to most local officials and agencies (Scanlon, 1979)" (Quarantelli, 1980b:82).

IVB2. Correlates of Community Response

Even less explored than organizational systems are the qualities of community structure that might alter warning response. However, some general guidelines have been suggested. Based largely on individual response studies of the type discussed above, community planners can be advised of six factors that will alter public responses:

1. The warning must be clear;
2. The warning must convey what is the appropriate response;
3. The warning must be perceived as coming from a credible source;
4. The warning must be reinforced socially and at the local level;
5. The medium used to disseminate the warning is important; and,
6. The type of appeal must be considered and assessed. (Adapted from Illinois Department of Transportation, Division of Water Resources, 1980:27.)

But what characteristics of communities might impact warning responses? Here the literature is sparse. The few factors suggested have some striking parallels to those identified above regarding individual response variation.

IVB2.1(H) The greater the frequency of a disaster agent, the greater the effectiveness of the community warning system.

This hypothesis is based on numerous conclusions appearning in the literature, but it awaits a systematic testing wherein a multi-community design is employed (see Ralph H. Turner, 1976:182; Anderson, 1969a). As I noted regarding other system levels, however, "past experience" is a complex variable. Thus, the specification of various conditionals wherein various forms of "past exerience" are more or less valid awaits detailed study.

IVB2.2(H) "The effectiveness of the performance of the warning function varies directly with the range of past error in the predictability of the disaster agent" (Mileti, Drabek, and Haas, 1975:41).

IVB2.2a "Familiarity with a particular hazard leads to an expertise in recognizing mounting danger. . . . Unfortunately many of the worst disasters are suffered by communities that have traditionally been peripheral to hazard-prove areas. [p. 176] . . . In such locales, it may also be difficult to generate public interest even when warnings have been issued. Darwin, Australia, had often received tropical cyclone alerts or warnings. Normal storm paths, however, saved the city from disaster on many occasions and little cyclone damage had been suffered since 1937. As a result, when cyclone warnings were issued on Christmas Eve 1974, most residents believed that, as usual, the city would be spared and so continued their normal festivities (Haas, Cochrane, and Eddy, 1976) [pp. 176–177]'' (Foster, 1980:176–177).

Disasters rarely happen at convenient times. Community warning systems reflect a variety of complications that reduce their effectiveness. Reviewing warning responses in several Colorado communities that were flooded during the mid-1960s, Worth and McLuckie (1977) concluded that ''. . . a continuum seemed to develop from an administrative vacuum on one end to an unsanctioned assumption of authority leading to a duplication of effort on the other end'' (Worth and McLuckie, 1977:72). They were not able to test the factors that might have produced this variation, but their case study data did suggest that several types of influences were operating. Among these were: ''[1] leaders were gone from the community and unable to return, or in some instances, isolated on the field and not in easy communication with relevant organizations; . . . [2] a lack of clear conception of what a particular leader's role should be by both he and others; . . . [and 3] personality factors of particular leaders and between leaders'' (Worth and McLuckie, 1977:72).

VB. Society System Level

The research literature reviewed contained few referents to warning systems for entire societies. In part, this may reflect the search process. Relatively few of the academic journals included through my procedures are publication outlets for analyses of warning systems designed for war—the very disaster on which national level warning systems are most likely to focus. But this absence also reflects the decentralized nature of American society. While several federal agencies play important roles in many disaster warnings—most notably National Weather Service offices—the fundamental responsibilities reside with local government. Thus, a clear void exists in the research data base and this situation should be corrected. The few observations I coded can be divided into two groupings: (1) warning systems within the U.S.A. and (2) warning systems outside the U.S.A.

VB1. Warning Systems within the U.S.A.

Two key ideas are worth noting. First, the complex series of processes or functional requirements that constitute a warning system have been dissected (see Mileti, 1975b). These appear to have transferability to other system levels. Thus, they may fit a society, community, or organization with equal applicability.

> VB1.1 "An integrated system actively incorporates three basic processes: 1. *evaluation*, the detection, measurement, collation, and interpretation of threat data (typically referred to as prediction and forecast); 2. *dissemination*, the decision to warn, message formulation (when warning is not accomplished by purely technical means such as sirens), and message conveyance; and 3. *response* by those who receive the warnings" (Mileti, 1975b:xiv).

But what *ought* to exist does not. At least the major cross-site study completed by the University of Minnesota team (Leik *et al.*, 1981) certainly suggested many important holes in the interorganizational networks they analyzed. While their sites may not represent the entire nation state, their data base provides the best available global assessment of the national picture, from a behavioral—as opposed to a normative—standpoint.

> VB1.2(H) "Despite the widely accepted concept of an integrated warning system, actual capability and practice at the local level represent a fragmented, poorly linked and frequently ineffective communication system" (Leik *et al.*, 1981:427).

Among the specific findings they offer that are supportive of this overall conclusion are the following.

> VB1.2a(H) ". . . serious gaps exist in the communication systems currently in use in our 22 study sites. . . . over half of the organizations we interviewed were unaware that warnings had been issued during the height of the natural hazard threat" (Leik *et al.*, 1981:71).

> VB1.2b(H) ". . . EOC's [Emergency Operations Centers] tend to become isolated enclaves which operate to inhibit coordination between different governmental jurisdictions" (Leik *et al.*, 1981:76).

Attaining a level of precision heretofore not available, this research team provided the first evidence documenting variability in network performance at differing developmental states of the warning process. Thus, networks varied in the degree to which planned contacts were implemented.

> VB1.2c(H) "The negative correlation between watch and warn phases for the percent of planned contacts actually made suggests considerable inconsistency in the system as a hazard approaches and develops. How well a site performs during early phases does not necessarily predict how it will continue to perform throughout the hazard" (Leik *et al.*, 1981:428).

Finally, they concluded that community size might be a critical determinant of warning system functioning. As with their other conclusions, however, this must be regarded as an important *hypothesis* since the 22 cases studies are far from being an adequate sample to generalize further, either across communities or to the larger society system as a whole.

VB1.2d(H) ". . . large sites with local WSO [Weather Service Office] and an integrated warning system appear to adhere more closely to emergency plans during the warning phase. If the watch phase is examined, all three site properties correlate negatively with percent of planned contacts actually made. Thus in smaller sites without WSO's and without integrated systems, early phase activities appear to fit plans better" (Leik *et al.*, 1981:429–430).

VB2. Warning Systems Outside the U.S.A.

Here again the void was striking and was exacerbated by my conceptual bias. As perusal of the bibliography indicates, there are a few case studies of a *descriptive* nature wherein some aspects of national warning systems are described. But such descriptive detail is not the type of *relational* material I sought to identify.

One study suggested that urban-rural differences existed in hazard perceptions—a point we will explore in detail in the chapter on mitigation (Chapter 9). Thus, the following hypothesis is suggested.

VB2.1(H) Warning system effectiveness covaries with the degree to which intrasocietal differences in hazard perception are recognized explicitly in the planning process.

VB2.1a ". . . not only was warning effective at the village level, but that in general terms at least the villager had a better appreciation of what a cyclone meant to him than urban dwellers (especially newcomers) in developed parts of the world that are cyclone-prone" [Tonga] (Oliver and Reardon, 1982:33).

The coming decade probably will be marked with several administrative experiments to incorporate earthquake predictions into the national warning system. Progress to date is summarized in several publications (e.g., Mileti, Hutton, and Sorensen, 1981). But clearly, the evolving Chinese system (see Gimenez, 1976) appears to be in sharp juxtaposition to those developing in Japan or the U.S.A. We will return to this topic in Chapter 9 (mitigation) since earthquake prediction technology represents a specific adjustment option like hazard insurance or use of building codes (see VIH3.11).

VB2.2(H) Earthquake prediction technologies will be absorbed into societal warning systems in accordance with prevailing political and economic ideologies.

While this hypothesis has not been pursued to date, the implications for community planners are extensive. The following brief summary by Blundell (1977) conveys the scope and potential that may be on the horizon as further progress is made in prediction technology.

". . . early on 4 February 1975, the seismic network recorded a swarm of earthquakes with unusual characteristics and closely grouped within the expected epicentral region. This was correctly interpreted as a fore-shock sequence, which is known sometimes to precede a major shock. By midday the local authorities had been alerted and the general public were set in a state of preparedness, moving elderly and infirm to places of safety, livestock out of their barns into the fields, and congregating in open spaces. The main earthquake occurred at 7.36 p.m. that evening and was of magnitude 7.3. Because most people were in the open, cas-ualties were very slight even though damage to buildings was severe. In one village of 3000 population no-one was killed even though 82 dwellings out of some 800 collapsed completely and many others were severely damaged. In another, one child died, from a population of about 3500, where 90% of the houses were destroyed. The Chinese ascribe this success in preventing disaster as much to the education and mobilisation of the public at large as to the monitoring programme. They claim to have suc-cessfully predicted and taken effective preventive measures for 10 earth-quakes, although Haicheng has been the most spectacular'' [China] (Blundell, 1977:44).

VIB. International System Level

International warning systems, be they cooperative weather watches or what have you, have not been researched by behavioral scientists (see Committee on International Disaster Assistance, 1978a, 1979; World Me-teorological Organization, n.d.). At least, the literature search processes I implemented did not identify studies with such a focus. The single ex-ception was Brown's (1977) analysis of the Sahel drought—a type of warning issue not commonly considered by most sociologists who have focused almost exclusively on warning systems for more rapidly developing events. (For detailed discussion of this event see Glantz, 1976.)

> VIB1.1(H) "The United Nations did not move quickly to take the lead in alerting the international community to the Sahelian disaster. Three critical factors emerge as central problems in response to the crisis: (1) lack of information and a weak reporting system; (2) lack of experienced personnel; and (3) lack of adequate authority to act upon information received'' [Africa] (Brown, 1977:146).

Brown's conclusion is evaluative, which may or may not be acceptable to others who might propose different criteria or assumptions about in-tervention. What it illustrates, however, is the complex research agenda that this entire topic represents.

Selected Bibliography

Anderson, William A. [1969] "Disaster Warning and Communication Processes in Two Communities." *The Journal of Communication* **19** (June):92–104.
Breznitz, Sholomo [1984] *Cry Wolf: The Psychology of False Alarms*. Hillsdale, New Jersey, and London: Lawrence Erlbaum Associates, Publishers.

Carter, T. Michael [1980] "Community Warning Systems: The Relationships among the Broadcast Media, Emergency Service Agencies, and the National Weather Service." Pp. 214–228 in *Disasters and the Mass Media: Proceedings of the Committee on Disasters and the Mass Media Workshop, February, 1979,* Committee on Disasters and the Mass Media. Washington, D.C.: National Academy of Sciences.

Christensen, Larry, and Carlton E. Ruch [1980] "The Effect of Social Influence on Response to Hurricane Warnings." *Disasters* 4 (No. 2):205–210.

Drabek, Thomas E., and John S. Stephenson III [1971] "When Disaster Strikes." *Journal of Applied Social Psychology* 1 (No. 2):187–203.

Hammarstrom-Tornstam, Gunhild [1977] *Varningsprocessen.* (Warning Process). Disaster Studies 5. Uppsala, Sweden: University of Uppsala.

Ikeda, Ken'ichi [1982] "Warning of Disaster and Evacuation Behavior in a Japanese Chemical Fire." *Journal of Hazardous Materials* 7:51–62.

Illinois Department of Transportation, Division of Water Resources [1980] "Notifying Floodplain Residents: An Assessment of the Literature." Chicago: Illinois Department of Transportation, Division of Water Resources.

Irish, J. L., and B. Falconer [1979] "Reaction to Flood Warning." Pp. 313-329 in *Natural Hazards in Australia,* R. L. Heathcote and B. G. Thom (eds.). Canberra: Australian Academy of Science.

Janis, Irving L., and Leon Mann [1977] "Emergency Decision Making: A Theoretical Analysis of Responses to Disaster Warnings." *Journal of Human Stress* 3 (June):35–48.

Leik, Robert K., T. Michael Carter, John P. Clark, and others [1981] "Community Response to Natural Hazard Warnings: Final Report." Minneapolis: University of Minnesota.

Mileti, Dennis S. [1975] *Natural Hazard Warning Systems in the United States: A Research Assessment.* Boulder, Colorado: Institute of Behavioral Science, The University of Colorado.

Mileti, Dennis S., Janice R. Hutton, and John H. Sorensen [1981] *Earthquake Prediction Response and Options for Public Policy.* Boulder, Colorado: Institute of Behavioral Science, The University of Colorado.

Moore, Harry Estill, Frederick L. Bates, Marvin V. Layman, and Vernon J. Parenton [1963] "Before the Wind: A Study of Response to Hurricane Carla." National Academy of Sciences/National Research Council Disaster Study #19. Washington, D.C.: National Academy of Sciences.

Okabe, Keizo, and Shunji Mikami [1982] "A Study on the Socio-Psychological Effect of a False Warning of the Tokai Earthquake in Japan." A Paper presented at the Tenth World Congress of Sociology, Mexico City, August.

Perry, Ronald W., and Marjorie R. Greene [1983] *Citizen Response to Volcanic Eruptions: The Case of Mount St. Helens.* New York: Irvington Publishers.

Perry, Ronald W., and Marjorie R. Greene [1982] "The Role of Ethnicity in the Emergency Decision-Making Process." *Sociological Inquiry* 52 (Fall):309– 334.

Perry, Ronald W., Michael K. Lindell, and Marjorie R. Greene [1982a] "Crisis Communications: Ethnic Differentials in Interpreting and Acting on Disaster Warnings." *Social Behavior and Personality* 10 (No. 1):97–104.

Perry, Ronald W., Michael K. Lindell, and Marjorie R. Greene [1982b] "Threat Perception and Public Response to Volcano Hazard." *Journal of Social Psychology* 116:199–204.

Perry, Ronald W., Michael K. Lindell, and Marjorie R. Greene [1981] *Evacuation Planning in Emergency Management*. Lexington, Massachusetts, and Toronto: Lexington Books.

Perry, Ronald W., and Alvin H. Mushkatel [1984] *Disaster Management: Warning Response and Community Relocation*. Westport, Connecticut, and London: Quorum Books.

Sorensen, John H., and Philip J. Gersmehl [1980] "Volcanic Hazard Warning System: Persistence and Transferability." *Environmental Management* **4** (March):125-136.

Turner, Ralph H. [1976] "Earthquake Prediction and Public Policy: Distillations from a National Academy of Sciences Report." *Mass Emergencies* **1**:179–202.

4
Evacuation and Other Forms of Pre-impact Mobilization

As emphasized previously, the lines that demark human responses across the life cycle of a disaster are blurred. Yet, once the earliest warnings have been issued, additional forms of mobilization occur. Other sectors of the community beyond those involved in the initial aspects of the warning process gradually begin to monitor the impending threat with more concern. These responses take somewhat different forms depending upon the system level studied.

The disaster impact period is difficult to define with precision, especially when events of slow onset are included within the data base, e.g., droughts. Most sociologists, however, have studied events with relatively short impact periods. How long does it take a tornado to ravage a Kansas town? A flood to crest in central Illinois? These stand in sharp contrast to the years of suffering experienced in the Sahel drought, for example. As a consequence of this skewed sample of events, a whole series of research issues pertaining to the issue of generalizability have been ignored.

Having noted this issue, but lacking analysis of it, I simply divided the response phase into two subtopics: (1) evacuation and other forms of pre-impact mobilization and (2) post-impact emergency actions. The first complements the discussion of warning responses. Clearly, precise separation simply is not possible, given the tight interdependency. The second topic—the subject of Chapter 5—will move us into the issues of recovery; this boundary also lacks precision. But we will jump across the actual impact period as if it was instantaneous, knowing full well that it isn't. Thus, we will ignore a host of questions implied regarding response variations that might be evoked by events with variable qualities. Thus, once again, the limits of the existent knowledge base stare us in the face.

IC. Individual System Level

Upon reviewing the large number of findings pertaining to individual behavior during the pre-impact mobilization phase, four related themes were apparent: (1) pre-evacuation responses; (2) evacuation rates and reasons; (3) receiver qualities; and (4) message qualities. As will become evident quickly, however, this section was difficult to separate from the next one that focuses on groups. This is because most people evacuate within family units whenever possible.

IC1. Pre-evacuation Responses

After receipt of a warning message, the response patterns that are evoked will vary with the numerous qualities identified in Chapter 3. Thus, initial responses of disbelief and denial are commonplace, followed by varied forms of confirmation-seeking behavior. Panic—except in highly specialized contexts that exist rarely—is not a modal response. These insights set the stage for additional behavior patterns that occur prior to the arrival of disaster.

Before proceeding, however, an important distinction must be noted. Traditionally, as implied in the above paragraph, evacuation is a term used to refer to withdrawal behavior prior to impact. For example, families might leave beachfront homes prior to arrival of a hurricane. But there are other possibilities. These have appeared in the literature over the years. For example, during a study of search and rescue responses (Drabek *et al.*, 1981), I became acutely aware of the multiple forms of evacuation and found a typology formulated by Perry, Lindell, and Greene (1981) to be a helpful tool. "By cross-classifying these two important dimensions of evacuations, [i.e., timing and period of evacuation] one may generate a tentative classification format for distinguishing four kinds of evacuations: preventive, protective, rescue, and reconstructive" (Perry, Lindell, and Greene, 1981:4). To date, however, most of the research focus has been on short-term, pre-impact evacuation forms. That is, studies focus on evacuations which are preventive, rather than protective (pre-impact, long-term), rescue (post-impact, short-term), or reconstructive (post-impact, long-term).

> IC1.1 ". . . in pre-impact stress situations there is a tendency to act in familiar ways (Demerath, 1957; Kilpatrick, 1957; Glass, 1970; Anderson, 1969a)" (as summarized in Mileti, Drabek, and Haas, 1975:49). (See also Oliver and Trollope, 1981:47; Frazier, 1979:344–345; Society for the Be-

havioral Science of Disaster, 1978; Paulsen, 1981:14; Chandessais, 1966:452.)

As noted in Chapter 3, panic responses do not occur when disaster warnings are issued. We'll pursue this matter later as there are some special conditions that may evoke panic (see ID1.7). During the pre-impact phase, however, it is important to realize that the mechanisms of denial remain strong, (see Quarantelli, 1954, 1964, 1981b; Frazier, 1979:347; Mileti, Drabek, and Haas, 1975:43).

IC1.2 "A better focus of concern would be what might be considered the reverse of panic—inaction, denial, a fear of appearing foolish by overreacting, the need to investigate before leaving a burning building, re-entry of it, or persistence in fighting a fire too large to control rather than promptly leaving" (Paulsen, 1981:13).

IC1.2a "The Beverly Hills Supper Club fire in Southgate, Kentucky on May 28, 1977, in which 165 people died, is a case where a superficial look might lead one to ascribe many fatalities to panic. Sime quotes a British newspaper report with the headline 'Panic Kills 300.' (125,[1] p. 63). Contrary to this, researchers agree that panic, in the sense of aggressive behavior which would add to the danger to self and others presented by the fire itself, did not occur" (Paulsen, 1981:12).

IC1.2b " 'Research of fires shows that people need sufficient information about a fire before they can or are prepared to leave a building. There is growing evidence that the delay in warning people in a number of major fires has been a primary reason why people have been unable to escape in time. An emphasis on avoiding "panic" contributes to delays.' (126,[2] p. 214)" (Paulsen, 1981:12–13).

Although rare, some case materials reveal instances when fear levels have been heightened to the point that victims were immobilized—at least temporarily (e.g., see Quarantelli, 1981b, 1980b, 1954). In a review of a draft of this chapter Quarantelli noted that there are at least two kinds of immobilization: (1) from fear, which is rather rare, and (2) from redefinition of the situation as one requiring immobility, as seen in some mine or aircraft disasters (e.g., Lucas, 1969). To date, however, precise measurement of such responses at either the behavioral or subjective levels remains a neglected research topic. Thus, our knowledge of disaster-produced "fear" remains a near void.

---

[1]125: J.D. Sime, "The Concept of 'Panic.' " Pp. 63–81 in *Fires and Human Behaviour*, David Center (ed.). New York: John Wiley and Sons, 1980.

[2]126: J.D. Sime, "The Concept of 'Panic in Fires': A Brief Appraisal." Pp. 211–214 in *Second International Seminar on Human Behavior in Fire Emergencies, October 29–November 1, 1978—Proceedings of Seminar*. National Bureau of Standards Report No. NBSIR 80-2070. Issued June, 1980. NTIS Order No. PB 80 204738.

Of course, for some events—a winter blizzard, for example—one's home may be the safest place to stay. Curiously, most studies have focused on evacuation responses prior to hurricanes or floods rather than events wherein staying home may be the best bet. If you were warned that an approaching blizzard might preclude shopping for a couple of days would you buy an extra can of soup? Data from an Ohio blizzard (1977–78) are among the few analyses of such events that I uncovered. Stockpiling— or might it be labeled hoarding?—behavior was documented. What we don't know is how far to generalize these findings, and thus they imply an important series of hypotheses meriting follow-up under varied conditions that ought to be specified very carefully.

> IC1.3(H) "The day before the impact of the blizzard, which began in the early morning hours of January 26, 1978, a number of warnings were issued. . . . 72.2 percent, did hear that there might be a blizzard and had some time to make additional preparation. Of these, 82, or 53.5 percent, did make additional preparation. . . . Fifty percent obtained extra food and 15 percent prepared an extra water supply. The other preparatory activities received very little attention" (Neal, Perry, and Hawkins, 1982:71).

IC2. Evacuation Rates and Reasons

During the last two decades, several studies conducted on evacuations from floods and hurricanes have provided a partial picture of the evacuation process and the prime reasons that potential victims offer regarding their decisions to leave. Clearly, that picture, as detailed in Chapter 3, is one of adaptive response. When warned properly, significant proportions of threatened populations do relocate temporarily. While there are exceptions, most people respond in a reasonable manner. Despite official and public expectations of traffic accidents, researchers documented low rates (see Quarantelli, 1980b).

> IC2.1 When warned adequately of approaching natural disasters, approximately 50% of the threatened population will evacuate upon receipt of official advisories. (Based on Quarantelli, 1980b; Perry, Lindell, and Greene, 1981.)

These rates are variable, however, and unique events may skew the curve, although not as much as might be anticipated. Thus, Stallings (1984:11) concluded that despite intense media coverage in the Three Mile Island accident (March, 1979), evacuation "did not differ significantly from those taking place in natural disasters." To date, calculation of these variations and even the analytic qualities that produce them await specification.

> IC2.1a "In the volcanic eruption studies here, [i.e., Mount St. Helens] 11.1% of the citizens at risk failed to evacuate. For natural disasters this

is a low proportion of nonevacuees and has been explained in terms of the uniqueness of the disaster and the high levels of community emergency preparedness in the affected communities. The more commonly seen figure is that for the flood communities where about half of those who received a warning failed to evacuate (Quarantelli & Dynes, 1972). At TMI, where only an evacuation advisory for pregnant women and young children was issued, it is estimated that 144,000 people, 39% of the total population within 15 miles of the reactor, evacuated'' (Perry, 1983:43).

IC2.1b ''. . . the high level of so-called 'spontaneous' evacuations around TMI appears to be related to the public's perception of high personal risk. Although there were numerous parallels between the nuclear case and the volcano and flood evacuation, in the nuclear case citizens apparently believed themselves to be at relatively greater risk of danger. Thus, the perceived negative consequences associated with failing to undertake a protective action, or doing so too late, were extremely high'' (Perry, 1983:46).

IC2.1c [Based on telephone interviews with 1505 individuals who lived within 55 miles of TMI.] ''Results indicate that severity, susceptibility, barrier and cost variables were, as suggested by the model, related to evacuation behavior''. [However, it appeared that ''conflicting'' or ''confusing'' information may have increased the evacuation rate in this case, as compared to non-nuclear instances.] (Houts et al., 1984:27).

Why do people say they evacuated their homes? Again the knowledge base is limited, but the studies point toward several factors with reasonable consistency.

IC2.2 ''. . . situational danger and advisories from officials were cited most frequently as critical reasons for evacuating in both the nuclear emergency and the natural disasters. Indeed, these two reasons alone account for more than 55% of the volcano evacuees, 82% of the flood evacuees, and nearly 45% of the TMI evacuees'' (Perry, 1983:41).

IC2.2a The four most important reasons for evacuating were: (1) saw eruption (29.1%); (2) officials urged departure (26.6%); (3) relatives urged departure (20.3%); (4) neighbors left (12.7%). (Adapted from Perry and Greene, 1983:89; see also Perry and Greene, 1982a:345.)

IC2.2b ''Concerning our sample's reported behavior during the accident period (28th March–11th April 1979), 71% evacuated with 85% of these travelling to points outside a 25 mile radius around the plant. The reasons which were most commonly given for evacuation were (in rank order) the need to remove one's family from danger, the fear of the unknown, and being told to leave by authorities'' (Goldsteen and Schorr, 1982:51).

Of course, those choosing not to evacuate have their reasons too. As yet these remain researched minimally. Certainly, the next decade should provide an improved knowledge base regarding this issue.

IC2.3 ''Among nonevacuees at TMI, the presence of conflicting messages and the absence of an official evacuation order were frequently cited reasons for staying. In the natural disasters people also reported that they chose to stay so that they could protect their homes from the environmental threat. Unlike the natural disasters, fear of looting was given as a reason for not evacuating at TMI'' (Perry, 1983:43).

IC2.3a "The Niigata earthquake occurred in the daytime on a weekday. We found evidence of the operation of the three factors mentioned above in keeping people from evacuating. In asking why they hesitated to leave their homes, 37 percent felt deeply attached to their household effects; 13 percent worried about their family, especially children in school; and 33 percent thought little of the hazard. Moreover, only about half of the victims (50 percent of the males, 47 percent of the females) could decide what course of action to take; 17 percent of the males and 30 percent of the females did as neighbors did; others waited for directions from authorities" [Japan] (Ohta, 1972:176).

IC2.3b "Villagers tend to leave their homes after flood warnings only as a last resort because they believe that thieves in boats will steal their belongings. . . . villagers required personal persuasion by community leaders to evacuate their homes" [India] (Schware, 1982:215).

Given population densities in many coastal areas, especially in sections of Texas and Florida, the option of "vertical evacuation" has been considered recently as an alternative to the more traditional "horizontal evacuation." As you drive through areas like Clearwater Beach, Florida, or Galveston Island, Texas, the capacity of the roadways can be seen as an obvious constraint. Based on two recent experiments, Ruch (1984) concluded that if individuals have a "vertical shelter" as an option it will not delay or inhibit them from evacuating horizontally. Since the samples were very small and the experimental procedure did not allow for group decision making—the more common experience of most evacuees—Ruch expressed caution regarding these results. But certainly the questions raised merit further research, given the increasingly expanding coastal populations. Furthermore, as Ruch noted:

"If the respondents had been exposed to a positive promotional campaign favoring the wide-scale use of 'vertical shelters' or if 'vertical shelters' were described as being located within walking distance of each residence, the result may have been different. Presently, 'vertical shelters' are largely unknown quantities to their potential users" (Ruch, 1984:399).

In short, while much progress has been made regarding the human side of evacuation during a wide variety of potential threats, the available base must be extended to many specific issues such as this one if further policy is to be guided by scientific knowledge rather than folklore.

IC3. Receiver Qualities

As with warning responses, numerous researchers have investigated a large number of variables that might impact evacuation behavior. Quarantelli's (1980b) review highlighted this variation. Unfortunately, differing studies have not always produced uniform results. At a fairly general level, however, several categories of variables can be identified. These still await precise testing among multiple events with differing analytic qualities, however, before the limits of generalization can be specified.

> IC3.1 "People's vigilance and propensity to evacuate is dependent on three pieces of information. They need to know that there is high probability of a disaster to occur, that the disaster will have rather bad consequences, and that there is great risk of an individual being stricken by the bad consequences given that the disaster occurs" [Sweden] (Hultaker, 1976:8).

Carrying this general conclusion to a more precise level, Perry, Lindell, and Greene have proposed the following summary.

> IC3.1a ". . . three variables which are critical in the individual's evacuation decision-making process: (1) the definition of the threat as real (that is, the development of a belief in the warning), (2) the level of perceived personal risk (beliefs about the personal consequences of disaster impact), and (3) the presence of an adaptive plan (being acquainted with a means of protection). . . . research on evacuation performance in natural hazards suggests three social variables: the family context in which the warning is received, the network of kin relationships in which the family is enmeshed, and the level of community involvement" (Perry, Lindell, and Greene, 1980:40). (See also Perry, 1985:90-92.)

Thus, it is clear that a multivariate model will be required to make more precise predictive statements. It is equally clear that quite independent of event qualities, various characteristics of the *receiver* of warning messages, and the context in which they are received, also affect evacuation behaviors. What is unclear is the precise extent of such effects and the variations among alternative clusters of variables. Let's examine a dozen or so of these qualities and review evidence related to each.

> IC3.2 ". . . a greater probability of evacuation exists when personal risk is perceived to be high and when perceived threat is at least moderate" (Perry, Lindell, and Greene, 1981:151). (See also Perry, 1982:64.)

Personal risk and perceived threat are concepts used by Perry and his colleagues in several publications. While not the same as "expectation of damage" or "confidence in weather forecasting" the basic idea is that the emergent perception of the hazard and the individual's assessment of potential vulnerability are keys to understanding the propensity to act—or not to do so. Related conclusions are as follows.

> IC3.2a "People who believe that weather reports are usually accurate were more likely to evacuate than people who do not believe in forecasts, [p. 14] . . . knowledge about hurricanes and hurricane safety rules were consistently not found to be associated with evacuation behavior. . . . Respondents who could give their elevation within one foot accuracy were considerably less likely to evacuate than people who either over-

estimated or underestimated their elevation [p. 16]" (Baker, 1979:14, 16). (See also Mileti, Drabek, and Haas, 1975:49; Perry, 1985:90–92; Perry, 1983:36; Perry, 1979b:34.)

The point to be stressed here, and throughout this section, is that the threat is in the eye of the beholder. That is, "correctness" of the perception is not the issue. Rather evacuation behavior reflects what people perceive. This seems to be most notable in chemical and nuclear disasters wherein public familiarity is low (Quarantelli, 1980b:63).

In making an assessment of vulnerability, a key factor appears to be *timing*.

> IC3.3 "The shorter the time period during which a disaster is threatening, the greater, *ceteris paribus,* the probability that a warning about the disaster increases an individual's vigilance and propensity to evacuate" [Sweden] (Hultaker, 1976:9).

> IC3.3a ". . . the variable of time is of central importance in explaining behavior elicited by warnings in predisaster settings. . . . Situational context, perceived warning certainty, and warning content were not related to warning confirmation as postulated. Again referring to the immediateness of the situation, perhaps the heretofore predictors of confirmation do not hold relevance when response must be almost immediate" (Mileti and Beck, 1975:44).

Similarly, *past experience* has been found to affect evacuation behavior, although not consistently. Certain types of disaster experiences appear to reinforce definitions of relative invulnerability. What we lack is research that identifies the forms of past experience and the conditions under which this has been relevant (see Quarantelli, 1980b:41–42).

> IC3.4 "People have a tendency to believe that history will repeat itself, and it is often very difficult to persuade people that a new disaster will be different from an earlier one" [Sweden] (Hultaker, 1976:10–11).

> IC3.4a ". . . presence or absence of previous experience, *per se,* is unrelated to evacuation. The same is true with respect to the number of hurricanes experienced, recency of one's experience, and whether damages or injuries were suffered by one's household. . . . Residents who had evacuated in previous hurricanes were also the most probable to evacuate in Carla" (Baker, 1979:17).

> IC3.4b "Several researchers note that individuals are inclined to judge the probable destructive effects of an incoming hurricane upon the basis of the last one that affected the area, and consequently are often not inclined to evacuate (Moore *et al.,* 1963; Wilkinson and Ross, 1970[3])" (Quarantelli, 1980b:40).

---

[3]Kenneth P. Wilkinson and Peggy J. Ross, "Citizens' Responses to Warnings of Hurricane Camille." Report No. 35. State College, Mississippi: Social Science Research Center, Mississippi State University, 1970.

In contrast to these findings are those of other researchers who have reported that past disaster experience—especially if the event was severe—increased the propensity toward evacuation.

> IC3.4c "Prior severe flood experience was significantly related to evacuation for the population as a whole, and for younger persons (16–59 years). This experience measure was not related for older persons (60 + years)" (Hutton, 1976:265). (See also Mileti, Drabek, and Haas, 1975:50; Perry, Lindell, and Greene, 1981:153.)

These inconsistencies imply the necessity of multivariate models wherein "prior experience" is proposed as one factor within a causal network.

> IC3.4d "The greater the individual's perception of real threat (warning belief), the greater the probability of evacuation. a. Prior experience with similar disasters increases the likelihood of developing a warning belief. b. The more detailed the warning message content, the greater the likelihood of developing a warning belief. c. As the number of warnings received increases, so does the degree to which the threat is perceived as real. d. Receipt of a warning from a credible source increases the degree to which the threat is perceived as real. e. The presence of environmental cues associated with a disaster increases the extent to which the threat is perceived as real. f. Successful confirmation of a warning message increases the extent to which the threat is perceived as real" (Perry and Greene, 1982b:326–327). (See also Perry and Mushkatel, 1984:52.)

In contrast to timing and whatever might be implied by "prior experience," it is clear that physical location and other *site characteristics* also impact evacuation behavior. It is likely that these factors in their various forms are critical in the formation of perceptions of vulnerability. What is important here is not a researcher's perception of these elements, however, but an understanding of how they are perceived by those threatened.

> IC3.5(H) Propensity to evacuate varies directly with selected site characteristics and physical proximity to predicted impact areas. (Based on Mileti, Drabek, and Haas, 1975:50; see also Guard Police Psychology Research Society, 1971b.)

> IC3.5a(H) "Elevation of the respondent's home above mean sea level exhibited one of the strongest associations with evacuation produced by any of the four studies. The relationship was clearly monotonic with people living in lowest-lying areas being the most likely to leave" (Baker, 1979:19).

> IC3.5b(H) "Age of the house was not associated with evacuation, but people living in two-story structures were less prone to leave than people living in one-story buildings" (Baker, 1979:19).

> IC3.5c(H) "[Mobile home] dwellers were the most probable to evacuate" (Baker, 1979:19).

IC3.5d(H) ". . . people who had lived at the same address . . . for less than five years were slightly more likely to evacuate than people living at the same address five years or more" (Baker, 1979:18).

Quite different than these variables are more traditional demographic qualities of the receiver—education, sex, age, and ethnicity, for example. The research base contains many inconsistencies. For example, neither educational level nor income has been found to impact evacuation behavior in a uniform manner. Indeed, Quarantelli (1980b:42–45) has questioned the wisdom of studies limited to a few demographic variables that are evaluated one at a time.

IC3.6 "For most other findings in this area, studies are either inconsistent, fail to provide positive evidence, or the results are ambiguous . . . For example, educational level has been asserted by some to have a greater bearing on evacuation decision-making than does income or occupational status (e.g., Moore *et al.*, 1963:80–83). But, while education was found to be correlated with the greater probability of withdrawal in the Three Mile Island nuclear incident (Flynn and Chalmers, 1980), education has not been found to be a significant variable in other research (Lachman *et al.*, 1961). [p. 43] . . . Studies dealing with demographic characteristics and evacuation are simply not conclusive [p. 44]" (Quarantelli, 1980b:43, 44). (See also, Mileti, Drabek, and Haas, 1975:30, 50; Zeigler, Brunn, and Johnson, 1981:3.)

Age, however, for reasons that may have to do with receipt of warning (Drabek and Boggs, 1968:448) rather than stereotypic assumptions of rigidity, has been found by many, although not all, to correlate with evacuation behavior.

IC3.7(H) As age increases, the propensity to evacuate decreases. (Based on Mileti, Drabek, and Haas, 1975:52; Friedsam, 1962; Moore *et al.*, 1963; Okabe *et al.*, 1981a; Guard Police Psychology Research Society, 1970.)

IC3.7a(H) "Families headed by aged persons, or extended family households containing aged, are less likely to evacuate in response to hazard warnings. a. As age increases, the frequency of contacts with kinsmen decreases. b. As age increases, the level of community participation decreases. c. In general, with other factors constant, as age increases, the number of warnings received decreases" (Perry, 1979b:35). (See also Perry, Lindell, and Greene, 1981:156–157; Perry, 1985:91.)

IC3.7b(H) "Death among older persons in the Rapid City flood plain occurred disproportionately. [p. 262] . . . in Rapid City there was no significant relationship for either age and warning receipt or for age and evacuation [p. 265]" (Hutton, 1976:262, 265).

Similarly, gender or sexual role differences in evacuation decisions appear to have reasonable consistency.

IC3.8 "Men tend to be the passive type in evacuating, while women tend
to be the positive type. [i.e., men indicate they will evacuate only when
the dangers approach or when ordered to do so.] [Japan] (Guard Police
Psychology Research Society, 1970)." (As summarized in Yamamoto
and Quarantelli, 1982:A-86.) (See also Guard Police Psychology Research
Society, 1971b; Mileti, Drabek, and Haas, 1975:52; Society for the Behavioral Science of Disaster, 1978.)

It appears that ethnic minority groups will exhibit less propensity to
evacuate. Only Blacks and Mexican-Americans have been studied thus
far, however. And recent work by Perry, Greene, and Mushkatel (1983)
reveals that these response patterns are complex and probably intertwined
with other factors like those discussed above and in the chapter on warning
(Section IB).

IC3.9 Ethnic minorities are less likely to evacuate than Whites. (Based
on Perry, Lindell, and Greene, 1982a:97; Drabek and Boggs, 1968:447;
Perry, Lindell, and Greene, 1981:157–158; Perry and Mushkatel,
1984:106).

IC3.9a(H) "Blacks who perceive risk to be low are more likely to undertake some protective action as warning belief increases, but the majority still do not evacuate. Among Whites and Mexican-Americans, when
risk is believed to be low, increases in level of warning belief do not
affect the modal warning response—which is to continue a normal routine" (Perry and Mushkatel, 1984:215–216).

IC3.9b(H) "Blacks and Whites who defined risk to be high evacuated
even when level of warning belief was less than high. High risk-high
warning belief Mexican-Americans evacuated, while those with lower
levels of warning belief engaged in a protective action" (Perry, Greene,
and Mushkatel, 1983:280).

IC3.9c(H) "A positive relationship was found between message specificity
and level of perceived personal risk among all three ethnic groups, although the magnitude of the correlation was weaker among Mexican-
Americans than Blacks or Whites. Furthermore, Blacks appear to be
slightly more sensitive to increases in message specificity. That is, among
Blacks a smaller increase in specificity is associated with a larger increase
in perceived risk than is the case among Whites" (Perry and Mushaktel,
1984:218–219).

Although still controversial, in part because of a design flaw in the original study, a personality quality of "fate control" may relate to evacuation
decision making.

"Although admittedly based upon only a small sampling of behavior of
a small number of respondents, these findings and interpretations may
be relevant to the disproportionately higher death rate from tornadoes
in the South. Fatalism, passivity, and perhaps most important, lack of

trust in and inattention to society's organized systems of warning constitute a weak defense against the terrible strike of the tornado" (Sims and Baumann, 1972:1391).

Critics have argued that timing, not "fatalistic" attitudes, may account for these results, however. That is, more tornadoes in Southern states occur after dark than elsewhere (Mileti, 1983, personal communication). Yet, others have validated the relevance of this personality characteristic. A good example was provided by Hodge, Sharp, and Marts (1979).

"The flow of lava began on 23 September, [1977] heading toward the village of Kalapana. For several days the flow continued toward Kalapana, and on 29 September the decision was made by Civil Defense officials, with the assistance of Hawaiian Volcano Observatory scientists, to evacuate the town. There was little doubt in their minds that the 150-m-wide river of lava would eventually inundate the town and flow into the ocean. However, many of the local residents perceived the situation differently. Pele remains an honored and respected goddess in the minds of many of Kalapana's people, and the belief that she harms no one who has not harmed her justified their defiance of the initial evacuation order. Although most of the residents were eventually evacuated, their faith in Pele was upheld when the lava flow suddenly stopped about a quarter mile above the nearest residents on 1 October, causing those who believed in Pele to become even more steadfast in their faith" (Hodge, Sharp, and Marts, 1979:242–243).

IC3.10(H) "Individuals characterized by an external locus of control are less likely to evacuate or engage in any type of protective action" (Perry and Greene, 1982b:327), (See also Perry, 1985:91; Perry and Mushkatel, 1984:112–115, 132.)

IC3.10a " . . . citizens characterized by a primarily internal locus of control were far more likely to engage in some adaptive planning than citizens with neutral or primarily external locus of control. Although the majority of our respondents across all three ethnic groups showed a primarily internal locus of control, there was a slightly greater tendency among minority citizens to be external than among Whites. Also, lower income respondents were more likely to report a primarily external locus of control than Whites. When statistical controls for income level were introduced, the relationship between ethnicity and locus of control did not disappear. . . . both ethnicity and socioeconomic status have an independent effect upon locus of control *and* ethnicity is also correlated with income (minority citizens tend to have lower incomes), consequently having an indirect effect upon locus of control through income" (Perry, Greene, and Mushkatel, 1983:282).

Shifting from demographics and personality attributes, it appears that the presence of a plan—not for the community, but one designed by the individual—affects the propensity to evacuate. Perry and his associates have reported this relationship in several studies.

IC3.11 "The more precise an individual's adaptive plan, the higher the probability of evacuation. a. Prior experience with similiar disasters increases the chance that an individual will develop an adaptive plan. b. The more detailed the warning message content, the more likely it is to provide the elements of an adaptive plan. c. Individuals characterized by an external locus of control are less likely to develop adaptive plans" (Perry and Greene, 1982b:326). (See also Perry, 1979b:34; Perry, Lindell, and Greene, 1981:152.)

Finally, group context and the degree to which an individual is integrated into the community affect evacuation decision making. Neither of these dimensions has been explored with adequate precision, but consistent results reported to date suggest that both are critical.

IC3.12 "To the extent that family members are together at the time of warning or otherwise accounted for, the probability of evacuation is increased. . . . The nature and frequency of kin relationships is related to the definition of family members who need to be accounted for in emergencies" (Perry and Greene, 1982b:327). (See also Drabek and Stephenson, 1971; Society for the Behavioral Science of Disaster, 1978; Perry, 1979b:35.)

IC3.13 ". . . the more frequent a person's contacts with community organizations, the more likely is compliance with an evacuation warning. . . . a positive relationship exists between frequency of contact with voluntary associations and the number of warnings received" (Perry, Lindell, and Greene, 1981:156). (See also Perry, 1979b:35; Perry, 1983:36.)

IC4. Message Qualities

As with warning responses, evacuation behavior appears to be related to certain characteristics of message qualities. These relationships have been less studied than warning responses. As with receiver characteristics, however, sets of message qualities may impact evacuation behavior. Thus, multivariate analyses are required.

IC4.1 The greater the credibility of the warning message source, the greater the propensity to evacuate.

IC4.1a "Experience has shown that the credibility of public advices may depend, in part, upon whether the advices are identified with anonymous sources or with an individual or a few highly visible individuals to whom the public can relate. Credibility tends to diminish as the anonymity of the source increases" (Simpson and Riehl, 1981:290).

IC4.2 ". . . as the specificity of message content increases, so does the likelihood of evacuation" (Perry, Lindell, and Greene, 1981:152).

The message source, and perhaps mode of dissemination, quite apart from issues of credibility, have been found to impact evacuation decisions in a fairly uniform manner. In most cases, the number of warning messages, consistency among them, and receipt of other types of environmental cues increase evacuation rates. In a sense, these are forms of confirmation. Thus, initial responses of disbelief are blunted as evacuation by some spurs others to do likewise.

> IC4.3 "Information derived from official sources has also consistently been shown to be related to the undertaking of evacuation behavior (Clifford, 1956; Moore *et al.*, 1963; Drabek, 1969; Wilkinson and Ross, 1970;[4] Worth and McLuckie, 1977)" (Quarantelli, 1980b:73).

IIC. Group System Level

Three themes depict group responses during the pre-impact phase: (1) group interactions; (2) families as evacuation units; and (3) shelter selections. The presence of, and potential roles performed during this period by, emergent groups, and especially work groups, is a conspicuous void. Without negating the importance of family and neighbor group systems, it is essential that the focus of future studies be broadened. Furthermore, there may be important continuities with more general social processes that have been documented for non-disaster-related movements of human population. Thus, certain parallels may exist between disaster-induced evacuation and migration. To date, however, this matter has not been pursued beyond some insightful conjecture offered by Aguirre (1983).

IIC1. Group Interactions

As with the warning process, group interactions play a vital role in the behavioral dynamics that comprise community evacuations. Thus, upon receiving threat information people initiate a variety of confirmatory efforts—that is, of course, if they are motivated to act at all. Typically, a "wait-and-see" posture is common. For example, when Mississauga residents first learned of the train car derailment (1979) and the threat of chlorine gas, most began monitoring the media; many of those nearby tried to get a look. "People beyond Zone A began to think that they might have to evacuate but by and large made no emergency preparations for their home to be left or for their family to be housed, until they were given definite information. They appeared instead to spend some time trying to see the accident for themselves" [Canada] (Whyte, 1980:19).

---

[4]Kenneth P. Wilkinson and Peggy J. Ross, "Citizens' Responses to Warnings of Hurricane Camille." Report No. 35. State College, Mississippi: Social Science Research Center, Mississippi State University, 1970.

IIC1.1 "Also implicit in much of the literature is the idea that if a family
is ambivalent about evacuation, they will seek information about what
neighbors plan to do. If neighbors evacuate, the family is more likely to
do so. However, if the majority of the neighborhood is not inclined to
leave the area the family will often choose to 'ride it out.' (Killian, 1954;
Moore et al., 1963; Baker, 1979)" (Quarantelli, 1980b:48).

During such periods, as on a day-to-day basis, many will have communications with kin. And as with the daily pattern, the speed, propensity,
and intensity of these interactions vary among families. Some are quicker
to contact kin than others. Thus, in their studies of Washington State
communities, Perry, Lindell, and Greene reconfirmed the role of relatives
in augmenting officials as warning sources. "Face-to-face warnings delivered either by officials or relatives were cited in Sumner, Fillmore, and
Valley as very important in the decision to leave by large proportions of
the evacuees" (Perry, Lindell, and Greene, 1981:158).

If event qualities were held constant, I would hypothesize that pre-
disaster kin interactional patterns would determine this behavior pattern.
Available evidence suggests this although there are complexities—situational factors offset or intensify the roles of kin.

IIC1.2(H) "The closer one's relationship to extended kinsmen, the more
likely one is to evacuate" (Perry, 1979b:35). (See also Perry, 1985:91–
92; Perry, Lindell, and Greene, 1981:55; Okabe et al., 1981a).

There are qualities of families, however, that affect evacuation behavior.
As such, they point toward the greater specificity and multivariate modeling required. Two concepts that illustrate this point are the presence of
young children and ethnicity.

IIC1.3 "One of the propositions about which there is most agreement is
that withdrawal movement does seem to be associated with the presence
of young children in the household. Some of the very earliest (e.g., Moore
et al., 1963:77) and some of the very latest studies (e.g., Brunn et al.,
1979;[5] Flynn and Chalmers, 1980) tend to agree on this observation"
(Quarantelli, 1980b:42–43).

IIC1.4 ". . . Mexican-Americans received substantially greater proportions of warning information from relatives than did whites" (Perry, Lindell, and Greene, 1981:157–158).

IIC2. Families as Evacuation Units

When people evacuate they commonly do so as group members—most
typically the group is a family unit (Drabek, 1983b). This means that evac-

---

[5]Stanley Brunn, James Johnson, and Donald Zeigler, *Social Survey of Three Mile Island
Area Residents*. East Lansing, Michigan: Department of Geography, Michigan State University, 1979.

uation planners at any level of government must explicitly recognize this social webbing and seek to design plans that complement it, rather than trying to neutralize it.

IIC2.1 ". . . one disaster researcher after another has reported that evacuation is almost always by family units, not solitary individuals" (Dynes and Quarantelli, 1976:235). (See also Drabek, 1983b.)

As with kin interaction rates and their impacts on evacuation behavior, however, this generalized pattern does not hold universally. There are exceptions, although these have not been studied systematically. Of special significance, I suspect, is the degree to which work settings are disrupted by the evacuation and the length of departure time that is anticipated.

IIC2.1a ". . . while the majority of evacuees left in complete family units, the proportion of partial families fleeing the disaster was larger than would be expected from the conclusions of natural-hazard research. . . . partial families composed one-third of all evacuation units, but in the sample communities beyond fifteen miles from the plant, evacuation units were more likely to be partial families than complete families. Within six miles of the plant, complete families outnumbered partial families by more than three to one" (Zeigler, Brunn, and Johnson, 1981:4–5). (See also Quarantelli, 1980b:46.)

Thus, there are times that family members are physically separated when warnings are given. If time permits, they will exhibit a delay action; they will sit tight until all members are present—or at least accounted for. Both qualities—a propensity to delay leaving and trying to account for others—have been documented in several studies.

IIC2.2 ". . . families either evacuate as units or otherwise account for missing members before leaving home" (Perry, Lindell, and Greene, 1981:45). (See also Perry, 1982:64; Perry and Greene, 1983:86; Akimoto and Ohta, 1980:88; Quarantelli, 1980b:67.)

IIC2.2a ". . . most of the evacuees had a strong tendency to wait to leave until they could evacuate with their families (93% left with their families)" [Japan] (Ikeda, 1982:53).

IIC2.2b "Most people evacuated with all of their family members (93.0%). This explains the fact that most people evacuated after 6:00 p.m. in spite of an earlier evacuation order (at 3:30 p.m.) [Japan] (Okabe et al., 1981b)" (as summarized in Yamamoto and Quarantelli, 1982:A-174).

When they leave, American families typically do not leave on foot. Rather, again reflecting their normal daily routine, they drive to a shelter location. Depending on the anticipated length of the evacuation period and the place selected initially, they may not remain at their first choice. Regardless of this, they most commonly move in private vehicles.

IIC2.3 "The overwhelming majority (84%) of families left in their own cars . . . for destinations outside of Mississauga [p. 13] . . . Overall, 35%

of the evacuees moved twice and 10% moved three times [p. 14]'' [Canada] (Whyte, 1980:13, 14). (See also Perry, Lindell, and Greene, 1981:159; Perry, Greene, and Lindell, 1980a:443).

It is quite likely that social class and community size differences may affect this pattern. Hultaker's (1977) analysis of World War II evacuations suggested this.

> IIC2.3a ''. . . the economic status of the families determined how the families evacuated, and this is more conclusive from our results than from Boyd's. The poorest families evacuated under the government's scheme more often than other families; this was cheaper than private evacuation. The richest families evacuated privately more often than other families'' [England] (Hultaker, 1977a:7).

While noted in the literature earlier, Whyte's (1980) analysis of the 1979 Missassauga evacuation provides documentation of the social definition of "a family unit." For many people, pets are "family." They too, therefore, frequently will be in the car if a family evacuates, although dogs are more apt to be there than snakes or birds. When left behind, it is my impression that pressure to return quickly is intensified—sometimes even prior to impact. Hence, many seasoned practitioners I have discussed this with have indicated that they urge families to arrange for pet care prior to leaving.

> IIC2.4 "The evacuation of some 40,000 households, half of which had at least one pet, involved some 30,000 pets in addition to 260,000 people. Abandoned in the evacuated area were cats, birds, fish and small mammals . . . Dogs were generally taken with the family when they left (88%) but cats present a different problem. Many could not be found when the family were leaving and searches had to be made. Less than half the cats were evacuated" [Canada] (Whyte, 1980:21).

Finally, it is clear that family composition and point in the life cycle— qualities that interact with individual attributes like age—also structure evacuation behavior. Based on a telephone survey of adults and a questionnaire survey of high school students living near Three Mile Island at the time of the nuclear power-generating plant incident (March, 1979), the following linkages were documented.

> IIC2.5 "The data collected show that living near the plant (absolute or perceived proximity), younger age and lower grade level of the adolescent respondent, presence of pre-school age child in the home, lower parent's or adult's education, and evacuation of all or part of the family were all associated with a stronger negative affective response to the accident and with the likelihood of having evacuated the area" (Bartlett et al., 1983:19).

Similarly, following Hurricane Frederic (1979), results from 429 family interviews in Alabama highlighted the response variability associated with family composition—a matter rarely examined prior to this study.

IIC2.6 ". . . the manner in which residents decide to evacuate differs depending on the structural characteristics of the household. Results show that the complete nuclear family—father, mother, and children—appears to respond much more like relatively isolated groups, relying on their own interpretation of warning information, in contrast to what may be labelled as incomplete nuclear families—married couples without children and single residents living alone—who rely on their prior perceptions of risk and their social contacts with other significant persons" (Carter, Kendall, and Clark, 1983:95).

IIC3. Shelter Selections

When they leave, where do families go? To some extent this depends on event qualities, especially length of forewarning and anticipated evacuation time. If advised that a gas leak in the neighborhood will be repaired in an hour or so, it is unlikely that many families will head for a relative's home located 200 miles away. Yet, when a hurricane approaches they just might.

IIC3.1 ". . . when kin are within a reasonable distance of the disaster site and some forewarning is possible, evacuees clearly prefer the homes of relatives as shelter" (Perry, Lindell, and Greene, 1981:160). (See also Barton, 1969:194–195.)

This overall pattern has been documented repeatedly in both techno-logical and natural disasters (Drabek, 1983b). The rates will vary some-what, in part, reflecting such factors as event quality, community size, and proximity to other areas. Illustrative of the range of more specific findings reported are the following.

IIC3.1a Where people evacuated (after a warehouse fire): Evacuation place designated by the city (32.0%); houses of their friends or relatives (59.6%) [Japan] (Okabe et al., 1981a). (Based on summary in Yamamoto and Quarantelli, 1982:A-174.)

IIC3.1b "On leaving their homes, people went mainly to the homes of neighbours or friends or relatives living close to the flood affected areas. Few went to relief centres. If they did not have friends or relatives living close to their area, they went to the homes of relatives living further away" [Australia] (Short, 1979:452). (See also Society for the Behavioral Science of Disaster, 1978.)

IIC3.1c "Most families went to stay with relatives and friends through private arrangements (84%)" [Canada] (Whyte, 1980:16).

IIC3.1d "The homes of relatives and friends proved to be the preferred evacuation quarters among both the actual and the potential evacuees. The MSU survey found that 81 percent of the evacuees stayed with rel-atives and friends. The comparable figures were 78 percent in the NRC study and 74 percent in the Rutgers study. These proportions exceed those characteristic of evacuations from natural disasters" (Zeigler, Brunn, and Johnson, 1981:9).

Some families are more likely to seek refuge in public shelters than others. While the matter has not been researched with much precision, most electing this option are lower-income families.

> IIC3.2 ". . . there is a definite relationship in American society between socio-economic level and seeking refuge in mass shelters. A majority of those who go to such shelters are from the lower end of the socio-economic scale, researchers noting that white collar and skilled trade workers tend to view the need to seek public shelters as stigmatizing, (Moore *et al.*, 1963)" (Quarantelli, 1980b:126).

Conversely, families with other demographic characteristics—the aged and ethnic minorities, for example—are more likely to seek out relatives. Thus, multiple patterns coexist, with the result that relatives *and* public shelters are more likely to be evacuation points for the poor, the elderly, and ethnic minorities. The whereabouts of the more wealthy remains unknown, although second homes and commercial units may absorb those not seeking out homes owned by relatives or friends. From a policy perspective, these types of findings have much significance; if public shelters had to take the full responsibility for all families evacuated, the task would be enormous.

> IIC3.3 "The lower the social class of the family, the greater the tendency to evacuate to homes of relatives" (Drabek and Boggs, 1968:447).

> IIC3.4 "The older the family member, the greater the tendency to evacuate to homes of relatives" (Drabek and Boggs, 1968:448).

> IIC3.5 "Spanish-American families will evacuate to homes of relatives more frequently than Anglos" (Drabek and Boggs, 1968:447).

My study of the 1965 flood in Denver, Colorado, provided new insights into the social processes whereby relatives emerge as prime evacuation locations. During the confirmation process, many families indicated that they received invitations from kin to "come on over here till we see how this thing is going to develop." (See Drabek, 1969.) Frequently, it was not a belief that they were at risk that precipitated evacuation behavior; rather, their behavior reflected invitations offered by kin. More recently, Perry and his colleagues have documented this process for about one-quarter of the families who evacuated following the May, 1981, eruption of Mount St. Helens.

> IIC3.6 ". . . this process [i.e., evacuation by invitation] apparently operated in Toutle/Silverlake where 24.4 percent of the evacuees report that they were first contacted by someone at their destination. This finding supports Drabek's contention and adds the qualifier that the effect is intensified in communities where advance warning is possible and community disaster preparedness is high" (Perry and Greene, 1983:94). (See also Perry, Lindell, and Greene, 1981:160.)

Thus, as this pattern suggests, much of the group behavior during the evacuation phase of disasters is prefigured by normal daily routines. Wherever they might be—with relatives, friends, or in a school building managed by a Red Cross volunteer—family units persist and members remain guided in their action choices by the norms and values that did so previously. Sometimes labeled "emergent norm theory," these observations provide context and perspective for grasping the behavioral, rather than a mythical, reality of human response to disaster. "During the threat period all married people or people with children played traditional sex and family roles . . . thus the care and evacuation of family members were their initial concern. . . . Women were nurturant and protective toward children, and they expected protection, leadership, and orders from men" (Wolf, 1975:408).

IIIC. Organizational System Level

In contrast to individual and group system responses during the pre-impact phase, more complex systems have been examined by relatively few researchers. But case studies underscore both the policy significance of the topic and the difficulties future researchers will have in sutdying it. For example, after his extensive literature review, Quarantelli (1980b) concluded that:

> ". . . organizations typically have serious problems with the movement of institutionalized populations such as in hospitals, jails, nursery homes, mental hospitals. . . . When hospitals have had to be evacuated as in the Wilkes Barre flood (Blanshan, 1975),[6] or jails as in a propane threat in Everett, Washington, questions arise as to who can be released, how 'difficult' cases can be transported, where those moved can be taken, what facilities are necessary at the new relocation place, etc." (Quarantelli, 1980b:123).

Certainly, this single topic alone—that is, evacuations of specialized populations such as prisoners or nursing home residents—merits extensive study. Similarly, practically nothing is known about the behaviors within manufacturing plants or other private sector organizations when threatened with disaster. But such domains represent difficult challenges for researchers, in part for reasons inherent in the very phenomena requiring study. Quarantelli's recent case study of a chemical tank explosion in Taft, Louisiana (December, 1982) illustrates this point well.

---

[6]Sue Blanshan, "Hospitals in 'Rough Waters': The Effects of a Flood Disaster on Organizational Change." Dissertation. Department of Sociology. Columbus, Ohio: The Ohio State University, 1975.

"In what way and for how long the situation in the plant developed into
a dangerous possibility is presently cloaked in corporate secrecy. At the
time DRC did its field work in the area, stories were circulating among
some public officials that the problem had been known for hours, if not
days, before the explosion. However, no one was able to cite any hard
information or verifiable source to back up the stories. What is concretely
known is that around 11:00 p.m. on Friday, December 10, plant officials
had become sufficiently concerned to evacuate employees from the
southern portion of the plant. This does suggest that there must have
been some awareness of a problem earlier, but this is only an inference"
(Quarantelli, 1983b:26).

Such difficulties also were implicit in Westgate's (1975) analysis of a
large explosion in England. Obviously, when potential culpability is at
issue, researchers are entering difficult areas—both in terms of the type
of cooperation that can be expected and ethical dilemmas more typically
confronted by investigative reporters or sociologists studying certain forms
of deviance.

In contrast to these issues that occupy an important niche within the
research agenda of the 1990s, three other topics were addressed by the
findings I coded within this category: (1) organizational leadership in
evacuations; (2) organizational structure and evacuation effectiveness; and
(3) media organization responses. While each topic is important substantively, none has been penetrated systematically.

IIIC1. Organizational Leadership in Evacuations

Most researchers argue that improved disaster planning can increase the
effectiveness of emergency responses. Thus, statements like the following
one by Scanlon and Massey Padgham are typical: "The evacuation of Mississauga was successful because of the pre-planning, training, experience,
and nature of the Peel Regional Police Force, the availability of assistance
from close at hand and the characteristics of Mississauga, its people and
the surrounding area [216,935 evacuated, plus three hospitals, within a
24-hour period]" [Canada] (Scanlon and Massey Padgham, 1980:102).

But they take us one more step and offer an important hypothesis which
their case study confirmed.

IIIC1.1(H) ". . . the Peel police plan was not only a good plan, it was
known to members of the force. The requirement that all officers know
the plan in order to pass promotional examinations is rare if not unique,
and effective" [Canada] (Scanlon and Massey Padgham, 1980:101).

On the negative side, several factors have been identified that might
distract from effective performance. Thus, as detailed in Chapter 2 a belief
in a public response of panic has been noted by several researchers in
varying nations. Precise testing awaits us, however.

IIIC1.2(H) "Fear of generating panic is one of the main reasons people
in positions of responsibility hesitate to issue an evacuation order when

natural disaster threatens. [see also Clifford, 1956 (Mexico); Quarantelli, 1977 (Italy)] When Florence was on the verge of being flooded, the local Italian authorities saw the danger of panic as greater than the danger of floods, and no alarm was issued (Quarantelli, 1977)'' [Japan] (Hirose, 1979:61).

Similarly, while the picture is changing within the U.S.A., evacuation performance may be hampered because organizational officials lack awareness of domain expectations by specialized agencies like the Red Cross or may sense political pressure. Available evidence relegates such observations to the status of interesting hypotheses, however. We really don't know the limits of generalization nor do we have much insight into factors that account for whatever variation there is.

IIIC1.3(H) "Groups without experience and knowledge of disasters typically will overestimate the number of evacuees who will need housing, not realizing most people seek refuge with friends and relatives; even worse, they may not be aware that other agencies such as the Red Cross have certain formal responsibilities for emergency sheltering and thus will not attempt to exchange information about housing needs" (Quarantelli, 1980b:91).

IIIC1.4(H) ". . . organizational decision makers sometimes feel self projected pressure to withhold decisions because of the possible political and legal ramifications of recommending or ordering an evacuation" (Quarantelli, 1980b:85).

IIIC1.5(H) "Business interests are sometimes said to be unofficially important in the official decision making process, although explicit documentation of this is rather rare (Killian, 1954; Hirose, 1979)" (Quarantelli, 1980b:85).

IIIC2. Organizational Structure and Evacuation Effectiveness

Despite the obvious importance of this topic—both theoretically and administratively—little has been published about it. What factors would enhance mobilization speed? Beyond the insights offered earlier by Barton (1969) and Dynes (1970a), my review captured only a few additional ideas.

IIIC2.1(H) ". . . the greater the continuity between disaster roles and the normal responsibilities of an organization, the less problematic disaster mobilization is likely to be" (Mileti, 1975b:23).

IIIC2.2(H) ". . . as the role conflict of organizational members increases, the ability of the organization to mobilize decreases" (Mileti, Drabek, and Haas, 1975:53).

IIIC2.3(H) ". . . information about threats or the need for immediate withdrawal often reaches an organization's intermediate or lower levels rather than its top decision making levels. In other words, organizations may obtain appropriate information but it will not necessarily quickly get to those in positions of authority. In many transportation accidents involving hazardous chemicals, we have often found that both first responders from emergency agencies or on-site company personnel realize that they will have to make a decision regarding evacuation of the nearby area" (Quarantelli, 1980b:83).

It does appear that the interorganizational network affects not just mobilization speed, but other performance qualities too. Furthermore, participation in an emergency operations center may contribute a good deal to increased effectiveness, if all other things are equal.

> IIIC2.4 ". . . coordination is considerably facilitated if interacting organizations all use the same EOC, or at least are at a point where information converges" (Quarantelli, 1980b:92).

IIIC3. Media Organization Responses

For certain types of emergencies, such as toxic chemical spills, for example, media organizations may play relatively minor roles since the forewarning period is so short and response time so minimal. Based on DRC studies in numerous communities confronting such fast-moving threats, Gray (1981:363) concluded: "Mass media units rarely play a role in the initial evacuation of a population group since the movement occurs so rapidly. At best, radio and television stations serve as a means of secondary confirmation of initial warnings."

But in other types of events the media have been found to perform critical roles. Consistently, in flood, tornado, and hurricane evacuations, large segments of the threatened populations indicate that they were alerted through these organizations. Yet, the behavioral dynamics both within and among these organizations remains an unknown. Earlier research did document, however, various types of problems related to overlapping listening areas. The continued presence of this problem, its scope, and the effectiveness of various forms of corrective policies await the attention of future researchers.

> IIIC3.1 ". . . in studies of both Hurricane Carla and Hurricane Camille, it is noted that due to overlapping radio listening areas, information broadcast for one area was heard in others. This not only led to confusion, but influenced what people took into account in deciding whether or not to evacuate (Moore et al., 1963; Moore, 1964; Wilkinson and Ross, 1970[7]). The same problem of overlapping radio listening areas with subsequent problems for the evacuation process has also surfaced with other kinds of disaster agents ranging from floods (Worth and McLuckie, 1977) to chemical disasters (Albert and Segaloff, 1962[8])" (Quarantelli, 1980b:59).

---

[7]Kenneth P. Wilkinson and Peggy J. Ross, "Citizens' Responses to Warnings of Hurricane Camille." Report No. 35. State College, Mississippi: Social Science Research Center, Mississippi State University, 1970.

[8]Michael Albert and Louis Segaloff, *Task Silence: The Post-Midnight Alarm and Evacuation of Four Communities Affected by an Ammonia Gas Release*. Philadelphia, Pennsylvania: University of Pennsylvania, Institute for Cooperative Research, 1962.

IVC. Community System Level

Even to the most casual observer, it is clear that community responses during the pre-impact phase vary considerably. Yet, the types of comparative community studies that have documented other social processes— be they differential power distributions or impacts of industrial plant relocations—have yet to be completed so as to provide a precise accounting of pre-disaster mobilization. Findings clustered into three themes: (1) community dynamics; (2) disaster subcultures; and (3) public shelter use.

IVC1. Community Dynamics

When disaster warnings are issued, what types of community level responses can we anticipate? As we saw previously, overall, there is a propensity to deny the threat initially, seek confirmation, and to try and normalize things as much as possible.

> IVC1.1 ". . . persons tend to assimilate news from the media in such a way as to make it conform to their own view of reality" [Canada] (Scanlon, 1976:114).

> IVC1.1a ". . . they tend to distort the information to suit their own view of reality as they pass messages along from one person to another. . . . persons often check what they heard from another source, usually a media one; furthermore, individuals who learned first from someone else or from the radio are most likely to turn to another media source" [Canada] (Scanlon, 1976:114).

> IVC1.1b "About half the people who heard the rumor that a dam had burst fled immediately. But even under such conditions 42.8 per cent tried to get official confirmation before fleeing" [Canada] (Scanlon, 1976:115).

After cross-checking, and perhaps receiving an invitation from a relative to "come on over here," further information from officials may be transformed. "If the matter really is serious, they must be 'ordering' us to leave." Thus, several researchers have documented varying rates of "spontaneous" evacuations within communities. It is important to recognize that while legally ordered evacuations may occur, most within the U.S.A. have been in the form of advisories, at least technically. Of course, some local officials have blurred this line—intentionally, or not.

> IVC1.2 ". . . statements by public authorities about the seriousness of a threat, are frequently interpreted as 'orders' to leave" (Quarantelli, 1980b:120).

Also reflecting both a "normalization" quality and possible interpretations of mandatory evacuation, departing families do so with relative calmness and orderliness. Images of mass hysteria and countless auto accidents simply are not validated by the research completed to date.

What remains unknown are the conditions that might alter this response mode, however.

> IVC1.3 "The absence of traffic accidents and orderly motor movement characterizes both pre- and post-impact evacuation movements" (Quarantelli, 1980b:110).

> IVC1.3a "One study specifically looked for and found only 0.6 percent of evacuees involved in a major pre-hurricane evacuation either witnessed or were involved in traffic accidents or automobile breakdowns, the latter mostly due to broken fan belts or a flat tire (Moore *et al.*, 1963). Only one minor accident was similarly reported in a flood situation where with only two roads out of town, 3,500 cars left in one and a half hours with a minimum of congestion (Pierson, 1956,[9] p. 109)" (Quarantelli, 1980b:110).

> IVC1.3b "Both in Hurricane Carla where over a half a million people left coastal areas (Moore *et al.*, 1963), and in the Mississauga, Canada toxic chemical incident where 250,000 persons moved in less than 24 hours, no traffic fatalities occurred. In a study which collated reports of 64 different disastrous incidents and which involved the evacuation of over one million individuals, a total of only 10 deaths could be associated with the withdrawal movements and seven of these occurred in connection with a single helicopter crash (Hans and Sells, 1974:8[10])" (Quarantelli, 1980b:110).

Within the community system, the pre-impact period does bring important interactional shifts among responding organizations. Case studies offer useful hypotheses that should be explored empirically through carefully selected cross-community and cross-event comparisons.

> IVC1.4(H) "During the pre-impact phase, . . . both the horizontal and vertical ties are strengthened, i.e., they become more extensive and intensive. [p. 33] . . . Immediately following the impact, . . . the horizontal ties tend to be strengthened. . . . During the early post-impact period, . . . the vertical ties are weakened. . . . Soon, however, the vertical ties begin to increase in number and intensity [p. 34]" (Wenger, 1972:33, 34).

Up to this point, the discussion of findings and hypotheses conveys a rather positive image of the community response pattern. But these are not the whole picture by a long shot. Numerous studies have concluded that the required interagency linkages to move threatened populations are lacking. This is especially true when the time is short as it is following toxic chemical spills or accidents. Of course, there is variation; what we

---

[9]Stanley Pierson, *The Big Flood: California 1955*. Sacramento, California: California Disaster Office, 1956.

[10]Joseph M. Hans, Jr. and Thomas C. Sells, *Evacuation Risks—An Evaluation*. Washington D.C.: U.S. Government Printing Office, 1974.

need to know are the factors associated with it and the relative effectiveness of alternative intervention strategies.

> IVC1.5(H) If there has been little contact among agencies prior to a disaster, then the degree of coordination during the warning period will be minimal. (Based on Quarantelli, 1980b:90.)

> IVC1.5a(H) "The fact, as a current DRC study shows, that chemical plants or industries usually have very poor or few ties with local civil defense and other public emergency agencies means that evacuation is frequently delayed and not efficiently organized when a nearby or surrounding community is threatened by a toxic chemical cloud from an inplant fire or explosion" (Quarantelli, 1980b:26–27).

IVC2. Disaster Subcultures

Dating back to the seminal work of Harry Moore (1956, 1958), the topic of disaster subcultures has fascinated numerous researchers (e.g., Hannigan and Kueneman, 1978). While not the same as "previous disaster experience," it parallels much of what that variable frequently implies at the individual system level. Yet, as with individuals, experience alone is not a sufficient condition to generate the complex of normative understandings that this concept has come to represent. Wenger has summarized the themes well.

> ". . . in fully developed subcultures, the local community may not even perceive or define the impact of a disaster agent as being 'disastrous.' Some communities have institutionalized their mode of response to the point where they view such events as floods as simply nuisances, or possibly even look forward to the flood period as a time of 'carnival' " (Wenger, 1972:39).

> IVC2.1 ". . . the latent disaster subculture contains both facilitating and debilitating factors relevant to emergency response" (Wenger, 1972:40). (See also Wenger, 1978:41–43.)

> IVC2.2 ". . . communities tend to specialize in their disasters, and the subsequently developed subcultures tend to be keyed to a specific type of agent" (Wenger, 1972:39).

> IVC2.3 "There is great diversity among disaster subcultures [p. 42] . . . [e.g., some emphasize] technological and organizational elements. [Others reflect] the valuative, normative, attitudinal, legendary and mythological elements of the culture [p. 43]" (Wenger, 1972:42, 43). (See also Perry, 1982:64.)

IVC3. Public Shelter Use

It is clear that variations in reported shelter use reflect the characteristics of both the event and the community. But as pointed out above (Section

IIC), most evacuees go to the homes of relatives and friends. That point cannot be overemphasized. Thus, when trying to untangle the respective impacts of event or community structure variables on shelter use patterns, it is well to remember that we are referring only to a minority of potential victims, often a very small minority. This holds true for both U.S.A. studies and those I have encountered from other nations. For example, ". . . community shelters have limited capacity to accomodate a large number of persons with provisions for food and adequate sanitation. The interview data suggest that the overwhelming majority of the respondents usually shunned this response unless absolutely necessary" [India] (Schware, 1982:215).

> IVC3.1 ". . . 'the smaller the scope of the community disaster, the more probable is the kin group the major source of help' (Quarantelli, 1960a:264)" (Quarantelli, 1980b:124).

Beyond scope of impact, some case studies reveal rather unusual cir-circumstances that alter shelter use. For example, with the memory of Cyclone Tracy etched in their memories, many living in Darwin at the time of Issac's arrival may have responded within that context. Clearly, the massive airlift of significant portions of the Darwin population to distant points within Australia was an atypical case. Britton's case materials illustrate the complexity of the conceptual problem confronting researchers who must go beyond "scope of impact" in future analyses.

> ". . . the call 'go to shelter', issued by the Cyclone Warning and Information Service's 'go to shelter' public radio broadcast tape, plus an unauthorized 'volunteer source', prompted a significant number of people to leave the relative safety of their homes and move into the public cyclone shelters. [p. 28]) . . . 7,500 people were estimated to have sought refuge in public shelters (15% of Darwin's estimated 1981 population) [p. 41]" [Australia] (Britton, 1981a:28, 41).

Taking us beyond case materials, Perry, Lindell, and Greene (1981) have offered the following proposition.

> IVC3.2 "The use of public shelter increases when community preparedness is high, when the entire community must be evacuated, and when the evacuees anticipate that the necessary period of absence will be long. Even under these conditions, however, public shelters seem to attract only about one fourth of the evacuees at a given site" (Perry, Lindell, and Greene, 1981:160). (See also Perry and Greene, 1982a:349.)

When persons do go to public shelters, it is clear that they may not remain there as long as the disaster might require. Thus, once there, they often begin to search for an alternative location, although the dynamics of that have not been investigated thoroughly.

> IVC3.3 ". . . public shelters are apparently used as stops on the way to some other place (Perry, 1979c). Home-to-eventual shelter is not always a straight line (Drabek and Boggs, 1968). There are indications that at

Three Mile Island, the few evacuees that used a public shelter in a sports arena stayed only a day or two while they made arrangements to withdraw to houses of relatives or friends outside of the locality of the nuclear reactor (Flynn and Chalmers, 1980). The same seems to have happened at Mississauga'' (Quarantelli, 1980b:127).

Quite independent of where they may have taken up temporary shelter, evacuees will seek to return home as soon as possible. It is clear from case study material, however, that the social processes that operate herein are as complex as those that move persons out of their residences initially. To date, the focus has been on the social routes that resulted in getting people out; thus, relatively little is known about the variations that might exist regarding their return.

IVC3.4 ''. . . evacuees tend to decide themselves when they will attempt to return . . . this process does not always correspond to organizational perceptions and decisions'' (Quarantelli, 1980b:130). (See also Quarantelli, 1983b:38.)

VC. Society System Level

Almost no findings were coded within this area of the taxonomy. Thus, the limits inherent in the search processes I used became evident. Despite the fact that some researchers (e.g., Ian Davis) have explored limited aspects of this area, generalizations about total societies during the pre-impact period should command the attention of future researchers. The findings disclosed through my literature search pertained to either: (1) natural disaster evacuations or (2) war-caused evacuations. This is not to imply inherent differences between evacuations caused by agents of these two types. Rather the content of the findings suggested this division.

VC1. Natural Disaster Evacuations

Cross-event comparisons are informative for many reasons. At times, particular comparisons are most helpful in defining the scope of a problem. For example, while evacuations due to some type of threat are rather frequent, it turns out that the larger numbers of evacuees are almost always responding to hurricane threats. Of course, there are exceptions, like the massive Mississauga chlorine gas episode (e.g., see Scanlon and Massey Padgham 1980; Whyte, 1980). But, in general, larger evacuations have been hurricane related.

VC1.1 [Based on a review of 228 events wherein evacuation occurred, it was found that] ''hurricane evacuations account for the majority of evacuees and that the average hurricane evacuation has involved about 40,000 evacuees as compared with about 4,000 in other types of disasters'' (Strope, Devaney, and Nehnevajsa, 1977:4).

How might societies vary in their responses before disaster strikes? Two of our earlier hypotheses provide limited insight.

> VC1.2(H) "Sjoberg has suggested that when 'catastrophe is thought to be engendered primarily by spiritual forces, man can himself do little to alter the course of events apart from recourse to religious and/or magical practices' (1962:363). In societies where such beliefs prevail, magical practices may be the only actions taken before impact" (as summarized in Mileti, Drabek, and Haas, 1975:54).

> VC1.3(H) "McLuckie found that strongly established patterns of centralized decision-making may delay preventive actions prior to impact, while the Instituut Voor Sociaal Onderzoek Van Het Nederlandse Volk Amsterdam (1955) has found that a disaster in which no agency or set of bureaucratic institutions exist creates problems for system mobilization" (as summarized in Mileti, Drabek, and Haas, 1975:54).

VC2. War-Caused Evacuations

My coding captured only two major conclusions; both stemmed from Hultaker's reanalysis of data on WWII bombing responses in England. It could be useful to search specifically for related studies of wars since the 1940s. My search process just didn't get to them.

> VC2.1 ". . . many persons evacuated the days before the outbreak of the war, although not more than one million and a half used the official evacuation program. This was only 35 per cent of the number for which the government had planned, but more than two million people evacuated privately. The right number of persons left the evacuation areas, but they were partly others than those for whom the government had planned" [England] (Hultaker, 1977b:7–8).

> VC2.2 "We have only discussed the three largest evacuations in this summary. The government tried to evacuate people during other periods as well, but those attempts failed almost totally. People had no information on when the air raids would come, and too long periods of threat will decrease people's propensity to evacuate" [England] (Hultaker, 1977b:9–10).

> VC2.2a(H) "People evacuate when they believe that a war will have extremely bad consequences, and when they think that there is great risk of being hurt. This risk is the joint probability of the occurrence of a disaster and the probability of an individual being hurt given that the disaster occurs" [England] (Hultaker, 1977b:10).

VIC. International System Level

Only two relevant studies were coded for this area of the taxonomy. Both were directed at cross-national contrasts rather than the international system *per se*, however. In that sense they really are extensions of the questions posed above. That is, how do societies vary? Using different search procedures, it would be helpful for some scholar to prepare a synthesis akin to mine, although my impression is that the bulk of the available literature is descriptive rather than analytic.

For example, upon reviewing a draft of this chapter, Quarantelli noted several citations to reports completed by staff members associated with the Agency for International Development (AID). Given my search procedures, these were not captured and probably illustrate a large collection of additional fugitive writings. Thus, acquisition and codification of such materials would be a useful augmentation to my review. (Among the citations provided by Quarantelli were the following titles; the Agency for International Development, Office of U.S. Foreign Disaster Assistance, is listed as both author and publisher: *Bangladesh: A Country Profile; Case Report: Bangladesh—Floods July–October 1974; Case Report: Honduras—Hurricane and Floods, September–October 1974; Case Report: Nicaragua—Earthquake, December 1972; Case Report: Sahel Region (Senegal, Mauritania, Mali, Upper Volta, Niger and Chad) Drought—1972 to 1975; Chad: A Country Profile; Honduras: A Country Profile; Nicaragua: A Country Profile.*)

VIC1.1(H) "Where the family institution is dominant there will be more reluctance to evacuate and to seek official public shelters" [Italy, Japan, U.S.A.] (McLuckie, 1977:97).

VIC1.2(H) "Rural populations are more reluctant to evacuate than urban populations" [Italy, Japan, U.S.A.] (McLuckie, 1977:97).

VIC1.3(H) "One factor that will separate Swedish families to a higher extent than e.g. American ones is that a high proportion of the Swedish mothers are gainfully employed. [p. 8] . . . It was found that 42 per cent of the children had to stay at the nursery-home more than eight hours each day [p. 9]" [U.S.A. and Sweden] (Hultaker and Trost, 1976:8, 9).

While the existent knowledge base provides a basic understanding of many aspects of individual and small-group behavior just before disaster strikes, the paltry amount of information on organizational systems, and those of greater structural complexity, is disappointing. The implications for the research community are clear.

Selected Bibliography

Baker, Earl J. [1979] "Predicting Response to Hurricane Warnings: A Reanalysis of Data from Four Studies." *Mass Emergencies* 4:9-24.

Bartlett, Glen S., Peter S. Houts, Linda K. Byrnes, and Robert W. Miller [1983] "The Near Disaster at Three Mile Island." *International Journal of Mass Emergencies and Disasters* 1 (March):19–42.

Carter, T. Michael, Stephanie Kendall, and John P. Clark [1983] "Household Response to Warnings." *International Journal of Mass Emergencies and Disasters* 1 (March):95–104.

Chandessais, Charles A. [1966] *La Catastrophe de Feyzin* (The Feyzin Catastrophe) (in French). Paris: Centre d'Etudes Psychosociologiques des Sinistres et de Leur Prévention.

Drabek, Thomas E. [1983] "Shall We Leave? A Study on Family Reactions When Disaster Strikes." *Emergency Management Review* 1 (Fall):25–29.

Drabek, Thomas E. [1969] "Social Processes in Disaster: Family Evacuation." *Social Problems* 16 (Winter):336–349.

Flynn, C. B., and J. A. Chalmers [1980] *The Social and Economic Effects of the Accident at Three Mile Island.* Tempe, Arizona: Mountain West Research, Inc. with Social Impact Research, Inc.

Hirose, Hirotada [1979] "Volcanic Eruption and Local Politics in Japan: A Case Study." *Mass Emergencies* 4:53–62.

Hodge, David, Virginia Sharp, and Marion Marts [1979] "Contemporary Responses to Volcanism: Case Studies from the Cascades and Hawaii." Pp. 221–248 in *Volcanic Activity and Human Ecology,* Payson D. Sheets and Donald K. Grayson (eds.). New York: Academic Press.

Hultaker, Orjan E. [1977] *Evakueringar i Stobritannien under Andra Varldskriget.* (Evacuations in Great Britain during World War II) (in Swedish with an English summary). Disaster Studies 3. Uppsala, Sweden: University of Uppsala.

Hultaker, Orjan E. [1976] *Evakuera* (Evacuate) (in Swedish with an English summary). Disaster Studies 2. Uppsala, Sweden: University of Uppsala.

Hultaker, Orjan E., and Jan E. Trost [1976] *The Family and the Shelters.* Disaster Studies No. 1. Uppsala, Sweden: Uppsala University.

McLuckie, Benajmin F. [1977] "Italy, Japan, and the United States: Effects of Centralization on Disaster Responses 1964–1969." The Disaster Research Center Historical and Comparative Disasters Series, No. 1. Columbus, Ohio: Disaster Research Center, The Ohio State University.

Mileti, Dennis S., and E. M. Beck [1975] "Communication in Crisis: Explaining Evacuation Symbolically." *Communication Research* 2 (January):24–49.

Ohta, Hideaki [1972] "Evacuating Characteristics of Tokyo Citizens." Pp. 175–183 in *Proceedings of the Japan–United States Disaster Research Seminar: Organizational and Community Responses to Disasters.* Columbus, Ohio: Disaster Research Center, The Ohio State University.

Oliver, John, and D. H. Trollope [1981] *Hurricane Allen: A Post-Impact Survey of a Major Tropical Storm.* Disaster Investigation Report No. 3. Townsville, Queensland, Australia: Centre for Disaster Studies, James Cook University of North Queensland.

Perry, Ronald W. [1985] *Comprehensive Emergency Management: Evacuating Threatened Populations.* Greenwich, Connecticut, and London: JAI Press, Inc.

Perry, Ronald W. [1983] "Population Evacuation in Volcanic Eruptions, Floods and Nuclear Power Plant Accidents: Some Elementary Comparisons." *Journal of Community Psychology* 11 (January):36–47.

Perry, Ronald W., Michael K. Lindell, and Marjorie R. Greene [1981] *Evacuation Planning in Emergency Management.* Lexington, Massachusetts, and Toronto: Lexington Books.

Quarantelli, E. L. [1983] "Evacuation Behavior: Case Study of the Taft, Louisiana Chemical Tank Explosion Incident." Columbus, Ohio: Disaster Research Center, The Ohio State University.

Quarantelli, E. L. [1980] "Evacuation Behavior and Problems: Findings and Implications from the Research Literature." Columbus, Ohio: Disaster Research Center, The Ohio State University.

Quarantelli, E. L. [1964] "The Behavior of Panic Participants." Pp. 69–81 in *Panic Behavior,* D. P. Schultz (ed.). New York: Random House.

Scanlon, T. and Massey Padgham [1980] *The Peel Regional Police Force and the Mississauga Evacuation.* Ottawa, Ontario: Canadian Police College.

Schware, Robert [1982] "Official and Folk Flood Warning Systems: An Assessment." *Environmental Management* 6 (May):209–216.

Strope, Walmer E., John F. Devaney, and Jiri Nehnevajsa [1977] "Importance of Preparatory Measures in Disaster Evacuations." *Mass Emergencies* 2:1–17.

Whyte, Anne [1980] *Survey of Households Evacuated during the Mississauga Chlorine Gas Emergency November 10–16, 1979.* Toronto: Emergency Planning Project, Institute for Environmental Studies, University of Toronto.

Zeigler, Donald J., Stanley D. Brunn, and James H. Johnson, Jr. [1981] "Evacuation from a Nuclear Technological Disaster." *Geographical Review* 71 (January)1–16.

5

Post-impact Emergency Actions

Immediately after a tornado has cut through Lubbock, Texas, or Topeka, Kansas, or Xenia, Ohio, what happens? What behavioral responses are evoked by individuals or the more complex social systems in which they participate? These actions are the focus of this chapter. Obviously, there is a blurred line between these and the early portions of the recovery phase. But in general, conclusions that are summarized here pertain to human activities within the initial few hours after impact. In some instances, the findings deal with emotional responses that were manifested within a few days, but the major focus is on immediate emergency actions. As in the preceding chapters, our assessment is organized by system levels. We will begin by examining the responses of individuals and systematically move across levels of increased structural complexity—from groups and organizations to communities and total societies.

ID. Individual System Level

As is evident with the large number of findings included in this chapter, we are beginning to obtain a fairly well-documented picture of individual response patterns immediately after disaster strikes. Yet, this expanded data base has a curious consequence—more refined research questions are now identifiable. Pursuit of these is essential if emergency managers are to do their jobs better. While this research base has provided documentation of numerous behavioral response sets that have proved invaluable to many managers who structure their planning on scientific evidence rather than myth, the job really has just begun.

Although a research agenda was not my task here, I stress this point and thereby emphatically disagree with those colleagues who suggest that we know enough about this area and should "check it off." Certainly more is known than is being used, but that is a different problem. Future research that *builds* on this existent base, rather than ignoring it, can help emergency managers do their jobs better. And in so doing, lives may be saved and victim trauma may be reduced. To "check it off" is not only premature, but exceedingly unwise.

Three general topics can be differentiated that collectively summarize the empirical evidence regarding individual responses to disaster during the initial emergency period: (1) victim reactions; (2) non-victim actions; and (3) emotional responses.

ID1. Victim Reactions

When victimized by disaster—be it a flood, tornado, or earthquake—most individuals evidence behavioral continuity and remarkable composure.

> ID1.1 "Disaster victims react in an active manner, not passively as implied in the dependency image. They do not wait around for offers of aid by organizations" (Quarantelli, 1960b:73). (See also Quarantelli, 1965 and 1976.)

The first point to be made about individual responses is the presence of control and continued rational behavior—rational here meaning that it is guided by existent roles. But not everyone behaves identically—the invisible strings of socialization continue to guide groups of people differently, just as in everyday life. Unfortunately, the existent data base does not penetrate this matter very far.

> ID1.2 [There is a] "tendency of people in fires to do the familiar: they use familiar exits; they assume familiar roles" (Paulsen, 1981:13).

> ID1.2a "Behaviors in accordance with traditional male/female roles have been identified by several researchers. . . . 'Females are more likely to warn others and wait for further instruction . . . they will close the door to the room of fire origin and leave the house. In both cases, females are most likely to seek assistance from neighbours. Male occupants are most likely to fight the fire. Male neighbours are more likely to search for people in smoke and attempt a rescue.' (38,[1] pp. 120, 122)" (Paulsen, 1981:14). (See also Research Committee of the Miyagiken Oki Earthquake, 1979.)

---

[1]D. Canter, J. Breaux, and J. Sime, "Domestic, Multiple Occupancy, and Hospital Fires." Pp. 117–136 in *Fires and Human Behaviour,* David Canter, (ed.). New York: John Wiley and Sons, 1980.

Adding precision to these themes are the behavioral patterns identified by Abe (1981) through extensive study of responses to building fires. The patterns were refined even more through a series of studies reported by Bryan (1983).

> ID1.3 [Seven behavioral tendencies during evacuation in building fires:] "(1) people choose the way out they know best, (2) people run away from smoke, (3) people who are not familiar with the setting tend to blindly follow a leader, (4) people evacuate toward brighter places such as windows or the like, (5) people who recognize the sign of an 'emergency exit' will safely evacuate, (6) people tend to follow other peoples' behavior, and (7) some people will shut themselves up in a room after they have been successful in escaping [Japan] (Abe, 1981)" (as summarized in Yamamoto and Quarantelli, 1982:A-33–34).

> ID1.3a "The conclusions and results of both Project People studies indicated the sterotyped accounts of individuals panicking and competing for escape from the fire incidents buildings, did not occur within these primarily residential and health care occupancy study populations.[2] Examples of altruistic behavior, involving the notification of others of the incident, evacuation assistance to others, and reentry into the fire incident structure to assist others were documented" (Bryan, 1983:199).

I do not want to imply that people remain unfrightened. Fear is present—more or less, depending on the circumstances. People do realize they are in danger, sometimes in real danger. But to date, the consistent pattern reported by the researchers who have interviewed *survivors* is that they kept their wits and responded in a reasonable manner. Although a few studies have been completed (e.g., Gruntfest, 1977), responses by those who have perished remain relatively unknown.

In short, despite fear of varying intensity, the behavioral response is relatively controlled and often very adaptive. For example, Takuma (1972) documented that many Japanese families experiencing earthquakes quickly turned off fuel outlets thereby reducing subsequent fires. As noted below, however, there was variability in the proportions who did so.

> ID1.4 "One-fourth of the subjects felt their lives were in danger, and all of them were frightened. Those who lived in wooden houses felt a greater degree of fear than those who lived in reinforced concrete houses. Those who were outdoors or in automobiles were more afraid than those who were indoors" [Japan] (Takuma, 1972:185).

---

[2]John L. Bryan, *Smoke as a Determinant of Human Behavior in Fire Situations, (Project People)*. Washington, D.C.: Center for Fire Research, National Bureau of Standards, NBS-GCR-77-94, June 30, 1977; John L. Bryan and James A. Milke, *The Determination of Behavior Response Patterns in Fire Situations, Project People II. Final Report—Health Care*. Washington, D.C.: Center for Fire Research, National Bureau of Standards, NBS-GCR-81-343, September, 1981.

ID1.4a "The response 'rush out of houses or building' was given by 60 percent of the subjects. Most of them carried nothing with them. There were only 13 percent who went outdoors *after* turning off all fuel outlets, and only 7.3 percent carried something from their houses" [Japan] (Takuma, 1972:185).

ID1.4b "Nearly 80 percent of the subjects returned to their homes within 10 minutes after the quake ended. Their purposes were different: 15.1 percent of the subjects returned to turn off the fuel outlets; 28.7 percent returned to get certain things; 26.3 percent returned to see the degree of damage; and 29.8 percent returned without any particular purpose. Men returned primarily to see the degree of damage, whereas women returned to get things" [Japan] (Takuma, 1972:186).

Unfortunately, we have limited comparative data. How might U.S.A. responses, or those from other nations strickened by earthquakes, for example, differ? To what extent can such adaptive responses be modified by public information campaigns? These are but two of a host of important questions that these conclusions direct us to ask.

From California, however, I did find another form of variation on our first principle (ID1.1) regarding victim reactions. What might happen to mental patients following an earthquake? Evidence from one study suggests a parallel response pattern—obviously one that should be subjected to replication.

ID1.5(H) [February, 1971, earthquake in the San Fernando Valley, California] ". . . 131 patients with psychiatric problems walked to safety in an orderly and controlled fashion after being tossed out of bed and cast into darkness, challenged by the destruction of exits, and withstanding the terrifying rumble of the earth's motion and the screeching of shifting walls" (Stein, 1974:34).

Finally, it appears that having a feeling of responsibility for the well-being of others may act as a barrier to negative effects of fear and aid one in adaptive responses. While consistent with broader theories of human behavior that highlight the integrative consequences of being embedded in social groups of various forms, the idea has not been studied carefully.

ID1.6(H) ". . . a sense of official duty has an effect on their action. For example, a teacher of a kindergarten class felt no fear at all during a severe earthquake although she was usually afraid of even a slight one. At that time she was more concerned about the safety of her small pupils than of herself" [Japan] (Takuma, 1972:194).

These six propositions are in sharp contrast to what many believe; recall the disaster myths documented by Wenger and his colleagues that I summarized in Chapter 2. Probably the most commonly believed myth about disaster responses has to do with panic. So let's examine this matter in detail. The first point to be noted is the ambiguity of the term. Quarantelli (1981b) has dissected the problem as well as anyone to date, and emphasizes the multiple meanings that laypersons and researchers alike may attribute to it. Within the context of this discussion, by the term "panic" I mean—following Quarantelli (1954, 1957)—acute fear coupled with flight or attempted flight. Thus, when a person replied that they looked at a restaurant bill and "panicked," they are using the term in but one of many ways that I am *not*.

More precisely, Quarantelli has offered the following differentiation.

> "Panic behavior is characterized by six features, three of a covert nature and three of an overt nature. . . . Covertly, panic involves fear, not anxiety, a projection into the future rather than a view of the past, and a perceived place of danger rather than a generalized threat. [p. 342] . . . Overtly, panic involves directional rather than purely random flight, nonsocial rather than antisocial activities, and nonrational rather than irrational behavior [p. 344]" (Quarantelli, 1977:342, 344). (See also Quarantelli, 1981b; Mileti, Drabek, and Haas, 1975:58.)

These distinctions provide the context for the conclusion by disaster researchers that panic rarely accompanies disaster.

> ID1.7 Victim responses rarely involve panic flight behavior (Quarantelli, 1954, 1957, 1981b; Fritz and Marks, 1954; Fritz, 1961:671; Martin, 1964; Form and Nosow, 1958:90; Drabek, 1968:3; Instituut Voor Sociaal Onderzoek Van Het Nederlandse Volk Amsterdam, 1955).

Following numerous lectures wherein I have made this point—and in my university course—I have been challenged repeatedly. Often the questioner will refer to Orson Welles' radio broadcast "War of the Worlds." It is amazing how mythology is reinforced by media sources at times (see Quarantelli and Dynes, 1972). More recently, a Swedish case provided a remarkable parallel—media reports again reinforced the panic mythology.

> ID1.7a "In 1974 there was a radio broadcast in Sweden which made reference to a nuclear plant accident which generated a radioactive cloud drift. As in the instance of the 'Invasion from Mars' broadcast, this too was purely a fictional account. News accounts described fleeing and hysterical persons. . . . A team of Swedish sociologists decided to make an intensive study of the reactions of the population in the affected area.[3] They undertook an intensive interview sample of the population in the affected area, examined records, police reports and thoroughly looked into all the behavioral reactions. *They found not one single case of flight in their sample*" (Quarantelli, 1977:340–41).

There are instances of what might be labeled "stampede behavior," however. A rock concert provided a good example a few years ago.

---

[3]K. Rosengren, *The Barseback Panic*. Lund, Sweden: University of Lund, 1974.

". . . a large number of young people were congregated outside a small door opening to an auditorium where a concert had begun in Cincinnati, Ohio. In the rush to get into the concert hall, many young people apparently died of suffocation and were trampled by the crowd. . . . the following conditions existed: immediate, severe danger in seconds or minutes; a limited number of escape routes; escape routes believed closing but not yet closed; lack of leadership; and lack of information'' (Hargreaves, 1980:683).

While emphasizing the rareness of such behavior, Singer (1982) identified parallel cases. He failed to differentiate between panic flight and instances of stampede behavior, however.''

". . . panic is *not* a common response to the trauma of disaster. Reports from numerous disasters reveal that most victims—to the extent they are able—display constructive, goal-directed behavior. When panic does occur, however, it can be contagious and may lead to uncontrolled mass flight. Drayer *et al.*[4] have described how on a sinking ship over-crowded lifeboats were stormed by terrified passengers who seemed oblivious to the fact that there were other boats with more room nearby. Similarly, in the Iroquois Theater fire in Chicago, the risk of being crushed to death did not deter people from stampeding a single exit, even though nine other exits were available''[5] (Singer, 1982:247).

Reviewing numerous cases like these, Quarantelli has formulated the most precise statement to date as to the social conditions most likely to generate panic responses.

ID1.8 ". . . there are two contextual and three immediate conditions that are responsible for the phenomenon [i.e., panic flight]. . . . *Contextual Conditions.* . . . [1.] the existence of a pre-crisis definition of certain kinds of crisis settings as having high potential for evoking panic flight. . . . [2.] the absence of pre-crisis social ties among the potential participants. . . . *Immediate Conditions.* . . . [1.] a perception of possible entrapment. [2.] a sense of powerlessness or impotency in the situation. [3.] a feeling of social isolation or sole dependency upon oneself in the crisis'' (Quarantelli, 1977:347–348).

Thus, while panic is rare, Quarantelli presents a portrait of the conditions that *may* produce it.

"In about 20 years of studying, of trying to find examples of where the social, the strongest social ties are broken, I have been able to find only a handful of situations . . . [e.g.,] where a mother abandoned her child.

---

[4]C. S. Drayer, D. C. Cameron, W. D. Woodward, and A. J. Glass, "Psychological First Aid in Community Disasters." *Journal of the American Medical Association* 156 (1954):36–41.

[5]D. Robinson, *The Face of Disaster.* New York: Doubleday, 1959.

But it does occur. That is why I say it does represent the end of a continuum of human behavior. [p. 109] . . . What is essentially involved in
panic flight? There is an acute fear reaction. . . . the person involved
sees the situation as highly and personally dangerous. . . . It is a fear for
self but it also tends to have a specific threat associated with it. . . . the
panic flight is linked to a specific place of danger. . . . people just do not
flee in panic. They always flee *from* something [p. 108]'' (Quarantelli,
1976:108, 109).

This conclusion is not limited to the U.S.A. research base—it has been
validated by researchers working within other cultural settings (Mileti,
Drabek, and Haas, 1975:58). Given the case study method used, however,
I regard these as important *hypotheses* that merit future retesting.

ID1.8a(H) With the degree of the damage controlled, the major factors
which affect the occurrence of panic were as follows: 1. Source of information: the greater the number of sources, the more likely panic is to
occur. 2. Confirming behavior: the failure to confirm information led to
panic. 3. Anxiety: the larger-the anxiety, the greater the possibility of
panic. 4. Sources of information: those who obtained information from
their neighbors, passers-by, or relatives are more likely to panic than
those who obtained information from co-workers or friends. 5. Experiences: those who had experienced no earthquake were more likely to
panic than those who had not [Japan] (Abe, n.d.) (adapted from summary
in Yamamoto and Quarantelli, 1982:A-36).

ID1.8b(H) ". . . (i) that relatively homogeneous groups were facing in
the same direction, (ii) that neighbouring groups faced in opposite directions, (iii) that in the vicinity of the groups in flight, other people were
standing still and calm and watching the photographers. This analysis
justified the assertion that panic is localized. . . . Analysis of the pho-
tographs was done by recording on tracing paper the orientation of faces
in the crowd. . . . Lima Stadium panic (Peru, 25 May 1964)'' [France]
(Chandessais, 1980:226).

ID1.8c(H) "All those interviewed agreed that fear was intense, as demonstrated by cries and a rush towards the exits; there was no real dangerous panic, no spreading of terror, no confused behavior; small natural
groups played an important role in mutual aid, passing information and
decision-taking; leadership of boys and submissiveness of girls was general: it was notable that in all cases boys let girls go first to the exit. . . .
The fire in a dance hall (St. Laurent du Pont Isère, 1 November 1970)''
[France] (Chandessais, 1980:226).

ID1.8d(H) [Generally speaking, earthquakes are not accompanied by this
collective phenomenon. (i.e., panic behavior). Hasty flights were subsequently reported during some of the strongest of the other 420 quakes
which were reported in Friuli during the second half of 1976 and in 1977.]
[Italy] (Boileau *et al.,* 1978:144). (See also Withey, 1976:130; Demerath
and Wallace, 1957; Barton, 1969:81.)

In an effort to systematize the literature on panic-producing conditions, Ponting (1976) offered a more precise series of hypotheses. Many of these have parallels to the above themes but I have listed several since they provide good examples of the type of conceptual precision needed. The next obvious step is the formulation and testing of a multivariate model.

> ID1.9 "Panic can occur only if the participants define the situation to be highly and personally dangerous" [Canada] (Ponting, 1976:48).
>
> ID1.9a(H) "The greater the individual's level of anxiety, the greater the likelihood that that person will engage in panic behaviour" [Canada] (Ponting, 1976:35).
>
> ID1.9b(H) "Panic participants will undergo a psychological change from a vague anxiety to a fear of a *specific* agent which threatens their life" [Canada] (Ponting, 1976:38).
>
> ID1.9c(H) "The greater the degree of fear that another explosion might occur, the greater the likelihood that a person will engage in panic behaviour" [Canada] (Ponting, 1976:42).
>
> ID1.9d(H) "Panic can occur only if the threat is perceived as immediate rather than distant" [Canada] (Ponting, 1976:51).
>
> ID1.9e(H) "The threat agents which give rise to panic are usually perceived by the participants as uncontrollable" [Canada] (Ponting, 1976:53).

OK. So victims rarely panic; but what do they do? Based on numerous case studies we know that *they react*.

Their actions are guided by choice and efforts to help those around them that may require it. They don't wait for officials to get there and tell them to which hospital they should take their injured child. They will go to the nearest hospital or source of medical assistance they know about, often the one they might have selected in a non-emergency situation.

> ID1.10 "Victims don't wait for orders from authorities or for someone to give directions; they react immediately, attending to their own well-being and helping those nearby (Quarantelli and Dynes, 1972:68; Form and Nosow, 1958:66, 76; Fritz and Williams, 1957)" (as summarized in Mileti, Drabek, and Haas, 1975:59).
>
> ID1.10a ". . . the patient's choice in a chaotic situation is to identify with stable, already existing sources of medical care. . . . 62.4% of those who sought medical help went to a private physician. The most frequent reason why they chose that particular source of care was because it was their *regular* source of care" (Smith, Traum, and Poole, 1977:23).

In addition to providing help to those around who might require it, victims commonly seek information. In part, this probably stems from a desire to know if the danger has passed and an acute need to define the situation.

Of course, as they contact others or turn to the media, the information received may not be totally consistent.

> ID1.11(H) After attending to self and injuries of those nearby, victims engage in a wide variety of information-seeking actions.

> ID1.11a(H) "Information-search behaviors after a quake[:] 1. Most people tried to obtain information through television rather than radio. 2. People in their 20s are more likely to rely on radios. 3. Women are more likely than men to rely on T.V. [Japan] (Abe and Kazama, 1979)" (as summarized in Yamamoto and Quarantelli, 1982:A-47).

> ID1.11b(H) "The transistor radio was used as the main source of information by 30 to 50 percent of the people in Niigata and served to check rumors and calm the people. [p. 166] . . . The transistor radio did not decide the final action of individuals . . . They are mostly influenced by passers-by, . . . This tendency is shown more clearly in women [p. 167]" [Japan] (Abe, 1972:166, 167).

Some disaster victims die upon impact, others do so within the next few hours. Of course, events vary considerably in the degree to which this ultimate human cost is extracted. Most disasters within the U.S.A. take few lives. While a few American communities have experienced disaster death tolls in the hundreds, those exceeding two or three thousand are nonexistent. The distribution of disaster-releated deaths is not random, however. In part, this is because some social categories of persons have a greater likelihood to be in potentially dangerous areas.

In 1975, we looked for data to document this assumption and found little beyond the conclusion of Bates and his colleagues: "As socioeconomic status decreases, the probability of dying increases (Bates *et al.*, 1963)" (as summarized in Mileti, Drabek, and Haas, 1975:62). Since then the data base has changed some, but it still lacks adequate precision.

> ID1.12 Disaster-related deaths are distributed differentially according to socioeconomic status, age, sex, and locational variations.

> ID1.12a ". . . the vast majority of deaths and injuries occurred in the lower income and slum areas of the city . . . where the structures were again of adobe with heavy tile roofs" [Guatemala] (Olson and Olson, 1977:75).

> ID1.12b "In the Bangladesh typhoon of 1970, age-specific death rates showed a bimodal distribution: 29% and 20% respectively in the 0–4 and over 70 year age groups, compared with 6% in the 35–39 year age group" [Bangladesh] (Lechat, 1976:424).

> ID1.12c The elderly were more likely to be injured in the storm than others and likewise were more likely to have experienced a storm-related death in their household. (Based on Bolin and Klenow, 1982–83.)

> ID1.12d "Among the casualties [from two earthquakes] women and children predominate. In the Ashkhabad earthquake 47% of the dead were

women, 35% were children and 18% were men. Within those districts of Tashkent that were most affected by the earthquake there were 20% more women than men (Zilper and Savitskayai, 1968[6])" [U.S.S.R.] (Beinin, 1981:143).

ID1.12e [From earthquakes it] ". . . is to be expected the death toll is higher in urban than in rural areas. Thus in Ashkhabad the number of dead made up 13.5% of the population while in the nearby rural district of Geok-Tepens the equivalent figure was 11.3%" [U.S.S.R.] (Beinin, 1981:143).

In contrast to demographic characteristics of victims, some deaths reflect actions taken—or not taken. Certainly, we need to go far beyond the insightful observations offered by Abe.

". . . [Those] who survived and those who died in the fire behaved differently. Three kinds of survival behavior were noted: [(1) Prior knowledge, (2) return to habit, (3) chance location near exit. Three death patterns were: (1) escape route led to dead end, (2) crowd followed authority to central area with killing smoke, and (3) jumpers.] . . . survival behavior can be affected by prior knowledge. . . . people often return to the familiar and to habit in times of crisis" [Japan] (Abe, 1976:120).

As an illustration of the immediate applicability of behavioral research, and its lifesaving potential, the conclusions of Glass and his associates (1980) following the Wichita Falls, Texas, tornado is hard to match. By carefully documenting the death and injury rates among those who remained in their automobiles, the National Weather Service and others responsible for tornado warnings have the insight needed to save lives. Media broadcasts instructing those in cars and mobile homes to seek alternative shelter may save many in the years ahead. A "nugget" of this type demonstrates the social significance of this research area.

ID1.12f "Twenty-six (60 percent) of the 43 traumatic deaths and 30 (51 percent) of the 59 serious injuries occurred in people who, despite ample warning, went to their cars to drive out of the storm's path" (Glass et al., 1980:735).

Finally, it is now clear that some disaster-related deaths occur as secondary consequences. Available data are less dramatic than the tornado casualty rates just cited, but research over the next decade should provide the precision needed to precipitate more informed policy actions.

ID1.12g "The total number of deaths was significantly higher (8%) in a 'blizzard week' than in the preceding and subsequent (control) weeks

---

[6]Zh. Z. Zilper and L. A. Savitskayai, "Trauma and Heart Attacks as the Direct Health Hazards of the Tashkent Earthquake." Anthology of material from the 3rd Scientific Conference of Young Scientists from the Tashkent Medical Institute, Tashkent, 1968, pp. 314–315.

(114.1 vs. 105.3 deaths per day). Deaths from ischaemic heart-disease
(I.H.D.), which rose significantly by 22% in the blizzard week from 36.7
to 44.6 deaths per day, accounted for 90% of the excess total deaths.
The increase was greater in males than in females (30% vs. 12%), and
in both sexes there was no difference in the distribution of deaths by age
between the blizzard and control weeks. I.H.D. deaths were increased
for 8 days after a snowstorm, suggesting that the effect was related to
activities such as snow shovelling rather than the storm itself'' (Glass
and Zack, 1979:485). (See also Faich and Rose, 1979:1050.)

These twelve general propositions provide a portrait of victim behavior
that impacted the training of many emergency managers. Researchers like
Dynes, Quarantelli, and many others have reached many responsible for
designing and implementing such training, especially in the U.S.A. Yet,
when turnover is considered, and the number and complexity of the emergency management systems is considered, even within the U.S.A., it is
obvious that the job barely has been started. And equally important, while
numerous highly significant insights have been obtained, the base lacks
precision. Ranges of generalization rarely are specified; weak conceptualization precludes integration with larger bodies of social psychological
theory. Thus, the most researched area within the entire conceptual taxonomy presented in Chapter 1 still represents a pressing research agenda.

Before turning to our next topic—responses by non-victims—I want to
add a final note. At the outset of the last chapter, I emphasized that most
disaster research conducted by sociologists has centered on events of relatively short duration. The general propositions just presented illustrate
this. Turton's case study of responses to drought conditions adds further
support to the normalization thesis that underlies these. But it adds another
dimension. When disaster impacts are prolonged—years of hunger, rather
than minutes to escape from a fire—people may reorder their priorities.
Survival for the day may force redefinition of commitments to longer-
term expectations. The implicit hypothesis awaits empirical study.

> "During this period of hunger, i.e., 1971–73, however, people began call-
> ing in debts and pressing claims which, in less difficult times, they might
> have left dormant. Particularly significant here is the fact that there was
> even a tendency for cattle which had been paid in bridewealth to be
> recalled—or rather, taken back by force. It was as though it was no longer
> possible to wait for reciprocity to be achieved in its own time. The Mursi
> had lost confidence in the natural order of things and they had, so to
> speak, lost confidence in their social order as well. They therefore began
> turning their long term, intangible assets—claims on the property of other
> based on kinship, affinity and past exchanged—into short term, tangible
> ones'' [Ethiopia] (Turton, 1977:285).

ID2. Non-Victim Actions

As pointed by Taylor (1983) and others, the line between victims and
non-victims is not as obvious as might appear at first glance. Thus, beyond

those who have been hurt physically—or have incurred losses of possessions—are a wide variety of "hidden victims." Parents whose child died
in a school bus accident or spouses who were widowed when a jumbo jet
crashed are but the more obvious examples. While we need to know much
more about responses to and impacts of disaster on such hidden victims,
I will use the term more narrowly here. Thus, when referring to non-
victim actions here, I mean those who were not *directly* impacted in a
physical sense. Obviously, scars to the psyche may have occurred to many.

But what do they do? Consistent with victim behavior, there is an overall
pattern of continuity and a rapid response to first define the situation and
then a propensity to take action.

> ID2.1 ". . . non-victims, not unlike victims, seek to 'structure' the sit-
> uation and 'normalize' it, i.e., integrate the novelty of the disaster into
> conceptual schemes used in everyday life (Anderson, 1968)" (as sum-
> marized in Mileti, Drabek, and Haas, 1975:63).

At times, to some observers at least, the behavioral response seems
like mass chaos. From the perspective of those streaming into a devastated
tornado area, however, the actions make sense and are guided primarily
by a motivation to help (Killian, 1954; Fritz, 1961).

> ID2.2 "Persons who confront a disaster situation seek to structure it
> through using previous roles and norms as guides. But most of these are
> not much assistance, other than providing a general motivation and desire
> to help. So they actively seek role definitions that will enable them to
> engage in behaviors that they can define as being helpful" (Mileti, Drabek,
> and Haas, 1975:65). (See also Taylor, Zurcher, and Key, 1970.)

This desire to help is intense and defines one of the most significant
dimensions of the overall response.

> ID2.3 "The helpers' response to a disaster is characterized by solidarity.
> This is expressed by emergence of core values, the strengthening of pre-
> existing and emergent networks, and the actions of counter-disaster, vol-
> untary and other organizations. The emergence of core values is observed
> in the consensus on priorities, altruistic behavior and the disappearance
> of many barriers between individuals" [Australia] (Leivesley, 1977b:214).
> (See also Mileti, Drabek, and Haas, 1975:65; Martin, 1964; Kutak, 1938;
> Menninger, 1952.)

This massive helping response is extensive. Based on a carefully selected
sample of victims following the tornado in Wichita Falls, Texas (population: 94,201), for example, we found that: "Nearly three-fifths (59%) of
all uninjured victims we interviewed rendered aid to someone else within
minutes after the tornado passed. Projecting this to the estimated population at risk (21,000), it is possible that upwards of 10,000 individuals
may have been helping to search through the rubble that minutes earlier
had been their neighborhoods." (Drabek *et al.*, 1981:97). How this might
vary across events and among societies constitutes an important research
agenda item.

ID2.3a(H) "It is now known that within 30 minutes of a major disaster, such as an earthquake, up to 75% of the healthy survivors are actually engaged in efficient rescue activities" [Belgium] (Lechat, 1976:422).

Additional insight on rates of helping behavior comes from a survey directed by Nakamura (1981) following the eruption—for the first time in human history—of Kiso no Ontakesan (October 28, 1979). Since no major damage occurred, however, he put the questions hypothetically. Within the context of a rather surprising event—although it was one causing minimal damage—we learn a bit about what people *say* they will do, if needed—or if asked.

ID2.3b [To a question "If the eruption became more severe and if your relatives and friends were in distress, do you think you would help?", more than 75 percent of the total survey population (number of returned questionnaires was 548) answered positively; while a little more than 14 percent answered that they would probably help if asked.] [Japan] (Nakamura, 1981:188).

Not all persons are as quick to help as others, however. We have some clues as to the factors that affect this, but the matter has not yet been pinned down with precision.

ID2.4 "Many factors have been found to affect the possibility of an individual's participation in rescue activity." (Wenger, 1972:56). These include: (1) location; (2) knowledge about the welfare of significant others; (3) extent of injury; (4) degree of identification with the community; (5) relevance of training for emergency situations; and (6) membership in emergency-oriented organizations. (Adapted from Wenger, 1972:56; see also Nakamura, 1981:183–184.)

ID2.4a "Older persons are less likely than younger ones to engage in behavior oriented toward individuals and groups beyond self and family in rescue and immediate post-impact phase (partially supported only; Friedsam, 1962)" (as summarized in Mileti, Drabek, and Haas, 1975:65).

ID2.4b "In contrast to women, men are more likely to help persons they do not know personally, and will remain with rescue activities longer (Form and Nosow, 1958:70–71)" (as summarized in Mileti, Drabek, and Haas, 1975: 65). (See also Nakamura, 1981:176–177.)

ID2.4c ". . . rates of devotionalism (a measure of the intensity of religious organizational participation) are positively related to the performance of helping behavior. . . . devotionalism was a predictor of three of the four types of ordinary helping behavior examined while church attendance consistently predicted emergency helping behavior. . . . effect of church attendance on emergency helping behavior is found to be primarily through churches' provision of organizational means for participation" (Nelson and Dynes, 1976:47).

ID2.4d ". . . those who provide emergency aid are typically individuals whose predisaster role performance included similar types of helping behavior. [p. 267] . . . The findings consistently demonstrate continuity in helping roles from ordinary to emergency situations. The more diversified an actor's program of ordinary helping behavior, the more likely is the actor to have performed emergency helping activities of all the types tapped in the study [p. 269]'' (Nelson, 1977:267, 269). (See also Raphael, 1979:331.)

ID2.4e [*The aid most rapidly provided was given by people who were closest to the scene.*] [France] (Chandessais, 1966:465). (See also Nelson, 1973.)

A few early researchers, especially Killian (1952), proposed that helping behavior might be curbed at times by forms of "role conflict." That is, persons might experience conflicting obligations (Moore *et al.,* 1963). Killian, in particular, argued that disasters would leave many with conflicts between family and organizational responsibilities. But subsequent research has recast the matter significantly (Mileti, Drabek, and Haas, 1975: 67–68). The conclusions of Dynes and Quarantelli appear to be on target (see also, the Proceedings from an NIMH–FEMA sponsored conference, *Role Stressors and Supports For Emergency Workers,* 1985).

ID2.5 "In our experience over the years, in over 100 disasters and in the course of interviewing over 2,500 different organizational officials, we found that role conflict was *not* a serious problem which creates a significant loss of manpower. . . . In fact, we have had difficulty in finding any illustrations of the phenomena, let alone documenting the pervasiveness of it" (Dynes and Quarantelli, 1976:237).

ID2.5a(H) [Three propositions as to why role abandonment is not found empirically:] "[1.] The total role structure, thus, becomes more coherently organized around a set of value priorities and, at the same time, irrelevant roles which could produce strain are eliminated until the emergency is over. [p. 239] . . . [2.] Because of the assurance that these organizational members on duty will remain, other organizational members not on duty have the reassurance that they have time to check personal and familial damage and also to engage in limited amounts of non-occupational role behavior before reporting. [p. 240] [3.] . . . family units can make internal allocative decisions which facilitate the assumption of various emergency roles on the part of various family members [e.g., wife may go to EOC with husband and serve as secretary] [p. 240]'' (Dynes and Quarantelli, 1976:239–240). (See also Dynes, 1970a:154–155; Instituut Voor Sociaal Onderzoek Van Het Nederlandse Volk Amsterdam, 1955; Form and Nosow, 1958:102.)

Despite the influx of non-victims into disaster areas, researchers repeatedly have documented an absense of looting behavior. This pertains both to the immediate emergency period and, as we will see in the next chapter, to the early stages of recovery, except under highly specialized circumstances. Media reports of organizational actions taken to prevent looting are commonplace, however, as unfortunately are quotes from persons at the scene who claim knowledge of actual looting incidents. No doubt some looting behavior occurs, but it is minimal at worst and entirely nonexistent, at best.

> ID2.6 "After the collision of an airliner and another aircraft over San Diego on September 25, 1978, in which 144 persons died, a report circulated of looting at the crash site. The San Diego chief of police was disturbed enough by this rumor, which he said couldn't be traced, to write to a national newsmagazine: 'There is absolutely no evidence that any looting occurred at the crash site or in the immediate vicinity' " (Frazier, 1979:351).

> ID2.6a "Sixty-two per cent of those interviewed said they refrained from entering the cordoned off area, however, 37% said they entered the area to view the damage. . . . No looting or other such activities occurred in the commercial district following the tornado contrary to early national media reports" (Hodler, 1982:48).

As a final note, I noticed the consistency between this portrait of helping behavior and certain "counterriot" activity. Thus, even in the hostile confrontations of ghetto riots, some emerged as helpers trying to avert further physical harm and violence. This topic, like many others related to rescuer activity, however, presents a complex research agenda.

> "Counterriot activity is viewed here as measures taken by black civilians to dissuade other blacks from engaging in violence. . . . The Kerner Commission made no attempt to draw analytical distinctions between counterrioters. It chose instead to discuss only the typical counterrioter. On the basis of our interviews with individuals involved in peace-restoring activities, we suggest that the term counterrioter does not represent a single category. At least four fairly distinct types can be observed: opportunistic, moral, functionary, and political counterrioters" [Opportunistic refers to peace-restoring activities that are viewed as opportunities to realize some personal aim or goal.] (Anderson, Dynes, and Quarantelli, 1974:52).

ID3. Emotional Responses

How do disaster victims respond emotionally? There is a clear consensus on the question; statements like the following summary by Singer are typical.

> ID3.1 "In contrast to some of the popular assumptions about human behavior in disasters, reports of actual experiences reveal that most persons respond in an adaptive, responsible manner. Those who show manifestly inappropriate responses, including panic and psychotic behavior, tend to be in a distinct minority. At the same time, most people do show some signs of emotional disturbance as an immediate response to a disaster, and these tend to appear in characteristic phases or stages" (Singer,

1982:248). (See also Mileti, Drabek, and Haas, 1975:60; Kentsmith, 1980:409).

While limited data are available, the range, intensity, and duration of such "temporary symptoms" have not been well specified across the spectrum of disasters. Thus, I suspect that certain experiences, like confronting large numbers of disfigured dead or body fragments, would produce higher rates than a slowly rising flood that took no lives. But that remains conjecture, not a conclusion backed by precisely designed studies.

> ID3.1a(H) "Nearly three-quarters (72%) of the subjects stated they had psychosomatic problems. The medical survey compared the affected population of Feyzin with that of the non-affected community of Irigny. A total of 1967 persons responded to the questionnaire for themselves or for their children under 12. . . . The symptoms identified included nervousness (49%), anxiety (56%), sleeping difficulties (27%), fatigue (18%) and digestive problems (13%). Of these, the first three symptoms are generally combined and form a characteristic 'triad.'" [On 4 January 1966, a fire at the 'Rhone-Alpes' refinery caused many tanks of gaseous propane to explode.] [France] (Chandessais, 1980:224–225).

There was a time when researchers argued a very different position on this matter, however. And no doubt, some observed—or perhaps had reports from—victims who were overwhelmed by the disruption of a disaster. Thus, "the disaster syndrome" was created. Wallace (1956) defined it as:

> ". . . a psychologically determined defensive reaction pattern consisting of these stages: (1) people appear dazed, stunned, apathetic, passive, immobile or aimlessly puttering around; (2) extreme suggestibility, altruism, gratitude for help, personal loss minimized, concern for family and community; (3) euphoric identification with the damaged community, enthusiastic participation in repair and rehabilitation; and (4) euphoria wears off and 'normal' ambivalent attitudes return (full course of the syndrome may take several weeks) (Wallace, 1956). (See also Killian, 1954:68; Menninger, 1952:129; Wallace, 1957:24; and Wilson, 1962.)" (As summarized in Mileti, Drabek, and Haas, 1975:61.)

Although his report failed to identify the data source to which he was referring, Hocking's conclusion illustrates how this concept got used— maybe a bit abused—in the literature of the 1960s.

> "Although rapid recovery is the rule, about one-third of survivors display what has been called the 'disaster syndrome', and for the next few hours they are dazed and withdrawn, and wander around in an aimless fashion. Over the next few days, insomnia, digestive upsets, anxiety and tremulousness are common. These symptoms usually subside, . . ." (Hocking, 1965:479).

Reflecting more current studies and improved data collection techniques, most would concur with the tone and substance of the following conclusions offered by Dynes, Quarantelli, Oliver, and Reardon.

ID3.2 "There is some limited evidence of what has been called a 'disaster syndrome' (i.e., a state of shock leading to regression in normal cognitive processes). However, it appears only in the more traumatic and sudden kinds of catastrophes, is confined to the post-impact period, . . . at most only 14 percent of all respondents may have manifested some of the initial stages of the syndrome" (Dynes and Quarantelli, 1976:235).

ID3.2a "Disaster shock still remains a controversial matter. . . . despite the undoubted personal hardships widely experienced, a few days after the cyclone our visits to different parts of Tonga, even to the severely disrupted Sopu area, did not reveal any readily apparent disorientation or psychological disturbance" [Tonga] (Oliver and Reardon, 1982:64).

In short, few, if any, victims, even in the worst disasters studied to date, evidence the types of zombie states reported by a few earlier researchers. Most will experience varying degrees of short term "upset," however. But what factors might predict the distribution of the symptom pattern? Here we have many conclusions but an insufficient degree of study or consistency to feel that we have a good handle on the matter. Thus, we have numerous *hypotheses,* a lot of argument among the experts, and a shortage of rigorous designs and measures.

Some researchers argue that the qualities of the "stressee" matter little—that is, "every person has a breaking point." What is critical then is the nature of the stressor. Of special significance, I suspect are matters of probable reoccurrence—for example, earthquake aftershakes—and uncertainty about possible long-term health impacts. Thus, fears of exposure to contaminants—be it radioactive dust or buried cans of chemicals—are secondary consequences of some events that may evoke differing symptom patterns than those emerging from hurricane or tornado damage.

ID3.3(H) "A review of wartime psychiatric casualties fails to reveal individual characteristics which predispose a person to breakdown. The duration of the stress seems to be the most critical factor" (Kentsmith, 1980:411). (See also Barton, 1969:80; Wilson, 1962.)

ID3.3a(H) [In the Friuli case, we had the situation, not contemplated in the literature on disasters, of a repetition of the destructive event. The earthquakes which occurred on 11 and 15 September, somewhat less intense than those of May, struck a community which, for 4 months, had been experiencing the "recovery" phase . . . The psychosocial reactions to the quakes of September are thus completely different from those of May; in place of the normal sequence of dumbfounded stupor, there is ferocious activity as the reactions of fear, depression, flight burst forth immediately, . . .] [Italy] (Boileau *et al.,* 1978:153).

ID3.3b(H) "The NRC survey showed a higher level of stress symptoms for those persons living closer to TMI at the time of the accident for all fifteen indicators: stomach trouble, headache, diarrhea, constipation, frequent urination, rash, abdominal pain, loss of appetite, overeating, trouble sleeping, sweating spells, feeling trembly and shaky, trouble thinking clearly, irritability, and extreme anger'' (Flynn and Chalmers, 1980:50, 51).

ID3.3c(H) ''. . . the breakdown rate was directly related to the degree of stress to which the soldier was subjected, so that infantry regiments in combat had 12 times the rate of those in quieter areas,'' (Hocking, 1965:479).

In contrast, are those researchers who argue for subject heterogeneity. That is, not all victims are the same and some will respond differently to disaster-caused stressors than others. Thus, as would be expected, the variable selected reflects the theoretical orientation of the researcher. Among the qualities proposed by some are ''stable'' personalities and birth order. Others have looked for sex, age, and ethnic differences—and to some degree, at least, claimed to have found them. Those more socially oriented have examined previous disaster experiences and social context. For example, were persons alone when the event occurred?

ID3.4(H) ''. . . persons reporting pre-disaster higher levels of psychological instability . . . react in more maladaptive manner after impact'' [Italy] (Pelanda, 1979:1). (See also Wilson, 1962:126–127.)

ID3.4a(H) ''Perhaps a measure of a person's mental well-being can be seen in his capacity to block off immediate acute anxiety reactions. The ability to lift this repression after the acute danger is past would indicate the flexibility of one's defensive systems. Under this schema a 'mature' man would function in an emergency (effective repression) and feel terror later when it was safe (no need to continue the repression). This resembles the war-time phenomenon of pilots who were not flooded with fright during dangerous missions, but who had many anxiety equivalents and who only revealed the enormity of their anxiety when they were treated in convalescent centers'' (Greenson and Mintz, 1972:19).

ID3.4b(H) ''For a number of depressed patients, the earthquake seemed to act as a brief shock treatment that enabled them to respond to directions, get out of the building, and help others. One patient had been hospitalized a few hours before the earthquake, and was so hyperactive and uncontrollable that he was placed in restraints—a practice used only in extreme situations. At the time of the earthquake, a nurse disengaged his restraints, and told him that an 18-year-old catatonic girl could not get out of the building without help, and it was up to him to direct her. He escorted her safely out, remained coherent for a few hours, then regressed'' (Stein, 1974:40–41).

ID3.5(H) ''Considering the entire sample, birth order was unrelated to anxiety or affiliation for both sexes'' [only respondents who were alone when the quake struck ($N = 112$)] (Hoyt and Raven, 1973:123). (See also Strumpfer, 1970:267–268.)

ID3.6(H) [About twice as many women as men reportedly suffered from emotionally-related problems after the catastrophe.] [France] (Chandes-

(Chandessais, 1966:478). (See also Strumpfer, 1970:267–268; Abe and Kazama, 1979; Hoyt and Raven, 1973:124–125; Barton, 1969:86.)

ID3.6a(H) "Women were prevented from seeing these bodies in most instances by relatives, and this was often reinforced by Police. Despite support from the counselling team suggesting that viewing should be made possible for some at least, this unwritten rule remained throughout the period. Many women, especially young wives and mothers, suffered further distress, confusion and anger because of this" [Australia] (Raphael, 1979–80:215).

ID3.6b(H) "Those who thought TMI was a very serious threat at the time of the accident were younger, female, more highly educated, and of high income. Pregnant women were much more likely (64 percent) than average to view it as a very serious threat and much less likely to think it was no threat at all" (Flynn and Chalmers, 1980:50).

ID3.7(H) "Older persons are more likely to become physical casualties and experience more intense sense of deprivation than younger ones (Friedsam, 1961; 1962)" (as summarized in Mileti, Drabek, and Haas, 1975:62). (See also Strumpfer, 1970:267–268; Abe and Kazama, 1979.)

ID3.7a(H) ". . . we found the elderly not to suffer disproportionate material losses in the storms. They did however evaluate their situation as worse than those around them, a finding which supports Friedsam's (1962) relative deprivation hypothesis" (Bolin and Klenow, 1982–83:294).

ID3.8(H) "If we can extrapolate these results to disasters we could expect less fear and anxiety from those people who are not alone during the impact of a natural disaster" (Glenn, 1979:27). (See also Mileti, Drabek, and Haas, 1975:62.)

All of these *hypotheses* offer insight; none, in my judgment, should be accepted as "proven." Indeed, what the variety suggests to me is the acute need for a more comprehensive multivariate model wherein both qualities of the stressor and the stressee would be tested systematically in a comparative manner. Until research designs are employed that permit this greater degree of precision, results will continue to accumulate that preclude integration.

And as I emphasized above, among the concepts requiring more theoretical elaboration and empirical documentation is the term "victim." Extending the pioneering work on behavioral responses during mine disasters—such as that illustrated by Lucas's (1969) study—Harvey and Bahr's (1980) exploration of responses by women waiting to learn if their husbands would be rescued from the tragic fire that occurred in the Sunshine Mine (near Cour d'Alene, Idaho; May 2, 1972) underscored this point. Their interviews provided further documentation of the continuity thesis I have described above. Also, the utility of an emergent norm perspective is further verified. That is, behavioral responses reflect continuity in underlying values and the emergence of normative guidelines that are adaptations to specific aspects of the event. When the duration of impact is prolonged, as in cases of trapped miners, for example, these phenomena become more pronounced.

> ID3.9 "During the week's search for the missing men, several types of patterned behavior evolved, and sometimes there was social pressure in support of the emergent norms" (Harvey and Bahr, 1980:8).

> ID3.9a "During the week of search the mine site took on aspects of hallowed ground, and three-fourths of the widows-to-be made one or more pilgrimages there. [p. 8] . . . A second norm that quickly emerged was that people and organizations should 'do something.' Even the wives of the missing men, who themselves needed assistance, contributed to the effort [p. 10]" (Harvey and Bahr, 1980:8, 10).

> ID3.9b ". . . over 95 percent of subjects in all three groups noted anxiety as a personal attribute during the week of search for the missing men. Next to anxiety in frequency was a 'need to pray,' reported by over 85 percent of the women. . . . Compared to the other women, the widows cried more, felt more resentment or hostility, were less able to make decisions, had more difficulty in responding to family needs, and said they had more difficulty acting constructively. Widows also had less need to talk to others about the fire. . . . physical reactions (typically insomnia, loss of appetite, headaches, or combinations of these) were reported by 80 percent of the widows, 62 percent of survivors' wives, and 59 percent of the other miners' wives" (Harvey and Bahr, 1980:15).

In addition to these forms of coping came blame assignation, a topic I will discuss further in Chapter 7 (see Section IVF1). Thus, some events are demarked by this fundamental process that sometimes starts before the impact period has ended. How this process impacts the ways individuals cope—both in the short term, and months thereafter—constitutes an important research issue. We have just begun to get limited insight into both the process and its consequences.

> ID3.9c "While between 68 and 72 percent of the women said that those around them were blaming someone for the fire, usually the company, they were apt to say that they themselves did not hold anyone responsible for the fire during that first week. Only 27 percent of the widows, 24 percent of survivors' wives, and 26 percent of the miners' wives said that they blamed anyone for the disaster initially. Those who did generally blamed the Sunshine Mine officials" (Harvey and Bahr, 1980:29).

IID. Group System Level

As emphasized in the previous section dealing with group responses prior to impact, families are a prime source of constraint for many individuals during normal times. And post-disaster periods are no different. Similarly— and to a greater degree, actually—small groups frequently emerge as various lifesaving tasks are identified. Unfortunately, neither of these two types of groups have been studied adequately under post-disaster emergency conditions. Thus, while we know of their presence and can make some predictions about probable activities, the specifics regarding their dynamics and variability await future investigators.

IID1. Family Responses

IID1.1 ". . . the helping response is determined by pre-existing networks and norms, with an emphasis on family and friends" [Australia] (Leivesley, 1977b:214).

This proposition has been supported repeatedly in the case studies of disaster for three decades now (e.g., Fritz, 1961; Quarantelli, 1960a:263). As stressed in the previous section, many will contact—or be contacted by—relatives and go to their homes prior to impact. If they didn't get there prior, they will try to get there afterwards. Thus, a major form of kin aid is to provide shelter.

IID1.1a "During the first night following the disaster, the majority of the victims stayed with relatives" [Sweden] (Edberg and Lustig, 1983:60). (See also Bjorklund, 1981:10; Drabek, 1969; Drabek and Boggs, 1968; Young, 1954; Moore et al., 1963:124; Dacy and Kunreuther, 1969:142; Loizos, 1977:232.)

Beyond stating that this form of aid can be expected, however, we can only hypothesize several factors that may constrain the pattern across events and victim samples. Thus, kin will more likely be help sources as the scope of the disaster decreases (Quarantelli, 1960a:264) and their distance decreases (Instituut Voor Sociaal Onderzoek Van Het Nederlandse Volk Amsterdam, 1955).

Based on case studies conducted during the 1950s, it appeared that male–female responses differed during and right after impact. Furthermore, as Barton (1969) suggested, people responsible for children, or other types of dependents, evidenced response differences. More recent data, however, indicate that these patterns are not totally consistent, although it is not clear why (e.g., Perry, Hawkins, and Neal, 1983:186).

IID1.2(H) "After impact the males in the impact area were much more active in rescue and relief than the females, and those men with dependents more than men without. The effect of dependency was reversed among the females—those with dependents were the least active of all in providing help to people outside the family" (Barton, 1969:83).

IID1.2a(H) "Research on the post-impact period has shown that men are more likely than women to help persons not known to them personally. This finding was not supported. Only one significant difference between men and women was found; that women were more likely to receive help from strangers than men" (Perry, Hawkins, and Neal, 1983:186).

IID1.2b(H) "Research on the post-impact period has also shown that younger persons are more likely than older persons to give aid beyond the immediate family. It was found, in this study, that there was no difference in whether or not young, middle-aged, or older persons helped their relatives. Younger persons were more likely to help friends and strangers than older persons. Nor were persons in different age categories more or less likely to receive help from their relatives or strangers. Both the young and the old were more likely to receive help from their friends than the middle-aged" (Perry, Hawkins, and Neal, 1983:186).

Despite these and other ambiguities that remain in our knowledge base today, it is clear that right after impact—whatever the duration may be—the major task of searching for and rescuing victims is prime. All family members must be accounted for, and any missing become focal points for active searching. Failure to anticipate and appreciate the intensity of these motivations can further exacerbate official rescue efforts. Parents searching for missing children will not be stopped easily—if at all.

IID1.3 "Absent family members returned to their destroyed houses and they accepted great risks in their search for missing family and neighbours. All traffic to the disaster site was stopped by the police who did not, however, succeed in preventing victim families and their kin from entering the area" [Sweden] (Edberg and Lustig, 1983:59).

IID1.3a "The Problem of People at their Offices. . . . About 56 percent found their families, who had not been evacuated, waiting at home. About 27 percent could not find out where their families had been evacuated to . . . The person whose family has been evacuated experiences anxiety and confusion, not knowing where the family has gone" [Japan] (Takuma, 1978:163). (See also Henderson, 1977:189.)

During this period, most family members—and friends of possible victims—engage in searching actions of various forms. If missing members are not found, relatives may be canvased in the hope that they might have news. This is true for general information about the disaster too.

IID1.4 "Many of those who had been at home when the slide occurred left the area immediately afterward, while the family members who had been elsewhere returned to the area to look for them. It was difficult to obtain information as to who had been lost and who had been rescued and where they had been taken. Many people searched the area for hours . . . When the family members could not find a victim within the slide area they went to a relative or friend whom they hoped the victim would contact" [Sweden] (Bjorklund, 1981:9). (See also Quarantelli, 1982b:8; Scanlon, Dixon, and McClellan, 1982:8).

Thus, post-event responses are structured to a large degree by family groups. When word arrives that members may have been victims, group cohesiveness heightens—if only temporarily.

IID1.5(H) "It was this spirit of cohesiveness that provided the stability required by the fragmented subsystem of relatives and friends. This supports the generalization that 'high group morale and cohesiveness will generally minimize the disaster effects of impact' " (Grossman, 1973:41).

Apart from reducing the physical impacts by providing temporary shelter, food, and other forms of aid, it is likely that these groups perform important emotional support functions. While many interviews document the perceived significance of these activities for family members, the extent, form, and differential distribution of such involvements remain imprecisely measured. Variations in grieving, for example, both among families and their respective members, is a critical topic that should be examined carefully.

IID1.5a(H) "We assessed the grief reactions of the families for potential complications. In some families, there would be a single family member who showed little emotion. The danger for such a person was a delayed or repressed grief reaction which might later express itself through psychosomatic disease or depression. . . . We were also concerned about those people who did not express their grief directly, but who spent time and energy helping others. . . . A third reaction that concerned us was an extreme and profound expression of guilt. One family member said over and over, 'I killed her—if I hadn't been gone, she would be alive!' " (Ciuca, Downie, and Morris, 1977:456).

Finally, we have very little insight into cross-cultural variations. Upon reviewing a translation of the Akimoto and Ohta (1980) text—*Cities in Disaster*—I encountered the following finding that illustrates the complexities that such comparisons will reveal in the next decade as more cross-national comparisons are made.

[After the Miyagi Prefecture Offshore Earthquake, gas was the last of the essential utilities sustaining city life to be restored. Those who had gas-heated baths had to use public bath houses or baths at someone's house for a month. The so-called naked relationship—sharing the same bath water—tended to be established with relatives, even if they lived far away, rather than nearby neighbors. It makes us think about the influence of social distance (this may have to be explained to American scholars who grew up with western-style bath where the hot water is drained each time someone takes a bath).] [Japan] (Akimoto and Ohta, 1980:95).

IID2. Emergent Group Responses

Augmenting family responses are those of small emergent groups. While some headway has been made in studying these short-lived responses, a much firmer understanding is required. Their actions are quick and often lifesaving. Yet, too few emergency officials really grasp or understand the range of important contributions made by such groups.

IID2.1 [Once individuals themselves and their families are safe, they form little groups and try to help as many people as possible.] [Italy] (Boileau *et al.*, 1978:145).

But what conditions give rise to these groups? In what types of disasters might their presence be more widespread? To date we have a wide variety of clues, but no firm answers.

IID2.2 "After disaster a portion of the community acts as if usual status roles were held in suspension: people adopt a kind of 'role moratorium.' During this period new and ephemeral roles—helping roles—may be taken on, only to be dropped again during the post-crisis period" (Taylor, 1972:112). (See also Forrest, 1972:170.)

IID2.2a(H) "The greater the size, density, and proximity of community populations to the impact area, the more complex the milling processes and the greater the development of emergent groups which perform disaster-relevant activities. . . . [Also hypothesized as an independent variable is] intensity and scope of impact" (Kreps, 1978:80–81).

IID2.2b(H) Factors that encourage formation of emergent groups: (1) emergency demands exceed community capability; (2) low interorganizational coordination; (3) authority lapse; (4) low community preparedness; (5) lack of prior experience; and (6) crisis remains inadequately defined. (Summary of findings listed by Mileti, Drabek, and Haas, 1975:72–73, based on Palmer and Sells, 1965; Quarantelli, 1966; and Parr, 1970.)

Once formed, the internal dynamics of such groups may result in shifts in structure or task changes. Yet, empirical case studies of these groups are rare, despite a few exceptional instances like the dissection by Taylor, Zurcher, and Key (1970) of the rescue and recovery group which emerged following the 1966 tornado in Topeka, Kansas. E. L. Quarantelli and staff of the Disaster Research Center were engaged in empirical studies of several such groups at the time I was writing this review (e.g., Stallings and Quarantelli, 1985). Undoubtedly their findings will do much to lay the groundwork for subsequent investigators.

IID2.3 "The groups studied in this research did emerge in a crisis situation. Faced with a common threat (a natural disaster) group participants were drawn closer together, cooperation was voluntarily extended and tasks were conscientiously carried out" (Forrest, 1974:92). (See also Kates *et al.*, 1973:986; Mileti, Drabek, and Haas, 1975:74–75.)

IID2.3a(H) As the size of an emergent group increases, there is (a) an expansion in the number of formally designated positions; (b) expansion in the size of the administrative component; (c) both a qualitative and quantitative expansion in task specialization and in the number of specifically designated structural subunits; (d) an expansion in the number of hierarchical authority levels; and (e) a specific normative structure that develops to integrate group activities. (Adapted from Forrest, 1974:97.)

IID2.3b(H) "Previous interaction patterns identify and recruit specific actors for emergent group participation" (Forrest, 1974:98).

In contrast to rescue groups that emerge, a few researchers have examined victim groups. How might a collection of coal miners (e.g., Lucas, 1969) or shipwrecked passengers behave? While many predictions might be offered based on small-group theory, only a handful of empirical case studies appear in the literature. These accounts—although subject to possible embellishment—are powerful testimonials to the tenacity of the human spirit.

> ". . . the [1906] Courrières disaster, which claimed 1,100 lives (1,057 Frenchmen and 43 Belgians), was unprecedented and undoubtedly constitutes one of the world's worst recorded pit disasters. [p. 33] . . . twenty days after the explosion, thirteen men effectively rescued themselves . . . This self-rescue was the most remarkable event of the Courrières disaster, and assuredly one of the most incredible feats of human survival in mining history. . . . the men had wandered aimlessly for miles through the complicated system of galleries, before eventually making their way to the bottom of shaft No. 2. . . . [They] had kept themselves alive by drinking their own urine and stagnant water, and by eating a combination of putrefying horse meat, bark stripped from pit props, oats found in underground stables, and provisions taken from the bodies of their former workmates. . . . they had retained their mental faculties and were still able to walk into the blinding daylight. [pp. 38–39] . . . [In contrast,] twenty-five days after the explosion, another miner, Auguste Berthon, was discovered alive . . . At one point he had lost confidence and had unsuccessfully searched for a hatchet in order that he might amputate a hand and bleed to death. It had been purely by chance that he had been found; he had seen a light, cried out, and fortunately was heard by rescuers. When discovered, Berthon was in a dazed state and seemingly unaware of his plight or the length of time he had been trapped [p. 40]" [France] (Neville, 1978:33, 38–40).

These processes were documented with more precision in the study by Henderson and Bostock (1977). Their findings are consistent with small-group responses to various forms of stress, but must be viewed as hypotheses at present since they lack subsequent validation.

> IID2.4(H) Interviews with 7 men who survived a ship wreck after 10 days in a rubber raft and 3 days on land (3 crew members died at various times throughout this period) revealed 5 behaviors they saw as critical to group morale: (1) Attachment ideation, (2) Drive to survive, (3) Modelling, (4) Prayer, and (5) Hope [Australia] (adapted from Henderson and Bostock, 1977:16).

> IID2.4a(H) "The use of hope by these men leads us to conclude that as a coping behaviour, it has the following characteristics: (1) It consists of anticipating relief from distress either by one's own action or through intervention by others. (2) Within a group, hope is likely to be more

powerful if it is verbalized, since this increases its potency through suggestion and confirmation. (3) A leader may use hopeful statements to sustain morale while not necessarily himself believing in what he says. (4) The principal function of hope is to control mood, which in turn determines what other behaviours a survivor will undertake to increase his chances of rescue'' [Australia] (Henderson and Bostock, 1977:18).

IID2.4b(H) "Throughout the ordeal, the most conspicuous behaviour was the men's preoccupation with principal attachment figures such as wives, mothers, children and girl friends. We have termed this 'attachment ideation' and consider it to be of considerable theoretical importance. Every one of the survivors reported it as the most helpful content of consciousness which they experienced. . . . The existence of a strong social bond between the survivor and his kin provides him with affective sustenance on the one hand and acts additionally as a force motivating him towards reunion'' [Australia] (Henderson and Bostock, 1977:16).

Finally, as I pointed out above, the urge is strong to return home immediately after the emergency. Based on scattered case study observations, it appears that this process may be as complex as those depicting departures. Unfortunately, to date, the research base deals almost exclusively with departure, rather than return.

IID2.5 "Many people, eager to return home, tried to enter the evacuation zone before they were told to" [Canada] (Whyte, 1980:21). (See also Guard Police Psychology Research Society, 1971b).

IIID. Organizational System Level

How do organizational systems respond after receiving word of disaster? What are the consequences of disaster-generated demands on organizational structures and participants? What special types of problems are confronted by medical and media organizations? Research sheds much light on these and numerous other questions. Thus, a solid foundation has been laid; what the future requires are highly focused studies that will take each of the many strands identified herein and provide depth.

Six topics captured the major ideas generated by this collection of findings: (1) initial responses; (2) emergent organizations; (3) stress effects; (4) correlates of effectiveness; (5) media organization responses; and (6) medical organization responses. Curiously, both media and medical organizations have been studied much more since our 1975 inventory was completed (Mileti, Drabek, and Haas), but police, fire, public works, military, and other first-responder organizations have not been pursued much. Thus, the Disaster Research Center monograph series and the collection of articles published in the *American Behavioral Scientist* (1970) remain the best summary available.

IIID1. Initial Responses

When confronted with the unexpected, many strands of continuity remain. Organizational systems do not dissipate instantly; nor are they immediately transformed into some alternative structural form. Rather, these systems—like the individuals comprising them—reflect initial responses that are rooted within long-standing normative guidelines. For example, in Westgate's (1975) analysis of a plant explosion in England, fleeing workers might be viewed as panic participants behaving in a random or totally disorganized manner. Yet, as we would expect from the preceding section, some would risk their own safety to help the injured.

> "Although a minority of respondents indicated making this response, [i.e., help to injured] the response is governed by whether, 1. the respondent's flight path led him into contact with injured colleagues, 2. the respondent was with anybody at the time he began his flight, who, if found to be missing later, could perhaps have been injured during his own flight, 3. the respondent knew of the location of any colleagues within certain parts of the plant deemed by him to have experienced damage at the hands of the explosion" [England] (Westgate, 1975:13).

In short, the theme of continuity is the logical starting point for trying to understand organizational responses immediately after disaster impact. People do not abandon their social histories when confronted with adversity—and organizational systems reflect it.

> IIID1.1 "Many pre-impact or Time One factors carried over into the trans- and post-impact periods or Time Two, supporting the general proposition derived from disaster studies that there is considerable continuity in social behavior in the two time periods" [Italy] (Quarantelli, 1979:211).

Case study materials validate this general conclusion; what is lacking are specifications of degree. That is, for example, under what conditions do fire department officials seek to extend their domain?

> IIID1.1a "Fire department officials generally do not seek to extend the domain of their organization following disasters" (as summarized in Mileti, Drabek, and Haas, 1975:83, based on Warheit, 1970).

> IIID1.1b "They [authority problems] do not stem, as is sometimes thought, because authority lines break down within organizations. Studies show that this simply does not occur if, in pre-impact times, there was exercise of authority. . . . if authority is very weak in the first place, as is true of much county government authority in normal times in the U.S., it can completely disappear at the time of an emergency. . . . instead of power being grabbed by the military or anyone else, there is a tendency for authority not to be fully exercised. Instead, authority problems in disasters tend to be of two kinds. They can stem from old jurisdictional issues, or from new tasks" (Quarantelli, 1982b:10).

Case studies suggest that planning, and the degree of event predictability, are related to the amount of response continuity. But the *hypothesis* has not been tested precisely.

> IIID1.2(H) The greater the degree of planning and predictability of the event consequences, the less the degree of emergence and improvisation in response.

Bardo's (1978) study of a public works unit (identified as being in a middle-size city in the central section of the East Coast of the United States) after Hurricane Agnes, June, 1972, illustrates this type of case study.

> "Following Brouillette and Quarantelli's lead, we also focused on a public works department. . . . Following the 1969 floods caused by Hurricane Camille, the city had greatly modified its disaster plans. [p. 92] . . . During this portion of the disaster response, the only part of the formal structure that failed to function as specified in the disaster plan was the communication channel between the E.O.C. and the Chief of the Bureau of Operations. Because of a mechanical failure, the two-way radio used to link them broke down. Since no backup communications system was provided, the Chief relayed communiques through a nearby policeman's patrol car radio. [p. 99] . . . no long term organizational change occurred. All responses to the disaster episode were short-run adaptations to a temporarily modified environment; no structure/function patterns initiated at T2/T3, T4a, or T4b were ongoing at T5 [p. 101]" (Bardo, 1978:92, 99, 101).

With increasing frequency, transportation accidents involving toxic substances have challenged first responders. Here again, our research base indicates the theme of continuity—despite its costs. As greater awareness of this problem emerges over the next decade, I suspect that a wide variety of planning efforts will alter the range of responses captured by researchers during the 1970s. But such is the nature of social phenomema—it does change over time.

> IIID1.2a "As the nature of the chemical threat becomes clearer, however, there is a tendency to try to adjust organizationally to the newly recognized situation. Prior experience with emergencies is likely to positively influence the adjustment process. Yet, there is usually an ad hoc quality to much that is done, or at best very gross moves towards attempting to implement disaster plans" (Gray, 1981:360).

Attacking an important aspect of this problem, Dombrowsky (1983) formulated the idea of "solidarity in disasters." Based on qualitative interviews (2–3 hours) with 40 professionals in German disaster relief organizations that had responded to two severe winter blizzards, he sought to recast Durkheim's fundamental notion of "organic solidarity."

> "Durkheim's 'organic solidarity' is characterized by the socially prescribed existence of seemingly useful functions and function holders,

which become accomplices through their mutual application. But nothing will remain of these silent accomplices when disasters destroy their objective functioning and cut off their application's background. That's the problem with Durkheim's conception: How must a 'solidarity' be conceived which doesn't collapse in the disaster, but on the contrary, which is stimulated or even induced by disaster?'' (Dombrowsky, 1983:193).

IIID2. Emergent Organizations

Often, fairly complex social systems are created by persons—with varying degrees of awareness and conscious design—as they struggle with the demands of the disaster. The literature is filled with descriptions like the following.

"Although rescue operations began with creditable, and even remarkable speed, they had to be set up largely on an *ad hoc* basis because of the lack of previously constituted organisations to deal with such emergencies. Helicopters lacked the means of direct contact with police controllers on the ground and messages had to be relayed through RAF stations" [Scotland] (Symons and Perry, 1979:11).

IIID2.1 "At the organizational level, the period of post-disaster utopia is often characterized by the emergence of ephemeral social organizations which incorporate utopian values. Sometimes these appear as completely new organizations; sometimes they grow within the framework of pre-existing organizational structures" (Taylor, 1972:112). (See also Quarantelli, 1979:211.)

Such emergent systems were recognized in the earliest disaster studies. But Quarantelli (1966) and Dynes (1970a) recognized several important variations. By cross-tabulating two dimensions—tasks and structure—a fourfold typology is produced. Tasks are either regular or nonregular; structure is old or new. Thus, four types of organized behavioral responses are derived: (1) established (regular, old); (2) expanding (regular, new); (3) extending (nonregular, old); and (4) emergent (nonregular, new). (See Dynes, 1970a.) This typology—one that many have found useful—permitted Stallings (1978) to derive a series of highly insightful hypotheses that case study materials had implied.

IIID2.2 "The more severe the disaster, the more different types of organizations involved" (Stallings, 1978:91). (See also Gillespie, Perry, and Mileti, 1974, for a series of hypotheses linking stressful events and emergent systems.)

IIID2.2a(H) "Established organizations seldom experience stress since they generally avoid undertaking non-traditional tasks" (Stallings, 1978:91).

IIID2.2b(H) "Expanding organizations undergo greatest stress because their structures and functions change simultaneously, their boundaries are vague and permeable, and their emergency role is frequently ill-defined" (Stallings, 1978:91).

IIID2.2c(H) "Extending organizations have greater difficulty mobilizing than do either established or expanding organizations, but since they are not as central to the disaster response effort their difficulties have little impact on the overall response" (Stallings, 1978:91).

IIID2.2d(H) "Emergent groups tend to appear where people are isolated from emergency organizations and where there is a lack of information, control, and coordination. [p. 91] . . . Operations groups tend to emerge where the lines of communication among organizations intersect. . . . Coordinating groups emerge as a result of a perceived need for overall coordination and where information is problematic [p. 92]" (Stallings, 1978:91, 92).

Despite their importance, we still lack much insight into the internal dynamics of these emergent organizations. To date, Forrest's work is the most helpful I have encountered. Among the propositions he has formulated are the following. Note his emphasis on continuity.

IIID2.3(H) "As the size of an emergent group increases, there is a corresponding structural expansion" (Forrest, 1978:112).

IIID2.3a(H) "Prior interaction patterns identify and recruit specific actors for emergent group participation" (Forrest, 1978:115).

IIID2.3b(H) "Previous structural and procedural patterns are utilized to establish a set of functional interdependencies in emergent groups" (Forrest, 1978:115).

Many disaster victims are surprised at times by the quick responses exhibited by some religious organizations. Often these organizations are "expanding"—in the sense indicated by the Dynes–Quarantelli typology. That is, regular tasks—helping members in need—are accomplished by new structures. Other times, they may reflect the properties of "extending" organizations, i.e., nonregular tasks performed by preexistent structures. Although few have penetrated this issue, Smith's (1978) analysis of 86 congregations that responded following the Xenia, Ohio, tornado (1974) is especially insightful.

IIID2.4 Congregations most involved in disaster responses will reflect greater disaster demands, normative/structural characteristics most adaptive to disaster functioning, higher pre-disaster rates of participation, and larger amounts of disaster-relevant resources. (Based on Smith, 1978:135-137.)

IIID2.4a " . . . the distance of the church building from the impact area is significantly related to both emergency and long-term disaster response" (Smith, 1978:136).

IIID2.4b "Emergency response is significantly associated with the percentage of households with major damage" (Smith, 1978:137).

IIID2.4c "Both emergency and long-term disaster responses tend to be associated with the normative characteristics of a more liberal theology . . . , a more positive community involvement . . . , higher levels of benevolence giving . . . , a more social (vs. spiritual) role . . . , and a more active disaster role definition" (Smith, 1978:137).

IIID3. Stress Effects

What effects on organizational structures and personnel can be anticipated immediately after disaster strikes? Researchers have provided many leads which have been reconfirmed in several settings. The broad outlines are now clear—except at the participant level. There, little is known. Based on contacts I have had with a few rescuers after some especially horrifying events involving body recovery, e.g., the 1978 San Diego aircraft crash, I am convinced that this topic should be studied intensively.

IIID3.1 " . . . organizational decision making in crises has several distinguishing characteristics. The rate of decision making increases, as does the number of decisions made, particularly at lower levels of the organization. There seems to be less consultation among organizational members, and such individual autonomy means that organizational personnel and resources are committed quickly, often outside the organization's previous domain of competence. Organizations usually lose autonomy when coming under the control of new 'coordination' arrangements; within organizations, sectors with high crisis relevance gain decision making autonomy" (Dynes and Quarantelli, 1977:24). (See also Quarantelli, 1970a:389; Drabek and Haas, 1969; Haas and Drabek, 1973:250–256; Yamamoto, 1981b:66.)

IIID3.2 "The mode of adaptation to disaster by an organization will be influenced by: (1) pre-existent bureaucratic structure, (2) the emergency capability, and (3) the perceived effectiveness and efficiency of the emergency response (Brouillette and Quarantelli, 1971)" (as summarized in Mileti, Drabek, and Haas, 1975:79).

Waxman's (1972) study of fire department responses during civil disturbances brings us to the more precise analytical level that is required. Thus, once a series of studies like this have been completed on samples of organizations with different goals, e.g., police, public works, and the like, we can begin to cut across other analytic variables that most organizational theorists would suggest are more important—qualities like technology, size, or environmental stability. Of course, whether or not these pattern shifts have applicability to natural disaster responses remains problematic too, since Waxman's data were limited to civil disturbance incidents.

IIID3.3(H) "These patterns show in clear relief how the fire department, a complex bureaucratic structure made up of numerous interrelated sections or components, adapted to the conditions imposed upon it by the civil disturbance. [p. 59] . . . [These adaptations included:] [1.] retain their pre-emergency structure and their pre-emergency functions. [None of the sections studied did this although more peripheral sections like finance and budget may have.] . . . [2.] emergence of a new structure and the continuance of the regular functions. Fire suppression ideally fits this case. The regular task of extinguishing the numerous fires continued to be the main function of the fire suppression section but its structure underwent changes. [p. 57] . . . [3.] change in the functions and the continuance of the regular structure. The communication section underwent this change. . . . [4.] change in both the structure and the functions of a section. This applies generally to the fire prevention section. . . . Structurally, it lost its form and disappeared as a distinct section [p. 59]" (Waxman, 1972:57, 59).

IIID3.4(H) "All other things being equal, following impact there will be a heightened sense of 'morale' and organizational solidarity" (as summarized in Mileti, Drabek, and Haas, 1975:84, based on Demerath and Wallace, 1957; Dynes, 1970a).

Despite such hypothesized increases in organizational solidarity, some types of events may extract heavier tolls from organizational personnel than has been recognized. Careful analyses of short-term stress effects on rescuers, for example, have not been completed although some observations have been offered.

IIID3.5(H) "The principal psychiatric symptom mentioned in the record of the Big Thompson flood of 1976 was burn-out among a few pivotal law officers. [p. 326] . . . the burn-out syndrome, a state of exhaustion, irritability, and fatigue which may creep up on an individual unrecognized and undetected, and markedly decrease his effectiveness and capability. . . . Symptoms include confusion; slowness of thought; inability to make decisions, to think of alternatives or to assign priorities; negative feelings about self and others; cynical dehumanizing attitudes; depression, irritability, overexcitability, extreme mood swings; physical and sleep disturbance [p. 324]" (Hartmann and Allison, 1981:324, 326).

IIID4. Correlates of Effectiveness

Organizational effectiveness is viewed by many sociologists as being a problematic concept (see Drabek *et al.*, 1981:249). Yet, managers of emergency organizations—not unlike those directing units with other goals—remain concerned with improving performance. And most related to such improvements is an explicit recognition that the emergency period of a disaster response alters the level of interdependence among participating organizations. As emphasized repeatedly in Chapter 2, this insight is a key ingredient to effective disaster planning. Interorganizational arrangements that work during routine emergencies do not fit the requirements of large-scale disaster. Thus, from the vantage point of each single

organization, its own effectiveness is determined in part by the emergen
multiorganizational system.

> IIID4.1 ". . . a disaster event reduces the autonomy of each organization
> since it no longer has the same control over its environment" (Dynes
> and Warheit, 1969:12). (See also Quarantelli and Dynes, 1967; Dynes,
> 1970a:170; Ponting, 1974:12; Mileti, Drabek, and Haas, 1975:81.)

> IIID4.1a "The simultaneous shifting of the boundaries of many secondary
> organizations means that none is clear about what to expect from others,
> or what others expect of it" (Thompson and Hawkes, 1962:279).

> IIID4.1b "Many organizations will confront surpluses of volunteers who,
> while highly motivated to help, cannot be easily integrated into the or-
> ganizational task structure (Dacy and Kunreuther, 1969:94; Dynes,
> 1970a:179)" (as summarized in Mileti, Drabek, and Haas, 1975:85).

> IIID4.1c(H) ". . . chemical company personnel often fail to promptly
> notify local authorities about fixed installation accidents even when the
> development of a threat outside the plant grounds appears imminent"
> (Gray, 1981:361).

Furthermore, qualities of the event and the degree to which the organizational mission is disaster-related may affect effectiveness, although
these notions have not been tested carefully. Useful hypotheses have been
proposed by Kreps and Adams.

> IIID4.2(H) "The greater the continuity between these roles [disaster roles
> and normal responsibilities], the less problematic is disaster mobilization
> likely to be" (Adams, 1970a:166).

> IIID4.2a(H) "The greater the relevance of the pre-disaster charter of an
> established organization, the more routine the organized disaster response
> and the more adaptive the organization in making non-routine solutions
> when demands exceed capabilities. [Two other independent variables
> hypothesized are: 1.] The greater the level of disaster experience . . .
> [and 2.] The higher the ratio of cadre to voluntary personnel . . ."
> (Kreps:1978:80).

Obviously, some internal characteristics of responding organizations
may correlate with effectiveness levels. Some too may be significant for
some types of events and not others. While the following hypotheses are
insightful, they really do little more than introduce the topic.

> IIID4.3(H) Selected internal characteristics of organizations will constrain
> the speed of adaptation and improvisation, and hence response effec-
> tiveness. (Based on Mileti, Drabek, and Haas, 1975:83; see also Gillespie
> and Perry, 1976:309; Quarantelli, 1979:210.)

> IIID4.3a(H) "The more centralized the authority structure of an estab-
> lished organization, the more routine the organized disaster response but
> the less adaptive the organization in making non-routine solutions when
> demands exceed capabilities" (Kreps, 1978:80).

IIID4.3b(H) "The greater the number of boundary spanning roles and personnel of an established organization, the more non-routine the organized disaster response but the more adaptive the organization in making non-routine solutions when demands exceed capabilities. [Two other independent variables hypothesized are: 1.] The greater the complexity . . . [and 2.] The more professionalized . . ." (Kreps, 1978:80).

IIID4.3c(H) "[As] . . . Form and Nosow (1958:112) point out, the effectiveness of the rescue activity of an organization may depend upon the flexibility of its structure and its ability to adapt its procedures to the ongoing activity" (Wenger, 1972:56–57).

IIID5. Media Organization Responses

As indicated at the outset of this section, two organizational task types had numerous findings related to them—media and medical organizations. This division is not meant to imply that these findings lack relevance to other organizational systems. Given our present embryonic knowledge base along these lines, however, I believe that it will be helpful to encourage researchers to pursue *both* cross-cutting designs wherein hypotheses are tested using heterogeneous samples of organizations *and* strictly homogeneous samples for other issues for which these are more appropriate. This section and the next reflect this assumption.

IIID5.1 "There was almost universal condemnation by other organizational personnel of mass media representatives" [Italy] (Quarantelli, 1979:209). (See also Chandessais, 1966:498; Larson, 1980:119.)

This conclusion applied to a single case study. But as will be clear from what follows, it is not unique to this event. Based on a detailed review of national television coverage of the TMI accident, for example, Nimmo (1984) concluded that differences existed regarding the techniques of news gathering and reporting, especially concerning "the weaving of fables."

". . . CBS narrated a tale of responsible political and technological elites, ABC a nightmare of common folk victimized by elites, and NBC a story of resignation and demystification. [Compared to how they report other crises, the TMI coverage by all three networks consistently constructed] . . . rhetorical visions of reassurance, threat, and primal assurance" (Nimmo, 1984:115).

After an extensive review of literature for a committee of the National Academy of Sciences, Kreps articulated the tone of the existent literature.

". . . [There is] a long-standing assumption among disaster researchers that the media are deficient in disaster reporting. The media have been accused of inaccurately reporting disaster impacts, of giving undue emphasis to the sudden and dramatic, and of conveying false images about disaster behavior. [pp. 40–41] . . . There is also a more positive conventional wisdom among disaster researchers in discussions of the mass media, one that presupposes that the media can be a constructive force in mitigating the effects of disasters. [pp. 44–45] . . . Until recently, however, mass media activities and their effects in disaster warning have not been systematically studied [pp. 45–46]'' (Kreps, 1980:40–41, 44–46).

Kreps' point regarding positive functions is well taken. A recent study (Goltz, 1984) of earthquake coverage by two California newspapers (Alaska, 1964; Imperial Valley, California, 1979; Algeria, 1980; and Italy, 1980) questioned a linkage that had been inferred by some researchers. As noted previously (e.g., see Section IA4 in Chapter 2), public belief in a disaster mythology has been documented as has the role of the media as a primary information source. But Goltz's findings indicated that we had best refrain from making any generalizations that attribute the development of this mythology to routine media coverage of disaster events. Of course, Goltz (1984) stresses the limits of generalization of his own data base, limited as it was to two newspapers. But his work underscores the real limit of our research base on these issues. Rightly or wrongly, however, it appears that significant portions of the public, and even larger segments of emergency managers, are distrustful of media coverage.

IIID5.1a "These statistics indicate a considerable degree of suspicion on the part of the public. Organizational officials . . . were even more critical of the media's coverage of destruction. Sixty-two percent of them believed that the media tend to exaggerate. . . . Even 33.3 percent of the media representatives . . . agree that media reports tend to overstate the devastation" (Wenger, 1980:253).

Pursuing this matter—just a bit at least—several have offered suggestions as to the basis for these negative evaluations. Some stress excessive sensationalism, others emphasize rumor circulation or factual inaccuracies. Still others—like Scanlon (1982)—indicate the distortive quality of disaster-related content, i.e., excessive emphasis on the impact period and a propensity to ignore stories of hazard mitigation.

IIID5.1b "A qualitative survey of 42 newspapers from around the country showed that the vast majority covered the accident in much the same way as the major suppliers of news, such as the wire services, the broadcast networks, *The New York Times,* and *The Washington Post.* A few newspapers, however, did present a more frightening and misleading impression of the accident. This impression was created through headlines and graphics, and in the selection of material to print" (President's Commission on the Accident at Three Mile Island, 1979:58).

IIID5.1c ". . . the Terrace flood study suggests: . . . [1.] in a disaster the media will concentrate on the impact period and ignore stories relating to possible hazard mitigation . . . [2.] the media's initial stories will be inaccurate. . . . [3.] media coverage will ignore certain aspects of disasters, thus distorting the information that flows to policy makers. . . . these distortions or omissions are duplicated by the official flow of information. . . . [4.] the media . . . may serve as the central focus of data collection, as the agency that synthesizes what is going on and puts it in perspective" [Canada] (Scanlon, 1980:262). (See also Harvey and Bahr, 1980:17; Britton, 1983:187–188.)

IIID5.1d "The general impression left by media accounts was, on the whole, accurate. [p. 69] . . . We identified 23 specific and verifiable factual errors in the reports we examined. All 23 were in accounts that contained no attribution, no information about the source. The media, apparently, either produced figures out of thin air or did not consider it important to inform their audiences of the source of their data. [p. 71)] . . . On the whole, however, it tends to confirm most of what scholars have reported. The media were inaccurate, confused and contradictory. And they appear to act as Wright suggested—as open carriers of information without regard to source [p. 72)]" [6 disasters, 1973–1976] [Canada] (Scanlon, Luukko, and Morton, 1978: 69, 71, 72). (See also Scanlon and Frizzell, 1979:316–317.)

In contrast to assessments of *media outputs,* others have sought to examine the internal dynamics of media organizations and the types of specialized problems they confront during the immediate disaster aftermath. For example, after a rather unique event like the eruption of Mount St. Helens, I suspect that there was a flurry of activity by media personnel as they attempted to learn more about the earth-science aspects of volcanic eruptions. Thus, as has been documented following the accident at the Three Mile Island nuclear power plant, linkages to segments of the scientific community are ignited.

IIID5.2 "Many [reporters] had no scientific background. Because too few technical briefers were supplied by NRC and the utility, and because many reporters were unfamiliar with the technology and the limits of scientific knowledge, they had difficulty understanding fully the information that was given to them. In turn, the news media had difficulty presenting this information to the public in a form that would be understandable" (President's Commission on the Accident at Three Mile Island, 1979:58).

IIID5.2a "The reporters who were given this technical assignment fell into four categories, judging by responses to questionnaires we handed out. About a third were frankly bewildered. They relaxed when the questioning turned momentarily nontechnical, took frantic verbatim notes when the going got rough, and stopped writing altogether when it got rougher still. . . . Only a handful of reporters knew much about nuclear power before they reached T.M.I. . . . Nearly a quarter of the reporters had a single expert on tap—a source from an earlier story, a science writer back in the office, or a paid consultant on the scene. . . . The rest of the reporters made *themselves* into experts—fast" (Sandman and Paden, 1979:54). (See also Scanlon, Dixon, and McClellan, 1982:29, 30.)

Apart from examining this particular linkage, it is clear that numerous other forms of organizational adaptation may emerge. In this regard, as proposed below, the shifting structure of media organizations may reflect certain aspects of the patterned coping responses documented among units with different tasks.

IIID5.3 "These studies suggest that local media, like most organizations in the immediate disaster area, often improvise considerably in performing what they and others define as their disaster-related functions" (Kreps, 1980:62).

IIID5.3a ". . . the fire caused major changes in the organization under disaster conditions, including (1) an increased specialization of work roles, (2) a reduction in the number of formal positions, and (3) an increase in the number of persons working for the station" (as summarized in Larson, 1980, based on Adams, 1974[7]).

IIID5.3b "1) Whereas during normal operations the radio newsmen were the controllers of the major gate in the news flow, during local disasters these and other gatekeepers were replaced by an emergent norm that opened all gates.
   2) Whereas during normal operations news was what newsmen made it, during local disasters news was what the public made it.
   3) Whereas during normal operations there was little feedback between public and station, during local disasters there was massive and instantaneous public feedback" (Waxman, 1973:758).

It is important to note, although few have made the distinction, that "the media" is comprised of a highly heterogeneous category of organizations. Certainly the print media have significant differences from the electronic. And too, locally based organizations are distinctive from the national media regardless of form. Differences in disaster response among them and the nature of the interaction and exchange transactions await detailed study.

IIID5.4(H) The news-gathering efforts of the national media differ markedly from those used by local media organizations. (Based on Larson, 1980.)

IIID5.4a(H) "The news-gathering efforts of the two groups . . . are different. . . . the national media are generally less interested in details . . . than in unique aspects of a particular disaster or in human interest elements in the event" (Larson, 1980:87).

IIID5.4b(H) ". . . local media invariably report disasters . . . from the perspective of the formal social control agencies in the community, particularly the law enforcement organizations" (Larson, 1980:87).

---

[7]D. Adams, *A Description and Analysis of a Radio Station Operation during a Forest Fire.* Preliminary Paper 14. Columbus, Ohio: The Ohio State University, Disaster Research Center, April, 1974.

Following this more behavioral emphasis, an exceptional study by Singer and Green (1972) introduced a series of very precise analyses of functional shifts in the operations of a radio station. While too concrete to be linked to more generalizable organizational concepts, they point the direction for future researchers.

IIID5.5(H) During the emergency period, task processes and the environment contacts of media organizations will change to emphasize event-related priorities.

IIID5.5a ". . . after the blizzard transformed the city, there was a corresponding shift in the kinds of issues brought to the open line show. There was a psychological shift from the abstract to the concrete; there was a concomitant temporal shift, for an emergency forces individuals to be concerned with the 'here and now' and minimizes the amount of energy expended on future speculation. Localism prevails as a spatial shift occurs, from issues of international and national concern to those occurring at the community's own doorstep [e.g., transportation calls; normal = 10%, emergency period = 32%; social problems calls; normal = 18%, emergency period = 0% except for talk of storm]" (Singer and Green, 1972:9–10).

IIID5.5b "There is a change in the sex ratio of radio callers before and during the storm. During the 'Open Line' program it is the females who place the majority of the calls (58.2 per cent) but this dropped to 41.5 per cent during the emergency operation. Male representation rose from 41.8 per cent to 58.5 per cent" [Canada] (Singer and Green, 1972:42).

Scanlon and his colleagues completed impressive studies of media responses to several hostage situations. Based on detailed case comparisons, Scanlon (1981) proposed that there is a sequential process that frequently characterizes these responses. Furthermore, it appears that several of these response patterns have some degree of continuity with natural disasters. For example, Scanlon and Alldred (1982) juxtaposed their hostage case studies against what they observed following the May, 1981, Mount St. Helens eruption.

IIID5.6 Much of the media behavior at Mount St. Helens paralleled media behavior at a number of Canadian hostage incidents. A sequential model of media response is proposed: 1. The media will hear of an event; try to obtain more information; use its files to add to the story; dispatch reporters to the scene. 2. As information becomes available it will be reported and will spread from medium to medium. The media will attempt to fit the news into a framework. 3. To give the news form and structure the media will demand official news conferences at which official statements can be recorded. 4. The various media—radio, television, and print—will act differently. 5. Despite these differences the foreign press tend to support each other and often antagonize local media. 6. The media will make demands on communications, transportation, and other local resources. 7. The media will operate in cycles focusing on news highs, then searching for less dramatic material to fill in less spectacular periods. 8. In a truly major incident almost all reporters will share what they have. 9. The media—whatever techniques they use to obtain information—will not publish it if they decide it would be harmful. 10. The media will also cooperate with official requests that certain information be withheld. [U.S.A. and Canada] (Adapted from Scanlon and Alldred, 1982:14–18.)

IIID6. Medical Organization Responses

As with the media, medical organizations also come in many shapes and forms. The heterogeneity among them is recognized explicitly by organizational theorists, but as yet, disaster studies have not attained that level of precision. Thus, most conclusions refer to "hospitals" as if there were minimal variation. With this caution stated, let's examine the major types of substantive conclusions that have been published.

First are matters of organizational intelligence. Case studies repeatedly demonstrate that most hospitals lack effective monitoring systems. Thus, when disaster strikes, most do not secure quick, accurate, or comprehensive information regarding the demands produced.

> IIID6.1 "Hospitals rarely have an accurate picture of the total scope of impact, victim dispersal, or rapid alert (Quarantelli, 1970a)" (as summarized in Mileti, Drabek, and Haas, 1975:84).

And as one consequence, victims typically are distributed among hospitals in a highly uneven manner. This issue will be pursued further in the community system section—see Section IVD5; emergency medical systems.

> IIID6.1a "Lack of a communication system also results in an uneven distribution of the load among hospitals and in hospitals not knowing how many casualties to expect" (Eldar, 1981: 114).

Such uneven patient distributions are not totally reflective of inadequate inter-hospital communication systems, however. As stressed in the individual response section (Section ID), victims and those nearby do not wait for authorities. They act quickly and one result is that most victims arrive at hospitals after a disaster through unofficial means. Neighbors, friends, or others who just happen to be there gather injured persons and rush to a hospital.

> IIID6.2 ". . . the first patients were at hand before anyone at the hospital could decide whether additional staff was needed, whether blood donors should be activated . . . the entire decision-making process at the Civic Hospital was delayed for an 11-minute period. This delay meant that no action was taken during this period by the hospital to prepare to receive disaster victims" [Canada] (Scanlon and Taylor, 1975:4). (See also Gray, 1981:364.)

IIID6.2a "One quarter of those at the hospital first learned of the tornado from the victims themselves; another 24 percent first heard the news from a fellow hospital employee; and 21 percent actually saw the storm as it passed within four blocks of the hospital. In contrast, half of those not at the hospital at the time first learned from radio and television news reports while another 13 percent witnessed the storm. In short, personnel at the hospital at the time the disaster occurred knew of the emergency much sooner but had less specific information on the number of casualties than did those who were elsewhere at the time" (Stallings, 1975:50).

There are instances, of course, wherein hospital organizations have been impacted directly. Few studies have been published on these instances, however. To date, Blanshan's (1978) analysis remains one of the most insightful explorations of this issue.

IIID6.3 "The flooded hospital actually faced temporary 'organizational death'. During the activation and the evacuation influx stages, organizational adaptation and innovation were at a premium. New tasks were suddenly introduced and, in order to carry them out, the division of labor was simplified; job specialization between administration, medical, and support staffs was blurred; work hours were expanded; decision-making was decentralized; and communication patterns become more informal and less hierarchical" (Blanshan, 1978:196).

IIID6.3a "Debureaucratization was the major response to the problems of the post-impact emergency stage. The non-flooded hospital and the field hospital were responding to highly inflated demand levels for their services. Therefore, as they mobilized resources and personnel and coordinated their responses, the standard bureaucratic mode was, for the most part, ignored. However, in the recovery stage, the overriding organizational concern was one of returning to the 'old routine', and as this occurred, pre-disaster patterns were reinstated" (Blanshan, 1978:197).

Given the daily routine of hospitals, a cadre of resources can be mobilized. Of course, apart from official requests to personnel, many staff may try to see if they are needed. If telephone contact is not possible, some can be anticipated to show up. Once there, most are willing to assume new roles as might be needed. The altruistic mood is not limited to volunteers.

IIID6.4 "A steady build-up took place throughout the entire five-and-a-half hour emergency period, although the pace tapered off slightly after about two hours. But employees were still coming in as late as 9.00 and 10.00 p.m." (Stallings, 1975:51). (See also Hargreaves *et al.,* 1979:269.)

IIID6.4a "Forty-two percent (95) of the participants in the disaster response were already at the hospital when the tornado struck. Another 18 percent (40) were contacted by switch-board operators and others at the hospital and requested to report for duty, while fully 40 percent (89) of those involved reported to the hospital voluntarily after learning of the disaster" (Stallings, 1975:49).

IIID6.4b ". . . a questionnaire was mailed to the 106 students enrolled
in the associate nursing degree program at Mid-western State University
in Wichita Falls . . . [75 responded] 49.2 percent of those who responded
to the questionnaire had rushed to work in the disaster units or the hospitals" (Palmer, 1980:680).

Finally, like others who comprise the "rescue force," some hospital
personnel may become part of the troop of "hidden victims." While I
would emphasize again a picture of rational response—as with victims
directly impacted—there will be some for whom stress will take its toll.
To date, only a few studies of this matter have been completed.

IIID6.5 "Major stresses for the nurses during the disaster were found to
be excessive physical demands and concern for their own and their patients' safety. Most of the nurses (16 or 59 percent) coped with their
anxiety while on duty" (Laube, 1973:343). (See also Raphael, 1979–
80:217.)

IVD. Community System Level

The classic sociological tradition in disaster studies—illustrated by Prince's
(1920) analysis of the massive explosion that ripped through Halifax's
shipping docks (Nova Scotia; 1917), many of the NORC studies of the
1950s (e.g., Fritz and Marks, 1954), and numerous Disaster Research
Center case studies (e.g., Drabek, 1968; Yutzy, 1970; Wenger, 1978)—
reflects a community system orientation. That is, communities are viewed
as the appropriate units of analysis and the immediate, post-impact period
commonly is the temporal slice selected for scrutiny. Obviously, as this
book documents, that tradition has been augmented by a far more complex—and complete—definition of the research task.

As I examined the array of findings coded into this cell of the taxonomy,
six major topics emerged: (1) global community response patterns; (2)
correlates of effectiveness; (3) community solidarity; (4) interorganizational
relations; (5) emergency medical systems; and (6) handling of the dead.
There is considerable variation, however, in the degree to which each has
been explored.

IVD1. Global Community Response Patterns

Throughout this section, I again will refer to disasters—with few exceptions—in the aggregate. As I have stressed, we are not yet able to do
otherwise although it is clear that we must. Warheit's (1976) conclusion
underscores the differentiations that future research must strive to clarify.

IVD1.1(H) ". . . differing types of stressful agents produce contrasting
kinds of community responses. . . . these differential responses can be

attributed to the characteristics of the events, i.e., the amount of warning given, their scope and duration, and to the normative context produced by the emergency [e.g., civil disturbances intensify basic community dissensus]" (Warheit, 1976:136).

Ignoring this point for now, what can we say in general terms about overall community responses—realizing that these patterns fit the typical natural disaster and may take important, and yet undefined, convolutions in events with differing analytic properties (Drabek, 1970). Based on the responses documented above, i.e., for individual, group, and organizational systems, the answer should not be surprising. There is continuity; there is action; there is altruism.

IVD1.2 ". . . research shows that disaster victims will continue to attempt to cope with their disaster environment in the same way as they did with their pre-impact environmental conditions, and they will use whatever tangible and intangible resources are at hand" (Quarantelli, 1981d:4).

Numerous case studies document these patterns—and the false assumptions that in part may form the motivational structures that produce them. But not everything can be done at once. Building on the insights of numerous community sociologists, and earlier disaster researchers like Yutzy (1970), Wenger (1972) has provided an important synthesis that outlines typical shifts in functional priorities.

IVD1.3(H) Functional priorities shift in communities following disaster in a patterned manner reflecting the prevailing value structure.

IVD1.3a "The priority of functions is somewhat as follows. . . . The *production–distribution–consumption* function is drastically altered. Production units are shut down except for those which produce essential commodities, or are viewed as not possessing disaster relevant resources in a highly focalized disaster" (Wenger, 1972:31–32).

IVD1.3b "*Socialization* activities associated with formal structures are reduced to a minimum" (Wenger, 1972:32).

IVD1.3c "The *social control* function is altered in that certain norms and procedures become more important than they were in normal times, while others recede in importance. Traffic and parking violations are ignored unless clearly flagrant. Laws concerning domestic disputes, drunkenness, disturbing the peace, and so forth are normally not enforced" (Wenger, 1972:32).

IVD1.3d "Many of the normal, organized channels for *social participation* are terminated after a disaster event" (Wenger, 1972:32).

IVD1.3e "*Mutual support* functions assume great prominence" (Wenger, 1972:33).

Reflecting this priority shift, a desire to help, and a variety of other motives—especially curiosity—disaster scenes are points of convergence. Early NORC studies documented this response pattern; since that time it has been observed in numerous other countries.

IVD1.4 "As virtually a universal phenomenon, within minutes after impact, 'mass convergence' to the scene begins, initially from areas contiguous to the site, and of three major forms: personal, informational, and material" (Fritz and Mathewson, 1957:4). (See also Scanlon, 1979:142.)

IVD1.4a "Reflecting varied motivational patterns, five types of personal convergees can be differentiated: (1) the returnees, (2) the anxious, (3) the helpers, (4) the curious, and (5) the exploiters" (Fritz and Mathewson, 1957:29).

IVD1.4b [The Friuli disaster saw the immediate intervention of the army inasmuch as a large contingent is stationed there, undoubtedly more than 60,000 troops. Among those who "converged" on the area we find rescue volunteers, press representatives, some who are just seeking news, and the merely curious.] [Italy] (Boileau et al., 1978:147). (See also Cattarinussi and Tellia, 1978:253).

IVD1.4c ". . . the 'convergence' phenomenon identified by American researchers (Fritz and Mathewson, 1957) was experienced in full measure, with messages, people, material and money pouring into the disaster area in such abundance that its organisational resources, caught completely unprepared, came near to collapsing under the strain. The Tasmanian disaster experience fully supported this item of the developing social theory of disaster. Equally it supported the general finding that two other problems, panic and looting, which loom large in disaster mythology and often secure the heavy commitment of resources, prove in the event to be of relatively minor significance (Quarantelli, 1954; Dynes and Quarantelli, 1968)" [Australia] (Wettenhall, 1979b:433). (See also Leivesley, 1977b:214.)

The above samplings from Italy and Australia are representative of numerous other case studies wherein similar observations are made. Scanlon and his associates have sought to trace this pattern in more detail so as to provide a far more precise understanding of its dynamics.

IVD1.5 "Speed of Learning [and Convergence] . . . one out of every five persons became aware of the blast immediately. Another one of every seven was to learn within the first ten minutes. . . . Nearly two-thirds of the sample, 64%, knew about the explosion before half an hour passed" [Canada] (Scanlon and Taylor, 1975:6).

IVD1.5a "Assuming that the sample was reasonably representative this means that somewhere between 3,000 to 4,000 were at the site within the first hour. . . . What brought these people there? Of those who went, about 45% said they went from simple curiosity. Another 33% said it was simple routine. Only a small per cent—8%—said they went because their jobs took them there" [Canada] (Scanlon and Taylor, 1975:9).

IVD1.5b "There has been some suggestion in earlier studies that early media information might be guided in such a way as to prevent convergence and that reports might be delayed until it becomes clear what should be or could be helpful. Clearly, the Carleton–North Bay findings do not support this idea at all. The problems of convergence in North Bay appear to have been caused almost entirely by extremely high-speed word-of-mouth communication from direct observation of the disaster" [Canada] (Scanlon and Taylor, 1975:11).

Using the logic of the Dynes–Quarantelli organizational typology that I summarized in the previous section, another dimension of the convergence pattern can be articulated with far greater precision. Dynes and Quarantelli devised a typology of volunteers based on field observations of helping behavior in a wide variety of disaster situations. Two questions form the typology: (1) was the volunteer guided by emergent norms, or by norms operative in the pre-disaster situations? and (2) did their behavior occur mainly in the context of emergent social relationships or would it also occur in pre-disaster relationships? This classification produces four different types of volunteering: (1) organizational volunteers (established relationships, enduring norms); (2) group volunteers (established relationships, emergent norms); (3) volunteers in expanded roles (emergent relationships, enduring norms); and (4) volunteers in new roles (emergent relationships, emergent norms) (see Dynes and Quarantelli, 1980:348).

To date, however, we lack specification as to the rates and contributions of volunteers of these different types. Nor do we know how event qualities might alter this mode of participation. Thus, these topics, like those listed below regarding emergent leaders—type unspecified—await the attention of future disaster researchers.

IVD1.6 "The appearance of the emergent leader in the early stages of disaster is a frequent and significant phenomenon" (Killian, 1954:69). (See also Taylor, Zurcher, and Key, 1970; Bates et al., 1963.)

IVD1.6a "Persons who end up as emergent leaders usually have any one of the following characteristics: (1) well-defined role responsibilities, (2) previous disaster experience, (3) the possession of disaster-related skills, and (4) absence of strong ego involvements in the disaster (Fritz, 1957)" (as summarized in Mileti, Drabek, and Haas, 1975:89). (See also Instituut Voor Sociaal Onderzoek Van Het Nederlandse Volk Amsterdam, 1955; Demerath and Wallace, 1957.)

When I have entered disaster-stricken communities, one theme has been consistent and pronounced. While stated in different ways, the message comes through loud and clear. "Problems, you bet! Communications— we had no communications." Elsewhere I have argued that this issue is misunderstood; what is perceived as a "communications problem" often is a problem of control and managerial autonomy (see Drabek, 1979). Thus, a conclusion like the following from Gray is commonplace. It is as much a part of the community response as convergence behavior, unfortunately.

> IVD1.7 ". . . communication about an acute chemical hazard tends to diffuse slowly and erratically. . . . [e.g.,] when fire department personnel have correctly identified the particular chemical agent, they are usually so site-oriented that they often fail to communicate this information to other responding groups" (Gray, 1981:361).

At times these communication failures are exacerbated by equipment malfunctions, but typically that is not the case. Thus, while a matter of degree—some communities do handle the task better than others—community systems experience communication difficulties; only the specifics vary. As emphasized by Scanlon, links to external help sources are especially crucial.

> IVD1.7a [The Darwin response to Tracy demonstrated] "the crucial role of community communications in the wake of crisis. [p. 147] . . . The city leaders needed to report their problems to the outside and needed contact with the outside to establish the possibilities for future action. In Darwin on Christmas Day those were difficult tasks [p. 145]" [Australia] (Scanlon, 1979:145, 147).

One specific aspect of this very broad problem is the matter I introduced above—rumors. Typically disaster scenes are hotbeds for rumor. All the structural conditions that foster their origin and persistence appear to be there. But curiously, we know relatively little about the specifics of the dynamics of rumor transmission or arrest in disaster settings. Scanlon's work provides some useful groundwork, however. He completed a detailed tracing of a rumor regarding the death of a two-year-old girl in a windstorm and confirmed several hypotheses reported by earlier researchers.

> IVD1.8(H) Rumor transmission reflects constraint patterns of socioeconomic status, sex, and ethnicity, and a general process of leveling. (Based on Scanlon, 1977.)

> IVD1.8a "Rumors are normally passed between those of the same socioeconomic status" (Scanlon, 1977:125).

> IVD1.8b "Rumors are . . . levelled [i.e., some details eliminated], sharpened [i.e., focus on a particular detail], and assimilated [i.e., detail is added]" (Scanlon, 1977:125).

> IVD1.8c "Rumors rarely break sex lines except where persons in the same families are involved" (Scanlon, 1977:125).

> IVD1.8d "Rumors are normally not carried across language barriers" (Scanlon, 1977:125).

Pursuing this matter just a bit further, it is clear that available technologies alter community communication patterns dramatically. For example, Jefferson and Scanlon (1974) discovered that citizens' band radio was used to create an improvised multiorganizational communication system. Thus, CB radio augmented an existing network which was highly inadequate.

> " 'Without citizens' band radio we would have been really up against it.' . . . The citizens' band radio organization, React, set up a communications system throughout the entire community in two ways. First a CB base radio station was placed at the police station, and CB radio cars were placed at all critical points such as the police, the fire department outlets, the hospitals, the R.C.M.P., the Sydney Academy, the power company, etc. Second, citizens' band radio cars were sent out on a patrol basis throughout the entire community so that damage reports could be brought in and assessed. . . . in the minds of the emergency officials, the critical element in the communication system was the rapidly assembled and mobile citizens' band radio system" [Canada] (Jefferson and Scanlon, 1974:11).

I encountered a more specialized example of improvisation along these lines in the response to a tornado that demolished the northern portion of Cheyenne, Wyoming, in 1979. Here, amateur radio members—as opposed to CB'ers—provided important linkages among operations personnel that greatly increased the communications capability of the overall response network (see Drabek *et al.*, 1981/82).

The most detailed study of CB use following a disaster is the case study I and several associates completed in the Grand Forks region which was threatened with very serious flooding in the Spring of 1978 (Drabek, Brodie, Edgerton, and Munson, 1979). There we documented that alternative use patterns of CB radios reflected structural features of the three types of communities studied.

> IVD1.9(H) Improvised use patterns of radio equipment—or other technologies—will covary with structural characteristics of communities.

> IVD1.9a ". . . the pre-existing structure of emergency services reflected minimal pre-planning for the use of CB radio" (Drabek, Brodie, Edgerton, and Munson, 1979:vii).

> IVD1.9b ". . . interview data clearly revealed three distinctly different emergent patterns of CB use. . . . All seemed to reflect the pre-existing social organization of three types of communities, . . . Pattern One: Cooptation and Absorption. [p.15] . . . Pattern Two: Emergent Multiorganizational Communication Network. [p.16] . . . Pattern Three: Latent Telephone System [p. 17]" (Drabek, Edgerton, Munson, and Brodie, 1979:15–17).

> IVD1.9c ". . . perceptions of costs and benefits of CB use varied minimally across different sectors of the user community, which overwhelmingly attested to various positive contributions and minimized costs . . ." (Drabek, Brodie, Edgerton, and Munson, 1979:vii).

Certainly, this general area merits further attention from the research community. Beyond specialized radio equipment, studies should be made of cable television use. Similarly, the adoption and use of various types of computers appears to me to be a top-priority research issue. It will be interesting to see if a future volume of this type will inform us of these significant social forces.

IVD2. Correlates of Effectiveness

As with organizational systems, most managers are interested in knowing more about factors that might increase emergency response effectiveness. Curiously, the literature I reviewed rarely addressed this in a direct manner. There are many relevant insights, however, as demonstrated by the two sections that follow. Community solidarity and interorganizational relations are highly salient. Yet, only a few researchers have proposed relational statements wherein community effectiveness was the dependent variable.

> IVD2.1 "Communities with prior emergency experience were better able to handle the emergency demands imposed upon them than were those communities which lacked previous experience" (Warheit, 1968:123). (See also Cattarinussi, 1978:4; Wenger, 1978:24.)

I have referred to "disaster subcultures" several times. In our case study (Drabek *et al.,* 1981) of the response to Hurricane Frederic (1979), it became very evident that subcultural elements had intensified following an earlier visitor—Camille (1969). While some elements of disaster subcultures may actually neutralize response effectiveness, e.g., hurricane parties, most appear to have positive impacts (see Hannigan and Kueneman, 1978; Wenger, 1978).

Beyond this variable, Dynes' observations remain reasonable interpretations that ought to be refined and tested.

> IVD2.2 "Dynes (1970a) has argued that community effectiveness may be reduced because of lack of overall coordination, which is often retarded because of: (1) task interdependence, i.e., accomplishing one task requires achievement of another, and (2) pluralistic decision-making which typifies many communities. Thus, communities with prior planning and pre-existing arrangements among organizations will most likely respond more effectively" (Mileti, Drabek, and Haas, 1975:95).

Paralleling several of these themes, Warrick and his associates stated the issue in the negative.

> IVD2.3 "There were three major hindrances to community response efforts, as noted consistently by key officials. . . . [1.] *conflicting information,* which caused a great deal of confusion and uncertainty with respect to the effects of volcanic ash and what to do about them. [p. 114] . . . [2.] *communities had some difficulty in disseminating information*

because of limited communications capabilities. . . . [3.] *coordination
between state and local levels left much to be desired* [p. 115]'' (Warrick
et al., 1981:114, 115).

Obviously, this is a matter that deserves more discussion than these
few observations permit. Despite the conceptual difficulties with the concept of effectiveness, practitioners deserve much more than this from the
research community.

IVD3. Community Solidarity

As a specialized aspect of the overall community response pattern,
heightened levels of solidarity have been reported repeatedly.

> IVD3.1 "Communities struck by natural disasters will experience
> heightened levels of internal solidarity and intolerance for outsiders
> (Barton, 1969:71; Dynes, 1970a:85; Dacy and Kunreuther, 1969:100)"
> (as summarized in Mileti, Drabek, and Haas, 1975:96).

One important manifestation of this process is the reduction of social
distance, especially across class lines, albeit only temporary.

> IVD3.2 "Previous intergroup differences are lessened, cooperation and
> social solidarity are heightened in the first post-impact period; followed
> by a reversal of these trends as time goes on (Demerath and Wallace,
> 1957)" (as summarized in Mileti, Drabek, and Haas, 1975:93).

> IVD3.2a ". . . the immediate post-impact period in the Yungay area was
> characterized by considerable social solidarity and cooperation. The crisis
> had an immediate status-leveling effect on the adjacent community of
> survivors which it had created" [Peru] (Oliver-Smith, 1979a:44).

In part, these shifts reflect relationships among victims—social class
makes little difference when sharing a foxhole. But equally important are
attitudes toward victims held by those who escaped. The rise of these
sentiments was modeled by Barton (1969) in an imaginative effort. He
formulated 72 hypotheses that seemed to provide a framework explaining
this very important network of processes. Using case study materials from
the Feyzin disaster (France), Chandessais (1966:469–473) selected 36 of
Barton's propositions. While many were not relevant to the specifics of
this event, he concluded that his data were consistent with Barton's model.
For example, Barton's proposition to the effect that sympathy grows with
the emergence of victims was verified for both firemen and people residing
in neighboring towns.

In contrast to these processes are examples like the one noted by Haas,
Cochrane, and Eddy (1977) in their analysis of Cyclone Tracy: " . . .
inmates of a prison farm outside of Darwin escaped Christmas Day, spent
the next week in volunteer clean up work, and subsequently received full
pardons" [Australia] (Haas, Cochrane, and Eddy, 1977:48).

Thus, there is a complex network of forces operating. Some have to do with reactions to victims, others reflect emergent attitudes toward helpers—even escaped inmates. Shifting to a more specialized dimension of this rather global process, let's note that conflict, including that among organizations, appears to be reduced somewhat, again temporarily. Dynes (1970a) put it well.

> "It will be argued here that disasters create unity rather than disorganization. The consequence of a disaster event on a locality is in the direction of the 'creation' of community, not its disorganization, because during the emergency period a consensus of opinion on the priority of values within a community emerges; a set of norms which encourages and reinforces community members to act in an altruistic fashion develops; also, a disaster minimizes conflict which may have divided the community prior to the disaster event" (Dynes, 1970a:84).

Consistent with Dynes' interpretation, numerous case studies contain statements somewhat paralleling the following observation from Italy.

> IVD3.3 "Together with the decrease of conflict the authors register a growth in interal solidarity that gives rise to an altruistic 'mood', based on cooperation and mutual help" [Italy] (Cattarinussi, 1978:5).

> IVD3.3a "Conflict in a disaster community is minimized because: (1) the precipitating event is outside the community system, (2) a consensus on a hierarchy of values quickly emerges within the community, (3) emergency period problems require immediate and apparent actions, (4) disasters produce a 'present' orientation which minimizes previous memories of and future opportunities for conflict, (5) disasters reduce status differences, (6) disasters tend to strengthen community identification (Dynes and Quarantelli, 1971). (See also Dynes, 1970a:98.)" (As summarized in Mileti, Drabek, and Haas, 1975:96.)

Of course, it is highly likely that this pattern is not experienced uniformly. Few have pursued this question, although Stallings has proposed an interesting hypothesis.

> IVD3.3b(H) "The legitimacy of organizational domains in disaster is greatest for established organizations, less so for expanding organizations, less still for extending organizations, and least for emergent groups. [p. 96] . . . The probability of interorganizational conflict is directly related to the degree of difference in perceived domain legitimacy between organizations [p. 97]" (Stallings, 1978:96, 97).

There is another matter that the temporarily intensified community solidarity affects that has been of special interest to emergency managers—looting. Recall that in Chapter 2 I emphasized the significance of the work by Wenger and his colleagues which demonstrated that the public and many local officials believed in a mythology. One element of this mythology is an assumption of widespread looting behavior following disasters. It is clear that occasional instances of looting will occur, and to date no one has specified the conditions that encourage such actions, although a few hypotheses have been put forward. What we know is—like panic flight—the behavior is rare; and yet many officials still excessively allocate precious organizational resources to insure its absence. A sampling of the conclusions from various case histories are as follows.

> IVD3.4 "... in most disaster studies, there exists a common paradox that community officials, particularly those charged with problems of order, become concerned with the prevention of 'looting' while careful studies indicate that looting is infrequent, if not non-existent in disaster situations" (Wenger, 1972:67).

> IVD3.4a "... conforming to research findings, public order did not dissolve and there was little panic or looting" [Guatemala] (Olson and Olson, 1977:76).

> IVD3.4b "... many had heard of rumours about families who had lost their belongings. Some of the things reported as stolen had been collected by rescue workers and brought to a police station where the victims later received their belongings. Nevertheless, certain things disappeared in such a way thefts cannot be totally ruled out" [Sweden] (Edberg and Lustig, 1983:60).

> IVD3.4c "... the possibility of looting ... In Friuli only four thieves were discovered, coming from the outside, and immediately prosecuted" [Italy] (Cattarinussi, 1978:6).

> IVD3.4d "... the looting of the sea-damaged Custom's Shed at Nuku'alofa, may be viewed more as the outcome of the changing of a traditional society in an urban context than a consequence of the cyclone's effect" [Tonga] (Oliver and Reardon, 1982:64).

A synthesis offered by Quarantelli is consistent with the case materials I encountered, although it too fails to speak to the issue of variability. That is, under what conditions will looting behavior become more pervasive? We will return to this topic in the next section, since these concerns become more heightened as the emergency ends and thoughts of recovery begin.

> IVD3.5 "Many stories of looting will circulate, but actual instances will be rare and if they occur will be done by outsiders rather than the impacted population itself. . . . pro-social rather than anti-social behavior is a dominant characteristic of the emergency time period of a disaster. Crime rates will drop and exploitative behavior is only likely to be seen in relatively rare instances of profiteering after the immediate emergency period is over" (Quarantelli, 1982b:8).

In short, the matter of community solidarity has many side streets. Collectively all point to one central conclusion—there is a temporary focus on the event which precipitates a pulling together, albeit short-lived. Various forms of antisocial behavior, especially one commonly anticipated—looting—are suspended for the most part. While this overall portrait has been documented repeatedly, we lack understanding of the dynamics of its origin or of the processes that guide its demise.

IVD4. Interorganizational Relations

One feature of community life that may hold the key to improving an understanding of the shifts in community solidarity just discussed is the relationships among organizations. Several researchers have suggested that this focus will provide an approach whereby many of these issues can be pursued with greater precision without losing site of the community as the system to be studied (Warheit, 1968).

> IVD4.1 "Studies have shown that disaster-stricken communities exhibit a high degree of solidarity. Part of this cohesion stems from the sharing of externally imposed problems, and participation in collective efforts to solve them" (Mileti, 1975a:11). (See also Wenger, 1978:35.)

But we need to back up just a bit. For, as with individuals, often agencies require some structuring time. A complete definition, or even a partial one that evokes a perception of "disaster," does not happen instantly. Sometimes considerable time is required. Unfortunately, we don't have a good fix on this microprocess or how "event definition" might vary among disasters with alternative features. Britton's (1983) case study of the Tasmanian bushfires (February, 1982) has many parallels in the literature. What we lack, however, are precise hypotheses that would account for variations in these "event definition" processes.

> "It appeared to the Regional Officer that none of the organizations which were presently involved in the fire-fighting were fully aware of the extent of the fire situation: they appeared only aware of the fires and the situation as they affected their own interests or areas of jurisdiction. It also appeared that this individualistic approach to the fire threat would have continued right through the emergency period had it not been for the Special Emergency requiring some form of combined cooperation and a pooling of resources which were required by law under the State Disaster Plan and the Emergency Services Act 1976" [Tasmania] (Britton, 1983:85).

> IVD4.2(H) "There is an 'authority lapse' right after impact; frequently, the mayor or city manager, and others in power, do not assume control of the disaster activities until the initial emergency period is over (Parr, 1969a)" (as summarized in Mileti, Drabek, and Haas, 1975:90).

Quickly, however—and where planning has laid the foundation it may be very quick—organizational officials recognize that the fragmentation among agencies must be reduced. While enhancing agency autonomy, and permitting routine emergency response with a modicum of efficiency, a disaster requires restructuring. This restructuring is not necessarily smooth, met with consensus, or easy to document. But typically some type of command post does emerge, often more than one.

> IVD4.3 "In reaction to fragmentation, the community takes on a more than normal amount of interdependence, allocating resources into a synthetic organization which can employ computational decision processes" (Thompson and Hawkes, 1962:275). (See also Form and Loomis, 1956.)

> IVD4.3a ". . . a new emergent structure develops more effectively to meet the demands created by the disaster event. Among the characteristics of this structure are functional priorities, maximized values, normative altruism, increased autonomy, and a greater centralization of the decision-making processes. This structure is temporary" (Wenger, 1978:39).

> IVD4.3b "As the response becomes more protracted and as more agencies or groups become involved, primary responders usually find it necessary to activate a facility for purposes of central decision-making and information exchange. In most cases, the command post is informally organized, under-equipped in terms of communications hardware, and lacks clear leadership" (Gray, 1981:363).

Based on comparisons among ten community responses wherein mass casualities resulted from disaster, Wright reconfirmed the rarity of centralization as a quality of the first response. Focusing on the emergency medical system (EMS), he tried to carry the analysis an additional step. Thus, he asked: "What conditions might increase the likelihood of greater centralization?"

> IVD4.4 Centralization is relatively rare during the initial response to disaster. (Based on Wright, 1977.)

> IVD4.4a(H) "As the magnitude of the task increased, a centralized response was less likely" (Wright, 1977:190).

> IVD4.4b(H) "As interorganizational expertise was more available, a centralized response was more likely" (Wright, 1977:190).

> IVD4.4c(H) ". . . centralized responses tended to occur in smaller communities (with limited resources) and in which such cooperation would be necessary. The largest cities (with vast resources) tended to cooperate badly, and centralized responses were nonexistent" (Wright, 1977:194).

Yamamoto (1981a) has developed a very insightful theoretical statement that extends these insights a great deal. Using case study materials as a grounding basis for hypothesis generation, he developed a theoretical model that has parallels in earlier Japanese studies regarding the variations in interorganization coordination and the factors that might be correlated.

> IVD4.4d(H) Based on case studies of two earthquake responses (Izu-Oshima Kinkai, January, 1978, and Miyagiken Oki, June, 1978), Yamamoto proposed that more decentralized/diffused types of interorgan-

izational coordination will emerge in disaster responses within urban settings (vs. rural) because of larger: (a) amount of tasks, (b) size of interorganizational field, (c) variety of resources, and (d) average size of organizations. [Japan] (Based on Yamamoto, 1981a:9–15; see also Guard Police Psychology Research Society, 1973.)

Dissecting this topic further, Dynes (1978) identified several factors that appear to affect the speed and form of this restructuring process. These are not the same as those noted above that were based on Wright's (1977) analysis of the EMS, but there are several parallels.

IVD4.5(H) Interorganizational relationships during a disaster response are constrained by prior communication patterns, personal friendships, and the differential decision-making needs.

IVD4.5a(H) "Interorganizational contacts prior to a disaster . . . contribute to the legitimation of the organizations involved in the emergency" (Dynes, 1978:52).

IVD4.5b(H) "Because the community is normally pluralistic, it requires structural modifications for more unified decision-making. . . . [Typically, two groups emerge:] [a.] an 'operations group' [i.e.,] A small group of individuals forms an operations center near communications lines and gradually becomes the source for information and requests for aid. . . . [and b.] one that can deal with overall problems of coordination and resource allocation, typically emerges in widespread disasters" (Dynes, 1978:61).

One critical task of this emergency period is the searching for and rescuing of victims—SAR. As I stressed above, a critical aspect of this activity is the interface between formal organizations and individuals and families who are acting rather autonomously. Mileti put the matter well.

". . . studies have consistently shown that initial search and rescue work is carried out by persons who are in the impact area and that formal rescue organizations become involved at a later point . . . The family functions as a basic rescue group. . . . Socially isolated victims—such as the aged living alone or persons in far-flung areas—are often overlooked by those persons who are concerned with helping relatives and friends, and constitute a problem in providing emergency aid during the initial emergency period" (Mileti, 1975a:9).

Early case studies often concluded that organizational responses—in contrast to those of families and neighbors—were not well organized. Some, like Kennedy (1970:359), proposed that there were understandable reasons for this. For example, following large disasters this task is overwhelming, especially if large numbers of casualities are involved. Also, SAR actions occur immediately, often as organizational mobilization is in process. Typically no single organization has been assigned the SAR task prior to a disaster.

In contrast, Syren (1981) concluded that at least one Swedish example provided a point of contrast.

"International literature usually claims that the supervision and coordination of rescue activity is often a cause for serious problems at a disaster. Experience from the Tuve landslide does not give the same picture.
During the acute period there were no rescue activities that counteracted
each other. This is explained by the fact that the authority carried by the
head of the fire-brigade was effectively used" [Sweden] (Syren, 1981:14).

In an attempt to fill this void somewhat, I directed field studies of SAR
responses in six major disasters including the Wichita Falls, Texas, tornado
(April 10, 1979); Hurricane Frederic, which hit the Gulf Coast in August,
1979; and the May, 1980, eruption of Mount St. Helens. To date, these
case histories are the most thorough analyses of multiorganizational responses to search and rescue demands following disaster. Among the major
conclusions were the following.

IVD4.6 "We identified the key operational problems in each of the SAR
responses. . . . four themes appeared time after time [interagency communications, ambiguity of authority, poor utilization of special resources,
and unplanned media relationships]" (Drabek et al., 1981:240). (See also
Drabek, 1985; Drabek, 1983a.)

Note the parallels in these problem areas to those noted by Neff (1977).

IVD4.6a [Based on four case studies] "three . . . interrelated problems
stand out . . . [1.] Minimal Coordination of On-site EMS Activities. . . .
[2.] Breakdown in the Existing Communications Network. . . . [3.] Lack
of Coordination Between the Mass Casualty Site and the Receiving Hospitals" (Neff, 1977:186–187).

IVD4.7 Multiorganizational coordination was positively associated with:
(1) high domain consensus, (2) a multiagency association, (3) frequent
simulation exercises, (4) absence of interpersonal cleavages, (5) team
approach to decision making. (Based on Drabek, Adams, Kilijanek, and
Tamminga, 1979:9–15).

Upon comparing the six disaster events, plus data gathered in a study
of one routine SAR mission, we identified several points of similarity and
important variations among these emergent multiorganizational networks—
systems we called EMONS. The task ahead is to address the question of
the correlates of this patterned variation.

IVD4.8 Similarities among EMONS: multiorganizational, diversity, improvisation, emergence and loose coupling. (Based on Drabek et al.,
1981:237–238).

IVD4.9 "The seven EMONS we studied differed in five important ways
[planning, unregulated communication flows, flattened decision and control structures, EMON stability, and perceptions of performance]" (Drabek et al., 1981:238).

Obviously, these specifications are just a start. But there are other clues
scattered throughout the literature that subsequent research should seek
to integrate, test, and refine. For example, the SAR mission study I re-

ferred to above—a search for a lost photographer on Washington State's Mount Si—gave us several ideas that I believe emergency managers would do well to implement now. Here we saw a well-coordinated multiagency response. (See also Drabek, 1985.)

> IVD4.10(H) Multiagency coordination will increase to the degree that each of the following factors are operative.
>
> IVD4.10a(H) "Domain Concensus . . . There was domain consensus. Each knew the purpose of the network. And more importantly, each entered it with at least a general understanding of what others expected from their unit" (Drabek, Adams, Kilijanek, and Tamminga, 1979:12).
>
> IVD4.10b(H) "King County Search and Rescue Association (KSARA) . . . most units reported at least monthly interactions with many of the others. Much of this was stimulated by KSARA meetings" (Drabek, Adams, Kilijanek, and Tamminga, 1979:13).
>
> IVD4.10c(H) "SAR Simulation Exercises. All of the units comprising the Mount Si EMON had participated in SAR simulation exercises" (Drabek, Adams, Kilijanek, and Tamminga, 1979:13).
>
> IVD4.10d(H) "Decision-making Style . . . a team approach" (Drabek, Adams, Kilijanek, and Tamminga, 1979:13).

These factors complement those proposed years ago by Fritz and Williams (1957), and reconfirm several they proposed.

> IVD4.11 "Factors which mitigate against coordination are: (1) the physical disorganization of the stricken area; (2) darkness if rescue is done at night; (3) convergence effects; (4) great sense to act urgently; (5) lack of pre-existing plans; (6) ambiguity about what agency has authority; (7) absence of an agreed upon division of labor; (8) rumors; (9) lack of systems reconnaissance; or (10) lack of central coordination mechanism (Fritz and Williams, 1957)" (as summarized in Mileti, Drabek, and Haas, 1975:90).

Similarly, the last factor they list—that is, lack of a central coordination mechanism—reappears time and time again, in our case, studies and those done by others (e.g., for a Japanese case, see Yamamoto, 1981b). When an emergency operations center has not been established ahead of time, usually one will appear in some form and with varying degrees of operational effectiveness. This much we do know without a doubt. The altered degree of cross-agency interdependency simply requires it.

Given expanded planning efforts, wherein the vital functions of an EOC are stressed, I would hope that few researchers in the U.S.A., Japan, Canada, or other industrialized nations would be able to find cases for study like the emergent EOC described by Kueneman (1973).

> [An emergent EOC, established and directed by state (Provincial) level agency:] [1.] ". . . the EOC was not a preplanned phenomenon. As a

result, most people did not know each other nor did they know who was
in charge of each task area, . . . [2.] The decentralized structure of the
EOC was also problematic especially in the early stages. . . . [3.] Once
the division of labour which EMO had established was learned and once
decisions for task allocations were deferred to EMO, the EOC began to
function more smoothly. . . . [4. Personal leadership ability, i.e.,] his
decisions may have been respected not so much because they came from
an EMO officer but rather because they came from him. . . . [5.] EMO
became legitimate in the EOC and in the community very early in the
emergency. The Mayor put the city departments 'under the umbrella of
EMO' and encouraged the public to listen to the EMO'' [Canada]
(Kueneman, 1973:11).

Yet, as recent Disaster Research Center studies of chemical incidents
have documented in the U.S.A., this lesson may not be learned as thoroughly as we could hope. And the consequences for coordination continue
to be reconfirmed.

IVD4.12 "While an on-site command post is often set up in chemical
incidents, it is extremely rare for an emergency operating center (EOC)
to be activated. The absence of an EOC can affect the quality and quantity
of information disseminated to the public" (Gray, 1981:363).

In contrast to the organizational focus that I have emphasized throughout
this section, Kreps has begun a new line of research that I believe will
be most productive. It complements my portrait of community disaster
responses as being organizationally based by adopting a *process* approach.
Kreps (1982, 1983, 1985) has been reanalyzing hundreds of interviews
stored within the Disaster Research Center archives and has demonstrated
the empirical utility of this approach. "The study of process during disasters requires that major attention be given to the *response itself* (rather
than some organization) as the *unit of analysis*. I identify four key properties of *any* organized response: *(1) domain, (2) tasks, (3) human and
material resources, and (4) activities"* (Kreps, 1982:15).

Of most importance to this work is to make problematic the notions of
"rationality" and organizational boundary. Rather than assume the constraint of either, Kreps' process approach encourages the analyst to allow
for variation and permit the data to demonstrate the presence or absence
of both.

IVD4.13 "The Weberian interpretation of rationality . . . suggests the
dominance of domain initiated patterns, [i.e., domain defines task, which
in turn specifies human and material resources that result in activities.]
[p. 17] . . . Sixteen of the 24 logical possibilities are documented at least
once. Even though the interviews are skewed toward the actions of disaster relevant bureaucracies, note that only 32% of the responses are
DRTA patterns, i.e., those most consistent with a Weberian interpretation
of rationality [p. 25]" (Kreps, 1982:17, 25). (See also Kreps, 1983:450–
455.) [In a later publication (Kreps, 1985:147), Kreps revised his con-

clusion and indicated that 21 of the 24 logical possibilities had been found within this data set.]

Among 18 conclusions derived from model testing, Kreps's 423 cases of organized disaster responses indicated the following factors were related to maintenance and suspension.

IVD4.13a(H) The greater the magnitude and scope of impact, the larger the size of the unit, the greater the degree of formal disaster preparedness, the greater the relevance of military resources in the social network of the enacting unit, and the more complex the social network at the origins of organization, the greater the degree of substantive rationality at the maintenance state. (Adapted from Kreps, 1985:189–190.)

IVD4.13b(H) The greater the degree of substantive rationality at the maintenance of the organization, the greater the magnitude and scope of impact, and the greater the degree of disaster experience of the impacted community, the less likely is the organization to reach the terminal state. (Adapted from Kreps, 1985:198.)

While the full implication of this line of inquiry will await review in a subsequent compilation of this type, maybe a decade from now, it is my belief that our understanding of the community level system dynamics of disaster responses will be enhanced by it.

IVD5. Emergency Medical Systems

One form of an interagency network that Disaster Research Center researchers and others have dissected recently is emergency medical systems (EMS). The boundary between SAR and EMS is not precise. Yet, here we have two overlapping constellations of multiagency systems that merit much further attention, given their strategic location in the lifesaving aspect of disaster management. Analytically speaking, it makes sense to compare EMS systems across events with different demand characteristics. To some degree that has been done as the findings below will indicate. A next step is to shift abstraction levels one more notch and compare EMS, SAR, and other multiagency networks. This will bring disaster research to more general theories of interorganizational behavior. While some efforts at that level of integration appear in the literature now, the payoffs, in both directions, will be greatest if the future reflects acceleration of this trend.

What can we conclude about EMS? Let's begin by emphasizing a point made earlier, because it is fundamental.

IVD5.1 "Even in the most extensive disasters the formal agencies contact but a relative fraction of all victims" (Quarantelli, 1960b:74). (See also Drabek, 1968; Dynes, 1970a:120; Drabek et al., 1981.)

This response reflects a value pattern that agencies ought not to bemoan.

Rather they must mold their own response capability to capitalize on it rather than be in opposition. Lives are saved because neighbors and relatives react. Taking us one step toward understanding the complexities of the needs assessment task which the EMS must accomplish rapidly are the following insights from Golec and Gurney (1977).

> IVD5.2 Factors which exacerbate problems of needs assessment: (1) uncertainty, e.g., the disaster site may be very large or there may be several disaster sites; (2) the initial assessment, facilitated by a lack of rumor control, is the one which prevails; (3) control and centralization at the site rarely occurs; (4) lack of integration of the medical component into the community response. (Adapted from Golec and Gurney, 1977:174–176.)

As a consequence of these difficulties and others, an overall assessment of EMS performance by Tierney and Taylor (1977:154–156) revealed numerous deficiencies. After adding to this data base, so as to have 21 separate field surveys, Dynes (1979) offered the following observations regarding operational problems that reduce the effectiveness of the EMS within the U.S.A.

> IVD5.3 Emergency medical systems had the following problems: (1) lack of coordination among those providing EMS in disasters prevails; (2) poor inter- and intraorganizational communication; (3) the extrication and transportation of disaster victims is generally very poorly handled and appears at times to contribute to additional medical damage; (4) meaningful triage is seldom attempted in actual disaster situations; (5) casualties are treated and admitted simply because they were persons involved in a disaster, and not because of the severity of injuries they have suffered; (6) in some instance, care being given to regular hospital patients falls below acceptable standards because of the attention given to providing EMS to disaster victims. (Adapted from Dynes, 1979:57.) (See also Golec and Gurney, 1977:172–174.)

IVD6. Handling of the Dead

Unlike the other topics pursued in this section of this chapter, relatively little is known about how the dead are handled. I chose to highlight it as a specialized topic, however, because it is a matter that has grave significance to those managers who may be called upon to deal with a mass casualty situation. Despite the fact that norms of efficiency might encourage a simple mass burial of large numbers of bodies, whose deteriorating state represents severe health hazards to the living, research demonstrates that other values often—but not always—will prevail. Mass burials followed both the large explosion (November, 1984) and massive earthquakes (September, 1985) in Mexico City, for example.

But within the U.S.A. there is a strong need, as Quarantelli has put it, to bury a person, not an object. Thus, what might appear to be an administrative expedient will clash with powerful sentiments about rotting bodies. They are not perceived as such by those who loved the self that has departed; sense of closure must be attained. "Americans not only value open-casket funerals; more basically, they require that each body be named, buried separately, and some form of 'ceremony' precede the burial. 'Mass burial,' though a highly efficient and expeditious method for handling mass casualties, runs counter to these values" (Wenger, 1972:59).

> IVD6.1 "Pre-impact factors, especially certain cultural values and norms, also were very important in how the dead were handled" [Italy] (Quarantelli, 1979:208).

Beyond this highly abstract statement, we have limited insight into the behavioral sequence that mass casualty events produce. Following the Rapid City, South Dakota, flash flood (1972) in which 237 people died, Hershiser and Quarantelli (1976:198) documented that the overall community response "was coordinated by an ad hoc group composed of a county commissioner, the county sheriff, a local national guard representative, a local judge, and a probation officer." However, "there emerged three other well-defined groups: a missing persons group headed by the probation officer, an identification group headed by the judge, and a seven-man search-and-recovery group headed by a national guard officer" (Hershiser and Quarantelli, 1976:198).

With this study as context, Blanshan and Quarantelli examined the way in which the dead were handled following the Big Thompson (near Loveland, Colorado) flash flood that left 139 dead, four years later. Three features characterized this aspect of the community response.

> IVD6.2 "The overall response is characterized by three features. When a mass disaster occurs, there is an initial quick response to doing something about the dead. Rapid efforts are made to find bodies, to collect them, and to prepare them for later handling. [p. 7] . . . The second major characteristic of the overall response is its primarily symbolic or non-instrumental nature. That is, in many disasters, objectively, it would be often easier to leave bodies where the person was killed. Instead, labored and extended efforts are almost always made to dig bodies out from underneath debris, rubble, earth or mud. . . . Finally, although the initial, rapid, overall response is unplanned, it relatively quickly assumes an organized form. A division of labor in the process of handling the dead tends to emerge. In the Loveland flash flood, for example, there were both professional and volunteer body handlers who engaged in relatively few overlapping tasks [pp. 7–8]"(Blanshan and Quarantelli, 1979:7–8).

Thus, the job progressed with a curious emergent pattern wherein professionals and volunteers formed a division of labor. More precisely, this division of labor was differentiated across eleven specific tasks.

> IVD6.3 "In sequential order the new tasks are search for the bodies, recovery of the corpses, their transportation out of the disaster stricken

area, clean-up of cadavers and initial identification. Therefore, the body handlers in a mass casualty disaster carry out eleven discernable tasks although the six ones necessary during ordinary times are not necessarily carried out in the normal sequence after major disasters'' [six normal tasks are: embalming; storage; positive I.D.; death certification; distribution; and presentation] (Blanshan and Quarantelli, 1979:12).

Through detailed analysis of how these tasks were accomplished, Blanshan (1977) offered the following insights. These are the most thorough and perceptive understandings of this facet of the community response that I encountered.

IVD6.3a "In a mass casualty situation professional body handlers are immediately called upon for assistance as public servants rather than as small business persons who have been contacted by the families of the deceased. . . . additional body handlers are sought from medical, safety, and identification organizations. These volunteers are recruited due to the relative 'goodness-of-fit' between their everyday occupations and the body handling tasks'' (Blanshan, 1977:257).

IVD6.3b "In the division of labor rather striking contrasts are seen between the professionals and the volunteers. The professional body handlers by virtue of their expertise and comfort with body handling are able to carry out very complex tasks, e.g., embalming, while the volunteer body handlers at all stages of the process deal with simplified tasks created through minute specialization and task segmentation. In the overall division of labor it is most noteworthy that the professional body handlers exercise considerable control over the body handling process as they retain the tasks to which they are accustomed and delegate the alien tasks to the volunteers'' (Blanshan, 1977:257).

VD. Society System Level

Consistent with the scarcity of conclusions that pertain to society level systems during the preparedness and pre-impact stages, my review of the emergency period responses yielded little. The Three Mile Island nuclear power plant incident in March, 1979, evoked a general assessment of the federal response, and how it interfaced with actions taken by state and local agencies. As evidenced by administrative reorganizations and major planning emphases since that time, this response was judged to be deficient along several lines.

"At all levels of government, planning for the off-site consequences of radiological emergencies at nuclear power plants has been characterized by a lack of coordination and urgency. . . . Interaction among NRC, Met Ed, and state and local emergency organizations in the development, review, and drill of emergency plans was insufficient to ensure an adequate level of preparedness for a serious radiological incident at TMI'' (President's Commission on the Accident at Three Mile Island, 1979:39).

While useful as case materials, conclusions of this type do not really provide a comparative analysis. To date, relatively few *relational* statements have appeared in the literature and most of these were provided by McLuckie (e.g., 1970). His untimely death deprived the disaster research community of an important resource. The few hypotheses available pertain either to possible intersocietal differences in response or to internal shifts in societal functioning during disaster response. Those pertaining to intersocietal comparisons will be reviewed in the next section. But in neither case do we have more than the vaguest of hints.

Two levels of issues were raised by Oliver and Reardon (1982) in their case study of the impacts of Tropical Storm Isaac on Tonga: (1) internal organizational features which left some more vulnerable than others and (2) changes in response planning. Regarding the latter point they concluded, for example, ". . . the central government found it desirable in the emergency phase after *Isaac* to re-examine the structure of the disaster organisation and to introduce a revised pattern" [Tonga] (Oliver and Reardon, 1982:84).

Numerous characteristics of a society might be hypothesized as contributing to the vulnerability of specialized segments of its citizens. In Tonga, Oliver and Reardon were impressed with the impact of migration, especially as it affected persons who were recent urbanites. Similarly, linkages among villages and urban centers may reflect differential trade or exchange patterns that denote varying dependency levels. Such economic pathways dissect one important feature that highlights the heterogeneity found within most societies. And heterogeneity among intrasocietal subsystems may predictably result in different disaster responses and impacts. The following case material from Oliver and Reardon's study illustrates the challenge ahead.

> ". . . Tonga is experiencing, albeit on a very small scale, some of the difficulties that town growth has brought to many Third World countries. In the more individualistic and less integrated social structure of the town self-sufficiency, family help, traditional customs and standards are vulnerable. An urban dweller is more dependent on others for many essential services and food supplies. . . . Recent migrants to the town or its periphery, for example those who have recently established themselves in the Sopu area, are more vulnerable in disaster. [p. 10] . . . Whilst the villages are less subject to this 'crisis of dependency' (Bayliss-Smith 1977, p. 5[8]), it is none the less commencing in villages on Tongatapu which are readily accessible to Nuku'alofa, so that these villages have different

[8]T. P. Bayliss-Smith, "Hurricane Val in North Lakeba: the View from 1975." In *The Hurricane Hazard: Natural Disaster and Small Populations,* H. Brookfield, (ed.). Island Reports No. 1. Canberra, Australia: Man and the Biosphere Programme, Project 7, The UNESCO/ UNFPA Population and Environment Project in the Eastern Islands of Fiji.

problems and needs when it comes to the organisation of both relief and
reconstruction after a disaster [p. 11]'' [Tonga] (Oliver and Reardon,
1982:10, 11).

Similarly, in their case study of the response following the massive
earthquake that struck Nicaragua in December, 1972, Kates and his colleagues were able to identify three key features of social organization that
they believed affected the nature of the response.

> "... there are three principal observations that help in understanding
> the social response in Managua. The first is that there was a highly cen-
> tralized government, thin on human and material resources and operating
> in a delicate political matrix. Second, the tradition of the extended family
> was still very strong in this urban setting. Finally, there was wide disparity
> in socioeconomic status among the population, combined with high vis-
> ibility of these differences. . . . the more centralized the power structure
> of such governments, the less dependable and effective will be the civil
> service units that do exist. When communications break down and di-
> rectives from the sole source of power are not being received as usual,
> the actions of usually subservient organizations become less predict-
> able. . . . Within the family unit, all sorts of help, including social and
> psychological support, are available because the well-being of the family
> is usually given exceedingly high priority. Individuals survive and recover
> in large measure because of this strong tendency to seek out, help, and
> protect members of one's own family first'' [Nicaragua] (Kates *et al.*,
> 1973:987).

Generally speaking, these observations are consistent with what we have
seen in the documentation of the U.S.A. responses. The family focus was
there—it just was accented in the Managua response. But there was one
important point of divergence—looting behavior. As we will see in the
next chapter, however, there has been one circumstance wherein extensive
looting behavior has been documented within the U.S.A. experience—
the so-called ghetto riots of the mid-sixties (see Section IVE4). Thus,
where extreme social class differences exist in a society, or as in the
American riot case, may be temporarily heightened in awareness, the typical normative constraints that mitigate against looting behavior may be
set aside. This temporary suspension, or short-lived redefinition of property rights, may neutralize constraints so that many strike out at those in
power (see Quarantelli and Dynes, 1970:169, 176–179).

> "When, then, in the middle of the night the walls came tumbling down
> and windows shattered and the affluent, in the form of hired guards or
> the National Guard, were not there to protect these much-desired pos-
> sessions, the result was almost inevitable. The overwhelming evidence
> suggests that people took what they could get from homes, shops, su-
> permarkets, department stores, and even warehouses. . . . The com-
> munity normative structure provided a justification, if not positive sup-
> port, for the taking of unguarded property. [p. 988] . . . Looting began

almost immediately and was apparently widespread. Commandeering of private property (for example, automobiles and trucks) took place to an unknown extent without any effort at record-keeping or promise of compensation [p. 986]" [Nicaragua] (Kates *et al.,* 1973: 986, 988).

Shifting to a more analytic mode, the following hypotheses offer limited insight regarding societal responses.

VD1.1(H) "The amount of system stress varies inversely with the predictability of the disaster agent (McLuckie, 1970)" (as summarized in Mileti, Drabek, and Haas, 1975:97).

VD1.2(H) "Prior disaster experience may affect the amount of stress experienced by the social system (McLuckie, 1970)" (as summarized in Mileti, Drabek, and Haas, 1975:97).

VD1.3(H) "The political institution becomes more dominant during disaster than in normal pre-disaster times (McLuckie, 1970)" (as summarized in Mileti, Drabek, and Haas, 1975:98).

VID. International System Level

Two categories of conclusions summarize the findings I coded for this system level: (1) societal response differences and (2) international system responses. As with the societal level just reviewed, relatively little headway has been made here. If the formulations proposed by McLuckie were eliminated, the base would be near nonexistent.

VID1. Societal Response Differences

As Durkheim's analyses of suicide rates demonstrated so well, various characteristics do differentiate clusters of societies. Following this tradition, Dynes (1975) has proposed that various structural features identify three generalized societal types; each type appears to have differing forms of vulnerability and response patterns. In summary form his analysis proposes the following.

VID1.1(H) Disaster impacts and basic response patterns covary among societal types.

VID1.1a(H) "In Type I societies, [i.e., small population base, economic base dependent on food gathering, social structure centered on kin] . . . The effects of disasters can often be very disruptive of existing social relationships. Because these disruptions are often impossible to 'repair,' adaptation and change within the structure is often the only alternative" (Dynes, 1975:30). (See also Dynes, 1972:252–253.)

VID1.1b(H) "In Type II societies, [i.e., larger population base, agricultural economic base and initial industrialization] the structural problem resides in the poor articulation between the family and village structure where disaster impact is felt and the superior resources of the national, political, and governmental structure. Often the political units find it difficult to mobilize their superior resources in a fashion which facilitates coping with the disaster at the local level'' (Dynes, 1975:30). (See also Dynes, 1972:252–253).

VID1.1c(H) "In Type III societies, there is the growth of structural complexity, involving the elaboration of governmental structure, the development of voluntary associations, and the emergence of individualism. Emergent groups often appear in response to 'gaps' within the structure. There is complexity in the bases of authority for various elements. All of this provided the base for problems of coordination, particularly in the immediate post-impact period'' (Dynes, 1975:30). (See also Dynes, 1972:252–253.)

Dynes' formulation has not been without critics, however. Torry (1978a, b), in particular, has criticized his proposals by arguing that the resiliency of folk societies has not been appreciated adequately. (See also VIF2.5.) But, more precisely designed research and expanded data bases will be the tools of resolution, not academic conjecture.

Returning to McLuckie's hypotheses—many of which are consistent with Dynes' more generalized formulation—we see the challenge of the research agenda. Aside from a study by Fischer (1980) wherein he juxtaposed two emergency responses—U.S.A. vs. Norway—McLuckie's work remains the most penetrating inquiry into these exceedingly complex issues.

VID1.2(H) "The proportion of time necessary to achieve coordination varies directly with the extent of functional differentiation (McLuckie, 1970)'' (as summarized in Mileti, Drabek, and Haas, 1975:98).

VID1.2a(H) ". . . the *lack of a priori roles* for accident management by all of the actor types involved. For both Bravo and TMI even the Accident Response Actors were not prepared for immediate active involvement both on and off-site'' [U.S.A. and Norway] (Fischer, 1980:337).

VID1.2b(H) ". . . the necessity for a *centralized organizational form* as near to the scene as possible for responding to accidents. The TMI accident showed the confusion and loss of political and public credibility that can occur from a decentralized system that is at varying distances away from the actual accident. . . . the Bravo accident demonstrated that a centralized system where accident response actors and normal regulators are merged together into one body can be a workable arrangement'' [U.S.A. and Norway] (Fischer, 1980:338–339).

VID1.3(H) "Time and its associated cultural patterns affect the performance of disaster response functions (McLuckie, 1970)'' (as summarized in Mileti, Drabek, and Haas, 1975:99).

VID1.4(H) "The greater the degree of dominance of the family institution in a society, the more frequently conflicts will emerge between social

members and representatives of formal organizations'' (as summarized
in Mileti, Drabek, and Haas, 1975:98, based on McLuckie, 1970; Roth,
1970).

VID1.5(H) ''The priority given to specific technological resources varies
directly with the technological level of the society (McLuckie, 1970)''
(as summarized in Mileti, Drabek, and Haas, 1975:99).

A final point illustrates the rich potential this area has for social theory.
Elsewhere in this chapter I emphasized various forms of volunteer participation. Event qualities appear to impact the rate and type of such involvements, although we don't have hypotheses regarding specifics. Similarly, there may be great variations among nation states. Upon reviewing
translated portions of *Cities in Disaster* (Akimoto and Ohta, 1980), I encountered this point—one that illustrates nicely the need for increased
international collaboration among disaster researchers. The authors propose (pp. 117–119) that volunteer activities during post-disaster rescue
efforts are virtually absent in Japan—in contrast to the U.S.A. experience.
Yamamoto (1981b:59) also made this same observation. He suggested that
this absence of volunteer activities reflects an integration of volunteer
behavior into residential organizations in Japanese regional communities.
The degree to which event differences may affect this differential remain
unknown. But certainly their suggestion regarding this differential rate of
volunteer involvement merits careful follow-up.

VID2. International System Responses

I suspect that there are file cabinets filled with reports prepared by agencies
like UNDRO, for example, that could provide a great wealth of information
on this topic. Given the search processes I adopted, these were not included. Certainly this facet of the typology has more substance than reflected in the research journals reviewed. I suspect that the bulk of what
may be available, however, is descriptive case material, rather than carefully designed hypothesis-testing studies.

I encountered two case studies, each dealing with a different event.
Both raised several very insightful points, especially regarding the complex
coordination problem such international responses reflect. We will pursue
this topic in the next chapters since it is in the recovery phase that international responses occur most dramatically (see Sections VIE3 and
VIF1). Yet, I know of numerous instances of international search and
rescue responses, for example. These do occur with some regularity, but
to date have yet to catch the eye of the research community.

Foreign volunteers responding to the Sahel, West Africa, drought (1968–
1974) were found to have many deficiencies. Among these were:

1. ''Volunteers came from ten countries, with more than ten percent
   each from Norway, United Kingdom, Belgium, Switzerland and Can-

ada. While para-medical workers made up 35 percent of the volunteers, physicians 14 percent and nutritionists 8 percent, more than 40 percent of the volunteers were without qualification in the medico-nutritional field.''

2. ''A majority of the volunteers had no prior experience in developing countries. In fact, only 14 percent had two or more years of experience. Furthermore, only 15 volunteers had had prior exposure to Black Africa. Volunteers were as a whole rather young (81 percent between 22 and 35 years old, of whom 28 percent were less than 26 years old).''

3. ''. . . mission heads thought that more than half of the personnel should be refused for future similar activities. . . . Singled out was the immaturity of many volunteers, regardless of age, as well as temperament, excessive individualism and a 'St. Bernard' tendency'' [Sahel] (Wauty, de Ville de Goyet, and Chaze, 1977:106).

The degree to which these observations might characterize other responses remains unknown. In contrast, I discovered a different coordination problem addressed by researchers studying responses to the Andhra Pradesh cyclone.

"Inaccurate reports during a disaster can lead to deployment of scarce relief resources to low-priority sectors. Three days after the Andhra Pradesh cyclone, for instance, ABC News reported 'Cholera has broken out in three villages.'[9] Cholera deaths had occurred, it turned out, but the number of deaths was later found to be about average for normal circumstances. Yet scarce cholera vaccines were flown to Andhra Pradesh immediately and mass inoculations carried out, at the expense of more important relief measures" [India] (Committee on International Disaster Assistance, 1979: 32–33).

Again the limits of our knowledge base are highlighted. It is obvious to me that heightened interdependencies among nation states, currently being accelerated by rapid adoption of many technologies, such as satellite-based communication systems involving voice- and computer-based information exchanges, will alter the range and form of disaster responses. Reflecting varying motivations, international disaster assistance programs may be expanded. The question of major concern is whether or not the behavioral research community will be encouraged to respond. To the degree that we are not, the capability represented by our use of the scientific method will remain unused. And emergency managers will continue to flounder within administrative practices reflective of mythology at best, total ignorance at worst.

---

[9]See E. Rogers and R. Sood, ''Mass Communication in Disasters: The Andhra Pradesh Cyclone as an Example of Mass Media Coverage of a Disaster.'' Paper presented at a meeting of the Committee on International Disaster Assistance, National Academy of Sciences–National Research Council, Washington, D.C., May 1–2, 1978.

Selected Bibliography

Abe, Kitao [1976] "The Behavior of Survivors and Victims in a Japanese Nightclub Fire: A Descriptive Research Note." *Mass Emergencies* 1:119–124.

Akimoto, Ritsuo, and Hideaki Ohta [1980] *City In Disasters: Toshi to Saigai* (in Japanese). Tokyo: Gakubunsha.

Bardo, John W. [1978] "Organizational Response to Disaster: A Typology of Adaptation and Change." *Mass Emergencies* 3:87–104.

Blanshan, Sue A. [1977] "Disaster Body Handling." *Mass Emergencies* 2:249–258.

Boileau, A. M., B. Cattarinussi, G. Delli Zotti, C. Pelanda, R. Strassoldo, and B. Tellia [1978] *Friuli: La Prova del Terremoto* (in Italian). Milan, Italy: Franco Angeli.

Britton, Neil R. [1983] *The Bushfires in Tasmania, February 1982: How the Disaster Relevant Organizations Responded.* Disaster Investigation Report No. 6. Townsville, Queensland, Australia: Centre for Disaster Studies, James Cook University of North Queensland.

Cattarinussi, B., and B. Tellia [1978] "La Risposta Sociale al Disastro: il Caso del Terremoto in Friuli" (Social Response to Disaster: The Friuli Earthquake) (in Italian). *Studi di Sociologia* (April–June):236–254.

Dombrowsky, Wolf [1983] "Solidarity during Snow-Disasters." *International Journal of Mass Emergencies and Disasters* 1 (March):189–206.

Drabek, Thomas E., Harriet L. Tamminga, Thomas S. Kilijanek, and Christopher R. Adams [1981] *Managing Multiorganizational Emergency Responses: Emergent Search and Rescue Networks in Natural Disasters and Remote Area Settings.* Boulder, Colorado: Institute of Behavioral Science, The University of Colorado.

Dynes, Russell R. [1978] "Interorganizational Relations in Communities under Stress." Pp. 49–64 in *Disasters: Theory and Research,* E. L. Quarantelli (ed.). Beverly Hills, California: Sage.

Dynes, Russell R. [1975] "The Comparative Study of Disaster: A Social Organizational Approach." *Mass Emergencies* 1:21–31.

Dynes, Russell R., and E. L. Quarantelli [1976] "The Family and Community Context of Individual Reactions to Disaster." Pp. 231–245 in *Emergency and Disaster Management: A Mental Health Sourcebook,* Howard Parad, H. L. P. Resnik, and Libbie Parad (eds.). Bowie, Maryland: The Charles Press.

Forrest, Thomas R. [1978] "Group Emergence in Disasters." Pp. 105–125 in *Disasters: Theory and Research,* E. L. Quarantelli (ed.). Beverly Hills, California: Sage.

Glass, Roger I., Robert B. Craven, Dennis J. Bregman, Barbara J. Stoll, Neil Horowitz, Peter Kerndt, and Joe Winkle [1980] "Injuries From the Wichita Falls Tornado: Implications for Prevention." *Science* 207:734–738.

Gray, Jane [1981] "Characteristic Patterns of and Variations in Community Response to Acute Chemical Emergencies." *Journal of Hazardous Materials* 4:357–365.

Henderson, Scott, and Tudor Bostock [1977] "Coping Behaviour after Shipwreck." *British Journal of Psychiatry* 131 (July):15–20.

Kreps, Gary A. [1985] "Structural Sociology, Disaster, and Organization." Williamsburg, Virginia: Department of Sociology, College of William and Mary.

Larson, James F. [1980] "A Review of the State of the Art in Mass Media." Pp.

75–126 in *Disasters and the Mass Media: Proceedings of the Committee on Disasters and the Mass Media Workshop, February, 1979*, Committee on Disasters and the Mass Media. Washington, D.C.: National Academy of Sciences.

Leivesley, Sally [1977] "Toowoomba: Victims and Helpers in an Australian Hailstorm Disaster." *Disasters* 1 (No. 3):205–216.

Nakamura, Y. [1981] "Helping Behavior in a Disaster" (in Japanese). Pp. 165–194 in *Socio-Scientific Approach to Disasters*, Hirotada Hirose (ed.). Tokyo, Japan: Shinyosha.

Neff, Joan L. [1977] "Responsibility for the Delivery of Emergency Medical Services in a Mass Casualty Situation: The Problem of Overlapping Jurisdictions." *Mass Emergencies* 2:179–188.

Nelson, L. D. [1977] "Continuity in Helping Roles: A Comparison of Everyday and Emergency Role Performance." *Pacific Sociological Review* 20 (April):263–278.

Oliver, John, and G. F. Reardon [1982] *Tropical Cyclone 'Isaac': Cyclonic Impact in the Context of the Society and Economy of the Kingdom of Tonga*. Townsville, Queensland, Australia: Centre for Disaster Studies, James Cook University of North Queensland.

Perry, Joseph B., Jr., Randolph Hawkins, and David M. Neal [1983] "Giving and Receiving Aid." *International Journal of Mass Emergencies and Disasters* 1 (March):171–188.

Quarantelli, E. L. [1981] "Panic Behavior in Fire Situations: Findings and a Model from the English Language Research Literature." Pp. 405–428 in *Proceedings of the 4th Joint Panel Meeting, The U.J.N.R. Panel on Fire Research and Safety*. Tokyo: Building Research Institute.

Quarantelli, E. L. [1979] "The Vaiont Dam Overflow: A Case Study of Extra-Community Responses in Massive Disasters." *Disasters* 3 (No. 2):199–212.

Scanlon, T. Joseph with Rudy Luukko and Gerald Morton [1978] "Media Coverage of Crisis: Better Than Reported, Worse Than Necessary." *Journalism Quarterly* 55 (Spring):68–72.

Smith, Martin H. [1978] "American Religious Organizations in Disaster: A Study of Congregational Response to Disaster." *Mass Emergencies* 3:133–142.

Stallings, Robert A. [1978] "The Structural Patterns of Four Types of Organizations in Disaster." Pp. 87–103 in *Disasters: Theory and Research*, E. L. Quarantelli (ed.). Beverly Hills, California: Sage.

Syren, Sverker [1981] *Organiserad Aktivitet efter Tuveskredet* (The Tuve Landslide—Organized Activities) (in Swedish with an English summary). Disaster Studies 10. Uppsala, Sweden: Uppsala University.

Takuma, Taketoshi [1978] "Human Behavior in the Event of Earthquakes." Pp. 159–172 in *Disasters: Theory and Research*, E. L. Quarantelli (ed.). Beverly Hills, California: Sage.

Tierney, Kathleen J., and Verta A. Taylor [1977] "EMS Delivery in Mass Emergencies—Preliminary Research Findings." *Mass Emergencies* 2:151–157.

Wauty, E., C. de Ville de Goyet, and S. Chaze [1977] "Social Integration among Disaster Relief Volunteers: A Survey." *Mass Emergencies* 2:105–109.

Waxman, Jerry J. [1973] "Local Broadcast Gatekeeping during Natural Disasters." *Journalism Quarterly* 50 (Winter):751–758.

Wright, Joseph E. [1977] "The Prevalence and Effectiveness of Centralized Medical Responses to Mass Casualty Disasters." *Mass Emergencies* 2:189–194.

6
Restoration

As I have emphasized throughout, disastrous events vary in many important ways and so too do the human responses to them. Yet, it is only recently that researchers have begun to explore the implications of this variation in an explicit manner. Today we are far from specifying in a detailed and precise manner the dimensions of taxonomic criteria that might facilitate comparisons, identify commonalities, and highlight response differences.

I stress this point here again, because as we move into the recovery phase, this issue takes some important convolutions. Why? That answer is not available. But at least a few researchers recognized the issue explicitly in their data collection designs. As will be emphasized later in this chapter, many of the conflicting results that have been reported undoubtedly reflect some of these dimensions.

The point is this. If you are in a building that is on fire, your evacuation and initial behavioral responses may vary primarily by characteristics of the event and your proximity to it. These are the types of taxonomic dimensions many have proposed previously (e.g., Barton, 1969; Dynes, 1970a). And given the research focus on this phase, that is understandable. It is of minimal importance to you whether the fire resulted from an "Act of God" or a deranged individual. During such emergency responses your behavior may not be affected much by thoughts about causation. Your prime concern is personal safety for self and others.

When we examine the recovery process, however, this dimension is reflected by, but not limited to, a "natural" vs. "man-made" dichotomy. Indeed we are now seeing how complex such a dichotomy really is, especially when examining social perceptions. Flood victims, like those suffering in many Utah communities bordering the Colorado river during the 1983 Spring runoff, may redefine what constitutes an "Act of God." Indeed, the American experience of the past three decades seems to be one wherein God is losing ground very rapidly. Increasingly, disaster victims engage in a blame assignation process. And when a culprit has been identified, their interpretations of the event and its impacts on them and those involved in recovery may reflect processes that do not occur when they view their plight as "God's doing."

This issue has now been articulated as one requiring concentrated effort by the research community (Kreps, 1984b). It is but one aspect of the more general taxonomic problem that disaster events pose to the social theorist. Nuclear, as opposed to non-nuclear, events are another strand of the same problem. Yet, to date, as will be clear in most of this chapter, very few have tried to incorporate such distinctions into their work or conclusions. In my judgment, the question is *not,* "are floods the same type of event as a nuclear power plant accident?" While evacuation behavior may occur following each, that is only one of the hundreds of microprocesses that such events produce. Disciplined analysis, as opposed to political or ideological polemics, must reflect a recasting. The questions must be those of "to what degree?" and "under what analytic conditions?" In short, "What conditionals circumscribe the limits of generalizability for the particular proposition under examination?"

As indicated in Chapter 1, this chapter too has a fuzzy temporal split. The discussion here of "short-term recovery"—what I have labeled restoration—will be followed by analyses of "long-term" recovery or reconstruction in Chapter 7. Operationally, I used a criterion of six months to separate the studies reviewed in these two chapters, although this varied somewhat with the scope of the event. Recovery processes may evolve at a faster pace in events of more limited scope, although no one has ever tried to test this judgment systematically. Hence, while the classification of some studies left me feeling perplexed, this criterion was used as systematically as possible.

IE. Individual System Level

Two broad topics emerged when I reviewed the wide range of findings related to individual responses during the initial phases of the recovery process: (1) victim perceptions of the recovery process and (2) victim health status. It is my judgment, although relevant data are lacking, that these two dynamics may be somewhat interdependent. That is, certain aspects of victim health, especially matters of a psychological nature, may be related to their definitions of loss, type, and extent of self-help they evidenced, adequacy of helping behaviors initiated by others, and victim

appraisals of the degree of altruism that motivated those extending offers
and acts of assistance.

IE1. Victim Perceptions of the Recovery Process

Depending upon the nature and scope of the event, many case studies
have documented the gradual demise of the helping relationships that fade
quickly as emergency actions are completed. Thus, after families have
been reunited, medical treatment has been provided, and temporary shelter
made available, victims experience the next phase in the process. In part
it is a period of disengagement—a time for the kids to leave Grandma's
house; in part it is confronting the reality of more permanent reconstruction. And this reality has a quality of bureaucracy that often stands in
bold relief to the spontaneous outpouring of help experienced earlier. Thus,
victims are left with a new experience to put into the context of their
broader life history. At times fears may linger—fears of recurrence and
fears of matters like a potential suit. Unfortunately, we know relatively
little about these perceptions, even those related to how victims view
mitigation actions that might reduce the chances for recurrence.

> IE1.1 "Spontaneous helping relationships dissipate and the work of relief
> is increasingly assumed by bureaucratically organized units who reflect
> concerns, actions, and requirements that are a sharp contrast—indeed
> an insult—to the mood of the therapeutic community" (Mileti, Drabek,
> and Haas, 1975:101).

> IE1.1a(H) "What had not been reported previously, however, were the
> legal concerns of some helpers. At Lake Pomona, Wichita Falls, Chey-
> enne, and in the Texas Hill Country, a few expressed concern about their
> legal liability should victims or their families sue them. These concerns
> were expressed voluntarily; they were not responses to questions we
> asked. [p. 242] . . . when we asked managers about the legal protection
> and/or insurance coverage of their personnel, it was clear that their
> knowledge of the situation was limited [p. 243]" (Drabek *et al.,* 1981:242,
> 243).

Obviously such processes are not uniform, and here is where disasters—
and also, perhaps, their impacts—may again differ from each other. Within
the same event, however, there appear to be differentials among both
victims and helpers, although neither has been pinned down well. These
differentials have to do with the characteristics of both helpers and forms
of aid that varying types of victims seek and use differentially. As indicated
in IIE1.4 (see below), however, a recent national survey of disaster victims
indicated that these differentials may not be as pronounced as studies of
individual disasters had documented.

> IE1.2 "The researcher has concluded that 'on the whole, the people who
> tended to continue longest in the helping process, particularly on a vol-

unteer basis, were middle-aged women not in the work-force and of relatively high educational status'. These people were probably involved the longest simply because they had no other commitments which could not be postponed until after the emergency" [Australia] (Short, 1979:457).

Some evidence suggests that these processes may reflect differential perceptions of loss. But as the findings below indicate, this matter is a complex one and existing inconsistencies suggest that more refined queries will be required to sort the matter out.

IE1.3(H) ". . . [the elderly] did not appear to be more anxious about their financial state than younger flood victims. To the question 'Do you feel that you are no longer financially secure as a result of the flood?' fewer of the elderly answered in the affirmative than did the younger flood victims . . . Apparently the elderly felt confident in being able to survive in spite of their financial losses" (Huerta and Horton, 1978:543–544). (See also Cochrane, 1975:83; Friedsam, 1962.)

IE1.3a(H) ". . . older victims regarded the loss of exterior items and house related damage as being more important. In contrast, younger victims placed primary emphasis on the loss of personal belongings and interior items. One-third of the elderly victims also indicated the loss of sentimental items" (Kilijanek and Drabek, 1979:564–565).

The degree to which persons evaluate the losses of others, *relative* to their own, was proposed by Barton (1969) as a key to understanding such patterns. Yet, this lead still awaits careful study, although it has been supported.

IE1.3b(H) [One who has suffered from a disaster evidences a feeling of relatively low deprivation when he compares his own losses with those of others: . . . the villagers usually asserted that the situation was much worse in the neighboring village.] [Italy] (Boileau *et al.,* 1978:156).

Finally, seasoned practitioners of the recovery process do discuss, informally at least, a shift into "the bitch phase." Here, it seems, many victims—maybe nearing the end of their rope so to speak—have a need to lash out. And those who are near receive the brunt of their hostility—even though they may be there solely to help, even though they may be undeserving of the sharp language. While observed, however, case study reports have not really dissected the extent, differentials, or major contributors to such actions.

IE1.4 "Frustrated with their efforts to regain a sense of stability, and fed up with a 'fish bowl' existence, increasing proportions of victims begin to turn against those who are trying to help them. The non-victims, confronted with this emergent hostility, may retreat even further into bureaucratic regulations for protection. While the intensity of this type of conflict and others surely varies depending on many as yet unspecified factors, the contrast to the mood immediately after impact is significant"

(Mileti, Drabek, and Haas, 1975:107). (See also Form and Nosow, 1958:118; Bates *et al.,* 1963).

IE2. Victim Health Status

What do we know about the health impacts of disaster? Presently, the picture is a blurred one. Inconsistencies among findings preclude overall summaries of a simplistic nature. To some extent, these reflect differences in the events studied *and* the types of indicators selected for measurement. I have sorted out the key conclusions to highlight this mix and some of the factors that may account for it. Thus, I have grouped the findings so as to cluster those stressing a return to normalcy, those reporting positive changes, those indicating differential change patterns—both positive and negative fluctuations—and, finally, those emphasizing negative impacts.

Before turning to the issue of victim impacts, however, there is a related matter that should be differentiated. To what extent will victims seek out mental health assistance if its availability is announced? Based on my interviews with a small number of practitioners, I have concluded that this varies—the event itself makes a difference as do various qualities of the population impacted. I suspect that the occurrence of aftershocks following an earthquake, or the continued presence of a threat like what Mount St. Helens represents for many today, may encourage more victim solicitation. And too, some communities are far more accepting of psychological counseling in its various disguises than others. Thus, following the 1976 Big Thompson flood in Colorado—a horrifying event, but one that ended quickly with little likelihood of immediate recurrence—relatively few victims accepted the outreach efforts of mental health specialists (Drabek and Key, 1984:186–188). The impacted population was not overly accepting. Yet, the 1971 responses to the programs offered to California victims are not to be denied. This juxtaposition highlights the limits of our understanding.

> IE2.1(H) Events characterized by high recurrence potential and horrification experiences, impacting populations with higher use rates of mental health services, will elicit greater degrees of victim participation in psychological counseling if it is available and advertised.

> IE2.1a [Hurricane Agnes, 1972, Wilkes-Barre area, Pennsylvania] "Most persons who needed psychiatric treatment, including medication and follow-up therapy, would not have consulted any mental health worker during this crisis. Most of them thought they were just shocked by the flood, that they would get over it, and that they did not have any long-standing emotional problems requiring psychiatric help. . . . Depression was the major symptom seen, especially among persons who felt that they were too old to start over again" (Knaus, 1975:299).

> IE2.1b "Before dawn, on February 9, 1971, a magnitude 6.4 earthquake occurred in the San Fernando Valley of California. On the following day,

the San Fernando Valley Child Guidance Clinic, through radio and newspapers, offered mental health crises services to children frightened by the earthquake. Response to this invitation was immediate and almost overwhelming. During the first 2 weeks, the Clinic's staff counseled hundreds of children who were experiencing various degrees of anxiety. . . . For about 90 percent of the families seen in groups, a single 90-minute session provided sufficient support for families to reestablish their own ability to cope and return to their predisaster adjustment level. About 10 percent of the children seen in the groups continued to show signs of distress. These children returned to the Clinic and attended four desensitization group sessions in which they were taught how to relax under conditions resembling those that had brought on the fear'' (Howard, 1980:190).

Many conclusions that reflect an overall "return to normalcy" thesis have been published. These can be grouped into a sequence with an emergent picture of short-term and relatively minor reactions that follow a decay curve. That is, over a few weeks nearly all victims come to terms with their plight and resume lives much like those they had before. Obviously, this conclusion is not referring to the outer extremes of the impacted population—those suffering acute physical injury or those who may now be the sole survivor in a household of four or five. Rather these findings reflect typical victims within events having short-term traumatization periods.

IE2.2(H) "Disasters do not cause any appreciable instance of psychiatric illness (Gilbert, 1958)" (as summarized in Mileti, Drabek, and Haas, 1975:103). (See also Takuma, 1978:169.)

IE2.2a "It appears that many of the psychosomatic indicators of stress have been reduced to their pre-accident levels over time. Goldsteen's data indicate that feelings of demoralization increased sharply during the emergency period, but these indicators of stress were short-lived. Data from the NRC survey show a similar pattern for similarly measured indicators: overeating, loss of appetite, difficulty in sleeping, feeling trembly or shaky, trouble thinking clearly, irritability, and extreme anger. However, the more somatic symptoms, such as rash, headache, stomach trouble, diarrhea, constipation, frequent urination, cramps, and sweating spells continue to affect a small percentage of the population" (Flynn and Chalmers, 1980:65–66).

IE2.2b "Adult respondents were also asked about changes in their use of alcohol, tobacco, sleeping pills, and tranquilizers. While such changes are not direct responses to the crisis, they can be seen as efforts to deal with the anxiety associated with an uncertain situation. Generally, increases were seen in the use of all four substances, though only for the period of the crisis; use of all four substances quickly returned to baseline levels" (Bartlett et al., 1983:30).

While conveying an overall image of a return to normalcy, and emphasizing that only small segments of the population evidence persisting impacts, some populations *may* be more vulnerable than others, e.g., children, persons with previous instabilities.

IE2.2c(H) [A survey of community leaders conducted by two pediatricians following the 1975 Omaha tornado indicated:]

[1.] "The directly involved children who reacted showed transitory emotional upsets as manifested by insomnia and restless sleep, clinging to parents, more dependency, and fear of storms, wind, or dark clouds. With some children, these reactions persisted and parents sought professional advice. . . .

[2.] Those not directly in the tornado path had only minimal fear and anxiety. Severe reactions were rare. . . .

[3.] Children who had previous emotional imbalances or came from disrupted families exhibited more anxiety and needed more help and reassurance. . . .

[4.] There was no remarkable change in school performance noted by the educators, . . ." (McIntire and Sadeghi, 1977:703). (See also Perry and Perry, 1959; Blaufarb and Levine, 1972:17).

IE2.2d(H) "The pathologic reactions appear only in a small number of persons (on examining 200 students a few days after the earthquake, we found pathological reactions in only 5% of them). The above data show that seismic psychic traumata alone cannot produce reactive psychotic or neurotic states. [p. 187] . . . In the group of postseismic reactions, the evolution largely varies from one case to the other: some of the cases registered complete recovery or improvement (61.83%), while others had a prolonged evolution (stationary 23.66% and worsened 14.5%), especially those with previous psychiatric disorders [p. 188]" [302 total (166 with previous psychic disorders; 136 who were assumed to have been healthy prior to 1977 earthquake in Romania which left 1,570 dead and 11,300 injured)] [Romania] (Predescu and Nica-Udangiu, 1979:187, 188).

Other researchers have emphasized conflicting data patterns. That is, many victims were able to cope well, whereas others were not. Thus, the overall portrait of relative normalcy might mask large numbers of victims who are evidencing various symptom patterns. Research to date indicates that age and sex differences may be documented, but as yet such conclusions must be viewed as promising hypotheses at best.

IE2.3(H) "Three types of reaction to the disaster were observed . . . [1.] those storm victims who were able actively to engage in the reinstatement processs. They adapted to the damage of their homes, made temporary repairs where possible, contacted their insurance companies immediately for assessment and attempted to secure tradesmen to carry out the necessary repairs. . . . [2. Those] who were able to function but suffered at the same time from significant emotional distress. . . . The reaction was expressed in excessive hostility and anger directed towards insurance representatives, assessors, tradesmen and other people in the street who received what was defined as 'preferred treatment.' [p. 212] . . . Depression was also observed as periods of listlessness. Housewives and their husbands reported how they found themselves unable to summon the energy to continue with the reinstatement process. . . . [3. Others had] symptoms which directly interfered with daily activities, including severe depression in the form of apathy, listlessness, limited movement within the home; agitation which appeared in unconnected disoriented attempts to alleviate stress; uncontrolled tears and expressions of sorrow over the damage done to home and garden; and incessant worry about reinstatement [p. 213]" [Australia] (Leivesley, 1977b:212, 213).

IE2.3a(H) "Scores on the Anxiety subscale showed a significant sex difference after the disaster: scores for girls decreased and scores for boys increased (table 2). This effect did not occur in the comparison period" (Burke *et al.*, 1982:1012).

IE2.3b(H) " . . . the elderly flood victims did not show excessive feelings of personal disorganization as a result of losing their homes and possessions. . . . the younger respondents experienced a greater emotional burden as a result of the flood than did the older people. To the questions 'Many people feel that they will never recover from the effects of the flood. Do you feel this way?', 42% of those under age 65 said 'yes' while only 29% of the older respondents felt that way . . . Resilience and fortitude is much more apparent among the elderly with the younger respondents expressing more despair" (Huerta and Horton, 1978:543). (See also Bell, 1978:539; Gerontology Program, 1976:125; Burke *et al.*, 1982:1012.)

A few researchers have detected various pattern changes that might be labeled "positive." These have not been large in number, however. It is my judgment that the reason for this is more a function of the definition of the problem than a reflection of what exists. It may well be that far more types of positive changes in victim health status would be identified if they were searched out. Both of the conclusions below are suggestive of a wide-ranging set of hypotheses that might be explored.

IE2.4(H) [Cases of suicide and homicide decrease: . . . During the 6 months following the May quakes, very few cases of suicide were reported and no homicide.] [Italy] (Boileau *et al.*, 1978:156).

IE2.5(H) ". . . the disaster reinforced their desire to pursue their nursing education. The universal comment was that suffering through this natural disaster deepened their commitment to nursing" [survey of 75 nursing students in Wichita Falls, Texas] (Palmer, 1980:682).

In contrast to this perspective are those reports which have identified a wide variety of symptom patterns that clearly indicate the negative face of disaster. Future work must be directed toward identifying the types of conditionals that may specify those events and those victim groups that are most vulnerable. As yet, we have a very mixed bag, both regarding the events studied and the quality of data obtained.

IE2.6(H) ". . . 67 survivors of cyclone Tracy who had been evacuated
to Sydney were studied by an objective test, the General Health Questionnaire, which has been found to be a reliable and valid instrument in
determining non-psychotic psychological disturbance. Fifty-eight percent
of these Darwin Evacuees scored as 'probable psychiatric cases' when
tested five to eight days after the cyclone. Psychological disturbance increased with age and was more pronounced in females" [Australia] (Parker, 1975:650). (See also Okura, 1974:24; Grant, McNamara, and Bailey,
1975:652; Leivesley, 1977a:321.)

Others have emphasized the costs of guilt. Reflecting a psychoanalytic
emphasis, they report victim feelings of guilt that seem to stem from a
variety of potential sources.

IE2.7(H) "There is also the element of what is called 'survivor guilt'.
Each individual experiences a sense of some, perhaps very small, relief
that it was not he or she that died. [pp. 303–304] . . . People with minor
injuries, or who travelled on the train and escaped uninjured, may have
periods of anxiety. Once the initial period of feeling gratitude for surviving
passes, previously mentioned feelings of 'survivor guilt' sometimes come
to the surface, or there may be a free-floating sense of anxiety or dread
[p. 305]" (Raphael, 1977:303–305). (See also Singer, 1982:246.)

IE2.7a(H) "Grief over the loss of friends and shipmates was expressed
as depression or anger. A great deal of anger was expressed toward the
ship owners and toward their dead Captain, whom they blamed for causing
the explosion through unsafe welding practices. This anger at the Captain
in turn fueled survivor guilt. . . . Only at this point did feelings of survivor
guilt really come forth. [Group meeting, shortly after being rescued.]
One man had been holding a lifeline when the ship suddenly listed and
he lost his comrade over the side forever. Several others said that, in
their haste to save themselves, they had left men to die whom they later
thought they might have been able to save. The mere sharing of this
mutual experience seemed to ease the burden" (Carlton, 1980:115).

Another type of potential negative impact that merits further study is
heightened tensions among family members. Faced with a demolished
home, some may respond by turning their rage inward, perhaps others
lash out at loved ones. Undoubtedly the modes of coping are varied and
multiple. Thus, rather than broad and encompassing conclusions—for example, disasters have negative mental health consequences; or they do
not—researchers of the future must define the problem with far greater
precision.

IE2.8(H) "One-fourth of the victims felt that the tornado had created
some interpersonal strain among family members. In contrast, almost
three-fourths reported an increase in subjective distress that usually was
associated with tension, nervousness and anxiety, and minor somatic
complaints. Nevertheless, the vast majority of the victims who reported
some psychological distress in themselves or their families expressed the

belief that these emotional reactions were natural and would pass in time, especially as financial problems were resolved and as they experienced less destructive storms. Clearly, the victims did not associate the post-tornado emotional reactions with a need for assistance from a mental health professional. Much of the emotional distress experienced by victims resembled that commonly seen in otherwise healthy individuals who experience some type of personal crisis" [n = 26; Joplin, Missouri; tornado; 1973] (Penick, Powell, and Sieck, 1976:67–68).

At the boundary of my search process—one not penetrating the medical literature very far—I uncovered a few conclusions that indicate the need for further study of potential physical health impacts.

IE2.9(H) "It appears that earthquakes have a serious effect on cardio-vascular disease. . . . According to data provided by Umidova et al. (1968)[1] during the period of heaviest underground tremors the number of cases of myocardial disease in Tashkent was 2.5 times the average number of such cases during the period 1961–1965. Mortality among patients with myocardial disease in Tashkent in 1965 was 29.3%. This rose in 1966 and mortality for this disease was 34.8%" [U.S.S.R.] (Beinin, 1981:145). (See also Dirks, 1979.)

In short, the literature to date, especially that of the past decade, has taken us far into the exploration of a series of very important issues. But at this time, the conflicts among many of the substantive findings require that we accept a situation of uncertainty. Numerous hypotheses can be proposed, but few firm conclusions are available. There appear to be important contours of differential responses and simultaneously existing impact patterns that are inconsistent in direction and content. Hopefully, the coming decade will provide an expanded base that gives greater clarity and precision.

IIE. Group System Level

While other types of group systems have been studied in the earlier phases we have examined, e.g., emergent search and rescue units, this phase has been dominated by family research. Yet, there are a variety of other issues that such a focus ignores. For example, my interviews with victims have left me with the strong suspicion that retelling "their story" to relatives, friends, and neighbors results in the emergence of a standardized version. One's own experiences may be remembered differently, in fact, as the opportunity to construct an interpretation takes place.

---

[1] Z. I. Umidova, A. A. Aripdzhanov, G. P. Korolev, Z. K. Timbekova, A. G. Mukhamedzhina, and S. M. Burleva. "Pecularities of the Course of Heart Attacks during the Tashkent Earthquake 1966–1967. *Cardiology* 2 (1968):25–27.

One observer described what might be called the "group story manu-facturing process" as follows:

> ". . . the post-threat period was one in which procedures of reality inter-pretation and reconstruction occurred in group networks of intense com-munication. These procedures were the means by which the chaos of the threat period was transformed and placed into the cognitive framework of everyday order with which people could deal. Such a transformation included the convergence of multiple individual experiences and per-ceptions toward a set of more or less coherent group perspectives, a common reality construction involving the formation of judgmental and normative statements regarding the event" (Wolf, 1975:412).

In contrast to this and a host of related issues that might not be restricted to family behavior, the literature is filled with case reports like the following wherein the vital functions of families, both nuclear and extended, are emphasized.

> "For the next months people lived in conditions of heavy overcrowding, usually with very close relatives; but often with co-villagers who were not so close kin. There was an initial period when food and money were shared freely. Perhaps suprisingly, in view of the frightened children and disorder, there seems to have been an almost holiday atmosphere for the first few days, produced by the unusual contact with other people and the freedom from normal work" [Cyprus] (Loizos, 1977:232).

Shifting to a more analytic level, four major topics have been explored: (1) differential participation in the therapeutic community; (2) relatives as help sources; (3) shelter behaviors; and (4) correlates of family recovery.

IIE1. Differential Participation in the Therapeutic Community

Some families receive more help from various sources than others. Yet, documentation of neither the extent of this variation, nor its correlates, has been completed.

> IIE1.1(H) ". . . persons who were non-white, those with lower incomes, and especially elderly victims, were less likely to be aided by external groups. And more isolated families—those with minimal linkages to kin or other social groups—were less frequently sought out as the therapeutic community began to emerge in Topeka" (Drabek and Key, 1984:109). (See also Erickson *et al.,* 1976:214.)

> IIE1.2(H) [The emergency being ended, the official organizations furnish only assistance of the "bureaucratic" type, and for the thousand diffi-culties, practical and psychological, of everyday living, the principal source of help is that of friends, fellow townsmen and religious peo-ple. . . . Among those who claim to have received some form of help, half mention friends and more than a fourth speak of the members of religious orders.] [Italy] (Boileau *et al.,* 1978:233–234).

IIE1.3(H) "Elderly victims are more likely not to have household disaster insurance in comparison to other victims. . . . Lower socioeconomic status families are less likely to have household disaster insurance than higher SES families. . . . High income victims are more likely to have adequate insurance coverage than lower income victims. Having household disaster insurance is positively associated with both economic and emotional recovery of victims" (Bolin, 1982:239). (See also Drabek and Key, 1984:115–116; Bolin and Klenow, 1982–83:291).

IIE1.4(H) "The social distribution of aid appears to be quite even, with older households and more affluent households appearing slightly less likely to receive aid than their younger and poorer counterparts" (Rossi et al., 1983b:9).

IIE2. Relatives as Help Sources

As reflected in Loizos' (1977) material that was quoted above, relatives often perform extremely critical roles in the recovery process following disaster. Limited documentation has been reported regarding the extent, types, and variability.

IIE2.1 ". . . the time following a disaster is characterized by an outpouring of help to victims. Most (77%) families indicated that they received assistance from at least one of the help sources listed. Over half (58%) reported that they were aided by two or more external groups. . . . Relatives were the most frequent source of help reported; over half (54%) of all victim families received help from kin" (Erickson et al. 1976:205). (See also Leivesley, 1977b:209.)

IIE2.2 "The more severe the impact of a disaster on a family, the less likely will that family rely solely on extended kin for recovery aid" (Bolin, 1976:275). (See also Bolin and Bolton, 1983.)

IIE2.3(H) "The later a victim family is in the life cycle, the less likely will it utilize kin-based aid for recovery" (Bolin, 1976:275).

IIE2.4(H) ". . . nearly all help was offered, not requested. . . . the impressionist evidence of 'the therapeutic community' that has been reported by many (Fritz and Mathewson, 1957; Taylor, Zurcher and Key, 1970; Barton, 1969) is supported by these data" (Erickson et al., 1976:205).

IIE2.5(H) "Certain types of help were supplied by only one or a few sources. For example, most shelter was provided by relatives. Other kinds of help were provided by a variety of sources, e.g., food and clothing" (Erickson et al., 1976:214).

Thus, relatives, as opposed to others, are a frequent source of temporary housing. Of course, this may vary by culture and nation state. But we lack the comparative data base required to specify the extent of variation.

The highest rate I encountered was from Central America. It contrasted sharply to data from Japan, for example.

> IIE2.5a(H) "The extended family system coped with over 95% of all refugees" [Nicaragua] (Davis, 1975:46).

> IIE2.5b(H) "Where they evacuated [during recovery period]
> a) their parent's house or relative's house (30.6%)
> b) another house on their own land (25.6%)
> c) apartment or rented house (24.4%)
> d) temporary houses for evacuees built by the city government (5.8%)
> [Japan] (Yasuda and Sato, 1979)" (as summarized in Yamamoto and Quarantelli, 1982:A-206).

We know little about the family dynamics and stresses produced by such short-term adaptations. Unfortunately, the types of family adjustment patterns that researchers of the 1953 Holland Flood (e.g., Instituut Voor Sociaal Onderzoek Van Het Nederlandse Volk Amsterdam, 1955) began to document have not been pursued. Nor do we really know if families seeking out homes of relatives adapt better in the long run than those who select some other option. Some very early studies suggested this might be the case along some dimensions at least.

> IIE2.5c(H) "Social adaptation of children and mothers to the place they evacuated to was better if they went to relatives than any other place (after bombing) (Bernert and Ikle, 1952)" (as summarized in Mileti, Drabek, and Haas, 1975: 108).

IIE3. Shelter Behaviors

How might a short-term public shelter experience impact a family? Curiously—and maybe because so many evacuees do take refuge with relatives or friends—we know little about this beyond observations offered prior to 1973.

> IIE3.1(H) "Females' roles are affected adversely more than male roles by evacuation to a temporary site (Stoddard, 1961)" (as summarized in Mileti, Drabek, and Haas, 1975:108).

> IIE3.2(H) "Groups of families tend to form spontaneously in shelters, in addition to groups formed on the basis of age, place of residence, and occupation (Moore et al., 1963)" (as summarized in Mileti, Drabek, and Haas, 1975:108).

IIE4. Correlates of Family Recovery

Using data from families impacted in 1972 by either the deadly Rapid City flood or the massive earthquake in Managua, Nicaragua, Bolin pieced together a series of propositions that give us some penetrating insights into the recovery process and why some families may fare better than others.

> IIE4.1 "The more severe the impact of the disaster on a family's resources and the more residential dislocation it experiences, the more likely will that family seek recovery aid from community agencies if it is available" (Bolin, 1976:275).
>
> IIE4.2 "The more a family utilizes institutional aid sources, the more likely will that family recover or reestablish housing equivalent to that lost in the disaster" (Bolin, 1976:275).
>
> IIE4.3 "The higher the socioeconomic status of a victim family, the more likely will that family reestablish housing equivalent to that lost in the disaster" (Bolin, 1976:275).
>
> IIE4.4 "The later a victim family is in the life cycle, the less likely will that family reestablish housing equivalent to that lost in the disaster" (Bolin, 1976:275).
>
> IIE4.5 "Families that rely solely on aid from extended kin groups are less likely to reestablish housing equivalent to that lost in the disaster" (Bolin, 1976:275).

In contrast to these aspects of physical recovery, Bolin also drew several conclusions about something less tangible—"an emotional sense of recovery." In general, the same independent variables—SES, age, and so forth—were proposed as being predictive of the likelihood of a "perceptual and emotional sense of recovery" (Bolin, 1976:275).

We need to know much more about parental interactions with children who have been disaster victims. Some case materials imply that parents may have strong denial processes at work that preclude acceptance of problems, i.e., "Nothing is wrong with my kid."

> "Despite the significant behavior changes found in parent ratings of the 93 specific items, on the first presentation of the overall question, not a single parent indicated that the child's behavior had worsened, and on the second presentation of the question, only one parent indicated a worsening of the child's behavior. . . . This study provides additional evidence of parents' denial of their child's problems. When parents were queried generally, they twice denied changes; when queried with a list of specific items of behavior, they reported that behavior changed significantly in several areas" [Israel] (Burke *et al.*, 1982:1012–1013).

Finally, as we will examine in detail in Chapter 9 when we review a wide-ranging set of findings pertaining to attitudes toward various types of hazard adjustments, there does seem to be a process of redefinition. Once victimized, people do evidence a tendency to increase their insurance, for example. As we'll see in the next section, this attitude shift and its behavioral manifestation—actual purchases increase—persist in the years ahead. But we know relatively little about any differentials that may exist among victim populations—do ethnic minorities shift in the same way as Whites, for example? Similarly, event qualities that may retard or spur behavioral shifts remain unclear too.

> IIE4.6(H) "The proportion of victims with household insurance will in-
> crease after a disaster, but it will not increase for non-victims in the same
> community" (Bolin, 1982:239; see also 187–189). (See also Drabek and
> Key, 1984:113–116.)

✗ IIIE. Organizational System Level

Four major themes convey the major insights learned to date about organizational systems during this first part of the recovery process: (1) the recovery environment; (2) emergent vs. routine task structures; (3) mental health impacts; and (4) media responses. These four topics take us far beyond where the literature was a decade ago, but each is little more than a door through which the research community has just begun to enter.

IIIE1. The Recovery Environment

Organizational environments are complex and influential. Indeed, the organizational studies literature of the late 1970s reflected a total redirection in analysis so as to portray the organizational environment as not only a major determinant of internal structural forms, but the very crux of survival—both birth and death. Disaster researchers have long been sensitive to the shifting community environments in which recovery personnel are nested. For example, important shifts in victim attitudes were noted above (IE1.4). Having experienced the outpouring of help that typically characterizes the post-event environment, bureaucrats are now much harder to take.

> IIIE1.1 "The more bureaucratic and impersonal that aid organizations
> are in their field operations, the more they will be negatively evaluated
> by victims" (Bolin, 1982:238). (See also Taylor, Zurcher, and Key,
> 1970:125–127.)

One study—which obviously does not settle the matter—did find that the many administrative streamlines adopted by the Red Cross during the past decade may have paid off. Also, their eligibility policies appeared to be accepted. Thus, in contrast to some earlier case studies that emphasized victim distaste for bureaucratic rigidities among some Red Cross staff (e.g, Taylor, Zurcher, and Key, 1970), more current studies indicate a shift. The best data available come from the national survey conducted by Rossi and his colleagues (1983b) (approximately 1,400 questionnaires were received from 2,600 households who indicated in a telephone survey—n = 13,000—that they were disaster victims between 1970–1980).

IIIE1.1a "The American National Red Cross apparently earns its high reputation for responsiveness to natural hazard events; in one study, it registered high levels of contact in connection with each type of event. Indeed, one in four of the households experiencing a serious flood event claimed that it was contacted by the Red Cross" (Rossi *et al.,* 1983b:160).

Furthermore, most victims receiving such aid indicated relative satisfaction with the agency. Thus, while not all agencies had the same high percentages of "satisfied customers" as the Red Cross, or the Mennonites who had even a higher proportion reporting high satisfaction, the overall pattern was clear—and encouraging. With this national profile as a context, what we need to know are the factors associated with variation in agency satisfaction levels.

IIIE1.1b ". . . clear pluralities, upward of two in three, were highly satisfied with their contacts with the national relief organizations and local agencies. About one in two registered the same high degree of satisfaction with federal agencies. In no case were there large proportions who claimed to have a low level of satisfaction with their contacts with any of the agencies" (Rossi *et al.,* 1983b:165). (See also Leitko, Rudy, and Peterson, 1980:739.)

A second issue pertaining to the recovery environment is the matter of volunteers. While victims have tired of their fishbowl existence, many volunteers have now experienced excitment and involvement. The potential for conflicts now is exacerbated as staff begin to need the volunteers less and less. Agency failures to effectively integrate volunteer groups and individuals continue to show up in case studies, but the dynamics await precise mapping.

IIIE1.2 ". . . a major community resource which some organizations will use more than others is volunteers. But such a resource may or may not be integrated into the organization effectively—even under non-disaster circumstances" (Mileti, Drabek, and Haas, 1975:110).

Pointing toward a different agenda are assessments of small-business response to disaster. As might be anticipated, the key variable proposed to matter is managerial personality.

IIIE1.3(H) ". . . the effectiveness of a small organization's response to its environment appears to depend to a large extent on the coping behaviors of its key manager. These coping behaviors appear to result more from personal characteristics of the decision makers than from objective environmental demands or from available organization resources, at least under conditions of stress" (Anderson, Hellriegel, and Slocum, 1977:271).

IIIE1.3a(H) "The use of class I (problem solving) coping behaviors by the owner-managers was strongly related to organizational effectiveness. . . . the use of class II (emotion centered) coping behaviors was inversely related to the effectiveness of the organizations. . . . Managerial personality, as evaluated through the internal–external control construct, accounted for a large percentage of the explained variance in coping behaviors. . . . levels of applicable resources were relatively unimportant contributors to the coping strategies used in recovery" (Anderson, Hellriegel, and Slocum, 1977:270).

IIIE2. Emergent vs. Routine Task Structures

During the recovery period, organizational responses vary across the dimensions proposed by Dynes and Quarantelli (see Chapter 5, Section IIID2). Thus, there are emergent organizational forms, both among and within organizations, as well as numerous adaptive responses that are made by organizations with more bureaucratic structures. Syren (1981), for example, examined organizational responses to the 1977 landslide north of Gothenburg and discovered that their typology aided a great deal in sorting out the varied response forms.

> IIIE2.1 During the disaster recovery process, selected organizations will assume new tasks and, at times, modify the ways in which previously accepted tasks are performed. (Based on Syren, 1981; see also Hewitt and Burton, 1971; McComb, 1980:78.)

> IIIE2.1a "The Land-Development Department is an example of an organization that is not expected to become involved in a disaster, but an organization that quickly and informally mobilized important resources for the people affected (organization type III)" [Sweden] (Syren, 1981:18).

For established organizations that have task domains that are disaster-relevant, we have a variety of insights regarding performance. Researchers have offered conclusions regarding structural features that aid in effectiveness, definitions that guide their involvement, and internal shifts in structure and staff orientations. These fragments do not comprise an integrated theory, but they do point to many important dimensions from which a primitive model might be deduced.

> IIIE2.2(H) Disaster recovery frequently brings new expectations regarding organizational functioning that require adaptation in structure. (Based on Leivesley, 1977b; Adams, 1977.)

> IIIE2.2a(H) "For salaried organization members there was a shift in compliance structure. That is to say, members whose participation in work is normally calculative and controlled by remuneration were suddenly faced with pressure of work which required a normative commitment, and staff in the government departments of Toowoomba worked long hours and adapted to difficult role changes to provide a service to the victims" [Australia] (Leivesley, 1977b:215).

IIIE2.2b(H) ". . . the problems local Red Cross organizations typically experience in the performance of their emergency mass care tasks . . . the assignment of area-staff personnel to the disaster operation, the addition of walk-in volunteers, and the mobilization of trained volunteers. . . . their elaboration in 'membership' during a disaster, at the top of the staff structure and at the bottom of the volunteer structure, has certain negative consequences for the capacity of the Red Cross to perform its emergency tasks" (Adams, 1977:47).

IIIE2.2c(H) "The character of natural disaster is such that new expectations sometimes emerge at variance with the established one, which put pressure on the military to assume a different role (emergent norms). When this happens, military organizations attempt to adapt to the new expectations without 'outwardly' breaking the old ones, for military authorities recognize that once the immediate emergency is over, their performance may be judged in retrospect by the prior established norms, rather than the emergent norms (Anderson, 1970b)" (as summarized in Mileti, Drabek, and Haas, 1975:111–112).

IIIE2.3(H) The greater the similarity between pre-impact operations and tasks performed during the recovery period, the fewer the number of adaptations. (Based on Mileti, Drabek, and Haas, 1975.)

IIIE2.3a(H) "Departments of public works operate well in disasters because (1) in a disaster the tasks are similar to pre-impact operations, (2) DPW personnel expect to become involved in emergency activities, (3) DPW's normally have excess trained personnel, (4) DPW's have a high degree of interchangeability of personnel, (5) the expectation that a DPW will become involved in community emergencies results in a rapid personnel mobilization, (6) DPW's usually have extensive resources, (7) because DPW's operate as an entity in the pre-emergency period, personnel have experienced working as a work group, (8) DPW's have usually coordinated activities with other community agencies, (9) a DPW can work autonomously and a lack of complete interorganizational coordination does not hurt its functioning to any large extent (Brouillette, 1970)" (as summarized in Mileti, Drabek, and Haas, 1975: 112).

IIIE2.3b(H) "The Salvation Army functions well in a disaster because it (1) can mobilize quickly, (2) is adaptable to different situations, (3) it has a lot of experience, (4) it has the equipment and facilities, (5) it has formalized associations with its volunteers, (6) it has many social relations with other organizations in non-disaster times, (7) it also has a very good public image (Ross, 1970)" (as summarized in Mileti, Drabek, and Haas, 1975:113).

In contrast to organizations *per se* are emergent linkages to others. The recovery period frequently requires new alliances among organizations. By focusing on a single organization, these linkage sets can be mapped. Few, however, have tried to do so; a notable exception is Ross's (1980) effort.

IIIE2.4(H) "The first phase in the emergence of an organization set is the *crystallization* of the focal organization. [p. 28] . . . the commitment to a course of action by the members of the newly forming organization. . . . The second phase, *recognition,* represents the attempts on the part of the newly emergent focal organization to acquire legitimacy through interaction with organizations in its environment. . . . The last phase, *institutionalization,* is most distinguishable from the earlier phase by the 'business-as-usual' nature of the contacts between the focal organization and its organization set [p. 29]" (Ross, 1980:28, 29).

IIIE2.5(H) As these organizational sets passed through each phase they exhibited similar characteristics. . . . (1) the size of the organization set; i.e., a tendency to decrease in size as they became institutionalized; (2) the hierarchical level of personnel engaged in boundary-spanning activity; i.e., by the time the institutionalization phase had been reached, most interorganizational contact was being made by middle- and lower-level personnel; (3) standardization of interorganizational contacts; and (4) specialization of boundary positions increased. (Adapted from Ross, 1980:30–31.)

Totally new organizations come into being following some disasters, especially severe ones. At times their emergence reflects new tasks. As these are identified, managers within established organizations may seek to expand their domain so as to stake a claim. If extracommunity resources are expected to be forthcoming—for example, in the form of a federal grant—I suspect that such expansion appears far more attractive. The following case material from Italy illustrates this theme.

[From these situations emerged formal organizations which in some cases can be traced back to preceding historical conditions: The tent city committees seemed to revive and reproduce the ancient forms of neighborliness. These committees' functions were exceptionally positive, particularly: (1) by offering many persons the possibility of self-expression and for the first time engaging in the political process (this was especially true of women who had always remained on the sidelines); (2) favoring integration movements; (3) avoiding the spread and adoption of attitudes of passive acceptance of the situation, of fatalistic abandon, of community disinterest and of a welfare type of mentality.] [Italy] (Cattarinussi and Tellia, 1978:246–247).

IIIE3. Mental Health Impacts

Mental health impacts may be found among both victims and helpers. We do not have a good fix on either, however. Instead, the literature to date consists of a few very vague conclusions and a great amount of case material wherein researchers like Raphael (1977, 1979), for example, have described worker reactions. Based on several years of talking with disaster responders, I am convinced that many have suffered from the trauma of their experiences. As clinician–researchers like Mitchell (1982) gather more data, the relative effectiveness of varied treatment interventions may be documented. The following quotation illustrates the present base, although a few more quantitatively oriented studies have appeared (e.g., Taylor and Frazer, 1980; Krell, 1978).

"Through liaison, the writer was able to attend and provide support during a debriefing session held by one of the major rescue teams. This voluntary group of well-trained men from one of the severely affected towns used the session to talk through the experience, the difficulties and stress, both then and subsequently. . . . Many defensive jokes appeared as well as discussion of their team's strengths: but they were able to ventilate, with encouragement, many of their fears, painful memories and subsequent stress. . . . Several members of the group showed levels of persisting distress, with symptoms, and were offered the opportunity for further support" [Australia] (Raphael, 1979–80:222–223).

IIIE3.1(H) "The researchers had reports of psychological and physical tension, irritability, fatigue, anxiety, despair, heightened sensitivity and preoccupation with death. These symptoms were not debilitating and the effects were ministered by a week's leave on return, psychological and logistical debriefing. With a small minority some short term counselling was needed on a voluntary basis and one person did not accept this offer even though he appeared to need help. [p. 311] . . . the recovery of 204 complete bodies and 139 part bodies, belongings and aircraft instruments was completed . . . [p. 312]" [DC-10 crash on Mt. Erebus, Antarctica; 29 of 42 rescue workers interviewed] [New Zealand] (Taylor and Frazer, 1980:311, 312).

IIIE3.1a(H) "The outcome revealed that about a third of the subjects [n = 180] experienced some transient problems initially, and about one-fifth after three months. At a 20-month follow-up there was still some evidence of subjects being under stress. In this study, disaster stress was seen as a complex interaction between environmental and task stressors, job competency, perceptual and emotional defenses, management and follow-up support" [DC-10 aircrash on Mount Erebus, Antarctica] [New Zealand] (Taylor and Frazer, 1982:4).

IIIE3.1b(H) ". . . the experience of Boston City Hospital during the aftermath of a 1973 airline crash in which 88 of the 89 passengers and crew were killed immediately. [p. 148] . . . four days and nights of continuous service to approximately 150 distraught relatives, friends, and family representatives who crowded into the hospital . . . A number of staff evidenced grief reactions comparable to those of family members. . . . staff members were reluctant to be relieved for rest breaks and showed extremely hostile reactions when asked to turn family members over to other colleagues . . . the staff members developed the following short-term reactions: severe depression and periods of crying, migraine headaches, withdrawal from social activities in private life, and irritation with the trivial activities associated with daily living and their jobs [p. 149]" (Krell, 1978:148, 149).

As I emphasized above in the discussion of individual victims, however, not all impacts are negative. For example, organizational personnel, proud of a job well done, may emerge from such trauma as stronger selfs. Unfortunately, few researchers have examined such possibilities.

> IIIE3.2(H) "Personal experience, especially of a highly emotional kind, provides significant opportunities for growth through self-reflection and feedback. In this situation members of the staff revealed qualities that had never before surfaced. This produced increased mutual respect" (Grossman, 1973:44).

In contrast to helper stress is that experienced by victims. Here again we have a very blurred picture of when such stress may legitimately require counseling assistance and of what forms. Yet, a few recent events have suggested—to me at least— that there may be interventions that could prove beneficial. For example, following the "coliseum crush" at a concert ("The Who") in Cincinnati, Ohio (1979), the media response was to blame the victims—"young barbarians."

> "It appeared that the community's major voice was blaming precisely those survivors most in need of an empathic understanding of their helpless predicament. Blame was provoking rage, and rage was accelerating the severity of the stress reactions. Members of the Disaster Assessment Team contacted three major television networks and two local newspapers to inform the public about the acute stress response syndromes survivors might expect, the nature of group behavior under stress and the numerous stories of heroism shared by those contacting the crisis service. . . . it became clear that a major site of difficulty would be a suburban high school where there had been three deaths and where the reactions of faculty and students were intense. With the assistance of the Clinic's school liaison educators, the team contacted the high school and provided immediate individual and group services to special educators, students and faculty" (Lindy and Lindy, 1981:18).

This type of perceptive intervention may well set the standard for the future. For example, following a school bus accident that forced many students to face their own mortality, now that a large number of classmates were dead, officials sought advice. (See also Klingman and Ben-Eli, 1981:529.)

> "Two divergent group opinions developed, one wanting to close the school for the first 2 days of the following week which would then lead to the beginning of the Easter vacation. The other group wanted the school open, with 'business as usual.' We recommended that school remain open as a means of actively helping students deal with this catastrophe, rather than closing school and implying an abdication of responsibility for the uninvolved students. . . . Our plan was to keep this a nonmental health function and prevent the unnecessary labeling of the student as 'patients' " (Tuckman, 1973:153).

Most disaster victims within the U.S.A., at least, will not accept mental health services even when offered. Whether this is because they are evidencing denial of their problems, doubt the efficacy of such interventions, or simply don't need such services remains unknown. As the following findings indicate, the research results are inconsistent, but clearly lean toward suggesting that relatively small proportions of victims will accept such services. On the other hand, five to twenty percent of an impacted area still represents a major demand for most human service networks, which typically are overtaxed normally. Bolin's interpretation of the Wichita Falls, Texas, post-tornado response makes the point well.

"It is not an exaggeration to say that the notion of mental health counseling carries a certain stigma with it for many of the citizens of north central Texas. Part of the problem in getting victims in need of crisis counseling to utilize services available through the Mental Health Center in Wichita Falls was making them understand that, within broad parameters, stress reactions to the storms were normal and nothing to be ashamed of. Some reluctance to utilize crisis counseling was also an outgrowth of sloganeering that emerged in the aftermath. The phrase 'Wichita Falls is Coming Back Strong and Fast' found its way onto innumerable bumper stickers and posters. As several crisis counselors told interviewers, some of their clients admitted hesitation in using counseling services because they saw it as a sign of weakness on their part, i.e., *they* weren't coming back strong and fast" (Bolin, 1982:178–179).

IIIE3.3(H) During the recovery period, mental health organizations will not experience sharp increases in demands for services; even with aggressive outreach efforts, less than one-fourth of the victims will accept their services. (Based on Bolin, 1982; Lindy and Lindy, 1981; see also Fraser and Spicka, 1981:259–260; Richard, 1974:217; Bromet and Dunn, 1981:14.)

IIIE3.3a(H) [Following the Beverly Hills Supper Club fire (1977, Kentucky)] "In the first week, 40 survivors telephoned. Clinicians responded to each of these calls, and 15 cases began treatment. . . . a Fire Aftermath Center . . . was designated with several principles in mind, gained from the experience of the 'Interfaith Council' following the Xenia tornado of 1974: 1) a new organization was to be formed, not specifically tied to a traditional mental health agency and uniquely charged with the task of assisting survivors in the emotional aftermath of the fire; 2) the center would be strictly time-limited in function for the period of the aftermath; 3) clergy would play a major role in its formation and function; 4) broad community sanction would be gathered. . . . Through this Center, 147 survivors were followed over a two-year period" (Lindy and Lindy, 1981:18).

IIIE3.3b(H) "A total of 39% of the Wichita Falls victims ($n = 79$) utilized community crisis counseling programs. In Vernon 30% ($n = 9$) of the victims did likewise. . . . In Wichita Falls 32% of the control families

indicated emotional 'problems' with at least one family member due to
the tornado. In Vernon the figure reached 50% for the controls; however,
only one control family sought counseling. This indicates either that the
problems were relatively minor and easily gotten over, or that non-victims
either didn't know about or did not want to use the crisis counseling that
was available'' (Bolin, 1982:179).

As noted above, a primary exception to this overall pattern was the
very pronounced response by California parents following the 1971 earthquake. Why this response is so much at variance with the others reported
to date remains unclear, although as I suggested above, the presence of
aftershocks and intense media campaigns may be a partial explanation.

"On the day of the earthquake the clinic's director of clinical services
went on the radio to offer help to parents and children who were frightened
by the quake. . . . Of the eight hundred parents who phoned, most only
needed reassurance that they were reacting appropriately. The workers
gave them advice about helping their children unwind by talking with
them, giving them some warm milk or hot chocolate at bedtime and reading to them, using a night light, and reminding the children they were
safe and the parents would take care of them'' (Blaufarb and Levine,
1972:17).

IIIE4. Media Responses

Given the fact that we know very little about shifts in public attitudes that
disasters may evoke, I decided to make this a separate category. This is
not because so much is known, however. Rather, it is my suspicion that
in addition to many other functions the media perform within such contexts, they also mold and partially shape the interpretations the public
gives to the recovery period and those involved in it.

"The first lesson to be drawn from press coverage of the Italian floods
of 1966 is that the preoccupations and preconceptions of writers will often
tend to divert them from straightforward accounts of events—perhaps
toward a lengthy and tenuous comparison with events elsewhere. Second,
there is frequently a strong tendency for reports to decline into cozy
accounts of exaggerated human drama—'how the ordinary people are
coping'—which further distort the picture. It is clear that journalists will
write about the kind of events that they imagine will interest their readers.
Thus, in Italy the artistic losses took second place to the human and
environmental effects; but they are paramount among the British reporting, which may perhaps have been addressing a public that thinks
of Florence primarily as a museum of the Renaissance and has but a hazy
idea of accelerated soil erosion'' [Italy] (Alexander, 1980:33).

In contrast is a detailed review completed on 50 days of coverage by
The Hindu and The Indian Express regarding the Andhra Pradesh Cyclone

(November, 1977). While limited to these data, the issues raised open the door of a very complex research agenda.

> IIIE4.1(H) "Trends in the issues reported, and their subsequent oscillations are as would be expected, with political factors probably receiving slightly more attention than usual due to the imminent State elections in March 1978; political capital is being made by the parties at each other's expense out of the disaster. [p. 159] . . . The reporting generally takes an 'objective' factual nature with no editorially expressed opinions, so that even when criticism of the Government's policy by 'international experts' is contained in planned interviews, the power of the press is not used to follow the points raised, and to pursue relief and reconstruction issues [pp. 159–160]" [India] (Caldwell *et al.*, 1979:159–160).

> IIIE4.2(H) ". . . there was little attempt on the part of the Indian press to acknowledge the activities of international relief agencies in the first 4 weeks following the disaster . . . in the later weeks some attention is paid to the problems of the distribution of relief goods. . . . This aspect generally receives little reporting and is largely of a 'back page' nature" [India] (Caldwell *et al.*, 1979:160).

IVE. Community System Level

Many of the findings I coded that pertained to reconstruction reflected a community focus. After considerable sorting and resorting of the finding cards coded for this niche in the taxonomy, I arrived at seven major subject categories: (1) dynamics of the mass assault; (2) rise and demise of the synthetic community; (3) community conflict patterns; (4) looting; (5) recovery differentials; (6) pressures for normalcy; and (7) social impacts.

IVE1. Dynamics of the Mass Assault

Since the NORC studies of the 1950s, case studies have documented the initial phase of the recovery period as one of "a mass assault."

> IVE1.1 Shortly after impact, there is a massive influx of protective agencies, supplies, equipment, volunteers, and other types of resources. (Based on Taylor, Zurcher, and Key, 1970; Barton, 1969.)

> IVE1.2 "The separate formal organizations become highly dependent on one another in disaster, but they may lack experience, plans, and facilities for coordinating their activities under the unexpected conditions and needs of disaster, so that their joint output is far below what it should be" (Barton, 1962:226).

And as might be expected, when so many people, representing so many organizations, are trying so hard to be helpful, things do not always reflect the functioning of a well-oiled machine. Thus, upon reviewing over two hundred field reports of varying types, Dynes extracted the following picture.

> IVE1.2a ". . . such supplies: (1) normally arrive in volumes far in excess of the actual needs; (2) in large proportion they are comprised of unneeded and unusable materials; (3) they require the services of large numbers of personnel and facilities which could be used for more essential tasks; (4) they often cause conflict relations among relief agencies or among various segments of the population; (5) they materially add to the problem of congestion in and near the disaster site; and (6) in some cases they may disrupt the local economy" (Dynes, 1970a:188–189).

Unfortunately, we don't have the next step. That is, while a summary portrait has been provided, we lack an empirical base for knowing the range of variation in such features or the factors that may affect their relative distribution. In short, while many researchers have noted clear examples of duplication, poor coordination, or unneeded actions, I did not find any study that had attempted cross-event comparisons that would specify potential causal factors. As instances of undesired immunization programs illustrate, many researchers have focused on documenting the presence of the problem, not identifying structures that might lead to *variable rates* of its presence (see Changnon *et al.*, 1983:71–82).

> IVE1.2b "Seven suspected disease outbreaks or environmental health hazards were reported in the 10 days after the storm, ranging from fears of chicken-pox and food poisoning at temporary shelters to questions of fecal contamination of drinking water and housing in flooded areas. No outbreaks of disease and no evidence of sewage backup could be found. Several unverified reports of disease outbreaks were widely circulated immediately after the storm when investigations were not conducted, but these ceased when epidemiologic verification became available" (Glass, O'Hare, and Conrad, 1979:1047–1048). (See also Greco *et al.*, 1981:405; Lechat, 1976:424; Coultrip, 1974:881.)

What we do know is that many arrive to help. At times, and in ways that we are just beginning to get some limited parameters on, helping efforts are not well integrated. Indeed, Dudasik (1980) has proposed that additional victims may be created in this helping process.

> IVE1.3(H) "My purpose is to demonstrate the need to examine differential victimization in the disaster process and to recognize as possible victims persons outside the area of impact" [Peru] (Dudasik, 1980:329).

> IVE1.3a(H) "A number of entry victims reacted in quite different ways. Rather than withdraw physically or psychologically from the stressful situation, they plunged into the tasks of rescue and relief with seemingly unbounded energy. Working from the early morning hours until late at night, these volunteers from outside the stricken area pushed themselves to the edge of exhaustion and kept up their frenetic pace without food and rest" [Peru] (Dudasik, 1980:336).

After reviewing the history of the U.S.A. experience during the initial recovery phase and numerous case histories, Mileti (1975a) offered the following observations.

> IVE1.4(H) "Many factors operate to complicate and reduce the effectiveness of relief and rehabilitation after disaster: (1) the lack of complete coordination between all involved relief organizations and groups, such that there may be a duplication of efforts in some areas of responsibility, or, of much greater significance, neglect of other areas; (2) the temporary, but extreme, work overload of local relief agencies; (3) built-in bureaucratic inflexibility which results in some inability to cope with unusual, or non-uniform, events; and (4) the lack of requisite legislation for required funds and necessary operations for relief, and more specifically, for rehabilitation" (Mileti, 1975a:19–20).

Shifting to a more specific subtopic, we encounter such microprocesses as damage assessment. A few researchers have examined single case incidents of this process, but the entire issue remains poorly understood. Yet, it is but one of the multitude of microprocesses that comprise the restoration phase. These have yet to even be conceptualized adequately for societal level systems.

> IVE1.5(H) There is a tendency to overestimate the extent of damage; difficulties encountered in the completion of damage assessment are not uniform. (Based on Dacy and Kunreuther, 1969:138.)

> IVE1.5a(H) "According to the Prefecture officials, among the 16,000 claims, there were about a hundred contested cases, in which the claimed damage was nearly double of the really suffered one. . . . On a total of 288 shops and inns, 8% claimed a damage more than the 40% over the ascertained one" [Italy] (Cattarinussi, 1978:6). (See also Cattarinussi and Tellia, 1978:242, for discussion of conflicts regarding damage assessment.)

> IVE1.5b(H) "In Toowoomba, elderly people had difficulty in assessing the extent of damage to their homes as they were unable to climb onto roofs. They also had difficulty in making temporary repairs and understanding the procedures required by their insurance companies. Single women had similar difficulties to the elderly" [Australia] (Leivesley, 1977b:209).

In contrast is the microprocess whereby mental health services are delivered. This has been examined in some detail through a series of studies conducted at the Disaster Research Center, beginning with a detailed assessment of the emergent mental health delivery system after the Xenia, Ohio (1974) tornado. The researchers concluded:

> "The actions of several groups and organizations, many from outside the local community, along with other exogenous cultural factors, led to a perceptual definition within the established system that there would be a change in demands for mental health services as a result of the disaster.

The definitional perception of the situation being advanced indicated that there was going to be both a quantitative increase in demands for services as well as a qualitative change in the kinds of mental health services which would need to be met by the established system. . . . the system made an initial attempt to respond by mobilizing a large-scale effort to deliver its traditional kinds of more clinically based services. This effort was a total failure, particularly because there were no demands for such services. . . . the ongoing system for delivering mental health services simply could not meet the anticipated changes in disaster-related demands for services through its existing capabilities. Furthermore, the system was unable to mobilize new and different capabilities. The consequence, given the continuing demand, was the emergence of a new system to deliver mental health related services to disaster victims'' (Taylor, Ross, and Quarantelli, 1976:249).

This is in sharp contrast to an underutilization view that others have advanced.

''The writers contend that there was in Wilkes-Barre an underutilization of social work expertise except for delivery of concrete services and some response to individual emotional needs. This phenomenon was not peculiar to Wilkes-Barre but exists broadly. Local leaders tend not to be familiar with the role social work can play in the recovery efforts following a natural catastrophe'' (Birnbaum, Coplon, and Scharff, 1973:551).

To date, the most thorough examination we have of this issue is the work completed at the Disaster Research Center. Early on, they discovered the area to be one meriting study because of important misperceptions as to victim needs (Baisden, 1979b). This conclusion and the others based on these studies provide many answers, but certainly are not the final word. Currently, this is where the matter stands.

IVE1.6(H) ''Overall, the delivery of organized mental health services in disasters is *characterized* by: a) A lack of preparedness planning at the local community level. b) Considerable extra-community influence, even pressure, exerted on the local mental health sector immediately after the disaster, to initiate a relevant service program. c) An attempt to derive quantitative estimates of mental health service (MHS) needs in the postemergency period despite the almost certain impossibility of obtaining anywhere near accurate figures. d) The establishment, usually one to three months later, of a new program to provide nontraditional MHS services to victims. e) A tendency, nevertheless, toward aspects of an inappropriate medical service model in the delivery effort. f) The eventual provision of primarily information services instead of treatment or clinically oriented counseling. g) A consistent absence of demands for traditional mental health services. h) Little evidence of the effects on clients of whatever services are delivered. i) Few indications of long-term consequences on the functioning of local mental health agencies. j) A slow and erratic diffusion through the mental health sector of relevant findings by disaster researchers and of lessons learned by mental health practitioners in actual disaster situations" (Baisden and Quarantelli, 1981:198).

IVE2. Rise and Demise of the Synthetic Community

Closely related to the above topic, and to some extent reflecting aspects of it, is the observation that emergent interorganizational networks spring out of the woodwork, so to speak. These emergent interorganizational linkages form what Thompson and Hawkes (1962) labeled "the synthetic organization."

> IVE2.1 "In reaction to fragmentation, the community takes on a more than normal amount of interdependence, allocating resources into a *synthetic organization* which can employ computational decision processes" (Thompson and Hawkes, 1962:275).

Many have noted that one element of this restructuring often involves the emergence of a modified network of organizational relationships. This process appears to parallel what we examined previously regarding emergent multiorganizational systems by which search and rescue tasks are accomplished. What differs are the agencies participating and the tasks associated with recovery. Syren's (1981) case study is a good illustration.

> "From the very moment that the landslide occurred until 10.30 PM the same evening it was the head of the fire-brigade who had the ultimate responsibility. After 10.30 PM and for the next five days the County Government Board was responsible after which the responsibility again became that of the fire-brigade for the following three weeks. The responsibility for the long-term reconstruction work was then assigned to a special supervisory group within the Gothenburg Commune" [Sweden] (Syren, 1981:14).

Stated more generally, however, and reflecting numerous case reports, Thompson and Hawkes (1962) offered the following interpretation.

> IVE2.2(H) "Recognition of a central headquarters, to which the several organizations attribute authority, results in the funneling of additional information to that headquarters. The disaster gradually is defined more precisely, the roles of the several organizations are more clearly delineated, and their interrelationships are refined" (Thompson and Hawkes, 1962:281).

Others have examined some of the factors that may affect the composition of intergovernmental recovery systems and their relative effectiveness. The best work completed to date is that of Rubin (1981) and her associates (1985). Based on 14 study jurisdictions, they concluded that recovery processes in local communities are impacted by four categories of "strategic choices." That is, community recovery will reflect the political aspects of post-disaster intergovernmental relations. Thus, the speed and scope of recovery depends upon the degree to which local government officials have the: (1) ability to act; (2) reason to act; (3) knowledge of what to do; and (4) political awareness and astuteness (Rubin and Barbee, 1985:59–62).

> IVE2.3(H) "Of those communities that had experienced frequent floods (annual or more often), the local officials were better prepared to respond" (Rubin, 1981:8).
>
> IVE2.3a(H) ". . . some communities pursue external contacts and connections more aggressively than others, thereby facilitating their access to external resources. Those communities that have cultivated and maintained wide contacts with external agencies appear to have fared better during the recovery period" (Rubin, 1981:9).
>
> IVE2.3b(H) "The belief that form of government would be a useful indicator of existing local public capacity from which forecast capability under stress [could be predicted] did not hold true. A form of government that appeared well-organized and efficient, in fact, did not ensure a capable, effective response. . . . local leaders did emerge—sometimes from unexpected places—and take charge during the period when leadership was most needed" (Rubin, 1981:10).
>
> IVE2.3c(H) ". . . familiarity in normal times with the intricacies of various program requirements—as well as benefits and limitations—paid off during the turmoil of the recovery phase" (Rubin, 1981:12).

A tangential topic, but one that is very important from the standpoint of constituency building, is the matter of changing role definitions. Thus, normal—as opposed to disaster—role definitions may be viewed differently by organizational members located at different structural points within the community. In part, different leadership skills may be required; in part, the domains of organizations may be altered somewhat—at least temporarily.

> IVE2.4(H) ". . . citizens' definitions of local officials' everyday role were incongruous with definitions of their disaster role, while officials maintained the same definitions for both environments. Citizens' disaster definitions were for a much more active role while they favored a custodial orientation in the everyday situation. Officials saw their roles as basically custodial in the disaster and everyday environments" ["Citizens" were members of two *ad hoc* groups which emerged within a few days after the event.] (Wolensky and Miller, 1981:484).
>
> IVE2.4a(H) "Different leadership skills are required during different phases of the disaster. Initially, effective leaders are decisive and action oriented, but as the situation becomes more stabilized, effective leaders tend to be those who are more intellectually oriented (Bruning, 1964)" (as summarized in Mileti, Drabek, and Haas, 1975:123).

Finally, a few observations have been offered about the demise or death of these emergent systems. But the death process has not been documented; rather researchers just point out that it occurs. The dynamics await study. (For elaboration, see Drabek, in press).

> IVE2.5(H) "As the bases for normal relationships gradually are restored, the system withdraws resources from the synthetic organization and gradually returns to pluralistic processes for allocation and integration decision" (Thompson and Hawkes, 1962:277).

IVE3. Community Conflict Patterns

Early case studies emphasized altruism and the propensity of would-be helpers to rapidly arrive at the disaster scene. In their site visits many were impressed with countless stories of organizational cooperation and humanitarian acts. As documented in the previous chapter, this portrait has been validated further by more recent case studies.

> IVE3.1(H) "For a short time, the ancient fault line (conservative/liberal split) that had for so long divided the citizens of Waco was cemented by overwhelming and unifying emotions of fear, anxiety, sympathy, and fellowship" (Moore 1958:33). (See also Fritz and Williams, 1957; Instituut Voor Sociaal Onderzoek Van Het Nederlandse Volk Amsterdam, 1955.)

But note that there is a qualifier; the absence of conflict is only "for a short time." As the recovery phase progresses, many seasoned operational personnel have advised me of a turning point. "The bitch phase" they label it sometimes. Thus, in contrast to a view wherein conflict is absent, others have sought to broaden the perspective (see Tuckman, 1973:156). Indeed, at least one researcher—Klinteberg (1979)—has voiced strong concern regarding an overly rosy view of disaster that seems to pervade in too many of the case studies and has presented a series of *hypotheses* regarding "uprooted communities."

> IVE3.2(H) Once one or several forms of deprivation have pushed a community to a certain point, most or all of the following signs begin to be noticeable:
> • General disorientation about the present situation.
> • Inability of leaders and traditional institutions to cope.
> • Reduction of social control.
> • Weakening of the system of rights and obligations dictating the individual's role in the community.
> • Breaking-up of certain of the traditional groupings which provide the framework for the individual's loyalties and security.
> • Practical and emotional inability to plan for the future.
> • Reduction of openness to innovations. (Adapted from Klinteberg, 1979:64–65.)

Thus, we know these occur sometimes. What is unclear are the factors that may precipitate increased degrees of conflict. Several interesting hypotheses have been offered.

IVE3.3 ". . . while there frequently is a period of high solidarity, morale and consensus immediately after a disaster, as time passes, new disagreements and conflicts generated by the relief effort as well as pre-impact group, organizational and community differences, cleavages and hostilities surface again" (Quarantelli, 1981d:5). (See also Instituut Voor Sociaal Onderzoek Van Het Nederlandse Volk Amsterdam, 1955:35; Leivesley, 1977b:215, 216; Boileau *et al.*, 1978:148; Angotti, 1977:327.)

IVE3.3a(H) "A week after the landslide, an emergent group was established in order to co-ordinate the interests of the victims from different housing areas within the disaster site. The group was formed because victims believed themselves to be in a similar situation and to have common interests. Nevertheless, conflicts arose and the group was almost dissolved before accomplishing its tasks" [Sweden] (Edberg and Lustig, 1983:61).

IVE3.3b(H) "Austin civic life has been enlivened for some years by skirmishes and battles between those who wish to encourage population and economic growth and those who see such growth as threatening the urban and suburban amenities they hold dear. Consequently, it was not surprising that voices were heard, soon after the waters subsided, charging that unbridled 'development' was the major cause" (Committee on Natural Disasters, 1982:28).

Turning to the issue of variability, Quarantelli and Dynes (1976) have offered the most insightful leads I have encountered. They have proposed that there are numerous reasons why community conflict tends to be dampened in responses to *natural* disasters.

IVE3.4(H) Seven factors are associated with the absence of community conflict in natural disaster situations: (1) natural disasters involve an external threat; (2) the disaster agent can generally be perceived and specified; (3) there is high consensus on priorities; (4) disasters create community-wide problems that need to be quickly solved; (5) disasters cause a focusing of attention on the present; (6) there is a leveling of social distinctions; (7) disasters strengthen community identification. (Adapted from Quarantelli and Dynes, 1976:141–143.)

Similarly, they have identified three factors that may exacerbate conflict. As noted, a wide variety of case study data supports their proposals. Given this range of ideas, it seems that a series of cross-event and cross-national comparisons should be initiated wherein precise hypotheses could be formulated to guide data collection efforts.

IVE3.5(H) Three factors amplify conflict: (1) In-group–out-group political lines, e.g., local community officials may be from one political party, but state and national officials represent another; (2) an ideological component, e.g., charges that relief and rehabilitation administration has discriminated against various disadvantaged groups such as Blacks; (3) vested interests, e.g., competition between the newly emergent and the more established organizations in the community. (Adapted from Quarantelli and Dynes, 1976:148–149; see also Demerath and Wallace, 1957; Adams, 1970b:399.)

IVE3.5a(H) "Playing the helper role permitted the entry victim to cope with conditions in the earthquake area, but it also led to a sense of alienation between the outsiders and residents. The outsiders not infrequently perceived themselves as self-sacrificing humanitarians, an attitude expressed in interaction with residents. Projects were pushed through to completion despite all obstacles, and aid recipients themselves were often blamed for the failure of the programs. Irritability grew in proportion to frustration and anxiety, so that the relationship between relief agents and residents was in some cases a negative one" [Peru] (Dudasik, 1980:336). (See also Zarle, Hartsough, and Ottinger, 1974:313; Hammerstrom, Hultaker, and Trost, 1980:8.)

IVE3.5b(H) "Individual aid in disaster situations is inevitably a source of friction in a highly stratified system. [p. 8] . . . urban survivors, who had lost everything in the avalanche, saw themselves as far more deserving of aid than the peasants who had suffered only the effects of the earthquake. The fact that this further category of social differentiation seemingly went unrecognized in the distribution of relief to refugees in general insulted and enraged the urban survivors almost as much as being placed on an equal level with people of lower social categories. [p. 7] . . . Aid which was directed toward the rehabilitation of community structures and services tended to be less divisive in general and on the whole, was met with a greater degree of acceptance by the receptor population [pp. 9–10]" [Peru] (Oliver-Smith, 1977a:7–10). (See also Oliver-Smith, 1979a:46.)

IVE4. Looting

As discussed in the chapter on planning, one of the commonly believed *myths* about disaster responses pertains to looting behavior (see Section IA4).

IVE4.1 ". . . the number of verified cases of actual looting in recent peacetime disasters, both in the United States and in foreign countries, is small" (Dynes and Quarantelli, 1968:101).

Of course, this is not to say that no form of looting behavior exists. Case studies have documented a few cases at various disasters (Mileti, Drabek, and Haas, 1975:120).

IVE4.1a(H) [Looting: despite the watchful eye of the military, many houses were likewise relieved of money, precious articles, equipment and other property, even though difficult to carry. There were also thefts in churches. . . . However, these actions are surely quantitatively insignificant compared with the innumerable acts of spontaneous and unselfish assistance.] [Italy] (Boileau *et al.,* 1978:156).

One creative response to curb looting, which I have not seen replicated, occurred following Tropical Storm Tracy in Darwin, Australia. Here was a unique allocation process.

> "The head of the local food committee, himself a leading food wholesaler in Darwin, put into effect the simplest of all possible arrangements— have the supermarkets open up their doors and let the 'customers' cart away as much food as they wished. This went on for more than three weeks, until January 20, 1975. There were only a few instances of reported hoarding. The government paid the store owners for the difference between predisaster and post January 20 inventory figures" [Australia] (Haas, Cochrane, and Eddy, 1977:47).

In contrast to looting *behavior,* however, are public *perceptions.* Recall the documentations of these when I discussed evacuation behavior. (See IC2.3 in Chapter 4.) Thus, officials must act in terms of these perceptions. It would be illogical for a County Sheriff to tell disaster victims that no security system was in place at the tornado site because sociologists have proven that looting would not occur. That, I would suggest is a serious misreading and misapplication.

> IVE4.2(H) "Little looting goes on in a disaster, but the belief that it will exists; this results in a major deployment of police in disasters. Thus, police are concerned with non-existent problems while other realistic tasks may not be attended to because of the lack of manpower (Kennedy, 1970)" (as summarized in Mileti, Drabek, and Haas, 1975:119).

In contrast to this data base, however, are marked exceptions. As numerous American cities experienced rampages during the hot summer months of the late 1960s, Quarantelli and Dynes expanded our understanding of looting behavior and extended the notion that I have sought to convey repeatedly—that is, that "disaster" does not represent a single and uniform conceptual entity. Thus, civil disorders may have important parallels from the standpoint of emergency organization operations, but may differ greatly along other lines. And clearly, one of these lines is looting behavior.

> IVE4.3 "To summarize: looting in civil disorders is widespread, collective and public, being undertaken by local people who are selective in their activity and who receive community support for their actions. In contrast, looting in natural disasters is very limited, individual and private, being engaged in by outsiders to the community taking advantage of certain situations they find themselves in, but who are strongly condemned for their actions (Quarantelli and Dynes, 1969:284)" (as summarized in Mileti, Drabek, and Haas, 1975:120).

Quarantelli and Dynes tried to identify a set of specifics that give several points for contrast.

> IVE4.3a(H) "Looting in disasters is done by individuals, in civil disorders it is done in groups (Quarantelli and Dynes, 1969)" (as summarized in Mileti, Drabek, and Haas, 1975:120).

IVE4.3b(H) "Looting in disasters is situational, in civil disorders it is 'selective' (Quarantelli and Dynes, 1969)" (as summarized in Mileti, Drabek, and Haas, 1975:120).

IVE4.3c(H) "Looting in disasters is a private act, in civil disorders it is of a public nature (Quarantelli and Dynes, 1969)" (as summarized in Mileti, Drabek, and Haas, 1975: 120).

IVE4.3d(H) "Looting in disasters is by outsiders, in civil disorders it is done by local residents (Quarantelli and Dynes, 1969)" (as summarized in Mileti, Drabek, and Haas, 1975:120).

Finally, their interpretations were supported through a field study in Curaçao following a series of rather violent acts. There, Anderson and Dynes (1975) recognized an important dimension—looting behavior, perhaps like acts of terrorism, may reflect political stresses. When other avenues of communication and institutional change are thwarted, looting behavior, like revolution, may emerge.

IVE4.3e(H) ". . . the violence that did occur in Curaçao on May 30 can best be interpreted as communicating a message from an underclass to the larger society. Thus massive looting can be seen as one form of the group protest. . . . In certain types of crowd situations, looting becomes widespread and looters come from all segments of the population, not just the criminal element. The looting is not done by outsiders nor by isolated opportunists. Looters often work in pairs, family units, and small groups. . . . The public character of looting is striking since goods are taken openly and in full view of others—bystanders, coparticipants, and often even security forces. During this time there is not only little sanction *against* such behavior, there is even strong immediate support *for* it" [Curacao] (Anderson and Dynes, 1975:126).

IVE5. Recovery Differentials

Why do some communities "recover" from a disaster quicker than others? Despite the importance of the question, few answers are available. Two broad categories of factors can be identified: (1) qualities of the community and (2) qualities of the event. To date, however, researchers have offered minimal speculation, much less precise empirical testing.

IVE5.1(H) "If placed on a continuum representing degrees of recovery, the Teton case probably falls near the extreme positive end. In spite of extensive material loss and social disruption other factors were probably optimal for recovery: 1) brief but marginally adequate warning; 2) low death rate and physical injuries; 3) relatively autonomous, homogeneous and highly integrated population; 4) effective local disaster response; 5) supportive network of personal relations intact post-disaster; 6) financial compensation; and 7) large surplus of resources available for temporary assistance" (Golec, 1983:273). (See also Golec, 1982; Demerath and Wallace, 1957; Warrick *et al.,* 1981:121.)

In contrast to this question are a host of issues regarding differential participation in the emergent therapeutic community. Some will be sought out and aided more quickly than others, but we are just beginning to accumulate a sufficient data base so as to grasp the parameters of this community process both at primary group and organizational levels. Data from a few individual disasters indicate some degree of inequity (see Brinkmann, 1975:39; Hodler, 1982:47). A national survey completed by Rossi and his colleagues (1983b), however, suggested that these may be exceptions rather than reflective of the overall pattern.

> IVE5.2 ". . . the patterning of financial aid does not spell out a serious degree of inequity through the lack of access to financial help. The major pattern that emerges is that the probability of financial help rises with the amount of damage experienced. We have a bit of a hint that such help is not always an unmitigated blessing, because the more affluent families appeared to be less likely to receive financial aid (or to ask for it). Perhaps the major bias is against renting families, possibly through the more usual lack of insurance coverage among that group" (Rossi *et al.*, 1983b:156).

> IVE5.2a(H) ". . . a 'pattern of neglect' was most evident. That is, older victims who incurred intensive damage received aid from community resources far less frequently than did other age groups. Only 8% were assisted by five or more sources compared to 32% of victims 39 years of age or younger. And nearly one out of every five elderly victims received no aid whatsoever from any of the nine common help sources. Such differential participation in the emergent therapeutic community . . ." (Kilijanek and Drabek, 1979:565).

When relocation is required, opportunities for differential recovery processes are greater. Thus, socioeconomic characteristics of the community and of the relocation site may impact the recovery process.

> IVE5.3(H) ". . . a direct relationship exists between one's economic means and the available choices. The flood did not wash away that reality. People who had more options available before the flood were in a position of having more desirable choices when dealing with the system after the flood. . . . When mobile homes became available, the people with fewer options had to accept them, though the sites were densely populated and frequently located in a remote area. However, land owners could put their mobile homes on their own land. . . . Rentals were scarce and those who could afford to pay more had a greater number from which to choose" (Feld, 1973:48).

IVE6. Pressures for Normalcy

As the recovery process moves forward, victims press for a return to normalcy. They want to return home, or at least have the issues of location settled so that they can begin making plans.

IVE6.1 ''. . . the vast majority relocate back to their old location, often rebuilding on the same spot they occupied in preimpact times. However, this seems more true of homeowners than renters. Renters not only take longer to obtain permanent housing, but sometimes they never return to the same location. In addition, in the communities studied, there was actual resistance to the development of multi-family housing designed as rental property'' (Quarantelli, 1982a:78).

IVE6.1a(H) ''Strong sentiment to restore the canyon emerged soon after the disaster. A survey conducted in October, 1976, showed that about half of the residents expressed a desire to rebuild on the same location, while a majority of the rest favored a combination of some rebuilding with construction of parks. Approximately one-half (53%) of the victims were unwilling to sell their land to the government, one-third would sell at pre-flood values, and 16% would sell at post-flood prices. Not surprisingly, almost everyone surveyed wanted U.S. Route 34 reconstructed along its pre-flood route'' (Cochrane et al., 1979:21).

There may be important differences among events regarding the return home and subsequent rebuilding processes, however. Thus, the speed of the process and important constraints on rebuilding as mitigation opportunities are reviewed may produce significant variations.

IVE6.2(H) [What should be rebuilt first? . . . there are some differences between the men and the women: houses, schools and medical services have the same order of importance, but the third item is requested more by the men than by the women; in successive indications, the order of importance expressed by the women favors job opportunities (more than the men: symptom of feminine desire for greater participation?), the church, services for the elderly, while that expressed by the men includes jobs, services for the elderly, and, on an equal basis, recreational and fraternal services . . .] [Italy] (Boileau et al., 1978:244).

Regardless of the variation, however, I suspect that few victim families ever feel that the return home is quick enough. Thus, the relativity of this matter must be kept in mind. But so too must the potential for differential impact. I suspect that victim perceptions of the recovery process, especially related to the degree to which uncertainties were *perceived* as being excessive, may take its toll. Longer-term impacts then may vary significantly not only by event and emergency response qualities, but also by features of the initial recovery phase.

IVE6.3(H) ''An added factor that made difficult the planning for rebuilding was the uncertainty about which areas would be designated for demolition. As a result, hope and optimism waned. People were working many additional hours in reopening businesses, families were feeling cramped and trapped in their mobile homes with minimal space for movement or storage, and children experienced isolation from friends and boredom from the lack of recreational facilities. Depressive reactions became more manifest'' (Birnbaum, Coplon, and Scharff, 1973:547).

IVE6.3a(H) "As the reconstruction process continues, community level decisions can affect the hierarchy of return. . . . One need only look at the Wichita Falls city council's indecisions on the placement of mobile homes. Victims didn't know from week to week whether the trailers they had placed on their house lots were legal or illegal, or for that matter whether FEMA might confiscate them. That such uncertainty in the early stages of recovery was stressful was readily apparent from interviews with victims. The city council, however, had to consider both the early return to normalcy and the longer-term consequences of their decisions. In their rush to take decisive action to help victims by permitting mobile homes on private lots, they acted so quickly that they then reversed themselves repeatedly until they returned to their original decision" (Bolin, 1982:62).

Similarly, if the threat continues, the desire to return *and* stay home may be complicated a great deal. During the Spring of 1977—a little more than six months after the second quake struck the Friuli region—Geipel (1982) and his colleagues received 6,568 usable questionnaires from 39 impacted communities (15,688 had been distributed). Although a significant proportion of the respondents (42.3 percent) were 60 years of age or older, the survey results clearly documented the propensity to "stay with the home spot."

IVE6.4 [The results indicated] ". . . that the people who wanted to rebuild were more frustrated by the beginning of winter than by the initial events, and that 70 per cent had not yet begun to rebuild. The next question will reveal that a large group of people affected is either not ready or not able to rebuild in the future. . . . This question, which was perhaps the most important, showed that at the time of the study the determination to rebuild (40.9 per cent) and an attitude of resignation (43.1 per cent), as far as our questions could get at them, were almost evenly balanced among the respondents. The number of people (102, or 1.6 per cent) who wished to leave Friuli either for a time or for good was remarkably small, which may, of course, be due simply to the ages of the people questioned, among whom many could no longer take these alternatives" [Italy] (Geipel, 1982:59–62). (See also Boileau *et al.,* 1978:241.)

While discussed briefly in the previous chapter, I want to again emphasize the point here. Certainly one of the most important issues among the "pressures for normalcy" is a sense of closure regarding the dead.

". . . the organizational structure—which provided mechanisms for the flow of information among the particular task groups (e.g., the computer to correlate the information from two groups assigned different but complementary tasks, or the policy to preserve identifying characteristics as a supplementary task in the transport and burial preparation groups) and specific groups associated with specific tasks—contributed to the effective response. But perhaps most importantly, each of the groups, by simply affecting an efficient operation, demonstrated and accomplished the value of respect for the dead and living. . . . Compromises were needed, e.g., the decision to carry three rather than just one body at a time, or the decision to reduce the number of burial choices. There is certainly a balancing situation being accomplished. . . . The balancing of the efficiency and respect goals does present a problem in a specific situation. But it seems that as a practical problem the solutions can be worked out in accordance with the particular desires of the community involved. What occurred in Rapid City was simply that the problem (though never expressly stated) was addressed—usually with a high priority given to the 'proper' completion of the task'' (Hershiser and Quarantelli, 1976:205).

IVE7. Social Impacts

What types of system impacts can be anticipated during the initial recovery period? By this I am referring to a wide variety of social indicators that might be identified that parallel those used commonly in efforts to assess the community impacts of a large plant relocation or mining venture. Curiously, the so-called "social impact literature" has not been juxtaposed with community disaster studies. It appears to me that such a juxtaposition would greatly strengthen the quality of future disaster studies and could provide some initial conceptual frameworks that would enhance the theoretical integrity of the work. As it is, we have a series of scattered topics that have little relationship to one another—or seemingly to much of anything else. Use of a social impact assessment framework could guide future inquiries that would produce more cumulative statements.

One of the most elaborate studies that sought to examine these possibilities was completed by a team of researchers at Northwestern University. Using an elaborate time-series analysis methodology, they identified several short-term impacts in four communities: (1) Yuba City, California (flood, 1955); (2) Galveston, Texas (hurricane, 1961); (3) Conway, Arkansas (tornado, 1965); and (4) Topeka, Kansas (tornado, 1966). They became acutely aware of how difficult it is to hold other factors constant. Thus, to claim that "the disaster" was the sole force in operation requires the type of quasi-experimental design they employed. But even then, there are serious methodological problems, as they point out in detail.

> IVE7.1(H) [There were several short-term effects, e.g., one-month increase in deaths and decrease in divorces. Thus the aftermath period: 1.] "is characterized by instantaneous destruction. We saw that deaths in Topeka, for example, increased sharply in the month of the disaster only. The next month, there was a slight, off-setting spike which is typical of this aftermath effect. We saw the same effect in divorce applications for Galveston and new claims for unemployment compensation in Yuba City. . . . [2.] is characterized by a decaying effect. We saw in both Yuba City workforce and Galveston assaults a persistence of effect beyond the initial destruction. . . . [3.] is characterized by delayed effects. We saw in a number of instances that the second or third months of aftermath were worse (or better!) than the first month. . . . In the case of Galveston marriages, for example, the aftermath effect may be due initially to a

closing of government offices. . . . [4.] is characterized in rare cases by substantial periods of instability. With Galveston unemployment, we hypothesize that instability results from overcompensation, as for example, when too many outside workers are brought into the community'' (Friesema *et al.*, 1979:139–140).

Two other topics that have been reviewed somewhat are prices and media output. Unfortunately, neither has been studied enough to give us firm conclusions. But the following findings illustrate the broad range of issues that might be examined.

IVE7.2(H) ''During normal times, an increase in demand for an item accompanied by a decrease in supply would lead to some increase in the item's price. Yet the prices remained stable following the earthquake (Alaska, 1964), despite the apparent existence of the two conditions'' (Dacy and Kunreuther, 1969:114).

IVE7.2a(H) ''There is an inflated market price in all goods and services immediately after a cyclone rake off period. . . . [For example,] the property market increases dramatically in prices, caused partly by scarcity, high priced materials, wages and general price increases. [p. 66] . . . The scarcity of goods and services immediately after a disaster induces retailers and other business houses, who can supply these scarce goods, to invest in premises, etc. within the disaster area. The high turnover figures and the probably higher margin of profit tends to itself to increase as the inflow of Government relief and rebuilding capital comes into the market place [p. 68]'' [Australia] (Walters, 1978:66, 68).

IVE7.2b(H) ''. . . small-scale disasters do not affect unit repair costs much. The probable reason is that the demand for repair is small compared to the market's capability. . . . some small disasters actually reduce repair costs. When 400 homes were flooded in McCombs, Miss., a local lumber company enlarged its supply capability and sold lumber at a discount . . . Both Camille and Agnes created conditions that escalated unit repair costs'' (Yancey *et al.*, 1976:276).

IVE7.3(H) Disasters alter media content. (Based on Singer and Green, 1972.)

IVE7.3a(H) ''Newspapers display a rapidly rising interest in disaster, but lose interest very quickly as the dramatic aspects of the situation are replaced by the prosaic activities of replanning and rebuilding'' (Moore *et al.*, 1963:126).

VE. Society System Level

Consistent with the scarcity of macrosystem studies of the other phases of disaster response, issues related to short-term recovery have received minimal attention. Again, I remind the reader that there may be large bodies of information and reports of various types that were not captured through the search process used. But within the standard sociological research journals the matter is clear—few have broached this area.

The scattered findings I did locate reflected two themes: (1) relief differentials and (2) relocation.

VE1. Relief Differentials

As will be detailed a bit further in the next section of this chapter, the early phases of recovery require various forms of damage assessment (see Section VIE1). And one issue that crops up repeatedly is the fear of an epidemic. At times the damage assessment task may be complicated, especially when requests are directed toward the international system. While a case study may document the problem well, what we lack is any understanding of its scope and of factors that might alter its intensity. Yet, as the following case material indicates, distinguishing between routine maintenance needs and disaster relief is not always easy.

> VE1.1(H) "Fears of typhoid, dysentery or other epidemics are often exaggerated in a disaster situation and sometimes lead to distorted relief priorities. . . . Major requests were made for medical supplies and drugs to overseas donors and to the World Health Organisation. Such requests tended to be inflated and to go beyond the immediate needs of the emergency. It is not suggested that exaggerated request lists were assembled irresponsibly. Rather they demonstrated clearly the difficulty that a developing country finds in distinguishing between the needs of disaster relief and those related to maintenance or improved development of services" [Tonga] (Oliver and Reardon, 1982:60).

Similarly, there are some hints that disaster relief processes are not distributed uniformly throughout nation states. For example, insurance coverage for wind damage appears to vary within the U.S.A. across socioeconomic strata. Not all families are covered, but the proportions vary by income groupings.

> "Only 50% of the homes damaged in the Lubbock tornado (1970) were estimated to be covered by insurance, and the average coverage was 40% of the home's value (Kunreuther, 1973a[2]). The Eastern Area tornadoes (April, 1974) showed a similar pattern of coverage. The American Red Cross estimated that the average number of homes covered in the six states affected was 80%" (Cochrane, 1975:90).

> VE1.2(H) "The lowest income group shown was discovered to have approximately 53% of their homes insured at an average coverage of 54% of the house value. In contrast, 85% of the highest income group was insured for 84% of the structure's value" (Cochrane, 1975:91).

May's (1985) analysis of Presidential declarations indicated another potential variable—use of community disasters by those running for election.

---

[2]Howard Kunreuther, "Insurance." Summary Report presented at Natural Hazard National Conference, Estes Park, Colorado, 1973.

His data precluded a motivational conclusion, however. He noted that he could only point out the associational relationships.

> VE1.3(H) "A greater percentage of requests were granted in presidential election years than in off-election years under the Nixon and Ford Presidencies. Under the Carter administration, the pattern was reversed" (May, 1985:112).

> VE1.4(H) "With respect to the more specific hypothesis that politicians' efforts in providing for federal assistance in the aftermath of disasters are rewarded with favorable votes on election day, the results are mixed. In many of the instances reported here politicians are rewarded in the sense that electoral gains (or losses) in disaster-affected counties are greater (or in the case of losses, less) than the corresponding changes in nondisaster-affected counties. Yet this is not always the case, as voters sometimes seem to withhold support for politicians who are either closely associated with what is perceived to be a less-than-adequate federal response to the disaster or who do not fulfill citizen expectations about the role of elected officials in the aftermath of disasters" (May, 1985:122).

In contrast, it appears that both the issues of relief and axes of differentiation may vary by nation state. But such speculation rests solely on limited case study data.

> VE1.5(H) "The reassessment was instrumental in unveiling the 'double standard' by which some victims of a disaster attract sufficient attention to become relatively privileged compared to the nonaffected population. The preliminary analysis strongly suggested that at the time of the survey, nomads, most of them from foreign origin, were better off than the sedentary, (Nigerian) population, which confirmed several reports from external observers and Red Cross teams. The relief effort—at its peak of efficiency—was mostly directed to the nomads . . . Measures were immediately taken to extend food and medical relief assistance to neighbouring sedentary villages" [Niger] (de Ville de Goyet et al., 1977:226).

Finally, when future researchers do pursue such matters, they should note the strengths present in less developed societies. These may not be obvious at first glance. Thus, any efforts at variable specification, and especially measurement, ought to be informed by these case study data.

> VE1.6(H) "A village society provides a form of welfare service by its very nature, being a more cohesive and integrated group. In Tonga there is no strongly developed formal government, centralised, welfare infrastructure" [Tonga] (Oliver and Reardon, 1982:74).

VE2. Relocation

Issues of relocation are very complex and several case studies, especially those completed by Davis (e.g., 1975, 1977), highlight many of these. But one issue that comes through very clearly is the matter of consistency. When people must be relocated, they will avoid, if possible, settings,

structures, and interactions that are inconsistent with their cultural traditions.

> VE2.1(H) "In a situation with extreme housing deficits, all temporary
> housing becomes permanent. Any housing, to be effective, must be cul-
> turally acceptable to Nicaraguans. The obvious examples of housing that
> do not appear to fit are the igloos and possibly the expensive housing
> for FUNDECI made out of Asbestos Cement" [Nicaragua] (Davis,
> 1975:46).

> VE2.2(H) "In Skopje 150,000 left the city within the first three weeks.
> However, families did not like being split up, children could not speak
> the language of different Yugoslav republics and the net result was that
> within 2½ months they had virtually all returned" [Yugoslavia] (Davis,
> 1977:33).

Undoubtedly reflecting the structure of the search net I used, only a
few studies pertained to war-caused relocations or analyses of refugee
flows. Here is another subtopic of immense complexity that merits thorough review and perhaps a good deal of empirical study. For example,
what parallels may there be between war-caused relocations and those
resulting from natural disasters? Using data from Nicaragua (earthquake)
and India, Cuny (1977) has proposed the following.

> VE2.3(H) ". . . differences between a major relief operation following a
> natural disaster and one for war refugees residing in a foreign country
> . . . First, in the former case there is only one type of camp; there are
> no phases as in the latter. Second, the government, for political reasons,
> must respond itself to the consideration by local authorities, and more
> government resources will be available to camp builders. . . . A third
> difference relating to camps is that the number of refugees following a
> natural disaster is constant. This enables the planner to design a camp
> for an ultimate capacity, facilitating selection of both a plan and a site. . . .
> social services within the camp are geared to getting the refugee back
> into the mainstream of national life, while a government will usually re-
> strict foreign refugees to activities within their own camps and prohibit
> them from meaningful work outside" [Nicaragua and India] (Cuny,
> 1977:129).

Obviously, we have just opened the door to a complex series of research
agendas. Matters of societal responses—even federal level agency behavior
within the U.S.A.—have yet to be studied. When more specialized issues
like cultural acceptance of relief efforts, including temporary housing, and
war-caused refugee flows are considered, the scope of the research agenda
is both clarified and magnified.

VIE. International System Level

Three general topics were reflected in the findings coded within this section
of the taxonomy: (1) public health myth; (2) societal response differences;
and (3) international system responses. As will be quite evident from the

discussion below, however, none of these have been examined in detail. Rather, what we again have is a small number of isolated studies that collectively do little more than provide food for thought.

VIE1. Public Health Myth

As was just noted in the preceding section, damage assessment never is easy and is complicated greatly when the task is assigned to one unfamiliar with the impacted peoples. Thus, in reviewing various studies and documents pertaining to international disaster assistance efforts, one National Academy of Sciences committee emphasized the potential difficulties. Case study data illustrate the specifics. Of course, the extent of such difficulties and the relative effectiveness of various corrective policies and training programs remain unknown.

> VIE1.1(H) "Experts from industrialized countries have difficulty distinguishing disaster-related needs from chronic problems characteristic of developing countries. They may overstate emergency requirements because they falsely attribute to the disaster deficiencies in basic services and infrastructure, such as sanitation and water supplies, that were there long before. They also may impose standards wholly inappropriate for a developing area" (Committee on International Disaster Assistance, 1979:3).

> VIE1.1a(H) ". . . the ultimate example of a lack in communication and resulting misperception involved the sending of food to Guatemala for distribution in the rural areas. . . . various canned foods (from hams to peaches) [were] fed to dogs or pigs because, for an Indian, what comes in a can is not 'food' " [Guatemala] (Olson and Olson, 1977:78).

> VIE1.1b(H) "Although international aid was prompt and extensive, donor agencies continued to provide assistance that conflicted with cultural preference or actual needs of the people in this region. . . . unfamiliar canned food, along with the tons of donated medical supplies, were either sold for animal food or stored away probably never to be used again . . . villagers were suspicious that the food might contain pork or pork by-products. This is taboo in the Islamic society of Turkey. Western style womens' dresses were also a wasted donation" [Turkey] (Mitchell, 1977:239).

A recurring issue that may be confounded by such perceptual mismatches has to do with the fear of potential epidemics. Indeed, somewhat paralleling fears of looting, there appears to be an important public health mythology that can now be debunked. Careful testing of the following hypotheses within cross-hazard research designs is a first step.

> VIE1.2(H) "There have been no reported epidemics of communicable diseases after several recent natural disasters. [p. 184] . . . Rumours of epidemics were rife by the 2nd and 3rd weeks after the earthquake. At

various times, outbreaks of measles, typhoid fever, typhus, anthrax, rabies, hepatitis, influenza, and dysentery were reported in the disaster area. More than 30 reports of outbreaks were investigated and proved to be without foundation [p. 182]'' [Guatemala] (Spencer *et al.*, 1977:182, 184). (See also Greco *et al.*, 1981:405; Committee on International Disaster Assistance, 1979:63.)

VIE1.2a(H) "During the beginning of the evacuation, there was considerable interest in administering a variety of immunizations, such as cholera, typhoid fever, and yellow fever, to the refugees. This concern resulted from the widespread belief that disease epidemics commonly accompany human disasters and that mass immunizations could easily prevent these outbreaks" [Guam] (Shaw, 1979:309).

Obviously, like looting behavior, certain conditions may cause epidemics. What we now need is two things: (1) communication to countervail the myth and (2) further study directed toward specification of conditions that most likely will produce actual, rather than feared, epidemics.

VIE1.3(H) "The creation of an epidemic or a rise in disease incidence requires one or more of the following triggers: 1) the disaster must introduce a disease agent to a non-immune population (this may occur through migration of carriers or through the migration of susceptibles); 2) there must be an increase in the disease susceptibility of the population such as is caused by malnutrition; 3) there must be an increase in disease transmission through one or more of the mechanisms charted in Figure 1, such as overcrowding or vector proliferation" (Paulozzi, 1980:142–143).

VIE2. Societal Response Differences

As noted in the last chapter, cross-national response differences may covary with fundamental structural features such as the degree of centralization of authority. Unfortunately, the matter has been considered by only a few scholars, in particular, McLuckie. Most of his hypotheses dealt with emergency responses, however. But a couple have relevance to recovery.

VIE2.1(H) "A centralized society reacts to disasters in ways that are different from a decentralized society, i.e., fewer positions are responsible for decision making and these positions are at a higher level in a centralized society" (McLuckie, 1975:8).

VIE2.1a(H) ". . . in the more centralized societies there is a tendency for military organizations to become involved in disaster relief activities in a leadership role rather than a supportive capacity" (Anderson, 1969b:252).

VIE2.1b(H) "Disaster response in the United States involves the private sector to a greater extent than in either Japan or Italy (McLuckie, 1970)" (as summarized in Mileti, Drabek, and Haas, 1975:126).

A second criterion of differentiation, also emphasized in Chapter 5, is the degree of commitment to kin. Thus, one variable that appears to impact the recovery phase a great deal is the degree to which this structural feature is present.

> VIE2.2(H) "Clifford suggested that the Mexican community tended to share certain characteristics with other Latin American countries. Among these characteristics were (1) a greater emphasis on ascriptive criteria, such as age, sex, class, and kinship in ordering social relationships; (2) a greater emphasis on personalized relationships; and (3) a greater dependence on people rather than positions. Consequently Clifford found that, in the Mexican community, there was a greater dependence on the kin group as a source of advice and help. There was a greater reluctance to accept 'official' warnings and aid. There was a greater resistance to cooperative relationships among disaster-related agencies and a greater tendency to depend upon 'heroic' personalized leadership rather than on 'rational' authority and cooperation" (Dynes, 1972:236–237). (See also Clifford, 1956.)

A third variable is less precise, but has to do with the prevailing religious structure. For example, several scholars have argued that the degree to which fate control is prevalent and reinforced by the dominant religion, as opposed to dependency upon the supernatural, is critical. Similarly, Cattarinussi and Tellia (1978:244) have proposed that in Italy the Catholic church is particularly important since it can count upon a national capillary structure that permits prompt aid in support of victims. Furthermore, especially in smaller communities, the charismatic position occupied by the clergy places them in a strategic role. But observations such as these coming from the response to the Friuli earthquake (1976) have not been juxtaposed against case studies from other nation states wherein the influence of the Catholic church, or any other, is comparable.

> VIE2.3(H) "In pre-industrial urban societies and pre-literate ones, characteristic responses might be resignation to one's fate and/or recourse to magic. 'When catastrophe is thought to be engendered primarily by spiritual forces, man can do little to alter the course of events apart from recourse to religions and/or magical practices' (Sjoberg, 1962:363)" (as summarized in Mileti, Drabek, and Haas, 1975:126).

VIE3. International System Responses

Of the few studies I encountered concerning the international system response during the initial recovery phase, most emphasized coordination difficulties. This parallels the portrait of fragmentation and high levels of organizational autonomy that characterizes the U.S.A. response pattern during the emergency period. Indeed, the National Academy of Sciences committee cited above suggested that the coordination was so riddled with problems as to render the term "system" problematic. Using this conclusion as a hypothesis, what we now need are several cross-event response comparisons with acceptable types of measures so as to ascertain more precisely the degree to which this may in fact be the case and the conditions under which it varies.

VIE3.1(H) "In any major disaster, this diverse involvement virtually guarantees problems of coordination among international donors and between the donors and the disaster-stricken society. To talk of an international disaster response *system* is inappropriate, because that concept implies relatively high levels of mutual awareness, interdependence, and coordinated activity that presently do not exist" (Committee on International Disaster Assistance, 1978b:5).

VIE3.1a(H) ". . . the international relief effort was clearly instrumental in helping the people [p. 107] . . . it included priceless vital services such as air transportation, professional evaluation, specialized expertise, and prompt provision of fully equipped hospitals. But on the other hand it also involved the dumping of useless 'donations' such as expired medical samples, nylon underwear, and unmatched ladies shoes—help that was counterproductive, especially since the fuel for each aircraft's return flight was paid for by the assisted country [p. 108]" [Guatemala] (de Ville de Goyet *et al.*, 1976:107, 108).

VIE3.1b(H) ". . . there were severe problems in gathering and distributing information and in co-ordinating relief activities. In the case of the UN system, the inability of UNDRO to assume co-ordination responsibility led to a search for a focal point and the creation of OSRO within FAO. The delay caused by having to create a new relief co-ordination point hampered effective action by and co-operation among all donors during the initial stage of relief operations. Further problems in developing a disaster relief response focus on (a) lack of funds; (b) lack of pre-disaster contingency plannings; and (c) difficulty in accurately assessing needs" [concerning Sahel drought] [Africa] (Brown, 1977:147). (See also El-Khawas, 1976:93.)

Taking the matter a different direction, the NAS committee broached the sensitive issue of "motive." To what degree are disaster relief efforts consciously used as "political weapons" by donors? A complex range of research studies is implied by the committee's conclusion.

VIE3.2(H) "Nor can one assume that both offers of and requests for external assistance are guided purely by humanitarian motives. The Committee cannot document the extent to which the seeking or offering of assistance is politically motivated or competitive. However, we believe that the present pattern of international disaster assistance has elements of both competition and cooperation and that both selfless and and selfish motives operate" (Committee on International Disaster Assistance, 1978b:5).

Twisting coordination issues yet another direction, we come to those who have questioned the "politics" of aid distribution. Do those com-

munities with better "connections," for example, receive a disproportionate share of the aid offered?

> VIE3.3(H) ". . . a failure to understand local political operations is likely
> to prevent the accomplishment of a goal such as the equitable distribution
> of disaster relief supplies to those who need them most. . . . the more
> significant kinship ties that a community had with individuals directly
> involved in the division of relief resources, the better it fared. [p. 269] . . .
> those Mortlock communities with more political power in Truk District
> and Trust Territory politics fared better than those communities with
> comparatively less power [p. 268] [Micronesia] (Marshall, 1979:268, 269).

As I noted in Section VE2, Davis conducted a series of studies wherein
he documented numerous types of problems regarding relocation, especially those pertaining to temporary housing. In various events, he has
found a remarkably consistent pattern—underuse of structures donated
by other nations.

> VIE3.4(H) Externally manufactured structures provided to disaster vic-
> tims for temporary housing will be underused. (Based on Davis, 1977.)

> VIE3.4a(H) "In the town of Masaya, outside Managua, igloos provided
> by the West German Red Cross were one of the only forms of rent-free
> housing. Despite this, only 75 out of the 310 units were occupied (Davis,
> 1975). An analysis of provision in other situations tends to confirm the
> fact that low occupancy is more likely to be the norm than the exception.
> The A.I.D. [Agency for International Development] wooden houses in
> Managua were only 35% occupied eleven months after the disaster (A.I.D.
> paper, 1974)" [Nicaragua] (Davis, 1977:32).

> VIE3.4b(H) "In Chimbote the multiple family units built by the Peruvian
> government and A.I.D. were again little used, as were the United Nations
> shelter units (Marking, 1971³). In Skopje seven months after the earth-
> quake only 179 families were living in the Nissen huts and quonset huts
> provided by the British and Americans (*Your Aid to Skopje,* 1963⁴). The
> capacity of these units was at least four times this total" [Peru and Yu-
> goslavia] (Davis, 1977:32).

Why? The answer is far from clear, but Davis had offered the following
insights.

> VIE3.5(H) "Reasons for this underuse may include: overestimates of the
> homeless population; excessive volumes of aid; the location of the units
> (often away from bus routes, a vital requirement as work gets back to
> normal); cultural rejection of unusual forms of housing; the almost uni-
> versal hostility to multi-family units; and finally, the fact that as more

---

[3] G. Marking, "Emergency Housing Peru." *Architectural Design* (May, 1971): 264–265.
[4] *Your Aid to Skopje July-December, 1963.* Committee for Reconstruction and Development
of Skopje.

permanent housing becomes available, this is seen as a better alternative''
[Nicaragua] (Davis, 1977:32).

Finally, the wisdom of policies directed toward temporary shelter of
any kind has been challenged by Davis. That is, given the pattern of underuse, and the costs involved, it may be more efficient to strive for permanent housing as an initial goal rather than follow the practices used.
With only a short delay, victim families might be aided in a way that
would be far less disruptive in the longer run. As noted before, much
evidence suggests a strong pressure for resolving uncertainties—a desire
to get a sense of closure so that life can go on. We don't know, however,
the extent to which Davis's conclusions may apply across the broad range
of events that occur annually.

> VIE3.6(H) ''The cost of temporary donor provisions using western tech-
> nology may be higher than that of permanent housing. In Gediz, precise
> costs of permanent housing are not available, but it is highly probable
> that the igloos costing about $31 per square metre, were more expensive
> than the new prefabricated units'' [Turkey] (Davis, 1977:34).

Selected Bibliography

Alexander, David [1980] ''The Florence Floods—What the Papers Said.'' *Environmental Management* **4** (January):27–34.

Anderson, Carl R., Don Hellriegel, and John W. Slocum, Jr. [1977] ''Managerial
Response to Environmentally Induced Stress.'' *Academy of Management
Journal* **20** (No. 2):260–272.

Angotti, Thomas [1977] ''Playing Politics with Disaster: The Earthquakes of Friuli
and Belice (Italy).'' *International Journal of Urban and Regional Research*
1:327–331.

Baisden, Barbara, and E. L. Quarantelli [1981] ''The Delivery of Mental Health
Services in Community Disaster: An Outline of Research Findings.'' *Journal
of Community Psychology* **9** (July):195–203.

Bartlett, Glen S., Peter S. Houts, Linda K. Byrnes, and Robert W. Miller [1983]
''The Near Disaster at Three Mile Island.'' *International Journal of Mass
Emergencies and Disasters* **1** (March):19–42.

Beinin, L. [1981] ''An Examination of Health Data Following Two Major Earthquakes in Russia.'' *Disasters* **5** (No. 2):142–146.

Brown, Barbara J. [1977] ''The United Nations and Disaster Relief in the Sahel,
1973–75.'' *Disasters* **1** (No. 2):145–150.

Burke, Jack D., Jr., Jonathan F. Borus, Barbara J. Burns, Kathleen Hannigan
Millstein, and Mary C. Beasley [1982] ''Changes in Children's Behavior after
a Natural Disaster.'' *American Journal of Psychiatry* **139** (August):1010–1014.

Caldwell, Nick, Andrew Clark, Des Clayton, Kuldip Malhotra, and Dag Reiner
[1979] ''An Analysis of Indian Press Coverage of the Andhra Pradesh Cyclone
Disaster of 19 November 1977.'' *Disasters* **3** (No. 2):154–168.

Committee on International Disaster Assistance [1979] *Assessing International
Disaster Needs*. Washington, D.C.: National Academy of Sciences.

Committee on International Disaster Assistance [1978] *The U.S. Government Foreign Disaster Assistance Program*. Washington, D.C.: National Academy of Sciences.

Dacy, Douglas C., and Howard Kunreuther [1969] *The Economics of Natural Disasters*. New York: The Free Press.

Davis, Ian [1977] "Emergency Shelter." *Disasters* 1 (No. 1):23–40.

Davis, Ian [1975] "Disaster Housing: A Case Study of Managua." *Architectural Design* (January):42–47.

Edberg, Anna-Karin, and Britt-Inger Lustig [1983] *Solidaritet och Konflikt* (Solidarity and Conflict) (in Swedish with an English summary). Disaster Studies 14. Uppsala, Sweden: University of Uppsala.

Erickson, Patricia E., Thomas E. Drabek, William H. Key, and Juanita L. Crowe [1976] "Families in Disaster: Patterns of Recovery." *Mass Emergencies* 1:203–216.

Hammarstrom, Gunhild, Orjan E. Hultaker, and Jan E. Trost [1980] *Ett Forgiftat Samhalle* (A Poisoned Community) (in Swedish with an English summary). Disaster Studies 8. Uppsala, Sweden: Uppsala University.

Huerta, Faye, and Robert Horton [1978] "Coping Behavior of Elderly Flood Victims." *The Gerontologist* 18 (December):541–546.

Krell, George I. [1978] "Managing the Psychosocial Factor in Disaster Programs." *Health and Social Work* 3 (August):139–154.

Leitko, Thomas A., David R. Rudy, and Steven A. Peterson [1980] "Loss Not Need: The Ethics of Relief Giving in Natural Disasters." *Journal of Sociology and Social Welfare* 7 (September):730–741.

Leivesley, Sally [1977] "Toowoomba: Victims and Helpers in an Australian Hailstorm Disaster." *Disasters* 1 (No. 3):205–216.

Lindy, Jacob D., and Joanne G. Lindy [1981] "Planning and Delivery of Mental-Health Services in Disaster—The Cincinnati Experience." *Urban and Social Change Review* 14 (Summer):16–21.

Mitchell, William A. [1977] "Partial Recovery and Reconstruction after Disaster: The Lice Case." *Mass Emergencies* 2:233–247.

Palmer, Ellen L. [1980] "Student Reactions to Disaster." *American Journal of Nursing* 80 (April):680–682.

Paulozzi, Leonard J. [1980] "Great Myths in Disaster Relief—Epidemics." *Journal of Environmental Health* 43 (No. 3):140–143.

Penick, Elizabeth C., B.J. Powell, and W.A. Sieck [1976] "Mental Health Problems and Natural Disaster: Tornado Victims." *Journal of Community Psychology* 4 (January):64–68.

Quarantelli, E. L. [1982] "Sheltering and Housing after Major Community Disasters: Case Studies and General Conclusions." Columbus, Ohio: Disaster Research Center, The Ohio State University.

Quarantelli, E. L., and Russell R. Dynes [1976] "Community Conflict: Its Absence and Its Presence in Natural Disasters." *Mass Emergencies* 1:139–152.

Quarantelli, E. L., and Russell R. Dynes [1969] "Dissensus and Consensus in Community Emergencies: Patterns of Looting and Property Norms." *Il Politico* 34:276–291.

Raphael, Beverley [1979–80] "A Primary Prevention Action Programme: Psychiatric Involvement Following a Major Rail Disaster." *Omega: Journal of Death and Dying* 10 (No. 3):211–226.

Ross, G. Alexander [1980] "The Emergence of Organization Sets in Three Ecumenical Disaster Recovery Organizations—An Empirical and Theoretical Exploration." *Human Relations* 33 (January):23–39.

Rossi, Peter H., James D. Wright, Eleanor Weber-Burdin, and Joseph Pereira [1983] *Victims of the Environment: Loss from Natural Hazards in the United States, 1970–1980*. New York: Plenum Press.

Taylor, A. J. W., and A. G. Frazer [1980] "Interim Report of the Stress Effects on the Recovery Teams after the Mt. Erebus Disaster, November, 1979." *New Zealand Medical Journal* 91 (April 23):311–312.

Taylor, James B., Louis A. Zurcher, and William H. Key [1970] *Tornado: A Community Responds to Disaster*. Seattle: University of Washington Press.

Taylor, Verta with G. Alexander Ross and E. L. Quarantelli [1976] *Delivery of Mental Health Services in Disasters: The Xenia Tornado and Some Implications*. Disaster Research Center Book and Monograph Series No. 11. Columbus, Ohio: Disaster Research Center, The Ohio State University.

7

Reconstruction

Long-term recovery—frequently referred to as the reconstruction phase—brings the response cycle into issues of mitigation. When this phase can be assumed to have "ended," remains, like a host of other questions, both theoretically and methodologically perplexing, however. When we completed our earlier review (i.e, Mileti, Drabek, and Haas, 1975), we emphasized the relative scarcity of findings concerning such matters. Our knowledge base has expanded greatly since then, as will be very evident from the discussion that follows.

It is my view, however, that *we lack an adequate base to draw many firm conclusions* at this point regarding most long-term responses. Frequently, available findings are inconsistent. The research methods used are woefully inadequate on several scores. Results are offered with little or no discussion of fundamental design flaws. In relatively few studies are control samples contrasted to those impacted by a particular disaster. In only one (i.e., Drabek and Key, 1984), or possibly a handful of others depending on leniency of interpretation, have pre-event data been available or have efforts been made to take subsequent life stresses into account. Small sample sizes, made worse by high attrition levels between the measurement points, are noted by many investigators, but only noted. Typically, measures used lack much sophistication. On the positive side, the past five years have brought increased recognition of this situation and some efforts to remedy it.

Detailed critique of each study reviewed in this section could comprise a book by itself. Obviously, such was not my objective, although, from time to time, I have offered notes of criticism. But generally, I have pre-

sented the findings as they have been reported in the literature. By des-
ignating nearly all as hypotheses, however, I have indicated my position.

For most disasters studied—aside from a few cases that appear to have
important differentiating qualities—the overall picture is one of mixed,
but relatively minor, ripples in the long-term developmental cycle. Thus,
impacts are mixed, in the sense that some could be regarded as negative,
others as positive. They are minor, in that consistency, rather than total
redirection, emerges. Resiliency is high for most, but *not all systems* impacted. For example, a tornado killing seven people may evidence no
discernible impact on the total community, but the families from which
these seven were lost will be disrupted severely. And if the same death
toll stemmed from corporate negligence—actual or perceived—the recovery process may shift in important ways for all systems impacted.
Thus, the taxonomic problem I have highlighted throughout this book must
be seen as more complex than simply a listing of event characteristics.
As reflected in the system distinctions I have used, forms of social structure
must be included as well.

IF. Individual System Level

While many investigators have examined more complex social units, the
largest concentration of studies have been of individual impacts. As will
be very clear from the studies discussed below, the results available preclude a single answer. Thus, my assessment is consistent with those offered
by Perry (1979a, 1985) and Quarantelli (1980b), although I would emphasize
more that recent research points toward both positive and negative impacts
being registered.

> "Two general conclusions may be drawn regarding the controversy: (1)
> the frequently used 'after-only' survey design reflects inappropriate con-
> ception of what the research question should be; and (2) there are probably
> some short-term psychological consequences of natural disasters, but
> research designs have been inadequate to effectively determine whether
> the consequences are wholly positive or negative, or whether they persist
> into the long run" (Perry, 1979a:176).

> "The great majority of the research argues that disasters do not bring
> about serious or long lasting psychological consequences. Stress may be
> experienced, but it is not said to result in psychoses, severe mental illness,
> or even functionally disabilitating behaviors. It is acknowledged that a
> significant number of disaster victims do manifest minor symptoms such
> as sleeplessness and listlessness, and in some cases, victims acquire a
> hypersensitivity to cues signalling a possible recurrence of disaster. Most
> such psychological difficulties, however, appear to be transient and sit-
> uational, attributable not so much to the threat or impact of the disaster,
> as to quite reasonable frustrations and annoyances arising from dealing

with impersonal and sometimes inefficient emergency and relief organizations'' (Quarantelli, 1980b:144).

After struggling with the diverse and voluminous array of findings cards
for some time, I arrived at six major substantive categories that I believe
best convey the present state of the literature: (1) findings of continuity
and positive impacts; (2) findings of negative impacts; (3) findings suggesting variation in impact; (4) children as victims; (5) secondary victims;
and (6) treatment orientations.

IF1. Findings of Continuity and Positive Impacts

Looking across ten studies of disaster victims, Baisden (1979a) noted a
consistent portrait—aside from the results coming from Buffalo Creek,
West Virginia. Key findings from that event—a horrifying flash flood (1972)
that left over one hundred residents of a tiny Appalachian community
dead—will be summarized below.

> IF1.1(H) "Victim populations do seem to undergo considerable stress
> and strain and *do* experience varying degrees of concern, worry, depres-
> sion, anxiety, together with numerous problems in living and adjusting
> in time to disaster. . . . Except for the Buffalo Creek study, none of the
> research [10 studies reviewed] found a link between disaster and severe
> psychopathology" (Baisden, 1979a:328). (See also Gilbert, 1958; Bates
> *et al.*, 1963; Moore and Friedsam, 1959.)

In general, this portrait was consistent with what William Key and I
discovered three years after a tornado had cut a diagonal path through
Topeka, Kansas (1966). Unlike all other studies cited in this section, however, we had the luxury of both pre- and post-event data for both victims
and non-victim community residents.

> IF1.1a(H) "*Within our own data base, there was no evidence of long-
> term negative impacts no matter how we rearranged it,* when *both* the
> pre and post-tornado and non-victim comparisons were made. [p. 366]
> . . . We reviewed a large assortment of data ranging from expectations
> about the future . . . attitudes of alienation and despair . . . and self-
> perceptions of physical health [p. 365]" (Drabek and Key, 1984:365, 366).

> IF1.1b(H) "There was a subtle change in outlook. [p. 383] . . . First, *an
> element of fear remained*—fear of another tornado, especially among
> children. [p. 384] . . . [second, many] expressed a heightened conscious-
> ness about storms—tornadoes, in particular. *Rather than emphasizing
> only their fear, however, they stressed action.* [pp. 384–385] . . . Third,
> *others stressed memories and appreciation of the therapeutic community*
> . . . Fourth, *several suggested a tone of anti-materialism.* [p. 385] . . .
> Finally, *a few expressed an evaluation of actual profit* [p. 386]" (Drabek
> and Key, 1984:383–386).

Consistent with these outlines and extending the details further are findings from tornadoes in Xenia, Ohio, and Omaha, Nebraska, and a nightclub fire in Southgate, Kentucky.

> IF1.2(H) "Omaha's tornado produced neither serious psychopathology nor social disorganization. Milder problems were evident in the form of child weather fears and adult problems of daily life. . . . responses by the tornado victims strongly suggest that they did not perceive themselves and their lives as having been substantially changed. 22 percent of the respondents indicated that their mental health had worsened since the tornado while 15 percent said that it had improved; the remainder felt that their mental health was unchanged" (Rosenberg, Fine, and Robinson, 1980:24). (See also Cohen and Poulshock, 1977:264.)

> IF1.2a(H) "According to the survey, 38 percent of the victims sampled thought that half or more of Xenians had mental problems related to the disaster. Asked how they felt emotionally after the disaster, 58 percent said good or excellent, 33 percent said only fair, and 9 percent reported their mental state was poor. About half the population admitted to being more nervous or excited at some time since the tornado, and half said they had felt depressed on occasion. Other symptoms were exhibited by smaller percentages of the population. For example, 27 percent of the population reported having trouble sleeping, and 25 percent reported headaches" (Taylor, 1977:94).

> IF1.2b(H) "Unlike our experience at Buffalo Creek, we found that many survivors of the fire, while moderately stressed at the time, were not impaired when they saw us, particularly those contacted via our telephone team" [Beverly Hills Supper Club Fire, May, 1977] (Lindy, Grace, and Green, 1981:475).

Behaviorally, some victims may resort to various mood-altering substances to cope with the stresses produced by the event and the restoration of their homes. But available evidence suggests that such indulgence is not excessive and may be reversed among some.

> IF1.3(H) "Rapid City, as a community, did not experience a major mental health crisis after the flood. There was no rash of attempted suicides, no line of distressed victims at the door of the mental health center, and there was not even an increase in prescriptions for tranquilizers" (Hall and Landreth, 1975:59).

> IF1.3a(H) ". . . the Three Mile Island incident did produce stress in people . . . [but these effects were] shortlived, not severe enough to manifest themselves in dramatic indicators like psychiatric admissions or suicide . . . was well within the limits of stress that occur annually in that local population from stress inducing events like the occurrence of a major holiday" (Mileti et al., 1984:89).

> IF1.3b(H) "Only 1 percent of the population had considered suicide at any time after the tornado; only 3 percent reported any increase in drink-

ing, whereas 7 percent of Xenians claimed they consumed less alcohol—
a report substantiated by the State Department of Liquor Control, which
found that the number of gallons of liquor sold in Xenia actually went
down significantly after the disaster" (Taylor, 1977:94).

In subsequent research, adverse physical health effects may be found
to follow events with certain qualities. But research designs must meet at
least quasi-experimental standards. The following conclusion illustrates this
point well and points to several potential stress effects that merit pursuit.

> IF1.4(H) "These cancer data seem to indicate that the increase in leukemia
> and lymphoma rates occurred in all three river valleys and that the rates
> for these approximately 100,000 people were about 35 percent higher
> than would be expected, starting from about 2 years after the flood. [p.
> 353] . . . When we matched the names of these residents and of the con-
> trols with names on the list of evacuees, we found no evidence of an
> association between leukemia and lymphoma and evacuation. However,
> our failure to find an association may have been due to the small numbers
> involved. [p. 354] . . . Examination of reproductive statistics for the four
> counties for 1970–77 (table 3) showed that there had been a statistically
> significant ($p < 0.01$) excess of spontaneous abortions in 1973 as compared
> with the average of the other yearly rates. Except for 1973, the year
> following the flood, the spontaneous abortion rates in these four counties
> were consistently lower than for the rest of upstate New York. [pp. 353–
> 354] . . . When names of these matched pairs were compared with names
> on the evacuation list, there was no evidence of an increased risk of
> spontaneous abortion associated with the evacuation, but again, this
> conclusion is based on small numbers [p. 354]" (Janerich *et al.*, 1981:353–
> 354).

In contrast to researchers oriented toward the pathological, investigators
must look for "positive" alterations too. Here the literature is more sparse,
although Fritz argued for such a perspective over two decades ago.

> IF1.5(H) "Disaster provides an unstructured social situation that enables
> persons and groups to perceive the possibility of introducing desired in-
> novations into the social system, [p. 685] . . . disasters . . . become col-
> lective representations or symbols by which past, present, and future
> happenings become rated and dated [p. 691]" (Fritz, 1961:685, 691). (See
> also Quarantelli and Dynes, 1972:69.)

For some, as our interview data from Topeka, Kansas, indicated clearly
(Drabek and Key, 1984), recovery from disaster may bring expanded and
more favorable views of self. To confront a challenge and conquer it does
build self-esteem.

> IF1.6(H) ". . . a sizeable number of individuals actually experienced
> positive changes in their lives or emotional functioning as a result of
> events subsequent to the flood. In the older age group, 25 (34%) reported
> that their functioning had improved on at least one item of the two scales.

Almost identical findings were evident for the younger aged group (n = 17, 33%). Thirteen of the 18 adults who were permanently relocated due to extensive flood damage directly attributed their healthier functioning to an improved living situation" (Ollendick and Hoffmann, 1982:162).

IF1.6a(H) ". . . there was an extremely low rate of severe mental illness, if any at all, as a consequence of the tornado. On the contrary, it [a study by the Disaster Research Center, Ohio State University] concluded that a large percentage of the people had *extremely positive reactions* to the disaster. Eight-four percent of the people claimed that their experiences had shown them they could handle crises better than they thought; and 69 percent reported that they felt they had met a great challenge and were better for it. A year and a half later, there were still few cases of severe pathological disturbances as a direct result of the disaster" [Xenia, Ohio; tornado; 1974] (Taylor, 1977:93).

IF1.6b(H) "Others registered the emotional impacts of the storm, but tried to find some positive things in their experiences. One Wichita Falls respondent sounded a common theme: 'It is a once in a lifetime experience and makes you place more importance on human relationships and less on material possessions.' Others frequently used the phrases, 'it brought many people closer together,' or 'we feel closer as a family.' Families and individuals can come away from experiences such as the tornadoes emotionally affected, but not necessarily in a dysfunctional sense" (Bolin, 1982:131).

Finally, and perhaps good or bad depending on one's personal views, disaster victims report increased religiosity. The only voluntary associations in our Topeka data set that registered increased participation were churches. (Drabek and Key, 1984:346–358). Others have noted parallel shifts in life orientations—materialist emphases are weakened, broader perspectives on life are reported.

IF1.7(H) "The dominant forms of coping appear to be sociable behaviors, especially talking about feelings and with family, relating to others, reading, and especially being thankful. [pp. 47–49] . . . nearly half of the people interviewed changed their level of being thankful, with almost all of them increasing their thankfulness. [p. 49] . . . people affected by the mountain are sharing their feelings, engaging in social activities, being thankful, planning for the future, and believing in God much more than they did before the May 18 eruption. Most of those increases continue through the second six month period. Very little negative behavior is evident in the responses [pp. 47–50]" (Leik *et al.*, 1982:47–50).

IF1.7a(H) "In the older aged group of adults, 86% considered themselves to be religious persons. Of the group, 17 (23%) reported that their religiosity had increased following the flood . . . Forty-five (88%) of the younger aged group considered themselves to be religious. Eleven (22%) reported that their religiosity had increased" (Ollendick and Hoffmann, 1982:162).

IF1.7b(H) "Eighty-four per cent of the reactors and 56 per cent of the non-reactors reported changes in attitude and life style after the cyclone. They had become more religious, concerned and attached to their families. Twenty-three per cent also reported withdrawal from social life and 3 per cent had become alcoholics" [Sri Lanka] (Patrick and Patrick, 1981:214).

IF2. Findings of Negative Impacts

In direct contrast to the portrait just outlined, others have emphasized the negative. A sampling of such statements conveys the tone and variations in emphasis. As indicated by the multiple citations listed, many more negative than positive findings have been reported.

IF2.1(H) "Although the literature on the subject is sparse, and research studies differ in focus and methodology, there does seem to be mounting evidence that disasters produce or influence emotional problems" (Cohen and Ahearn, 1980:36). (See also Hocking, 1965:480; Heffron, 1977b:108; Chamberlin, 1980:238.)

Among one of the more stressful events studied was a shipwreck wherein seven men survived after spending ten days at sea and three on land. Three crew mates died. Follow-up interviews 12-24 months later revealed much that was negative; yet, a glimmer of light did show through.

"Of the seven men, five have developed formal psychiatric disorders for the first time in their lives. It is equally important to note that one man claims to have benefited from the experience, seeing himself as more resourceful and having more enjoyment from his marriage and family, while the seventh is coping well with increased responsibility" [Australia] (Henderson and Bostock, 1977:18).

As noted above, the single natural disaster that has produced the most evidence of negative impacts occurred in Buffalo Creek, West Virginia, in 1972. This flash flood had many atypical qualities. It was a horrifying event that struck a population already stressed, and there was evidence of culpability. These qualities were developed brilliantly by several scholars, most especially Lifton and Olson (1976), Erikson (1976a), Titchener and Kapp (1976), and Gleser, Green, and Winget (1981, 1978). The substance of their conclusions is illustrated by the following quotations.

IF2.2(H) "The claim of 'psychic impairment' in the lawsuit against the Pittston Company, whose Buffalo Mining Company subsidiary had built the dam, was based on the effects on the survivors' psychological well-being of the flood experience itself as well as the destruction of the community. The lawsuit was settled out of court in August 1974 for 13.5 million dollars, approximately half of which was based on 'psychic impairment.' . . . The psychological impact of the disaster has been so extensive that no one in Buffalo Creek has been unaffected. The overwhelming evidence is that everyone exposed to the Buffalo Creek disaster has experienced some or all of the following manifestations of the general constellation of the survivor (Lifton, 1968,[1] pp. 479-541)'' (Lifton and Olson, 1976:1). (See also Titchener and Kapp, 1976.)

IF2.2a(H) "Some 615 survivors of the Buffalo Creek flood were examined by psychiatrists one and one-half years after the event, and 570 of them, a grim 93 percent, were found to be suffering from an identifiable emotional disturbance. [p. 58] . . . Virtually everyone on Buffalo Creek had a very close encounter with death, either because they felt doomed themselves or because they lost relatives and friends or because they came into contact with dead bodies. . . . Where one finds death on so large a scale one also finds guilt. It is one of the ironies of human life that individuals are likely to regret their own survival when others around them are killed in what seems like a meaningless and capricious way, in part because they cannot understand by what logic they came to be spared. [p. 59] . . . a second trauma, a collective trauma, followed closely on the first, immobilizing recovery efforts and bringing a number of other problems into focus [p. 61]''(Erikson, 1976c:58, 59, 61).

IF2.2b(H) "Our scaled data yield convincing evidence that the adult survivors of the Buffalo Creek disaster continued to suffer from symptoms of anxiety, depression and hostility–belligerence with social isolation, disruption of daily routine, and somatic concerns over 2 years after the disaster. These symptoms were of a severity comparable to that seen in the typical psychiatric outpatient clinic. Furthermore, individual differences in severity showed some stability over a period of 9 months despite differences in interviewers and their attendant biases, differences in the format and setting of the interviews, and differences between raters'' (Gleser, Green, and Winget, 1978:216).

Another event that stands alone in the U.S.A. disaster experience is the Three Mile Island nuclear power plant incident of March, 1979. For days, the eyes of the nation watched a complex drama unfold as various corrective actions were discussed and implemented. While official reports documented only minute radiation releases, *threat* of a serious disaster was etched in the memories of an alarmed populace. And in the months ahead, various types of surveyors sought to capture the human consequences.

IF2.3(H) "The major health effect of the accident appears to have been on the mental health of the people living in the region of Three Mile Island and of the workers at TMI. There was immediate, short-lived mental distress produced by the accident among certain groups of the general population living within 20 miles of TMI. The highest levels of distress were found among adults a) living within 5 miles of TMI, or b) with preschool children; and among teenagers a) living within 5 miles of

---

[1] R. J. Lifton, *Death in Life*. New York: Random House, 1968.

TMI, b) with preschool siblings, or c) whose families left the area. Workers at TMI experienced more distress than workers at another plant studied for comparison purposes. This distress was higher among the nonsupervisory employees and continued in the months following the accident" (President's Commission on the Accident at Three Mile Island, 1979:35). (See also Houts *et al.*, 1980:27.)

IF2.3a(H) ". . . during this [13 month] period, 33% of TMI mothers and 14% of Beaver County mothers reported one or more episodes of anxiety or depression. . . . compared to their controls, the rate of clinical episodes of depression and/or anxiety following the TMI accident was more than twice as high among TMI area mothers. When asked about events that might have triggered their disorder, more than half of the TMI mothers spontaneously mentioned the accident; none of the control mothers made this attribution" (Bromet and Dunn, 1981:13).

IF2.3b(H) [Based on a survey (n = 391) of a community within five miles of the TMI reactor conducted at two points in time, i.e., October–November, 1979, and October–November, 1980] "The findings of the study indicate that: 1) the community can be characterized as distressed at Time I and at Time II; and 2) in general, perceived threat to physical health is more highly associated with distress than personal or demographic characteristics" (Goldsteen, Schorr, and Goldsteen, 1984:369). (See also Schorr, Goldsteen, and Cortes, 1982.)

But these two events are far from the limits of the data base. Various manifestations of stress adaptations have been discovered following floods in the U.S.A. and Australia. While the range of stress effects varies, at least at the level of self-perceptions regarding their physical health, many victims have reported altered symptom patterns and persisting mental distress.

IF2.4(H) "Although there were no significant differences in the number and nature of the illnesses experienced by the flood and non-flood respondents, there were significant differences in the duration of illness and self-perceived influence of the flood on the health of the two subsamples of respondents" (Melick, 1978a:335).

IF2.4a(H) ". . . victims of the flood were assigned to various subgroups based upon their perception of stress during the recovery period. [p. 75] . . . stress arising from the flood experience is significantly associated with both mental and physical health problems measured 5 years after the flood [p. 76]" (Logue, Hansen, and Struening, 1981:75, 76). (See also Logue, Melick, and Struening, 1981:239; Logue, Hansen, and Struening, 1979:502.)

IF2.4b(H) "Study of symptomatology and surgery attendances following the Brisbane floods of the Australia Day weekend 1974 showed significant health changes in the flooded group (N = 695) as compared to non-flooded controls (N = 507). Headaches, irritability, nervous tension, depression,

worrying, fatigue, sleeplessness, and loss of weight, digestive disturbances, shortness of breath and rheumatism, were more frequent at the
0.001 level. Flooded women showed an equally significant increase in
sleeping tablet and 'nerve tablet' consumption. Significantly more males
and females rated their health temporarily and permanently worse following the flood'' [Australia] (Raphael, 1979:331). (See also Abrahams
et al., 1976:936.)

Behaviorally too, there is limited evidence that some victims will resort
to stress-reducing substances. Note how the following findings contrast
to those from Rapid City that I cited above (IF1.3). It is clear that this
entire matter needs careful follow-up so that we can get a more precise
measurement of such actions and their pattern of variability. So too does
the matter of occupational and other behavioral shifts that may be disaster-
related.

IF2.5(H) ''Tranquilizers or other sedatives were used by one-third of the
respondents in the flood group but by only 9 percent of the controls.
More than 50 percent of the flood group found alcoholic beverages helpful,
in contrast to 16 percent of the controls'' (Logue, Hansen, and Struening,
1979:498).

IF2.5a(H) ''. . . the psychic distress experienced by many of the Buffalo
Creek victims was crippling to the extent of interfering with effective
daily functioning . . . among those followed as long as 4–5 years post-
disaster, over 30% continued to suffer debilitating symptoms. . . . 30%
indicated increased alcohol consumption; 44% increased cigarette smok-
ing, and 52% increased use of prescription drugs. As expected, these
increases tended to occur in families in which the adults displayed the
more severe symptoms, particularly with regard to anxiety and depression
. . . Over three-fourths of the respondents admitted having difficulty in
getting to sleep or staying asleep during the week preceding the interview,
more than 2 years after the disaster. Approximately one-third of the respondents needed to use medication at least 'sometimes' in order to get
to sleep, and more than two-thirds 'sometimes' or 'often' had nightmares.
These percentages are very much higher than those found in general population surveys'' (Gleser, Green, and Winget, 1981:141).

IF2.5b(H) ''Surviving crewmembers may be severely affected, even to
the point that they are unwilling or psychologically unable to continue
in their occupations. [p. 159] . . . Both these flight attendants received
professional help for their mental health problems and wanted to return
to flying; both expressed fear of another accident [p. 160]'' (Duffy,
1978:159, 160).

In a similar and equally complex manner, limited data on psychiatric
admissions suggest disaster impacts. Presently, however, it is my judgment
that the complexities involved in such data analyses require that we have
additional studies like Ahearn's (1981) before we reach a firm conclusion.

Evidence of a limited nature indicating these types of delayed responses was reported following floods both in Romania and Australia.

> IF2.6(H) "Admissions did not increase in the months following the earthquake. Both Managua and the adjacent areas moved in tandem in the first months after the calamity showing only slight changes, and then recording sharp rises in the second post-disaster year. For the years 1974 and 1975, both regions significantly exceeded their estimated trend rates. On the other hand, the rural area had a sharp fall-off of admissions in the year after the earthquake, then rose strongly in 1974 before beginning a gradual decline. One may conclude, therefore, that rates of psychiatric admissions will increase for an area destroyed by a catastrophe, but not in the first post-disaster year" [Nicaragua] (Ahearn, 1981:25). (See also Ahearn and Castellón, 1978.)

> IF2.6a(H) [. . . the depressions found in the 87 patients observed were caused by the floods of May 1970. A small part of these conditions did not set in immediately but several weeks or months later, and in some even after they had managed to largely do away with material losses. One case detailed began 8 months afterwards during which time the patient (male) had built a new house for his family. [p. 113] . . . Sex differences were pronounced; 62% female, 38% male, which held in all age categories. [p. 110] [Romania] (Grecu, Csiky, and Munteanu, 1972:110, 113).

> IF2.6b(H) ". . . while the flood does not appear to have increased the number of hospital admissions or deaths, it may have affected the pattern of admissions. . . . in the case of those whose houses were severely flooded . . . the number of male admissions doubled and the number of female admissions halved. A disproportionate increase in male ill-health (though not nearly as marked as in the present study), was also found by Bennet (1970)[2] in his Bristol research, and by Abrahams et al. (1976) in Brisbane. [p. 3] . . . Although there was no overall change in total numbers of deaths in the two years, deaths from heart disease increased in statistically significant terms in the year following the flood for the whole of Lismore [p. 4]" [Australia] (Smith, Handmer, and Martin, 1980:3, 4).

As I emphasized above, most events studied have not been at the far extreme either in terms of horrification or death tolls. Buffalo Creek probably is the most extreme natural disaster studied in terms of impact ratio, i.e., scope of damage versus community size and the recovery capacity reflected by the value pattern of Appalachia. But for individuals that lose family members in a disaster, the impacts may be far different than for those whose losses are limited to material objects. This hypothesis should be pursued through a series of studies so as to extend the line of inquiry introduced by Bahr and Harvey (1979). (See also Harvey and Bahr, 1980.)

---

[2] G. Bennet, "Bristol Floods 1968, Controlled Survey of Effects on Health of Local Community Disaster". *British Medical Journal* 3 (1970):454–458.

IF2.7(H) "From interviews with 44 widows of victims of the 1972 Sunshine Mine disaster (Idaho) and comparison samples of wives of survivors
of the fire and of miners employed in other mines two types of loneliness
were identified—one (personal loneliness) referring to whether respondents felt 'very lonely and remote from other people' and the other (community underinvolvement) to whether they felt as involved in community
life as they wanted to be. The widows manifested very high levels of
personal loneliness but not of perceived community underinvolvement.
An hypothesized link between loneliness and low income did not appear,
but education was related to both kinds of loneliness [i.e., higher the
education, the lower the loneliness]. Participation in organizations seems
related to low personal loneliness. Contacts with friends and relatives,
belonging to a variety of voluntary organizations, having satisfying daily
employment, and participating in religious organizations are related to
satisfaction with level of involvement in community. Both types of loneliness are inversely related to high morale, happiness, and perceived
high quality of life among widows. [p. 367] . . . among the widows the
lonely are the ones who had such a relationship [i.e., close friendship
relationship with husband] and lost it. . . . However, feelings of underinvolvement in the community show no relation to perceived quality
of personal relationship to husband [p. 382]" (Bahr and Harvey,
1979:367, 382).

We need longitudinal designs that go far beyond the typically used one-
to two-year period. Thus, the four-year contrast made by Harvey and
Bahr is commendable—but unfortunately, exceptional. I did encounter
one study from Germany that reported ten-year follow-up interviews with
11 miners who were discovered in a chamber ten days after an initial cave-
in. They were saved four days later through a difficult and dangerous
rescue action.

IF2.8(H) Follow-up interviews ten years after the event revealed the following. (1) All but one of the survivors reported: phobias that occur in
situations which reflect the threat, bothersome crowding memories and
nightmares dealing with the threat. "Severe" for four and "moderate"
for four. (2) The symptoms are intensified in situations that trigger
thoughts of the disaster (talks, queries, the season of the disaster in Oc-
tober/November). (3) Phobias do not occur if there is particularly successful defense against fear during disaster; this was accomplished here
by hallucination or the permanent group leader position. (4) Youth at the
time of the trauma, followed by subsequent maturation of the personality,
appears to check the development of symptoms. Memories are present
but they are not bothersome. (5) Psychogenic symptoms that existed before the disaster are intensified by traumatization. [Germany] (Adapted
from Ploeger, 1974:139–142.)

Finally—and pinpointing a voluminous series of studies that I have not
reviewed—there are even longer-term follow-ups on the atomic bomb victims of Hiroshima and Nagasaki. In 1981, an English edition was published

of the massive report completed by the Committee for the Compilation
of Materials on Damage Caused by the Atomic Bombs in Hiroshima and
Nagasaki (Japanese publication, 1979). Complete integration of the
hundreds of findings culled from nearly one thousand separate studies
tabulated by the Committee was beyond the scope of my effort here, especially since the bulk of them pertained to physical and medical effects.
But there were several findings of *sociological* significance. For example,
thirty-year follow-up studies now question the continuity of trend lines
and projections made within shorter-term time frames, "shorter-term"
here referring to 15 or 20 years. These two events continue to perplex
researchers examining such social processes as marriage rates and the
plight of a unique type of secondary victim—the "orphaned elderly."

> IF2.9(H) "Contrary to Lifton's expectation (1967),[3] in the life cycle of
> thirty years since the bombing there has been, rather, a relative decrease
> in the second generation of the A-bomb survivors' community; and this
> decrease is the principal cause of the aging of that community as a whole"
> (Committee for the Compilation of Materials on Damage Caused by the
> Atomic Bombs in Hiroshima and Nagasaki, 1981:427).

> IF2.9a(H) "The 1960 national census recorded marriage rates of 60.8
> percent for males and 56.7 percent for females; the rate for married A-
> bomb victims, especially males, was higher than national levels; and
> among these, those severely affected by the bombings stand out. Ac-
> cording to R.J. Lifton's assessment of these records, 'A-bomb victims
> show a high rate of marriage and must be assumed to have given birth
> to many children' (Lifton, 1967[4])" (Committee for the Compilation of
> Materials on Damage Caused by the Atomic Bombs in Hiroshima and
> Nagasaki, 1981:424).

> IF2.9b(H) "If the results of the Ministry of Health and Welfare's 1965
> nationwide survey and national census figures for the same year are
> combined and adjusted for age composition, the nationwide [marriage]
> rate for males is 73 percent against 72.8 percent for male A-bomb victims;
> comparable figures for females are 67.4 percent against 62.7 percent.
> Victims' rates are lower generally than national rates, and particularly
> for males aged twenty-five to twenty-nine (aged five to nine at bombing
> time) and for females aged twenty to thirty-four (birth to fourteen at
> bombing time)" (Committee for the Compilation of Materials on Damage
> Caused by the Atomic Bombs in Hiroshima and Nagasaki, 1981:424–
> 425).

> IF2.10(H) "The 'orphaned elderly' were older persons who, whether or
> not they themselves were A-bomb victims, lost their spouses and children
> and thus were completely without anyone on whom to depend. Some of

---

[3] R. J. Lifton, *Death in Life—Survivors of Hiroshima*. New York: Random House, 1967.

[4] See note 3 above.

them had one or more grandchildren but no one else to rely upon; others had some surviving family members but were forced, for some reason, to live apart in the same conditions as the fully orphaned elderly. Both the quasi-orphaned and the fully orphaned came to be called the 'orphaned elderly' " (Committee for the Compilation of Materials on Damage Caused by the Atomic Bombs in Hiroshima and Nagasaki, 1981:444).

IF2.10a(H) ". . . the employment rates for men victims age seventy and over and for women victims of all ages are well above national levels . . . Here, then, is a countervailing image of some elderly A-bomb victims getting up each day and forcing their aged and sometimes infirm bodies to work in order to support themselves" (Committee for the Compilation of Materials on Damage Caused by the Atomic Bombs in Hiroshima and Nagasaki, 1981:445).

IF2.10b(H) "Of the 347 elderly persons without relatives, 158 (45.5 percent) felt their daily lives lacked any joy or pleasure; and a startling 250 (72 percent) had come to feel their lives were not worth living. Their spiritual props had fallen away, and they faced their remaining days without purpose" (Committee for the Compilation of Materials on Damage Caused by the Atomic Bombs in Hiroshima and Nagasaki, 1981:447).

While not easily separated from mental health impacts, several researchers have examined various aspects of physical health following natural disasters. While we found no such symptom shifts among the individuals surveyed three years after the Topeka tornado (Drabek and Key, 1984), other events with different victim populations and data collection procedures have registered such impacts as the following.

IF2.11(H) ". . . the respondent rated her own health and the health of every member of her immediate family at the time of the survey, using a six-point scale ranging from 1 (excellent) to 6 (very poor). Statistically significant flood versus non-flood differences were noted [p. 240] . . . flood group respondents were more likely than non-flood respondents to state that their present health status was poorer than a year ago . . . In addition, flood group respondents more frequently cited specific effects that the flood had had on their health, . . . while non-flood respondents overwhelmingly (94 percent) stated that the flood had no influence on their general health [p. 241]" (Logue, Melick, and Struening, 1981:240, 241). (See also Janney, Masuda, and Holmes, 1977:33, for parallel results in Peru following an earthquake.)

IF2.11a(H) "With respect to the respondent, statistically significant . . . flood versus non-flood differences were noted regarding severe headaches, bladder trouble, and the occurrence of at least one condition. A significant difference was noted in the incidence of hypertension for the husbands of the respondents. Finally, with respect to the entire family, a number of significant differences were noted: gastritis, frequent constipation, severe headaches, bladder trouble, disease of the bone or cartilage, conditions pertaining to the cardiovascular and digestive systems, and the

occurrence of at least one condition. In each of these cases, the flood
group experienced greater incidence rates than the non-flood group''
(Logue, Melick, and Struening, 1981:241–242). (See also Logue, Hansen,
and Struening, 1981:71, 74; Logue and Hansen, 1980:28, 32.)

IF2.11b(H) "The incidence of ulcers increased somewhat from before to
after the flood . . . For men ulcers increased from 7.6% to 8.8%, for
women they increased from 6.5% to 9.4%. . . . hypertension in the Buffalo
Creek sample showed a dramatic increase after the flood. Prior to the
flood, 5 men and 21 women had been diagnosed hypertensive; following
the flood, this increased to 19 men and 44 women" (Gleser, Green, and
Winget, 1981:69).

Finally, apart from the intensification of weather and storm consciousness that has been found in several studies (see IF1.1b), others have noted
attitude shifts of a far more negative nature. Among these are "survivor
guilt," fears of recurrence, and desires to relocate. While such negative
attitude sets have been reported, various design flaws preclude full acceptance of these conclusions until further study has been completed. For
example, in the follow-up work on the Three Mile Island nuclear power
plant incident, interviewees were queried on the anniversay date, surely
a time when community consciousness levels would be heightened. Similarly, most data from Buffalo Creek were collected within a context of
litigation. Thus, until additional studies are completed wherein these and
other methodological issues are resolved better, these findings are best
viewed as important hypotheses.

IF2.12(H) ". . . it seems not uncommon for the survivor to believe there
was an overriding reason why he survived, when others did not. Three
flight attendants who were in catastrophic accidents in which many died
expressed belief that there was some reason they were not 'taken.' In
some cases this apparently was an impetus for a change in values or goals
for the survivor. This change could cause a stress on the relative–survivor
relationship, and thus increase the possibility of social conflict for both"
(Duffy, 1978:161). (See also Miller, Turner, and Kimball, 1981:114.)

IF2.13(H) "The principal finding to be noted with regard to perceived
danger of living near a nuclear power facility is that the large majority
of residents feel that it is dangerous, although the percentage declines
over time. When asked about TMI, however, the percentages are even
higher, and they are constant over time. . . . when asked specifically
about fear of living near TMI, nearly half of the residents at Time One,
Time Two, and Time Three reported that these fears occurred fairly or
very often. [pp. 12–13] . . . An increasing proportion of the population
perceived that their chances of getting cancer have gone up due to the
TMI accident, from 39 percent six months after the accident to 58 percent
one and one-half years after the accident [p. 13]" (Schorr, Goldsteen,
and Cortes, 1982:12–13).

IF2.13a(H) ". . . public trust levels are very low for all categories of
government with the percentages saying they do not trust state and federal

officials increasing over time. The only group of officials who are significantly regaining the public trust are the local officials" (Schorr, Goldsteen, and Cortes, 1982:16).

IF2.13b(H) ". . . the average respondent has lived in this community for 17.43 years. Nearly half of the respondents would move to another house more distant from a nuclear power generating station. This figure is fairly constant at all three points in time" (Schorr, Goldsteen, and Cortes, 1982:17).

In short, if our total evidence base was limited to that contained in this single section, disasters would be viewed as bringing dire consequences for nearly all victims. But as I stressed above, other data offer a contrasting portrait. It is my judgment that elements of both are correct, depending upon a series of specifics. That is, not all disasters are the same, either as physical events or in terms of the social interpretations given to them by victimized populations of varying types. Similarly, the range of altruistic behaviors that comprise the emergent therapeutic community response of helpers—both formal and informal—may have significant consequence for longer-term victim impacts (Barton, 1962, 1969; Fritz, 1961). Thus, once again the basic taxonomic issue is evident. Let's examine some specifics.

IF3. Findings Suggesting Variation in Impact

Many investigators have offered interpretations of their results that imply a belief in differential impacts. A few have tried to explicate qualities that may have deflected the results. Buffalo Creek provides an excellent illustration.

". . . the Buffalo Creek disaster is related to certain characteristics specific to this situation: (1) . . . suddenness [p. 8] . . . The general principle, in Buffalo Creek and elsewhere, is that the suddenness and terror of a disaster intensify both its immediate and long-range human influences. (2) *The relationship of the disaster to callousness and irresponsibility of other human beings.* [p. 9] . . . (3) *The continuing relationship of survivors to the disaster.* . . . the people of Buffalo Creek for the most part still work in the mines of the company whose policies and actions led to the flood [p. 10]" (Lifton and Olson, 1976:8–10).

I formulated hypotheses that explicate eight qualities that may produce differential impacts. Future research designs must seek to establish the relative degree that these qualities define alternative parameters for generalization. A multivariate matrix should be constructed that defines the taxonomic niches into which future disasters must be classified. Depending upon in which niche a subsequent event fell, we could then better estimate long-term impacts on victims. The listing below provides a primitive specification of what such a future taxonomy of disasters might resemble. I suspect that the taxonomic qualities appropriate for establishing the limits of generalization within the recovery phase may not be the same criteria required for response or preparedness.

More theoretical work is needed along the lines initiated by Perry and Lindell (1978:108–114) when they tried to integrate findings from numerous studies of psychological impacts. They proposed three classes of variables: (1) characteristics of disaster impact: forewarning, duration, and scope of impact; (2) characteristics of the social system: level of community preparedness, presence of a disaster subculture, development of the therapeutic community, destruction of kin networks and friendship networks, the extent of property damage, and presence of institutional rehabilitation; and (3) characteristics of the individual: pre-impact psychological stability and grief reactions.

> IF3.1(H) The greater the severity of the event, the greater the long-term victim impacts. (Based on Gleser, Green, and Winget, 1981; see also Lindy and Lindy, 1981:19–20; Western and Milne, 1979:495.)

"Severity" has been defined in numerous different ways. The Buffalo Creek flood illustrates several forms of "severity," ranging from the death of loved ones to survival despite a life-threatening experience.

> "Over half the sample had lost someone at least as close to them as a dear friend, and more than a fourth had lost one or more extended family members. Indeed, one man claimed he lost 27 relatives in the flood. On the other hand, relatively few of our sample (32 or 8.4%) has lost members of their immediate family in the flood, and only 17 families were thus affected. . . . Approximately 42% of the men and 32% of the women had come close to death themselves or watched helplessly while others they knew were carried to their death" (Gleser, Green, and Winget, 1981:45).

> IF3.1a(H) "Those victims—men, women, and children—who suffered the traumatic loss of family members, relatives, and friends were more severely disturbed than those who lost only material possessions. . . . Those who barely escaped from the flood waters were more impaired psychologically than those who left well before the water reached them" (Gleser, Green, and Winget, 1981:143).

> IF3.1b(H) ". . . those directly hit reported higher levels of storm anxiety than did the comparison group. [p. 117] . . . The incidence of bad dreams is lower among the controls at both sites . . . Strong associations were found for both victim samples for two variables: the number of neighbors injured and the number of friends killed. That is, having had four or more neighbors injured, or having had a friend killed was clearly associated with reporting bad dreams [p. 118]" (Bolin, 1982:117, 118).

Thus, while complex, it is clear that event severity must be calibrated in a multidimensional manner including assumptions regarding probable recurrence (see Leik et al., 1982:43, 45; Patrick and Patrick, 1981:215), secondary consequences like increased indebtedness (Rossi et al., 1983b), and uncertainty about safety (see Goldsteen and Schorr, 1982:57). While his cases did not require these multiple dimensions, Hocking (1965:480) concluded that the "key" factor that predicted pathologies among Norwegian resistance fighters was the degree of stress experienced. He reached the same conclusion regarding 34 survivors from the crews of two ships involved in a collision and subsequent explosion. Similarly, he interpreted differential illness patterns among prisoners of war as reflective of the severity of their experiences. Thus, event severity in its many forms is a critical dimension. (See also Kinston and Rosser, 1974:446.)

> IF3.2(H) Intentional events produce greater long-term victim impacts than those attributed to accidental or non-controllable causes. (Based on Gleser, Green, and Winget, 1981.)

Although intentionality was mentioned frequently as a criterion that might differentiate among events, I did not find a single study wherein an investigator had made empirical comparisons. The closest finding was litigant versus non-litigant data from Buffalo Creek. Recovery may have been facilitated among litigants because they had taken actions designed to rectify the injustice experienced.

> IF3.2a(H) ". . . the litigants as a group displayed to a substantial degree symptoms of anxiety, depression, somatic concerns, belligerence, agitation, social isolation, and changes in their daily routine and leisure time activities. Considerable alcohol abuse was noted among the males. . . . Evidence that the litigants, who were the main source of our data, were not unique, and that the litigation was not prolonging their suffering, was obtained by a comparison of their responses to the symptom checklist and the family psychosocial disruption questionnaire with those of a small group of nonlitigants . . . nonlitigants . . . were suffering more symptomatology than litigants" (Gleser, Green, and Winget, 1981:140).

> IF3.3(H) The slower the speed of recovery and the more disruptive the process, the greater the long-term victim impacts. (Based on Erikson, 1976b.)

Erikson's (1976b) analysis of Buffalo Creek has advanced the idea of "two disasters" most forcefully. That is, many events are transcended by recovery efforts that compound the stress levels of already traumatized victims.

Of special significance are repeated relocations, especially any involving mobile homes. The following quotations are illustrative of a larger pool of similar conclusions (see Ahearn and Castellón, 1979:66; Tierney and Baisden, 1979:30; Heffron, 1977a:111; Instituut Voor Sociaal Onderzoek Van Het Nederlandse Volk Amsterdam, 1955:52; Logue, Melick, and Struening, 1981:256; and Parker, 1977:548).

> IF3.3a(H) "The greater the number of post-disaster residential moves victims make, the more likely they are to report reduced leisure, emotional 'upsets', and strains in family relations. [p. 236] . . . Negative emotional/

family impacts of disasters may be expected to persist in a significant portion (40–60%) of victim families for a year or more [p. 237]" (Bolin, 1982:236, 237).

IF3.3b(H) "Victims who were forced to live outside the canyon reportedly suffered more psycho-physiological symptoms and used more drugs than victims who could move back to the canyon following the flood" (Miller, Turner, and Kimball, 1981:115).

IF3.3c(H) ". . . having studied the evidence, it is my conviction that the total traumatic effect on the Non-Returned Evacuees was the resultant of two sets of factors: the primary impact, and the alienation from the social and physical environment to which they had become adapted. I also believe that what the Stayers *gained,* and what the Non-Returneds *missed,* was the *therapeutic effect* of being inside the post-disaster community" [Australia] (Milne, 1979:121).

IF3.4(H) The lower the recovery capacity of the community, the greater the long-term victim impacts. (Based on Drabek and Key, 1984; Erikson, 1976a.)

A future disaster taxonomy must take into account community differences if victim impacts are to be understood. As we proposed following our analysis of the Topeka tornado, while Xenia, Ohio, and Omaha, Nebraska, paralleled our study site, Buffalo Creek did not (Drabek and Key, 1984). Erikson emphasized the atypical quality of this community: ". . . the people of Buffalo Creek had to face the effects of the flood with reflexes that had already been dulled by a more chronic catastrophe, a catastrophe that is part of the Appalachian heritage" (Erikson, 1976a:132).

Despite low questionnaire response rates (52% victims and 21% controls) and the inability to control for demographic qualities, Logue, Hansen, and Struening (1981) offered a parallel interpretation regarding the long-term impacts of Hurricane Agnes.

IF3.4a(H) "More recently, however, it [the Wyoming Valley] had been subjected to high unemployment, the migration of young people to other areas offering better opportunities, and the aging of its population. It is likely that the Wyoming Valley population was less able to adapt to the flood and the changes that it caused because of the social problems the population had experienced before the flood" (Logue, Hansen, and Struening, 1981:78).

IF3.5(H) "A strong tendency of females to report emotional upset more often than males . . ." (Moore and Friedsam, 1959:138).

This conclusion has been reported by others who have combined it with educational and income variables that may act in concert. Others have reported that gender alone did not differentiate health impacts (see Smith *et al.,* 1979:137–138).

IF3.5a(H) [High-risk populations:] ". . . women with lower educational levels and incomes are high risk candidates, regardless of age, concerning their long-term health status. The group at highest risk, however, are women under 65 years with lower levels of education and income" (Logue, Melick, and Struening, 1981:261).

IF3.5b(H) [Low education levels and middle to advanced age, in particular in the case of the women, identify the stratum of greater risk of maladjustment in the long run. . . . The fact that a person is a woman, significantly predicting greater preconstituted socio-economic vulnerability and a greater degree of psychological instability prior to the impact, enhances the probability of greater maladjustment. Sex turns out to be an important discriminant in the type of response to the "extreme" environment created by the disaster.] [Italy] (Strassoldo and Pelanda, 1980–81:466).

IF3.6(H) "Positive consequences of disaster experience are also reported in studies of the elderly after the Wilkes-Barre flood, many of whom were evacuees. It was found that large numbers of the aged developed new church and club associations. Settling into new neighborhoods and/ or reestablishing ties in old ones was not problematic. Some of the evacuees had a greater number of social contacts than before (Poulshock and Cohen, 1975; Cohen and Poulshock, 1977). Although not as strongly, studies of the aged in the Omaha tornado also showed a broadening of post-impact social ties (Bell, Kara, and Batterson, 1978:79)" (Quarantelli, 1980b:140).

Unfortunately, we have contradictory results regarding age (e.g., Cohen and Ahearn, 1980:9; Kinston and Rosser, 1974:445; Smith *et al.,* 1979:139). It is not clear what might explain these. Bolin and Klenow's (1982–83) results from the Wichita Falls, Texas, tornado (1979) indicated that the elderly fare as well as, if not better, than younger victims. Conquering previous stress-producing challenges may or may not better equip the older person; the conclusion depends on which writer one selects. My personal view is to side with the potentially positive value of experience.

IF3.6a(H) "Elderly victims exhibited a lower incidence of emotional and family problems than did the younger victims. The rate of emotional recovery for the elderly was not significantly different from the comparison group in spite of the preceding finding. Both groups reported significant levels of lasting emotional effects of the storms. [p. 294] . . . the elderly can handle the stress of disasters better than those who are younger, particularly in terms of emotional coping [p. 295]" (Bolin and Klenow, 1982–83:294, 295). (See also Ollendick and Hoffmann, 1982:164–165; Kilijanek and Drabek, 1979:565; Boileau *et al.,* 1978:156.)

IF3.6b(H) "The more stress the victim has in the past experienced, the greater are the adverse effects of subsequent victimizations. The age of the victim, insofar as development of identity and maturity of moral judgment are concerned, can strongly influence the severity and duration of the effects of stress, as well as the probable behavioral responses to stressful experiences. Younger, less identity-secure victims are more susceptible to adverse effects of stress. . . . Conversion, or the 'Stockholm Syndrome,' seems unlikely when the terrorist is humiliating a mature victim and distinctly differentiating the victim as a different species of being from the captor" (Fields, 1980:83).

IF3.7(H) The duration and severity of disaster victim impacts covary with the intensity of their participation in social support systems. (Based on Fields, 1980; Henderson, 1977.)

Based on hostage studies (Fields, 1980) and one Australian disaster (Henderson, 1977), this argument can be advanced. We will pursue it further in the subsequent section of this chapter when we examine group level phenomena.

Finally, several researchers have tried to identify personality qualities that might characterize the more resilient. Two have been proposed, although evidence for neither is very solid.

IF3.8(H) The greater the degree of victim stability and internal fate control prior to a disaster, the less the long-term impacts. (Based on Anderson, 1977.)

IF3.8a(H) "Ninety entrepreneurs participated in two data collection phases over a 2½-year interval following the effects of a major disaster. Internals were found to perceive less stress, employ more task-centered coping behaviors, and employ fewer emotion-centered coping behaviors than externals. Successful internals became more internal, whereas unsuccessful externals became more external [Success was measured by pre-flood and post-flood business credit ratings.]" (Anderson, 1977:446). (See also Thurber, 1977:160.)

IF3.8b(H) ". . . another at-risk group . . . includes those who, at the time of the disaster, were experiencing certain life crises. Members of this group might include, for example, people who have recently been widowed or divorced and those who have recently undergone major surgery" (Cohen and Ahearn, 1980:10).

IF3.8c(H) [Persons reporting higher pre-disaster levels of psychological instability] ". . . report more intense psychosomatic symptoms 2 years after the impact" [Italy] (Pelanda, 1979:2). (See also Cattarinussi et al., 1981:149; Strassoldo and Pelanda, 1980–81:456.)

Those who were hospitalized because of mental disorders prior to a disaster present a mixed picture, although data are most limited. The following two findings serve only to place the matter on the research agenda.

IF3.8d(H) "They [psychiatrists] observed varieties and intensities of anxiety from acute panic to apparent indifference. They saw regressive phenomena as well as evidences of progress. For most patients, this cataclysmic event resulted in an eventual deepening and enrichening of the therapeutic experience'' [Los Angeles earthquake; February 9, 1971] (Greenson and Mintz, 1972:7).

IF3.8e(H) ''. . . favourable evolutions were more frequent in patients without previous psychiatric disorders, the differences being statistically significant in the group of the improved cases. Likewise, the number of the worsened cases was bigger in the patients with previous psychiatric disorders, without being, however, statistically significant. [p. 186] . . . The most frequent postseismic [1½ years later] pathological reactions were anxiety reactions, reactive depression, phobic-obsessive reactions, psychotic reactions (confusional, manic, paranoid) being encountered only in a small number of cases. [p. 188]'' [302 total (166 with previous psychic disorders; 136 who were assumed to have been healthy prior to 1977 earthquake in Romania which left 1,570 dead and 11,300 injured)] [Romania] (Predescu and Nica-Udangiu, 1979:186, 188).

These eight clusters of variables reflect qualities of differentiation. Hopefully, the coming decade will bring extended taxonomic work, theoretical multivariate modeling, plus field studies using comparative designs. Only through such efforts can we extend our level of understanding.

IF4. Children as Victims

Three decades ago Perry, Silber, and Black (1956) emphasized the resiliency of children caught in disaster, especially if their families were strong and remained a source of social support. Thus, the overall portrait many accepted might parallel the following.

IF4.1(H) ''The general conclusion is that children rarely need specialist psychiatric treatment but that they do benefit from an opportunity to ventilate their anxieties to a sympathetic adult. Those most at risk are between 8 and 12 yr, have a previous history of physical or emotional illness, and come from unstable homes'' [based on extensive literature review.] (Kinston and Rosser, 1974:445).

But about the middle of the 1970s the tone began to change as researchers began to scrutinize the matter more carefully. Certain elements, especially fears of subsequent events and sleep disturbances, began to be reported.

IF4.2(H) ''Although a variety of emotional and mental health disturbances in children have been reported following disasters, the most prominent seem to be phobias concerning the natural elements and future disasters, sleep disturbances, and a lack of personal responsibility'' (Frederick, 1977:47). (See also Newman, 1976:312; Howard, 1980:190.)

IF4.2a(H) ''For the total group of children then, 34 to 54 (63%) had temporary problems, while 23 to 54 (43%) had continued problems [e.g., fears, sleeping problems, etc.]'' (Ollendick and Hoffmann, 1982:164).

IF4.2b(H) "Separation anxiety refers to fears the children have of being away from home during cloudy/stormy weather. In Wichita Falls both victim and control families with children report separation anxieties at relatively high, but declining rates. Victim rates were apparently 25% higher and showed a smaller decline at Time 2, indicating a relatively persistent phenomenon. In Vernon rates are similar to those in Wichita Falls but, as with other measures, both victims and controls have increasing rates" (Bolin, 1982:120–121).

IF4.3(H) ". . . the worst effects of disaster occur when there is separation from or loss of parents, when the children's parents themselves have major (often preexisting) psychological problems, or when there are other anxiety-creating factors in their backgrounds (e.g., child abuse or parental alcoholism)" (Singer, 1982:247).

This hypothesis has been mentioned by several other writers (e.g., Boyd, 1981:747). Severe consequences of parental separation were documented following the earthquake in Skopje, Yugoslavia (1963).

[632 children (aged 6–16) from 20 elementary schools were placed into three homes that were visited by a psychiatric team 5–7 months afterwards. Nearly one-fourth (24%) of the children had changed homes 3, 4 or more times following the earthquake. The formal reason for such a long separation was the demolished condition of houses and apartments which were unusable; only 5% lost both parents in the quake. Most children, of course, never left their parents or if so, the separation was brief but these children remained institutionalized months afterwards with episodic parental visits. The children evidenced a variety of reactions that were interpreted as 'defensive' by the 4 member psychiatric team, e.g., a fear of hunger, most probably a synonym of a fear of emotional hunger— of abandonment. The children were allowed to eat all they wanted but frequently carried bread away and hid it under their pillows. Destructiveness was another reaction. It was an epidemic in the Crikvenica home where children broke electric plugs, destroyed furniture and removed 700 window catches. . . . Based on various psychological testings, the authors concluded that 69% of the children had psychological disturbances . . . The authors concluded that changing homes, especially more than once had a significant impact on the occurrence of the disturbances, *rather than* the children's presence in Skopje during the earthquake. . . . But "place changes" probably caused the occurrence of insecurity and the feelings of rejection. Every change of institution brought the children close to the point of panic—they expressed fear that they would again lose their parents.] [Yugoslavia] (Moric-Petrovic, Jojic-Milenkovic, and Marinkov, 1972:53–64).

Far less pathology was reported among older children in Italy who had been evacuated from earthquake areas (Boileau *et al.*, 1978:226). Yet, fears remained. Hopefully, the coming decade will provide more insight into these processes and strategies of mitigation.

IF5. Secondary Victims

As noted previously, rescuers and family members of victims are impacted by disasters. Like personnel in emergency organizations—a topic that will be noted later (Section IIIF5)—such individuals constitute a portion of the "hidden victims" of disaster. Unfortunately, we know little about such impacts but I decided to form this separate section so as to highlight this topic as a research need.

> IF5.1(H) ". . . following a rail disaster in Sydney, Australia, . . . January . . . 1977, in which 83 people were killed . . . follow-up study was performed 15 to 18 months later to assess the level of functioning of the bereaved relatives. . . . They included 15 widows, nine widowers, 11 mothers, and eight fathers who had lost children. The trends were for the bereaved spouses to have done better than bereaved parents; the widowers to have done better than the widows; those with a supportive network to have done better than those without one; those who saw the body to have done better than those who did not; and, in addition, there was a tendency for those who had bereavement counseling to do better than those who had no such intervention" [Australia] (Singh and Raphael, 1981:203).

> IF5.2(H) [Random sample of 124 adults, interviewed eight months after Rochester, Minnesota, flood.] "A total of 68% of the sample reported they were at least somewhat more depressed after the flood than before" (Ollendick and Hoffmann, 1982:161).

IF6. Treatment Orientations

What treatment modalities and orientations are appropriate for disaster victims? Obviously, such a question is beyond the scope of this book. Those responsible for such would do well to consult a handbook like the one prepared by Cohen and Ahearn (1980). But we do have a few findings that ought to be pursued so as to better arm those with these responsibilities.

> IF6.1(H) Victim social networks should be maintained to the greatest extent possible. (Based on McBride, 1979.)

> IF6.2(H) Disaster victims should not be defined as mentally ill or in need of psychotherapy. (See Peter McDonald, 1979:132; Okura, 1975:143.)

Some researchers—for example, Maley (1974)—reacted strongly to analyses of victim survivor guilt. But opinions aside, relevant data were very scarce among the documents captured in my review.

> "It's not merely that I object to such theories, perhaps the more important problem is the effect such language has on the behavior of professional intervention strategists. For example, the concept of 'survivor guilt' as

an explanation of increasing numbers of car accidents following disasters is probably wrong, but more important is the problem that the concept implies psychoanalytic treatment is needed and this is nonsense" (Maley, 1974:75).

IF6.2a(H) ". . . 147 survivors or approximately 6%, responded to several different outreach methods and could be differentiated with regard to their degree of risk at the fire and their impairment levels one year later. Of these, 51, or one-third, were at continuing risk for long-term psychological impairment one year following the fire. Continuing risk was defined as exposure to severe threat to life or bereavement *and* moderate to severe impairment on a quantified interview scale (the Psychiatric Evaluation Form, Endicott and Spitzer) one year after the fire. . . . 24, or one-half of the continuing high-risk survivors elected psychotherapy. Those choosing psychotherapy were markedly improved two years following the fire on the basis of standardized measures (SCL-90, PEF). Those not choosing therapy also improved, but to a lesser extent" [Beverly Hills Supper Club fire, Kentucky, 1977] (Lindy and Lindy, 1981:19). (See also Sank, 1979:337.)

Looking back over this voluminous collection of rather inconsistent findings, it seems as if little progress has been made. Yet, when I recall the near void that this area represented just a decade ago, I am encouraged. Indeed, it may well be that the taxonomic requirements required to order this mixture of discrepant findings will provide a model for the other response phases.

IIF. Group System Level

While the number of new studies focused on this niche of our taxonomy of system responses remains relatively small, the past decade has extended our data base and theoretical understanding a great deal. All of the studies are restricted to family groups, however. Although highly interrelated, three topics convey the central lessons learned to date: (1) disaster impacts on family functioning; (2) alterations in recovery capacity; and (3) correlates of family adjustment.

IIF1. Disaster Impacts on Family Functioning

IIF1.1 [Families tend to develop greater internal solidarity: Not only does the family unit become stronger from the trials of natural catastrophes but solidarity is also extended to friends and relatives.] [Italy] (Boileau *et al.,* 1978:155). (See also Fritz, 1961:687; Bates *et al.,* 1963; Crawford, 1957.)

Several studies have reported similar conclusions. As a *general pattern,* I suspect it will continue to be verified in future studies. But many complications emerge when the topic is pursued. First, it is clear that there are important exceptions—the response is not uniform among all families, although we are just getting to the point of having some useful *hypotheses* that might inform future studies on the matter. Second, concepts like internal solidarity are complex and not unidimensional; the patterns of adaptation are multiple and not inherently consistent. Thus, the following conclusions should be pursued as hypotheses so that we can penetrate this adaptive mode far more extensively.

> IIF1.1a(H) ". . . internal family life among victims appeared altered only slightly. However, three trends emerged: (1) victims tended somewhat more frequently to rate their marriages as less happy than did controls; (2) husbands and wives in victim families tended to go out together without their children more frequently than did controls; and (3) victim respondents more often spent their evenings at home than did controls, but were no different regarding weekend time spent together. Thus, there appeared to be some signs of 'pulling-in'— of altered interaction patterns reflecting a 'tighter' family group" (Drabek and Key, 1972:101).

> IIF1.1b(H) ". . . all four sets of respondents were asked during the Time 2 interviewing if they thought family ties were strengthened during hard times. For all the samples, 90% or more of each answered in the affirmative. This indicates, if nothing else, that many of those queried feel that family ties *should* be strengthened by adversity. These data, however, show lingering disruptive effects that fail to support this normative sentiment at least for a portion of the victim samples. . . . the effects of heavy disaster impacts may be observed in the Wichita Falls victims; there, 11% more high damage victims reported family strains. It is important to note that even a year and a half after the disaster, 50% of the victims with high losses reported family strains" (Bolin, 1982:112).

Separate from internal or nuclear family bonding is the matter of relationships with kin. As noted above (i.e., IIF1.1), many investigators have included this observation in general comments regarding social solidarity. Based on these, and the overall quality of the Topeka, Kansas (e.g., Drabek and Key, 1984) and Wichita Falls, Texas (Bolin, 1982) data sets, I regard this conclusion as firm, at least *for these types of events and victim populations*. That is, it holds when victims: (1) experience physical damage from which recovery is rapid; (2) have kin who comprise an important facet of an extensive emergent therapeutic community response; and (3) reside in communities with high stability.

> IIF1.2 "*Kin linkages,* however, *were changed.* Most affected were victim perceptions of relatives as resources to be used when future family problems or money problems might occur. While shifts in interactional and exchange transaction data were inconsistent, the overall pattern was clear. *These bonds were much tighter*" (Drabek and Key, 1984:367). (See also Drabek *et al.,* 1975:481.)

> IIF1.2a "In Vernon and in Wichita Falls the high-damage group has the highest rate of increase in visitation [with kin]. This reflects the help

offered by kin to victims. This increase in contact continued to the 8-month point, a time when most families were relatively well recovered" (Bolin, 1982:105).

IIF1.2b "Apparently a response to widowhood among these women was a reestablishment and strengthening of ties to relatives . . . a modest increase in kinship interaction for the widows, an increase more notable because they were slightly less likely than women in the other groups to have close relatives living nearby" (Harvey and Bahr, 1980:45).

Also distinct from adaptations within the nuclear family are tentacles extending to friends and neighbors. Here the existing data are less clear. In part, as I will pursue below, this may be because of multiple and simultaneous adaptations occurring among victim families with differing social characteristics. It appears that links to friends may be tightened just a bit, while those with neighbors are weakened. In the Kansas data, our sample size allowed us to control for relocation and the pattern persisted. Thus, the slight weakening in neighbor bonds was not due totally, although it was in part, to relocation. It also occurred among those who did not move from their homes following the tornado (see Drabek and Key, 1984:310–342).

IIF1.3(H) "Regardless of their socioeconomic status, a slightly larger proportion of *families victimized by the tornado had tighter linkages to groups of friends. . . . bonds to neighbors were weakened*" (Drabek and Key, 1984:367). (See also Drabek and Key, 1976:96–99; Horige and Oura, 1979.)

IIF1.3a(H) "Visitation frequencies remain unchanged for both victims and controls when measured one year after impact. [p. 102] . . . Vernon victims in the high damage (i.e., home 100% destroyed) category exhibited an increase in visitation frequencies with friends, while those in the lower damage category did not. In Wichita Falls . . . High damage victims, on the other hand, show a steady increase in visitation frequencies [p. 104]" (Bolin, 1982:102, 104).

For those who are widowed, this process has several important variations. Linkages to friends and neighbors become part of the overall struggle to maintain the social status of the family unit. Yet, as singles, many now find their presence among married couples as problematic. Findings from the Idaho mine widows that I discussed above (see IF2.7) and Shamgar-Handelman's (1983) study of Israeli war widows are very revealing. They recast this conclusion regarding heightened bonding, and thereby illustrate my next point—the idea of differential adaptation.

IIF1.3b(H) "Change in friends among the widows was far more frequent than the expected rate noted above: almost half of them (48 percent) said their group of friends had changed since the fire. . . . The primary reason given was not that their friends have moved or that they have been lost in the fire, but rather that they no longer saw their married friends any-more'' (Harvey and Bahr, 1980:47).

IIF1.3c(H) [Israeli war widows used three methods to curb the erosion in status formerly accorded them through their late husband.] ''None of them succeeded in preventing erosion in the status of the widow and her family. Over time, the place of the family within the various social groups and categories to which it had belonged was lost, due to the weakened position of the widow in her social network. [p. 153] . . . This study revealed three patterns of attempts to construct a substitute status [p. 156] [(1) adopting the new status of war widow; (2) preservation of former family status; and (3) construction of a self-achieved status (pp. 156–169)]'' [Israel] (Shamgar-Handelman, 1983:153, 156–169).

Finally, family integration within more secondary types of associations requires further study. Reflecting the general concept of ''solidarity,'' it is clear from the Kansas data, at least, that there are important, and per-haps patterned, *differential adaptations*. Family linkages to religious or-ganizations may be increased at the expense of others.

IIF1.4(H) ''There was *a slight deterioration in their participation* in a wide variety of *social and civic groups,* ranging from lodges and fraternal organizations, to hobby groups and those oriented toward political action. Only tentacles leading to one type of voluntary association seemed un-touched. Indeed, it—*the church*— *appeared to have become more central.* More victims reported church affiliation; and among those indicating membership, victims reported more frequent attendance. Thus, their linkages to external groups were altered both positively and negatively'' (Drabek and Key, 1984:367).

Again, the study of the Idaho Sunshine Mine widows provides an im-portant contrast, both regarding their participation in voluntary organi-zations and their church involvements.

IIF1.4a(H) ''In every case but two, widows' rates for organizational af-filiation are slightly higher than those for the survivors' wives''(Harvey and Bahr, 1980:53).

IIF1.4b(H) ''The influence of the disaster both to increase and to decrease church attendance parallels its influence on perceptions of the importance of religion in the women's lives. . . . while the widows attend church more frequently than the other women, a substantial number of them (30 percent) say that since the disaster they attend church less than formerly. On the other hand, both among the widows and the survivors' wives a sizeable proportion (between one sixth and one fifth) report that they attend church more frequently now than they did before the disas-ter''(Harvey and Bahr, 1980:62).

There were two additional ideas that merit follow-up. First, the matter of potential shifts in perceptions of and commitment to establishing a family ought to be examined. Following a disaster in Cyprus from which recovery was very slow, Loizos (1977) observed important shifts in attitudes toward marriage. To my knowledge, no investigator has ever examined potential impacts of this type on other cultures.

> IIF1.5(H) ". . . the meaning of marriage had changed. Previously to marry was a sober decision crowning years of educational and economic investment in a stable future; it now approached more closely an act [of] desperation—a short-term seeking for self-esteem in an uncertain world" [Cyprus] (Loizos, 1977:235).

Equally important are the insights from research on families stressed by Mount St. Helens. Using detailed interviews and a new "stress graph methodology," a team from the University of Minnesota Family Study Center documented important inconsistencies among family members. These data suggest that households wherein teenagers reside constitute variable social worlds. Thus, the dynamics of family life may well require far more precise dissection than heretofore has been done by those examining disaster impacts.

> IIF1.6(H) ". . . results consistently show evidence of stress due to a considerable amount of negative experience with Mt. St. Helens. In contrast, both experience and stress vary within families, across families in the same location, and across locations. It is by no means evident that there is a single theoretical explanation behind the diversity of relationships between experiences, stress levels and decisions. . . . Husbands, wives and teenagers did not perceive or react to the threat of the volcano in the same way" (Leik et al., 1982:151).

IIF2. Alterations in Family Recovery Capacity

Limited evidence suggests an increased recovery capacity for many victim families. To date, however, neither this complex concept nor appropriate data have been pursued sufficiently to give us firm conclusions. The most thorough work is Bolin's (1982:210–234) path modeling based on data from the Wichita Falls, Texas, tornado; this effort extended his earlier study of Rapid City and Nicaragua families (e.g., Bolin and Trainer, 1978).

Among the many dimensions of family recovery capacity that have been examined are insurance and house quality. Limited evidence indicates that disaster victims tend to increase their protection in the latter months of the recovery period by expanding their insurance coverage. While income differentials remain, the pattern has been found among victim families within both higher- and lower-income samples.

> IIF2.1(H) ". . . disaster victims increased life insurance purchases after the disaster. . . . Prior to the flood the average family had $2,800 in cash value [insurance] while two years later that amount had risen to $4,000" (Vinso, 1977:211). (See also Drabek and Key, 1984:115–116.)

Both perceptually and based on various more objective measures of household quality, many victim families come out ahead. For example, interview data contain many references to planned repairs or remodeling dreams that were made possible by insurance settlements (e.g., see Drabek and Key, 1984:386). While far from uniform—obviously many victim families are left worse off—this pattern appears in the literature with enough frequency that it ought to comprise the basis of a systematic study.

> IIF2.2(H) Improved housing quality—both objectively and perceptually—will be gained by varying proportions of disaster victims.

> IIF2.2a(H) "For a great part of the households the new permanent dwelling offered an improved standard of living" [after landslide in Tuve] [Sweden] (Bjorklund, 1981:11).

> IIF2.2b(H) ". . . two years after the completion of housing for hurricane victims in Honduras . . . ninety percent or more of the housing recipients found their house, location, and neighborhood equal or better than their pre-disaster situation. In Comparison Project I, the exception, fifteen percent felt the location was less satisfactory and thirty-seven percent felt the house was less satisfactory" [Honduras] (Snarr and Brown, 1978:249).

But there may be a latent consequence that few researchers have examined. With improved housing may come expanded indebtedness. In part, this may reflect purchases of household goods on credit. But more costly may be the indebtedness incurred through refinancing packages or replacement home loans. The national disaster victim survey completed by Rossi and his associates (1983b:9-10) documented this as a general pattern, thereby validating Vinso's (1977) pioneering work.

> IIF2.3(H) ". . . two years later the level of assets for this average household had not only returned to preflood level but in fact was higher. Debt, on the other hand, had also increased. . . . After two years the debt to equity ratio was 0.36 and the debt 26% of total assets. Not only were these levels very much higher than desired by the households (as compared to preflood levels) but, in fact, were even higher than the households experienced *after* the disaster but before recovery" (Vinso, 1977:213).

IIF3. Correlates of Family Adjustment

Why do some families emerge from the ruins of a disaster as winners and others appear to be devastated? A complete answer is lacking but several important hypotheses have been explored. Also, disaster studies are now being integrated with those focused on other sources of family stress (e.g., McCubbin, Olson, and Patterson, 1983; Bolin, 1982:11–16; Drabek and Key, 1984:19–27). This more theoretical orientation appears to offer much potential.

IIF3.1 "Victims with heavy losses are more likely to experience a decrease in neighboring than are moderate loss victims. Victims with heavy
losses are the most likely to experience post-disaster increase in visitation
frequencies with kin, reflecting a primary group support response" (Bolin,
1982:236).

Thus, degree of loss *as experienced at the microsystem* level appears
to be crucial. Disasters may differ dramatically in the degree of concentration and dispersal of damages. When measured at the community system
level, a cluster of events may appear to be very similar, but when viewed
from the vantage point of the microsystem impacted, they may vary considerably. This is especially true regarding the matter of relocation. Thus,
related to, but not totally a function of, the extent of damage, families
will experience an event differently depending upon the number and types
of relocations experienced. Recall Erikson's (1976a) "two disaster theory"
and the impacts attributed to life in temporary housing units, especially
mobile home parks, that I summarized above (see IF3.3).

IIF3.1a(H) "In both sites, the public provision of temporary housing offered low-rent shelter in the early months. However, in both cities the
solution provided also created further disruption to social networks and
in the daily activities of persons actually living in these settlements. In
some ways these programs retarded the reintegration of families into established neighborhoods" [U.S.A. and Nicaragua] (Trainer and Bolin,
1977:55).

IIF3.1b(H) "Most of the families had not one, but several temporary
homes and during the time of temporary housing the 58 households lived
in a total of 175 homes. The main reason for the frequent moves was
that families were not satisfied with the accommodation they were offered
and they moved as soon as something better could be arranged" [Sweden]
(Bjorklund, 1981:10).

Beyond event qualities, and such secondary effects as relocation, limited
evidence indicates important differential modes of adjustment. Based on
cross-cultural comparison, Bolin and Trainer (1978:237) proposed that at
least three recovery modes could be differentiated: (1) autonomous; (2)
kinship; and (3) institutional. Not all families will select the same pathways
for recovery. There are important variations within a population of families
within a single community regarding longer-term impacts or adaptations.
These are constrained by qualities of age, social class, and other such
social differentiators. But to date, we have just begun to penetrate the
area with enough depth to grasp the complex mazeway of differential adaptation.

IIF3.2(H) ". . . we identified evidence suggesting differential modes of
adaptation. . . . Reflecting differences in their developmental cycles or
constraints stemming from ethnic discrimination and income availability,
the tentacle selected may vary. . . . while some will retract a bit from

neighbors and focus their time in activities with members of their immediate family, others will seek tighter bondings with friendship groups''
(Drabek and Key, 1984:374).

IIF3.3(H) "Elderly victims, [rural victims and large families] will tend
to score lower on economic recovery indices than other victims" (Bolin,
1982:240). (See also Crawford, 1957:290; Bell, Kara, and Batterson,
1978:76–77; Instituut Voor Sociaal Onderzoek Van Het Nederlandse Volk
Amsterdam, 1955.)

IIF3.3a(H) "The more traditional the family, the more disruptive the
effects of these processes [i.e., public agency intervention in disaster
relief] on the family-leader's self-image" [Italy] (Pelanda, 1979:3).

IIF3.3b(H) "The victim of a catastrophe recovers fastest from an accident
if he lives in a family, meaning that he shares responsibility for other
family members, and if he has kept his job. Landholding—that is, attachment to one's house and ground—is a powerful motive for reconstruction. Younger persons, on the contrary, who have no household of
their own, feel more caught in a state of flux. They still have a greater
range of choices open. After a certain age threshold (pensioned status),
willingness to get involved in reconstruction decreases" [Italy] (Geipel,
1982:78).

IIF3.3c(H) "Because of the importance of the loans [SBA] in allowing
victims to reconstruct their homes, these problems were associated both
with emotional stresses and housing recovery delays. The poor and the
elderly could not qualify for SBA loans and, as a consequence, were
denied an important recovery resource" (Bolin, 1985:712).

Beyond these types of qualities, one feature has been proposed as critical—that is, pre-stress solidarity. Families that were strongest prior to
such stresses as war-caused separations or unemployment appear to fare
best. So too, there is limited evidence indicating that families evidencing
the highest degree of internal solidarity before a disaster better readjust
afterwards.

IIF3.4(H) ". . . persons from families which are relatively intact have
better chances to get adjusted than evacuees who are not together with
their whole family at their evacuation address" (Instituut Voor Sociaal
Onderzoek Van Het Nederlandse Volk Amsterdam, 1955 (Vol. IV):50).

Similarly, this quality of pre-stress integration may extend to external
family relationships as well. Those who have built linkages to other social
groupings—be they relatives or friends—appear to be better able to meet
the demands of a disaster, receive more aid via these pathways, and register even stronger linkage patterns in the years following.

IIF3.5(H) ". . . *these data provide considerable support to the therapeutic
community hypothesis.* . . . Those who had received help from friends
or relatives were far less alienated, had better self perceptions about

their health, rated their marriages happier, and more frequently participated in both friendship and neighbor groups, voluntary associations,
and their churches. [p. 377] . . . those whose recovery from this tornado
was facilitated through larger numbers of help sources, three years afterwards reported intensified social solidarity. For the most part, both
their *personal and their social systems appeared to have been strengthened by the experience* [p. 379]'' (Drabek and Key, 1984:377, 379). (See
also Instituut Voor Sociaal Onderzoek Van Het Nederlandse Volk Amsterdam, 1955.)

While my search procedures did not identify more than a few of the
studies pertaining to the family impacts of the Viet Nam War, there is an
important stream of work that is relevant to this theme of differential adaptation to stress. For example, McCubbin and several colleagues at the
Center for Prisoner of War Studies (University of Minnesota and the University of Wisconsin-Madison) have extended Hill's earlier analyses which
were based largely on the trauma produced by World War II.

> "The underlying hypothesis for this investigation was that when a family
> is called upon to adapt to the absence of a husband/father listed as missing
> or a prisoner of war, the occurrence of family role changes and hardships
> (in the broadest sense) can be anticipated as part of the natural history
> of the situation.
>
> The length of absence of these men extended from less than one year
> to over nine years. One hundred thirty-nine (64.6 percent) of these ab-
> sences were extended over a period of three to six years'' (McCubbin,
> Olson, and Patterson, 1983:77).
>
> IIF3.6(H) ''In examining the interaction of family resources and percep-
> tion through the study of family coping, we begin to identify a range of
> factors which families found beneficial to them in managing the crisis
> and working towards adjustment. The family's adaptive resources iden-
> tified in this longitudinal study were (a) self-reliance and self-esteem, (b)
> family integration, (c) social support, (d) social action, and (e) collective
> group supports. The factors associated with the family's perception and
> meaning were (a) religious beliefs, (b) the ability to redefine the hardships,
> and (c) endowing the situation with meaning'' (McCubbin, Olson, and
> Patterson, 1983:87).
>
> IIF3.6a(H) ''Time, interacting with circumstances, appeared to have a
> profound impact on the family system and its members. In our initial
> interviews conducted in 1972 and 1973, we found changes in wives' as-
> sessments of their marriages. The majority (79.8 percent) of the wives
> in retrospective assessments of their marriages prior to their husbands'
> casualty (loss or capture), rated their marriages as being either satisfactory
> or very satisfactory. In contrast, less than half of the group (44.2 percent)
> felt the same degree of satisfaction with their marriages at the time of
> the follow-up interviews.
>
> Wives, functioning in the role as head of the household, appeared also
> to mature and become more independent and self-confident'' (McCubbin,
> Olson, and Patterson, 1983:78–79).

Carrying this framework to a more specific level of analysis, Boss (1983) examined the matter of ambiguity in family boundary, as evidenced by "missing-in-action" spouses. The point is that "psychological father presence" (PFP)—or absence—is a behavioral reality that may yield significantly different consequences depending upon the interpretations given by family members. Father absence resulting from war-caused death or detention may not parallel the consequences of divorce, for example, or death caused by a flood or hurricane. Yet, there may be some consistencies in coping processes. As Boss points out so well, we really don't know at the present time; and can't know until these types of juxtapositions are made carefully. Her work with families who either had a member "missing-in-action" or were divorced or separated produced several insightful hypotheses that she hopes to pursue through comparisons to other situations that remove a family member—like incarceration.

> IIF3.7(H) "Keeping an absent parent psychologically present is more directly dysfunctional for the spouse than it is for the children in the family. That is, the spouse may be able to perform family role responsibilities even though she is personally preoccupied and psychologically involved with her missing spouse. Thus family functioning is not always in congruence with the psychological health of the remaining spouse" (Boss, 1983:71).

> IIF3.7a(H) "Coping strategies used by various populations experiencing separation will fall into both individual and group (family) variables. It is proposed that both individual psychological and group variables will be significant predictors of families who are coping in situations of father absence. Specifically, it is proposed that both a development of independence/self sufficiency in the remaining spouse and family cohesiveness are necessary for family functioning under the stress of family separation. It is in fact a dialectical balance between family and individual strategies that makes for successful family coping under stress of separation" (Boss, 1983:71).

IIIF. Organizational System Level

As with the other two system levels we have reviewed thus far within the reconstruction period, the research base regarding organizations has been extended beyond that summarized in our earlier review (Mileti, Drabek, and Haas, 1975:135–136). While progress has been made, however, it has been far less than what we have seen above. I grouped the findings into five categories so as to accent the directions that have been explored with the hope that others will pursue each of these in the decade ahead. The topics are: (1) organizational change: global patterns; (2) organizational change: adoption of innovations; (3) organizational change: image alterations; (4) emergent organizations; and (5) mental health needs assessments and impacts.

IIIF1. Organizational Change: Global Patterns

Based on field reports that had been gathered since the 1950s, as well as those produced at the then newly formed Disaster Research Center, Quarantelli and Dynes offered the following ideas. To date, however, no research has been completed linking any of these potential "problems" to specific rates or types of changes in organizational structures.

> IIIF1.1(H) "Disaster creates unanticipated organizational change due to increase in organizational personnel, which in turn precipitates problems of: (1) planning for new tasks; (2) interorganizational communication; (3) authority relationships; (4) decision-making; (5) definition of organizational boundaries (Quarantelli and Dynes, 1967)" (as summarized in Mileti, Drabek, and Haas, 1975:136).

Anderson's (1970a) detailed assessment of organizational shifts following the 1964 Alaskan earthquake remains the most helpful theoretical inquiry regarding global structural changes in emergency organizations. His augmentation of this analysis by using data from three other disasters has laid the groundwork (Anderson, 1972). Hopefully, the coming decade will bring other researchers who will pursue the line of inquiry he initiated so that these hypotheses can be validated, qualified, or perhaps reformulated with greater precision.

> IIIF1.2(H) "In several organizations the disaster generated new patterns of change and in others it merely accelerated pre-existing patterns" (Anderson, 1970a:96).

> IIIF1.2a(H) "Long-term change seems not to have occurred in organizations that did not have to adapt to a new set of environmental circumstances, or when potential changes were of low priority in relation to other organizational concerns" (Anderson, 1970a:96).

> IIIF1.2b(H) "Conditions under which maximum disaster-related long-term change occurred in an organization seemed to be as follows: (1) a number of changes were planned in the organization or were in the process of being realized when the disaster occurred, and these changes became more relevant because of the disaster; (2) new strains were generated or old ones were made more critical by the disaster; (3) the organization experienced so great an alteration in its relation to its environment that new demands were placed on it; (4) alternative organizational procedures and norms were suggested by the disaster experience; and (5) increased external support was given to the organization following the disaster" (Anderson, 1970a:115).

While Anderson focused exclusively on change patterns within public emergency response organizations, they are but one segment of the universe that could be impacted. Work like that of Douty (1977) points to an entire range of organizational units that have yet to receive much attention from the disaster research community.

IIIF1.3(H) "The conditions produced by the earthquake do not seem to have affected the organizational structure of the labor market. The splitting of the City Front Federation may have been a result of the disaster, but this cannot be said with certainty. Even more tenuous is the connection of the disaster with the demise of the Carmen's union. As noted above, several unions did not survive the earthquake, due chiefly to the displacement of the employees concerned" (Douty, 1977:260).

One of Geipel's students—Rudolf Stagl—based his Master's thesis project on 95 interviews with planners in 45 of the communities most affected in the Friuli earthquakes (1976) (see Geipel, 1982:163–164). His results illustrate a broad range of questions regarding the consequences of the recovery process on the perceptions of organizational personnel. The planners he interviewed perceived that certain groups, like industry and families who owned several homes that could be rented, profited from the earthquake. The elderly and those who fell through the cracks of the relief network were *perceived* as "disadvantaged." Thus, both structural as well as perceptual organizational characteristics have been identified as changing because of disaster.

IIIF2. Organizational Change: Adoption of Innovations

This topic, like the one that follows, is implicit in Anderson's work, but it reflects a type of narrowing in focus. This increased specificity seems to me necessary in order to deal with measurement problems. Thus, what we really need are a series of studies directed at several such potential impacts that are, as these studies illustrate, integrated both with general organizational theory and various structural features of the organizations selected for study.

Case materials like those offered by Forrest (1979) can be used for data sources.

"Hurricane Betsy had a strong impact upon the long-term operational adjustments of the organizations [p. 125] . . . the likelihood that organizations will make these changes may be dependent upon whether their communities are faced with recurrent threats. [p. 130] . . . [Among the many specific organizational changes documented were: 1.] *Civil Defense:* . . . the addition of new personnel, the relocation of an official, and the adoption of an emergent organizational structure which proved satisfactory and could be used in future disasters. [p. 125] . . . [2.] *Salvation Army:* . . . acquisition of new resources [pp. 126–127] [3.] *Red Cross:* . . . the number of shelters was increased from 15 to 50. Accompanying this increase was a corresponding increase in additional personnel and supplies [p. 127]" (Forrest, 1979:125–127, 130).

But these must be translated into networks of more abstract relationships like those offered by Weller (1974) and Ross (1978).

IIIF2.1(H) "Comparisons among our three populations of organizations suggest that these innovations are strongly influenced by normative, exogenous and episodic conditions" (Weller, 1974:98).

IIIF2.1a(H) "In some cases these innovations were adopted without a clear definition of how they would operate or what problems they would solve. The preponderant influence of normative as compared with merely cognitive definitions is supported by these patterns in our data. Organizations appear to innovate when they 'should' rather than because they have 'learned' of a problem or a new way of operating. . . . The organizations that actually adopted innovations, however, were those for which a normative expectation of preparedness was an important element of their domains" (Weller, 1974:99).

IIIF2.1b(H) "In cases where new normative elements are acquired from the organizational reference system, strain is introduced (Haas and Drabek, 1973:273). The strain may be resolved by innovations changing the organization to conform with current social network norms. This is precisely what appears to have happened in the two social networks that included police departments and fire departments. The social networks became mobilized with regard to the problems of controlling civil disturbances. Through a variety of interactive processes new normative expectations about what police and fire departments should be and do were created" (Weller, 1974:101).

IIIF2.2(H) ". . . when tabulated for all seventy-four organizations at once, none of the relationships between the independent variables and the three types of innovation was statistically significant. . . . In the three natural disaster settings only one significant relationship appeared between the independent variables and innovation. For the twenty organizations in New Orleans, complexity was found to be positively related to resources change [p. 223] . . . On the other hand, in the single technological disaster, the Indianapolis Coliseum explosion, four significant relationships were present. As in New Orleans, [1.] complexity was related positively to resource change . . . [2.] Autonomy exhibited a positive relationship with structure change . . . [3.] Size was also found to be a significant variable— the larger the organization in terms of total personnel, the more likely was resource change . . . [4.] general organizational function was significantly related to change in structure [i.e.,] welfare organizations were the most likely to change. [p. 224] . . . the most feasible answer relates to the characteristics of the disaster agent itself. With the exception of the Coliseum explosion, all the disasters were of wide scope, affecting the entire community in which they occurred. In contrast, Indianapolis experienced a disaster with a very limited and specific focus. . . . variables which account for innovation in normal, non-disaster situations were operative only in the less disrupted Indianapolis setting [p. 226]" (Ross, 1978:223, 224, 226).

IIIF3. Organizational Change: Image Alterations

Like adoption of innovations, disasters may impact community definitions of organizational images. Similar to occupational niches, organizational domains are comprised of prestige expectations that managers seek to protect as much, perhaps, as they do those expectations that define the limits of autonomy and economic security (see Haas and Drabek, 1973:178–183). The research question is not, "Do disasters impact these?" Rather, the issue must be recast so that we ask instead, "Under what conditions are organizational images altered—positively or negatively?" and "For which classes of organizations and within what constituencies are such modifications most likely?"

Similarly, we need to know what ranges of strategies managers may seek to employ to counteract or encourage such alterations. Unfortunately, the structural imagery implicit in the available findings renders managerial behavior as irrelevant or inert. While that may be the case at times, my experience is different. Good managers act; at times their actions are motivated by the desire to enhance the image of their agency. Of course, they remain constrained by the structural features that characterize their agency and the web of structured strains in which they are embedded. But they do act.

IIIF3.1(H) ". . . variations in organizational prestige can be tied to the changes in task saliency over time after a disaster. [pp. 208–209] . . . Organizations associated with early disaster tasks, such as security, decline in prestige while organizations associated with tasks such as social services, which assume greatest importance later, rise in prestige [p. 209]" (Wright, 1978:208–209).

IIIF3.2(H) "*Persons, in general, have highly positive opinions of the relief provided by agencies. This finding contradicts evidence from previous disaster studies.* However, there is a strong indication that persons in the Moderate Impact Zone (San Fernando Valley excluding Sylmar and San Fernando) and/or persons in the Low Impact Zone who suffered moderate amounts of damage and injury are less likely to have contact with agencies and more likely to have unfavorable opinions about the way in which agencies and officials conducted themselves" (Bourque *et al., 1973:ii).

IIIF3.3(H) ". . . the literature has traditionally been consistent in demonstrating that the Red Cross suffers from a negative image among disaster victims. [p. 56] . . . the severe negative evaluations of the Red Cross reported in the short-run following disasters do not persist in the form of an organizational legacy over longer periods of time. [p. 58] . . . findings clearly indicate that the previous literature, by concentrating on more immediate disaster reactions, may have misconstrued the Red Cross' true public image among disaster victims [p. 59]'' (James and Wenger, 1978:56, 58, 59).

IIIF4. Emergent Organizations

After some disasters, especially those wherein culpability is perceived, new organizations may be born and coalitions among preexisting units may be strengthened (Drabek, in press). Disasters may provide rallying points that at times may serve the purposes of some concerned about very different issues. Studies currently in process at the Disaster Research Center should provide an important new data base on this topic in the years ahead (see Stallings and Quarantelli, 1985).

Case studies, like Walsh's monitoring of two groups that emerged out of the scare produced by the incident at Three Mile Island in March, 1979, are necessary first steps. Hopefully, in the coming decade we will gain a far better understanding of these dynamics.

> IIIF4.1(H) "The leadership and organizational structure of ECNP remained essentially the same after the accident as it had been before. While there were a few cadre changes as a result of the accident, a temporary mushrooming of monthly attendance, and a considerable increase in financial contributions for the coalition, the pre-accident leader . . . remained firmly in charge. [ECNP = Environmental Coalition on Nuclear Power] . . . TMIA, in contrast to ECNP, experienced sweeping leadership and structural changes as a result of the accident. The organization was transformed from a cluster of intermittent activists mailing out occasional newsletters to the largest protest organization in the area with a seven-member steering committee, a 30-member planning council, and 12 community group affiliates [TMIA = Three Mile Island Alert]'' (Walsh, 1981:7).

> IIIF4.2 "In the case of the TMI mobilization process, background variables, preaccident solidary networks, preaccident ideology, and issue-specific discontent each made its own significant independent contribution toward explaining who did, and who did not, become actively involved'' (Walsh and Warland, 1983:779).

> IIIF4.2a ". . . the activists were in higher educational, occupational, and income categories than the free riders'' (Walsh and Warland, 1983:774).

> IIIF4.2b ". . . the activists [were] much more likely than the free riders to report liberal political sympathies (51% vs. 13%) prior to the accident and mobilization processes. The activists were also more opposed, even before the accident, to commercial nuclear power in general, TMI in particular, and the increased production of nuclear weapons'' (Walsh and Warland, 1983:775).

In contrast to the work of Walsh and Warland are studies completed by Soderstrom and his associates at the Oak Ridge National Laboratory.

Rather than focusing exclusively on those opposing the restart of TMI-1 (the undamaged nuclear reactor), they also studied an emergent group that favored restart—a position also voiced by the area Chambers of Commerce. Thus, through a series of focused group discussions, they probed the perceptual worlds of participants in these opposition organizations. While there were parallels in membership characteristics, both evidenced selective perception.

> IIIF4.3 "All groups, however, are very similar in the 'types' of people who are members and leaders. Members are, for the large part, middle to upper-middle class, perhaps typical of interest groups in general. Leaders tend to be reflective of the general social status of the groups, largely professionals and business persons or skilled bluecollar workers (e.g., plumbers)" (Soderstrom et al., 1984:235).

> IIIF4.4 "Despite uncertainty over source of commitment, we see strong evidence of selective perception shaping pro- and anti-restart group perceptions of risk. . . . groups favoring restart conceptualized the issue primarily in economic terms, choosing to ignore potential health risks. Anti-restart groups did exactly the opposite by focusing on health risks and largely ignoring economic impacts" (Soderstrom et al., 1984:242).

Through comparisons of the antinuclear organizations that delayed a restart of the undamaged reactor at TMI to the less successful efforts of local groups that were spawned by the 1969 oil spill at Santa Barbara, Walsh (1984) highlighted the importance of nationally based social movements. His work suggested the following hypothesis.

> IIIF4.5(H) The greater the interaction between emergent local organizations and nationally based social movement organizations, the greater the longevity and probability of success of the locally based emergent organization. (Based on Walsh, 1984.)

IIIF5. Mental Health Needs Assessments and Impacts

Following the observations offered in earlier chapters, e.g., Chapter 2, Section IVA5, it is clear that precise conclusions regarding probable demands for mental health services cannot be made with the present information base. Available data indicate, however, some general guidelines—and cautions—for those with administrative responsibilities. As I emphasized in the planning chapter, mental health providers would be well advised not to overreact. Most disaster victims will not accept outreach efforts, maybe because there are other avenues of healing available. Among those coming forward, the needs may not be what traditional crisis intervention training might suggest (see Tierney and Baisden, 1979; Cohen and Ahearn, 1980).

This entire issue is a very complex one and must be assessed within the taxonomic orientation toward disasters that I have proposed throughout this book. Mental health needs within a victim population suffering from displacement caused by a slowly rising river probably differ significantly from those precipitated by events of a different quality. Rather than accept premature closure on this very important topic, I suggest that we view the matter as being on hold until a more substantial data base has been generated.

> IIIF5.1(H) Mental health needs during the reconstruction period will vary with disaster severity and other characteristics; but generally such services will be accepted only by small percentages of the victim population. (Based on Lindy, Grace, and Green, 1981; see also Wettenhall, 1979a:242.)

Furthermore, practitioners should be forewarned that once programs are initiated, pressures to demonstrate legitimacy may deflect from original goals and expectations.

> IIIF5.2(H) "When a project [i.e., Mental Health Programs, Section 413] is funded, particularly with public money, pressure is exerted to justify it by means of a detailed, quantitatively documented needs assessment. [p. 8] . . . outreach can become an effort aimed more at attaining a magic number, delivering the types of service committed to, rather than searching out those in need and providing the services required [p. 9]" (Baisden and Quarantelli, 1979:8, 9).

In contrast to service demands from the public-at-large is another matter I raised in the chapter on planning within the context of "hidden victims" (e.g., see Taylor, 1983). That is, what may be the long-term health impacts on rescue personnel? Certainly this is a topic that should be examined carefully in the coming decade (e.g., see Mitchell, 1982). We must build on the insights provided by Jones and Fischer (1982) and seek to validate— or perhaps reformulate—their conclusions across the full disaster taxonomy. (See also Taylor and Frazer, 1980, 1982, and IIIE3.1.)

> IIIF5.3(H) ". . . a questionnaire survey of the emotional effects on the USAF personnel involved in recovering and identifying the mass suicide and murder victims from Jonestown, Guyana. Questionnaires were sent to 592 participants (225, 38%, responded) and to 352 controls (76, 22%, responded). . . . Short-term dysphoria was reported by 32% of the 'Guyana' respondents and 9% of the controls ($p < .001$); long-term dysphoric rates were 21% and 17% respectively (NS at the .05 level)" (Jones and Fischer, 1982:abstract).

> IIIF5.3a(H) "Among the Guyana respondents, significantly higher rates of dysphoria were found in those under 25 years old, blacks (as compared to whites), and enlisted (as compared to officers)" (Jones and Fischer, 1982:abstract).

> IIIF5.3b(H) "Higher rates were also noted among those reporting a greater exposure to the remains, more emotional support (who perhaps

sought it out), or inadequate emotional support" (Jones and Fischer, 1982:abstract).

IIIF5.3c(H) "Many reported that bodies of children evoked the strongest emotional responses" (Jones and Fischer, 1982:abstract).

IIIF5.3d(H) "Some felt that the entire experience led to a feeling of personal growth and an increased appreciation of life" (Jones and Fischer, 1982:abstract).

IIIF5.3e(H) "Group support and humor were mentioned as valuable supports through stressful times. . . . in future undertakings of this nature, younger personnel should be teamed with older for individual support. Open expression of emotional responses should be encouraged in individual conversations, by group process, and perhaps in final debriefings" (Jones and Fischer, 1982:abstract).

IVF. Community System Level

Numerous studies have been completed on several aspects of community system development during the reconstruction phase since our earlier review (i.e., Mileti, Drabek, and Haas, 1975:137–141.) Unfortunately, we still don't have enough cumulative evidence to draw many firm conclusions. To use an analogy, the area has expanded in a shotgun manner, rather than as if a rifle had been used.

Despite the wide array of specialized areas considered, I have clustered the findings into three very broad topics: (1) blame assignation processes; (2) disaster-induced community changes; and (3) housing and reconstruction planning problems.

IVF1. Blame Assignation Processes

Following some disasters, but not most, case studies have documented elaborate searches for "the guilty" (e.g., Drabek, 1968). When is this most likely to occur? Why are some public positions more apt to be seized upon than others? Building on the earlier observations of Bucher (1957), Quarantelli and I (1967) sought to make sense out of the community response in Indianapolis, Indiana, following a massive explosion that occurred in the coliseum (1963).

IVF1.1(H) ". . . blaming for disasters arises out of seeking a satisfactory explanation for something which cannot be accounted for conventionally. Once persons have defined the situation sufficiently to assess responsibility, blaming occurs when people are convinced that the responsible agents will not of their own volition take action to prevent a recurrence and the agents are perceived as in opposition to basic values" (Bucher, 1957:467).

IVF1.2(H) "This tendency to seek the cause in a *who*—rather than a *what*—is common after airplane crashes, fires, caveins, and other catastrophes not caused naturally. Personalizing blame in this way is not only a standard response, but well in harmony with the moral framework of American society. [p. 12] . . . Not only does individual blame draw attention from more functional causes, but it might actually give the illusion that corrective action of some sort is being taken [p. 16]'' (Drabek and Quarantelli, 1967:12, 16).

IVF1.2a(H) [Here we might take note of the comments made by Moore (1958) . . . Feyzin's situation before the catastrophe was analogous to the situation of Waco, Texas. Among the people there was a division along economic lines: a desire for ''modernization and rapid growth'' opposed to ''conservative economic interests.'' Following the Feyzin catastrophe, as in the case of Waco, this previous situation favored the choice of the town administration as a scapegoat: ''after the tornado this fundamental division was strongly felt at the political level. Once again a campaign was undertaken to change the form of the municipal government'' (in Waco).] [France] (Chandessais, 1966:489).

These interpretations were supported and extended further by Neal's (1984) examination of a grass-roots citizen organization that blamed a local company for air pollution to which these citizens attributed a variety of health problems. While the placement of blame both facilitated and distracted from the group's effectiveness, Neal (1984:251) concluded that the case clearly illustrated that the ''. . . placing of blame does not lead to structural change.''

IVF1.2b(H) ''The blaming process directed toward the company aided in the mobilization of the citizen's group but also prevented any immediate issue-oriented actions. As blame directed toward the company decreased within the group, solidarity within the group decreased. Yet, as blame decreased within the group, issue-oriented actions by the group increased'' (Neal, 1984:251).

Of course, others, rooted within a psychoanalytic framework still emphasize the irrationality of such actions, commonly labeled ''scapegoating.''

''. . . the anger is oftentimes directed in irrational ways, ways that may not be simply a function of the immediate crisis, but that reflect preexisting conflicts and hostilities. This phenomemon, often referred to as 'scapegoating,' may be directed toward specific individuals *and* groups, such as minority ethnic groups, the financially successful, civic officials, the government, and even rescue and relief personnel themselves.[5] After the Cocoanut Grove fire the Jews were blamed,[6] while after the Andrea Doria and Titanic disasters the Italians were the scapegoats''[7] (Singer, 1982:246.)

---

[5] T. E. Drabek and E. L. Quarantelli, ''Scapegoats, Villains, and Disasters.'' *Trans-Action* **4** (1967):12–17.

[6] E. Lindemann, ''Symptomatology and Management of Acute Grief.'' *Am. J. Psychiatry* **101** (1944):141–148.

[7] P. Friedmann and L. Linn, ''Some Psychiatric Notes on the Andrea Doria Disaster.'' *Am. J. Psychiatry* **107** (1957):426–432; W. Lord, *A Night to Remember.* New York: Henry Holt and Co., 1955.

We don't have a good fix on this matter at present, aside from knowing that instances of blame assignation do occur. Despite the interpretation Quarantelli and I offered regarding the Indianapolis case that seemed to parallel the responses to the three airplane crashes studied by Bucher, I would not suggest that all such activities are inherently "rational." More work along the lines of the case studies cited below should provide the data necessary to formulate more precise hypotheses for future testing.

IVF1.3(H) "The generalized belief that formal authorities in local government were unresponsive to the needs of specific citizens was central to group mobilization. There existed a 'gap' between what was expected and what was delivered. In response to this, certain constituencies felt unprotected and 'forced' to mobilize" (Wolensky and Miller, 1981:497–498). (See also Battisti, 1978b:206.)

IVF1.3a(H) [In the recovery phase, the population, often exasperated and pressed by precarious living conditions and the lack of short-term improvement, could tend to increase pressure on the local government by demanding rapid and incisive action to solve problems, by more insistently criticizing administrators believed to be incompetent and responsible for delays and lack of action, and by wanting to be more involved in the decision-making process. These behaviors, almost always linked to the power play between parties or individuals, can lead to crises in local governments such as actually happened in Friuli where mayors and entire councils were forced to resign, where majorities shifted, where commissioners from the Prefecture took over.] [Italy] (Cattarinussi and Tellia, 1978:250).

IVF1.3b(H) "Suddenly imposed (or abruptly realized) and continuing major grievances, attributable to human decisions or negligence, made sustained grass-roots protest mobilization more likely when the target collectivity is of working-class or higher socio-economic status" (Walsh, 1981:18).

IVF2. Disaster-Induced Community Change

Late in the 1970s, two large-scale projects were completed that appropriately received considerable attention. I emphasize "appropriately" because of two qualities. First, both reflected high standards of excellence in the research methods used. Second, each offered a conclusion that threatened some. Thus, when the University of Massachusetts at Amherst project members (Rossi et al., 1978; Wright et al., 1979) concluded that disasters produced no discernible long-term effects, some relief agency representatives were not sure how to respond. While reflecting very different research methods and data sets, this conclusion paralleled that reached at about the same time by a team at Northwestern University (Friesema et al., 1979). Thus, for a limited range of variables and across a broad sampling of natural disasters, the hypothesis of "resumption of normalcy" received substantial support for community level systems—counties and census tracts.

IVF2.1(H) "We find *no discernible effects* of either floods, tornadoes, or hurricanes on the changes in population or housing stocks experienced by *counties* in the period between 1960 and 1970. Additional analyses were also made of the effects of natural disasters on other characteristics of counties, including housing values, rents, age composition, educational level of population, and family income. While there were a few instances in which the disaster coefficients were large enough to be statistically significant, no coherent interpretable pattern emerged. In short, there appear to be no firm findings to indicate that natural disasters have any long-lasting effects on counties" (Wright *et al.*, 1979:24) (emphasis added). (See also Rossi *et al.*, 1978:126–127.)

IVF2.1a(H) "There are *no discernible net effects* of natural disaster events on growth trends in housing or population stocks for *census tracts* in the period 1960 to 1970" (Wright *et al.*, 1979:27) (emphasis added).

While lacking a comparative community data base, these conclusions are not consistent with the interpretations from many case studies. For example, while the overall net effects may have evened out the trend lines, more detailed analyses contained within several case studies emphasize fluctuations that appeared to be disaster-induced.

IVF2.1b(H) ". . . difference in the composition of San Francisco's population in 1910 as compared with 1900. The changes seem due primarily to the experience of the disaster. Particularly evident is the increase in the proportion of males in San Francisco's population aged 15 years and over, and the almost complete absence of growth in the number of children. Oakland experienced a more rapid growth of population increase than San Francisco, and this might have been expected, but the number of adult males grew disproportionately fast" (Douty, 1977:361–363).

IVF2.1c(H) "An increased birth rate occurred in Aberfan during the five years after the disaster there in 1966. It was not confined to the bereaved parents. [p. 303] . . . By 1972 the number of children killed in the disaster had been replaced and the birth rate had fallen to near the pre-disaster level. It had not, however, fallen to the level which would have been reached had the decline indicated by pre-disaster figures continued [p. 304]" [England] (Williams and Parkes, 1975:303, 304). (See also Boyd, 1981:748.)

Many criticisms were leveled against the methods developed by Rossi, Wright, and their associates. Thus, consistent with the taxonomic argument I have developed throughout this book, several expressed concern with the blurring of the concept of disaster. In order to secure a large sample size ($n = 1,140$ counties), Rossi and his associates included numerous events with limited damage levels. That is, to qualify as a "disaster," tornado damage, for example, had to exceed 50 using the following index: twice the number of houses destroyed + the number of houses with major damage. Is it reasonable to expect that tornadic destruction of two dozen farm buildings would alter the *countywide* housing values, for example, so as to register change in census data collected a decade apart?

But this criticism, like some of the others proposed (see Changnon *et al.*, 1983:83–104), is less relevant to the Northwestern study. They used four massive disasters and an elaborate time-series analysis technique. Upon reaching a "no effect" conclusion, however, they proposed an important interpretation that should be pursued—externalization. That is, most disaster-stricken communities within the U.S.A. receive sufficient levels of relief and are so tightly interdependent with regional economics that losses may be mitigated completely.

> IVF2.1d(H) ". . . none of these disasters [i.e., four studies via time-series analysis] led to major long-term economic losses to these communities. [pp. 176–177] . . . the American society and polity has become so knit together and the economy so integrated by the mid-20th century that most of the economic costs of natural disasters are externalized to the larger, carrying society [pp. 177–178]" [Dependent variables included: size of work force, unemployment level, number of businesses, e.g., restaurants, filling stations, retail sales, sales tax revenue.] (Friesema *et al.*, 1979:176–178).

In contrast to these analyses, researchers using limited case study data have offered observations regarding disaster-induced social change, both content and causal dynamics. It must be emphasized that none of these *hypotheses* are negated by the conclusions offered by the two 1979 studies. But these should serve as a springboard for future analyses that reflect the methodological rigor of the studies completed by the Rossi and Friesema teams.

> IVF2.2(H) "The observed changes in a community from a disaster represent an acceleration of already operating processes rather than the introduction of completely new directions into the normal change process (Bates *et al.*, 1963). (See also Prince, 1920 and Lessa, 1964:21)" (as summarized in Mileti, Drabek, and Haas, 1975:138).

Especially promising, it seems to me, is the more theoretical direction proposed by Pelanda (1982a). Thus, rather than the "raw empiricist" approach that dominated the tenacious efforts of the teams directed by Rossi and Friesema, a broader interpretative framework is needed. "The 'classical' problem of the long-term social effects of local disasters . . . could be rephrased in terms of differential trends based on different types of sociosystemic order" (Pelanda, 1982a:23).

> IVF2.3(H) ". . . we found that knowledge of at least three levels of predisaster social vulnerability was needed in order to explain the social dynamics in an impacted area. We found, in other words, that the whole disaster social process depends on the degree of actualization of three types of sociostructural vulnerability: [pp. 10–11]" [1. typological, i.e., includes both the technological and social factors which *directly* define the probability of avoiding or minimizing a *specific type*, or a set, of potentially destructive events; 2. specific, i.e., a complex measure of both socioeconomic development and cultural stability at the local level;

and 3. general, i.e., degree of socioeconomic, organizational, and technological development at the societal level. (See pp. 11–12.)] [Italy] (Pelanda, 1982a:10–12).

Review of case study materials provides much support for Pelanda's argument. These stand in sharp relief to statistical analyses of housing values, rent levels, age composition, and the like. Thus, the dynamics of healing—both dimensions of pain and joy—are revealed in less precise terms, but terms that may have far more theoretical import. A typical illustration is Miller's (1973) dissection of these healing processes following the Aberfan mine disaster.

> "As one studies the documents of the last six years, one becomes aware of the transformation that has taken place in this mining village. In an area in which communities are slowly disintegrating in the despair of a dying industry, Aberfan has shown a remarkable resilience and power of recuperation. . . . It may be that the fight to get the tips removed allowed Aberfan to work out this aftermath and left it free to receive the forces for rehabilitation that were at work there from the early days. . . . The people themselves say that they are different, that 'the community has been reborn,' that there is a new tolerance, a new pride in the place and that the community association has been 'a lifeline of sorts' " [England] (Miller, 1973:165).

As with case studies of organizations, various types of community level changes have been documented following certain events. For example, following a major landslide in Port Alice, British Columbia (1975), Scanlon, Jefferson, and Sproat (1976:57) documented a series of changes including modifications in the public warning system, public education, and public evacuation plans.

In a detailed case study of the decade following the destruction that Tropical Storm Agnes (1972) brought to Wilkes-Barre, Pennsylvania, which was contrasted to earlier disasters in Dayton, Ohio, and Galveston, Texas, Wolensky (1984) described three post-disaster changes. Two were political-organizational (local government reorganization and power structure realignment); the other reflected expanded flood mitigation. Consistent with the general theme that disasters may accelerate change processes already in motion, Wolensky (1984:50) concluded that ". . . the disaster triggered charter reform in Galveston." But had the disaster not occurred, this change would have been made eventually; the 1900 tidal wave-flood that killed over 6000 served as the catalyst to speed up the process. Hence, "The storm led to the first so-called reformed government structure of the Progressive Era, the commission" (Wolensky, 1984:45). In contrast, "Flood protection changes occurred in the Wilkes-Barre area including the raising of the levees an average of three feet, nonstructural flood plain measures such as flood proofing regulations on new buildings, and a major structural prevention in the city's Brookside section" (Wolensky, 1984:209). His work provides detailed dissection of multiple forces that collectively pushed these local communities.

Additional observations have been offered that also suggest "community learning" (see Kliman, 1973:333; Nolan, 1979:331). Based on case study data from the community responses to the eruption of Mount St. Helens in 1981, however, Kartez (1984) concluded that local government jurisdictions tended to adopt only a limited set of the insights that research studies produced. Thus, he underscored the complexity of the disaster planning process and urged further study of it. He argues rather effectively that a "contingent analysis" model might aid in the conceptualization of those technologies and strategies that might most likely be accepted and implemented by local governments. Such analysis methodology would juxtapose situational opportunities against institutional constraints and various types of response strategies such as the use of volunteers, commercial media, private contractors, or telephone centers.

> IVF2.4(H) Disasters tend to accelerate community planning efforts, when recurrence is perceived to be likely. (Based on Quarantelli, 1980b.)

> IVF2.4a(H) "We found that mental health and human service agency activity was affected *by disaster* in the six towns that we studied. [p. 87] . . . disaster communities are slightly better endowed with help giving resources of all kinds. While the number of resource agencies was about the same for both sets of towns, communities that have experienced large-scale emergencies tend to be organizationally richer, with their agencies offering more types of service more frequently, as measured by resource scores [p. 86]" (Tierney and Baisden, 1979:86, 87).

A few researchers have documented shifts in community status systems. Oliver-Smith's (1979a, b) analyses of a Peruvian earthquake, for example, suggest that these processes may be altered permanently, especially if there was a pre-crisis trend in motion.

> IVF2.4b(H) "In the case of Yungay, the disaster seems to have hastened or accelerated patterns of change which are occurring at slightly slower rates in other parts of Peru. . . . changes in informal political institutions and practices, altered status and role behaviour and expectations, and rapid social mobility" [Peru] (Oliver-Smith, 1979b:100).

Finally, several aspects of the economic organization of communities have been examined. Case studies give us a sense of the interdependencies among different aspects of potential economic impacts. The following quotations illustrate this point, and provide a sense of where this mode of analysis is at the present time.

> IVF2.5(H) "Adjacent to the town of Abuta but almost untouched by the volcanic eruption is the town of Toyoura. Before the eruption, the two towns were approximately equal in the scale of their municipal finances. . . . in FY 1977, during which the eruption occurred, and the next year in FY 1978, Abuta's revenues were nearly double those for Toyoura. [p. 8] . . . by FY 1980, three years after the disaster, the number of visitors had yet to regain its 1976 level. [p. 13] . . . even after Toyako-Onsen had become safe again, the tourists did not return. However,

through the process of recovering from the disaster, another change took place. Toyako-Onsen was transformed by being refurbished as a modern resort area. Although it must now enter the competition for tourists at the same level as other areas, the various new resources which it derived from the recovery process will undoubtedly give it a competitive advantage [p. 20]'' [Japan] (Hirose, 1982:8, 13, 20).

IVF2.5a(H) ''Prior to 1970, the non-monetary exchange of material and nonmaterial values, i.e. reciprocity, constituted the norm of the village, especially with respect to agricultural production, and payment of cash to workers was rare. . . . After the earthquake, many individuals in the community began to request money for services rendered, and, at first, they were usually people who had obtained salaried employment in Huaraz during reconstruction. . . . Even community members who wanted to adhere to traditional forms of labor exchange could not avoid becoming involved in new economic arrangements rapidly evolving'' [Peru] (Dudasik, 1982:35). (For parallel themes in Australia, see Butler, 1976:317; in El Salvador, see Sheets, 1979:559–560; and in Mexico, see Nolan, 1979:314.)

IVF2.5b ''On the basis of the San Francisco evidence, a localized disaster does not appear likely to alter long run economic trends; such trends almost surely were not changed in San Francisco. The disaster did stimulate population dispersal. It hastened the decline in the relative importance of manufacturing in the city's economy'' (Douty, 1977:369). (See also Mileti, Drabek, and Haas, 1975:140.)

IVF2.5c(H) [Three floods (1971, 1974, and 1976) had a cumulative impact.] ''For the tradespeople, business turnover quickly declined. . . . a succession of floods leads to lack of outside interest in investment in the towns. People who wish to move out cannot sell their businesses, but neither are they inclined to sink further capital in them'' [Australia] (Douglas and Hobbs, 1979:255).

Thus, important questions are being raised with a type of sophistication that was not found earlier. But we are a long way from having a good sense of the range of social and economic impacts that disasters may bring and how these may vary from case to case. While some have argued that short-term economic gains have produced mixed results among communities when longer-term trends are examined, these analyses do little more than help structure a series of important questions that merit detailed, cross-event comparison.

IVF3. Housing and Reconstruction Planning Problems

As the first six months after a disaster pass by, altruistic and heroic actions take on a dimness. People want to resume their lives. Indecisiveness, especially ambiguities related to housing alternatives, become thorns that grate on even the most patient.

Planners like Mader, Spangle, Blair, *et al.* (1980) have offered suggestions regarding pre-earthquake actions that could be taken ahead of time
and might smooth out the planning process that local government now
must do under great pressure. Such actions include:

1. preparing and keeping up-to-date realistic land-use, circulation, and
   public facilities plans;
2. enacting and enforcing land-use regulations, building codes, and project
   review procedures;
3. establishing a redevelopment agency and carrying out redevelopment
   or rehabilitation projects;
4. obtaining and using geologic and other natural hazard related information. (Adapted from Mader *et al.,* 1980:13.).

But, the reality often differs from the image conveyed in these recommendations, as the following two case studies illustrated very well.

"[The] Miami Valley Regional Planning Commission [report (*Xenia Rebuilds*)] offered three alternative land use-design proposals, one of which
was strongly recommended. That plan included three major elements
which would theoretically correct mistakes and thus enhance the design,
desirability, and image of the community [p. 17] . . . [It] was approved
by the city commission in June 1974, making the new zoning 'law.' But
the new plan was simultaneously accompanied by city commission ap-
proval of *overlay zoning*. This effectively assured that the new plan could
be modified by a process involving a hearing examiner reviewing all
properly prepared requests for rezoning. [p. 18] . . . Enough time has
passed in the rebuilding of Xenia to allow the judgment that the tornado
simply accelerated the major predisaster discard and assimilation forces
and thereby has perpetuated the principal elements of the psychological
geography of 'Ohio Town' [p. 24]" (Francaviglia, 1978:17, 18, 24).

"King[8] further states that the Cities Commission report may have created
a rift between the public and the planners, and the destruction of public
confidence contributed significantly to the failure of the planners' to bring
about changes in land use that were desirable (from the viewpoint of the
people, as perceived by the planners) and which could have been implemented. . . . By 1977, as reconstruction neared completion, 'land use
change in Darwin had, if anything, reinforced the pre-cyclone trends which
the planners had tried to halt. If judged against the statements of the
Cities Commission, the replanning of Darwin failed' (King, 1979:152)"
[after Cyclone Tracy, 1974] [Australia] (Britton, 1981a:17).

Further complicating the matter are the differences between emergency
and reconstruction processes. Upon completing his longitudinal study of

---

[8] S.A. King, "More than Meets the Eye: Plans for Land Use Change in Darwin." In *Two
Northern Territory Urban Studies*. Bulletin No. 5. Canberra, Australia: North Australia
Research Unit, Australia National University, August, 1979.

the 1976 Guatemalan earthquake, Bates (1982b) highlighted this issue very
well.

> IVF3.1(H) "Generally speaking, those organizations whose role in dis-
> asters is highly tied to the delivery of emergency services fall at the bu-
> reaucratically managed end of the continuum and those whose primary
> role before becoming involved in disaster was development tend to fall
> more towards the grass roots participation end of the scale. . . . Problems
> arise in disaster situations, however, at the interface between emergency
> and reconstruction activities. These two processes are not distinct in the
> real world, and activities carried on by both emergency and reconstruc-
> tion–development agencies are often mixed with respect to which process
> they relate to. As a consequence, a debate arises over how certain types
> of aid should be managed and delivered, not to mention the fact that
> there are arguments over whether it should be delivered at all" [Gua-
> temala] (Bates, 1982b:28).

Based on the Alaskan earthquake (1964) experience (Dacy and Kunreuther, 1969), it appeared that there was a tendency to overestimate
damages. Subsequent studies by Vinso (1977:209) and Leivesley
(1977b:211) have questioned the generalizability of these findings, however.

> "Dacy and Kunreuther suggest that there is a tendency to overestimate
> damage to public sectors in the post-impact period of disasters. The re-
> verse occurred in Toowoomba because of the lack of information on the
> extent of damage. Insurance companies continued to receive new claims
> several months after the hailstorm and early estimates gradually increased
> to a final pay-out figure of $15 million. The initial under-estimation was
> contributed to by the slow process of reinstatement, during which house-
> holders were not immediately aware of the contribution that had to be
> paid and were concentrating their attention on the protection of their
> houses from the heavy rains" [Australia] (Leivesley, 1977b:211).

From the victims' view, housing for family members is a first priority.
And many have noted the speed with which elaborate forms of temporary
housing have been erected. For example, Sarah Jane Hogg (1980) stressed
how rapid this process was, following earthquakes in May and September,
1976, in Italy.

> " . . . 98% of the prefabricated homes planned for Venzone parish were
> constructed by the end of March, 1977, and were ready for the return
> of the evacuees. By the end of April the full quota of 260 buildings were
> in use, providing 793 family units and housing a total of 2,320 people,
> 89.1% of those who had survived the earthquake" [Quakes occurred in
> May and September, 1976.] [Italy] (Sarah Jane Hogg, 1980:181).

She, like others, has pointed to a series of problems. It seems that at
times there has not been a good fit between the patterns and forms of
housing provided and victim cultures. Also, such arrangements may turn
out to persist long beyond the period expected initially.

IVF3.2(H) "The widespread introduction of prefabricated buildings in Venzone parish radically altered the character of the community as a whole and individual family lifestyles. For example, following relocation some wage earners have to spend more time and money commuting greater distances to work, or some people find their new neighbours incompatible" [Italy] (Sarah Jane Hogg, 1980:182). (See also Ciborowski, 1967.)

IVF3.3(H) " . . . I did observe that most of the earlier recommendations concerning physical arrangements of new villages, quality control of construction, indoor plumbing, water, animal shelters, and glass windows were not implemented . . . Consequently, as in the Gediz case, research in the Lice disaster area in 1979 or 1980 may reveal that many houses have been abandoned, and that villagers have returned to either their original or other villages. [p. 57] . . . why include water faucets, sinks, shower stalls, and indoor toilets if there is an extremely low probability that the house will ever have running water? Need houses be wired for electricity in economically depressed regions that have no electrical infrastructure within reasonable proximity? [pp. 57–58]" [Turkey] (Mitchell, 1976b:57-58). (See also Mitchell, 1977:246.)

Geipel's (1982) data from the Friuli earthquakes add important insights regarding the variability within these overall patterns, however. Not all families or communities recover with equal speed, especially when the scope of destruction has been so vast that many have been forced to evacuate their homesites. One of his study team members—Helene Voelkl—". . . sent 560 questionnaires to readers of the monthly *Fogolar* magazine in Germany and Switzerland, of which 141 (27.2 per cent) came back in usable condition" (Geipel, 1982:109). Questions probed their plans to return to their homeland. Of special importance was the ". . . fact that not one of the 141 respondents wanted to stay abroad for the rest of his life" (Geipel, 1982:109–110). But some envisioned returning home sooner than others. What factors differentiated the families?

IVF3.4(H) ". . . the actual background of emigration has no influence on propensity to return home. Social integration is also more important than economic: even with good living conditions and income in the host country, strong contact with Friulians and Italians indicates the feeling of being a stranger abroad. Encouraged in the 'duty' to go home by visits there, correspondence and remittances of money and goods there, and most of all by property destroyed in the earthquake, the people who first choose to go are mostly those who are most urgently needed at home— construction workers and mechanics . . ." [Italy] (Geipel, 1982:111).

Generally, disaster victims push to repair or rebuild at their original homesites. While some "extremists" representing varying ideological viewpoints can be expected to propose visions of redevelopment—including total community relocation—that are drastically different from the original pattern, few victims seem to maintain much interest. Certainly, the U.S.A. experience supports this conclusion as do fragments of the literature from other nation states.

[In some cases, the nature of the event may be such as to advise against the reconstruction of the stricken community and to move it elsewhere. In the Friuli case, it does not appear that anyone seriously thought about this possibility, even though a few urbanists attempted to support the hypothesis of making a clean sweep of the earthquake areas and concentrating the people into a "Greater Udine" and even though a few extremist fringes of pro-Friuli movements are accusing Rome of wanting to take advantage of the earthquake to destroy a troublesome ethnic group.] [Italy] (Boileau *et al.,* 1978:150). (For a parallel case in Peru, see Oliver-Smith, 1977b.)

While more recent years have seen some major examples of complete relocation, these remain exceptional cases. At times they may reflect mitigation efforts, e.g., relocation out of areas known to be highly flood-prone or seismically active. And a few instances have occurred because of contamination, e.g., Love Canal. The best study to date is that of Perry and Mushkatel (1984) who concluded that two factors distinguished the successful relocation of a small Arizona community: (1) the skills and planning strategies used and (2) ". . . several issues unique to relocations that occur as a function of natural hazards" (Perry and Mushkatel, 1984:181).

Based on this case they proposed five "principles of positive relocation": (1) the community must be organized; (2) those to be moved must participate in the decision-making process; (3) relocatees should understand the multiorganizational system that will be required; (4) personal and social needs must receive special attention; and (5) officials must be sensitive to the cultural and ethnic backgrounds of the movers. (Adapted from Perry and Mushkatel, 1984:183–194.)

The following Mexican case history highlights some of the tensions and difficult choices that such situations reflect.

"When the eruptions ended, the Mexican government encouraged the Zirosto Seca which was on the Uruapan–Los Reyes road. . . . In return for relocation, the people were promised an *ejido* grant, a 6-year school, bus service along the road, electricity, piped water, and street lights. A majority went to New Zirosto in 1953, but some adamantly refused to leave the old town. Brothers made different choices, placing strain on family relations and the solidarity of kinship networks. It is said in New Zirosto that the move would have been truly successful if all had gone together, taking with them the old bells that symbolized the community. In Old Zirosto, those who left are blamed. It is argued that if all had stayed, the Mexican government would eventually have rerouted the road, provided electricity, water, 6 years of school, and all the other benefits. In terms of social disruption Zirosto became, as is said locally, the town 'most destroyed by the volcano' " [Mexico] (Nolan, 1979:313).

The more common pattern of recovery, however, is to rebuild on sites used originally, reflecting an acceleration of pre-event developmental trends—if there is any change at all. The dynamics of these processes, motivations of involved parties, and factors resulting in exceptions, are not well understood. Most assume, however, that from the victim's standpoint the primary drive is a strong desire to get things settled so that life can go on.

> IVF3.5(H) "The major generalization supported by the Managua case study is that a large disaster in a dense urban area tends to accelerate, in accordance with predisaster patterns, those processes of residential development which were in motion before the disaster" [Nicaragua] (Bowden et al., 1977:144). (See also Douty, 1977:367–368).

Rubin and Barbee (1985) and their associates have examined factors that may affect the composition of intergovernmental recovery systems and their relative effectiveness (see also Rubin, 1981). Based on 14 study jurisdictions, they concluded that recovery processes in local communities are impacted by four categories of strategic choices. Thus, community recovery will reflect the political aspects of post-disaster intergovernmental relations. That is, the speed and scope of recovery depends upon the degree to which local government officials have the: (1) ability to act; (2) reason to act; (3) knowledge of what to do; and (4) political awareness and astuteness (Rubin and Barbee, 1985:59–62). The following were among 14 insightful "actionable propositions" that Rubin, Saperstein, and Barbee (1985) proposed for local government managers.

> "At the community level, vision of what the community could and should be after the disaster is an important attribute of effective leadership" (Rubin, Saperstein, and Barbee, 1985:49).

> "While some dependence on external resources is to be expected after a disaster, a heavy dependency on external resources (financial as well as specialized personnel) can cause a loss of local control and long delays" (Rubin, Saperstein, and Barbee, 1985:51).

> "Local officials in communities with known hazards, or ones at chronic risk, should determine before a disaster what procedures, requirements, and benefits are contained in the state and federal disaster assistance programs for response and recovery" (Rubin, Saperstein, and Barbee, 1985:53).

VF. Society System Level

As has been the case throughout this book, when we move to the societal level of analysis, the size and precision of our knowledge base drops dramatically. Since our earlier review (Mileti, Drabek, and Haas, 1975), only a few investigators have penetrated this research niche.

Reflecting his emphasis on the positive functions of disaster, Fritz's assertion remains a logical starting point.

VF1.1(H) ". . . disasters unify societies" (Fritz, 1961:683).

Obvious issues of measurement have precluded any from pursuing the matter empirically, although various observations have been offered that reflect aspects of his themes of integration and solidarity. I suspect that as we begin to get cross-national studies that examine large numbers of events, we will find patterns of contradiction and unevenness, as we have at less complex system levels. And we may find that adaptations made within one institutional sector will have very significant effects elsewhere. Thus, disasters may serve as useful tools for improving our understanding of how societies work, by providing better mappings of the degrees of interdependency among institutional subsystems.

VF1.1a(H) "Disasters however can be 'Acts of God' in a more positive sense: as opportunities to break the pattern of events which together hold people in the grip of increasing poverty. [p. 33] . . . 1. Disasters foster linkages . . . and local leadership . . . 2. Disasters lead to co-operation . . . 3. Disasters draw resources and personnel to the most needy areas . . . 4. Disasters introduce a process of selectivity [p. 34] . . . [and] 5. Disasters often lead to surveys . . . [e.g.] a comprehensive survey of vulnerable areas which provides a more complete understanding of the ecosystem, the basic unit in natural and resource management [p. 35]" [India] (Fernandez, 1979:33–35).

VF1.1b(H) ". . . the earthquakes have modified the outer-trappings of religious life without altering more deep-seated feeling about religion. . . . [For example] fires were lit on hilltops on the twelfth night before Christmas to bring good omens for the next year's crop. Before the quake, virtually all villages between Gemona and Cividale practiced this rite, but now it has nearly disappeared. The feasts of the patron saints that were held annually in every village have also been abandoned" [Italy] (Barbina, 1979:148).

As I pointed out in the previous section, victim housing needs are of prime importance. And, as we have seen above in the discussion of differing subsystem levels, such as families and communities, a desire to resettle at or near the original location is the primary pattern. That which was viewed as serving temporary needs may be used much longer. Some types of changes do occur; often the new housing is perceived as being better. New distributional patterns tend to be a reflection of trends present earlier; also, limited alterations may occur in building materials used to reduce future vulnerability. Studies by Bates and his associates (Bates, Farrell, and Glittenberg, 1979; Bates, 1982b) provide excellent examples.

". . . considerable change has taken place in housing characteristics in Guatemala since the 1976 earthquake. [p. 132] . . . When unassisted by agencies, 28 per cent of the people used tile for roofing, as compared to 18 per cent of those who were agency assisted. This difference is statistically significant. Nevertheless, both categories of people show a marked

reduction in the use of tile for roofing as compared to before the earthquake, when 64 per cent of all houses had tile roofs [p. 126]" [seven
communities] [Guatemala] (Bates, Farrell, and Glittenberg, 1979:126, 132).

VF1.2(H) Disaster-induced housing reconstruction will reflect: (a) pronounced site stability accompanied by an acceleration of preexisting developmental patterns; (b) a perception of improvement; (c) minor alterations in use of building materials so as to reduce future vulnerability;
and (d) longer than initially planned use of shelters intended as temporary.
(Based on Bates, Farrell, and Glittenberg, 1979). For somewhat parallel
findings from Honduras, see Snarr and Brown, 1980; and from New He-
brides, see Tonkinson, 1979.)

VF1.2a(H) "19.5 per cent of the 370 persons interviewed are living in
exactly the same house that they lived in before the earthquake. . . . Of
those who lived in different houses, 60.8 per cent live in a different house
located on the same site as their pre-earthquake dwelling and 14.9 per
cent live in a different house on a different site in the same town or
village where they resided before the earthquake" [seven communities]
[Guatemala] (Bates, Farrell, and Glittenberg, 1979:128).

VF1.2b(H) "Massive migration was predicted following the May earthquake, but it did not materialize. . . . As recovery proceeded, Friulians
began to display a preference for new settlement arrangements. The traditional rural model was that of dispersed terraced houses straddling both
sides of the main roads. What became popular now was the model of
small, single family home, a pattern which had already been spreading
over rural areas in the last ten years" [Italy] (Barbina, 1979:146).

VF1.2c(H) ". . . uniform prefabricated housing, intended as temporary
shelter, is still inhabited some 50 years—and three generations—later"
[Greece] (Hirschon and Thakurdesai, 1979:247).

As with community level status systems, some researchers have argued
that massive disasters may alter these structures for the entire society.
Urban/rural inequalities may be widened as may the gap between the rich
and the poor. Thus, in some cases, disasters seem to intensify, rather than
neutralize, previously existing status differences and patterns of social
inequality. Detailed documentation has been provided by Bates and his
associates using data on the 1976 Guatemalan earthquake (Bates, 1982b).
A wide variety of case study reports, however, clearly indicate how complex and relatively subtle such status-altering impacts may be. Holy's
analysis of the impact of a drought in the Sudan is a good illustration.

". . . the drought had a different effect on the domestic economy of the
rich households than it had on the poor ones. Wealthy households with
big herds of cattle, sheep and goats which were not completely decimated
during the long spell of dry years, were less affected by the drought as
their sources of cash income were not totally blocked. For the members
of poorer households with little or no livestock to sell, their labour became

the only possible source of cash income. [pp. 69–70] . . . [In the 1960s]
a wealthy man still had to participate himself in weeding his fields because
the supply of wage labour was considerably limited and he could not rely
on it alone. Nowadays, it is not only the poor Meidob who supply wage
labour but numerous poor Berti are only too eager to get hired for weeding
to earn the badly needed cash. [pp. 70–71] . . . While in the 1960s each
household represented to a greater or lesser extent a point of cash inflow
into the village, nowadays only the wealthy households are points of
cash inflow into the local community. Within it the cash is redistributed
to all the households through the establishment of the previously nonexistent intra-village labour market [p. 71]'' [Sudan] (Holy, 1980:69–71).
(See also O'Leary, 1980:326, for the impact of drought in Kenya.)

VF1.3(H) Disasters intensify preexisting status differences and social inequalities (Bates, 1982b). (See also Geipel, 1982:180; Killian, Peacock,
and Bates, 1982; Peacock and Bates, 1982. For parallel findings from
Nigeria, see Watts, 1979:102.)

VF1.3a(H) ''. . . conclusions [regarding] the social evolution of Senegal
over the last ten years, of which the drought/famine is one element . . .
Social, regional and national differences and inequalities have increased.
The urban-rural distribution of income is becoming more skewed. The
transfer of resources from agricultural production to the State budget is
accelerating'' [Senegal] (Copans, 1979:91).

VF1.3b(H) ''. . . selected changes in social relations or social institutions,
which were exacerbated by these natural and social upheavals, have become permanent aspects of daily life in the country. It is hypothesized
that disasters tend to exacerbate existing trends and patterns of instability
or inequality rather than initiate completely new forms of response. In
one sense, disasters may be said to attack the weakest link in a society
and may encourage changes which are already imminent in that society''
[Bangladesh] (Feldman and McCarthy, 1983:105).

A few scholars have tried to trace out longer-term economic consequences among a variety of individual disasters. Typically, certain forms
of reorganization that were in process earlier are said to have been accelerated. For example, Margolis, (1979, 1980) has made such an interpretation of frost impacts on Brazilian coffee growers.

"This paper will review the post-frost adaptive strategies of coffee cul-
tivators in southern Brazil. Following Sjoberg, it will demonstrate that
natural hazards '. . . bring to the surface changes in the system that actually were underway prior to the catastrophe' (Sjoberg, 1962). [p. 231]
. . . The 1975 frost clearly was a catalyst for rather rapid social and economic change in Parana's coffee zone. But the specific responses to this
natural disaster in each of the zone's three sub-regions were largely shaped
by conditions existing *prior* to it. [i.e.,] Land divisions, soil quality, water
resources, labor legislation, and the subsequent economic regimes in the
three sub-regions in question [p. 235]'' [Brazil] (Margolis, 1980:231, 235).

VF1.4(H) Economic transformations already in process will be accelerated
by disasters. (Based on Margolis, 1979; Osterling, 1979.)

Such matters are very complex, however, and clearly will require extensive
theoretical development before we will have the guidance needed to direct
the data collections necessary to empirically test such interpretations.
Since Bates has considered such matters more than any other American
sociologist, I would advise any trying to pursue this topic to give special
attention to his (1982b) conclusions.

> "To decide upon which direction the society is moving in and also to
> understand the dynamics of the change process, it is necessary to attend
> to certain broad issues raised by scholars who study development and
> by those who shape the disaster relief process. The most important among
> these issues are: (a) the cultural and technological appropriateness of aid
> and of aid delivery systems, (b) the issues of dependency, paternalism,
> and rising expectations, (c) the question of centralized professional man-
> agement of aid processes versus decentralized, grass roots participation
> and management" [Guatemala] (Bates, 1982b:32).

Documents compiled by the Committee for the Compilation of Materials
on Damage Caused by the Atomic Bombs in Hiroshima and Nagasaki
(1981) summarize the history of a unique emergent social movement. It,
like the event that gave it birth, occupies a special niche in our disaster
taxonomy. Hopefully, no other social systems will have their roots in a
parallel event. As I pointed out in discussion of the other system levels,
however, such emergent phenomena—be they social action groups mobilized to attain "equitable" victim restitution, to curtail nuclear power
plant development, or, as in this case, to seek to abolish the use, indeed
the very existence, of nuclear arms—have been documented as one of
the social effects of disaster.

> VF1.5(H) Disasters produce emergent social movements when recurrence
> is perceived as avoidable and when victim compensation is perceived as
> being just. (Based on Committee for the Compilation of Materials on
> Damage Caused by the Atomic Bombs in Hiroshima and Nagasaki, 1981.)

Without attempting to do any more than highlight the detailed social
history of various A-bomb victims' movements, let me note that:

> "If the A-bomb victims' movements are viewed in terms of organizational
> activity and the nature of their appeals and demands, and if their strength
> is measured by success in getting laws enacted and budgets allocated,
> then there appear to be three major periods" (Committee for the Com-
> pilation of Materials on Damage Caused by the Atomic Bombs in Hi-
> roshima and Nagasaki, 1981:563).

The three developmental periods were: (1) 1945–1956—largely victim
aid and treatment activities; (2) 1956–1966—proposals to press for an international agreement to ban all nuclear weapons and to establish an A-

bomb victims relief law; and (3) 1966–1978—shift from a social welfare emphasis to a push for victim pensions and formal acknowledgment of demands, including: (a) compensation for the past, (b) relief for the present, and (c) a pledge for the future—that is, ''That the government declare its commitment, to the A-bomb victims and the Japanese people, that there never be another 'Hiroshima' or 'Nagasaki' '' (Committee for the Compilation of Materials on Damage Caused by the Atomic Bombs in Hiroshima and Nagasaki, 1981:568).

As with other emergent social systems, not only do such mobilizations impact the subsequent development and responses of entire nations, but so too the participants may experience important forms of psychological change. In the face of future potential tragedies, they have acted. And in so doing, the very core of their reason for living may be transformed. Thus, according to the Committee:

> ''. . . the A-bomb victims see themselves as a 'chosen people'—hence, their sense of mission. The ideology of the A-bomb victims outlined here is not merely an expression of 'restored' and 'recovered' psychological functions. It represents a higher level of consciousness attained through the strenuous process of recovering those functions. For the A-bomb victims, the forging of this ideology has changed the vague and remote concept of 'mankind' into a real and close feeling for actual people. The view of human life held by most people is constricted, if not microscopic. Life in the A-bomb victims' ideology has expanded spatially to embrace all the living and chronologically to include all yet to be born'' (Committee for the Compilation of Materials on Damage Caused by the Atomic Bombs in Hiroshima and Nagasaki, 1981:500).

VIF. International System Level

Paralleling the scarcity of research focused on the international system level during the other phases of disaster response, I found far more questions than answers here. Several exceptional field studies of reconstruction responses were completed during the 1970s, however. And a few ties permitting cross-national collaboration were created. While empirical comparisons of two or three nation state responses are to be lauded, they are but the beginning. Among the findings I uncovered, two themes were present: (1) dynamics of the recovery process and (2) societal variations. Neither, however, has been developed very far.

VIF1. Dynamics of the Recovery Process

Extended study in Nicaragua, following the 1972 earthquake, enriched the insights that Kates had developed over several years. Upon juxtaposing these data with the historical records of earthquake recovery in Anchorage (1964) and San Francisco (1906), and field studies conducted in Rapid City following the deadly 1972 flash flood, Kates (1977) drew the following conclusions. While each requires further testing, and qualification regarding exceptional cases, these propositions represent the best insights we have regarding the dynamics of the recovery process.

> VIF1.1(H) "*The reconstruction process is ordered, knowable, and predictable*—All cities rebuild and, except for the smallest of urban places, do so on the same site" [U.S.A. and Nicaragua] (Kates, 1977:262).

> VIF1.2(H) "*Ambitious planning is counterproductive* [p. 267] . . . the characteristic finale to such expectations is bitterness and disappointment. Much of the comprehensive study is little utilized, and the change affected is always less than the change potential. . . . comprehensiveness of study, flexibility of planning, and innovativeness of design are all purchased in heavy postdisaster coin, a high cost in precious time and anxious uncertainty [p. 268]" [U.S.A. and Nicaragua] (Kates, 1977:267, 268).

In contrast to these conclusions is a theme that appears in the literature frequently—at times, with a sharp tone of social criticism. Several researchers have questioned the effectiveness of relief efforts made by outsiders who seem to be oblivious to the constraints of culture and local resources. As noted above (IVF3.3), Mitchell put the issue bluntly. Geipel's (1982) work in Friuli, Italy, underscored this concern.

> "Mitchell's example . . . has parallels in Friuli; for example, in respect to location along railroad lines and heavily traveled roads. Here, the planners obviously have overlooked the fact that the nightly passage of trains past the flimsy prefabs would give rise to similar conditions to those of the earthquakes in the shaking and the noise they made, and did not take seriously enough the traumatic experiences of their potential occupants" [Italy] (Geipel, 1982:118–119).

> VIF1.3(H) "Western, consumer-oriented society is inclined to think in terms of material solutions like tents, emergency housing, and some permanent housing, while persons in developing countries tend to prefer social mechanisms such as extended family accomodation coupled with accelerated reconstruction. The problem is one of understanding local conditions and developing appropriate solutions, rather than designing abstract solutions to assumed problems" (Committee on International Disaster Assistance, 1978a:2).

Such disregard for local culture has predictable consequences, as the following case study materials illustrate. The extent of such actions, and their motivations, however, remain undocumented.

> "Many villagers would move into the new houses, stay for a short time, then return to the old site and rebuild their damaged homes. Consequently the new houses are in many instances uninhabited, are deteriorating, and are not being paid for. Why? [p. 311] . . .
> [1.] Most villagers complained about the small size of the houses.

Traditionally, many kept animals on the first level and lived on the second. The new village houses are on one level, however, so there is no place for animals. In the old houses the animals provide some heat and in turn are themselves protected from the cold, making the arrangement practical. . . .

[2.] Many of the glass windows in the new houses had been replaced by boards in 1973. The planners suggested that children were breaking the glass windows and that glass was too expensive to replace. The villagers agreed with this, but they expressed a desire for windows much higher or closer to the ceiling than the new houses provided. Traditional houses in Kutahya Province often have no windows, or the windows are high on the wall [p. 312]" [Turkey] (Mitchell, 1976a:311, 312).

VIF1.4(H) The greater the disparity between local culture expectations regarding shelter placement and design and that provided by donors from other nations, the less the levels of acceptance and use.

VIF1.4a(H) [Following earthquake, 1970] "Old Gediz had an estimated population of 2,500 in 1976. This is due to (1) villagers occupying abandoned homes, usually buying or renting them from owners who now live in the new city, and (2) the elderly who were reluctant to move due to folklore (belief in the need to stay where ancestry lived) and parochial attitudes" [Turkey] (Mitchell and Miner, 1978:80).

VIF1.4b(H) "Finally, the vital matter of cultural acceptance must be reemphasized. In Bangladesh some families were reluctant to live in the 'A' frame units because of associations with local church forms" [Bangladesh] (Davis, 1977:33).

Others have been even more questioning. For example, based on her assessment of the Nicaraguan and Guatemalan reconstruction processes, Kreimer (1979) questioned the fundamental motivations among local officials.

"The categories of emergency, temporary, and permanent housing, used not only for postdisaster shelter but also for shelter under standard conditions, are in many cases a device to legitimize a lack of government regulation of the housing sector, to provide visibility to the agencies' activities, and to disguise a lack of government programs to prevent the serious decay of the physical and environmental conditions of human settlements" (Kreimer, 1979:361).

Most pointed have been critiques regarding many aspects of the response to the Sahel drought. Glantz (1976), for example, expressed dismay at the "on-again–off-again" quality of the response.

". . . for one reason or another—political expediency, lack of resources, lack of concern—the will of governments to cope with these pressing perennial problems of the Sahel surfaces only intermittently. Their will is strong when a crisis is new but fades as the crisis continues in time, especially when it becomes clear that solutions required to deal effectively with the problems are often difficult to implement and not without sacrifice on the part of the recipient and donor states" (Glantz, 1976:20–21).

Seaman and Holt (1980) voiced similar conclusions following their study of starvation tragedies in Bangladesh and Ethiopia. Of special significance in all of these events were the refugee populations produced. Refugee migration is not well studied, be it the result of threatened starvation or political upheaval. When people do move, however, field reports clearly indicate—as I pointed out with short-term pre-event evacuations—that their choices remain patterned by the anticipated presence of kin or friends. Such informal networks may do far more to pattern such movements of humanity than governmental policies or threatened dangers.

VIF1.5(H) Most refugee populations will migrate to locations occupied by kin and friends. (Based on Hansen, 1979:378; Neldner, 1979:393.)

VIF1.5a(H) "By 1972 there were approximately 20,000 Angolan refugees in Zambia. About 7,000 (35%) were housed in government refugee camps, while the rest had spontaneously resettled themselves in existing rural settlements, towns and cities. . . . Many Angolans had Zambian relatives, and some Angolans had previously lived in Zambia. . . . many Angolans were fleeing to known people and places, and these Angolans were accompanied by their relatives and friends" [Zambia and Angola] (Hansen, 1979:378).

More analytical than most other reports on the Sahel drought that I reviewed was the work of Brown, Tuthill, and Rowe (1976). Yet, they too underscored many shortcomings of the response—especially interagency coordination.

VIF1.6(H) "Many field personnel of the voluntary agencies are very aware of the need for increased interagency and host-country cooperation. This is manifested in their active support of such groups as SPONG. However, effective progress in development cooperation must occur at *both* the field and headquarters level to be productive. Without this kind of cooperation, the very special experiences and contributions of voluntary agencies in the development process may well lose their potential impact in improving the lives of those they most want to help" (Brown, Tuthill, and Rowe, 1976:VA24).

Speaking with the tone of a seasoned practitioner, Cuny's (1983) dissection of the international relief system response to numerous events elaborated on these themes and integrated them into a conceptual whole. "There are a number of major problems common to the relief system and the agencies and organizations within it" (Cuny, 1983:125). Among these are: decision-making and authority issues, accountability, the overloading of local organizations, competition, lack of coordination, and various obstacles to change, like the lack of a collective memory, failure to evaluate programs, and inadequate training (adapted from Cuny, 1983:125–137).

Reflecting the viewpoint of administrators from voluntary and private sector relief organizations, Cuny highlighted numerous "lessons from the past." Among these were the following:

VIF1.7(H) "Relief and reconstruction operations should be conducted within the context of development. [p. 103] . . . The lack of uniform reconstruction standards or policies (or failure of all intervenors to agree on basic approaches to relief) creates undue competition and leads to inequitable distribution of assistance. [p. 104] . . . Aid may inadvertently be provided in such a way as to inhibit the recovery process and create dependence [p. 104]" (Cuny, 1983:103, 104).

VIF2. Societal Variations

Returning to the study directed by Haas, Kates, and Bowden (1977), future researchers should try to build on the role of differential kinship emphases in disaster recovery. Contrasts among the coping pathways selected by Managuan families and those in Rapid City are most instructive.

VIF2.1 "Within the family, three pathways of recovery describe the range of familial coping for postdisaster homes and jobs: institutional, kin, and autonomous modes" [U.S.A. and Nicaragua] (Kates, 1977:264).

VIF2.1a ". . . Rapid City was characterized by very high reliance on institutional aid from public and private sources, supplemented by help from relatives. In Managua, familial aid from relatives was the major source" [U.S.A. and Nicaragua] (Kates, 1977:264).

VIF2.1b [Two factors account for these differences: 1.] "In Managua the extensiveness of the earthquake created a large victim population, while at the same time damaging a major part of the city's resource structure. . . . In Rapid City the damage was in a limited area and the community's resource structure received massive inputs in the form of federal aid. . . . [2.] Latin American normative structure specifies a reliance on kinship ties in times of crisis while in the United States it is typical to turn to the government in all but domestic crises" [U.S.A. and Nicaragua] (Bolin and Trainer, 1978:236).

VIF2.2 ". . . recovery processes in different cultures reflect different institutionalized mechanisms for the acquisition and distribution of resources for reestablishing, maintaining, or improving one's position within the social whole. . . . the processes of disaster 'recovery', whether judged successful or unsuccessful by those persons involved with promoting recovery, are not special cases of 'disaster behavior' but cultural values for the community or society under scrutiny" (Bolin and Bolton, 1983:143).

VIF2.2a ". . . Managua victim families were more likely to report being recovered eighteen months after the disaster if the head of household had been employed for all or most of the time since the disaster. The head of household was, in turn, more likely to have steady work if he or she was high on the measure of access to resources. It can be noted that recovery of one's predisaster level of income was not important enough to perception of recovery on the part of the head of household that it even remained in the revised model.

For Rapid City, continuity of employment is not an important factor in the perception of recovery. The recovery of an income level similar to or higher than the family's predisaster level has considerably more effect" (Bolin and Bolton, 1983:138–140). (See also Trainer and Bolin, 1977:55.)

Shifting levels, and contrasting two more comparable cultures, Kreimer (1978) underscored the importance of governmental structure.

VIF2.3(H) The degree of governmental centralization will constrain the recovery process. (Based on Kreimer, 1978.)

VIF2.3a(H) [Reconstruction policies and practices in Nicaragua were far more centralized than those in Guatemala. Two positive aspects were:] "1. *Emphasis on the utilization of recycled and recovered materials*. [p. 35] . . . 2. *Attempts by several agencies to implement self-help and training programs, and to promote the organization of cooperatives* [p. 36]" [Nicaragua and Guatemala] (Kreimer, 1978:35, 36).

VIF2.3b(H) "Two problems associated with the decentralized approach undertaken in the reconstruction were: 1. *Emphasis in the reconstruction of rural areas rather than urban areas*. . . . 2. *Lack of provision of comprehensive plans for development of infrastructure and social facilities for the communities*" [Nicaragua and Guatemala] (Kreimer, 1978:36).

Following the eruptions of Mount Usu and Mount St. Helens, Perry and Hirose (1983, 1982) collaborated in a study to compare the responses in Toyako-Onsen, Japan, and Cougar, Washington. While there were some minor response differences initially, both communities evidenced parallel restructuring. This reflected the similarities in their initial economic organization—tourist-based economies—and the impact brought by the threat of future volcanic activity. Thus, patterns of multilineal cultural evolution may have much relevance for sorting out cross-societal similarities and differences in cross-societal adaptations.

VIF2.4(H) Communities with comparable patterns of economic organization will tend to evidence parallel modes of differential adaptation when impacted by similar types of disaster, actual or threatened. (Based on Perry and Hirose, 1982, 1983.)

VIF2.4a(H) ". . . the post-impact recovery of tourist commerce was significantly affected by the perceptions of the public regarding the safety of the area after the eruption. The belief on the part of outsiders that the volcanoes posed some danger to visitors apparently inhibited tourism to the stricken towns for some time following the major erutpions. . . .

[Thus, the communities] experienced functional shifts of emphasis in local tourist economies. In each case, the tourist business became largely a day-time or day-trip affair, requiring local business to increase reliance upon selling souvenirs and catering to the needs of short-term visitors" (Perry and Hirose, 1983:247).

This line of reasoning was developed most fully by Dynes (1972, 1975) through the three clusters of societal types I summarized earlier (see VID1.1). Reflective of Sjoberg's (1962) earlier analysis, Dynes linked several key aspects of macro social theory and disaster field studies. Thus, extending to longer-term adaptations we have a hypothesis that parallels the one presented above.

VIF2.5(H) Type and mode of structural adaptation following disaster covaries with societal type. (Based on Dynes, 1975.)

As I noted above, however, Torry has challenged Dynes' implicit "developmental bias" (e.g., Torry, 1978a, b). Type I societies may have far greater adaptive potentials than Dynes acknowledged. Using village responses to famine in India, Torry (1979b) developed a complex hypothesis network. The logic of that network paralleled his earlier case materials from three dam impact studies on African tribes and reanalysis of anthropological field reports.

". . . the portrayal of traditional social system responses to extreme ecological stress as fragile, plastic or rigid, or encumbered by mystical constraints is unacceptable. Rather, recovery phase adjustments seem to assume the following pattern. Social activity is scaled down but not restructured. Routines that bear on the food quest and on physical security are stressed while many others are retrenched, substituted, simplified or merged. . . . Nowhere is retrenchment more pronounced than in the ceremonial sphere. This is perhaps because ceremonies draw heavily on food reserves and consume time while ostensibly contributing little to productive requirements. Political activity, however, is intensified to promote collective activities that enhance communal welfare" [Tikopia, Solomon Islands; Ghana; Nubia, United Arab Republic; Zambia; and Rhodesia] (Torry, 1978b:180).

More conjectural than empirical—at least as I use that term—are Barkun's (1974) notions about millenarianism. While I question whether or not subsequent empirical investigation will validate many of his hypotheses, I like the type of questions he raises. Implicit in his book is an entire research area that heretofore has escaped the traditional disaster research specialist. ". . . millenarian or chiliastic movements are social movements which expect immediate, collective, total, this-worldly salvation. They anticipate the complete destruction of the existing social, political, and economic order, which is to be superseded by a new and perfect society" (Barkun, 1974:18).

Given this definition, what types of disasters might give rise to such collective responses? Barkun answers this question in the negative.

VIF2.6(H) "There are four kinds of disaster situations from which millenarian movements are *not* likely to emerge: those that leave a substantial portion of the perceived primary environment intact, those where the environmental damage is quickly repaired, those indefinitely prolonged within the same social unit, and those which occur in the absence of ideas of future change" (Barkun, 1974:64).

Returning to the study with which we began this section, i.e., the work directed by Haas, Kates, and Bowden (1977), let's conclude this chapter with a final series of findings. They are follow-on products of this study, although published by two junior members of the research team. They represent the type of conceptual precision that I hope will characterize future cross-national disaster data banks. For only through analyses with this type of methodological rigor will we ever be able to unravel the complex mazeway that constitutes this social reality.

VIF2.7(H) "The case studies of the two cities indicate that the disruption of routine activities, including use of local facilities, neighboring, kin visitation, and leisure, was pervasive following the 1972 disaster at each site. Further, for some families alterations in daily life styles persisted, or were perceived to still exist, for periods of more than a year following impact" [U.S.A. and Nicaragua] (Trainer and Bolin, 1976:282).

VIF2.7a(H) "Visiting: . . . Managua: . . . About 60% reported they engaged in about the same amount of visiting as before. But 28% indicated they visited less with their relatives than they used to, and 31% reported less frequent visiting with friends than before the disaster. The in-depth interviews done with some of these families indicated that to a great extent decrease in visiting had to do with the dispersion of persons throughout the city. . . . Rapid City victim families also displayed a decrease in frequency of visiting. At Time 1 in Rapid City, 41% of the victim families interviewed indicated they visited their predisaster neighbors less, while 9% said they visited their relatives less than before the impact. [p. 284] . . . With respect to relatives, in Rapid City there was only a slight decline in visiting after the disaster, and most victim families reported normal visiting frequencies with kin by Time 2. This would indicate the greater saliency of kin networks over friendship networks to victim families in the recovery stage" [pp. 284–285]" [U.S.A. and Nicaragua] (Trainer and Bolin, 1976:284–285).

VIF2.7b(H) "Leisure Activities: At Time 2 in Managua, 32% of the heads of household were reported to no longer engage in what had been their favorite leisure time activity prior to the disaster . . . . While many respondents [in Rapid City] revealed a reduction in the amount of time available for leisure pursuits, when time was available most families (71%) continued to pursue their favorite preflood leisure activities" [U.S.A. and Nicaragua] (Trainer and Bolin, 1976:285).

Selected Bibliography

Ahearn, Frederick L., Jr. [1981] "Disaster Mental-Health—A Pre-Earthquake and Post-Earthquake Comparison of Psychiatric Admission Rates." *Urban and Social Change Review* **14** (Summer):22–28.

Anderson, William A. [1970] "Disaster and Organizational Change in Anchorage." Pp. 96–115 in *The Great Alaska Earthquake of 1964*, Committee on the Alaska Earthquake of the National Research Council (ed.). Washington, D.C.: National Academy of Sciences.

Bates, Frederick L. (ed.) [1982] "Recovery, Change and Development: A Longitudinal Study of the Guatemalan Earthquake." Athens, Georgia: Guatemalan Earthquake Study, University of Georgia.

Bolin, Robert C. [1982] *Long-Term Family Recovery from Disaster*. Boulder, Colorado: Institute of Behavioral Science, The University of Colorado.

Bolin, Robert C., and Patricia A. Bolton [1983] "Recovery in Nicaragua and the U.S.A." *International Journal of Mass Emergencies and Disasters* **1** (March): 125–152.

Britton, Neil R. [1981] *Darwin's Cyclone 'Max': An Exploratory Investigation of a Natural Hazard Sequence on the Development of a Disaster Subculture*. Disaster Investigation Report No. 4. Townsville, Queensland, Australia: Centre for Disaster Studies, James Cook University of North Queensland.

Cattarinussi, Bernardo, C. Pelanda, A. Moretti, in collaboration with M. Strassoldo, R. Strassoldo, and B. Tellia [1981] *Il Disastro: Effetti di Lungo Termine—Indagine Psicosociologica Nelle Aree Colpite dal Terremoto del Friuli* (The Disaster: Long-Term Effects—Sociopsychological Investigation in Areas Stricken by Friuli Earthquake) (in Italian). Udine, Italy: Editrice Grillo.

Cuny, Frederick C. [1983] *Disasters and Development*. New York: Oxford University Press.

Douty, Christopher Morris [1977] *The Economics of Localized Disasters*. New York: Arno Press.

Drabek, Thomas E., and William H. Key [1984] *Conquering Disaster: Family Recovery and Long-Term Consequences*. New York: Irvington Publishers.

Drabek, Thomas E., and E. L. Quarantelli [1967] "Scapegoats, Villains, and Disasters." *Transaction* **4** (March):12–17.

Erikson, Kai T. [1976] *Everything in Its Path*. New York: Simon and Schuster.

Forrest, Thomas R. [1979] "Hurricane Betsy, 1965; A Selective Analysis of Organizational Response in the New Orleans Area." The Disaster Research Center Historical and Comparative Disaster Series, No. 5. Columbus, Ohio: Disaster Research Center, The Ohio State University.

Francaviglia, Richard V. [1978] "Xenia Rebuilds—Effects of Pre-Disaster Conditioning on Post-Disaster Redevelopment." *Journal of the American Institute of Planners* **44** (No. 1):13–24.

Friesema, H. Paul, James Caporaso, Gerald Goldstein, Robert Lineberry, and Richard McCleary [1979] *Aftermath: Communities after Natural Disasters*. Beverly Hills, California, and London: Sage Publications.

Geipel, Robert [1982] *Disaster and Reconstruction: The Friuli (Italy) Earthquakes of 1976*. London: George Allen & Unwin.

Glantz, Michael H. (ed.) [1976] *The Politics of Natural Disaster: The Case of the Sahel Drought*. New York: Praeger Publishers.

Gleser, Goldine C., Bonnie L. Green and Carolyn N. Winget [1981] *Prolonged Psychosocial Effects of Disaster: A Study of Buffalo Creek.* New York: Academic Press.

Goldsteen, Raymond L., John Schorr, and Karen S. Goldsteen [1984] "What's the Matter with Those People: Rethinking TMI." *International Journal of Mass Emergencies and Disasters* **2** (November):369–387.

Grecu, G., K. Csiky and I. Munteanu [1972] "Studi Asupra Unui Grup de 87 Bolnavi cu Stări Depresive Declanşate de Inundatiile Din Mai 1970" (Study on a Group of 87 Patients with Depressive States Triggered by the Floods of May 1970) (in Romanian). *Neurologia, Psihiatria, Neurochirurgia* **17** (March):109–115.

Haas, J. Eugene, Robert W. Kates, and Martyn J. Bowden [1977] *Reconstruction Following Disaster.* Cambridge, Massachusetts, and London: The MIT Press.

Harvey, Carol D.H., and Howard M. Bahr [1980] *The Sunshine Widows: Adapting to Sudden Bereavement.* Toronto: Lexington Books.

Hogg, Sarah Jane [1980] "Reconstruction Following Seismic Disaster in Venzone, Friuli." *Disasters* **4** (No. 2):173–185.

Janerich, Dwight T., Alice D. Stark, Peter Greenwald, William S. Burnett, Herbert I. Jacobson, and Jane McCusker [1981] "Increased Leukemia, Lymphoma, and Spontaneous Abortion in Western New York Following a Flood Disaster." *Public Health Reports* **96** (July–August):350–356.

Jones, David R., and Joseph R. Fischer [1982] "Emotional Effects on USAF Personnel of Recovering and Identifying Victims from Jonestown, Guyana." Brooks Air Force Base, Texas: USAF School of Aerospace Medicine.

Kreimer, Alcira [1978] "Post-Disaster Reconstruction Planning: The Cases of Nicaragua and Guatemala." *Mass Emergencies* **3**:23–40.

Leik, Robert K., Sheila A. Leik, Knut Ekker, and Gregory A. Gifford [1982] "Under the Threat of Mount St. Helens: A Study of Chronic Family Stress." Minneapolis, Minnesota: Family Study Center, University of Minnesota.

Lifton, Robert Jay, and Eric Olson [1976] "The Human Meaning of Total Disaster: The Buffalo Creek Experience." *Psychiatry* **39** (February):1–18.

Lindy, Jacob D., Mary C. Grace, and Bonnie L. Green [1981] "Survivors: Outreach to a Reluctant Population." *American Journal of Orthopsychiatry* **5** (July):468–478.

Logue, James N., Mary Evans Melick, and Elmer L. Struening [1981] "A Study of Health and Mental Health Status Following a Major Natural Disaster." Pp. 217–274 in *Research in Community and Mental Health*, Roberta G. Simmons (ed.). Greenwich, Connecticut: Jai Press, Inc.

Mileti, Dennis S., Donald M. Hartsough, Patti Madson, and Rick Hufnagel [1984] "The Three Mile Island Incident: A Study of Behavioral Indicators of Human Stress." *International Journal of Mass Emergencies and Disasters* **2** (March):89–113.

Mitchell, William A. [1976] "Reconstruction after Disaster—Gediz Earthquake of 1970." *Geographical Review* **66**:296–313.

Moric-Petrovic, Slavka, Milica Jojic-Milenkovic, and Milica Marinkov [1972] "Mentalno-Higijenski Problemi Dece Evakuisane Posle Katastrofalnog Zemljotresa U Skoplju" (Mental Hygiene Problems of Children Evacuated after Catastrophic Earthquake in Skopje) (in Serbo-Croatian). *Anali Zavoda Za Mentalno Zdravlje* **4** (No. 1):53–64.

Oliver-Smith, Anthony [1979] "The Yungay Avalanche of 1970: Anthropological Perspectives on Disaster and Social Change." *Disasters* **3** (No. 1):95–101.

Ollendick, Duane G., and Sister Margeen Hoffmann [1982] "Assessment of Psychological Reactions in Disaster Victims." *Journal of Community Psychology* **10** (April):157–167.

Perry, Ronald W., and Hirotada Hirose [1983] "Volcanic Eruptions and Functional Change: Parallels in Japan and the United States." *International Journal of Mass Emergencies and Disasters* **1** (August):231–253.

Perry, Ronald W., and Michael K. Lindell [1978] "The Psychological Consequences of Natural Disaster: A Review of Research on American Communities." *Mass Emergencies* **3**:105–115.

Predescu, V., and St. Nica-Udangiu [1979] "Postseismic Reactions, Observations on a Group of Patients Displaying Psychic Disorders Determined by March 4, 1977 Earthquake in Romania." *Revue Roumaine De Médecine—Neurologie Et Psychiatrie* **17** (No. 3):179–188.

Ross, G. Alexander [1978] "Organizational Innovation in Disaster Settings." Pp. 215–232 in *Disasters: Theory and Research*, E. L. Quarantelli (ed.). Beverly Hills, California: Sage.

Rubin, Claire B. with Martin D. Saperstein and Daniel G. Barbee [1985] *Community Recovery from a Major Natural Disaster*. Boulder, Colorado: Institute of Behavioral Science, University of Colorado.

Strassoldo, Raimondo, and Carlo Pelanda [1980–81] "Quattro Anni Dopo la Catastrofe: Le Conseguenze Psico-sociodogiche—Alcune Risultanze di Una Ricerca sul Friuli Terremotato" (Four Years after the Friuli Disaster: The Sociopsychological Consequences—Some Results of a Research Study on the Friuli Earthquake) (in Italian). *Quaderni di Sociologia* (No. 3):447–480.

Walsh, Edward J., and Rex H. Warland [1983] "Social Movement Involvement in the Wake of a Nuclear Accident: Activists and Free Riders in the TMI Area." *American Sociological Review* **48** (December):764–780.

Wolensky, Robert P. [1984] "Power, Policy, and Disaster: The Political-Organizational Impact of a Major Flood." Stevens Point, Wisconsin: Center for the Small City, University of Wisconsin-Stevens Point.

Wright, James D., Peter H. Rossi, Sonia R. Wright, and Eleanor Weber-Burdin [1979] *After the Clean-Up: Long-Range Effects of Natural Disasters*. Beverly Hills, California: Sage.

8
Hazard Perceptions

While my literature search effort was structured so as to identify socio-logical studies of human system responses to specific *disaster events* of various types, early on I decided to include two chapters pertaining to disaster mitigation—one focused on hazard perceptions and another per-taining to hazard adjustments. In part, this reflects my belief that theories and public policies dealing with disasters—regardless of presumed cause—will be better informed if sociologists work within this broader context. Furthermore, if adopted and implemented, specific findings from disaster studies represent a form of mitigation—also a social process that can be improved through a better understanding of it. Thus, the mitigation phase completes the human response cycle.

While disasters *will* occur in the future, our responses to them can be made more effective through policy changes based on an improved knowledge base and better use of our existing one. But societies, like their respective subsystems, can mitigate. Actions can be taken to reduce the probabilities of occurrence, lessen the scope and intensity of impact, and enhance the quality and capacity for recovery. Knowledge of the human dimension regarding this aspect of disaster response can be as useful to the policy process as that pertaining to responses to disastrous events. Why? Because it can tell us why some social policies are more likely to be adopted than others; why some are destined to be implemented less effectively than others; and why many will never get beyond the talk stage until a certain mix of conditions emerge. In short, such research reveals the perceptions of hazards held by individuals, ranging from homeowners to national policy makers. These perceptions—both of the hazard and of various adjustment options—combine with other structural factors to form the invisible webs of constraint that place some people into settings wherein they have an increased probability of becoming disaster victims.

But the cautionary comments made in Chapter 1 must be reemphasized. I *did not* design a separate search for materials reporting disaster mitigation responses. Hence, this chapter and the one which follows *lack the comprehensive quality* that characterized those which precede. Literally, hundreds of studies were *not included* that would have been captured with different search procedures. Risk perception studies (e.g., Burton, Fowle, and McCullough, 1982; Covello, 1983) were not searched for separately. Nor were studies of various potential adjustments—be they structural devices, like dams, or nonstructural approaches, like flood insurance. Similarly, I did not make any effort to locate studies on plant safety programs, industrial security, corporate record storage practices, or a host of other topics that constitute this complex and multifaceted topic. While not comprehensive, I believe that this chapter, like the one that follows it, does convey an overall portrait of the larger literature base that is valid and balanced. But these two chapters *only illustrate* the range of research completed to date.

IG. Individual System Level

Three topics convey the emphases found within the findings I encountered regarding the hazard perceptions found among individuals: (1) hazard awareness and salience; (2) the role of experience; and (3) other correlates of hazard perception.

IG1. Hazard Awareness and Salience

Repeatedly, investigators have documented that the public lacks knowledge of and underestimates the hazardous quality of their environment (Covello, 1983). Some scholars resort to psychoanalytic interpretations of denial; others stress fundamental ignorance of earth-science principles, be they geologic, climatologic, or hydrologic in nature. My personal view emphasizes that people are people. That is, these underestimations reflect busy people. They are occupied with their own life priorities—day-to-day issues of living. Available leisure time easily is skewed elsewhere, given the enormous competition; after all, following the Rose Bowl comes the Super Bowl. Thus, aside from the matter of risks associated with nuclear energy—which appears to be an exception of the opposite extreme, except in terms of rampant public ignorance—the general pattern is underestimation. Clearly, there are variations on the theme; future study will provide the increased calibration needed—both regarding the risk estimation process and those factors associated with its patterned variation.

IG1.1 "Researchers have shown that experts and lay persons are typically overconfident about their risk estimates. . . . overconfidence leads people to believe that they are comparatively immune to common hazards" (Covello, 1983:288). (See also Murton and Shimabukuro, 1974:156; Jackson and Mukerjee, 1974:166; Lewis, 1975:29; Whyte, 1980:30; Hammarstrom, Hultaker, and Trost, 1980:7–8.)

IG1.1a ". . . the public tends to overestimate mortality rates from well-publicized hazards such as botulism, floods and tornadoes, it underestimates those from most chronic causes of death, such as diabetes, stomach cancer, and strokes (Fischhoff et al., 1978)" (Foster, 1980:32).

IG1.1b ". . . interviews indicate that the floodplain dwellers [n = 162] have no real appreciation of the flood danger and tend to minimize the extent of the damage that might result from a severe flood. [p. 25] . . . Floodplain users in Tucson in general are very satisfied with their neighborhoods and believe that the floodplain is an excellent place to live with no real disadvantages. A high proportion, 61%, do not appreciate that their area is in a flood danger zone while only 35% believe they would personally be affected. Those who are aware, consider that risk to life is low and expect to experience mainly property damage [p. 38]" (McPherson and Saarinen, 1977:25, 38).

IG1.1c ". . . the most striking aspect of these results is that perceived risk shows no significant correlation with the factor mortality. Thus, the variable most frequently chosen by scientists to represent risk appears not to be a strong factor in the judgment of our subjects" (Hohenemser, Kates, and Slovic, 1983:382).

As researchers have picked away at these perception sets, it has become clear that some very difficult methodological issues must be solved better (Covello, 1983). Questions worded differently do produce differences in results, and often in interpretation. Among the several issues that must be explored carefully are: (1) alternative measures of attitudes like hazard salience; (2) relative stability of such perception sets and the identification of factors that impact them; and (3) more precise assessment of the linkage between perceptions of hazard salience and awareness and adaptive action.

IG1.2 Relative to other community problems, natural hazards are named infrequently by the general public. (Based on Turner et al., 1979.)

IG1.2a Only two percent mentioned earthquakes when asked to name the three most important problems facing Southern California. Over sixty percent indicated that they were substantially frightened about the possibility of a damaging earthquake. Only ten persons (sample = 1450) indicated that they might move out of their current residence within the next five years because of fearing an earthquake. (Adapted from Turner et al., 1979:45, 47, 54–55.)

IG1.3(H) Among the public the relative salience of specific hazards varies over time; there is instability and change. (Based on Nigg, 1982; see also Moline, 1974:55.)

Evidence here is mixed, in part, I suspect because of the complex role that experience with a hazard plays. We'll pursue that matter in the next section, however.

> IG1.3a ". . . although the Minturn announcement contributed greatly to the overall trend of awareness, its effect was chiefly to exaggerate the loss of awareness between February and August 1977. The initial high levels of awareness, then, might be viewed as the consequence of unusual circumstances in 1976—the widespread media attention to earthquake prediction, major rumors in October and November of a destructive quake, and the widely publicized Minturn prediction in December. As the impact of these special circumstances wore off, the level of awareness seemed to decline'' (Nigg, 1982:76).

> IG1.3b " 'How certain are you that you now possess enough information to adequately protect yourself,' asked in April and then in August, 1980. These data indicate that people have become considerably *less* certain about whether or not they have sufficient information to protect themselves. [p. 105] . . . the respondents in Woodland have moved from a position of certainty—either likely or unlikely—to a position of relative uncertainty—i.e., even odds—regarding the likelihood that an eruption at Mt. St. Helens would affect their safety [p. 110]'' (Perry and Greene, 1983:105, 110).

Presently, we lack clarity regarding the relationship between hazard awareness—or other such attitudinal qualities—and many, though not all, forms of mitigative action. Recall discussion of this variable from the chapter on warning. We know, for example, that the propensity to evacuate when warned prior to a tornado or a hurricane increases directly with an accurate awareness and understanding of the hazard. Furthermore, limited evidence suggests that hazard perception is more helpful in understanding behavioral responses than simple measures of previous structural damage to one's home, for example.

In general, however, California data from several studies (e.g., Palm, 1981) are consistent with earlier results from Japan. That is, when victims were asked if they had given anti-earthquake measures any consideration when they purchased their home, 86% indicated that they had not (Yasuda and Sato, 1979). Thus, the percentages adopting any of the mitigative measures the investigators studied are relatively small. This too is true of self-reported actions taken toward such technologies as nuclear power plants—actions like writing a letter to a newspaper. Gardner and his associates (1982:187) reported that slightly over one-quarter (28.1%) of their sample ($n = 367$) had done so. And hazard perceptions appeared to be the key differentiating factor.

> IG1.4(H) "We would guess that the degree of personal action taken by Americans toward nuclear power is influenced directly by a large number of variables. Among the most important are its judged acceptability (both

in terms of desired restrictions and standards and desired level of deployment), attitudes towards relevant institutions, and several sociodemographic variables. Action is directly influenced, but to a lesser extent, by the perceived risks and benefits of nuclear power and perhaps also by qualitative risk and benefit characteristics and fatality estimates" (Gardner *et al.*, 1982:196). (See also Greene, Perry, and Lindell, 1981:61; Miller, Brinkmann, and Barry, 1974:84; Chandessais, 1980:228.)

IG1.4a(H) "[In 1976] . . . only 16% of those interviewed claimed they were informed of any possible earthquake hazards by the previous owner, developer, or landlord. However, the percentage had doubled from the 8% who said so in 1970. Furthermore, 55% (1976) as compared to 22% (1970) said they would inform future residents of potential earthquake hazards. . . . More significant than the change in attitudes was the increase in the percentage of residents who carried special earthquake insurance on their homes. This more than quadrupled from 5% in 1970 to 22% in 1976" (Saarinen, 1982b:14).

Several independent variables have been identified that appear to constrain attitudes toward and perception of hazards. A summary statement proposed by Gilbert F. White (1974b) over a decade ago still constitutes a reasonable interpretation of this literature base. Again I want to stress that the following discussion only *illustrates* the range of research that has been completed.

"Variation in hazard perception and estimation can be accounted for by a combination of the following: 1. Magnitude and frequency of the hazard; 2. Recency and frequency of personal experience, with intermediate frequency generating greatest variation in hazard interpretation and expectation; 3. Importance of the hazard to income or locational interest; 4. Personality factors such as risk-taking propensity, fate control, and views of nature. This variation is not related to common socioeconomic indicators such as age, education, and income" (Gilbert F. White, 1974b:5). (See also Murton and Shimabukuro, 1974:159.)

IG2. The Role of Experience

Experience with different hazards, as noted above, does impact our perceptions of them.

IG2.1 "Persons having more previous experience with the specific hazard (Kates, 1971; Burton and Kates, 1964; Roder, 1961; Saarinen, 1966), and those having a direct economic relationship to the hazard (a dry land farmer in relation to drought hazard), tend to have greater accuracy of hazard perception (Burton, 1962; Saarinen, 1966). Experiencing recent and intense impact by the hazard also seems to be associated with more accurate hazard perception (Kates, 1971)" (as summarized in Mileti, Drabek, and Haas, 1975:24). (See also Guard Police Psychology Research Society, 1977; Wenger, James, and Faupel, 1980:121; Cheney, 1979:88; Britton, 1983:141; Brinkmann, 1975b:41; Kunreuther *et al.*, 1978:241.)

Corroborating evidence has been published, reflecting a variety of additional types of natural hazards, since we formulated this proposition. The following conclusions illustrate this range of studies.

IG2.1a "*Prior* to its March activity, most respondents claimed to believe that volcanic activity was unlikely to affect their personal safety. . . . Once volcanic activity began in March, 1980, however, local residents became sensitized to their proximity to the volcano and to the increased probability of an eruption. . . . although awareness of the volcano hazard in general increased, people had some trouble identifying specific dangers—when asked to name specific threats, 31 percent of the total sample said they didn't know exactly what would threaten their safety" (Perry and Greene, 1983:30).

IG2.1b ". . . 54% of those interviewed had no idea when the most recent tornado occurred in the Kalamazoo area. Twenty-two per cent were able to correctly identify that a tornado had struck the county within the previous 2 years. . . . the basic mechanics of tornadoes were understood by the majority of the people. . . . Fewer correct responses were found pertaining to the rate a tornado moves across the landscape. . . . Some tornado folklore appears to be accepted as fact by over 70% of those interviewed. 'It is always calm just before a tornado hits' brought rapid agreement by many people" (Hodler, 1982:46).

Despite this overall pattern, "experience" is not uniform in its impact. Some people, perhaps reflecting a mythology akin to "lightning never strikes the same place twice," apparently twist their experience into a misplaced sense of invulnerability.

IG2.2 ". . . while the nature of past experience may be an important factor in forming people's perceptions of earthquake hazard, such experience is subject to a range of interpretation. Some respondents concluded that past damages provided evidence of likely future occurrence, while for others, simple awareness of local seismic risk was sufficient. Still another group strongly believed that, having sustained damages in the past, they were unlikely to do so again in the future" [Canada and U.S.A.] (Jackson, 1981:400–401). (See also Baumann and Sims, 1974:27.)

IG2.2a "One of the most alarming findings was the high rate of perceived 'past experience with hurricanes' among our respondents. When reviewing their claims and comparing them with actual occurrence, it became clear that most had experienced at best peripheral effects of storms, and many had encountered storms that were not even hurricanes. Our evidence shows that this 'experience' has led people to have greater confidence in their ability to survive another storm by taking the same minimal emergency measures they took in the past" [Survey in Sarasota, Florida] (Levy and Smith, n.d.:53).

IG2.2b ". . . approximately one half of those interviewed indicated they had never seriously considered the possibility of suffering flood loss prior to the flood of 1972. This lack of awareness of potential flooding was evidently based on the fact that in their memory (including for some 1936) no serious flooding had occurred on that section of Fishing Creek. . . . Even with the extensive damage that was experienced by many owners in the floods of 1972 and 1975, one half of those interviewed indicated that if they had it to do over again, they would still purchase the property. . . . Several factors seem to account for the relatively high satisfaction level with property in a proven flood hazard location. . . . [e.g.,] Most cottages had screen porches overlooking the Creek . . . friendship that has developed among the cottage people" (Johnson, 1968:8).

Such alternative interpretations are not unique to earthquakes, hurricanes, or floods. A follow-up study on the 1953 tornado that hit Flint, Michigan, provided an important insight.

[Follow-up interviews done in 1975 regarding awareness of 1953 tornado] "Responses in the interviews that were conducted with residents along the tornado path differed significantly from those of people involved in the random telephone survey drawn from a wider area. . . . awareness of this historic event is directly related to age, to length of residence at present address, and to length of residence in the county" (Perry O. Hanson, Vitek, and Hanson, 1979:23).

Thus, "experience" does matter, but one need not be a direct victim to have "experience."

IG2.3(H) "Only 10% of the respondents had suffered personal or family loss, injury, or property damage in the Flint tornado. [p. 281] . . . awareness of an event is higher in the immediate vicinity of the disaster and that awareness of an historical event does have an effect on people's response patterns. [p. 282] . . . it is *not* past experience with tornadoes that makes one more actively responsive to tornado warnings; there is no significant difference between those who have and those who have not experienced tornadoes in their patterns of response to warnings. It is awareness itself, not experience, that affects people's response to warnings [p. 280]" (Susan Hanson, Vitek, and Hanson, 1979:280–282).

Similarly, limited evidence suggests that views regarding causality—especially whether or not one believes that one personally can do anything to alter the outcome—are impacted by some disaster experiences. This, in turn, may affect both future hazard perceptions and the propensity to initiate various types of adaptive actions.

IG2.4 ". . . those whose homes had been destroyed attributed such outcomes more to luck and less to their own efforts, despite the fact that victims did not differ from nonvictims in actual efforts during the fire nor in characteristics of their homes. These results were interpreted as a naturalistic replication of previous findings regarding the illusion of control over chance events" (Parker, Brewer, and Spencer, 1980:454).

IG2.4a "Victims of the fire were significantly more likely to attribute such outcomes to luck and less to their own efforts than were those who had escaped major damage from the fire" (Parker, Brewer, and Spencer, 1980:459).

IG2.4b ". . . victims consistently did indicate higher probabilities for future fire damage then did nonvictims" (Parker, Brewer, and Spencer, 1980:459).

Independent of these aspects of the "experience" variable is the matter of frequency. Greater frequency increases awareness.

IG2.5 ". . . the perception of environmental problems and hazards is closely related to the frequency of such events. Hence, in Carlisle traffic noise and other local problems were seen as more important than flooding, which was spontaneously named by only 3 per cent of respondents as a disadvantage of the area. Conversely, flooding was specifically mentioned by 27 per cent of the floodplain residents in Appleby and was rated as the most important local environmental problem" [England] (Smith and Tobin, 1979:100). (See also Mileti, Drabek, and Haas, 1974:31; Shippee, Bradford, and Gregory, 1982:23.)

IG2.5a ". . . long intervals between individual cyclones may encourage people to be lulled into a sense of false security. . . . in an area in process of being opened up a considerable proportion of the population are relative newcomers frequently on the move. They have little or no experience of a cyclone, or if they have undergone a single storm they have no standards by which to judge their experiences. Those who have been on the periphery of a severe storm may well develop a false confidence in their capacity to cope with a cyclone" [Australia] (Oliver, 1975:109).

IG2.5b "The survey, conducted in May 1975, attempted to ascertain which facets of the physical environment of the Northwest Plain and the North Coast were perceived as hazards by residents in those areas. Flooding was recognised as a major hazard by a majority of persons interviewed. The level of perception was greater for the North Coast area . . . Droughts . . . are prevalent in both districts. However, the level of perception was markedly different between the coast and inland. . . . The low level of perception of droughts seems to be related to the magnitude of the geophysical event, not to its occurrence. The differences that exist between urban and rural distinction in both areas can understandably be due to the more direct dependence by the rural sector upon favourable conditions" [Australia] (N. S. McDonald, 1979:268).

Finally, the tornado study by Susan Hanson, Vitek, and Hanson (1979) that I cited above, and recent work on the Mount St. Helens eruption (May, 1980) illustrate the type of evidence we have indicating that the distance from the disaster site impacts subsequent perceptions. Also, at least for some types of hazards, there may be variations as to the exact nature of the threat that a more generalized form of questioning would blur. Thus, once again, "experience" turns out to be more complex than many of the measures used earlier had taken into account.

IG2.6 ". . . the two closer sites showed higher proportions of people who claimed prior knowledge of potential volcanic danger" (Greene, Perry, and Lindell, 1981:52). (See also Maderthaner *et al.,* 1978.)

IG2.6a ". . . the Woodland and Longview samples perceived themselves to be at considerably greater risk from mudflow/floods than the respondents in the Cougar sample. In Cougar 63.6% of the respondents reported the belief that mudflow/floods would produce no damage, compared to only 33.4% in Woodland and 40.0% in Longview" (Greene, Perry, and Lindell, 1981:59–60).

IG2.6b "The perception of risk from ash fall shows a different relationship with location. Respondents from the Cougar sample show the highest concern with damage from ash; 95.6% felt that at least slight damage would accrue from ash, with 69.6% fearing moderate–severe damage. The perception of moderate–severe ash damage declines as distance from the volcano increases. In Woodland 42.4% feared moderate–severe damage, with this figure decreasing to 23.5% in Longview" (Greene, Perry, and Lindell, 1981:59–60).

IG2.6c ". . . the level of perceived threat was noted, and related to the distance of the home from the threat source, either the river or the cliffs. It was found that the people who had formerly lived further away from the slopes and river banks thought little differently from those directly endangered. So, whereas locational differences between commune fractions (Braulins vs. Portis) can probably account for dissimilarities of perception, on the micro-level the whole commune seems to constitute a perceptual unit, but a smaller spatial area of 100 or 200 m does not." [Italy] (Geipel, 1982:152–154).

In short, at times—under conditions not yet specified—it appears that experience increases hazard perception, although not uniformly among all types of individuals. The factors that constrain this social process, giving it these variations in pattern, remain unclear.

IG3. Other Correlates of Hazard Perception

Seven additional variables were discussed in the literature I reviewed; each was presented as an independent variable that presumably acted to mold hazard perceptions in some way. Each variable should occupy a niche within a multivariate model that should be tested across a taxonomy of hazard types. Combined with various aspects of the disaster "experience" variable, the model should then be tested temporally so that ranges of stability can be ascertained. Once done, the research community will have derived a tool that many types of practitioners could use.

IG3.1(H) Hazard awareness varies directly with age; skepticism regarding personal vulnerability, due to natural hazards, varies directly with age. (Based on Turner *et al.,* 1979; Shimada, 1972.)

IG3.1a [When asked if they had heard any predictions of warning for earthquakes in Southern California, only 8 percent so indicated; however 59 percent indicated awareness of the "Palmdale Bulge". (pp. 9–11)] ". . . awareness of the Uplift [was lowest among] . . . young adults, those who live in households with school-aged children, the less educated and members of lower income strata, and non-white and non-Anglo groups . . . People over 50 years of age, people with especially strong attachment to their local communities, and those who live in especially vulnerable circumstances are most likely [aware of the Uplift] [p. 23]" (Turner et al., 1979:9–11, 23). (See also Perry O. Hanson, Vitek, and Hanson, 1979:23; Guard Police Psychology Research Society, 1967; Okabe et al., 1979a, b.)

IG3.1b ". . . survey on the awareness of the likelihood of an earthquake in the near future[:] . . . [1.] 85.2 percent of the respondents being aware to a certain degree. . . . [2.] proportion of those who are aware of the earthquake threat is higher (90%) among those in their 40s and 50s than in the 20s (75%)" [Japan] (Shimada, 1972:208). (See also Guard Police Psychology Research Society, 1970, 1976.)

While they may be more aware, the elderly tend to be more skeptical too (Hodge, Sharp, and Marts, 1979:228). That is, while they know more about the hazard generally, they are more likely to discount the threat: "It won't hit us." Additionally, but not only for this reason, it appears that the elderly disproportionately occupy many community floodplains within the U.S.A. (e.g., Smith, Traum, and Poole, 1977:21, document this for the Wyoming Valley in Pennsylvania; for the United Kingdom, see Harding and Parker, 1974:47).

IG3.2(H) Males evidence a greater degree of hazard awareness than females, but will report less fear or anxiety. (Based on Leik et al., 1982.)

IG3.2a "Throughout the analysis of risk, wives have been more bothered by the mountain than have their husbands. Again, if husbands and wives participated equally in a decision about moving, the wives would more often opt for leaving and the husbands would opt for staying" (Leik et al., 1982:76).

IG3.2b(H) "No significant difference between men and women in the degree of concerns about an earthquake" [although more women are anxious about an earthquake than men] [Japan] (Guard Police Psychology Research Society, 1977). (As summarized in Yamamoto and Quarantelli, 1982:A-118.)

In contrast to gender differences, a few researchers have hypothesized ethnic variations in hazard perception. For example, Turner's long-term study in Los Angeles revealed that " . . . Mexican Americans compared with Blacks express greater fear of earthquakes in general and in the future" (Turner et al., 1981:48). I suspect that this variation reflects additional variables, rather than being only a culturally produced difference.

Until the data base has been expanded, however, we really will not know. Certainly *ethnicity* should be retained as one of several independent variables, as cultural systems do impact hazard perceptions. Some evidence indicates that ethnic differences, like those associated with gender, may reflect lack of knowledge about the hazard.

IG3.3(H) Ethnic differences will impact hazard perceptions.

IG3.3a ". . . females were more likely to overestimate hazards than males, Filipinos and Portuguese more than other ethnic groups . . . The pattern of overestimation by females, Filipinos, and Portuguese is consistent with the lack of knowledge among these groups, as shown by the use of the 'no opinion' answer. With less information about a hazard, the tendency is to assume that it might occur. This also leads to greater fear; 52% of Filipinos, compared with 24% of all residents, described the general attitude toward Mauna Loa in their neighborhood as being at least somewhat fearful" (Hodge, Sharp, and Marts, 1979:241).

Several studies have indicated that people residing in rural areas have greater degrees of hazard awareness and more accurate perceptions (e.g., Saarinen, 1966). Most of these studies have focused on flood and drought issues, however, not the full range of hazards.

IG3.4(H) ". . . there is some evidence that rural people are more sensitive and responsive to hurricane cues than urban dwellers (Moore *et al.*, 1963) and that residents of coastal areas have more accurate knowledge of the relevant hazards than do flood plain dwellers (Burton *et al.*, 1965)" (Quarantelli, 1980b:59).

In part, this urban–rural variability may reflect familiarity with certain hazards that derives from work experience. Thus, as Greene, Perry, and Lindell (1981) learned following Mount St. Helens' eruption (May, 1980), loggers and their families tended to deny the risk represented by volcano more than others. Indeed, they suggested that these people may parallel the coal miners studied by Lucas (1969). Thus, while engaged in hazardous occupations and aware of the risks they ". . . tend not to define day to day exposure as continually life-threatening." (Greene, Perry, and Lindell, 1981:53). Lamson's (1983) study of Newfoundland fishermen buttressed this theme.

IG3.5(H) Hazard perceptions vary by occupation.

IG3.5a(H) "The survey suggests that fishermen accept and/or adapt to environmental hazards as a natural, to-be-expected feature of their occupation" [Canada] (Lamson, 1983:482).

In contrast to the conclusions of others (e.g., Turner *et al.*, 1979), Kunreuther and his colleagues (1978), like Islam (1974) and Gilbert F. White (1974b:5) earlier, ruled out aspects of socioeconomic status. But given much other research that documents the impact of SES on numerous attitude profiles, this variable should not be excluded from future work directed toward hazard perceptions.

> IG3.6(H) "Neither income nor education levels had any explanatory power in determining homeowners' perception of the seriousness of the hazard problem" (Kunreuther et al., 1978:242). (See also Brinkmann, 1975b:41; Islam, 1974:21.)

> IG3.7(H) Persons exhibiting internal-oriented personalities and less fatalist world views will have greater levels of hazard awareness and more accurate hazard perceptions. (Based on Simpson-Housley and Bradshaw, 1978.)

Evidence supporting the idea that hazard perceptions reflect personality differences is mixed, but several studies have demonstrated clear relationships with specific aspects of the myriad of variables that get lumped into the "personality" dimensions.

> IG3.7a(H) "The results clearly indicate the importance of personality variables in determining perceptions of natural hazards. [p. 71] . . . [A. Rotter's I-E Scale supported:] Preventive active measures to mitigate earthquake threat; . . . Expectation of household disruption by an earthquake; . . . [and] Expectation of a high degree of household earthquake damage is a positive function of internality. [p. 69] . . . [B. Repression–Sensitization Scale supported:] Preventive active measures to mitigate earthquake threat [and] . . . Expectation of a high degree of household earthquake damage is a negative function of repression and sensitization [p. 70]" [New Zealand] (Simpson-Housley and Bradshaw, 1978:69–71).

> IG3.7b ". . . three out of five people are fatalistic about the general impact of an earthquake, but fewer are fatalistic when it comes to the possibility of taking steps to protect themselves. [p. 68] . . . Only 8.5 percent of the respondents . . . claim[ed] . . . invulnerability. [p. 70] . . . The belief is overwhelming that something can be done for the groups in special danger [i.e., 85% agree]. When the issue is posed in this way, fatalistic attitudes are much less in evidence [p. 77]" (Turner et al., 1979: 68, 70, 77).

More so than others to date, Turner and his research team (1979) have captured the essence of the social process that I think is operational here.

> ". . . a great many if not all of these answers are a melding of physical frameworks with either a magical or a moralistic framework. This is an important observation. While people understand earthquakes overwhelmingly in physical terms, the physical frameworks they use are sometimes contaminated by other frameworks that are less compatible with science [p. 142]" [e.g., 21% indicated that psychics or mystics could predict earthquakes; 3% indicated that religious leaders could (p. 144)] (Turner et al., 1979:142, 144).

We need not go back to Weber's Protestant Ethic theme to find a logic for this reasoning. Certainly, some of the items that are included in so-called personality measures, e.g., fate control items on Rotter's I-E Scale, have a heavy ring of what others would label a "world view." Thus, paralleling Weber's argument that the tenets of Protestantism, especially as reflected in the version advocated by John Calvin and his followers, provided a more nutritive soil for the growth of capitalism than did other religious dogmas, so too one's view of various hazards are constrained by such abstract belief systems. Regardless of what they might be labeled, however, these dimensions merit further study with the model-building format I suggested above.

IIG. Group System Level

As with other informational areas—politics, religion, or what have you—primary groups impact individual hazard perceptions. People receive information about hazards from relatives and friends. At times, specific events that have been etched in the memories of those who were on scene may remain referent points that are shared with others for decades to come. This is especially true if no comparable event has occurred in the meantime. Thus, Westgate's (1978:255) interviews in the Bahamas in the mid-1970s revealed the 1929 hurricane as a key referent point—one element in a complex social calendar.

More detailed data have been provided by the former Washington State research team, i.e., Perry, Lindell, and Greene. Their studies documented the relative importance of primary groups as informational sources.

IIG1.1(H) Primary group members provide specific hazard information regularly to about two-thirds of the adult population. (Based on Greene, Perry, and Lindell, 1981.)

IIG1.1a "Approximately the same proportions of people in each sample reported receiving information from friends, neighbours and relatives: 69.6% in Cougar; 69.8% in Woodland; and 70.4% in Longview. [p. 56] . . . the proportions of people reporting direct contact with emergency officials (state, federal, county or local) declines sharply with increasing distance from the volcano. In the Cougar sample, 65.2% of the respondents reported such contacts, and this figure declines to 16.7% in Woodland and 9.3% in Longview [pp. 56–57]" (Greene, Perry, and Lindell, 1981:56–57).

IIG1.1b "After the first week of volcanic activity, almost half of the respondents felt that the likelihood of the mountain posing a serious threat to the safety of their families and property was 'even odds' or greater. . . . The high level of perceived threat was associated with a similarly high frequency of receipt of information. . . . Respondents were asked to indicate the sources from which they generally received information. Five sources were mentioned: television, newspapers, radio, friends or relatives, and emergency personnel. The mass media dominated, with 98% of the sample mentioning television as a source, 91% citing news-

papers, and 87% citing radio. [p. 201] . . . (70%) of the people reported
that they received hazard information from friends or relatives. Only 36
respondents (21%) had received information through direct contact with
either state, county, or local officials [p. 202]'' (Perry, Lindell, and
Greene, 1982b:201, 202).

IIIG. Organizational System Level

Three topics convey the central themes within the findings I reviewed
that depicted aspects of organizational system impacts on hazard perceptions: (1) hazard perceptions among organizational executives; (2) public
education efforts; and (3) media organizations: coverage and influence.

IIIG1. Hazard Perceptions Among Organizational Executives

In general, it appears that hazard perceptions among organizational executives parallel those of the general public, both in content and in pattern
variations. But this matter has not been documented with much thor-
oughness. Hazard experience appears to be the major variable impacting
awareness. And, as with the public, most executives demonstrate minimal
hazard awareness levels. Most research has been focused on the flood
hazard, however; thus, cross-hazard comparisons are in order.

IIIG1.1 "The perception of the flood hazard by the business community
proved essentially similar to that of the private residents" [England]
(Smith and Tobin, 1979:109).

IIIG1.1a "Awareness of the flood hazard by the business-men showed
a complex relationship. For instance, while all knew that the area had
been flooded in the past (64% in fact had personal experience of flooding)
there was a very low perception of future flooding. Only 21% suggested
that Carlisle would flood again in the next 25 years and 65% stated that
it would not" [England] (Tobin, 1979:219).

IIIG1.1b "In all cases the business-men with personal flood experience
showed greater awareness than the non-experienced group" [i.e., awareness of various amelioriation measures, e.g., new embankment] [p. 220]
. . . previously flooded business-men showed the greatest awareness of
the warning scheme, with 56% compared with only 25% of non-experienced respondents [p. 221]'' [England] (Tobin, 1979:220, 221).

While the public-at-large does affect the policy-making process, their
impact is mediated by agency executives. Thus, we need a much better
understanding of the types of hazard perceptions held by a range of organizational executives who play more direct roles in the public policy
process (see Drabek, Muskatel, and Kilijanek, 1983:197–198). Note the
several research leads in the following conclusions offered by Foster.

". . . it is the perception of hazards that shapes the legislation passed by politicians, the reactions of manufacturers, and the safety programs of professionals. That there is a divergence between actual and perceived risk has been demonstrated by numerous studies. Lawless (1974)[1] reviewed 45 major public alarms over technology and found that in over 25% of the cases opponents of development had overestimated the threat, while in more than 50% of the examples examined proponents had underestimated it. Professionals tend to selectively identify those hazards that they have been specifically trained to deal with (Sewell, 1971; Barker, 1977)"[2] (Foster, 1980:32).

The University of Delaware study that I discussed in Chapter 2 (Wenger, James, and Faupel, 1980) provided limited information whereby public perceptions can be contrasted to those held by local officials. The key differences are as follows.

IIIG1.2(H) ". . . officials tend to *underestimate* the level of public insight. . . . a larger percentage of the public is aware of the hurricane season and organizational responsibility for warning and evacuation than the officials realize" (Wenger, James, and Faupel, 1980:107).

IIIG1.2a(H) ". . . considering official perceptions: . . . there is less variation across the communities than was found for the public" (Wenger, James, and Faupel, 1980:130).

IIIG1.2b(H) [There is] ". . . a tendency for the officials to take a somewhat more optimistic view of these hazards. For example, a larger percentage of them believe that not only are the warnings fairly accurate, but the time for preparatory activity is longer" (Wenger, James, and Faupel, 1980:130).

Turning to one type of "human-caused" disaster—community disturbances—we have limited documentation of the perceptions held by agency heads. Nowhere did I encounter efforts to treat these types of perceptions as dependent variables. Thus, we do not know the degree of variability within this perceptual set, nor factors that pattern it.

IIIG1.3(H) "Social control agencies see individual actions in disturbances as being relatively unorganized and unplanned" (Quarantelli, Ponting, and Fitzpatrick, 1974:33).

IIIG1.3a(H) "Social control agencies view disturbances as emanating from one fairly specific event rather than from a series of sequential happenings" (Quarantelli, Ponting, and Fitzpatrick, 1974:31).

---

[1] E. Lawless, *Technology and Social Shock—100 Cases of Public Concern over Technology.* Kansas City, Missouri: Midwest Research Institute, 1974.

[2] W. R. D. Sewell, "Environmental Perceptions and Attitudes of Engineers and Public Health Officials." *Environment and Behavior,* **3** (1971):23–60; M. L. Barker, *Specialists and Air Pollution: Occupations and Preoccupations.* Western Geographical Series, 14. Victoria, British Columbia, Canada: University of Victoria, 1977.

IIIG1.3b(H) "Social control agencies view disturbance-generating events as the result of individual actions rather than as the consequences of social conditions" (Quarantelli, Ponting, and Fitzpatrick, 1974:32).

IIIG2. Public Education Efforts

Research suggests that merely increasing the frequency of public information campaigns does not produce sweeping change. Why? Saarinen's (1982b) summary of a series of experiments conducted by Slovic and his associates (1977) stated the matter well.

"Slovic *et al.*, (1977) came to three conclusions bearing on the issue of education for behavior change. A basic one is that people are resistant to change. Once initial impressions are formed they tend to structure and distort the interpretation of new evidence. Another is that making decisions about risky activities is difficult and humans may not be intellectually equipped to respond to that difficulty constructively. Instead, life's gambles are oversimplified to allow easy solutions, avoiding cognitive strain and emotional anxiety. A third conclusion is that otherwise intelligent individuals do not always have accurate perceptions of the risks to which they are exposed. Hazards that are easy to imagine or recall, that are certain to produce death, that take multiple lives, and have particularly dreaded consequences are overestimated, while risks from common, undramatic events involving only one person at a time are underestimated" (Saarinen, 1982b:16–17).

Although we know relatively little about the processes involved, certain approaches have limited impact. Broadly based, non-focused appeals are least effective (Illinois Department of Transportation, 1980). Thus, demonstration experiments should be completed. Program content and target populations should vary and reflect conclusions regarding the importance of such factors as community variations and characteristics of the threatened population (James, 1975). Among one of the better candidates for such experiments might be school-based curricular modifications. Given regional differences in hazard vulnerability, topics could vary. I found Regulska's (1982) observation rather disappointing, for example. I wonder if the same is true for areas more subject to tornadoes and earthquakes?

". . .'an assessment of the status of school-based hurricane instruction in the Gulf and Atlantic coastal states.' . . . found that 'in spite of the vulnerability of the Gulf and Atlantic coastal areas to major hurricane landfalls, almost none of the coastal states offered hurricane instruction beyond that found in conventional curricular materials.' State education department personnel interviewed in the study agreed that the need exists for additional school-based hurricane instruction in their states (Based on Geer, 1978[3])" (Regulska, 1982:58).

---

[3] Ira Geer, "Increase Hurricane Awareness through School-based Educational Activity." In *Hurricanes and Coastal Storms*, Earl J. Baker (ed.). Report No. 33. Gainesville, Florida: Florida Sea Grant College, 1980.

In the communities Wenger (1980) surveyed, he found that ". . . about 20 percent of the sampled residents in each community had received disaster-related educational information. . . . less than one third of those who had received information from public education programs mentioned them as a source of information" (Wenger, 1980:246). The implications of this are critical.

> "While about one-third of the residents of Hurricane City evidenced confusion about the concepts, the level of insight is still rather high. [i.e., hurricane warning vs. watch] [p. 98] . . . The National Weather Service must be aware that when they issue a 'tornado watch' about one-half of the public will not correctly interpret the message. The respondents, however, are more knowledgeable about the term 'tornado warning.' Almost two-thirds of the residents of Tornadoville know the correct meaning of this term. [p. 102] . . . About 50 percent of the respondents knew that the National Weather Service is responsible for forecasting river floods. . . . The results for evacuation are very similar. Once again, approximately one-half of the respondents are knowledgeable about which local organizations are responsible for evacuating the community [p. 104]" (Wenger, James, and Faupel, 1980:98, 102, 104).

> IIIG2.1(H) [Regarding forced awareness:] "study by McPherson and Saarinen (1977) indicates that discussions related to flood plain zoning do not necessarily lead to a rise in the level of public awareness even among the people in the area affected" (Saarinen, 1982b:12). (See also Illinois Department of Transportation, 1980.)

But, there are successes, at least of a limited nature. The following are illustrative of the types of interpretations I encountered that indicate some organizational impact on hazard perceptions. I have not seen a series of theoretical models that explicate rationales used or data substantiating relative effectiveness, however.

> "The Texas Insurance Information Center has prepared a media kit 'Hurricane Awareness Saves Lives and Property' containing materials developed particularly for the HAP, as well as news releases, maps and camera-ready materials. In the first mailing, the kit was sent only to the radio and television stations, editors, and insurance publications within the state. . . . Fifty respondents to this questionnaire agreed that materials are interesting and indicated that they will keep them in their reference files. Three-quarters of the respondents still have materials from previous mailings" (Regulska, 1982:64).

> "Waterstone (1978)[4] studied the effect of a brochure about flooding distributed by the Denver Urban Drainage and Flood Control District. . . . Hazard awareness was significantly higher for the population which had received the brochure. . . . A higher percentage of those re-

---

[4] Marvin Waterstone, *Hazard Mitigation Behavior of Urban Flood Plain Residents*. Natural Hazard Research Working Paper No. 35. Boulder, Colorado: Institute of Behavioral Science, University of Colorado, 1978.

spondents who had received the brochure had taken some form of mitigation action such as purchasing flood insurance, floodproofing their
residence, or developing an emergency plan, than in the population that
had not received the brochure. [p. 9] . . . the effects were apparently not
permanent. Only four to six weeks after the brochure was disseminated,
the rate for remembering receiving it was 62%. Only 37% of a group
interviewed about a year after the dissemination of information still remembered receiving it" [pp. 9–10]. (Saarinen, 1982b:9–10.)

IIIG3. Media Organizations: Coverage and Influence

During the 1970s, several researchers initiated studies of media responses
to hazards of various types. While this work has done little more than lay
the contours of a partially complete foundation, progress was made. We
now know, for example, that most people receive hazard information frequently. Indeed, one study indicated that 90% did so twice daily, or more
(Greene, Perry, and Lindell, 1981:57–58). Much of this barrage comes
from the media. As the previous section indicated, however, relatives,
friends, and other primary group members constitute an important source
of hazard information too. But they are in second place; the media rank
first. There is not a one-to-one correspondence, however, between what
the media transmit and what people remember.

IIIG3.1 ". . . the mass media were the most salient source of information
for all samples of respondents, *including those in communities that have
experienced disaster*. In each community, approximately 60 percent to
75 percent of the respondents reported that radio and television were
important sources of their disaster knowledge. Newspapers also were
important to a sizeable percentage. For many of the respondents, the
media were not only an important source of information, they were the
only source" (Wenger, 1980:243). (See also Greene, Perry, and Lindell,
1981; Saarinen, 1982b:15, 16.)

IIIG3.1a ". . . individuals seem to have only a rather vague and limited
awareness of the media's many predictions and announcements concerning the earthquake prospect. More people were convinced that there
would be a damaging earthquake than were able to specify particular
predictions, announcements, or cautions that led them to this conclusion"
(Turner, 1980:291).

IIIG3.1b [L.A. media coverage indicated: 1.] "Attention to politicized
controversies over dam, nuclear plant, and LNG terminal safety, while
emphasizing earthquake danger, does not stimulate attention to preparedness and safety in the local community and therefore probably does
not contribute toward public understanding of the local earthquake
threat. . . . [2.] The concern and compassion aroused by disastrous
earthquakes in foreign countries is not translated into attention to earthquake preparedness and safety in the local area, but remains focused on
the distant scene" (Turner *et al.,* 1981:15).

Implicit in several of these interpretations are notions about content and context. Analyses of newspapers provide some relevant clues about both matters. For example, Larson's (1980) literature review disclosed studies revealing that about two percent of all news items deal with accidents or disasters. Furthermore, ". . . the public perception of what was important in the news was not in direct proportion to the amount of space a story received in the paper or to the time it got on the air. When asked what was the most important item in the news yesterday or today, 22 percent of the respondents mentioned some story dealing with crime, and 11 percent mentioned accidents and disasters" (Larson, 1980:105).

Larson's own doctoral research also pointed to important variations in the American public's diet of TV news.

[The study] ". . . compared coverage of Third World and developed nations on U.S. network television, based on a content analysis of international news coverage by network television during the 5-year period from 1972 through 1976.[5] Among the major findings were the following: (1) Coverage of Third World countries contained a higher proportion of crisis stories than did coverage of developed nations. (Crisis themes included unrest and dissent, war, terrorism and crime, coups, assassinations, and disasters.) (2) The proportion of crisis stories was higher for all types of stories, but the difference in crisis orientation was most noticeable in the case of filmed reports from overseas" (Larson, 1980:102–103).

Other studies have examined different aspects of this broader issue. Thus, as illustrated by the following quotations, degrees of "sensationalism" that some have found may not be interpreted as such by all.

IIIG3.2(H) [In conducting] ". . . a detailed monitoring of news reporting by six major newspapers in the Los Angeles area for a 3-year period (1976–78) and a less intensive monitoring of television and radio coverage of earthquake news, we have been generally impressed with these media's highly responsible news treatment. If these media have erred, they have erred less in the direction of sensationalism than in the direction of underplaying threat and rumor" (Turner, 1980:282).

IIIG3.2a(H) "A second theme we find in media treatment of news about a prospective earthquake is a concern with protecting the public. Newspaper, television, and radio editors are anxious to avoid any reporting that may produce mass panic or other undesirable responses. Most media representatives share the popular misconceptions about the likelihood of mass panic" (Turner, 1980:283).

IIIG3.2b "Thus, in 1952–1953 and 1972–1974 the *Globe and Mail [established type]* had the smallest sensationalism quotient of any of the daily journals. This performance was in agreement with one of the hy-

---

[5] J. F. Larson, "America's Window on the World: U.S. Network Television Coverage of International Affairs, 1972–1976." Ph.D. dissertation. Stanford University, 1978.

pothesized characteristics of the emerging newspaper, that is, that the most cosmopolite papers would exhibit the smallest degree of unevenness, or sensationalism, in hazard news coverage . . . the extending papers tended to show a publication pattern of above average unevenness and sensationalism. Environmental crises at the local level are discussed enthusiastically for limited periods. [p. 533] . . . expanding newspapers produced an above average volume of hazard news that has regional ramifications" [pp. 533–534]" [Canada] (Needham and Nelson, 1977:533–534).

IVG. Community System Level

The small numer of findings I coded into this niche of the conceptual framework reflected two major themes: (1) community variations in threat perceptions and (2) disaster subcultures.

IVG1. Community Variations in Threat Perceptions

Survey data document important differences among communities regarding threat perceptions. These studies indicate that hazards vary widely in the relative degrees to which they are perceived to be a threat, regardless of available scientific evidence.

IVG1.1 Threat perceptions associated with different hazard types vary among communities. (Based on Petak and Atkisson, 1982.)

IVG1.1a "The risk model utilized in this study identified 101 of the respondent counties as being subject to significant losses from expansive soils, 100 as being subject to landslide, and 66 as being subject to earthquake losses. . . . only 4% of officials in the landslide communities were aware of this hazard, only 18% were aware of their expansive soils problems, and only 21% were aware of the earthquake threat" (Petak and Atkisson, 1982:405).

IVG1.1b "There is a widespread belief in the communities we studied that disasters involving hazardous chemicals are a community threat. . . . community officials ($N = 299$) were asked to indicate on a five point scale the probability of their area being impacted by one of 36 different natural and technological disaster agents, the five highest, in rank order, were chemical spills, multiple car wrecks, a major explosion in a chemical plant, a plane crash, and a sudden toxic substance release" (Quarantelli and Tierney, 1979b:459).

A large-scale study by Disaster Research Center staff (e.g., Helms, 1981; Quarantelli *et al.,* 1979; Quarantelli and Tierney, 1981) is one of the few that has been focused on community level variables that might be associated with different levels of threat perception. While these data were limited to one hazard type—chemical disasters—it represents an important step forward. Data were collected from key officials in 19 different communities.

> IVG1.2(H) ". . . respondents in small cities perceive the probability of
> a chemical disaster as significantly lower than their counterparts do in
> medium and large cities. However, there are no significant differences
> between medium and large cities in their ranking of the three chemically
> related disaster agents" (Helms, 1981:323).

Community size, however, is not the sole variable that structures such perceptions. Several variables were considered that might account for the differences found in the perceived threat represented by three potential types of chemical disasters, i.e., a sudden toxic release, a chemical substance spill, and a major chemical plant explosion. Two factors emerged as especially important, i.e., 88% of the variation in "perceived threat" was accounted for by these. Helms (1981) defined these as follows: (1) Threat 2—"existence or non-existence of a large chemical complex and/ or port facility within the community" (Helms, 1981:324, and (2) Public Expectations—". . .an assessment by organizational respondents of the public's expectations of a chemical disaster. Although it is a rather tangential measure of public awareness, it may more accurately reflect pressures to which officials are responding than would a general survey of the public." (Helms, 1981:324) Interestingly, an objective indicant of community vulnerability was not predictive (i.e., Threat 1—". . . an index of three equally weighted indicators: the number of chemical plants per square mile, the number of personnel employed by the chemical industry per total work force, and the number of accidents per square mile for 1971–1977 as a measure of transportation hazards by rail or truck" (Helms, 1981:324). This work suggests the following hypothesis.

> IVG1.3(H) Hazard awareness among community officials varies directly
> with their perceptions of public expectations. (Based on Helms, 1981.)

IVG2. Disaster Subcultures

The topic of disaster subcultures has been discussed in previous chapters. As Moore (1956) stressed three decades ago, the responses to and preparedness for selected disasters in some communities are best understood within this context. So too, hazard perceptions may be impacted greatly by disaster subcultures. But little of the literature captured through my search process dealt directly with the relationship between these two concepts. Reflecting on community surveys they designed to test the degree to which local officials and their publics believed in a disaster mythology (see Chapter 2, Section IA4), Wenger, James, and Faupel (1980) summarized several important impacts of disaster subcultures.

> IVG2.1 "There are disaster subcultures. The members of the public and
> officials in these communities possess a substantial body of instrumental

knowledge about effective disaster response that is focused upon their local hazard. Furthermore, this experience and knowledge appears to influence the manner in which they perceive various disaster agents" (Wenger, James, and Faupel, 1980:131). (See also Baker and Patton, 1974:34.)

IVG2.1a ". . . the knowledge base appears to be limited to instrumental and hazard perception elements—it does not extend to accurate knowledge of the social aspects of disaster. With respect to these latter beliefs, the residents of the subculture communities are only slightly more knowledgeable than people who live in non-disaster locales" (Wenger, James, and Faupel, 1980:131).

IVG2.1b ". . . the influence of prior experience and a subcultural setting appear to affect public perceptions of the nature of disaster agents far more than official perceptions of these characteristics" (Wenger, James, and Faupel, 1980:131).

But, as Moore (1956) and others have pointed out with such examples as hurricane parties, some elements of these subcultures function as threat denial mechanisms. To some degree these may reflect assumptions about preparedness levels, although humor and other social processes appear to operate too. At any rate, the consequence seems to be a tone of increased acceptance—"earthquakes come with the territory."

IVG2.2(H) Disaster subcultures dampen the threat dimension of hazard perceptions for specific disaster types for which these communities are more vulnerable. (Derived from Meltsner, 1978.)

IVG2.2a ". . . the longer one lives in California, the less one is likely to care about earthquakes. [p. 174] . . . About half of the long-term residents thought a serious earthquake was likely to happen, while over two-thirds of the newer residents had similar feelings: 22 percent of the long-term residents thought that a serious earthquake was unlikely, as compared to 10 percent of the newcomers [p. 173]" (Meltsner, 1978:173, 174).

IVG2.2b "Some respondents surveyed in the study believed there is no risk of a flood catastrophe due to the presence of the official warning system. . . . its mere existence had apparently created a sense of complacency among villagers" [India] (Schware, 1982:214).

VG. Society System Level

Consistent with the dearth of research on the other disaster phases that has been conceptualized at the societal system level, relatively few have documented hazard perceptions for total societal systems. Yet, as White and Haas (1975:8) stated so forcefully, all societies evidence continuing structural change, some of which may increase vulnerability. For example, they argued that the U.S.A.'s vulnerability to natural hazards was increasing because of four types of changes:

"1. Shifts in population from country and city to suburban and exurban locations. More and more people live in unprotected flood plains, seismic risk areas and exposed coastal locations.

2. More people live in new and unfamiliar environments where they are totally unaware of potential risks and the possible ways of dealing with them.

3. The increasing size of corporations enlarges their capacity to absorb risks, which may result in plants being located in high risk areas, or failure to adopt hazard-resistant building methods. The location of these firms attracts job-seekers and housing development to the same dangerous locations.

4. The rapid enlargement of the proportion of new housing starts accounted for by mobile homes means more families are living in dwellings which are easily damaged by natural hazards" (White and Haas, 1975:8).

But these are subtle, and the populace may be only vaguely aware of them. Only recently have researchers even tried to assess macro-level demographic shifts and their implications for hazard vulnerability. Yet, *perceptions* of threat or vulnerability may remain unchanged despite a social drift that intensifies risk levels. Kastenbaum (1974) stressed this theme and offered an interesting hypothesis.

VG1.1(H) ". . . conceptions of disaster and notions about successful intervention have some relationship to the ways in which events are defined and classified in the first place. . . . The danger of selective perception is increased by geographic, racial, and ethnic bias. We might even propose a Law of Inverse Magnitude: As physical and emotional distance is increased, so the magnitude of death and destruction must increase by an undetermined but powerful constant before the situation can be classified as disastrous and call forth appropriate relief efforts" (Kastenbaum, 1974:66).

Case study data and attitude surveys from other nations reinforce my overall suspicion. Thus, while we really don't have the type of longitudinal data bases to assess temporal shifts in hazard perceptions among societies, I suspect that it does occur, but relatively slowly. In part, this is because a society is a system. And major shifts in the perceptions or interpretative frameworks that define and make sense out of hazards—as a single element of human experience—must fit within the prevailing definitional structure. Ridington (1982) offered much insight into the costs involved in changing a perception. Unless a hazard becomes viewed as an extreme and certain risk to health, populations will tend to ignore it—often long after many cues signaling danger have been received.

"I will point out the contrast between values and perceptions of hunting and gathering people and those of people in industrial society. [p. 37]

> . . . It was a classic case of conflict between the testimony of personal
> experience and the authority of experts with vested interests in the overall
> industrial system that was responsible for the hazard in the first place.
> Nobody in Blueberry doubted that the well was a health hazard and a
> potential killer. . . . Now that the well has blown and nearly killed them
> all, they still find themselves in a conflict between their own informed
> intelligence that concludes the village site is no longer habitable, and the
> intelligence of 'experts,' hired by the oil company, who claim that the
> risk is negligible and that life in industrial society is inherently risky any-
> way [p. 41]'' (Ridington, 1982:37, 41).

Extending this line of reasoning—I think *not* to a ridiculous extreme—
is a view offered by Gilbert and Barkun (1981) who also argued that our
understanding of hazard perceptions must take on a much larger perspective. The cultural fabric of any society reflects interdependencies.
Thus, as interpretative frameworks regarding disaster causality, for example, shift toward more naturalistic explanations, attitudes toward other
events and behaviors may be impacted.

> "The equation of disaster and sexual sin had been simply one element
> in a larger scheme through which natural hazards were related to God's
> governance of an erring world. The assumption had been that messages
> of divine ill-favor would be sent via the destructive forces of nature. It
> was not clear that those forces were neither so destructive nor so prom-
> inent as they had once been. Further, they were being eclipsed by social
> changes of a kind that lay completely outside the old interpretive ap-
> paratus. Disasters were not being caused not by God through nature, but
> by other human beings. [pp. 10–11] . . . sexual fears intensified precisely
> because catastrophe seemed now much more related to the power of men
> to change the world for both good and evil. Industrialization and revo-
> lution were manmade and so was sexual sinfulness [p. 13]'' [England]
> (Gilbert and Barkun, 1981:10–11, 13).

The implications are significant. For example, within the U.S.A. there
is an increasing propensity to seek compensation for injury through litigation if another party can be held responsible. I have a suspicion that
issues of liability, be they pertaining to warning issuance or actions taken
during an emergency response, will be introduced with increased frequency
in the American court system in the coming decade (see Changnon *et al.*,
1983:157–172). Why? In part, because of some fundamental changes in
hazard perceptions. God is losing ground, when it comes to flooding, for
example. And if not God, then man.

VIG. International System Level

As will be evident by the brevity of this section, my literature search
procedure captured few studies wherein cross-national differences in hazard perceptions were compared. The best data base I uncovered was re-

ported by Burton, Kates, and White (1978). It included nearly 3300 households from 30 separate sites representing a dozen nations (Burton, Kates, and White, 1978:91–93). Following discussion of it and other cross-societal comparisons (Section VIG1), I will summarize a series of findings pertaining to media reporting (Section VIG2).

VIG1. Societal Comparisons

Looking across their study sites, Burton, Kates, and White (1978) attempted to identify common principles. Thus, they noted patterns in hazard perceptions and factors of constraint that tended toward the universal.

> VIG1.1 "People have difficulty in defining the future timing and significance of an extreme event in a fashion that is intelligible to others. Part of the problem is the difference among people in time horizon" (Burton, Kates, and White, 1978:96).

> VIG1.1a ". . . the financial arrangements and livelihood expectations range so widely that it is misleading to think of a given event as constituting the same hazard for everyone" (Burton, Kates, and White, 1978:97).

They nicely illustrated these propositions with case study data.

> "A real estate developer standing on the ground floor of a new apartment building on the floodplain of a creek in a Missouri Valley town was asked whether he thought he was taking any risk in locating a structure there. He replied to the contrary and, when pressed, observed further that he knew that the stream had many years earlier reached a stage at that point as high as his shoulders. How then could he say there was no risk? His answer was, 'There isn't any risk; I expect to sell this building before the next flood season' " (Burton, Kates, and White, 1978:96).

In general, it seems, people worldwide *underestimate* the risk confronting them that is due to natural hazards. Why? Burton, Kates, and White proposed that a common response pattern may be evident across many, if not most, societies.

> VIG1.2 "Faced with such masses of information, people may follow a process of 'anchoring' in which they begin with one rough estimate and then adjust it as more information comes in. They 'believe they have a much better picture of the truth than they really do' (Slovic *et al.*, 1974), and this generally leads to underestimation of the phenomena" (Burton, Kates, and White, 1978:98).

Urban-rural differences, as noted in the section on individual hazard perceptions, appeared to hold across their study sites.

> VIG1.3 "In general, urban dwellers appear to be less sensitive to the possibility of extreme events than rural people confronting the same phenomena" (Burton, Kates, and White, 1978:101).

So too, the role of experience loomed out as a predictive factor. Those who have been impacted more frequently are more accurate in their predictions. Oliver and Trollope (1981) made this point in their study of Hurricane Allen. Although there may be additional factors, Texans living along the Gulf from Corpus Christi to Brownsville evidenced much greater hurricane awareness "than that which characterises the Queensland coastal population" (Oliver and Trollope, 1981:52).

> VIG1.4 "The more frequent the experience of the individual with the extreme event, the more likely is the estimate of its recurrence to accord with the statistical probabilities. This, however, is subject to conditions imposed by factors of age, economic situation, and personality" (Burton, Kates, and White, 1978:102).

But economic considerations may impact these perceptions too. Thus, paralleling occupational differences in experience and corresponding definitions of "acceptable risk" found among individuals, societies may vary in collective interpretations.

> VIG1.5 "The acuity of perception of a hazard in nature is partly a function of the mix of the need for the resource and the social problems confronting people in that place. In the Ganga floodplain of India, where the sole source of income is from that land, the rising water may be a matter of the most intense concern. For owners of residential property along the Rock River in Illinois (U.S.A.) it is of secondary importance (Moline, 1974)" (Burton, Kates, and White, 1978:102).

There were differences, however. Thus, despite their emphasis on commonalities, Burton, Kates, and White reported one key contrast that provides another piece of evidence indicating that disaster researchers must begin to include in their net of independent variables the interpretative frameworks used by the populations being studied. As these six propositions indicate, this area of research has many potential corridors that represent important theoretical linkages to more general sociological theories.

> VIG1.6 "The sophisticated view—that it could happen any year—is the prevalent view especially in high-income areas. The deterministic view—consistent with the gambler's fallacy—that the phenomenon is grouped or regular in occurrence is less common but strong in pre-industrial societies and areas of yearly flooding" (Burton, Kates, and White, 1978:99–100).

> VIG1.6a ". . . persons in Puerto Rico and the United States differ importantly in the ways they anticipate responding to a hurricane both *before* and *after* its occurrence but are very similar in the behavior reported *during* the storm. . . . In Puerto Rico, 54 percent of the respondents see God as 'powerful and important' with respect to their lives, as opposed to 17 percent in the U.S. Contrariwise, 55 percent of those in the U.S. versus 21 percent in Puerto Rico see God as a benevolent protector. [p.

29] . . . in each case more Puerto Ricans give responses which recognize the importance of external forces—luck, God, economic development—in controlling their lives. In contradistinction, more Americans stress autonomy. Thus, for example, although equally religious, the two groups have quite different conceptions of the role of God in man's world. Puerto Ricans see him as directly involved in what happens to them, whereas Americans see him as benign but removed; their motto would be 'God helps those who help themselves' [pp. 29–30]'' (Baumann and Sims, 1974:29–30).

VIG2. Media Reporting

My search process uncovered two major studies that assessed media coverage of disasters from an international perspective. Each provides important insight into how hazard perceptions among nations may be influenced by media practices. Since very different research questions were addressed, however, we don't get much cross-validation.

Using the Sahel drought as his focal event, Morentz "examined the international communication about the drought of 14 organizations from September 1972 through August 1973. . . . The content of more than 750 wire service reports, special and mass media articles, and press releases also was analyzed.'' (Morentz, 1980:159).

VIG2.1 "Throughout the long period before the drought became an acknowledged issue, coverage by special interest media had virtually no influence on governments or international organizations. When the mass media became involved, however, they had a decided impact . . . The attention of the mass media and the subsequent development of the drought as an issue were largely responsible for the redefinition of the importance of the drought by government and international organizations. Even more directly, various information channels influenced government behavior'' (Morentz, 1980:181).

Pursuing this "agenda setting" function further, Rogers and Sood (1980) proposed that it is essential to differentiate among the roles played by different media. To treat "the media" as an entity limits our understanding.

VIG2.2 "The prestige press plays a more important role in a slow-onset disaster than in a sudden disaster. The prestige press can legitimize a slow-onset event as a disaster, as it sets the agenda of news for the other media'' [U.S.A., India, Senegal, France] (Rogers and Sood, 1980:155).

VIG2.2a "Although the local press in a developing country tends to give a disaster more coverage than the Western press does, local media tend to underplay negative aspects of a disaster and provide less perspective on the disaster than the foreign media do'' [U.S.A., India, Senegal, France] (Rogers and Sood, 1980:155).

VIG2.2b "Newspapers tend to follow and report on disaster related 'events,' whereas magazines wait for events to gain significance before they provide coverage" [U.S.A., India, Senegal, France] (Rogers and Sood, 1980:155).

Similarly, disaster type makes a difference. Providing further substantiation of my argument for the need to test hypotheses within and across a taxonomy of disasters, Rogers and Sood reported important differences in media coverage depending on whether the event was of slow onset like the Sahel drought or one that happened suddenly.

VIG2.3(H) Media reporting practices covary with the speed of onset of disasters. (Based on Rogers and Sood, 1980.)

VIG2.3a "Sudden disasters entail more uncertainty, fewer reliable data, and greater variation in severity estimates than do slow-onset disasters" [U.S.A., India, Senegal, France] (Rogers and Sood, 1980:153).

VIG2.3b "In sudden disasters, the severity is generally estimated through casualty and damage figures. In slow-onset disasters, the criteria for severity are the size of the affected population and the extent of the threat to that population" [U.S.A., India, Senegal, France] (Rogers and Sood, 1980:153).

The way in which hazards are perceived varies. These perceptions are ordered, however, and are subject to change—at least somewhat. But our interest in this perceptual process is not just academic. For beyond seeking to understand human responses to disaster events, we also want to know how these perceptions constrain the willingness to act prior to catastrophe. Thus, in the next chapter, we come full circle in the life cycle of a disaster through examination of attitudes toward various mitigative options.

Selected Bibliography

Burton, Ian, C.D. Fowle, and R.S. McCullough (eds.) [1982] *Living with Risk: Environmental Risk Management in Canada.* Toronto: Institute for Environmental Studies, University of Toronto.

Burton, Ian, Robert W. Kates, and Gilbert F. White [1978] *The Environment as Hazard.* New York: Oxford University Press.

Covello, Vincent T. [1983] "The Perception of Technological Risks: A Literature Review." *Technological Forecasting and Social Change* 23:285–297.

Hanson, Susan, John D. Vitek, and Perry O. Hanson [1979] "Natural Disaster— Long-Range Impact on Human Response to Future Disaster Threats." *Environment and Behavior* 11 (June):268–284.

Helms, John [1981] "Threat Perceptions in Acute Chemical Disasters." *Journal of Hazardous Materials* 4:321–329.

Hodge, David, Virginia Sharp, and Marion Marts [1979] "Contemporary Responses to Volcanism: Case Studies from the Cascades and Hawaii." Pp. 221–248 in *Volcanic Activity and Human Ecology,* Payson D. Sheets and Donald K. Grayson (eds.). New York: Academic Press.

Hohenemser, C., R. W. Kates, and P. Slovic [1983] "The Nature of Technological Hazard." *Science* 220:378–384.

Illinois Department of Transportation, Division of Water Resources [1980] "Notifying Floodplain Residents: An Assessment of the Literature." Chicago: Illinois Department of Transportation, Division of Water Resources.

Kastenbaum, Robert [1974] "Disaster, Death, and Human Ecology." *Omega: Journal of Death and Dying* **5** (Spring):65–72.

Lamson, Cynthia [1983] " 'I Think They're All Caught Up': An Inquiry of Hazard Perception among Newfoundland and Inshore Fishermen." *Environment and Behavior* **15** (July):458–486.

McDonald, N. S. [1979] "Hazard Perception in Northern New South Wales." Pp. 260–269 in *Natural Hazards in Australia*, R. L. Heathcote and B. G. Thom (eds.). Canberra: Australian Academy of Science.

McPherson, H. J., and T. F. Saarinen [1977] "Flood Plain Dwellers' Perception of the Flood Hazard in Tucson, Arizona." *The Annals of Regional Science* **11** (July):25–40.

Moline, Norman T. [1974] "Perception Research and Local Planning: Floods on the Rock River, Illinois." Pp. 52–59 in *Natural Hazards: Local, National, Global*, Gilbert F. White (ed.). New York: Oxford University Press.

Morentz, James W. [1980] "Communication in the Sahel Drought: Comparing the Mass Media with Other Channels of International Communication." Pp. 158–183 in *Disasters and the Mass Media: Proceedings of the Committee on Disasters and the Mass Media Workshop, February, 1979*, Committee on Disasters and the Mass Media. Washington, D.C.: National Academy of Sciences.

Needham, R. D., and J. G. Nelson [1977] "Newspaper Response to Flood and Erosion Hazards on the North Lake Erie Shore." *Environmental Management* **1** (November):521–540.

Oliver, John [1975] "The Significance of Natural Hazards in a Developing Area: A Case Study from North Queensland." *Geography* **60**:99–110.

Parker, Stanley D., Marilynn B. Brewer, and Janie R. Spencer [1980] "Natural Disaster, Perceived Control, and Attributions to Fate." *Personality and Social Psychology Bulletin* **6** (September):454–459.

Quarantelli, E. L., J. Rick Ponting, and John Fitzpatrick [1974] "Police Department Perceptions of the Occurrence of Civil Disturbances." *Sociology and Social Research* **59** (October):30–38.

Rogers, Everett M., and Rahul S. Sood [1980] "Mass Media Communication and Disasters: A Content Analysis of Media Coverage of the Andhra Pradesh Cyclone and the Sahel Drought." Pp. 139–157 in *Disasters and the Mass Media: Proceedings of the Committee on Disasters and the Mass Media Workshop, February, 1979*, Committee on Disasters and the Mass Media. Washington, D.C.: National Academy of Sciences.

Saarinen, Thomas F. (ed.) [1982] *Perspectives on Increasing Hazard Awareness*. Boulder, Colorado: Institute of Behavioral Science, The University of Colorado.

Simpson-Housley, Paul, and Peter Bradshaw [1978] "Personality and the Perception of Earthquake Hazard." *Australian Geographical Studies* **16** (April):65–72.

9

Attitudes toward and the Adoption of Adjustments

Following the framework and orientation developed by White and his associates (e.g., White *et al.*, 1975; Burton, Kates, and White, 1978), I find it useful to approach disaster research within an "adjustment" orientation. Thus, mitigation—as I defined it in Chapter 1—not only includes a perceptual dimension, but specific actions as well. White and Haas stated this quite well:

> "The nation and its component parts respond to extreme natural events either through adaptation in the organization and processes of the social system, or in specific and conscious adjustment intended to reduce the costs or increase the net benefits of the hazards. By *adaptation* is meant long-term arrangement of activity to take account of the threat of natural extremes. It is illustrated by farming systems in arid regions which endure a persistently dry climate . . . By *adjustment* is meant all those intentional actions which are taken to cope with the risk and uncertainty of natural events. These fall into three major classes: 1. *Modifying the causes of the hazard,* as in the case of reducing the velocity of a hurricane by cloud seeding, relieving the seismic stresses in an earthquake zone to prevent high-intensity movements, or heating an orchard to prevent freezing from cold air; 2. *Modifying vulnerability* to the natural event, as through constructing flood control dams, warning systems, building earthquake-resistant houses, or prohibiting construction in the path of a snow avalanche; and 3. *Distributing the losses,* as in the case of insurance, relief and rehabilitation operations, or individual loss-bearing" (White and Haas, 1975:57).

Thus, a diverse cadre of potential mitigative actions may become objects of study. Behaviorally, each represents a series of social processes that are operative at the differing systemic levels I have used throughout this book. For example, flood insurance constitutes the major social experiment of the last decade within the U.S.A. Analyses of community responses to this single adjustment could provide policy-relevant information that should be essential to the decision-making process. But our understanding will remain limited, until basic work is completed on adoption behavior by potential purchasers of such insurance. While individuals have been studied rather systematically we know much less about the *systems* typically involved. That is, most insurance purchase decisions are made by family groups and organizational executives, not isolated individuals.

The social processes whereby such groups receive information, process it, and then act, yet await the attention of the research community. I have a suspicion that family-focused studies of these processes will prove to be as central to our understanding of hazard mitigation adoption patterns as they did in warning response studies. Until the mid-1960s these too had been "individualistic" in focus. Today, we know better. Until we examine the *sociology*—that is, group and organizational behavior—of insurance purchasing and other mitigative actions, critical voids will persist in the policy-relevant information base.

Also, as White and Haas (1975:63) stressed a decade ago, the interdependencies among hazard adjustments must be mapped better. Failure to do so—and not to have this information used within the policy formulation process—will result in continued drift and untold cost.

IH. Individual System Level

Recall that my literature search was directed toward "disaster events," not attitudes toward flood insurance or any other hazard adjustment. As with the topic of hazard perceptions, my bibliography only *illustrates* the range of studies completed to date on this aspect of mitigation. I grouped the finding cards into four categories: (1) hazard adjustments: impacts and perceptual patterns; (2) adoption of hazard insurance; (3) attitudes toward earthquake predictions; and (4) other adjustments.

IH1. Hazard Adjustments: Impacts and Perceptual Patterns

Hazard adjustments do impact attitudes. Structural devices such as dams, for example, often engender a false sense of security.

> IH1.1 "Numerous such studies have shown that total reliance on such protection schemes builds a greater potential for catastrophe by inducing a buildup of vulnerable property and causing the people to have a false sense of security and protection. . . . A recent example was the Johnstown, Pennsylvania, flash flood of 1977. Many residents thought the dams and levees constructed since Johnstown's earlier flood disasters would

protect them from another" (Frazier, 1979:326). (For parallel findings in New Zealand, see Ericksen, 1974:64.)

Most people are aware that many adjustments could reduce their level of risk—at least for many types of hazards. But detailed studies of their perceptions of these options clearly demonstrate that their choice processes are bounded (Burton, Kates, and White, 1978:52, 88). Thus, across the range of adjustments available, relatively few are ever adopted (Slovic, Kunreuther, and White, 1974:190–191).

> IH1.2 ". . . all possible precautions and responses to an event were mentioned by at least one respondent. However, with the exception of insurance, no single adjustment was mentioned by more than 40% of the sample. . . . on an individual basis, respondents perceived a relatively narrow range of action for coping with earthquakes" [Canada and U.S.A.] (Jackson, 1981:403). (See also Jackson, 1977:278; parallel coping responses have been reported by Mileti, Drabek, and Haas, 1975:30.)

Adjustments that are adopted reflect several characteristics, including relevance to events that have recurred, and technological applications. Among Americans, especially, a quick fix through a technological remedy has high appeal. Individuals in other societies may be less activistic; some simply plan to bear most losses rather than trying to do much to reduce them. And, for Americans, at least, adjustment proposals that result in restrictions in their freedom of movement—like closing off a recreation area near a volcano—are less favored as their familiarity with the hazard increases.

> IH1.2a "Suggested user solutions were almost entirely technological involving channelization, dam construction, etc., and the residents feel that responsibility for handling the flood problem rests with government. [p. 25] . . . [162 residents living within the 100-year floodplain were surveyed.] The residents are aware of a very narrow and restricted range of adjustments to the flood hazards. Almost all consider the appropriate solution to be some form of engineering construction. For example, dams, levees or channelization. Few mentioned any type of individual adjustment and only a small percentage (14.5%) intend to purchase flood insurance [p. 39]" (McPherson and Saarinen, 1977:25, 39). (See also Ward, 1974:145; Earney and Knowles, 1974:174.)

> IH1.2b "Farmers were asked what they would do to mitigate the damages of a drought event . . . Virtually all of them indicated that their chief response would be simply to bear the losses, i.e., to suffer and starve until better times came along. An equal proportion would turn to God and pray to Allah or the traditional gods for help at such time. Beyond bearing the losses, 59 percent believe they could get help from relatives, 55 percent might look for work in the town of Yelwa, but not further afield, 84 percent would try to enhance their income by selling handicraft items, cut firewood, . . ." [Nigeria] (Dupree and Roder, 1974:117). (See also Jackson, 1981:403.)

IH1.2c "Those persons most familiar with the Mount Baker environment were the most strongly opposed to the closures. Finally, it was observed that expected future responses to possible new warnings differ between residents and recreationists. Concrete residents say that they would respond only to mandatory controls, not to warnings, whereas most recreationists say that they would either not visit the area if warnings were issued or would at least be uncertain as to their reaction" (Hodge, Sharp, and Marts, 1979:231).

Increased awareness of specific hazards results in more preparedness actions. This linkage is not a simple one, however, nor are all data consistent.

IH1.3(H) ". . . there is a generally applicable tendency for the people who are most aware of the Uplift to be best prepared for an earthquake. But the correlation is far from perfect and there are notable exceptions. Greater awareness is not converted into more extensive earthquake preparedness among people over fifty years of age, among college graduates, among people who fear earthquakes intensely, and among people who live in the most vulnerable housing. On the other hand, people living in households where there are minor children, and especially children of school age, are better prepared than people in households without children in spite of being less aware of the Uplift" (Turner et al., 1979:111).

In their surveys, Turner and his colleagues discovered ethnic differences. But as I have pointed out several times, this factor, like age and socioeconomic status, structures these perceptual sets in a rather complex manner. Important interaction effects probably exist among these variables.

IH1.4(H) ". . . findings suggest a widespread ambivalence toward government in the Black community. Blacks apparently look toward government to deal with the problem of earthquake hazards. But at the same time they have reservations about trusting government officials fully. [p. 45] . . . Mexican Americans look to American government officials to deal with earthquake hazard and have a more favorable view of official accomplishments than either White Anglos or Blacks [p. 48]" (Turner et al., 1981:45, 48).

IH1.5(H) ". . . high correlation between age and the tendency to adopt adjustments . . . suggests that the adoption of adjustments becomes habitual and is cumulative. It appears that the number of adjustments adopted increases over time because an adjustment once adopted forms a part of the individual's repertoire of habits and is rarely dropped. Insurance is a case in point. . . . The major effort involved in having an insurance policy is to be found in taking out the policy in the first place. After that, inertia is likely to operate: the cost of premiums usually becomes part of the expected expense, and the decision to renew is repetitive, while the decision to take out the policy in the first place is innovative and more resisted" [Canada] (Schiff, 1977:250).

These patterns may have some commonality across hazard types—and may even reflect a more generalized attitude–behavior syndrome.

> IH1.6(H) ". . . similar patterns of adopting adjustments for both natural and non-natural hazards. This suggests that the adoption of adjustments to natural hazards is part of a larger syndrome of adjustment behavior" [Canada] (Schiff, 1977:250). (See also James, 1968:368.)

Finally, as I discussed in the reconstruction phase, blame assignation following disasters is on the rise. While events *per se* may still be viewed as "Acts of God," it is my belief that greater segments of the public view certain types of damages as avoidable, *if* government will act.

Limited data indicate that this attitudinal shift is not unique to the U.S.A. Following the 1978 Miyagiken Oki earthquake in Japan, for example, respondents were asked if they viewed it as "an Act of God or a man-made disaster." Less than one in five (17%) attributed *the event* to "human failure." When asked who was *responsible for damages,* however, the responses took an important convolution.

1. Government is responsible (19%).
2. Real estate companies are responsible (32%).
3. People who had damages are responsible (4%).
4. No one; it was an Act of God (43%) (Horige and Oura, 1979; as summarized in Yamamoto and Quarantelli, 1982:A-68).

IH2. Adoption of Hazard Insurance

Recognizing the policy significance of the major nonstructural approach to hazard mitigation directed at flooding in the U.S.A.—namely, the National Flood Insurance Program (NFIP)—Kunreuther, Slovic, and several colleagues (e.g., Kunreuther *et al.,* 1978) initiated a series of studies that provided much insight into the behavioral dynamics of insurance purchasing. Their work established a model—both in terms of theoretical integration and methodological rigor—that others should emulate.

More recently, an Australian team, i.e., Britton, Kearney, and Britton (1983), working at the Centre for Disaster Studies, James Cook University of North Queensland, completed an extensive literature review. While they framed their conclusions at the more general level of "hazard insurance," most of the studies cited dealt with flood insurance, although a small portion were focused on earthquake insurance.

> IH2.1(H) The greater the salience of the hazard, the higher the probability of purchasing hazard insurance. (Based on Britton, Kearney, and Britton, 1983. For somewhat opposing interpretations, see Hansson *et al.,* 1979:423; Saarinen, 1982b:1; Lorelli, 1968:3–4.)

Britton, Kearney, and Britton (1983:268) identified six variables that are associated with hazard salience: (1) event frequency; (2) experience of events; (3) awareness/perception; (4) information; (5) proximity to hazard area; and (6) recency of hazard event. Each could be used to specify more precise propositions. Numerous opinions, a few study findings, and many quotations from our 1975 review (Mileti, Drabek, and Haas), were juxtaposed as evidence supporting each. Despite this and the relatively high plausibility of each variable, I suggest that the entire set be regarded as important hypotheses meriting careful empirical testing with comparative research designs. In many cases it is clear that the variable is relevant, but the precise nature of the relationship is ambiguous.

> IH2.1a "Of the 207 home owners, only 18 (8.7%) indicated that they had earthquake insurance, although 52 (29.3%) believed that a major earthquake will definitely or probably occur in the area while they are living there. Those who believe that a major earthquake is likely to occur while they are living in their present house are no more likely to purchase earthquake insurance [p. 56] . . . those aware of their location within a special studies zone were more likely to have purchased insurance than those not aware of their location [p. 57] (Palm, 1981:56, 57). (See also Britton, Kearney, and Britton, 1983:277.)

> IH2.2(H) The greater the level of information that individuals have about a hazard, the higher the probability of purchasing hazard insurance. (Based on Britton, Kearney, and Britton, 1983.)

While supporting this overall idea, Britton, Kearney, and Britton (1983) were quick to point out how complex this relationship is because of intervening variables. They arranged their very mixed set of conclusions around four themes: (1) lack of knowledge of hazard characteristics; (2) intellectual overload; (3) socioeconomic indices; and (4) underestimation of threats (Britton, Kearney, and Britton, 1983:280). Thus, several researchers have lamented the lack of knowledge about hazards that characterizes the public. And some, especially Kunreuther and his colleagues, have argued that people may be "overloaded" if they attempt to engage in "rational" decision making regarding insurance purchasing. Hazard knowledge was found to be limited among homeowners residing in hazard-prone areas, although those who had purchased insurance did show signs of being more knowledgeable—of having a higher level of information.

> IH2.2a(H) "Knowledge of Insurance: Most respondents in the field survey were aware that flood and earthquake insurance existed, but over 60 percent of the uninsured homeowners residing in hazard-prone areas said they were unaware that they were *eligible* to purchase coverage. . . . Approximately 25 percent of the uninsured in both the flood and earthquake surveys were unable to estimate the premium, even when prodded by the interviewer to offer their best guess" (Kunreuther et al., 1978:236).

> IH2.2b(H) "Knowledge of the Hazard: . . . Insured homeowners expect more damage from these disasters than do the uninsured group. . . . Homeowners were also asked to estimate the chances of a severe flood

or earthquake causing damage to their property during the next year. . . .
The insured homeowners generally have higher estimates of the chances
of a severe flood or earthquake than do the nonpolicy holders'' (Kunreuther *et al.,* 1978:236–237).

IH2.3(H) The higher the awareness of a hazard, the higher the probability
of purchasing hazard insurance. (Based on Britton, Kearney, and Britton,
1983:285.)

When they reviewed materials wherein "awareness" had been mentioned, Britton, Kearney, and Britton (1983:285–301) discovered much
diversity. They formulated seven variables that reflect differing aspects
of the complex property that is labeled "awareness": (1) risk-taking propensity; (2) defense mechanisms; (3) influence of significant others; (4)
land occupancy rate; (5) government policies and practices; (6) beliefs;
and (7) time horizons. Two of these were further categorized into additional
segments. For example, "defense mechanisms" was subdivided into 11
topics, including fatalism and locus of control; "influence of significant
others" had four subcategories, e.g., "group think" and "risky shift."
After reading all of the evidence assembled by Britton, Kearney, and
Britton (1983), I came to two conclusions. First, while all 11 of these
themes ought to be pursued, neither individually nor collectively do they
comprise a model that might be predictive of varied hazard awareness
levels. Second, in none of the instances are the available findings of sufficient consistency or reflective of adequate methodological designs to
conclude that we have any more than several rather vague hypotheses
that can point future researchers in directions of promise. Among those
that I suspect will prove to be most useful are the following.

IH2.3a(H) "The insured homeowner is he who has suffered damage from
a flood, who enjoys a relatively higher social class position, and who is
internally-oriented, that is, feels that the effects of the future on him are
determined by his own current behaviors. . . . Rotter's I-E Scale—'Internals' (those who feel they are in control of their destinies); 'Externals'
(those who feel their lives to be directed by outside forces); and those
in between. Sixty percent of the internal-oriented had purchased flood
insurance; 43 percent of those who scored midrange were insured; and
only 35 percent of the external-oriented were insured" (Baumann and
Sims, 1978:195). (For negative findings, see Schiff, 1977:246, 249; positive
findings also reported by Lorelli, 1968:3–4.)

IH2.3b(H) "A series of laboratory studies of insurance decision making
shows that people buy more insurance against events having a moderately
high probability of inflicting a relatively small loss than against low-prob-
ability, high-loss events. . . . people refuse to protect themselves against
losses whose probability is below some threshold" (Slovic *et al.,*
1977:237). (See also Kunreuther *et al.,* 1978:241.)

> IH2.4(H) The more extensive the experience with a hazard, especially
> actual losses because of it, the higher the probability of purchasing hazard
> insurance. (Based on Britton, Kearney, and Britton, 1983:302.)

In their review, Britton, Kearney, and Britton (1983:302) identified a large number of variables that might impact or be reflective of aspects of a broad dimension of "experience." Their listing included the following twelve categories: (1) assets at risk; (2) loss of previous assets; (3) tradition; (4) economic dependence on area; (5) attitudes toward mitigatory devices; (6) cost of mitigation practices; (7) additional community characteristics; (8) additional psychological characteristics; (9) biodata; (10) preferred risk level; (11) attitudes toward insurance; and (12) attitudes toward hazards. Obviously, the line between several of these is blurred—a reality that I am most appreciative of after the months I have spent in my own sorting effort. Also, several of these general categories are quite complex, e.g., "tradition."

> IH2.4a(H) "Most people show no interest in insuring themselves until
> they or their friends have been personally affected by a disaster (Kun-
> reuther, 1978:29[1])" (as summarized in Britton, Kearney, and Britton,
> 1983:316).

> IH2.5(H) The higher the premium cost and the more constraining company
> policies and selective actions by agents, the lower the probability of pur-
> chasing hazard insurance. (Based on Palm, 1981; see also Britton, Kear-
> ney, and Britton, 1983:318.)

As I detail in an upcoming section (see Section IIIH2), hazard insurance is an organizational product—or service, if you wish. Palm's (1981) study of California real estate agents penetrated deeply into the behavioral dynamics of house purchasing in seismically active areas. Through passage of the Alquist–Priolo Special Studies Zones Act, passed in 1972 and amended in 1975, the California legislature required "disclosure of the location of the special studies zone to persons considering the purchase of property within the zone" (Palm, 1981:7–8). But ". . . there was little measurable buyer response" (Palm, 1981:x).

Why? Primarily because of the third variable in the above proposition—selective actions by agents. Typically, "disclosure" was completed within the context of "closing" wherein prospective buyers were given a stack of papers for signature. Thus, they were required to sign a form; often as not, however, it was one among several sheets to be signed then. Rarely was much explanation given. This experience parallels what researchers discovered in Austin, Texas, following extensive flooding.

---

[1]H. Kunreuther, "Even Noah Built An Ark." *The Wharton Magazine*, (Summer, 1978):28–35.

"On the night of May 24–25, [1981] 528 residential and business structures suffered flood damage. Most were not covered by flood insurance. There appear to have been two main reasons for the low incidence of insurance: (1) a false sense of security and (2) lack of information and encouragement. . . . Interviews with insurance agents during this study indicated (1) that agents are not supported by their companies with informational and promotional campaigns designed to sell flood insurance, and (2) that the commissions allowed by government regulation are too low to bother with" (Committee on Natural Disasters, 1982:26).

In short, several issues have been pursued, and a series of variables have been identified. Significant headway has been made toward understanding the complex social dynamic that impacts the availability and adoption of various forms of hazard insurance.

IH3. Attitudes toward Earthquake Predictions

Early in the 1970s, the possibility of scientifically based earthquake predictions received widespread attention. A brief summary of those developments was prepared by Mileti, Hutton, and Sorensen (1981) as an introduction to their study of probable responses by families, organizational personnel, and societies. Since these were essentially conclusions about warning responses, I included them in those sections of Chapter 2. But, now, let's draw on a few quotations from their historical material to get a sense of one adjustment that has enormous potential consequence.

"In 1971, at an international scientific meeting in Moscow, Soviet scientists announced that they had learned to recognize some signs they believed were associated with impending earthquakes. This was the first widespread public knowledge of Soviet prediction research which has been initiated in the mid-1960's. Concurrently, prediction research was being conducted by the Japanese; in the late 1960's prediction efforts first received attention in the United States, and the Chinese Program began to be expanded" (Mileti, Hutton, and Sorensen, 1981:1).

"Several destructive earthquakes have been usefully predicted in China: the Haicheng earthquake, Liaoning Province, February 4, 1975; a pair of earthquakes 97 minutes apart, magnitude 6.9, near the China–Burma border, May 29, 1976; and a three-event cluster, magnitudes 7.2, 6.7, and 7.2, on August 16, 22 and 23, 1976, at Sungpan-Pingwu, Szechuan Province" (Mileti, Hutton, and Sorensen, 1981:4).

"In the United States, small events have been currently predicted in New York . . . and in South Carolina" (Mileti, Hutton, and Sorensen, 1981:4).

"The establishment of the National Earthquake Prediction Evaluation Council was announced on January 28, 1980. To be composed of not fewer than eight federal and non-federal earth scientists, the Council will review data collected by other scientists and recommend to the USGS director whether a formal earthquake prediction or advisory is warranted. Organization of the Council implements the provisions of the Earthquake Hazards Reduction Act of September, 1977, and of a plan developed by a White House working group. The Director of the USGS issued two earthquake hazard watches in 1980: one for Mammoth Lakes, and one for southern California'' (Mileti, Hutton, and Sorensen, 1981:8).

By the mid-1970s then, hazard researchers were being asked how people might respond to earthquake predictions, once they were made. Among the better judgments offered were those provided by a National Academy of Sciences study group chaired by Ralph H. Turner (see Panel on the Public Policy Implications of Earthquake Prediction, 1975). It concluded that responses to such warning messages might not differ much from those that had been documented for other types of disaster warnings. Of course, the matter of lead time—often a decade or more—had to be taken into account.

IH3.1(H) "As in the case of other disaster predictions and warnings, public officials responsible for issuing earthquake warnings are likely to delay until they are reasonably satisfied that the danger will actually develop. Officials will be concerned about what false alarms will do to their credibility and future effectiveness; they may also be concerned with the legal problems associated with erroneous predictions'' (Panel on the Public Policy Implications of Earthquake Prediction, 1975:51).

IH3.2 ". . . findings and guidelines from previous disaster-warning studies have general relevance to the earthquake prediction, warning, and response process. We would not expect most people to respond to the release of earthquake predictions and the issuance of earthquake warnings with panic, hysteria, or other nonrational or uncontrolled forms of behavior. On the contrary, a much more likely response derives from the so-called 'normalcy bias'[2]—i.e., the tendency for people to accept most readily any information that enables them to disbelieve the prediction, minimize the danger, and view the situation optimistically'' (Panel on the Public Policy Implications of Earthquake Prediction, 1975:49–50).

Since these opinions were published, Japanese researchers have reported empirical studies that are supportive.

IH3.2a [Following an earthquake prediction (August, 1976), and repeated reinforcement through the media by the scientific community, a three-wave panel study (15-month period) revealed that] ". . . levels of individual cognition of earthquake danger and earthquake anxiety showed a sort of stability. The relative stability of these factors provides some basis for concluding that there is very little chance that the sense of impending earthquake danger might suddenly flare up and ignite panic'' (Hirose and Ishizuka, 1983:110). (See also Abe, 1978.)

---

[2]Benjamin F. McLuckie, *The Warning System: A Social Science Perspective*, National Oceanic and Atmospheric Administration, United States Department of Commerce. Washington, D.C.: U.S. Government Printing Office, 1973, p. 22.

Turner's committee also speculated that, as with disaster warnings generally, responses would be differential—some would be less likely to receive, understand, or believe them.

> IH3.3(H) "On the basis of existing disaster studies, we expect the greatest
> difficulty in securing desirable responses to earthquake predictions and
> warnings from people outside the mainstream of society. . . . This group
> includes elderly people, the handicapped, those of lower socioeconomic
> status, and members of various ethnic and minority groups. People in
> these groups are especially likely not to receive, understand, or believe
> earthquake warnings" (Panel on the Public Policy Implications of Earth-
> quake Prediction, 1975:52).

Consistent with this idea are later findings from Japan that reflect differentials in awareness, knowledge, and trust. Thus, as with hazard perceptions generally, social factors appear to structure attitude sets. Unfortunately, our data base is limited at present, so we don't know if these
contours will apply across other study sites.

> IH3.4(H) "Women are more likely to think that scientific prediction of
> time is possible. Young women are more likely to trust the scientific
> prediction. People with more education, rather than people with less ed-
> ucation, tend to think that scientific prediction of earthquake is possible.
> In comparison with other categories professionals, managers, company
> or store owners, and clerical workers are more likely to think that pre-
> diction for the area is scientifically possible. . . . people who have a sci-
> entific attitude tend to think that predicting magnitude is not possible,
> but predicting area is possible [Japan] (Okabe, *et al.,* 1979b)" (as sum-
> marized in Yamamoto and Quarantelli, 1982:A-163).

> IH3.5(H) "Knowledge on earthquake and prediction methods
> A. The younger they are, the more they know.
> B. Men know more than women.
> C. Those who perceive the large possibility of danger are likely to know
>   more than those who perceive less [Japan] (Okabe, *et al.,* 1979a)"
>   (as summarized in Yamamoto and Quarantelli, 1982:A-169).

IH4. Other Adjustments

Scattered among the remaining finding cards that my literature search
produced were observations from several studies that offered limited insight into individual responses to other types of mitigative actions. Returning to the observations with which I began this chapter—White and
Haas (1975)—let's recall that one option applicable to many hazards is to
avoid them. People don't need to live in flood-prone areas. But then why
do they? White (1974b) hypothesized that four different types of justifi-
cations might be obtained from people. The distribution, stability, and
relative intensity with which these might actually serve as rationalizations
remain unknown today.

> IH4.1(H) "Human occupance that persists in areas of recurrent hazard
> is justified in the view of the occupants for the following reasons: 1.
> Superior economic opportunity; 2. Lack of satisfying alternative oppor-
> tunities; 3. Short-term time horizons; 4. High ratios of reserves to potential
> loss" (Gilbert F. White, 1974b:4).

James' research suggested that there may be a threshold level, beyond
which people will consider moving away. But other work emphasized the
propensity to remain (e.g., Nehnevajsa and Wong, 1977:151). Thus, the
$700 threshold level suggested by James may or may not be found to be
applicable to other study sites.

> IH4.1a(H) "The average out-of-the-pocket damage figure quoted by those
> flood-plain residents who consider an experienced flood loss as great
> enough to make them seriously consider moving away is $700" (James,
> 1973:1832).

Of course, rather than move away, some people will initiate some form
of flood-proofing. One study indicated that—as with other aspects of disaster response—primary group linkages are important. Also, the sequential
quality of such responses was evident.

> IH4.2(H) "People who adopt flood proofing are most likely to develop
> their plan by talking to neighbors and observing their adjustments"
> (Dexter, Willeke, and James, 1979:75).

> IH4.3(H) "Most individuals tried one idea and then another, until some-
> thing worked. This typical adjustment process, however, resulted in a
> less than optimal implementation strategy" (Dexter, Willeke, and James,
> 1979:75).

But, as I stressed above, available data clearly indicate that such actions
are taken by relatively small segments of the population at risk, even after
an event has taught them a lesson, so to speak.

> IH4.4 "The only action that most of the owners took following the 1972
> flood to protect their property from future flooding was to purchase flood
> insurance. . . . Only 13 percent carried out some flood-proofing, such as
> raising the level of the cottage, prior to 1972, while 25 percent floodproofed
> after 1975" (Johnson, 1968:9).

Surveys by Turner and associates in the Los Angeles area (Turner *et
al.*, 1979:93), which I have referred to many times, indicated that about
two-thirds of their respondents endorsed various structural safety measures. Thus, far more favored government focus here than on the more
problematic research area of earthquake prediction (two items garnered
28% and 26% in favor).

> IH4.5 ". . . in connection with structural safety, people are considerably
> less enthusiastic about providing loans to upgrade existing buildings than
> they are for strict enforcement of building codes. Nevertheless, the finding
> that more than 80 percent find it unqualifiedly important for government

to invest large sums of money in loans for upgrading unsafe structures
lends support to the previous findings concerning the building and safety
issue'' (Turner *et al.*, 1979: 93).

Finally, when all else fails, relief and rehabilitation actions will have to
be taken to aid victims. Generally, these receive public support—at least
in a comparative sense. Far better to be a disaster victim than a family
hit by some other form of tragedy that might qualify them for welfare
services. But even this form of mitigation has not been scrutinized adequately to give us a true sense of the behavioral dynamic.

IH4.6 ''. . . respondents were asked to rate disaster relief (helping victims
of hurricanes, floods, or other natural disasters) and welfare-relief (providing food, shelter and etc. for the poor and needy) . . . respondents
were more supportive of disaster than welfare services. Over half (60%)
of the respondents rate disaster services as very important compared to
one third (34%) who rated welfare services to be very important. [p. 735]
. . . Support for disaster relief is relatively stable across all categories.
[income, education, age, gender] [p. 736]'' (Leitko, Rudy, and Peterson,
1980:735, 736).

IIH. Group System Level

Prior to writing the preceding section of this chapter, I reviewed the few
finding cards that I had coded as pertaining to groups. Most contained
references to ''homeowners''; one indicated that neighbor behavior impacted hazard adoption. Given the discussion I had outlined for the preceding section, it seemed far better to fit these few conclusions into the
appropriate substantive areas there than to treat them in isolation here.

IIIH. Organizational System Level

Turning to research focused on organizational systems, my literature
search captured little. It did identify a few illustrations, however, that
introduce a complex research agenda that has remained almost totally
unexplored. I grouped the few available finding cards into four categories:
(1) hazard manager actions; (2) earthquake disclosure legislation; (3) hazard
insurance; and (4) public education.

IIIH1. Hazard Manager Actions

As a general portrait, Johnson's (1979) characterization is rather telling—
and discomforting. This image fits my own field experiences and impressions, except that I know of many atypical individuals. Thus, rather than
pursue questions framed within this critical perspective, we should seek

to identify the factors that might produce the exceptional cases and design experiments that could guide future interventions. But that is the future—Johnson's conclusions reflect a continuity with findings based on the general public.

IIIH1.1(H) "Hazard managers do not assess the full range of control alternatives" (Johnson, 1979:10).

IIIH1.2(H) "Hazard managers adopt control strategies which reflect those they perceive as being preferred by the public, rather than those which are technically most feasible" (Johnson, 1979:10).

IIIH1.3(H) "Hazard managers routinely fail to consider barriers to implementation, which often produce results quite different from those intended" (Johnson, 1979:11).

IIIH2. Earthquake Disclosure Legislation

Most prominent among the explorations completed to date is the study by Palm (1981) I alluded to above—assessment of the impact of the earthquake disclosure requirement enacted by the California legislature (see IH2.5). What behavioral consequence did this law appear to have, *given the way in which it has been implemented?*

IIIH2.1 ". . . the present disclosure law, while it may have affected the behavior of developers of large-scale new housing projects, seems to have little or no impact on individual home buyers. [p. 106] . . . fewer than half of the home buyers could remember a disclosure less than six months after the time it should have been made [p. ix]" (Palm, 1981:106, ix).

I noted that real estate agents played a critical role. Palm's (1981) insightful analyses pinned the matter down rather well—at least within the communities studied.

IIIH2.2 ". . . full information is not being provided because not all real estate agents understand the meaning and significance of the zones and also because the disclosure process itself minimizes the impact of the disclosure on the buyer and limits the amount of information conveyed" (Palm, 1981:x).

IIIH2.2a ". . . disclosure is not likely to take place at a time when it might most jeopardize the sale, that is, when the real estate agent is showing the house to the buyer, but rather at the time the buyer has already decided on the house, at the purchase contract time" (Palm, 1981:78).

IIIH2.2b "In Berkeley, disclosure on this form is simply a typed line stating 'in Alquist–Priolo zone' or 'in Alquist–Priolo district.' To the uninitiated buyer, such a statement might mean anything, most probably the names of the state legislators for the area. In Contra Costa County, the form includes a line stating 'special studies zone' and a box marked 'yes' or 'no.' This disclosure tells the buyer nothing about the *meaning* of the zones" (Palm, 1981:101).

IIIH2.2c "The third disclosure method is the signing of a contract addendum. This addendum, until recently, stated that 'the property *is or may be* situated in a Special Studies Zone' (emphasis added). No definition of the special studies zone is presented . . . The words 'seismic,' 'earthquake,' or 'fault' are not mentioned in the contract addendum" (Palm, 1981:101–102).

So? Once again we find evidence that the law enacted is not the law in action. While many questions remain, Palm's study demonstrated one type of contribution that behaviorally based research studies offer to the decision maker and the public policy process.

IIIH3. Hazard Insurance

As I pointed out above, hazard insurance is among one of the most significant nonstructural approaches to disaster mitigation that has been tried within the U.S.A., especially during the past decade through the National Flood Insurance Program (NFIP). But we are just now getting a few findings that point to the organizational behavior dynamics that constrain the effectiveness of such adjustment options. Available evidence suggests that disaster events stimulate sales. But we don't know the limits or universality of this relationship.

IIIH3.1 "The number of flood insurance policies increased from 36 to 202 the year after the flood. This is both helpful and detrimental. It will help people if they are struck again, but since it is available, it tends to encourage people to live in the canyon. The highway was rebuilt in the same location with federal financing. That also tends to orient life in the same pattern as before. Larimer County, however, courageously zoned the floodway. Prevention is certainly the best action to take, but the plans are based on a supposed 100-year flood level" (McComb, 1980:99).

Other findings from the 1976 Big Thompson flash flood in Colorado may or may not fit other communities, but certainly the possibility is there.

IIIH3.2 "A survey of insurance salespeople in Larimer County [following the Big Thompson flood (July, 1976):] . . . Eighty-three percent of the salespeople interviewed said that they perceived their roles as agents to sell flood insurance only when contacted by a customer requesting it. The same percentage indicated that the existing commission was fair" (Cochrane *et al.,* 1979:30).

IIIH3.3 "When asked why the concept of flood insurance has not caught on with the public, 70% of the agents interviewed offered one of two explanations: 1. premium payments were too costly for the home-owner,

or 2. the home-owner had a 'won't happen to me' attitude'' (Cochrane
et al., 1979:30).

Among disaster victims, claim filings vary by hazard type. Thus, Rossi
and his associates found, for example, that:

> IIIH3.4 "Claim filings were more frequent among those suffering from
> serious fires (93%), hurricanes (77%), and tornadoes (80%). Fewer claims
> were filed for floods (65%) or earthquakes (38%)'' (Rossi *et al.,*
> 1983b:131).

> IIIH3.5 "Virtually all serious fire claims were honored (99%), and close
> to all of the tornado (94%) and hurricane claims (89%) were also honored.
> Three out of four (77%) flood claims and a few more than one out of
> three (38%) earthquake claims were met with some payment'' (Rossi *et
> al.,* 1983b:131).

> IIIH3.6 "The major specific complaint made by those claiming unfair
> treatment concerned the size of the payment, two-thirds or more of the
> dissatisfied indicating that the payment was too small. For the hazards
> for which coverage was slight, complaints were registered that the claims
> were disallowed. Few claimed that the payments were too slow in coming
> or that insurance personnel acted impolitely'' (Rossi *et al.,* 1983b:134).

IIIH4. Public Education

Many organizations—schools, media, and the like—could provide far
greater amounts of hazard information than is done currently. As I discussed in the chapter on planning, this mitigative adjustment can save
lives.

> "Schwartz (1979)[3] has provided a graphic example of the value of such
> disaster education. In 1974, during a tornado outbreak in the United
> States, a seventh grade teacher reviewed severe weather safety rules
> with his class. After school, as one of the buses was taking pupils home,
> a tornado appeared in its path. The driver did not know what to do, but
> one of the recently briefed students did. He convinced the driver to pull
> over, get everyone out and far enough away so that the bus couldn't roll
> onto them. All passengers sought safety in a ditch. Although the tornado
> destroyed the bus, none of the pupils was injured'' (Foster, 1980:187).

I encountered the following observations that frame the types of matters
future research must define with more precision. Beyond these suggestions, it is clear that we need to gain a much clearer idea of the role played
by the media.

> IIIH4.1(H) ". . . public information campaigns have relatively high suc-
> cess potential—

---

[3]G. Schwartz, "Tornado!" *Journal of Civil Defense* **XII** (No. 2, 1979):10–13.

1. If they are planned around the assumption that most of the public will be only mildly interested or not at all interested in what is communicated.

2. If middle-range goals that can be reasonably achieved as a consequence of exposure to the messages are set as specific objectives.

3. If, after middle-range objectives are set, careful consideration is given to delineating specific targets in terms of their demographic and psychological attributes, their life-styles, their value and belief systems, and their mass media habits."[4] (Larson, 1980:121).

IIIH4.2 ". . . the 1952–1953 and 1972–1974 news coverage patterns were similar in being dominated by the modify the hazard category, that is, by adjustments that seek to rearrange or manipulate nature [p. 537] . . . A relatively large amount of coverage was devoted to adjustments designed not to control nature but to modify human behavior in the face of hazards. [during 1972–1974] Thus, government purchase and expropriation of land and property and land use controls were more common topics of the 1972–1974 hazard reporting. These two adjustments were the subjects of discussion in approximately 15 percent of the articles and 20 percent of the news volume . . . In contrast, in 1952–1953 only 6.61 percent of the articles and 6.68 percent of the news volume referred to adjustments in this modify the loss potential category [p. 538]" [Canada] (Needham and Nelson, 1977:537, 538).

IVH. Community System Level

While hazard adoption activities of communities have not been studied as frequently as those of individuals, three topics have been explored rather thoroughly. These areas are: (1) the impact of disaster experience; (2) correlates of community adoption of hazard mitigation adjustments; and (3) anticipating opposition.

IVH1. The Impact of Disaster Experience

Communities within the U.S.A., at least, are somewhat variable regarding the type and extent of hazard mitigation adjustments they have adopted. Numerous case studies provide documentation of community adoption of various forms of mitigative actions *after* a disaster has occurred. But the adoption process among those impacted is not uniform.

IVH1.1 "The correlation between experience and mitigative actions is not as clear as might be expected. For example, one community with a history of frequent coastal storms has paid minimal attention to mitigation, while another community, also subject to coastal storms but far less fre-

---

[4]H. Mendelsohn, "Some Reasons Why Information Campaigns Can Succeed." *Public Opinion Quarterly* **37** (1973):50–61.

quently, did take a number of significant, mitigative steps. Neither was
there a clear correlation between size of community and attention to
mitigation: the smallest community continuously engages in mitigation
planning, although it is dependent on external resources to accomplish
such measures" (Rubin, 1981:14–15). (See also Mileti, Drabek, and Haas,
1975:28; Anderson, 1970c.)

Sometimes the range of adjustments adopted are so pronounced that
researchers have argued that the aggregate represents a major aspect of
a "disaster subculture." I have described other research related to this
important concept in the chapters on planning and reconstruction. But
here I am referring to one of the impacts of disaster experience—an impact
that provides a nurturing soil, a community climate that is supportive of
the adoption of *certain* types of mitigative adjustments.

> IVH1.2 "With respect to the development of disaster subcultures, three
> factors appear to be of crucial importance. . . . [1.] repetitive disaster
> impacts must have been experienced by the community. . . . [2.] if the
> focal agent allows for some period of forewarning, [then subcultural de-
> velopment is more likely.] [p. 41] . . . [3.] subcultures are more likely to
> emerge when the repetitive disaster agent produces salient consequential
> damage [p. 42]" (Wenger, 1978:41, 42). (See also Panel on the Public
> Policy Implications of Earthquake Prediction, 1975:52.)

> IVH1.2a "Weller and Wenger have pointed out that the development of
> a subculture within a community is facilitated by three factors: repetitive
> disaster impacts, a disaster agent which regularly allows a period of fore-
> warning, and the existence of a consequential damage that is salient to
> various segments of the community.[5] Southern Manitoba meets all of
> these conditions as well as possessing certain contextual characteristics
> which have further contributed to the emergence of a disaster subculture"
> [Canada] (Hannigan and Kueneman, 1978:132).

This is not to suggest, however, that disaster events reverse or alter
severely the overall preexisting value patterns. Rapid adoption, or a short-
term time window wherein selected proposals may be considered, is really
the response—not wholesale or lasting priority shifts. Thus, adjustments
that are perceived to be consistent with broader trends and community
priorities appear to be those most likely to be adopted.

> IVH1.3 "Decisions which effectively reduce seismic risk are most likely
> to be made when they are consistent with other community objectives.
> Even after an earthquake, reducing seismic risk appears to have fairly
> low priority—certainly lower than quickly restoring the normal functioning
> of the community" (Mader *et al.,* 1980:7).

---

[5]Dennis E. Wenger and Jack M. Weller, "Disaster Subcultures: The Cultural Residues of
Community Disasters," Preliminary paper no. 9. Columbus, Ohio: Disaster Research Center,
The Ohio State University, 1973.

These processes, however, appear among experts too, not just the public. While the matter has not been studied explicitly, some researchers suggest that those responsible for making such decisions may, like the public, reflect strong propensities toward simplification. If flood-prone areas were to be used for recreation use, then they proceeded—typically without detailed evaluation as to whether or not this might uniformly be the best solution.

> IVH1.4(H) ". . . simplified strategies for easing the strain of making decisions about natural hazards may be used by experts and laymen alike. Although this hypothesis has not been studied systematically, a few relevant examples exist. Perhaps the simplest way to minimize the strain of integrating information is to avoid making decisions" (Slovic, Kunreuther, and White, 1974:197).

Finally, there is a decay curve. Unfortunately, it has not yet been mapped carefully. Thus, while there is evidence that disaster events do open up the constraint structures that typically restrain the adoption of mitigative adjustments, such effects are temporary. What we don't know is how temporary. Nor do we have much of a sense of how this may vary according to properties of the adjustment or community characteristics. Available evidence is limited to notions of enhanced invulnerability—we have weathered past storms—and a suggestion of gradual erosion and questioning of mitigative actions that were adopted when memories were fresh.

> IVH1.5 ". . . within 2 years of 'Althea' depressed prices for land and properties in coastal areas at risk from storm surges have recovered, and newcomers, who have purchased properties, are oblivious of the risks. Soon codes for improved building standards are questioned on the grounds of additional cost" [Australia] (Oliver, 1975:109). (For a parallel finding among Australian farmers, see Heathcote, 1974:133.)

With the implementation of some structural "solutions," the view may emerge that the problem simply no longer exists. We see examples of this at times with flood protection works. Control measures put in place after a flood may draw people back into the floodplain, and why not? The danger has been "eliminated."

> ". . . the scheme involved a combination of common engineering techniques used by river and water authorities in the 'prevention' of floods in urban areas in Britain. [p. 49] . . . There are plans for the redevelopment of the central area of Newtown, which is mainly on the flood plain, and this poses a potential problem which is difficult to handle in terms of public awareness and information. It is not surprising that the public and businessmen in Newtown regard the flood protection scheme as a 'solution' to the flood problem. Indeed it will be successful in all but the rarest flood events [p. 50]" [England] (Parker and Harding, 1978:49, 50).

Limited evidence, however, suggests that social factors influence these locational decisions, which at times may not really reflect an awareness of the risk they confront.

IVH1.6 "Those who move onto a flood plain unaware of the flood hazard fall into two broad groups. Some are in the lower end of the socioeconomic spectrum where other problems are too pressing for floods to be noted in a list of priorities. Such people usually react to flooding as an unavoidable act of God and continue as best they can without doing much to bring their plight to the attention of flood and drainage officials. Those in the second broad group who settle unawares are in the upper end of the socioeconomic spectrum and so preoccupied with their careers, clubs, civic activities, etc. that they don't look around their house enough to notice a creek until the water inundates their property. These people are not at all bashful at calling their situation to the attention of authorities and then using their influence (they have above average amounts) to get something done. They strongly favor a structural remedy (an unnoticed creek might just as well be concrete as natural). The activities of this group heavily bias the impression of flood control officials and the voices heard in public participation programs toward those who moved in unawares and now want structural protection" (James, 1973:1834).

IVH2. Correlates of Community Adoption of Hazard Mitigation Adjustments

As noted in Chapters 7 and 8, Rubin and her colleagues (1985) explored the dynamics of disaster recovery processes in communities through a comparative case study approach. One segment of this work focused on mitigative actions. As noted above (IVH1.1), Rubin (1981) discovered that neither disaster experience nor community size accounted for the range of variation observed. Both variables may, however, have interaction effects if included within a network of others.

IVH2.1(H) "Among the determinants of whether significant mitigative measures will be taken . . . are the following: [1.] *Regional area:* . . . [i.e.,] local public attitude and posture toward external organizations and other levels of government (especially federal). [2.] *Dependence vs. independence:* . . . (Either of these characteristics carried to the extreme becomes a problem of its own for state and federal emergency services personnel). [3.] *Understanding:* [p. 15] . . . [i.e.,] when economic and development pressures outweigh the benefits perceived from mitigation, the former wins over the latter [pp. 15–16]" (Rubin, 1981:15–16). (See also Rubin, Saperstein, and Barbee, 1985.)

With a focus on the National Flood Insurance Program (NFIP), Hutton, Mileti, and their associates (1979) added a very different dimension to the problem. After reviewing a large number of variables, they identified nine that characterized those communities that had adopted the emergency program of the NFIP. Generally speaking, these were consistent with previous research on the effects of community factors on policy adoption (see pp. C-25—C-28 of their report).

> IVH2.2 "Nine community characteristics were especially important in explaining why some communities adopted the NFIP under federal policy incentives, while others adopted only when sanctions for non-participation were added to the program. Positively related to adoption, that is, associated with program entrance under only incentive policy elements, were local government affluence, political activism of residents, urbanization, level of reform government, professionalism, and the size of local government. Negatively related to adoption were the level of government revenue generated out of local taxes (especially property taxes), a conservative citizenry, and centralization of local power" (Hutton, Mileti, *et al.,* 1979:C-29).

Using a single state as their study site, Luloff and Wilkinson (1979) divided Pennsylvania communities into two groups; 1,606 that participated in the NFIP and 857 who did not. They discovered that structural characteristics were less important than flood-relevant variables, however, when they subjected the data set to multiple regression analysis.

> IVH2.3 "The participating communities had more highly differentiated structures, as indicated by presence of selected organizations and services in the local area. Circulation ratios of local newspapers, treated as one measure of structural integration, were higher, on the average, in participating communities than in nonparticipating communities. Equality of educational attainment (the standard deviation of the educational distribution), which was a second measure of structural integration, was slightly greater in the participating communities than in the nonparticipating communities. [pp. 145–146] . . . [Multiple regression analysis indicated, however, that] Only the number of previous actions engaged in by the community and previous flood experience of the community appear to have substantial effects on participation in the flood insurance program [p. 148]" (Luloff and Wilkinson, 1979:145–146, 148).

Carrying these matters one step further, Burby and French (1980) tried to assess the effectiveness of the NFIP. Were mitigative actions, especially land-use requirements, having any real effect? To date, their work comprises the most rigorous quantitative examination of this issue. And it underscores the complexities that future theoretical models must reflect.

> IVH2.4 ". . . flood risk has a direct, positive relationship with both coastal and noncoastal communities' pursuit of land use management. Communities that have adopted the broadest management programs using the most different types of management measures tend to be those with a higher proportion of the community located in the hazard zone, with the greatest intensity of development in the hazard zone (coastal only), and

with higher value land uses (multifamily, office, commercial, industrial) at risk from flooding" (Burby and French, 1980:452).

Some communities viewed their program as more successful than did others. Burby and French (1980) identified several factors that differentiated these perceptions of effectiveness.

IVH2.5 Local officials vary regarding the perceived degree of effectiveness attained by implementation of the National Flood Insurance Program. (Based on Burby and French, 1980.)

IVH2.5a "Where communities had allowed more development to occur in the flood plain in the past, they tended to view their flood plain land use management program as less effective" (Burby and French, 1980:455).

IVH2.5b "Programs tended to be viewed as more effective where communities had more experience with land use management as a means of dealing with community problems" (Burby and French, 1980:455).

IVH2.5c "Programs were viewed as less effective where political support for the program was lacking" (Burby and French, 1980:455).

IVH2.5d "Direct state regulation of the flood plain was associated with positive local assessments of program effectiveness in preventing encroachment on natural areas" (Burby and French, 1980:455).

These and the other factors they identified may or may not be relevant to other adjustments. We really don't know the feasibility of a generic model that will predict the probable adoption of varied types of adjustments. Scattered within the literature I reviewed were a series of themes that may prove to be useful to those seeking to construct theoretical models.

First, among these is a theme of conservativism. It was stated well by Kirkby in her case study of the Oaxaca Mexican community.

". . . their conservative attitude to change further restricts their perceived alternatives. Their reverence for maize as the staple of life and their traditional view that a man should produce some of his family's own food provides considerable constraints on alternative modes of production. . . . membership of the community entails acceptance of its values even where these are in conflict with the ideal of personal advancement. The aims of the group transcend those of the individual. Community values include participation in religious rituals, the distribution of wealth or surplus within the community, and giving aid to other members of the group. [p. 126]

In Oaxaca, the variability of rainfall and the marginality of the area for dry farming has provided an extremely uncertain environment for peasants who have few reserves of capital or food. Without aid from the community, harvest losses from drought or flood would reduce many families to starvation each year. Village society in Oaxaca has therefore evolved a more formal system of providing mutual insurance than might be expected in a situation of less uncertainty or greater reserves to meet losses [pp. 126–127]'' [Mexico] (Kirkby, 1974:126–127).

Second is a theme developed by Barry Turner (1976b), who has stressed problem denial. Suggesting that researchers ought to focus more on the pre-event stage, rather than always starting their study after the plane has crashed, so to speak, he argued that there may be common behavioral sequences that depict certain types of pre-event responses. Thus, based on analysis of three disasters and the public inquiries into their causes, he proposed an "incubation stage" in pre-event sequences wherein large-scale intelligence failures occur.

"Common causal features are rigidities in institutional beliefs, distracting decoy phenomena, neglect of outside complaints, multiple information-handling difficulties, exacerbation of the hazards by strangers, failure to comply with regulations, and a tendency to minimize emergent danger" [England] (Barry A. Turner, 1976b:378).

Finally, there are a series of programmatic qualities that may define the conditions under which mitigation measures most likely may be adopted. Thus, while these have yet to be tested with a multiplicity of hazard mitigation programs, a review of over 200 studies revealed several guidelines. Collectively they comprise a set of basic principles that may have widespread applicability.

IVH2.6(H) Adoption of hazard mitigation measures will be increased if public education programs reflect selected principles of personalization, specificity, and reinforcement. (Based on Illinois Department of Transportation, Division of Water Resources, 1980.)

IVH2.6a(H) "Information should be personalized; that is, the information should be sufficiently specific to the residents' particular situation. The more personal the information, the higher the likelihood of adoption" (Illinois Department of Transportation, Division of Water Resources, 1980:28).

IVH2.6b(H) "Information must be clear, every effort should be made to reduce ambiguity of the message" (Illinois Department of Transportation, Division of Water Resources, 1980:28).

IVH2.6c(H) "Serious consideration must be given to the residents' perception of the credibility of the source of the information" (Illinois Department of Transportation, Division of Water Resources, 1980:28).

IVH2.6d(H) "The program should be designed to encourage social reinforcement of the information especially at the local level" (Illinois Department of Transportation, Division of Water Resources, 1980:29).

Shifting beyond cross-hazard comparisons, Frey (1983) brought us to a more theoretical, and sociological, definition of the problem. It is at this level of theory development that I would urge the hazard research community to push during the next decade. Starting with the assumption that public policy adoption at the subnational—or city—level may in part reflect the degree of match between certain attributes of the policy and those of the collectivity, Frey tested a series of hypotheses by comparing city adoption patterns for two federal programs—War on Poverty and National Flood Insurance Program (NFIP). Such cross-policy comparisons bring hazard research into the mainstream of sociological theory, and provide the breadth of perspective necessary to really attack the problem of policy adoption.

While Frey's data from his sample of cities (NFIP, $n = 43$ cities; War on Poverty, $n = 51$ cities) indicated that his hypothesized relationships did not explain everything, his model was validated partially. Four of his predictor variables accounted for 34.7 percent of the variation in pre-sanction adoption (i.e., city participation in the flood program prior to the enactment of federal government sanctions for non-participation).

> IVH2.7(H) "... if there is a match between attributes of a policy and those of a collectivity, then the probability increases that the policy will be adopted by the collectivity" (Frey, 1983:59).
>
> IVH2.7a(H) "Operationally complex policies or policies that reflect the structural dimension of differentiation tend to be adopted by collectivities with high differentiation" (Frey, 1983:62).
>
> IVH2.7b(H) "Redistributive policies or policies that reflect the structural dimension of fluidity tend to be adopted by collectivities with high fluidity" (Frey, 1983:62).
>
> IVH2.7c(H) "Policies initiated by a central government or policies that reflect the structural dimension of centrality tend to be adopted by collectivities with high centrality" (Frey, 1983:62).

IVH3. Anticipating Opposition

When a particular hazard mitigation adjustment is proposed, when is it most apt to be opposed? Case study data document repeated concerns with potential economic impacts. Thus, similar to earlier issues on the national agenda ranging from desegregation of housing to busing children so as to better integrate schools, some will wave the flag of economic loss: "If we adopt that policy our housing values will decline." While we lack a final answer on such matters, some studies have indicated that there is little basis for such fears: "... most of the evidence from the six study areas suggests that floodplain regulations have not had a significant dampening effect on residential land values in Oregon" (Muckleston, Turner, and Brainerd, 1981:66). (See also Hutton, Mileti, *et al.*, 1979.)

Apart from fears rooted in economic loss, a major contributor to opposition is ignorance. Britton's (1978) survey in New Zealand, for example, clearly revealed minimal knowledge levels regarding potential mitigation

actions related to the earthquake hazard. He concluded that lack of experience with actual quakes and a minimal knowledge regarding basic
earth-science facts about earthquakes contributed to the lack of adoption.
But as we have found elsewhere, hazard experience does not have a sin-
gular effect. Limited evidence indicates, however, that experience with
flooding reduces the propensity to resist proposed adjustments.

> IVH3.1 "Respondents in our survey were decidedly split on the role of
> government in flood control and relief. A sizeable minority (44 percent
> of those with flood experience and 37 percent of those without) objected
> to restrictions being placed on building on flood plain land. . . . 93 percent
> of those with flood experience agreed that real estate agents should be
> required to inform potential buyers about flood risks and 92 percent of
> this group indicated that they would contribute to a flood fund, if they
> themselves were not flooded" [Canada] (Hannigan and Kueneman,
> 1978:143).

After completing three case studies of emergent organized opposition
of attempts to reduce damaging hail through cloud seeding, Farhar (1976)
concluded that a single sequence of events may unfold in such cases.
Thus, an experience of high hail loss gives rise to a growing interest in
hail suppression and finally adoption. When this is followed by a *perceived
economic loss,* however, organized opposition may emerge. Her interpretation paralleled that of Brinkmann, Baumann, Beck, Krane, Murphy,
Sims, and Visvader, (1975).

> IVH3.2 "Opposition to hail suppression mainly arises when individuals
> and corporations believe that their economic interests may be threatened.
> Environmental groups rarely show active interest. In general, an over-
> whelming majority of people approve of modification projects (Haas,
> 1973). Under the South Dakota program, for instance, more counties
> officially requested participation than could be served, given the limited
> level of funding by the 1972 state legislature. By late 1972, two-thirds of
> the counties in the state had already requested participation in the 1973
> program" (Brinkmann, Baumann, Beck, Krane, Murphy, Sims, and Vis-
> vader, 1975:79–80).

Furthermore, Farhar concluded that greater degrees of dissensus among
scientists and higher levels of non-naturalistic religious belief would reduce
the likelihood of adoption.

> IVH3.3(H) The greater the uncertainty of the technology (i.e., scientific
> dissensus) and orthodox religious orientation, the less the probability of
> adoption of hail suppression. (Based on Farhar, 1976:320.)

These studies were consistent with conclusions reported earlier by Haas
(1973), who postulated several factors that might increase the possibility
of emergent opposition. Recasting these somewhat, I pieced together the
following set of hypotheses.

IVH3.4(H) Resistance to the adoption of hail suppression will be most likely when (1) in the past there has been economic loss (within or near the area) *attributed* by local residents to past weather modification efforts; (2) objective analysis indicates there is a high probability of some economic loss during the current weather modification effort; (3) negative, "unusual" weather events or conditions occur during the general time period in which the weather modification activity is going on; (4) there is evidence of significant antipathy by local power groups and/or community influentials toward the weather modifiers, their sponsors, or affiliated groups and organizations; (5) objective analysis indicates that within and near the area there are or will be some losers but few, if any, gainers as a consequence of the weather modification effort; (6) both the weather modifiers and their principal sponsors are external to the local area; (7) the losers have readily available economic resources or readily utilizable authority or interpersonal influence which could be used in support of losers' complaints; (8) objective analysis indicates that losers have high potential for mobilization. (Adapted from Haas, 1973:656.)

It is important to place these points into context, however. I don't want to leave the impression that most people oppose such experiments. While I have not seen recent national surveys that might speak to this point with precision, findings from the early 1970s indicated that a majority of Americans believed in the effectiveness of cloud seeding and generally favored its use (Brinkmann, Baumann, Beck, Krane, Murphy, Sims, and Visvader, 1975:80).

Shifting to the governmental policy level, we have limited case study data that support the hypothesis proposed by Olson and Nilson (1982) wherein they linked policy type to types of politics. For example, we examined the sequence of events wherein a federal agency tried to get the city of St. Louis to adopt a more stringent policy regarding building codes in seismic zones (Drabek, Mushkatel, and Kilijanek, 1983:93–105). The failure of the federal agency to have its proposed policy implemented seemed to be consistent with this policy–politics hypothesis.

IVH3.5(H) ". . . different types of policy (distributive, constituent, regulative, redistributive) have different types of politics (participatory, specialist, pluralist, elitist), and therefore, there will be different political strategies appropriate to each type of policy proposal" (Olson and Nilson, 1982:89).

Thus, we have several directions that future research should explore in the coming decade. Quite apart from the matter of inertia, it is clear that better understanding of when and why organized opposition may arise could be invaluable to those seeking to stimulate community adoption of hazard mitigation adjustments.

VH. Society System Level

What has been learned about the adoption of hazard mitigation adjustments at the societal level? We are far from having a complete picture of the complex social processes wherein varying layers and segments of government interact both with each other and with elements of the private sector so as to constrain the adoption and implementation of practices that might reduce the risks posed by hazards. After considerable reshuffling, I organized a very diverse collection of conclusions around six topics: (1) factors affecting vulnerability; (2) trends in mitigation policy; (3) evaluations of program outcomes; (4) predicting the adoption of risk mitigation adjustments; (5) disaster relief policies and outcomes; and (6) factors influencing research applications.

VH1. Factors Affecting Vulnerability

Several researchers have examined different aspects of vulnerability. Typically, the conclusion is reached that location decisions are putting more people at risk. This conclusion has been offered for hurricanes, floods, volcanoes, and chemical hazards within the U.S.A. Unfortunately, for entire nation states, as units, my search did not reveal much beyond the crude assessment completed by White and Haas (1975); thus, all of these estimates are based on poor data bases and do not permit aggregation across hazard types. (See Changnon *et al.*, 1983:178–180; Tubbesing, 1979.)

> VH1.1 Due to location decisions, the number of citizens within the U.S.A. who are at risk from natural and man-caused disasters has increased. (Based on Simpson and Riehl, 1981; White *et al.*, 1975; Warrick, 1975b; Quarantelli *et al.*, 1979).

> VH1.1a "The sharp rise in recent decades [in dollar losses due to hurricanes] reflects the increase in the property-at-risk that has accompanied the migration of population to seashores. The lack of effective land-use regulations and building practices in coastal zones significantly increases the hurricane damage potential. In many areas, protective dune lands at the oceanfront have either been removed to facilitate land development or have become the platforms upon which small structures have been erected without the foundational support of penetrative pilings. Either action reduces the natural protection afforded by the dunes and increases the potential for property losses" (Simpson and Riehl, 1981:21–22).

> VH1.1b "Newer and more concentrated chemical complexes tend to be built in industrial parks . . . as a result of zoning and land use policies, the newer complexes in industrial parks present less threat to surrounding areas than do older plants frequently located near residential neighborhoods" (Quarantelli *et al.*, 1979:15).

But the situation may be much worse than estimates like these imply. Why? Among the factors that have been explored are age-based migration trends and increased risk due to trends in the housing selected. Thus, the graying of the sunbelt and the rise in mobile home sales are two less visible trends that appear to be increasing risk levels for the U.S.A.

> VH1.2 [The fact that within the coastal population] ". . . the percent increase of the aged is larger than for the nation as a whole is of possible importance since it has been suggested that older persons are more likely to be among those killed or injured in a natural hazard . . . In states along the hurricane coast, mobile home sales have increased by 700% over the past ten years" (Brinkmann, Huszar, Baker, Baumann, and Sims 1975:15).

Changes in technological dependencies also may increase social vulnerability. A rather extreme position was advanced in Perrow's (1984) insightful, if grim, analysis. In order to examine a series of interorganizational and intergovernmental networks of systems whereby aircraft and ships are managed—as well as the electrical power produced by the nuclear facility at Three Mile Island—he created an analytical framework so as to view these and other high-risk technologies as varying in both complexity and coupling, i.e., subsystem interdependency. His framework forced him to conclude—a view not universally accepted, of course—that systems characterized by high complexity and tight coupling have inherent contradictions that produce unacceptable levels of risk. Thus, he concluded that "The case for abandoning nuclear power strikes me as very strong" (Perrow, 1984:347). Yet, neither his analysis nor those by others have produced adequate data sets or concepts to pin the matter down with much specificity.

> VH1.3(H) "A society becomes vulnerable to catastrophe when it becomes dependent upon complex, energy- and capital-intensive 'high' technologies which radically extend control over nature, but simultaneously increase the potential for catastrophic side-effects and social breakdown" (Orr, 1979:43). (See also McLuckie, 1970.)

Similarily as I noted above, attitudes toward flood protection works may reduce risk levels for events within a given range or scope, but exacerbate the threat potential for more catastrophic events (White and Haas, 1975).

> VH1.4 "The experience with Tropical Storm Agnes demonstrates that while the level of damage from the more frequent floods is curbed in protected flood plains, the probability of great catastrophes increases. Each stream reach protected by levees or dams is a candidate for a flood exceeding the design capacity of the planned control works. The design rarely attempts to cope with a theoretically maximum possible event. When an extraordinary event like Agnes occurs, the possibility of heavy property losses and broad systemic disruption is enhanced" (White et al., 1975:32).

After reviewing a complex series of responses to drought conditions over the Great Plains of the U.S.A. since 1890, Warrick (1983) offered two key hypotheses. These added a very different dimension to the conclusion of White *et al.* (1975) regarding flood control works.

VH1.4a(H) "... with increasingly elaborate technology and social organisation, the local and regional impacts of recurrent droughts of similar magnitude *lessen* over time. However, in lessening, the impacts change in form and shift—spatially and socially—to higher system levels" (Warrick, 1983:76).

VH1.4b(H) "... while local impacts from recurrent drought events of similar magnitude are lessened through an elaboration of technology and social organisation, the potential for *catastrophe* from events of rarer frequency is increased" (Warrick, 1983:78).

Outside of the U.S.A., researchers have proposed comparable developmental patterns and population shifts. These, however, have not been documented as well as the U.S.A. case. Thus, I regard each as a good hypothesis meriting follow-up through more quantitative methods.

VH1.5(H) "Urbanization has a decisive impact on an assortment of factors that govern hazard vulnerability. [p. 318] . . . the cities most migrants move to feature a high degree of seismic risk. In addition, migrants settle in vulnerable locations and occupy housing that is poorly equipped to withstand major seismic shocks [p. 325]" [Turkey] (Torry, 1980:318, 325).

VH1.6(H) "Regarding the siting of the projects, the Honduras Project clearly has one positive and one negative accomplishment in the cases of Santa Rica and Flores, respectively. San Jose is less clear but is certainly a much safer site than those formerly occupied by the residents, in that there is no danger of flooding. . . . Flores is located on a very poor site in reference to prevention and mitigation. It is located in a portion of the Sula Valley which is prone to flooding and, as mentioned before, was inundated by over 2m of water during hurricane Fifi" [Honduras] (Snarr and Brown, 1979:291).

VH1.7(H) [Based on experience in India] "These factors operating together increase the vulnerability of the disaster prone areas. They are not mutually self-correcting; on the contrary they mutually reinforce each other. They are present and operative long before a sudden increase in the pressure created by one factor (e.g. the failure of rains) brings about the physical event of death on a large scale. [p. 33] . . . [Factors are:] 1. . . . delivery systems are inadequate and inappropriate; . . . 2. Low productivity; [p. 32] . . . 3. Disaster prone areas have been in a centre–periphery relationships for centuries; . . . 4. Available resources untapped; . . . 5. Disaster prone areas are politically marginal; . . . [and] 6. Religion plays a dominant ideological role [p. 33]" [India] (Fernandez, 1979:32, 33). (For somewhat parallel conclusions from the Dominican Republic, see Jeffery, 1982.)

In contrast to these types of case study analyses, some progress has been made in the development of broad frameworks whereby fluctuations in societal risk levels might be assessed. To date, these have been limited and much controversy remains regarding a host of issues ranging from modes of aggregation to criteria used in establishing "acceptable" risk levels (see Kunreuther and Ley, 1982). As you might expect, "How safe is safe enough?" is not a simple question. Reflecting one dimension of this analytical problem, Fischhoff and his colleagues have examined many of the complications that technologically based hazards introduce into the emergent decision calculus. Especially insightful, for example, is their discussion of numerous types of constraints that they see hindering the effectiveness of hazard management efforts. This explication serves to help us understand better why no person or government official can wave a wand and eliminate the risk associated with a particular hazard.

> There are seven constraints on hazard management: 1. incomplete knowledge; 2. foregoing benefits; i.e., customarily the benefits are as clear and tangible as the risks are ambiguous and elusive; 3. a limited capacity to react; 4. the perception of hazards; i.e., there are systematic biases in people's perceptions of risks; 5. value trade-offs; i.e., reducing a hazard may conflict directly with some other widely held value or po- litical goal; 6. institutional weaknesses; i.e., perhaps the single greatest failing of our institutions has been their frequent inability to deal with the most important hazards first. Instead, massive attacks are often made on what are clearly problems of secondary importance; 7. the hazards of hazard management; i.e., the use of TRIS-treated pajamas, designed to reduce a fire hazard for children, created a new, unforeseen cancer risk. (Adapted from Fischhoff et al., 1978:20, 32–36.)

VH2. Trends in Mitigation Policy

White and Haas (1975) documented the major shift in mitigation policy that occurred in the U.S.A. during the 1960s and early 1970s. During this period there was movement away from a primary focus on technological or structural solutions to greater emphasis on nonstructural approaches (for analysis of tornado-related adjustments, see Wall and Webster, 1980:13–14). Thus, rather than proposing that more dams be built, experts argued for rezoning floodplains and providing flood insurance. Gradually, flooding was viewed as a natural process, not one to be eliminated com- pletely. Thus, flood prevention per se should not be the desired goal. As physical events, floods have many positive consequences that those rooted within a dam-building approach have neglected. Hence, the issue was re- defined; efficient use of flood-prone lands should be sought, not elimination of all flooding (Changnon et al., 1983).

Of course, in some places and for certain hazards, specific structural adjustments may bring immediate progress in risk reduction. Berberian (1979) argued this well regarding the threat posed by earthquakes in Iran. Similar arguments emerged following recent quakes in Central America, as documented in the chapter on recovery.

"During the last 78 years earthquakes caused a total death-toll of over 72,000 in the country. The large number of casualties in the Iranian earthquakes is mainly due to the immediate, total destruction of adobe and other improperly built houses and lack of reinforcement of aseismic building codes or any proper building control . . . Constructing the earthquake resistant houses enforced by the government is the only way to minimize the earthquake hazard and to stop the rapid increase in the casualty numbers due to Iranian earthquakes" [Iran] (Berberian, 1979:219).

Increasingly, however, the view emerged that it is a *mix* of structural and nonstructural options that should be sought (White *et al.*, 1975; Page, 1980). The interdependence among mitigation strategies was recognized. Roy Popkin—former Deputy Director, Disaster Services, American Red Cross—made the point very well.

"The steady growth of flood insurance coverage also impacts Red Cross disaster expenditures. Just as the advent of Homeowners Comprehensive Insurance reduced the need for Red Cross assistance following tornadoes, the expansion of flood insurance in recent years is beginning to have a comparable effect" (Popkin, 1978:51).

Within the U.S.A., the 1970s brought an increase in federal participation. While earlier disasters had occurred that were beyond the capability of the local and state governments affected—thereby defining them as national problems—the federal response was *ad hoc* and event specific. The Disaster Relief Act of 1974 (P.L. 93-288) changed all of that and opened the door for a greatly expanded federal role. Summaries of these and related developments are available in Mileti (1975a) and more recently Petak and Atkisson (1982) and May (1985).

Simultaneously with these changes occurring at the federal level, state capabilities were being modified too. Frasure (1972:41–42) summarized elements of the early actions that were precursors to a latter development that had far-reaching consequences—federally assisted state planning grants that became operative in all fifty states during the mid 1970s.

President Jimmy Carter implemented a major reorganization in 1979 through the creation of the Federal Emergency Management Agency, which today serves as the lead federal agency in natural and man-caused disasters. While many local and state officials favored a policy that provided "a single point of federal contact," some expressed concern with the expanding federal role. Many perceived increased assaults on local autonomy.

While these trends produced much rhetoric with strong political tones, the research community failed in trying to capture the behavioral dynamic. Thus, we really don't have much understanding of this process within the disaster-relevant intergovernmental sector, aside from a few case studies, such as those I coauthored with Mushkatel and Kilijanek (1983:93–105) wherein we traced the sequential steps that culminated in one federal agency backing off from a policy because of resistance from a local government that would have been impacted. One notable exception is a study by Rose (1980) of federal mandates. While important, this is obviously but one of a complex series of issues that comprise this area.

VH2.1 "A time series of all emergency service mandates and of disaster only mandates [revealed] a notable similarity in the two time trends, as both start off slowly with only a small number of mandates initiated in the period before 1966, level off, peak at 1975, and then trail off again. [i.e., federal mandates to local government] [p. 69] . . . Overall, . . . the number of emergency service mandates has decreased over time as a percentage of all federal–local mandates initiated [p. 70]" (Rose, 1980:69, 70).

These patterns set the context for assessments of the U.S.A. situation regarding mitigation costs. Petak and Atkisson (1982) proposed four key conclusions that defined the current scene—at least within their capacity to conceptualize and measure fragments of it.

1. "Annual expected losses from natural hazard exposures in 2000 may be reduced by more than 40% through application of currently available risk-reducing technologies and policy mitigations" [p. 318].
2. "Overzealous application of strengthened building codes and standards can substantially increase net annual natural hazard costs in the year 2000" [p. 319].
3. "Riverine and coastal area flood control facilities constructed in compliance with post-1936 economic criteria appear to be cost-effective methods for controlling losses at specified levels of hazard zone occupancy, but contribute to temporal increases in annual expected losses within the hazard zones" [p. 319].
4. "The large 'opportunity costs' associated with application of 'most effective' mitigations suggests that the use of such mitigations is not an economically justifiable approach for curbing the life loss associated with natural hazard exposures" [p. 320]. (Petak and Atkisson, 1982:318, 319, 320).

Extending these themes in a later article, Petak (1984:293–294) identified ten major barriers to policy adoption and implementation. These included such items as inadequate data bases, scarcity of mapping of hazardous zones (aside from riverine flood zones), inadequate coordination, and the like. On a positive note, however, and in explicit recognition of a movement that may be a significant long-term trend, he called for increased professionalization of the policy process. And as first steps toward this objective he proposed that the following actions be taken by those involved:

"1. Identify and address technical issues of fact. . . . 2. Formulate and develop model legislation and action. . . . 3. Form and educate natural hazard mitigation constituent support groups. [p. 299] . . . 4. Identify legislator interests and education needs. . . . 5. Increase professional status of staff at the local government level, and develop an appropriate recruitment, training, or regional cooperative program [p. 300]'' (Petak, 1984:299, 300).

VH3. Evaluations of Program Outcomes

Several researchers began the arduous task of trying to assess the outcomes of some of the policies and programs designed in the name of mitigation. Clearly, there is evidence that the net result has been positive for individuals serviced and the society as a whole. Warrick's conclusions regarding drought and volcanoes are among the most positive.

VH3.1 "When drought struck again in the early 1950s, the impact was much less severe [than in the 1930s]. The widespread financial distress, interstate migration, and regional disruption characteristic of the Dust Bowl era were largely absent. Though comparable in meteorological severity (even if not spatially uniform) the impact was moderated by the trends in adjustment, as well as by improved farm prices and a healthy economy. Again, attention was directed to drought adjustment and research. Strong emphasis was placed on water conservation and augmentation, on weather modification research, weather prediction and control, groundwater recharge, irrigation and river basin development, increasing runoff, evaporation control, desalination, phreatophyte control, and irrigation canal lining" (Warrick, 1975a:xiv).

VH3.2 ". . . the direct products of volcanic eruptions influence land use in ways compatible with the hazard risk. The agricultural benefits to be reaped from the fertilization effect are important in Hawaii, where the soils themselves are formed in lava and ash, and provide the basis for the agricultural economy of the island. . . . The soils east of the Cascades have benefited from the occasional falls of ash in the past. Generally, it would seem that most agricultural land uses are compatible with the risk . . . there is some evidence that urban development, in the form of expensive high-density vacation homes near rift zones in Hawaii, or encroachment into specific hazardous areas of Cascade river valleys subject to volcanic mudflows or floods, may be contributing to an increasing amount of undue damage potential" (Warrick, 1975b:56).

Turning to the earthquake hazard, especially in California, a rather different view was offered wherein a series of problems persisted, at least as of 1980. Since then, newer programs have been initiated, for example, the Southern California Earthquake Preparedness Project (SCEPP). Hopefully, these will address a mix of constraints.

VH3.3 "Observations of the strengths and weaknesses of the federal role under prior legislation has provided a basis for evaluating the adequacy of the present legislation and regulations as they apply to earthquake disasters. Seven problems are identified. 1. Lack of specific authorization and funding for redevelopment projects . . . 2. Lack of requirements, procedures and funding for planning and implementing plans for long-term reconstruction [p. 14] . . . 3. Disincentives for relocating public facilities or repairing and reconstructing facilities to improved standards not in force at the time of the earthquake . . . 4. Lack of guidelines for determining price to be paid for properties to be acquired as part of a post-earthquake redevelopment project or a planned relocation . . . 5. Little consideration of long-term hazard mitigation in administering disaster assistance . . . 6. Lack of explicit consideration in administering disaster assistance of opportunities to achieve other federal community development objectives [p. 15] . . . 7. Lack of flexibility in administering disaster assistance sometimes leading to federal/local conflict [p. 16]" (Mader *et al.*, 1980:14–16).

Land-use regulation received careful scrutiny by several researchers who sought to document the shifting patterns of intergovernmental relationships that put some people into risk areas like floodplains, and prevent others from building there. Historically, within the U.S.A., such decisions were regarded strictly as the providence of local governments. Today, they still are, except that state governments are playing much more active roles. Baker and McPhee (1975) noted this drift in their review which was completed in the mid-1970s. Unfortunately, little is known about the behavioral dynamics or consequences of such pattern shifts.

VH3.4 "State governments have typically delegated their authority to regulate land use to local units of government. Since the enabling acts were adopted permitting local units to regulate land use, almost all regulation has occurred at the local level. [p. 70] . . . The belief that local decision-makers should regulate land use is now giving way to the realization that few land use problems are truly local in nature. Many policies and actions affect an area larger than the local community [p. 80]" (Baker and McPhee, 1975:70, 80).

Starting with this point and examining case study data from seven local jurisdictions, Platt and his associates (1980) carried us far in unraveling the behavioral dynamics that constitute the type of intergovernmental relationships reflected by floodplain management. Their studies revealed that two basic mechanisms were used to achieve intergovernmental coordination.

VH3.5 1. ". . . assumption of certain floodplain management functions by *extra-local* public entities: federal, state, county, regional planning agency, and special district [and 2.] . . . direct *inter-local* arrangements or means of coordination: joint planning committees, agreements or contracts, litigation, and extraterritorial powers. Also included in the latter table are private interest groups. While they are not vested with governmental status, private groups in several case studies were important

catalysts to the achievement of an extra- or inter-local approach'' (Platt
et al., 1980:273).

Looking at the U.S.A. experience as of 1980, they offered the following
portrait—certainly one calling for policy intervention and redirection.

VH3.6 "Intergovernmental management of floodplains in the United
States is in a rudimentary phase. The concepts of nonstructural floodplain
management are themselves still novel and unfamiliar to many local public
officials. The notion that such measures as floodplain zoning and acquisition depend upon mutually compatible policies in all jurisdictions
sharing a floodplain is generally not yet recognized'' (Platt *et al.,*
1980:287).

VH3.6a ''. . . flood losses in the United States continue to escalate. A
disproportionate share of these losses occurs along minor streams and
creeks in the nation's metropolitan areas . . . These secondary streams
are generally uncontrolled by structural works and often are little noticed
in the process of metropolitan development'' (Platt *et al.,* 1980:288).

VH3.6b "Metropolitan watersheds and floodplains are further characterized by a multiplicity of jurisdictions. Urbanizing areas are rife with
odd-shaped municipalities, many of them growing haphazardly according
to the whims of annexation. Streams cross political and legal boundary
lines and also form boundaries themselves in many places, thus placing
opposite streambanks and floodplains in different jurisdictions. Fragmentation of authority over lands adjoining watercourses including
floodplains poses a serious threat to the nation's objective to achieve a
rational and uniform program for the management of floodplains'' (Platt
et al., 1980:288–289).

Similarly, the assessment of the National Flood Insurance Program
completed by Burby and French (1981) emphasized the paradoxical quality
of policy impact. Their study, like the work by Platt and his associates,
made it clear that the decentralized structure of the American political
system precluded a totally uniform application of this federal policy. And
most importantly, continued invasion of flood-prone areas means only
one thing—continued losses in the decades ahead.

VH3.7 "It often appears that the NFIP induces increased flood plain
development because the same factors which lead communities to participate in the NFIP are also associated with continuing flood plain invasion. These factors include past invasion of the flood plain and a need
for insurance and the potential for new construction in the hazard area
because of its attractiveness for development. . . . Flood plain land use
management regulations, including those required by the NFIP, have
had little effect on the rate of flood plain invasion'' (Burby and French,
1981:294).

VH3.7a ''. . . land use management programs were most effective in
protecting future development from flood damage (and also in protecting

natural areas and limiting flood plain encroachment) in Type A communities, where little flood plain development had occurred and where sites for new development were readily available outside the hazard area. As more flood plain development occurred and as sites for new development outside the flood plain became scarcer, program effectiveness steadily dropped. Land use management programs were least effective of all in Type D communities, where moderate to heavy flood plain development had occurred in the past and sites for new development outside of the flood plain were limited or unavailable'' (Burby and French, 1981:295).

VH3.7b "In April 1979, the Pearl River in Mississippi inflicted damage estimated at one-half billion dollars in the city of Jackson and surrounding areas. Most property damage accrued to development built in the floodplain since the previous major flood in 1961. . . . Issues for national flood policy posed by the Jackson experience include the need for (1) land use regulations as concomitants to flood control structures, (2) improved coordination between different levels and units of government sharing jurisdiction over floodplains, (3) consideration of inter-jurisdictional effects in the allocation of flood protection resources, (4) location of vital public services outside floodplains, and (5) revision of post-disaster recovery policies to encourage mitigation of future losses'' (Platt, 1982:219).

VH4. Predicting the Adoption of Risk Mitigation Adjustments

Apart from the issues involved in policy implementation and program outcomes, other researchers explored aspects of policy adoption. Why is it that some policies get adopted at certain times and others don't? Reflecting on a wide body of literature and responses to cases in England, Barry Turner (1979) proposed four hypotheses. In the aggregate, these help to underscore why most threats are ignored, especially technologically related hazards wherein powerful interest groups may have much to gain by even temporary delays in the adoption of mitigative requirements.

VH4.1(H) Hazard signs are denied initially and are recognized later only after several forms of constraint are overcome. (Based on Turner, 1979.)

VH4.1a(H) "Information warning of the hazard potential of particular events may be misunderstood because of erroneous assumptions'' (Turner, 1979:56).

VH4.1b(H) "Hazard signs may be overlooked or not responded to because of information handling difficulties'' (Turner, 1979:56).

VH4.1c(H) "Hazard signs may be overlooked because they are thought to be covered by discredited precautions or regulations'' (Turner, 1979:57).

VH4.1d(H) "Hazard signs are overlooked because of a feeling of invulnerability'' [United Kingdom] (Turner, 1979:57).

Continuing on the negative side of the adoption equation, Battisti's (1978a) assessment of the Italian experience also emphasized the historical context—actual disasters, not findings of study commissions or scientific reports, are critical to the adoption process.

> VH4.2(H) "The growth of a social and normative system of social assistance during disasters is not the result of a process of planned social reform but, on the contrary, it is the outcome of a series of historical experiences lived out as 'disasters' by the people and the governments of one nation" [Italy] (Battisti, 1978a:abstract).

As experimental work on individuals and small groups demonstrated, the human psyche tends to process threat information in disjunctive steps, rather than assess probabilities in a continuous manner (Slovic, Kunreuther, and White, 1974). Thresholds must be exceeded before actions are taken. Small losses, spread over time, are less likely to precipitate momentum for the adoption of mitigative adjustments than a single, but dramatic, event.

> VH4.3(H) "Hazardous events that produce multiple, rather than single, deaths and/or that inflict property damage on many rather than few persons tend to evoke more immediate and vigorous responses from policy makers and concerned publics than do the cumulatively larger losses that may be sustained by individuals one or two at a time as the result of less dramatic hazardous occurrences" (Petak and Atkisson, 1982:422–423).

These three ideas set the stage for four major research efforts; each reflected very different approaches. First, Mileti (1980) completed a broadly based literature review and expanded upon the community flood program adoption study I discussed above on which he had collaborated with Hutton and others (Hutton *et al.*, 1979). Reflecting his skill in theory construction, he produced an overarching model that specified linkages among an impressive array of key sociological concepts. In summary form, the core set of ideas are as follows.

> VH4.4 Higher levels of perceived risk are positively associated with: (1) ability to estimate risk, (2) causes of environmental extremes perceived as naturalistic, (3) experience with risk, (4) size of the unit of analysis, and (5) access to information; and negatively associated with: propensity to deny risk. (Based on Mileti, 1980.)

> VH4.5 Degree of risk-mitigating adjustment is positively associated with: (1) perceived benefits–costs of implementation of risk-mitigating policy and (2) image of damage (both of which are positively associated with perceived risk). (Based on Mileti, 1980.)

> VH4.6 Degree of risk-mitigating adjustment is positively associated with: capacity to implement policy; and negatively associated with: perceived costs of implemented policy. (Based on Mileti, 1980.)

VH4.6a Capacity to implement policy is positively associated with: (1) social differentiation, (2) power differentiation, (3) political differentiation, and (4) resources. (Based on Mileti, 1980.)

VH4.6b Perceived costs of implemented policy are positively associated with: (1) opposing values and (2) opposing interest group goals. (Based on Mileti, 1980.)

In contrast to Mileti's deductive approach, Rossi and his colleagues conducted a large-scale, national survey of local officials to ascertain how hazard mitigation adjustments were perceived. The message came through loud and clear. Relative to other community problems, state and local decision makers did not rank environmental hazards very high, although there was variability.

VH4.7 "For the most part, political decision makers in the states and local communities do not see environmental hazards as a very serious problem, particularly in comparison to the many other problems that these governmental units are expected to be doing something about. We asked each respondent in the sample to rate the seriousness of 18 potential state and local problems, including 5 environmental hazard problems. In all states and communities, the most serious problems are inflation, welfare, unemployment, and crime, and the least serious, at least in the minds of our respondents, are floods, hurricanes, tornadoes, and earthquakes" (Rossi, Wright, and Weber-Burdin, 1982:9). (See also Wright and Rossi, 1981:54.)

VH4.8 "The seriousness attributed to hazards problems varies across elite groupings in a predictable manner" (Rossi, Wright, and Weber-Burdin, 1982:10).

VH4.8a "Hazards specialists tend to see these problems as relatively more serious, real estate and land-development interests as less serious, with other elites arrayed between them" (Rossi, Wright, and Weber-Burdin, 1982:10).

Across a range of policy approaches, mitigation adjustments centering on structural adaptations were most favored, although here again, there was patterned variation.

VH4.9 ". . . most respondents are heavily attracted to traditional policy approaches. Of the options we presented to them, emphasizing structural mitigations was most favored; the second most-favored option was to emphasize postdisaster relief. Nonstructural approaches, in contrast, were rejected by a small majority, as was an approach emphasizing compulsory, government-subsidized hazards insurance" (Rossi, Wright, and Weber-Burdin, 1982:11–12).

VH4.9a ". . . those most favorable to such approaches [i.e., nonstructural] include what we call hazards specialists—persons whose positions involve them quite intimately and directly with environmental hazards (such as members of the Civil Defense or Red Cross)'' (Rossi, Wright, and Weber-Burdin, 1982:13).

But probing deeper, they discovered that at both state and local government levels, this attitude set appeared to be constrained by the viewpoints held by a relatively small number of "influentials." Of course, such cross-sectional data, despite the correlations revealed, do not necessarily provide evidence of causality. But certainly, the aggregated results suggest such an interpretation.

VH4.10 ". . . the index takes on a positive value if active, important, and influential elites in the community tend to favor nonstructural mitigations, and a negative value if the active, important, and influential elites tend to oppose such measures. This power-balance index is the single most important variable predicting the hazard-management views of local elected officials" (Rossi, Wright, and Weber-Burdin, 1982:20).

VH4.10a ". . . local elected officials—mayors and city councilmen in particular—are the key people in the local community when it comes to environmental-risk management issues. They are seen as the most active groups, the ones most important to have on one's side, the ones who most influence the views of others. In addition, they are seen as largely favoring land-use and building code approaches to natural hazards risk" (Rossi, Wright, and Weber-Burdin, 1982:19).

VH4.10b "The majority of state elites apparently do not favor land-use regulation in risk areas or tighter building codes to reduce damage and injury. Conservation groups, the state planning agency, the governor, and the Civil Defense director are the only ones seen as favoring such measures by more than 33% of the respondents" (Rossi, Wright, and Weber-Burdin, 1982:21).

In contrast to the survey approach used by Rossi and his associates, two political scientists—Wyner and Mann (1983)—completed detailed case studies of seismic safety as an issue on the policy agenda in 13 local government jurisdictions within California. These were selected so as to include seven with recent earthquake experience (Los Angeles County and the cities of Los Angeles, Burbank, Glendale, San Fernando, Simi Valley, and Santa Rosa) and six without (Alameda County and the cities of Berkeley, Fremont, Hayward, Oakland, and Salinas) (Wyner and Mann, 1983:70).

Upon reviewing their rich collection of case study materials they introduced into the literature several new themes. Most important among these were the following insights.

VH4.11 "By examining the way in which local jurisdictions have implemented land use and building code related seismic safety policy, it becomes clear that only a few jurisdictions have attained even some of their stated objectives. And it is important to remember that most land use objectives in the SSE's [Seismic Safety Element] were very modest, including such goals as collecting more information about the nature of seismic hazards. Resource allocation for implementation of seismic safety policy has been virtually nonexistent. Most jurisdictions have chosen not to allocate monetary or non-monetary resources in a manner that would permit fulfillment of the adopted goals; most jurisdictions have made only the slightest movement toward goal accomplishment. Whatever level of risk was accepted in the adoption of the SSE, very little has been done to make it a reality through policy implementation" (Wyner and Mann, 1983:321–322).

Thus, despite the relevance of the earthquake threat, Wyner and Mann documented a climate of relative neglect across these political agendas *during the time period* included in their case histories, i.e., 1969 to 1980. Their findings must be viewed within the context of that decade, however. During that time period, three qualities appeared to define the nature of the decision-making process. Developments since 1980, especially programs initiated through the 1977 Earthquake Hazards Reduction Act (P.L.95-124), probably have altered this situation somewhat.

VH4.12 "Risk level decision-making in local governments, then, is characterized by low visibility, incrementalism, and low priority" (Wyner and Mann, 1983:324).

Yet, there were instances of action; specific kinds of decisions were made indicating a policy process at its earliest stages in a temporal sense. So they tried to identify the key factors that differentiated the communities that had taken some actions. Initially, five qualities were identified; Wyner (1984) later summarized these into three core concepts.

VH4.13 ". . . five factors facilitate or influence the adoption and implementation of risk mitigation policies by local governments: state mandates, previous earthquake experience, staff ability, attitudes of local governmental leadership and staff, resources, and competition from other issues. State mandates are an initial condition affecting all local jurisdictions, while the remaining factors can explain why some jurisdictions have mitigated risk more than others" (Wyner and Mann, 1983:335).

VH4.13a "The most important aspects of seismic safety policy implementation in California are (1) the role of key governmental personnel, (2) the political environment surrounding the issue of seismic safety, and (3) the tractability of the issue itself" (Wyner, 1984:267).

Paralleling the Wyner–Mann studies, were two case studies I completed with two colleagues—Mushkatel and Kilijanek (1983). We selected two states—Missouri and Washington. Each had limited but important seismic histories. Among the many findings reported, the following are the most critical. First, as I referred to above regarding organizational analysis, we documented the behavioral dynamics of an implementation failure.

". . . a federal agency, the Department of Housing and Urban Development, tried to enforce seismic safety provisions for the rehabilitation of housing in the City of St. Louis. Citing the tremendous financial burden that would be placed upon the city, local officials and private interests successfully pressured HUD to back off. At the implementation stage, the policy met with failure" (Drabek, Mushkatel, and Kilijanek, 1983:209).

This sequence of actions reflected an important theme—policies may not be perceived uniformly, especially by officials in differing layers of governments (Olson and Nilson, 1982; Petak and Atkisson, 1982:404).

VH4.14 "The significance of overlapping policy characteristics is nicely illustrated by this case. HUD was attempting to implement a regulatory policy that, from its perspective, simply involved imposing stricter standards on rehabilitation of housing in seismic zone II areas. These standards also had a constituent policy element—they were partially designed by scientists and structural engineers. The presence of this constituent element suggests low levels of potential conflict, although the regulatory changes might involve more severe conflicts.

Officials from the City of St. Louis had a very different perspective on the matter. They saw the policy as not only regulative, but also of a redistributive nature. The redistribution would occur as developments which might have located in the city would choose not to because of the higher costs resulting from the seismic loading requirements. They perceived HUD officials to be asking the city to pay the costs of the policy. This would place St. Louis at a disadvantage when competing with other cities in trying to attract development dollars for rehabilitation" (Drabek, Mushkatel, and Kilijanek, 1983:100).

Second, while earthquake mitigation policy development was embryonic in Washington, this state was further along than Missouri. Three factors differentiated this evolutionary process.

VH4.15 "In Washington and, to a lesser extent, in Missouri during the 1970s, there was some action on mitigation, apparently for three main reasons. First, a key individual or group of individuals became concerned about the problem and had the legitimate authority to take some action. [p. 213] . . . Second, earthquake mitigation became part of the public policy process on the state or local level as a result of actions by one or more federal agencies. [p. 214] . . . Lastly, the earthquake hazard was linked sometimes to another issue confronting decision makers [p. 214]" (Drabek, Mushkatel, and Kilijanek, 1983:213–214).

Beyond these factors, we crudely tapped two more general ones that I suspect serve to constrain such specific social processes—the pattern of interorganizational relationships and degree of hazard awareness. If such benchmarks are reassessed a decade hence, they can provide the longitudinal data bases required to expand our understanding of such policy processes.

VH4.16 ". . . our data indicate that respondents believe seismic safety is an important issue, and that their agencies share this concern. Yet, only a small percentage of respondents' work time is spent on seismic mitigation matters. In addition, from their perspective, the communities and the state and federal governments have done little to aid local agencies in lessening the effects of an earthquake" (Drabek, Mushkatel, and Kilijanek, 1983:175).

VH4.17 "These data [in Washington state] show a contrast with the situation in Missouri. First, there were more reasons given for interorganizational interaction. . . . Second, the most common reason for contacts concerned controversies over seismic safety, e.g., the Skagit NPP siting, the Seattle Public Schools, and Northern Tier pipeline controversies. This was quite different from the basis for such contacts in Missouri, where the State Panel and FEMA Project had brought agencies together. Third, it appeared that local efforts predominate in Washington while state and federal efforts were more common in Missouri—at least during the last two years" (Drabek, Mushkatel, and Kilijanek, 1983:118).

VH5. Disaster Relief Policies and Outcomes

Disaster relief policy is complex, as are its outcomes. Among the types of issues that should be examined are those of equity and the degree to which relief may counteract subsequent mitigation. Neither have been pursued beyond the level of "issue-raising," however.

VH5.1(H) "If victims of a disaster were forced to bear the costs themselves, it has been shown above that they would have a larger incentive to protect themselves against future catastrophes. Current federal policy encourages individuals not only to continue to ignore these events in future but actually to take steps to profit from the next earthquake or flood. It was not unusual to hear that residents of the San Fernando Valley and Alaska were attempting to obtain the smallest down payment on their home mortgage and longest possible maturity so as to be in the best possible position to take advantage of the SBA policy should another earthquake hit the area" (Kunreuther, 1974b:213).

VH5.2(H) "From exploratory studies recently completed . . . there is reason to think that the poor receive a proportionately smaller share of the Federal assistance in relation to their losses than do flood victims in middle and upper-income groups. They probably also benefit less than others from public expenditures for protection and control. Flood protection does not affect all people equally, nor does public aid in relief and rehabilitation" (White et al., 1975:33).

VH5.3(H) "Under the current mix of policies, it seems clear that: (1) victims of one disaster may be treated differently than victims of another disaster; (2) proportionately higher reimbursement of natural hazard-induced losses is provided to the affluent than to the poor; and (3) preferential treatment is provided to individuals experiencing catastrophic losses in 'disaster areas' as contrasted to those experiencing such losses in other areas and at other times" (Petak and Atkisson, 1982:436).

As within the U.S.A., Australia has moved toward increased recognition that some disasters are beyond the capabilities of local governments. Hence, it appears that many policy issues have emerged that parallel the U.S.A. experience. Among these are the following.

(1) What are the alternatives to ad hoc organizational responses?

> VH5.4 "In Australia, the provision of government welfare services in disasters has been an *ad hoc* response to each disaster event. The aftermath of even a minor disaster such as the Toowoomba hailstorm shows that many problems arise from the lack of a systematic welfare policy. At present, the Commonwealth–State disaster agreements define the conditions for the provision of disaster funds but do not outline an organisational structure to administer material and financial resources to disaster victims. It is not feasible for either Commonwealth or State Governments to rely on local welfare organisations to make their own assessments and to command the resources to intervene effectively" [Australia] (Leivesley, 1977a:321–322).

(2) What are the consequences of shifting the relative funding levels provided by different layers of government and the private sector?

> VH5.5 "Absolute assistance by levels of government and relative proportions of total government assistance following the 1973–74 floods in Queensland:
> [1.] Australian Government   —55,494,795—88.66%
> [2.] Queensland Government— 5,797,010— 9.26%
> [3.] Local Government   — 1,198,545— 2.08%"
> [Australia] (Butler and Doessel, 1980:201).

(3) What types and degrees of equity can be expected from different administrative policies?

> VH5.6(H) ". . . government assistance to Queensland flood victims in 1973–74 was distributed in an inequitable manner under both schemes. By this we mean not only that flood victims in unequal economic positions were treated unequally but also that flood victims in unequal economic positions were treated equally. That is to say that the means tests applicable to both relief schemes violated the notions of horizontal and vertical equity as these notions apply in the context of natural disaster relief to individuals" [Australia] (Butler and Doessel, 1979:5).

Finally, while not restricted to issues of relief, the decade of the 1970s brought an increased awareness of a variety of legal issues, some of which pertain to actions taken in the name of mitigation. Rabin's report on the Buffalo Creek disaster illustrated four types of issues. For example:

> "It seems quite clear, however, that the dam violated both federal and state law. In preparing the lawsuit, Stern discovered that a state inspector had warned the Buffalo Mining Company on numerous occasions that it was violating West Virginia law by its failure to construct an emergency

spillway. The same inspector testified before a state investigatory commission that political pressure from the coal companies made it impossible to punish violations of the law" (Rabin, 1978:286).

VH5.7 The legal system provides four distinct responses to disaster situations: (1) administrative prevention techniques such as enforcement of safety standards; (2) private investment in safety stimulated by the likelihood of liability in tort; (3) administrative redress (e.g., FDAA responses through HUD); and (4) tort compensation suits. (Adapted from Rabin, 1978:289.)

Similarly, as Levine's (1982) careful documentation of the citizen response to the consequences of the chemical-waste-disposal site at Love Canal (a residential area of Niagara Falls, New York) demonstrated, emergent organizations may turn to the legal system in their efforts, first to gain disaster relief, and second to challenge existing assumptions and policies regarding technological procedures. Clearly, ". . . the Love Canal story would have been very different for the people and for our society, had there been no citizen's associations at Love Canal. . . . What began at Love Canal with one young woman knocking on doors grew into a force to be reckoned with by state and federal officials at the highest levels" (Levine, 1982:209).

This case, others like it, and recent examples of flooding in various parts of the U.S.A. may reflect a much broader social process wherein traditional assumptions about liability and negligence may be challenged. Descamps' (1972) analysis of several cases in France certainly suggested that such phenomena—both perceptually and behaviorally—are not unique to the U.S.A.

VH5.8(H) [When man creates his own living environment he takes over from nature. The increase in his technological ability brings under his responsibility the former act of God cases.] [France] (Descamps, 1972:389–390).

Support for this hypothesis is as follows:

[Thus, in France, the number of court cases related to various types of disasters has increased and new forms of legal structure are predicted to emerge given expanded definitions of human responsibility. Among numerous examples cited is the following: On 30 March 1963, after a storm, there was a collapse of the cliff which dominates Plan-du-Var quarter. Several tons of rocks in the course of their fall broke Vesubie canal, constructed along the shoulder of the hill. The water flooded the village and destroyed the building of the Société d'Entreprise de Travaux d'Alsace-Lorraine (SETAL). The latter appealed to the administrative court against the community for compensation. . . . Expert examination revealed that the cliff was unstable because of its varied composition. The community of Levens was declared responsible for the rocks that had fallen from the cliff, and, on the grounds that it had not taken the

necessary measures for strengthening and protection, was ordered to pay
187,984 francs in damages and interest, in accordance with article 1384
of the civil code. Thus, there is human responsibility even in an earth
collapse or slide because of failure to strengthen or warn.] [France] (Descamps, 1972:380).

But there is another side to this issue—one that questions both the wisdom and motivations of policies that encourage interventions. Waddell's
(1983:33–35) interpretation of a drought condition in New Guinea during
1972 could be paralleled by other critics who speak of "the disaster industry" in less than kind words. Morren (1983a) reinforced this reasoning
through his interpretations of the responses to two other droughts—one
in the United Kingdom and another in the Republic of Botswana. Both
cases, he argued, illustrate the possibility of "wrong" responses by government. Such "wrong" responses have the consequence of increasing
dependency and reducing the ability of "victims" to cope on their own.
Thus, we again come to the very core of the issue—with what criteria do
we define a social problem and how do alternative criteria used in this
definitional process constrain our perception of "reasonable solutions"?

VH5.9(H) "In summary, one began to suspect that perhaps the 'wrong'
characteristics of the 'wrong' responses and effects are related to the
'wrong' environmental problems and their characteristics! In fact, the
position most strongly reinforced by the studies of the Bushmen and the
British is that a wide range of environmental hazards may be viewed
most profitably as consequences of human activity—as 'unnatural' hazards!" (Morren, 1983a:65).

VH5.9a(H) "Implicit in the argument so far is the basic question, 'When
is a drought not a drought?', or more properly speaking, 'When is a problem "perceived" as drought, not a drought?' The Bushman case shows
the ambiguity of the question. They respond *as though* there were a
drought when, in our common understanding of that term, drought is not
the problem. Indeed, all else being equal, they seem very well able to
cope with rainfall scarcity. In ecological studies 'all else' is rarely equal.
The Bushmen, like other organisms and peoples, have multiple problems.
Responding to one problem reduces their ability to respond to other
problems" (Morren, 1983a:51).

VH5.9b(H) ". . . the drought and heat wave were not directly much of
a problem for most people in Britain until the late summer of 1976. There
had been a growing problem for farmers, graziers and stockmen in a
number of districts, as well as for some other rural functions, such as
firefighting, throughout 1975 and 1976. But the drought became a problem
for the general population when the national government made it a problem in August 1976" (Morren, 1983a:54).

In a synthesizing essay, Morren (1983b) extended this line of reasoning
and explicated a series of principles that challenge not only the wisdom
of theoretical frameworks like that used in this book, couched as it is

within a disaster-event orientation, but also that of government policies predicated on the assumption that such episodic events produce "victims" requiring assistance. In the coming decade, this position—one shared by other contributors to Hewitt's (1983) collection—will require serious review by sociologically oriented disaster researchers. Out of such confrontation will emerge expanded definitions of the research agenda that will have important policy implications. My personal concern, however, remains with disaster victims. For some may be forced to suffer excessively if conclusions like the following from Morren are used to justify policy changes.

> "We noted earlier the evidence that in the course of the San Francisco earthquake and fire the illegitimate insertion of federal troops, who forced mass evacuations, prevented individuals, including householders and business people, from protecting their property and otherwise salvaging belongings. In the same disaster it has been shown that most people who were left without shelter were able to arrange emergency accommodations on their own. They were permitted to do so because it took some time for locally and nationally supported shelter programmes to be organised. It is a typical feature of higher-level responses that individuals and groups otherwise capable of coping on their own are prevented from doing so. In the absence of de-escalation, the range of normal variability with which the people can cope on their own is permanently narrowed" (Morren, 1983b:294).

VH6. Factors Influencing Research Applications

Scientific research ought to be regarded as a form of disaster mitigation. Commonly it is not, however, especially if its focus is social behavior. Clearly, we know much more than is being used by those with operational positions. Hence, there is a need to improve our understanding of research utilization, including the social processes of information transfer, adoption, and implementation (Changnon et al., 1983:112).

To date, few have penetrated this matter, although key insights have been offered. For example, in 1975, White and Haas hypothesized the following.

> VH6.1(H) Four sets of characteristics associated with effective application of research findings are: (1) the researcher and research organization, i.e., they have extensive experience and display breadth of view; (2) the potential user and user organization, i.e., the research begins with approval of the effort by those top officials who have power to see that results are utilized; (3) the researcher–user relationship, i.e., users recognize the researcher as having relevant expertness and research skills and researchers see user problems as interesting and worthy of serious intellectual commitment beyond the theoretical implications for other scientists in the field; and (4) the research product, i.e., final report sets forth applications which are at least moderately feasible within ongoing

social, political, and economic constraints and is directly relevant to significant user problems. (Adapted from White and Haas, 1975:151–152.)

Yin and Moore (1985) have completed nine comparative case studies wherein they explored the processes by which earthquake and other natural hazards innovations have been used. These included such projects as (1) the Association of Bay Area Governments (ABAG) project on local governments' liabilities for injuries or losses due to earthquakes (Moore and Yin, 1983a); (2) the ABK Joint Venture (i.e., three Los Angeles-area engineering firms—Agbabian Associates, S.B. Barnes and Associates, and Kariotis, Kesler and Allys) focused on a cost-effective means to evaluate and retrofit unreinforced masonry buildings to withstand earthquakes (Moore and Yin, 1983b); and (3) the National Academy of Sciences (NAS) project that investigated the social, economic, political, behavioral, and legal consequences of earthquake predictions (see Panel on the Public Policy Implications of Earthquake Prediction, 1975; Moore and Yin, 1983c).

Comparative case study results indicated that utilization of the project results—innovations of sorts—reflected rather different social pathways and general models, although there were important parallels. Thus, despite some variations, the overriding theme is that ". . . social interactions may be the most important ingredient for utilization to occur." (Yin and Moore, 1985:24). The following conclusion from the ABAG case study illustrates the level of precision and theoretical rigor that characterized this work.

VH6.2 "The nature and extent of utilization of the ABAG project can be explained by comparing the pattern of events in the ABAG project with three models of the utilization process: the problem-solver model; the research, development and diffusion model; and the social interaction model. The utilization experience of the ABAG project follows most closely the social interaction model. Thus, the ABAG project staff and Advisory Committee members represented a diversity of 'social networks,' and engaged in a substantial amount of interaction with individuals in a number of different networks both during and after the research project. However, the ABAG experience also matched the problem-solver model in that the ABAG project was initiated to address a problem that had been predefined by a group of potential users. Finally, the ABAG experience was not consistent with the pattern of characteristics outlined in the RD&D model" (Moore and Yin, 1983a:36).

Based on their nine cases, Yin and Moore (1985) proposed that researchers would increase utilization of their study results if they: (1) joined and became active in associations whose membership included both knowledge producers *and* users; (2) identified specific potential user groups when designing new projects; (3) maintained flexibility in the research design during the course of the research; and (4) produced a major product aimed directly at user groups when the project results are available (adapted from Yin and Moore, 1985:80–81). For organizations interested in having project results utilized, they proposed several recommendations that included the following:

1. "Make sure that the research to be conducted addresses a practical or policy problem, preferably one specifically enunciated by a relevant, potential user group [p. 78].

2. "All other things being equal—especially without sacrificing the quality of the research to be done—make awards to investigators whose host organizations or agencies create direct and continual interactions between knowledge producers and knowledge users" [p. 78].

3. "Where the preceding type of host organization or agency is not the recipient of the award, determine whether the principal investigator has a positive record of prior communication with user groups" [p. 78]. (Yin and Moore, 1985:78.)

VIH. International System Level

As with the other phases, relatively few sociologists have examined mitigation issues at the international system level. Among the scattered findings I coded for this phase, three general topics emerged: (1) projections of disaster vulnerability; (2) disaster assistance; and (3) intersocietal comparisons.

VIH1. Projections of Disaster Vulnerability

Is the planet becoming a more hazardous place for human habitation? Given the inadequate disaster loss data bases for even those nations with a penchant for record keeping, crude answers for single hazard types are soft at best. A few efforts have been made to aggregate data so as to produce worldwide portraits, but the authors consistently lament the poor quality of the basic input (e.g., Thompson, 1982; Beyer, 1974; Nichols, 1974). Only recently have scholars ventured into the even broader issues of which natural hazards are but one element; that is projections of environmental trends that may be more critical to human survivability than more time-focused events, regardless of the magnitude of a single death toll (e.g., Holdgate, Kassas, and White, 1982; Kates; 1983).

Judgments appearing in the literature, based on the best data available, however, have a curious consistency—things appear to be getting worse. Why? Two reasons are cited often: (1) increased human settlement into areas known to be hazardous and (2) increased dependence on and use of technologies that are either hazardous or vulnerable to disruption or both (see Lewis, O'Keefe, and Westgate, 1977; Long, 1978).

Within this sea of gloomy projections, there are a few who point to social adaptations that lessen vulnerability, especially among less developed societies. While these adaptive strategies must be included in any overall accounting, and too often are not, they do not negate the death tolls that occur annually or the complex set of trends that appear to be placing more people at risk for massive catastrophes. By juxtaposing two interpretations we can sense the range of judgment reflected in the literature to date.

VIH1.1(H) "From the ethnographic literature, it is possible to distinguish some five devices commonly adopted to lessen vulnerability to such risks: 1) diversification of activities, rather than specialization or reliance on a few plants or animals; 2) storage of foodstuffs; 3) storage and transmission of information on what we can call famine foods; 4) conversion of surplus food into durable valuables which could be stored and traded for food in an emergency; 5) cultivation of social relationships to allow the tapping of food resources of other regions" (Colson, 1979:21).

VIH1.2(H) ". . . (1) peasants do possess a great deal of understanding of their environment and elaborate repertoires of 'adjustments' of daily practices which help them survive disasters; (2) these systems of understanding and adjustment become distorted—sometimes to the point of complete destruction—under the market conditions that characterise most underdeveloped countries; (3) distortion or destruction of the systems of 'peoples' science' produces a situation of 'decision pathology' on the part of peasants, which in turn explains apparently 'irrational' or 'non-adaptive' behaviour such as overgrazing in Africa, or refusing to evacuate a flood-plain in Asia; (4) increased vulnerability to disaster is the result of such a situation; (5) increased numbers of people suffering increased vulnerability to disasters explain why there has been a statistically significant increase in the number and severity of disasters in the past decade" (Wisner, O'Keefe, and Westgate, 1977:47).

Hall's (1983) critical assessment of the responses in Belize (a small former colony of Britain, located on the east coast of Central America) added another dimension to this issue—one that gained increased recognition during the early 1980s. He reviewed a variety of responses to both drought and hurricanes and concluded that current vulnerability reflected an unwillingness to recognize "the real problem." Presumably, this resulted primarily from a peasant agrarian system that was rooted in a colonial legacy. While some government aid was going to peasant farmers, there remained a bias toward commercial crops. "Private and foreign investors are granted or loaned millions of dollars while it is still almost impossible for peasant farmers to gain sufficient loans to acquire their own farms and equipment" (Hall, 1983:143). Thus, Hall concluded that ". . . an analysis of the overall extent of resource development in relation to natural hazards suggests that human activity, notably the history of the colony and biased attitudes of the national government, are also to blame for the form and degree of risk" (Hall, 1983:140).

Carrying this line of reasoning one step further—so as to provide a "radical" critique of the "dominant Western Model" of hazards research—Susman, O'Keefe, and Wisner (1983) argued that case study materials from such events as the 1976 Guatemalan earthquake and Hurricane

Fifi, which struck Honduras in 1974, pointed toward one conclusion: ". . . the underdevelopment process forces the peasantry into a more vulnerable position which, in turn, directs them to look for another source of live-lihood in areas where security may be less and hazard more severe or to change their resource use in ways that exacerbate vulnerability" (Susman, O'Keefe, and Wisner, 1983:278).

Using 245 disasters that had occurred in African and Latin American nations, Seitz and Davis (1984) brought this form of analysis to a new standard. (See also Davis and Seitz, 1982.) By dividing 50 nation states that had been impacted by earthquakes, floods, epidemics, droughts, or storms between the years 1964 and 1973 into one of three governmental categories or, to use their term, "patterns of authoritative allocation" (i.e., ethnic pluralism, corporatism, and egalitarianism), they explored linkages between these patterns and variations in hazard victimization rates (i.e., deaths, injuries, property damage).

While some hypothesized relationships were not supported or received only mixed support, their data underscored the utility and potential of this approach and the complex research agenda that it implies.

> VIH1.3(H) "The severity of their impact—in terms of numbers killed, amount of damages, and numbers of victims—can be traced in part to social, economic, and political contextual variables such as population density, literacy, industrialization, legislative effectiveness, and govern-mental instability" (Seitz and Davis, 1984:247, 249).
>
> VIH1.3a(H) [The earthquake data indicated] ". . . very high death rates for corporatist regimes and relatively modest ones for egalitarian and ethnic pluralist ones" (Seitz and Davis, 1984:243). (Pattern supported for floods and droughts, mixed for epidemics, and reversed for storms wherein death rates for ethnically pluralist nations were highest.)
>
> VIH1.3b(H) [Lower rates of damage to property were found among cor-poratist regimes for earthquakes, floods, droughts and storms, since] "ethnic pluralist states invest little in flood control [p. 245] [and] . . . corporatist regimes try to protect their much more developed and highly valued infrastructure [p. 247]" (Seitz and Davis, 1984:245, 247).
>
> VIH1.3c(H) Given an emphasis on human needs, it was expected that victimization rates would be lower in egalitarian nations than corporatist ones, except for storms. Data supported the hypothesis for earthquakes, floods, and droughts, including the expected reversal for storms. Pre-sumably, this reversal reflected the corporatist prophylactic property measures. (Adapted from Seitz and Davis, 1984:247.)

VIH2. Disaster Assistance

Through the search process I used, only two reports were uncovered that dealt with international disaster assistance from a mitigative standpoint. Among the issues raised were changing organizational roles and the ap-propriateness of certain technologies.

VIH2.1 "In the past 15–20 years the volume of international disaster assistance and the number of participants have greatly expanded. . . . the increased international attention devoted to disasters cannot be explained solely by the identification of victim needs in a few major disasters. The U.S. presence has grown, but so has that of other governments, voluntary agencies, the United Nations, and other international and regional organizations. Thus there has been an increase in the number of participants looking for meaningful roles to play" (Committee on International Disaster Assistance, 1978b: 4).

VIH2.1a ". . . historically the *largest number* of U.S. government disaster relief operations [in foreign disasters] have been in response to disaster agents that have rapid onset (e.g., earthquakes, tropical cyclones, hurricanes, and river floods), but the *largest amount of money spent* by the U.S. government has been for conflict disasters (e.g., civil strife or civil wars) and for the so-called creeping disasters (e.g., droughts and famines)" (Committee on International Disaster Assistance, 1978b:4).

VIH2.1b(H) ". . . the assumption that outside foreign assistance can be given quickly in most disasters should be seriously questioned. Foreign disaster assistance usually does not arrive in time to help during the immediate emergency, may not be relevant or usable when it does arrive, and its very presence may create further problems" (Committee on International Disaster Assistance, 1979:2).

VIH2.2 "One of the major myths to be dispelled is that Western technology can, if only it is tooled up for the task, provide an answer or fill a gap. All the evidence suggests that the reverse is true; ideally, the donor response is to support *what is already taking place,* and the technology will by definition be that of the locality" (Committee on International Disaster Assistance, 1978a:32).

Equally important, and just as complex of course, are issues related to impact. I discussed this issue in the chapter on reconstruction (see Sections IVF2 and VIF2.4) but raise it here again because of its relevance to mitigation. We must not only seek to identify the social processes that guide the flow of adoption of various mitigative adjustments, but we also must design research that better informs policy makers of the multiple impacts that such actions may have. Using a large number of anthropological case studies, Torry (1978a) advanced this argument most forcefully.

VIH2.3(H) ". . . disaster welfare frequently acts, itself, as an agent of disaster by nurturing long-term risks through short-term remedies" (Torry, 1978a:302).

VIH2.3a(H) "I consider two factors behind risk increment. First, sizeable capital outlays and institutional reforms attendant with state intervention weaken local support structures. Second, as the autonomy of local adjustments shrinks, concomitant dependencies on remote, unpredictable, and poorly devised bureaucratic solutions to disaster management prevail" (Torry, 1978a:302).

VIH2.3b(H) ". . . indigenous solutions, such as migration to host villages, would have enabled many victims to cope with little or no outside help" (Torry, 1978a:303).

VIH3. Intersocietal Comparisons

Societal variations in the adoption of various types of hazard mitigative adjustments is a research topic that a few scholars broached during the past decade. For example, within a rather elaborate theoretical interpretation of intrasocietal processes, Pelanda (1982a, b) proposed that subsequent analyses of societal adoption of disaster mitigation adjustments should be framed within a social change framework. Certainly, much can be said for this plea, as it affords yet another interface between the problems studied by disaster researchers and broader sociological theories of system change.

VIH3.1(H) ". . . the overall vulnerability of a social (sub)system is at a relative minimum when its structure is characterized by indeterminacy which swings between functional limits. Such a structural configuration maximizes the probability of absorbing a perturbation (or a threat) by generating both social change and increasing organized complexity" (Pelanda, 1982a:22).

VIH3.1a(H) [. . . local disasters produce diversified effects among communities within the same social system and among social entities belonging to the same community. These diversified effects are based mainly on the level of specific vulnerability in the pre-disaster period of the subsystem social entities (specific vulnerability is a capacity factor referred to the probability that the social entities involved maximize the adaptive behavior under hypothetic or real stress).] [Italy] (Pelanda, 1982b:516–517).

VIH3.1b(H) [This concept implies at least three sublevels of social vulnerability: general (Vg), of societal scale (for example: a nation), specific (Vs) and topologic (Vt), of subsystem scale (for example: regional area). The hypothesis is that if we only know one of these levels or if we measure them separately without connecting them, then it is not possible to measure the global vulnerability of the social subsystem being considered (for example: Irpinia, Friuli) or to predict or explain its behavior in the post-disaster period or its probability of avoiding destruction. In other words, knowing every type of vulnerability individually does not allow to predict or to explain the subsystems' social dynamics of the post-impact period. As a minimum requirement, only a triple and simultaneous measurement could have this predictive propriety at an acceptable level of reliability.] [Italy] (Pelanda, 1982b:517).

Less abstract than Pelanda's framework, and informed by field studies conducted in 18 nations, three social geographers—Burton, Kates, and White (1978)—provided key insights that future sociological theorists should seek to incorporate.

VIH3.2 "On the global scale, four factors are widely found to affect the mix of human response to hazard: (1) a few characteristics of extreme events; (2) the localized experience with hazard and success of adjustment; (3) the intensity of resource use; and (4) the level of material wealth attained" (Burton, Kates, and White, 1978:210).

VIH3.2a(H) "As nature constrains the modes of coping, so do the wealth, technological capacity, and organization of society. These modes vary by societal type . . . in a traditional or folk society, coping is characterized by a high absorptive capacity—a large number of adjustments widely shared among individuals and communities. These adjustments often involve patterns of behavior or of agricultural practices more cooperative with nature than controlling it" (Burton, Kates, and White, 1978:217).

VIH3.2b(H) "In the modern industrial state a different pattern emerges. Acceptance shifts from bearing loss personally, or sharing with kin, to sharing with the wider society by means of relief or insurance. The growing technological capacity to manage or manipulate the environment encourages the reduction of hazard by emphasizing policies for the control of nature." (Burton, Kates, and White, 1978:219).

VIH3.2c(H) "In the post-industrial society, . . . there is a marked shift to a broader coping pattern, a turning away from reliance on the control or modification of nature toward a comprehensive policy for lowering of the damage potential and a concern with the effects of disaster policies on the well-being of the people involved" (Burton, Kates, and White, 1978:220).

Emphasizing a perspective based more on conflict than that characterizing the work of Burton, Kates, and White, two economists—Kunreuther and Ley (1982)—have recommended that intrasocietal struggles must be reckoned with in these analyses, as with other studies of system change. Risks, risk assessment, and generalized notions of safety are social products, not absolutes. And as with most other social definitions, the legitimation of certain threshold levels may be more in the best interest of some than others. This theme was reflected also in an analysis by Drake and Long (1982).

VIH3.3 "Due to the lack of statistical data and standards that assessments must meet in order to be used as evidence, experts have few guidelines for restricting how they undertake risk assessments. Such broad degrees of freedom have created considerable problems for societal decision making processes" (Kunreuther and Ley, 1982:4).

VIH3.3a(H) "Several features of such risk problems can be underscored. [1.] . . . there are many different individuals and groups in society who are affected by a particular decision, each of which has its own goals and objectives, databases and constraints. . . . [2.] there is a limited statistical database on which to determine the risk associated with a specific project or activity. . . . [3.] the dynamic and sequential nature of the decision process" (Kunreuther and Ley, 1982:3).

VIH3.3b(H) ". . . it seems that different localities or countries may have different existing background risks and different attitudes toward acceptable safety. At the most local level, there is the danger that each town may ban all hazardous facilities but hope that they will be located nearby so their economic benefits may be enjoyed. Thus, the approach of decision making in a national or regional form appears to be the best solution" (Drake and Long, 1982:112).

Somewhat implied within these broader frameworks, but focused on more narrow problems, are the conclusions of several researchers. Thus, understanding the propensity to adapt certain mitigative strategies may be enhanced if societies are sorted across structural qualities. Among those proposed are technological development and religiosity.

VIH3.4(H) "The priority given to specific technological resources varies directly with the technological level of the society. . . . The number of points of vulnerability of a society varies directly with the dependency of the society on a complex technology" [Italy, Japan, U.S.A.] (McLuckie, 1977:96).

VIH3.5(H) "In societies where catastrophe is thought to be caused primarily by spiritual forces, man does little to alter the course of events apart from recourse to religious and/or magical practices" (Mileti, 1975b:23).

Shifting to a lower point on the abstraction ladder, some researchers have focused on a single adjustment type. For example, Huffman (1982, 1983) selected the matter of legal definitions of liability—both general and specifically for the external costs of earthquake predictions (Huffman, 1984). A theoretical model that might account for the types of variations he documented among a five-nation sample would be an important next step.

VIH3.6 ". . . the government in each of the five countries can be held liable for harm resulting from a significant range of government actions. There is little doubt that in every case the government may be liable for harm resulting from particular earthquake hazard mitigation activities" (Huffman, 1983:393).

VIH3.6a "The doctrine of sovereign immunity has been important in each country at some point in its recent history, although for varying reasons and not always under that name. The United States and New Zealand continue to rely on the doctrine of sovereign immunity to justify some limitations on government liability, while Japan, China and the Soviet Union have laws which justify limitations on liability upon other reasons" (Huffman, 1983:393).

VIH3.6b "In every country fault is a relevant factor in assessing government liability, although New Zealand's Accident Compensation Act makes fault irrelevant to the compensation of personal injuries. Fault is also irrelevant in all five countries to the extent that their welfare systems automatically compensate for particular types of harm like medical costs and loss of income'' (Huffman, 1983:393).

The degree to which different nations seek to protect their populations through such measures as building codes or regulations regarding land use varies greatly.

> ''. . . substantial differences have been observed between the hazard-mitigation policies of the several industrialized nations. For example, Wiggins and Moran (1971) have reviewed the earthquake-mitigation pro-visions of building codes in 14 nations, including the United States and have found substantial differences in the safety of structures required by such codes''[6] (Petak and Atkisson, 1982:94–95).

There is some evidence, although very limited at present, that suggests that this variation may reflect the relative degree of governmental cen-tralization. This structural quality, like any other, may of course vary over time as may the degree of unevenness or standardization of policy within a particular nation. Two examples of this line of reasoning are the following.

> VIH3.7 ''The 40 years after 1933 witnessed rapid growth in the assumption of the need for federal action in dealing with some major natural hazards in the United States. The trend was in the same direction in Canada, but to a much smaller degree'' (Visvader and Burton, 1974:220).

> VIH3.8(H) ''Where there exists a choice between handling risks indi-vidualistically (by the market, for instance) and handling them collectively (by regulation, for instance) both hermit and entrepreneur will favor the former. Both will be biased against institutions that collectivize risks, or convert voluntary into involuntary ones. They will instead tend to give their support to those more diffuse institutions that, directly or indirectly (but more likely indirectly), increase the areas of risk that are left to individual values and decrease the areas that are handled by social choice'' (Thompson and Wildavsky, 1982:158–159).

Finally, a few researchers have tried to sort out differential responses to the technology of earthquake prediction, in terms of both probable re-sponse patterns to actual predictions and the way the technology is in-tegrated within preexisting structures. To date, comparisons have been limited to those involving the U.S.A. and either Japan or China.

> VIH3.9(H) ''. . . a marked difference exists between Japan and the United States concerning earthquake prediction response. . . . a prediction in the United States would be responded to by organizations as an impo-sition. . . . [In Japan] a prediction would not be seen as an imposition but rather as an opportunity to make mitigation and preparedness ac-

---

[6]J. H. Wiggins and D. Moran, ''Earthquake Safety in the City of Long Beach Based on the Concept of Balanced Risk.'' Redondo Beach, California: J. H. Wiggins Company, 1971.

complishments that may have been hard to legitimate in the absence of a prediction'' [Japan and U.S.A.] (Mileti, 1983:410). (See also Mileti, 1982.)

VIH3.10(H) ''An admittedly tentative comparison between the possible consequences of earthquake prediction in China and the U.S. suggests that their respective systems of production and distribution, operating through their dominant forms of social organization, income distribution patterns, levels of employment, and access of individuals to nonmarket goods, are likely to have an enormous impact in structuring the possible social and economic consequences of [earthquake] predictions'' [China and U.S.A.] (Gimenez, 1976:339).

VIH3.11(H) There are at least four important differences between the U.S.A. and Chinese experiences with earthquake prediction technologies. (Based on Turner, 1978.)

VIH3.11a(H) ''The Chinese make political motives paramount in recruiting and sustaining amateur participation. American experience has shown that political or national concerns can be powerful incentives in periods of crisis, but that the service-interest—personal development motivation complex is quite adequate and probably more dependable as the incentive for volunteer and amateur participation in useful programs'' [China and U.S.A.] (Turner, 1978:159).

VIH3.11b(H) ''While the Chinese work through the local civil units in establishing their amateur network, autonomous and semi-autonomous organizational sectors in American society constitute a more appropriate medium'' [China and U.S.A.] (Turner, 1978:159).

VIH3.11c(H) ''While the Chinese program is chiefly crisis-oriented, an American program will, at least for the present, have to be organized on the basis of more sustained and less crisis-motivated activity'' [China and U.S.A.] (Turner, 1978:159).

VIH3.11d(H) ''. . . the Chinese plan conceives the earthquake amateur groups as single-purpose units. Since it will be difficult for people to feel deeply the importance of years of record-keeping without a significant earthquake, an amateur program is more likely to be effective if the earthquake-prediction observations are combined with other meaningful activities'' [China and U.S.A.] (Turner, 1978:159).

It is clear that future research must address the issues of intersocietal comparisons of mitigative adjustments within the emerging paradigms of societal change. Indeed, these embryonic theories may be enriched greatly through subsequent empirical study of the disaster case. Also, at the level of inter-nation collaboration there are numerous areas of potential application that could do much to lessen the probability of death and the degree of traumatization. The opportunities and challenges for future research are enormous.

Selected Bibliography

Baker, Earl J., and Joe Gordon McPhee [1975] *Land Use Management and Regulation in Hazardous Areas: A Research Assessment*. Boulder, Colorado: Institute of Behavioral Science, The University of Colorado.

Baumann, Duane D., and John H. Sims [1978] "Flood Insurance: Some Determinants of Adoption." *Economic Geography* **54** (July):189–196.

Britton, Neil, G.E. Kearney, and K. A. Britton [1983] "Disaster Response: The Perception of the Threat and Its Influence on Community Decision on Insurance." Pp. 260–332 in *Insurance and Natural Disaster Management:* Papers presented at a seminar, Townsville, July 1983, John Oliver (ed.). Townsville, Queensland, Australia: Centre For Disaster Studies, James Cook University of North Queensland.

Burby, Raymond J., and Steven P. French [1980] "The U.S. Experience in Managing Flood Plain Land Use." *Disasters* **4** (No. 4):451–457.

Butler, J. R. G., and D. P. Doessel [1981] "Efficiency and Equity in Natural Disaster Relief." *Public Finance* **36** (No. 2):193–213.

Butler, J. R. G., and D. P. Doessel [1979] *The Economics of Natural Disaster Relief in Australia*. Canberra: Centre for Research on Federal Financial Relations, The Australian National University.

Committee on International Disaster Assistance [1978] *The Role of Technology in International Assistance*. Washington, D.C.: National Academy of Sciences.

Descamps, Marc-Alain [1972] "Catastrophe et Responsibilité"(Disaster and Responsibility) (in French). *Revue Française de Sociologie* **13** (No. 3):376–391.

Drabek, Thomas E., Alvin H. Mushkatel, and Thomas S. Kilijanek [1983] *Earthquake Mitigation Policy: The Experience of Two States*. Boulder, Colorado: Institute of Behavioral Science, The University of Colorado.

Farhar, Barbara C. (ed.) [1977] *Hail Suppression: Society and Environment*. Boulder, Colorado: Institute of Behavioral Science, The University of Colorado.

Frey, R. Scott [1983] "The Structural Context of City Adoption of War on Poverty and National Flood Insurance Programs." *The Sociological Quarterly* **24** (Winter):59–74.

Hirose, Hirotada, and Tomoichi Ishizuka [1983] "Causal Analysis of Earthquake Concern and Preparing Behavior in the North Izu Peninsula." *Japanese Psychological Research* 25:103–111.

Huffman, James L. [1983] "Government Liability and Natural Hazard Mitigation in Japan, the Soviet Union, China, New Zealand and the United States." *International Journal of Mass Emergencies and Disasters* **1** (November):379–397.

Kunreuther, Howard, Ralph Ginsberg, Louis Miller, Philip Sagi, Paul Slovic, Bradley Borkan, and Norman Katz [1978] *Disaster Insurance Protection: Public Policy Lessons*. New York: John Wiley and Sons.

Kunreuther, Howard, and Eryl Ley (eds.) [1982] *The Risk Analysis Controversy: An Institutional Perspective*. Berlin, Heidelberg, New York: Springer-Verlag.

Levine, Adeline Gordon [1982] *Love Canal: Science, Politics, and People*. Toronto: Lexington Books.

Luloff, A.E., and Kenneth P. Wilkinson [1979] "Participation in the National Flood Insurance Program: A Study of Community Activeness." *Rural Sociology* **44** (Spring):137–152.

Mileti, Dennis S. [1983] "Societal Comparisons of Organizational Response to

Earthquake Predictions: Japan vs. the United States." *International Journal of Mass Emergencies and Disasters* **1** (November):399–414.

Mileti, Dennis S. [1980] "Human Adjustment to the Risk of Environmental Extremes." *Sociology and Social Research* **64** (April):327–347.

Olson, Richard Stuart, and Douglas C. Nilson [1982] "Public Policy Analysis and Hazards Research: Natural Complements." *The Social Science Journal* **19** (January):89–103.

Palm, Risa [1981] *Real Estate Agents and Special Studies Zones Disclosure: The Response of California Home Buyers to Earthquake Hazards Information.* Boulder, Colorado: Institute of Behavioral Science, The University of Colorado.

Panel on the Public Policy Implications of Earthquake Prediction [1975] *Earthquake Prediction and Public Policy.* Washington, D.C.: National Academy of Sciences.

Pelanda, Carlo [1982] "Disastro e Vulnerabilità Sociosistemica" (Disaster and Social Vulnerability) (in Italian). *Rassegna Italiana di Sociologia* **22**:507–532.

Perrow, Charles [1984] *Normal Accidents: Living with High Risk Technologies.* New York: Basic Books.

Petak, William J. [1984] "Natural Hazard Mitigation: Professionalization of the Policy Making Process." *International Journal of Mass Emergencies and Disasters* **2** (August):285–302.

Petak, William J., and Arthur A. Atkisson [1982] *Natural Hazard Risk Assessment and Public Policy: Anticipating the Unexpected.* New York, Heidelberg, Berlin: Springer-Verlag.

Platt, Rutherford H. [1982] "The Jackson Flood of 1979—A Public-Policy Disaster." *Journal of the American Planning Association* **48** (Spring):219–231.

Platt, Rutherford H. with the assistance of George M. McMullen, Richard Paton, Ann Patton, Michael Grahek, Mary Read English, and Jon A. Kusler [1980] *Intergovernmental Management of Floodplains.* Boulder, Colorado: Institute of Behavioral Science, The University of Colorado.

Rabin, Robert L. [1978] "Dealing with Disasters: Some Thoughts on the Adequacy of the Legal System." *Stanford Law Review* **30** (January):281–298.

Rossi, Peter H., James D. Wright, and Eleanor Weber-Burdin [1982] *Natural Hazards and Public Choice: The State and Local Politics of Hazard Mitigation.* New York: Academic Press.

Seitz, Steven Thomas, and Morris Davis [1984] "The Political Matrix of Natural Disasters: Africa and Latin America." *International Journal of Mass Emergencies and Disasters* **2** (August):231–250.

Slovic, Paul, Baruch Fischhoff, Sarah Lichtenstein, Bernard Korrigan, and Barbara Combs [1977] "Preference for Insurance against Probable Small Loss: Implications for Theory and Practice of Insurance." *Journal of Risk and Insurance* **44** (June):237–258.

Turner, Barry A. [1979] "The Social Aetiology of Disasters." *Disasters* **3** (No. 1):53–59.

Wyner, Alan J. [1984] "Earthquakes and Public Policy Implementation in California." *International Journal of Mass Emergencies and Disasters* **2** (August):267–284.

Yin, Robert K., and Gwendolyn B. Moore [1985] "The Utilization of Research: Lessons from the Natural Hazards Field." Washington, D.C.: Cosmos Corporation.

10

Disaster Research:
A Strategic Research Site

Independent of its utility as a guide to specific studies, this inventory provides a more generalized function. Given its scope, major directions within disaster research can be identified more clearly—so too can areas that thus far have been ignored. Similarly, certain topics that may have unique policy applications or have matured to a state of model development become more visible. In short, as Merton (1969) stated so well in his preface to Barton's (1969) synthesis that was based on the disaster literature of the 1950s, such reviews have important functions for sociological theory. Similarly, at times such syntheses may stimulate more informed social policy.

Within sociology, and the social sciences generally, at the dawn of the 1990s disaster research constitutes a strategic research site. Its strategic location within that complex and expansive tapestry that comprises human behavior in its variant displays and conditions becomes more evident when different dimensions are considered. The following six topics provide avenues of understanding: (1) the progress of a decade; (2) priorities for the future; (3) opportunities for policy and application; (4) candidates for model building; (5) areas requiring exploration; and (6) payoffs for sociological theory.

The Progress of a Decade

Table 10-1 displays the number of findings that were inventoried initially. As indicated, this included 1,250 specific findings, 751 major conclusions, and 153 general topics. Due to a length constraint, many findings were

Table 10-1. Inventory summary.[a]

Disaster phase	System level																	
	Individual			Group			Organizational			Community			Society			International		
	T	MC	SF	T	MC	SF	T	MC	SF	T	MC	SF	T	MC	SF	T	MC	SF
Preparedness																		
A. Planning	4	11	9	4	6	0	7	31	34	8	44	77	3	8	13	1	6	7
B. Warning	5	20	55	3	16	13	2	5	9	2	3	7	2	4	5	1	1	0
Response																		
C. Evacuation	4	24	57	4	17	26	3	11	0	3	13	25	2	5	1	1	3	2
D. Emergency	3	34	102	2	10	33	6	33	89	6	43	72	1	6	1	2	6	5
Recovery																		
E. Restoration	2	16	30	4	23	2	4	18	26	7	33	57	2	8	2	3	12	13
F. Reconstruction	6	35	79	2	16	37	5	16	26	3	20	40	1	5	17	2	16	37
Mitigation																		
G. Perceptions	3	16	54	1	1	2	3	6	17	2	5	7	1	1	0	2	10	13
H. Adjustment	4	26	37	0	0	0	4	14	3	3	23	23	6	51	45	3	20	41

[a] Grand totals: topics (T) = 153; major conclusions (MC) = 751; specific findings (SF) = 1,250.

deleted during final revision of this book. I noted these by the use of a "see also" format; thus, citation listings direct readers to additional relevant findings. Also, some new studies were integrated during the final revision process. Hence, Table 10-1 differs from the book summary presented in Chapter 1 (Table 1-2).

Certainly, the presence of these research products is a sign of progress. Despite the methodological weaknesses that have been underscored repeatedly—matters like design flaws, inadequate sampling, absence of control groups, and poor measurement—a legacy exists. It has its points of weakness but it provides a true foundation on which others may stand.

As with any other research area, however, this foundation remains uneven. Not all topics that the conceptual matrix reveals have received equal attention. As Merton (1957) noted years ago, sociological theory and research do not grow evenly or uniformly. Rather, theoretical breakthroughs emerge when topics are penetrated in depth, at times by a single but expertly executed study.

General points of concentration—and gaps—can be identified through a careful review of Table 1-2 or Table 10-1. That is, of all major conclusions inventoried, to which niche in the conceptual taxonomy do most relate? Since Table 10-1 presents the findings inventoried initially, rather than just those selected for quotation in the text, it provides a better basis for answering this question. Such an analysis is more easily pursued, however, when the category totals are transformed into percentages. These are presented as Table 10-2.

Clearly, more is known about certain topics than others. For example, the largest percentage of major conclusions deal with the adoption of hazard adjustments, primarily flood insurance, by societies (6.8% of the total). Relatively speaking, however, more major conclusions have appeared in the literature regarding community planning activities (5.9%) and emergency responses (5.7%) than other topics, although a goodly number have been documented regarding long-term impacts on individuals (4.7%), organizational responses during the immediate emergency period (4.4%), and organizational planning actions (4.1%).

Using the number of specific findings as an index indicates a somewhat consistent picture in that the following five cells ranked highest: individual (8.2%), organizational (7.1%), and community behavior (5.8%) during the emergency phase; long-term impacts on individuals (6.3%); and community planning activities (6.2%). Thus, in comparison to the other cells within the conceptual taxonomy, a bit more is known about these topics.

Refining the analysis just a bit, these same data were reorganized so as to examine the areas of concentration within each systemic level. Thus, as noted in Table 10-1, there are 423 specific findings pertaining to individuals, and of these, about one-quarter deal with the emergency period. To facilitate such an analysis, Table 10-3 was created. Note that the "percent by system level" listed in the "specific findings" column for individuals during the emergency phase is 24.1.

Table 10-2. Inventory summary: Percent by total.[a]

| | System level | | | | | | | | | | | | | | | | | |
| | Individual | | | Group | | | Organizational | | | Community | | | Society | | | International | | |
Disaster phase	T	MC	SF	T	MC	SF	T	MC	SF	T	MC	SF	T	MC	SF	T	MC	SF
Preparedness																		
A. Planning	2.6	1.5	0.7	2.6	0.8	0.0	4.6	4.1	2.7	5.2	5.9	6.2	2.0	1.1	1.0	0.7	0.8	0.6
B. Warning	3.3	2.7	4.4	2.0	2.1	1.0	1.3	0.7	0.7	1.3	0.4	0.6	1.3	0.5	0.4	0.7	0.1	0.0
Response																		
C. Evacuation	2.6	3.2	4.6	2.6	2.3	2.1	2.0	1.5	0.0	2.0	1.7	2.0	1.3	0.7	0.1	0.7	0.4	0.2
D. Emergency	2.0	4.5	8.2	1.3	1.3	2.6	3.9	4.4	7.1	3.9	5.7	5.8	0.7	0.8	0.1	1.3	0.8	0.4
Recovery																		
E. Restoration	1.3	2.1	2.4	2.6	3.1	0.2	2.6	2.4	2.1	4.6	4.4	4.6	1.3	1.1	0.2	2.0	1.6	1.0
F. Reconstruction	3.9	4.7	6.3	1.3	2.1	3.0	3.3	2.1	2.1	2.0	2.7	3.2	0.7	0.7	1.4	1.3	3.2	3.0
Mitigation																		
G. Perceptions	2.0	2.1	4.3	0.7	0.1	0.2	2.0	0.8	1.4	1.3	0.7	0.6	0.7	0.1	0.0	1.3	1.3	1.0
H. Adjustment	2.6	3.5	3.0	0.0	0.0	0.0	2.6	1.9	0.2	2.0	3.1	1.8	3.9	6.8	3.6	2.0	2.7	3.3

[a]T = Topic; MC = major conclusion; SF = specific finding.

Table 10-3. Inventory Summary: Percent by system level.[a]

	System Level																	
	Individual			Group			Organizational			Community			Society			International		
Disaster phase	T	MC	SF	T	MC	SF	T	MC	SF	T	MC	SF	T	MC	SF	T	MC	SF
Preparedness																		
A. Planning	12.9	6.0	2.1	20.0	6.7	0.0	20.6	23.1	16.7	23.5	23.9	25.0	16.7	9.1	15.5	6.7	8.1	5.9
B. Warning	16.1	11.0	13.0	15.0	18.0	11.5	5.9	3.7	4.4	5.9	1.6	2.3	11.1	4.5	6.0	6.7	1.4	0.0
Response																		
C. Evacuation	12.9	13.2	13.5	20.0	19.1	23.0	8.8	8.2	0.0	8.8	7.1	8.1	11.1	5.7	1.2	6.7	4.1	1.7
D. Emergency	9.7	18.7	24.1	10.0	11.2	29.2	17.6	24.6	43.6	17.6	23.4	23.4	5.6	6.8	1.2	13.3	8.1	4.2
Recovery																		
E. Restoration	6.5	8.8	7.1	20.0	25.8	1.8	11.8	13.4	12.7	20.6	17.9	18.5	11.1	9.1	2.4	20.0	16.2	11.0
F. Reconstruction	19.4	19.2	18.7	10.0	18.0	32.7	14.7	11.9	12.7	8.8	10.9	13.0	5.6	5.7	20.2	13.3	21.6	31.4
Mitigation																		
G. Perceptions	9.7	8.8	12.8	5.0	1.1	1.8	8.8	4.5	8.3	5.9	2.7	2.3	5.6	1.1	0.0	13.3	13.5	11.0
H. Adjustment	12.9	14.3	8.7	0.0	0.0	0.0	11.8	10.4	1.5	8.8	12.5	7.5	33.3	58.0	53.6	20.0	27.0	34.7

[a]T = Topic; MC = major conclusion; SF = specific finding.

In short, among all of the conclusions and findings reported for individuals, most pertain to either the emergency or reconstruction phases. In contrast, while group behavior looms high within these two cells as well, much higher percentages of the findings (23.0%) and conclusions (19.1%) pertaining just to groups deal with evacuation behavior than is the case for individuals. Among all of the organizational work, the emergency phase again accounts for the majority reported. Community studies have provided nearly as many conclusions and findings about planning as about the emergency phase. But in direct contrast, much larger proportions of the conclusions (58.0%) and findings (53.6%) pertaining to societies deal with hazard adjustments. Although the international system level reflects a parallel concentration, much work has been lodged within the reconstruction phase. Thus, to some extent, certain system levels have been more commonly studied within certain phases than others.

Turning the matrix on its side, so to speak, permitted analysis of the clustering produced by using the marginal totals across each phase. For example, across all system levels there are 27 subtopics pertaining to planning. When this figure and its counterparts for major conclusions (106) and specific findings (140) were used to calculate the percentages for each cell in the table, the relative patterning within each phase was identified. These data are given in Table 10-4. Thus, inspection of row number one—planning—reveals a concentration on communities (55% of all specific findings on planning and 41.5% of all major conclusions). In contrast, most research on warning has generated conclusions about individual responses, although some concentration has occurred with groups—primarily families. Evacuation studies reflect a parallel patterning.

Research conducted within the emergency phase has been concentrated at the individual, organizational, and community level systems. Relatively little has been completed on group systems and even less on response by total societies or international systems.

Research on recovery processes has been spread more evenly across system levels, although among all of the findings regarding the restoration period, nearly one-half pertain to communities. Few studies have been reported regarding responses by total societies.

As might be expected, the majority of the research on hazard perceptions has been conceptualized using individuals as the comparative units. However, some headway has been made, primarily through the efforts of social geographers, in the area of cross-national comparisons. This is in sharp contrast to studies of the adoption of hazard mitigation adjustments, which have been concentrated at the societal system level. Curiously, as noted in Chapter 9, practically nothing has been reported about the group dynamics of such decision processes.

In short, the behavioral knowledge base is spread across all phases of disasters and system levels. But there clearly have been concentrations; the progress is far from being uniform.

Table 10-4. Inventory Summary: Percent by Phase[a]

| | System level | | | | | | | | | | | | | | | | | |
| | Individual | | | Group | | | Organizational | | | Community | | | Society | | | International | | |
Disaster Phase	T	MC	SF	T	MC	SF	T	MC	SF	T	MC	SF	T	MC	SF	T	MC	SF
Preparedness																		
A. Planning	14.8	10.4	6.4	14.8	5.7	0.0	25.9	29.2	24.3	29.6	41.5	55.0	11.1	7.5	9.3	3.7	5.7	5.0
B. Warning	33.3	40.8	61.8	20.0	32.7	14.6	13.3	10.2	10.1	13.3	6.1	7.9	13.3	8.2	5.6	6.7	2.0	0.0
Response																		
C. Evacuation	23.5	32.9	51.4	23.5	23.3	23.4	17.6	15.1	0.0	17.6	17.8	22.5	11.8	6.8	0.9	5.9	4.1	1.8
D. Emergency	15.0	25.8	33.8	10.0	7.6	10.9	30.0	25.0	29.5	30.0	32.6	23.8	5.0	4.5	0.3	10.0	4.5	1.7
Recovery																		
E. Restoration	9.1	14.5	23.1	18.2	20.9	1.5	18.2	16.4	20.0	31.8	30.0	43.8	9.1	7.3	1.5	13.6	10.9	10.0
F. Reconstruction	31.6	32.4	33.5	10.5	14.8	15.7	26.3	14.8	11.0	15.8	18.5	16.9	5.3	4.6	7.2	10.5	14.8	15.7
Mitigation																		
G. Perceptions	25.0	41.0	58.1	8.3	2.6	2.2	25.0	15.4	18.3	16.7	12.8	7.5	8.3	2.6	0.0	16.7	25.6	14.0
H. Adjustment	20.0	19.4	24.8	0.0	0.0	0.0	20.0	10.4	2.0	15.0	17.2	15.4	30.0	38.1	30.2	15.0	14.9	27.5

[a] T = Topic; MC = major conclusion; SF = specific finding.

One final type of comparison cast these patternings somewhat differently. Using the disaster findings inventory published in 1975 (Mileti, Drabek, and Haas) as a referent point, Table 10-5 displays the growth pattern of the past decade. Thus, when the present inventory is contrasted to the distribution of findings ($n = 627$) gleaned from a much smaller number of publications ($n = 193$) published prior to July 1, 1973, priority changes in funding and deflections in the interests of researchers become clearer. As noted in a footnote to Table 10-5, changes in procedures and categories precluded exact comparisons. But the pattern of increases in available findings and conclusions reveal where this knowledge base has grown the most during the past ten years.

Because of my inclusion of some research completed by social geographers—albeit minimal—the most obvious increases are those listed in the first row of Table 10-5. Clearly, there have been many new findings pertaining to hazard mitigation, regarding both perceptions and attitudes toward adjustments. Since these were combined with the small number of findings dealing with planning in our earlier work, this large category reflects both sources of increase and thus the increase is harder to evaluate. My judgment is that the large difference is due to both the size of the category—it reflects three phases rather than one—and my inclusion of literature published by social geographers, economists, and others. Thus, the increase does reflect a real shift in emphasis, but it is exaggerated in this table due to these factors.

Independent of these areas, what other focal points emerged as key topics during the last decade? Long-term disaster impacts on individuals netted the biggest gain. The shift is from 16 to 114 findings, or a "difference" of 98, which represents 7.1% of the increases in findings. While I have stressed that this topic remains controversial as to conclusions, it clearly was "discovered" during this era.

A second focal point—largely reflecting work completed by staff members or graduates of the Ohio State University Disaster Research Center— was organizational responses during the emergency phase. Note the "difference" of 5%. Nearly as many new findings ($D = 4.7\%$) were reported for communities during this time period too. Of lesser magnitude, but still representing clear focal points in many research studies, were communities and groups during the reconstruction phase.

In short, while a crude method of comparison at best, the contrast summarized in Table 10-5 clearly demonstrates both continuity—many new findings appeared pertaining to the behavior of individuals, organizations and communities during the emergency phase—and the emergence of new areas of inquiry. Most significant of these were investigations of recovery processes and studies dealing with aspects of mitigation. The progress of the past decade clearly reflects a maturing field, one evolving toward better balance across a broader spectrum of research topics.

Table 10.5. Coded findings: 1973 vs. 1985.

| | | System level | | | | | | | | | | | | | | | |
| Disaster phase | Individual | | | Group | | | Organizational | | | Community | | | Society | | | International | | |
	1973	D^a	%	1973	D	%	1973	D	%	1973	D	%	1973	D	%	1973	D	%
Preparedness																		
A. Planning and mitigation[b]	33	120	8.7	11	−2	0.1	16	89	6.4	33	146	10.6	11	107	7.8	0	97	7.0
B. Warning	32	43	3.1	11	18	1.3	10	4	0.3	10	0	0.0	3	6	0.4	0	1	0.1
Response																		
C. Evacuation	30	51	3.7	14	29	2.1	10	1	0.1	15	23	1.7	4	2	0.1	0	5	0.4
D. Emergency	68	68	4.9	35	8	0.6	53	69	5.0	50	65	4.7	6	1	0.1	0	11	0.8
Recovery																		
E. Restoration	33	13	0.9	18	7	0.5	29	15	1.1	33	57	4.1	11	−1	0.1	0	25	1.8
F. Reconstruction	16	98	7.1	6	47	3.4	6	36	2.6	14	46	3.3	6	16	1.2	0	53	3.8

$^a D$ = The difference between the number reported for 1973 and the number listed in Table 10-1, i.e., the 1985 inventory.

^{b}Due to the format and emphasis of our earlier review, I had to combine the findings pertaining to planning with those included in mitigation, i.e., hazard perceptions and adjustments. The discrepant increase is due to the narrower focus of the earlier inventory which was limited primarily to materials located at the Disaster Research Center, Ohio State University. Also, two other qualifications should be noted. First, the number used for the 1985 base refers only to those listed in the text; thus it is slightly lower due to duplications that are referred to, but not quoted. Because of the revision process, it was not possible to reconstruct the actual number of coded findings. Second, a small number of findings selected for inclusion in the 1985 inventory appeared in the 1973 inventory. Rather than exclude these in the count, I included them so as to compensate for the underestimate just noted.

Priorities for the Future

After reviewing this morass of material, five future priorities emerged in my thinking. To those doing disaster research and especially those associated with funding it, I urge serious consideration of these matters (see Drabek, 1983c for elaboration).

1. *Automated information retrieval systems.* In Chapter 1 the procedures, assumptions, and limitations of this inventory were outlined and a prototype system was noted (Rogers, Nehnevajsa, *et al.*, 1984). Upon thorough critique and review of the prototype, researchers and other potential users should be surveyed regarding the content and formats they would find most useful. Rather than a single centralized system that may meet the needs of some, I urge the simultaneous development of several systems at multiple universities. Such a division of labor, both among the disciplines and across materials of different types, could bring this field forward in a single decade.

Through computer networking, researchers and practitioners throughout the nation, indeed the world, could have rapid access to subject matter listings that would direct them to relevant citations on highly specialized topics. Such systems would do more than any other action to bridge the present-day gap between the practitioner and research communities. Of course, the problems of synthesis, availability, and report format remain. But the first step is letting people know that a study has been completed on a topic of interest to them. Computerized information retrieval systems are required. These must be focused on the complex range of topics—many of which cut across multiple disciplines—that comprise the field of emergency management.

2. *Taxonomy of disaster events and response systems.* Throughout this book I have argued that the most basic scientific problem confronting social scientists studying disaster responses is the matter of taxonomy. Kreps' (1985, 1984b) work has pushed this matter further than others. I am not convinced that a single set of event-related criteria will do the job, however. Rather, researchers must carefully assess event properties across each of the disaster phases. Similarly, far greater specification must be made regarding the type of response system, regardless of disaster phase. Not all social systems are the same. Certainly, the criterion of system complexity has proved to be useful. Group responses do differ in important ways from those that typify community level systems or entire societies. Future analyses, however, must expand upon the number and range of system-related taxonomic criteria so as to incorporate aspects of such dimensions as permanence, technological certainty, degree of totality, and the like. And even greater is the need for improved measurement of the range and intensity of differential adaptations that are forthcoming.

In short, future integrations across studies must be done within more narrowly defined taxonomic niches. There may be "conditional universals" that characterize at least aspects of the human system response, but the *limits of generalization* must be specified. Broad common functional requirements can be specified that can guide planning efforts across hazard types. But the research community must address this fundamental issue if the next level of theoretical integration is to be attained.

3. *Cross-national data bases.* Although some progress has been made, as recent issues of the *International Journal of Mass Emergencies and Disasters* attest, relatively few researchers have had access to data sets that permit cross-national testing. Thus, nearly all of the findings recorded in this book originated within a single society and have never been subjected to cross-national testing. Construction of the requisite data sets will require a new level of cooperation among the international community of scholars. But many new mechanisms for data sharing and other forms of collaboration must be designed and funded if the field is to even begin to reflect its potential.

4. *Integration with theory.* There are many directions, perspectives, and orientations that define the legacy of disaster research. Certainly it would be ill-founded to argue that a single theoretical paradigm should be identified and promoted as "the theory." But researchers must be encouraged to push their work so that linkages can be made to broader theories of human behavior. Agencies responding to the search and rescue demands created by a tornado or hurricane are representative of a class of organizations about which specialists in several academic disciplines have something to say. The same is true for communities involved in recovery or seeking assessments of mitigation options. Thus, the points of interface are numerous. The challenge is clear.

5. *Increased practitioner–researcher interaction.* With full recognition of the risks and cautions raised by Hewitt (1983), I remain convinced that the quality of disaster research will be improved immeasurably if the interaction between practitioners and researchers is increased. As noted in Chapter 1, the emergence of the Natural Hazards Research and Applications Information Center (Boulder, Colorado) has pushed this development a great deal. So too has the use of advisory committees by many researchers. Additionally, the types of forums sponsored by the Senior Executive Policy Center at the Federal Emergency Management Agency's National Emergency Training Center (Emmitsburg, Maryland) provide another complementary direction. But additional mechanisms are required, as is a broader range of participation by the research community.

Opportunities for Policy and Application

During November, 1983, forty top-level policy makers from a broad spectrum of backgrounds—the private and voluntary sector; universities; federal, state, and local governments; and national public interest organizations—specified ten key policy issues in emergency management (Senior Executive Policy Center, 1984). Others might have produced a somewhat different mix, but certainly these issue areas reflect a significant portion of the challenges confronting any interested in emergency management. As such, these issue areas designate the broad contours into which future researchers must translate their work. Policy decisions are made daily by practitioners working at varied levels of government and in the private sector; scientifically based research will allow for more informed judgment.

The ten policy issue areas highlighted by this conference dealt with: liability, intergovernmental relationships, news media, management techniques, hazardous materials, nuclear facilities, public support, researcher–practitioneer interchange, disaster recovery fundings, and use of volunteers. Of course, each of these issue areas contains numerous more specific questions denoting both policy and research needs.

These areas overlapped somewhat with a series of issues that I presented in an opening address to these conferees. Cutting across all disaster phases I designated the following research areas as being top priorities for today's policy needs.

1. Integrated disaster loss data base
2. Training for and certification of emergency managers
3. Funding for integrated community warning systems
4. Liability for evacuation or not
5. Good Samaritan legislation
6. Mental health needs of first responders
7. Post-event mitigation efforts
8. Nuclear war as a planning problem
9. From flood to all-hazard insurance. (Adapted from Drabek, 1984:11–18.)

Shifting the level of abstraction, just a little lower on a couple of topics, brings us close to a project level. For example, within the training area, one topic that merits much attention is the use of simulation. Currently, selected local governments are testing their response capabilities through participation in rather elaborate simulation exercises conducted at the Emergency Management Institute—a component of FEMA's National Emergency Training Center. Rarely, however, are these experiences used for more basic research purposes. Such simulations, however, will reach only a small fragment of the potential clientele using only this single mode of delivery. A wide range of options, many of which can be transported to the field, must be developed. Research regarding the design, duration, frequency of repeat, and so on, is critical.

Similarly, the two major experiments in disaster policy require a series of assessments of their component parts—both short- and long-term impacts. The National Flood Insurance Program, like the Disaster Assistance Program, is complex and changing. Neither the individual nor the public assistance efforts have been examined by researchers who are external to the agency administration. As the NFIP is reoriented so as to shift greater portions of the cost to those electing to accept the risk of flood damage, the overall impact must be assessed. So too the interdependence between these two policy tools must be evaluated more precisely as must recent efforts at post-disaster mitigation requirements.

Additionally, the growing use of various technologies, including microcomputer adoption by emergency managers and satellite-based communications, opens an entire array of research issues (Congressional Research Service, 1984). During all four disaster phases, such technologies have widespread potential. Yet, little is known regarding their rate of adoption, use pattern, implementation difficulties, or organizational impacts. What policy changes will expanded use of these technologies produce in the years ahead?

Turning to a totally different topic—evacuation—the work reviewed in Chapter 4 regarding community evacuation highlighted another glaring need. Review of studies completed to date, plus a series of carefully designed cross-event assessments, could produce an evacuation-shelter estimation tool. Given values on a relatively small number of criteria, plus existent baseline population and land-use data, a local manager could obtain rather precise estimates of the sheltering requirements a specific event would entail. If programmed within a microcomputer, such a formula could be rather sophisticated, although the input data required at the time of decision-making need not be so. Welcome to the emergency management scene of the 1990s.

Candidates for Model Building

Another way to view the progress of the past decade is through an examination of theory development. In several topical areas, the state of information has changed dramatically. Studies have progressed from exploratory case histories to more focused surveys and beyond to multivariate formulations. Today there are several topics that are prime candidates for rigorous model-testing research designs of at least a quasi-experimental nature.

Among these, the following four illustrate the range of opportunities awaiting future researchers:

1. family evacuation behavior (see Chapter 4, Section IIC2)
2. post-event family adjustments (see Chapter 7, Section IIF3)
3. hazard insurance purchases (see Chapter 9, Section IH2)
4. community adoption of hazard mitigation (see Chapter 9, Section IVH2)

Of course, there are many other areas that are about at this stage of development, but these four illustrate the growth in theory construction that the past decade has produced. As such, they add another dimension to the way in which disaster research is at a critical intersection—it truly is a strategic research site.

Areas Requiring Exploration

Complementing a review of research concentrations, it is important to examine the holes. That is, which areas within the total spectrum of disaster phases and system levels have remained relatively ignored?

Throughout the text, I pinpointed numerous areas that had yet to be explored; these were very specific—some nearly at the project level. But let's be clear here. These are not necessarily topics that should be viewed as top priority for future funding. Indeed, building on the work to date by pushing further into the types of areas identified in the previous two sections strikes me as being equally important. Some of both is needed. The issue of criteria and a range of sociological topics, including extensive rationale for their priority designation, were summarized in a chapter prepared (Drabek, 1983c) as part of the multidisciplinary assessment of research needs on flooding (Changnon *et al.,* 1983).

With this clarification aside, what general research areas require exploratory study in the coming decade? The following listing highlights the major holes in our knowledge base as of 1985.

1. *Preparedness:*
   A. Family disaster planning activities.
   B. Cross-societal comparisons and analyses of international systems of disaster planning.
   C. Comparative analyses of organizational, societal, and international disaster warning systems.
2. *Response:*
   A. Cross-societal and comparative organizational studies of evacuation behavior, especially within private sector organizations.
   B. Uses and impacts of new technologies ranging from microcomputers to satellite communications.
   C. Cross-societal and international system responses during the emergency period.
3. *Recovery:*
   A. Cross-societal comparisons of reconstruction.
4. *Mitigation:*
   A. Group adoption of hazard adjustments, e.g., dynamics of family decision making regarding flood and earthquake insurance.
   B. Longitudinal and comparative study of community hazard policy formulation processes, especially within a multihazard perspective.
   C. Cross-societal analyses of hazard perception.

This is not to say that no work has been completed on any topic within these broad study areas. There are studies that are relevant to all of them. But in comparison to other niches within the conceptual framework, these areas are the least developed.

Payoffs for Sociological Theory

Disaster research is at a strategic intersection among several dimensions—public policy, user applications, and middle range theories. While we must do much more to articulate the shorter-term utility of policy and user applications, shifting our metric from decade to century underscores the more fundamental expectation—the real sociological promise. Only recently has disaster research emerged in some quarters as an identifiable specialty area within sociology—a topic that many still consider as bordering on the trivial. And lodged within the full spectrum of the social sciences, efforts at keeping the area locked within the structures of this single discipline are ill-advised at best, doomed to failure at worst. Expanded work in social geography—a legacy that parallels the evolutionary progress in sociology—is but one source of challenge. As I stressed in Chapter 1, every social science discipline—plus more practitioner-oriented areas like public administration—have now discovered disaster and hazards research. Under the rubric of "emergency management," entire new directions for application will emerge during the next decade.

Some developments, of course, probably will parallel previous intellectual and administrative fads—recall the growth cycle of criminal justice programs. But despite such short-term excesses, many scholars across all divisions of the social sciences are recognizing the unique opportunities for theory development that disaster studies permit. Thus, over the next several decades it will be through the fundamental strengthening of the theoretical cores of the various social science disciplines that disaster research will make its greatest contribution.

A forthcoming collection of essays edited by Dynes and Pelanda (in press) will provide elaboration on this theme. But as my final observation regarding disaster studies as a strategic research site, let's briefly examine two notions: (1) disasters as social laboratories and (2) disasters as social phenomena. From the standpoint of theory development, both orientations permit illustration of the potential—the promise for the future.

Disaster events represent unique laboratories; they are in this sense ethically acceptable natural experiments. For example, organizational theorists interested in basic questions of technological innovations—adoption, implementation, and impact—can find innumerable laboratories in disaster-relevant organizations. Community change specialists, like those who select total societies for analysis, could better test their current theories by invoking quasi-experimental designs of a longitudinal nature.

Populations of communities, like societies, could provide ongoing experiments wherein basic social processes could be dissected. Family sociologists, social psychologists, industrial and military sociologists, like those focused on schools, churches, and other institutional areas, could identify research opportunities permitted by disaster events. Thus, disasters present unique research opportunities to nearly all specialty areas within sociology if they are viewed as social laboratories.

Conceptualized at the higher level of abstraction, human system responses to stress can be dissected with precision and replicated under reasonably controlled conditions. The system level studied can vary from individuals to families or entire societies. Differential adaptations that emerge over the months following a tornado must be contrasted to those evoked by other stressors, be they spouses missing in action during a military conflict or what have you. Disaster events have and will continue to contribute to an emerging theory of human system responses to stress—both individual and collective.

Going beyond this "disaster as stress" orientation, Kreps (1985) has clarified the taxonomic problem in disaster research as a generalized problem in classical sociological theory. As progress is made in solving the problem here, the payoff for sociological theory generally may be of indefinable impact. His progress toward a taxonomy of emergent forms of association that characterize disaster responses illustrates a new conceptualization of structural sociology that integrates and extends the classical theories of Durkheim, Weber, Marx, Mead, and others.

In contrast to a view of disasters as social laboratories—settings wherein specialists pursue their unique research agenda—I propose that disasters also be viewed as distinctive social phenomena. As such, they constitute a legitimate topic of study in and of their own. At the application level, in contrast, there will emerge more curricular developments within a wide variety of formats and institutional settings under such labels as "emergency management." Within many social science departments, especially geography and sociology, the past decade has witnessed formal course offerings carrying such titles as "Hazard and Disaster Research" and "Community Responses to Natural Disasters."

As a research area viewed from a sociological vantage point, however, disasters represent types of uncertainties that display elementary forms of social process and structure. Thus, independent of tests of organizational or community theory *per se,* we must seek to build on the past efforts of sociologists like Fritz, Dynes, and Quarantelli, and integrate their insights with those of social geographers like White, Kates, and Burton. How do societies, and all of their attendant subsystems, respond to the hazards they confront? A theory of societal response thus becomes the major challenge of the future. And as Hewitt (1983) has stressed so pointedly, "response" includes mitigation actions, not just post-event assessments. The entire developmental cycle must be viewed as the object of study.

As such, it demonstrates the true promise of disaster research. Thus, the presence and clarity of this goal—that is, the formulation of an empirically verifiable theory of societal response to disaster wherein ranges of generalization for each of its component models are specified precisely through a taxonomic schema—is the most important manifestation of the strategic location of disaster as a research site.

Master Bibliography

Abe, Kitao [1981] "On Evacuation III." *Psychology* **12** (March):72–77.*

Abe, Kitao [1978] "Levels of Trust and Reactions to Various Sources of Information in Catastrophic Situations." Pp. 147–158 in *Disasters: Theory and Research,* E. L. Quarantelli (ed.). Beverly Hills, California: Sage.

Abe, Kitao [1976] "The Behavior of Survivors and Victims in a Japanese Nightclub Fire: A Descriptive Research Note." *Mass Emergencies* 1:119–124.

Abe, Kitao [1972] "Rumor Analysis in the Niigata Earthquake." Pp. 166–174 in *Proceedings of the Japan–United States Disaster Research Seminar: Organizational and Community Responses to Disasters.* Columbus, Ohio: Disaster Research Center, The Ohio State University.

Abe, Kitao [n.d.] "Social Disorder in a Disaster (Saigaiji-no Shakaiteki Knoran)."*

Abe, Kitao, and Ryoichi Kazama [1979] "Human Responses in Crises—A Social Psychological Analysis of the Izu-Oshima Kinkai Earthquake and Rumor (Kiki Bamen Ni Okeru Ningen No Hanno—Izu-Oshima Kinkai Jishin narabini Yoshin-Joho Dema no Shakai Shinrigakuteki Bunseki)." *Tokyo Gaikokugo Daigaku Ronshu* 29:211–234.*

Abe, Kitao, and Ryoichi Kazama [1978] "Social Psychological Research on the Influence of the Prediction of the So-called Kawasaki Earthquake (Iwayuru Kawasaki Chokka-Gata Jishin Yochi Joho no Shakai-Shinrigakuteki Telli)." *Tokyo Gaikokugo Daigaku Ronshu* 28:168–197.*

Abney, F. Glenn, and Larry B. Hill [1966] "Natural Disasters as a Political Variable: The Effect of a Hurricane on an Urban Election." *The American Political Science Review* **60** (December):974–981.

---

*Denotes a reference which was reviewed on the basis of a summary published in Yasumasa Yamamoto and E. L. Quarantelli, *Inventory of the Japanese Disaster Research Literature in the Social and Behavioral Sciences.* Columbus, Ohio: Disaster Research Center, The Ohio State University, 1982.

Abrahams, M.J., J. Price, F.A. Whitlock, and G. Williams [1976] "The Brisbane Floods, January 1974: Their Impact on Health." *The Medical Journal of Australia* **2** (December):936–939.

Abram, Harry S. (ed.) [1970] *Psychological Aspects of Stress.* Springfield, Illinois: Charles C. Thomas.

Adams, David S. [1977] "Policies, Programs, and Problems of the Local Red Cross Disaster Relief in the 1960s." The Disaster Research Center Historical and Comparative Disaster Series, No. 4. Columbus, Ohio: Disaster Research Center, The Ohio State University.

Adams, David S. [1970a] "Goal and Structural Succession in a Voluntary Association: A Constructed Type of the American Red Cross." Dissertation. Columbus, Ohio: The Ohio State University.

Adams, David S. [1970b] "The Red Cross: Organizational Sources of Operational Problems." *American Behavioral Scientist* **13** (January–February):392–403.

Aguirre, Benigno [1983] "Evacuation as Population Mobility." *International Journal of Mass Emergencies and Disasters* **1** (November):415–437.

Aguirre, Benigno [1976] "Problems of Method in the Development of Propositional Inventories in the Field of Disaster Research." Columbus, Ohio: Disaster Research Center, The Ohio State University.

Ahearn, Federico, and Simeón Rizo Castellón [1979] "Problemas de Salud Mental después de una Situación de Desastre" (Mental Health Problems Following a Disaster Situation) (in Spanish). *Acta Psiquiátrica y Psicológica de América Latina* **25** (March):58–68.

Ahearn, Federico, and Simeón Rizo Castellón [1978] "Problemas de Salud Mental después de una Situación de Desastre" (Mental Health Problems Following a Disaster Situation) (in Spanish). *Boletín de la Oficina Sanitaria Panamericana* **85** (July):1–15.

Ahearn, Frederick L., Jr. [1981] "Disaster Mental-Health—A Pre-Earthquake and Post-Earthquake Comparison of Psychiatric Admission Rates." *Urban and Social Change Review* **14** (Summer):22–28.

Akimoto, Ritsuo [1972] "Power Structure of Local Government in Emergencies." Pp. 196–207 in *Proceedings of the Japan–United States Disaster Research Seminar: Organizational and Community Responses to Disasters.* Columbus, Ohio: Disaster Research Center, The Ohio State University.

Akimoto, Ritsuo, and Hideaki Ohta [1980] *City In Disasters: Toshi to Saigai* (in Japanese). Tokyo: Gakubunsha.

Alexander, David [1980] "The Florence Floods—What the Papers Said." *Environmental Management* **4** (January):27–34.

Alldred, Suzanne, Robert Hiscott, and Joseph Scanlon [1982] "May Day at St. Joseph's: Fire and Evacuation at a Major City Hospital." Ottawa, Ontario, Canada: Emergency Communications Research Unit, Carleton University.

Anderson, Carl R. [1977] "Locus of Control, Coping Behaviors, and Performance in a Stress Setting: A Longitudinal Study." *Journal of Applied Psychology* **62** (August):446–451.

Anderson, Carl R., Don Hellriegel, and John W. Slocum, Jr. [1977] "Managerial Response to Environmentally Induced Stress." *Academy of Management Journal* **20** (No. 2):260–272.

Anderson, Jon W. [1968] "Cultural Adaptation to Threatened Disaster." *Human Organization* **27** (Winter):298–307.

Anderson, William A. [1972] "DRC Studies of Organizational Change." Pp. 74–88 in *Proceedings of the Japan–United States Disaster Research Seminar.* Columbus, Ohio: Disaster Research Center, The Ohio State University.

Anderson, William A. [1970a] "Disaster and Organizational Change in Anchorage." Pp. 96–115 in *The Great Alaska Earthquake of 1964: Human Ecology* Committee on the Alaska Earthquake of the National Research Council (ed.). Washington, D.C.: National Academy of Sciences.

Anderson, William A. [1970b] "Military Organizations in Natural Disaster: Established and Emergent Norms." *American Behavioral Scientist* 13 (January-February):415–422.

Anderson, William A. [1970c] "Tsunami Warning in Crescent City, California and Hilo, Hawaii." Pp. 116–124 in *The Great Alaska Earthquake of 1964: Human Ecology,* Committee on the Alaska Earthquake of the National Research Council (ed.). Washington, D.C.: National Academy of Sciences.

Anderson, William A. [1969a] "Disaster Warning and Communication Processes in Two Communities." *The Journal of Communication* 19 (June):92–104.

Anderson, William A. [1969b] "Social Structure and the Role of the Military in Natural Disaster." *Sociology and Social Research* 53 (January):242–252.

Anderson, William A. [1969c] *Local Civil Defense in Natural Disaster: From Office to Organization.* Columbus, Ohio: Disaster Research Center, The Ohio State University.

Anderson, William A. [1965] "Some Observations on a Disaster Sub-Culture: The Organizational Response to the 1964 Flood." Research Note 6. Columbus, Ohio: Disaster Research Center, The Ohio State University.

Anderson, William A., and Russell R. Dynes [1976] "Civil Disturbances and Social Change—A Comparative Analysis of the United States and Curaçao." *Urban Affairs Quarterly* 12 (No. 1):37–56.

Anderson, William A., and Russell R. Dynes [1975] *Social Movements, Violence and Change: The May Movement in Curaçao.* Columbus, Ohio: The Ohio State University Press.

Anderson, William A., Russell R. Dynes, and E. L. Quarantelli [1974] "Urban Counterrioters." *Society* 11 (March/April):50–55.

Angotti, Thomas [1977] "Playing Politics with Disaster: The Earthquakes of Friuli and Belice (Italy)." *International Journal of Urban and Regional Research* 1:327–331.

Bahr, Howard M., and Carol D. Harvey [1979] "Correlates of Loneliness among Widows Bereaved in a Mining Disaster." *Psychological Reports* 44 (April):367–385.

Baisden, Barbara [1979a] "Crisis Intervention in Smaller Communities." Pp. 325–332 in *The Small City and Regional Community, Proceedings of the Second Conference,* E. J. Miller and R. P. Wolensky (eds.). Stevens Point, Wisconsin: Foundation Press, Inc., University of Wisconsin.

Baisden, Barbara [1979b] "Social Factors Affecting Mental Health Delivery: The Case of Disasters." Pp. 238–241 in *Sociological Research Symposium IX,* E. P. Lewis, L. D. Nelson, D. H. Scully, and J. S. Williams (eds.). Richmond, Virginia: Department of Sociology, Virginia Commonwealth University.

Baisden, Barbara, and E. L. Quarantelli [1981] "The Delivery of Mental Health Services in Community Disaster: An Outline of Research Findings." *Journal of Community Psychology* 9 (July):195–203.

Baisden, Barbara, and E. L. Quarantelli [1979] "The Recovery Period in U.S. Disasters: Problems and Opportunities." In *Proceedings: National Public Policy Forum for Disaster Relief*. Racine, Wisconsin: National Voluntary Organizations Active in Disasters. (Disaster Research Center Reprint No. 127).

Baker, Earl J. [1979] "Predicting Response to Hurricane Warnings: A Reanalysis of Data from Four Studies." *Mass Emergencies* 4:9–24.

Baker, Earl J., and Joe Gordon McPhee [1975] *Land Use Management and Regulation in Hazardous Areas: A Research Assessment*. Boulder, Colorado: Institute of Behavioral Science, The University of Colorado.

Baker, Earl J., and Donald J. Patton [1974] "Attitudes Toward Hurricane Hazard on the Gulf Coast." Pp. 30–36 in *Natural Hazards: Local, National, Global*, Gilbert F. White (ed.). New York: Oxford University Press.

Baker, George W., and Dwight W. Chapman (eds.) [1962] *Man and Society in Disaster*. New York: Basic Books.

Baker, Randall [1977] "The Sahel: An Information Crisis." *Disasters* 1 (No. 1):13–22.

Barbina, Guido [1979] "The Friuli Earthquake as an Agent of Social Change in a Rural Area." *Mass Emergencies* 4:145–149.

Bardo, John W. [1978] "Organizational Response to Disaster: A Typology of Adaptation and Change." *Mass Emergencies* 3:87–104.

Barkun, Michael [1977] "Disaster in History." *Mass Emergencies* 2:219–231.

Barkun, Michael [1974] *Disaster and the Millennium*. New Haven and London: Yale University Press.

Bartlett, Glen S., Peter S. Houts, Linda K. Byrnes, and Robert W. Miller [1983] "The Near Disaster at Three Mile Island." *International Journal of Mass Emergencies and Disasters* 1 (March):19–42.

Barton, Allen H. [1969] *Communities in Disaster: A Sociological Analysis of Collective Stress Situations*. Garden City, New York: Doubleday and Company, Inc.

Barton, Allen H. [1962] "The Emergency Social System." Pp. 222–267 in *Man and Society in Disaster*, George W. Baker and Dwight W. Chapman (eds.). New York: Basic Books.

Bates, Frederick L. [1982a] "Methodological and Theoretical Problems in Cross-Cultural Field Research Related to Disasters." A paper presented at the Tenth World Congress of Sociology, Mexico City, Mexico, August.

Bates, Frederick L. [1974] "Alternative Models for the Future of Society: From the Invisible to the Visible Hand." *Social Forces* 53 (September):1–11.

Bates, Frederick L. (ed.) [1982b] "Recovery, Change and Development: A Longitudinal Study of the Guatemalan Earthquake." Athens, Georgia: Guatemalan Earthquake Study, University of Georgia.

Bates, Frederick L., W. Timothy Farrell, and JoAnn K. Glittenberg [1979] "Some Changes in Housing Characteristics in Guatemala Following the February 1976 Earthquake and Their Implications for Future Earthquake Vulnerability." *Mass Emergencies* 4:121–133.

Bates, Frederick L., Charles W. Fogleman, Vernon J. Parenton, Robert H. Pittman, and George S. Tracy [1963] "The Social and Psychological Consequences of a Natural Disaster." National Research Council Disaster Study 18. Washington, D.C.: National Academy of Sciences.

Battisti, Francesco [1978a] "Disasters and Social Change in Italy." A paper presented at the 9th World Congress of Sociology, Uppsala, Sweden, August.

Battisti, Francesco [1978b] "Some Conditions for the Social Perception of Pollution in Environmental Disasters." *Mass Emergencies* 3:201–207.

Baumann, Duane D., and John H. Sims [1978] "Flood Insurance: Some Determinants of Adoption." *Economic Geography* 54 (July):189–196.

Baumann, Duane D., and John H. Sims [1974] "Human Response to the Hurricane." Pp. 25–30 in *Natural Hazards: Local, National, Global,* Gilbert F. White (ed.). New York: Oxford University Press.

B'Chir, Mongi [1972] "Le Phénomène 'Gourbiville' dans les Villes Moyennes en Tunisie" (The Shanty-Town Phenomenon in the Middle-Sized Towns of Tunisia) (in French). *Revue Tunisienne de Sciences Sociales* 9:30–31, 139–150.

Beinin, L. [1981] "An Examination of Health Data Following Two Major Earthquakes in Russia." *Disasters* 5 (No. 2):142–146

Belardo, Salvatore, Kirk R. Karwan, and William A. Wallace [1984] "Managing the Response to Disasters Using Microcomputers." *Interfaces* 14 (March-April):29–39.

Belardo, Salvatore, Harold L. Pazer, William A. Wallace, and William D. Danko [1983] "Simulation of a Crisis Management Information Network: A Serendipitous Evaluation." *Decision Sciences* 14 (Fall):588–606.

Bell, Bill D. [1978] "Disaster Impact and Response: Overcoming the Thousand Natural Shocks." *The Gerontologist* 18 (December):531–540.

Bell, Bill D., Gail Kara, and Constance Batterson [1978] "Service Utilization and Adjustment Patterns of Elderly Tornado Victims in an American Disaster." *Mass Emergencies* 3:71–81.

Berberian, Manuel [1979] "Tabas-E-Golshan (Iran) Catastrophic Earthquake of 16 September 1978; A Preliminary Field Report." *Disasters* 2 (No. 4):207–219.

Bernert, Eleanor H., and Fred C. Iklé [1952] "Evacuation and the Cohesion of Urban Groups." *American Journal of Sociology* 58 (September):133–138.

Berren, Michael R., Allan Beigel, and Stuart Ghertner [1980] "A Typology for the Classification of Disasters." *Community Mental Health Journal* 16 (Summer):103–120.

Beyer, Jacquelyn L. [1974] "Global Summary of Human Response to Natural Hazards: Floods." Pp. 265–274 in *Natural Hazards: Local, National, Global,* Gilbert F. White (ed.). New York: Oxford University Press.

Birnbaum, Freda, J. Coplon and I. Scharff [1973] "Crisis Intervention after a Natural Disaster." *Social Casework* 54 (November):545–551.

Bjorklund, Birgitta [1981] *Skredet I Tuve: Familjen och Dess Bostadssituation* (in Swedish with an English summary). Disaster Studies 13. Uppsala, Sweden: Department of Sociology, Uppsala University.

Blanshan, Sue A. [1978] "A Time Model: Hospital Organizational Response to Disaster." Pp. 173–198 in *Disasters: Theory and Research,* E. L. Quarantelli (ed.). Beverly Hills, California: Sage.

Blanshan, Sue A. [1977] "Disaster Body Handling." *Mass Emergencies* 2:249–258.

Blanshan, Sue, and E. L. Quarantelli [1979] "From Dead Body to Person: The Handling of Fatal Mass Casualties in Disasters." (Preliminary Paper). Columbus, Ohio: Disaster Research Center, The Ohio State University.

Blaufarb, Herbert, and Jules Levine [1972] "Crisis Intervention in an Earthquake." *Social Work* **17** (July):16–19.

Blumer, Herbert [1939] *An Appraisal of Thomas and Znaniecki's "The Polish Peasant in Europe and America."* Bulletin 44. New York: Social Science Research Council.

Blundell, D. J. [1977] "Living With Earthquakes." *Disasters* **1** (No. 1):41–46.

Boileau, A. M., B. Cattarinussi, G. Delli Zotti, C. Pelanda, R. Strassoldo, and B. Tellia [1978] *Friuli: La Prova del Terremoto* (in Italian). Milan, Italy: Franco Angeli.

Bolin, Robert C. [1985] "Disasters and Long-Term Recovery Policy: A Focus on Housing and Families." *Policy Studies Review* **4** (May):709–715.

Bolin, Robert C. [1982] *Long-Term Family Recovery from Disaster.* Boulder, Colorado: Institute of Behavioral Science, The University of Colorado.

Bolin, Robert C. [1976] "Family Recovery from Natural Disaster: A Preliminary Model." *Mass Emergencies* **1**:267–277.

Bolin, Robert C., and Patricia A. Bolton [1983] "Recovery in Nicaragua and the U.S.A." *International Journal of Mass Emergencies and Disasters* **1** (March): 125–152.

Bolin, Robert C., and Daniel J. Klenow [1982–83] "Response of the Elderly to Disaster: An Age-Stratified Analysis." *International Journal of Aging and Human Development* **16** (No. 4):283–296.

Bolin, Robert C., and Patricia C. Trainer [1978] "Modes of Family Recovery Following Disaster: A Cross-National Study." Pp. 233–247 in *Disasters: Theory and Research*, E. L. Quarantelli (ed.). Beverly Hills, California: Sage.

Bollag, Ueli [1979] "Practical Evaluation of a Pilot Immunization Campaign Against Typhoid Fever in a Cambodian Refugee Camp." *Disasters* **3** (No. 4):413–415.

Boss, Pauline Grossenbacher [1983] "Family Separation and Boundary Ambiguity." *International Journal of Mass Emergencies and Disasters* **1** (March):63–72.

Bourque, Linda Brookover, Andrew Cherlin, and Leo G. Reeder [1976] "Agencies and the Los Angeles Earthquake." *Mass Emergencies* **1**:217-228.

Bourque, Linda Brookover, Leo G. Reeder, Andrew Cherlin, Bertram H. Raven, and D. Michael Walton [1973] "The Unpredictable Disaster in a Metropolis: Public Response to the Los Angeles Earthquake of February, 1971." Los Angeles: Survey Research Center, University of California, Los Angeles.

Bowden, Martyn J., David Pijawka, Gary S. Roboff, Kenneth J. Gelman, and Daniel Amaral [1977] "Reestablishing Homes and Jobs: Cities" Pp. 69–145 in *Reconstruction Following Disaster*, J. Eugene Haas, Robert W. Kates, and Martyn J. Bowden (eds.). Cambridge, Massachusetts, and London: The MIT Press.

Boyd, S.T. [1981] "Psychological Reactions of Disaster Victims." *South African Medical Journal* **60** (No. 19):744–748.

Bresenhan, Thomas P. [1968] "Strategy and Techniques to Accelerate the Reduction of Flood Hazards at Mobile Home Parks." *The Pennsylvania Geographer* **16** (December):11–18.

Breznitz, Sholomo [1984] *Cry Wolf: The Psychology of False Alarms.* Hillsdale, New Jersey, and London: Lawrence Erlbaum Associates, Publishers.

Brinkmann, Waltraud A. R. [1975] *Local Windstorm Hazard in the United States:*

A Research Assessment. Boulder, Colorado: Institute of Behavioral Science. The University of Colorado.

Brinkmann, Waltraud A. R. in collaboration with Paul C. Huszar, Earl J. Baker, Duane D. Baumann and John H. Sims [1975] *Hurricane Hazard in the United States: A Research Assessment.* Boulder, Colorado: Institute of Behavioral Science, The University of Colorado.

Brinkmann, Waltraud A. R. in collaboration with Duane D. Baumann, E. M. Beck, Sigmund W. Krane, Allen H. Murphy, John H. Sims, and Hazel J. Visvader [1975] *Severe Local Storm Hazard in the United States: A Research Assessment.* Boulder, Colorado: Institute of Behavioral Science, The University of Colorado.

Britton, Neil R. [1983] *The Bushfires in Tasmania, February 1982: How the Disaster Relevant Organizations Responded.* Disaster Investigation Report No. 6. Townsville, Queensland, Australia: Centre for Disaster Studies, James Cook University of North Queensland.

Britton, Neil R. [1981a] *Darwin's Cyclone 'Max': An Exploratory Investigation of a Natural Hazard Sequence on the Development of a Disaster Subculture.* Disaster Investigation Report No. 4. Townsville, Queensland, Australia: Centre for Disaster Studies, James Cook University of North Queensland.

Britton, Neil R. [1981b] "What Have New Zealanders Learnt from Earthquake Disasters in Their Own Country?" *Disasters* 5 (No. 4):384–390.

Britton, Neil R. [1981c] "What Have New Zealanders Learnt from Earthquake Disasters in Their Country?" Pp. 191–195 in *Large Earthquakes in New Zealand: Anticipation, Precaution, Reconstruction.* Wellington, New Zealand: The Royal Society of New Zealand Miscellaneous Series 5.

Britton, Neil R. [1978] "The Social Implications of Earthquake Predictions and Warnings On and For Organisations." *Bulletin of the New Zealand National Society for Earthquake Engineering* 11 (March):15–18.

Britton, Neil, G.E. Kearney, and K. A. Britton [1983] "Disaster Response: The Perception of the Threat and Its Influence on Community Decision on Insurance. Pp. 260–332 in *Insurance and Natural Disaster Management:* Papers presented at a seminar, Townsville, July 1983, John Oliver (ed.). Townsville, Queensland, Australia: Centre For Disaster Studies, James Cook University of North Queensland.

Bromet, Evelyn, and Leslie Dunn [1981] "Mental Health of Mothers Nine Months After the Three Mile Island Accident." *The Urban and Social Change Review* 14 (Summer):12–15.

Brouillette, John Robert [1971] "Community Organizations Under Stress: A Study of Interorganizational Communication Networks During Natural Disasters." Dissertation. Columbus, Ohio: The Ohio State University.

Brouillette, John Robert [1970] "The Department of Public Works: Adaptation to Disaster Demands." *American Behavioral Scientist* 13 (January–February):369–379.

Brouillette, John Robert, and E. L. Quarantelli [1971] "Types of Patterned Variation in Bureaucratic Adaptations to Organizational Stress." *The Sociological Quarterly* 41 (Winter):39–46.

Brown, Barbara J. [1979] *Disaster Preparedness and the United Nations: Advanced Planning for Disaster Relief.* New York: Pergamon Press.

Brown, Barbara J. [1977] "The United Nations and Disaster Relief in the Sahel, 1973–75." *Disasters* **1** (No. 2):145–150.

Brown, Barbara J., Janet C. Tuthill, and E. Thomas Rowe [1976] "International Disaster Response: The Sahelian Experience." Denver, Colorado: Graduate School of International Studies, University of Denver.

Brownstone, Jane, Elizabeth C. Penick, Stephen W. Larcen, Barbara J. Powell, and Ann F. Nord [1977] "Disaster-Relief Training and Mental Health." *Hospital and Community Psychiatry* **28** (January):30–32.

Bruning, James L. [1964] "Leadership in Disaster." *Psychology* **1** (No. 4):19–23.

Bruvold, William H. [1979] "Residential Response to Urban Drought in Central California." *Water Resources Research* **15** (December):1297–1304.

Bryan, John L. [1983] *Implications for Codes and Behavior Models from the Analysis of Behavior Response Patterns in Fire Situations As Selected from the Project People and Project People II Study Programs.* Washington, D.C.: U.S. Department of Commerce, National Bureau of Standards, Center for Fire Research, and U.S. Department of Health and Human Services.

Bucher, Rue [1957] "Blame and Hostility in Disaster." *American Journal of Sociology* **62** (March):467–475.

Burby, Raymond J., and Steven P. French [1981] "Coping with Floods: The Land Use Management Paradox." *Journal of the American Planning Association* **46** (July):289–300.

Burby, Raymond J., and Steven P. French [1980] "The U.S. Experience in Managing Flood Plain Land Use." *Disasters* **4** (No. 4):451–457.

Burke, Jack D., Jr., Jonathan F. Borus, Barbara J. Burns, Kathleen Hannigan Millstein, and Mary C. Beasley [1982] "Changes in Children's Behavior after a Natural Disaster." *American Journal of Psychiatry* **139** (August):1010–1014.

Burton, Ian [1962] "Types of Agricultural Occupance of Flood Plains in the United States." Dissertation. Department of Geography Research Paper #75. Chicago: University of Chicago.

Burton, Ian, C.D. Fowle, and R.S. McCullough (eds.) [1982] *Living with Risk: Environmental Risk Management in Canada.* Toronto: Institute for Environmental Studies, University of Toronto.

Burton, Ian, and Robert W. Kates [1964] "The Perception of Natural Hazards in Resource Management." *Natural Resources Journal* **3**:412-441.

Burton, Ian, Robert W. Kates, R. Mather, and R.E. Snead [1965] "The Shores of Megalopolis: Coastal Occupance and Human Adjustment to Flood Hazard." *Climatology* **18** (No. 3):3-17. Elmer, New Jersey: C.W. Thornthwaite Associates Laboratory of Climatology.

Burton, Ian, Robert W. Kates, and Gilbert F. White [1978] *The Environment as Hazard.* New York: Oxford University Press.

Butcher, J. N. [1980] "The Role of Crisis Intervention in an Airport Disaster Plan." *Aviation, Space, and Environmental Medicine* **51** (November):1260–1262.

Butler, J. R. G., and D. P. Doessel [1981] "Efficiency and Equity in Natural Disaster Relief." *Public Finance* **36** (No. 2):193–213.

Butler, J. R. G., and D. P. Doessel [1980] "Who Bears the Costs of Natural Disasters?— An Australian Case Study." *Disasters* **4** (No. 2):187–204.

Butler, J. R. G., and D. P. Doessel [1979] *The Economics of Natural Disaster Relief in Australia.* Canberra: Centre for Research on Federal Financial Relations, The Australian National University.

Butler, John E. [1976] *Natural Disasters*. Richmond, Victoria, Australia: Heinemann Educational Australia.

Caldwell, Nick, Andrew Clark, Des Clayton, Kuldip Malhotra, and Dag Reiner [1979] "An Analysis of Indian Press Coverage of the Andhra Pradesh Cyclone Disaster of 19 November 1977." *Disasters* 3 (No. 2):154–168.

Carlton, Thomas G. [1980] "Early Psychiatric Intervention Following a Maritime Disaster." *Military Medicine* 145 (No. 2):114–116.

Carr, Lowell [1932] "Disaster and the Sequence-Pattern Concept of Social Change." *American Journal of Sociology* 38:207-218.

Carter, T. Michael [1980] "Community Warning Systems: The Relationships among the Broadcast Media, Emergency Service Agencies, and the National Weather Service." Pp. 214–228 in *Disasters and the Mass Media: Proceedings of the Committee on Disasters and the Mass Media Workshop, February, 1979*, Committee on Disasters and the Mass Media. Washington, D.C.: National Academy of Sciences.

Carter, T. Michael, Stephanie Kendall, and John P. Clark [1983] "Household Response to Warnings." *International Journal of Mass Emergencies and Disasters* 1 (March):95–104.

Cattarinussi, Bernardo [1978] "Some Findings on Social Behavior after the Friuli Earthquake." A paper presented at the 9th World Congress of Sociology, Uppsala, Sweden, August.

Cattarinussi, Bernardo, C. Pelanda, A. Moretti, in collaboration with M. Strassoldo, R. Strassoldo, and B. Tellia [1981] *Il Disastro: Effetti di Lungo Termine— Indagine Psicosociologica Nelle Aree Colpite dal Terremoto del Friuli*. (The Disaster: Long-Term Effects—Sociopsychological Investigation in Areas Stricken by Friuli Earthquake) (in Italian). Udine, Italy: Editrice Grillo.

Cattarinussi, B., and B. Tellia [1978] "La Risposta Sociale al Disastro: il Caso del Terremoto in Friuli" (Social Response to Disaster: The Friuli Earthquake) (in Italian). *Studi di Sociologia* (April–June):236–254.

Chamberlin, Barbara C. [1980] "Mayo Seminars in Psychiatry: The Psychological Aftermath of Disaster." *Journal of Clinical Psychiatry* 41 (July):238–244.

Chandessais, Charles A. [1980] "The Work of Le Centre d'Etudes Psycho-Sociologiques des Sinistres et de leur Prévention (CEPSP) in France." *Disasters* 4 (No. 2):223–229.

Chandessais, Charles A. [1966] *La Catastrophe de Feyzin* (The Feyzin Catastrophe) (in French). Paris: Centre d'Etudes Psychosociologiques des Sinistres et de Leur Prévention.

Changnon, Stanley A., William C. Ackermann, Gilbert F. White, J. Loreena Ivens, Henry P. Caulfield, Jr., Thomas Drabek, Helmut E. Landsberg, Ray K. Linsley, G. Richard Marzolf, Jerome W. Milliman, William A. Thomas, and Flora Mae Wellings [1983] *A Plan For Research on Floods and Their Mitigation in the United States*. Champaign, Illinois: Illinois State Water Survey.

Cheney, N. P. [1979] "Bushfire Disasters in Australia 1945–1975." Pp. 88–90 in *Natural Hazards in Australia*, R. L. Heathcote and B. G. Thom (eds.). Canberra: Australian Academy of Science.

Christensen, Larry, and Carlton E. Ruch [1980] "The Effect of Social Influence on Response to Hurricane Warnings." *Disasters* 4 (No. 2):205–210.

Christensen, Larry, and Carlton E. Ruch [1978] "Assessment of Brochures &

Radio & Television Presentations on Hurricane Awareness." *Mass Emergencies* 3:209– 216.

Church, June S. [1974] "The Buffalo Creek Disaster: Extent and Range of Emotional and/or Behavioral Problems." *Omega: Journal of Death and Dying* 5 (Spring):61–63.

Ciborowski, Adolf [1967] "Some Aspects of Town Reconstruction (Warsaw and Skopje)." *Impact* 17:31–48.

Ciuca, R., C. S. Downie, and M. Morris [1977] "When a Disaster Happens." *American Journal of Nursing* 77 (March):454–456.

Clason, Christine [1983] "The Family as a Life-Saver in Disaster?" *International Journal of Mass Emergencies and Disasters* 1 (March):43–62.

Clifford, Roy A. [1956] "The Rio Grande Flood: A Comparative Study of Border Communities." National Research Disaster Study #7. Washington, D.C.: National Academy of Sciences.

Cochrane, Harold C. [1975] *Natural Hazards and Their Distributive Effects.* Boulder, Colorado: Institute of Behavioral Science, The University of Colorado.

Cochrane, Harold C., Eve Gruntfest, Marilyn Stokes, Heidi Burgess, Guy Burgess, and Lois Steinbeck [1979] "Flash Flood on the Big Thompson: A Case Study." Denver, Colorado: Western Governor's Policy Office, Institute for Policy Research, February.

Cochrane, Harold C., and Brian A. Knowles with Barbara S. Dunn and David W. Untermann [1975] *Urban Snow Hazard in the United States: A Research Assessment.* Boulder, Colorado: Institute of Behavioral Science, The University of Colorado.

Cohen, Elias S., and S. Walter Poulshock [1977] "Societal Response to Mass Dislocation of the Elderly: Implications for Area Agencies on Aging." *The Gerontologist* 17 (June):262–268.

Cohen, Raquel E., and Frederick L. Ahearn, Jr. [1980] *Handbook for Mental Health Care of Disaster Victims.* Baltimore and London: The Johns Hopkins University Press.

Colson, Elizabeth [1979] "In Good Years and in Bad: Food Strategies of Self-Reliant Societies." *Journal of Anthropological Research* 35 (Spring):18–29.

Columbia Area Mental Health Center [1974] "A Plan for Minimizing Psychiatric Casualties in a Disaster. *Hospital and Community Psychiatry* 25 (October):665–668.

Committee for the Compilation of Materials on Damage Caused by the Atomic Bombs in Hiroshima and Nagasaki [1981] *Hiroshima and Nagasaki: The Physical, Medical, and Social Effects of the Atomic Bombings.* New York: Basic Books.

Committee on Disasters and the Mass Media [1980] *Disasters and the Mass Media: Proceedings of the Committee on Disasters and the Mass Media Workshop, February, 1979.* Washington, D.C.: National Academy of Sciences.

Committee on Earthquake Engineering Research [1982] *Earthquake Engineering Research–1982.* Washington, D.C.: National Academy Press.

Committee on International Disaster Assistance [1979] *Assessing International Disaster Needs.* Washington, D.C.: National Academy of Sciences.

Committee on International Disaster Assistance [1978a] *The Role of Technology in International Assistance.* Washington, D.C.: National Academy of Sciences.

Committee on International Disaster Assistance [1978b] *The U.S. Government*

Foreign Disaster Assistance Program. Washington, D.C.: National Academy of Sciences.

Committee on Natural Disasters [1982] *The Austin, Texas, Flood of May 24–25, 1981*. Washington, D.C.: National Academy Press.

Committee on Socioeconomic Effects of Earthquake Predictions [1978] *A Program of Studies on the Socioeconomic Effects of Earthquake Prediction*. Washington, D.C.: National Academy of Sciences/National Research Council.

Committee on the Alaska Earthquake of the National Research Council (ed.) [1970] *The Great Alaska Earthquake of 1964: Human Ecology* Washington, D.C.: National Academy of Sciences.

Congressional Research Service, Library of Congress [1984] *Information Technology for Emergency Management*. Washington, D.C.: U.S. Government Printing Office.

Copans, Jean [1979] "Droughts, Famines and the Evolution of Senegal (1966–1978)." *Mass Emergencies* **4**:87–93.

Coultrip, Raymond L. [1974] "Medical Aspects of U.S. Disaster Relief Operations in Nicaragua." *Military Medicine* **139** (No. 11):879–883.

Covello, Vincent T. [1983] "The Perception of Technological Risks: A Literature Review." *Technological Forecasting and Social Change* **23**:285–297.

Cowley, R. Adams (ed.) [1979] *Collected Papers in Emergency Medical Services and Traumatology*. Baltimore: University of Maryland, School of Medicine.

Crabbs, Michael A. [1981] "School Mental-Health Services Following an Environmental Disaster." *Journal of School Health* **51** (No. 3):165–167.

Crabbs, Michael A., and Edward Heffron [1981] "Loss Associated With a Natural Disaster." *Personnel and Guidance Journal* **59** (February):378–382.

Crane, Billy G. [1960] "Intergovernmental Relations in Disaster Relief in Texas." Dissertation. Austin, Texas: University of Texas.

Crawford, Fred R. [1957] "Patterns of Family Readjustment to Tornadic Disasters: A Sociological Case Study." Dissertation. Austin, Texas: University of Texas.

Crawshaw, Ralph [1963] "Reactions to a Disaster." *Archives of General Psychiatry* **9** (August):157–162.

Crouch, Peter [1979] "Village Reconstruction in Lebanon." *Disasters* **3** (No. 2):126–129.

Cuny, Frederick C. [1983] *Disasters and Development*. New York: Oxford University Press.

Cuny, Frederick C. [1977] "Refugee Camps and Camp Planning: The State of the Art." *Disasters* **1** (No. 2):125–143.

Dacy, Douglas C., and Howard Kunreuther [1969] *The Economics of Natural Disasters*. New York: The Free Press.

Danzig, Elliott R., Paul W. Thayer, and Lila R. Galanter [1958] "The Effects of a Threatening Rumor on a Disaster-Stricken Community." Disaster Study #10. Disaster Research Group. Washington, D.C.: National Academy of Sciences.

Davis, Ian [1977] "Emergency Shelter." *Disasters* **1** (No. 1):23–40.

Davis, Ian [1975] "Disaster Housing: A Case Study of Managua." *Architectural Design* (January):42–47.

Davis, Morris, and Steven Thomas Seitz [1982] "Disasters and Governments." *Journal of Conflict Resolution* **26** (September):547–568.

Davis, Nancy Yaw [1970] "The Role of the Russian Orthodox Church in Five Pacific Eskimo Villages as Revealed by the Earthquake." Pp. 125–146 in *The Great Alaska*

Earthquake of 1964: Human Ecology Committee on the Alaska Earthquake of the National Research Council (ed.). Washington, D.C.: National Academy of Sciences.

Demerath, Nicholas J. [1957] "Some General Propositions: An Interpretive Summary." *Human Organization* **16** (Summer):28–29.

Demerath, Nicholas J., and Anthony F. C. Wallace [1957] "Human Adaptation to Disaster." *Human Organization* **16** (Summer):1–2.

Descamps, Marc-Alain [1972] "Catastrophe et Responsibilité" (Disaster and Responsibility). *Revue Française de Sociologie* **13** (No. 3):376–391.

de Ville de Goyet, C., E. del Cid, A. Romero, E. Jeannee, and M. Lechat [1976] "Earthquake in Guatemala: Epidemiologic Evaluation of the Relief Effort." *Bulletin of the Pan American Health Organization* **10** (No. 2):95–109.

de Ville de Goyet, C., E. Jeannee, M. F. Lechat and A. Bouckaert [1977] "Anthropometric Measurements in a Relief Programme in Niger: A Tool for Decision Making at the Community Level." *Disasters* **1** (No. 3):223–229.

Dexter, James R., Gene E. Willeke, and L. Douglas James [1979] "Social Aspects of Flooding." Pp. 65–80 in *Proceedings of the Specialty Conference on Legal, Institutional, and Social Aspects of Irrigation and Drainage and Water Resources Planning and Management.* Blacksburg, Virginia: ASCE.

Diggins, William, James D. Wright and, Peter H. Rossi [1979] "Local Elites and City Hall: The Case of Natural Disaster Risk Mitigation Policy." *Social Science Quarterly* **60** (September):203–217.

Diggory, James C. [1956] "Some Consequences of Proximity to a Disease Threat." *Sociometry* **19** (March):47–53.

Dirks, Robert [1979] "Relief Induced Agonism." *Disasters* **3** (No. 2):195–198.

Dombrowsky, Wolf [1983] "Solidarity During Snow-Disasters." *International Journal of Mass Emergencies and Disasters* **1** (March):189–206.

Douglas, Ian [1979] "Flooding in Australia: A Review." Pp. 154–161 in *Natural Hazards in Australia,* R. L. Heathcote and B. G. Thom (eds.). Canberra: Australian Academy of Science.

Douglas, Ian, and Jack Hobbs [1979] "Public and Private Reaction to Three Flood Events in North-Western New South Wales, 1971–1976." Pp. 251–259 in *Natural Hazards in Australia,* R. L. Heathcote and B. G. Thom (eds.). Canberra: Australian Academy of Science.

Douglas, Mary, and Aaron Wildavsky [1983] *Risk and Culture: An Essay on the Selection of Technological and Environmental Dangers.* Berkeley, California: University of California Press.

Douty, Christopher Morris [1977] *The Economics of Localized Disasters.* New York: Arno Press.

Drabek, Thomas E. [in press] "Emergent Structures." Chapter to appear in *Sociology of Disasters: Contribution of Sociology to Disaster Research,* Russell R. Dynes and Carlo Pelanda (eds.). Gorizia, Italy: Franco Angeli.

Drabek, Thomas E. [1985] "Managing the Emergency Response." *Public Administration Review* **45** (January):85–92.

Drabek, Thomas E. [1984] *Some Emerging Issues in Emergency Management.* Emmitsburg, Maryland: National Emergency Training Center, Federal Emergency Management Agency.

Drabek, Thomas E. [1983a] "Alternative Patterns of Decision-Making in Emergent Disaster Response Networks." *International Journal of Mass Emergencies and Disasters* **1** (August):277–305.

Drabek, Thomas E. [1983b] "Shall We Leave? A Study on Family Reactions When Disaster Strikes." *Emergency Management Review* 1 (Fall):25–29.

Drabek, Thomas E. [1983c] "Sociology Research Needs." Pp. 107–133 in *A Comprehensive Assessment of Research Needs on Floods and Their Mitigation,* Stanley A. Changnon *et al.* Champaign, Illinois: Illinois State Water Survey.

Drabek, Thomas E. [1979] "Communication: Key to Disaster Management." *Insight* 3 (July):3–4.

Drabek, Thomas E. [1970] "Methodology of Studying Disasters: Past Patterns and Future Possibilities." *American Behavioral Scientist* 13 (January–February):331–343.

Drabek, Thomas E. [1969] "Social Processes in Disaster: Family Evacuation." *Social Problems* 16 (Winter):336–349.

Drabek, Thomas E. [1968] *Disaster in Aisle 13.* College of Administrative Science. Columbus, Ohio: The Ohio State University.

Drabek, Thomas E. [1965] "Laboratory Simulation of a Police Communication System Under Stress." Dissertation. Columbus, Ohio: The Ohio State University.

Drabek, Thomas E., Christopher R. Adams, Thomas S. Kilijanek, and Harriet L. Tamminga [1981/82] "After The Wind: The Emergent Multiorganizational Search and Rescue Network Following the Cheyenne, Wyoming, Tornado of July, 1979." *Humboldt Journal of Social Relations* 9 (Fall/Winter):90–120.

Drabek, Thomas E., Christopher R. Adams, Thomas S. Kilijanek, and Harriet L. Tamminga [1979] "Multiorganizational Coordination: It Can Be Done!" *Search and Rescue Magazine* (Summer):9–15.

Drabek, Thomas E., and Keith Boggs [1968] "Families in Disaster: Reactions and Relatives." *Journal of Marriage and the Family* 30 (August):443–451.

Drabek, Thomas E., Donald Q. Brodie, Jessica Edgerton, and Paul Munson [1979] *The Flood Breakers: Citizens Band Radio Use during the 1978 Flood in the Grand Forks Region.* Boulder, Colorado: Institute of Behavioral Science, The University of Colorado.

Drabek, Thomas E., Jessica Edgerton, Paul Munson, and Donald Q. Brodie [1979] "CB Use in a Natural Disaster: Emergent Patterns and Perceptions of Outcome." *APCO Bulletin* 45 (June):14–20.

Drabek, Thomas E., and J. Eugene Haas [1969] "Laboratory Simulation of Organizational Stress." *American Sociological Review* 34 (April):223–238.

Drabek, Thomas E., and William H. Key [1984] *Conquering Disaster: Family Recovery and Long-Term Consequences.* New York: Irvington Publishers.

Drabek, Thomas E., and William H. Key [1976] "The Impact of Disaster on Primary Group Linkages." *Mass Emergencies* 1:89–105.

Drabek, Thomas E., and William H. Key [1972] "Meeting the Challenge of Disaster: Family Responses and Long-Term Consequences." Pp. 89–108 in *Proceedings of the Japan–United States Disaster Research Seminar: Organizational and Community Responses to Disasters.* Columbus, Ohio: Disaster Research Center, The Ohio State University.

Drabek, Thomas E., William H. Key, Patricia E. Erickson, and Juanita L. Crowe [1975] "The Impact of Disaster on Kin Relationships." *Journal of Marriage and the Family* 37 (August):481–494.

Drabek, Thomas E., Alvin H. Mushkatel, and Thomas S. Kilijanek [1983] *Earthquake Mitigation Policy: The Experience of Two States.* Boulder, Colorado: Institute of Behavioral Science, The University of Colorado.

Drabek, Thomas E., and E. L. Quarantelli [1967] "Scapegoats, Villains, and Disasters." *Transaction* 4 (March):12–17.

Drabek, Thomas E., and John S. Stephenson III [1971] "When Disaster Strikes." *Journal of Applied Social Psychology* 1 (No. 2):187–203.

Drabek, Thomas E., Harriet L. Tamminga, Thomas S. Kilijanek, and Christopher R. Adams [1981] *Managing Multiorganizational Emergency Responses: Emergent Search and Rescue Networks in Natural Disasters and Remote Area Settings.* Boulder, Colorado: Institute of Behavioral Science, The University of Colorado.

Drake, Elisabeth M., and Marian H. Long [1982] "Worldwide Standards and Practices for Siting LNG and LPG Facilities: A Comparison." Pp. 103–112 in *The Risk Analysis Controversy: An Institutional Perspective.* Howard C. Kunreuther and Eryl V. Ley (eds.). Berlin, Heidelberg, New York: Springer-Verlag.

Dudasik, Stephen W. [1982] "Unanticipated Repercussions of International Disaster Relief." *Disasters* 6 (No. 1):31–37.

Dudasik, Stephen W. [1980] "Victimization in Natural Disaster." *Disasters* 4 (No. 3):329–338.

Duffy, John C. [1978] "Emergency Mental Health Services and a Major Aircraft Accident." *Disasters* 2 (No. 2/3):159–163.

Dupree, Herb, and Wolf Roder [1974] "Coping With Drought in a Preindustrial, Preliterate Farming Society." Pp. 115–119 in *Natural Hazards: Local, National, Global,* Gilbert F. White (ed.). New York: Oxford University Press.

Dynes, Russell R. [1983] "Problems in Emergency Planning." *Energy* 8 (No. 8–9):653–660.

Dynes, Russell R. [1979] "EMS Delivery in Disasters." Pp. 56–58 in *Collected Papers in Emergency Medical Services and Traumatology,* R. Adams Cowley (ed.). Baltimore: University of Maryland, School of Medicine.

Dynes, Russell R. [1978] "Interorganizational Relations in Communities under Stress." Pp. 49–64 in *Disasters: Theory and Research,* E. L. Quarantelli (ed.). Beverly Hills, California: Sage.

Dynes, Russell R. [1975] "The Comparative Study of Disaster: A Social Organizational Approach." *Mass Emergencies* 1:21–31.

Dynes, Russell R. [1972] "Cross Cultural Studies of Disaster." Pp. 235–256 in *Proceedings of the Japan–United States Disaster Research Seminar: Organizational and Community Responses to Disasters.* Columbus, Ohio: Disaster Research Center, The Ohio State University.

Dynes, Russell R. [1970a] *Organized Behavior in Disaster.* Lexington, Massachusetts: Heath Lexington Books.

Dynes, Russell R. [1970b] "Organizational Involvement and Changes in Community Structure in Disaster." *American Behavioral Scientist* 13 (January–February):430–439.

Dynes, Russell R. [1966] "Theoretical Problems in Disaster Research." *Bulletin of Business Research* 41 (September):7–9.

Dynes, Russell R., and B. E. Aguirre [1979] "Organizational Adaptation to Crises: Mechanisms of Coordination and Structural Change." *Disasters* 3 (No. 2):71–74.

Dynes, Russell R., and Carlo Pelanda (eds.) [in press] *Sociology of Disasters: Contribution of Sociology to Disaster Research.* Gorizia, Italy: Franco Angeli.

Dynes, Russell R., and E. L. Quarantelli [1980] "Helping Behavior in Large-Scale Disasters." Pp. 339–354 in *Participation in Social and Political Activities,* David Horton Smith, Jacqueline Macaulay, and associates (eds.). San Francisco: Jossey-Bass Publishers.

Dynes, Russell R., and E. L. Quarantelli [1977] "Organizational Communications and Decision Making in Crises." Report Series #17. Columbus, Ohio: Disaster Research Center, The Ohio State University.

Dynes, Russell R., and E. L. Quarantelli [1976] "The Family and Community Context of Individual Reactions to Disaster." Pp. 231–245 in *Emergency and Disaster Management: A Mental Health Sourcebook,* Howard Parad, H. L. P. Resnik, and Libbie Parad (eds.). Bowie, Maryland: The Charles Press.

Dynes, Russell R., and E. L. Quarantelli [1975] *The Role of Local Civil Defense in Disaster Planning.* Columbus, Ohio: Disaster Research Center, The Ohio State University.

Dynes, Russell R., and E. L. Quarantelli [1971] "The Absence of Community Conflict in the Early Phases of Natural Disasters." Pp. 200–204 in *Conflict Resolution: Contributions of the Behavioral Sciences,* Clagett G. Smith (ed.). South Bend, Indiana: University of Notre Dame Press.

Dynes, Russell R., and E. L. Quarantelli [1968] "Redefinition of Property Norms in Community Emergencies." *International Journal of Legal Research* 3 (December):100–112.

Dynes, Russell, E. L. Quarantelli, and Gary A. Kreps [1972] *A Perspective on Disaster Planning.* Columbus, Ohio: Disaster Research Center, The Ohio State University.

Dynes, Russell R., and George Warheit [1969] "Organizations in Disasters." *EMO National Digest* 9 (April–May):12–13, 19.

Dynes, Russell R., and Daniel Yutzy [1965] "The Religious Interpretation of Disaster." *Topic 10: A Journal of the Liberal Arts* (Fall):34–48.

Earney, Fillmore C. F., and Brian A. Knowles [1974] "Urban Snow Hazard: Marquette, Michigan." Pp. 167–174 in *Natural Hazards: Local, National, Global,* Gilbert F. White (ed.). New York: Oxford University Press.

Edberg, Anna-Karin, and Britt-Inger Lustig [1983] *Solidaritet och Konflikt.* (Solidarity and Conflict) (in Swedish with an English summary). Disaster Studies 14. Uppsala, Sweden: University of Uppsala.

Edwards, J. Guy [1976] "Psychiatric Aspects of Civilian Disasters." *British Medical Journal* 1 (No. 6013):944–947.

Eldar, Reuben [1981] "A Multi-Hospital System for Disaster Situations." *Disasters* 5 (No. 2):112–119.

Eliot, Thomas E. [1932] "The Bereaved Family." *The Annals of the American Academy of Political and Social Science* 209 (March):1–7.

El-Khawas, Mohamed [1976] "A Reassessment of International Relief Programs." Pp. 77–100 in *The Politics of Natural Disaster: The Case of the Sahel Drought,* Michael H. Glantz (ed.). New York: Praeger Publishers.

Ericksen, Neil J. [1975] *Scenario Methodology in Natural Hazards Research.* Boulder, Colorado: Institute of Behavioral Science, The University of Colorado.

Ericksen, Neil J. [1974] "Flood Information, Expectation, and Protection on the Opotiki Floodplain, New Zealand." Pp. 60–70 in *Natural Hazards: Local, National, Global,* Gilbert F. White (ed.). New York: Oxford University Press.

Erickson, Patricia E., Thomas E. Drabek, William H. Key, and Juanita L. Crowe [1976] "Families in Disaster: Patterns of Recovery." *Mass Emergencies* 1:203–216.

Erico, Miguel Angel Gonzalez [1975] "Estructura y Desarrollo del Comercio Exterior del Paraguay: 1870–1918 (The Structure and Development of Foreign Commerce in Paraguay: 1870–1918) (in Spanish). *Revista Paraguaya de Sociología* 12 (September):125–155.

Erikson, Kai T. [1976a] *Everything in Its Path*. New York: Simon and Schuster.

Erikson, Kai T. [1976b] "Loss of Communality at Buffalo Creek." *American Journal of Psychiatry* 133 (March):302–305.

Erikson, Kai T. [1976c] "Trauma at Buffalo Creek." *Society* 13 (September/October): 58–65.

Faich, Gerald, and Richard Rose [1979] "Blizzard Morbidity and Mortality: Rhode Island, 1978." *American Journal of Public Health* 69 (October):1050–1052.

Farhar, Barbara C. [1976] "Hail as Sudden Disaster: Public Response to Hail Suppression Activity." *Mass Emergencies* 1:313–321.

Farhar, Barbara C. (ed.) [1977] *Hail Suppression: Society and Environment*. Boulder, Colorado: Institute of Behavioral Science, The University of Colorado.

Farhar, Barbara C., Jack A. Clark, Lynn L. Sherretz, Jerry Horton and, Sigmund Krane [1979] *Social Impacts of the St. Louis Urban Weather Anomaly*. Boulder, Colorado: Institute of Behavioral Science, The University of Colorado.

Feld, Allen [1973] "Reflections on the Agnes Flood." *Social Work* 18 (September):46–51.

Feldman, Shelley, and Florence McCarthy [1983] "Disaster Response in Bangladesh." *International Journal of Mass Emergencies and Disasters* 1 (March):105–124.

Fernandez, Aloysius [1979] "The Relationship Between Disaster Assistance and Long-Term Development." *Disasters* 3 (No. 1):32–36.

Fields, Rona M. [1980] "Victims of Terrorism: The Effects of Prolonged Stress." *Evaluation and Change*, Special Issue:76–83.

Fischer, David W. [1980] "Actors at Large-Scale Accidents: Lessons from the Bravo and Three Mile Island Accidents." *Scandinavian Political Studies* 3 (No. 4):321–345.

Fischhoff, Baruch, Christoph Hohenemser, Roger E. Kasperson, and Robert W. Kates [1978] "Handling Hazards." *Environment* 20 (September):16–20, 32–37.

Fischhoff, Baruch, Sarah Lichtenstein, Paul Slovic, Steven L. Derby, and Ralph L. Kenney [1982] *Acceptable Risk*. New York: Cambridge University Press.

Fisher, Brian E. [1978] "Mass Emergency Problems and Planning in the United Kingdom from the Perspective of the Police." *Mass Emergencies* 3:41–48.

Fitzpatrick, Jim [1977] "The Role of Emergency Grain Reserves." *Disasters* 1 (No. 3):217–221.

Flynn, C. B., and J. A. Chalmers [1980] *The Social and Economic Effects of the Accident at Three Mile Island*. Tempe, Arizona: Mountain West Research, Inc. with Social Impact Research, Inc.

Fogleman, Charles W. [1958] "Family and Community in Disaster: A Socio-Psychological Study of the Effects of a Major Disaster upon Individuals and Groups." Dissertation. Baton Rouge, Louisiana: Louisiana State University.

Form, William H., and Charles P. Loomis [1956] "The Persistence and Emergence of Social and Cultural Systems in Disasters." *American Sociological Review* 21 (April):180–185.

Form, William H., and Sigmund Nosow [1958] *Community in Disaster.* New York: Harper & Brothers.

Forrest, Thomas R. [1979] "Hurricane Betsy, 1965; A Selective Analysis of Organizational Response in the New Orleans Area." The Disaster Research Center Historical and Comparative Disaster Series, No. 5. Columbus, Ohio: Disaster Research Center, The Ohio State University.

Forrest, Thomas R. [1978] "Group Emergence in Disasters." Pp. 105–125 in *Disasters: Theory and Research,* E. L. Quarantelli (ed.). Beverly Hills, California: Sage.

Forrest, Thomas R. [1974] "Structural Differentiation in Emergent Groups." (Disaster Research Center Report Series No. 15). Columbus, Ohio: Disaster Research Center, The Ohio State University.

Forrest, Thomas R. [1972] "Structural Differentiation in Emergent Groups." Dissertation. Columbus, Ohio: The Ohio State University.

Foster, Harold D. [1980] *Disaster Planning: The Preservation of Life and Property.* New York, Heidelberg, Berlin: Springer-Verlag.

Foster, Harold D. [1976] "Assessing Disaster Magnitude—Social-Science Approach." *Professional Geographer* **28** (No. 3):241–247.

Francaviglia, Richard V. [1978] "Xenia Rebuilds—Effects of Pre-Disaster Conditioning on Post-Disaster Redevelopment." *Journal of the American Institute of Planners* **44** (No. 1):13–24.

Fraser, James R.P., and Douglas A. Spicka [1981] "Handling the Emotional Response to Disaster—The Case for American-Red-Cross–Community Mental-Health Collaboration." *Community Mental Health Journal* **17** (Winter):255–264.

Frasure, C. M. [1972] "State Disaster Legislation." *West Virginia Law Review* **75** (No. 1):32–49.

Frawley, Kevin [1979] "A Flood Hazard Case Study: Ingham, North Queensland, 1977." Pp. 173–188 in *Planning for People in Natural Disasters,* Joan Innes Reid (ed.). Townsville, Queensland, Australia: James Cook University of North Queensland.

Frazier, Kendrick [1979] *The Violent Face of Nature.* New York: William Morrow and Company, Inc.

Frederick, Calvin J. [1977] "Current Thinking About Crisis or Psychological Intervention in United States Disasters." *Mass Emergencies* **2**:43–50.

Frey, R. Scott [1983] "The Structural Context of City Adoption of War on Poverty and National Flood Insurance Programs." *The Sociological Quarterly* **24** (Winter):59–74.

Friedsam, H. J. [1962] "Older Persons in Disaster." Pp. 151–182 in *Man and Society in Disaster,* George W. Baker and Dwight W. Chapman (eds.). New York: Basic Books.

Friedsam, H. J. [1961] "Reactions of Older Persons to Disaster-Caused Losses: An Hypothesis of Relative Deprivation." *The Gerontologist* **1** (March):34–37.

Friesema, H. Paul, James Caporaso, Gerald Goldstein, Robert Lineberry, and Richard McCleary [1979] *Aftermath: Communities after Natural Disasters.* Beverly Hills, California, and London: Sage Publications.

Fritz, Charles E. [1961] "Disasters." Pp. 651–694 in *Contemporary Social Problems,* Robert K. Merton and Robert A. Nisbet (eds.). New York: Harcourt.

Fritz, Charles E. [1957] "Disasters Compared in Six American Communities." *Human Organization* **16** (Summer):6–9.

Fritz, Charles E., and Eli S. Marks [1954] "The NORC Studies of Human Behavior in Disaster." *The Journal of Social Issues* **10** (No. 3):26–41.

Fritz, Charles E., and J. H. Mathewson [1957] "Convergence Behavior in Disasters." National Research Council Disaster Study #9. Washington, D.C.: National Academy of Sciences.

Fritz, Charles E., Jeannette F. Rayner, and Samuel L. Guskin [1958] "Behavior in an Emergency Shelter: A Field Study of 800 Persons Stranded in a Highway Restaurant During a Heavy Snowstorm." National Academy of Sciences/National Research Council. Washington, D.C.: National Academy of Sciences.

Fritz, Charles E., and Harry B. Williams [1957] "The Human Being in Disasters: A Research Perspective." *The Annals of the American Academy of Political and Social Science* **309** (January):42–51.

Fujiyama, Yoshio, *et al.* [1979] "The Behaviors of Injured Persons in Earthquake Emergency—A Research on the Behaviors of Injured Persons in the 1978 Miyagiken-Oki Earthquake Emergency (Jishinji ni okeru Fushosha no Kodo)." *The Study of Sociology (Shakaigaku Kenkyu)* **38**:69-120.*

Gabor, Thomas [1981] "Mutual Aid Systems in the United States for Chemical Emergencies." *Journal of Hazardous Materials* **4**:343–356.

Gardner, Gerald T., Adrian R. Tiemann, Leroy C. Gould, Donald R. DeLuca, Leonard W. Doob, and Jan A.J. Stolwijk [1982] "Risk and Benefit Perceptions, Acceptability Judgements, and Self-Reported Actions toward Nuclear Power." *Journal of Social Psychology* **116**:179-197.

Geipel, Robert [1982] *Disaster and Reconstruction: The Friuli (Italy) Earthquakes of 1976.* London: George Allen & Unwin.

Gerontology Program, The [1976] *Service Priorities for the Aged in Natural Disasters.* Omaha, Nebraska: The Gerontology Program, University of Nebraska at Omaha.

Gilbert, Arthur N., and Michael Barkun [1981] "Disaster and Sexuality." *Journal of Sex Research* **17** (August):288–299. (Manuscript copy provided by author.)

Gilbert, J. E. [1958] "Human Behavior under Conditions of Disaster." *Medical Service Journal* **14** (May):318–324.

Gillespie, David F., and Ronald W. Perry [1976] "An Integrated Systems and Emergent Norm Approach to Mass Emergencies." *Mass Emergencies* **1**:303–312.

Gillespie, David F., Ronald W. Perry, and Dennis S. Mileti [1974] "Collective Stress and Community Transformation." *Human Relations* **27** (October):767–778.

Gimenez, Martha E. [1976] "A 'People's War' against Earthquakes." *Mass Emergencies* **1**:323–341.

Gist, Richard, and Stephanie B. Stolz [1982] "Mental Health Promotion and the Media: Community Response to the Kansas City Hotel Disaster." *American Psychologist* **37** (October):1136–1139.

Glantz, Michael H. [1976] "Nine Fallacies of Natural Disaster: The Case of the Sahel." Pp. 3–24 in *The Politics of Natural Disaster: The Case of the Sahel Drought,* Michael H. Glantz (ed.). New York: Praeger Publishers.

Glantz, Michael H. (ed.) [1976] *The Politics of Natural Disaster: The Case of the Sahel Drought.* New York: Praeger Publishers.

Glaser, Barney G., and Anselm L. Strauss [1967] *The Discovery of Grounded Theory: Strategies for Qualitative Research.* Chicago: Aldine Publishing Company.

Glass, Albert J. [1970] "The Psychological Aspects of Emergency Situations." Pp. 62–69 in *Psychological Aspects of Stress,* Harry S. Abram (ed.). Springfield, Illinois: Charles C. Thomas.

Glass, Roger I., Robert B. Craven, Dennis J. Bregman, Barbara J. Stoll, Neil Horowitz, Peter Kerndt, and Joe Winkle [1980] "Injuries From the Wichita Falls Tornado: Implications for Prevention." *Science* **207**:734–738.

Glass, Roger I., Philip O'Hare, and J. Lyle Conrad [1979] "Health Consequences of the Snow Disaster in Massachusetts, February 6, 1978." *American Journal of Public Health* **69** (October):1047–1049.

Glass, Roger I., and Matthew M. Zack, Jr. [1979] "Increase in Deaths from Ischaemic Heart-Disease after Blizzards." *The Lancet* (March 3):485–487.

Glenn, Christopher [1979] "Natural Disasters and Human Behavior: Explanation, Research, and Models." *Psychology: A Quarterly Journal of Human Behavior* **16** (Summer):23–36.

Gleser, Goldine C., Bonnie L. Green, and Carolyn N. Winget [1981] *Prolonged Psychosocial Effects of Disaster: A Study of Buffalo Creek.* New York: Academic Press.

Gleser, Goldine C., Bonnie L. Green, and Carolyn N. Winget [1978] "Quantifying Interview Data on Psychic Impairment of Disaster Survivors." *Journal of Nervous and Mental Disease* **166** (March):209–216.

Glittenberg, JoAnn K. [1982] "Reconstruction in Four Urban Post-Disaster Settlements." Pp. 634–707 in "Recovery, Change and Development: A Longitudinal Study of the 1976 Guatemalan Earthquake," Frederick L. Bates (ed.). Athens, Georgia: Guatemalan Earthquake Study, University of Georgia.

Golant, Stephen, and Ian Burton [1970] "A Semantic Differential Experiment in the Interpretation and Grouping of Environmental Hazards." *Geographical Analysis* **2**:120–134.

Goldsteen, Raymond, and John K. Schorr [1982] "The Long-Term Impact of a Man-Made Disaster: An Examination of a Small Town in the Aftermath of the Three Mile Island Nuclear Reactor Accident." *Disasters* **6** (No. 1):50–59.

Goldsteen, Raymond L., John Schorr, and Karen S. Goldsteen [1984] "What's the Matter with Those People: Rethinking TMI." *International Journal of Mass Emergencies and Disasters* **2** (November):369–387.

Golec, Judith A. [1983] "A Contextual Approach to the Social Psychological Study of Disaster Recovery." *International Journal of Mass Emergencies and Disasters* **1** (August):255–276.

Golec, Judith A. [1982] "A Contextual Approach to the Social Psychological Study of Disaster Recovery." A paper presented at the Tenth World Congress of Sociology, Mexico City, Mexico, August.

Golec, Judith A., and Patrick J. Gurney [1977] "The Problem of Needs Assessment in the Delivery of EMS." *Mass Emergencies* **2**:169–177.

Goltz, James D. [1984] "Are the News Media Responsible for the Disaster Myths? A Content Analysis of Emergency Response Imagery." *International Journal of Mass Emergencies and Disasters* **2** (November):345–368.

Grant, W.B., L. McNamara, and K. Bailey [1975] "Psychiatric Disturbance with Acute Onset and Offset in a Darwin Evacuee." *The Medical Journal of Australia* **1** (May 24):652–654.

Gray, Jane [1981] "Characteristic Patterns of and Variations in Community Response to Acute Chemical Emergencies." *Journal of Hazardous Materials* **4**:357–365.

Greco, D., A. Faustini, F. Forastiere, M. R. Galanti, M. E. Magliola, M. L. Moro, P. Piergentilli, F. Rosmini, M. A. Stazi, S. Luzi, L. Fantozzi, R. Capocaccia, S. Conti, and A. Zampieri [1981] "Epidemiological Surveillance of Diseases Following the Earthquake of 23rd November 1980 in Southern Italy." *Disasters* 5 (No. 4):398–406.

Grecu, G., K. Csiky, and I. Munteanu [1972] "Studiu Asupra Unui Grup de 87 Bolnavi cu Stări Depresive Declanşate de Inundatiile Din Mai 1970" (Study on a Group of 87 Patients with Depressive States Triggered by the Floods of May 1970) (in Romanian). *Neurologia, Psihiatria, Neurochirurgia* 17 (March):109–115.

Greene, Marjorie, Ronald Perry, and Michael Lindell [1981] "The March 1980 Eruptions of Mt. St. Helens: Citizen Perceptions of Volcano Threat." *Disasters* 5 (No. 1):49–66.

Greenson, Ralph R., and Thomas Mintz [1972] "California Earthquake 1971: Some Psychoanalytic Observations." *International Journal of Psychoanalytic Psychotherapy* 1 (May):7–23.

Griffin, Charles T., Charles L. Mulford, and Gerald E. Klonglan [1972] "An Analysis of Operating System Effectiveness: Focus on the Behavior of Local Coordinators." Ames, Iowa: Department of Sociology and Anthropology, Iowa State University.

Grossman, Leona [1973] "Train Crash: Social Work and Disaster Services." *Social Work* 18 (September):38–44.

Gruntfest, Eve [1977] "What People Did during the Big Thompson Flood." (Working Paper 32). Boulder, Colorado: Institute of Behavioral Sciences, The University of Colorado.

Guard Police Psychology Research Society (Keibi Shinrigaku Kenkyukai) [1980a] *Report on the Psychological Research for Countermeasures against Earthquake Disaster—The Drivers' Responses to an Earthquake Prediction Warning, Vol. 14 (Daishinsai Taisaku no tameno Shinrigakuteki Chosa Kenkyu—Keikai Sengen Hatsureiji ni okeru Jidosha Untensha no Ishiki to Kodo, Dai 14-ho).* Tokyo: Tokyo Metropolitan Police Board (Keishi-cho).*

Guard Police Psychology Research Society (Keibi Shinrigaku Kenkyukai) [1980b] *Report on the Psychological Research for Countermeasures against Earthquake Disaster—The Railway- and Subway-stations in Earthquake Warning, Vol. 15 (Daishinsai Taisaku no tameno Shinrigakuteki Chosa Kenkyu—Keikai Sengen Hatsureiji ni okeru Tonai Kakueki de no Jitai Yosoku, Dai 15-ho).* Tokyo: Tokyo Metropolitan Police Board (Keishi-cho).*

Guard Police Psychology Research Society (Keibi Shinrigaku Kenkyukai) [1977] *Report on the Psychological Research for Countermeasures against Earthquake Disaster—The Residents of the Areas More Vulnerable to Earthquake, Vol. 12 (Daishinsai Taisaku no tameno Shinrigakuteki Chosa Kenkyu—Dai Jishin ni Mottomo Kiken to Sareta Chiiki deno Ishiki Chosa, Dai 12-ho).* Tokyo: Tokyo Metropolitan Police Board (Keishi-cho).*

Guard Police Psychology Research Society (Keibi Shinrigaku Kenkyukai) [1976] *Report on the Psychological Research for Countermeasures against Earthquake Disaster, Vol. 11, Survey Research on People's Consciousness in the High-Rise Buildings (Daishinsai Taisaku no tameno Shinrigakuteki Chosa Kenkyu Vol. 11, Saigaiji ni okeru Koso Biru Riyosha no Ishiki Chosa.* Tokyo: Guard Police Psychology Research Society and Tokyo Metropolitan Police Department.*

Guard Police Psychology Research Society (Keibi Shinrigaku Kenkyukai) [1973] *On the Fire at the Kumamato Taiyo Department Store (Kumamoto Taiyo Depaato Kasai ni Kausuru Keibi Shinrigakuteki Chosa Kenkyu).* Tokyo: Tokyo Metropolitan Police Board (Keishi-Cho).*

Guard Police Psychology Research Society (Keibi Shinrigaku Kenkyukai) [1971a] *Report on the Psychological Research for Countermeasures against Earthquake Disasters—Earthquake and Human Behaviors. (Daishinsai Taisaku no tameno Shinrigaku teki Chosa Kenku—Jishin to Ningen Kodo).* Tokyo: Tokyo Metropolitan Police Board (Keishi-Cho).*

Guard Police Psychology Research Society (Keibi Shinrigaku Kenkyukai) [1971b] *Report on the Psychological Research for Countermeasures against Earthquake Disasters—On Evacuation Behavior to the Designated Evacuation Places, Vol. 6. (Daishinsai Taisaku no tameno Shinrigakuteki Chosa Kenkyu—Shitei Hinan Basho eno Hinan Kodo, Dai 6-ho).* Tokyo: Tokyo Metropolitan Police Board (Keishi-Cho).*

Guard Police Psychology Research Society (Keibi Shinrigaku Kenkyukai [1970] *Report on the Psychological Research for Countermeasures against Earthquake Disasters—On Evacuation Behaviors, Vol. 5 (Daishinsai Taisaku no tameno Shinrigakuteki Chosa Kenkyu—Hinan Kodo ni tsuite, Dai 5-ho).* Tokyo: Tokyo Metropolitan Police Board (Keishi-Cho).*

Guard Police Psychology Research Society (Keibi Shinrigaku Kenkyukai [1967] *Report on the Psychological Research for Countermeasures against Earthquake Disasters—How Should Tokyo Residents Respond to an Earthquake Disaster in Underground Shopping Malls or on Bustling Streets? Vol. 3.* Tokyo: Tokyo Metropolitan Police Board (Keishi-Cho).*

Guard Police Psychology Research Society (Keibi Shinrigaku Kenkyukai [1966] *Report on the Psychological Research for Countermeasures against Earthquake Disasters—How Do Companies, Schools, and Neighborhoods Respond to an Earthquake Disaster? Vol. 2 (Daishinsai Taisaku no tameno Shinrigakuteki Chosa Kenkyu—Kigyo, Gakko Chiiki wa Ikani Taisho Sureba Yoika? Dai 2-ho).* Tokyo: Tokyo Metropolitan Police Board (Keishi-Cho).*

Gurd, C., A. Bromwich, and J. Quinn [1975] "The Health Management of Cyclone Tracy." *The Medical Journal of Australia* 1 (May 24):641–644.

Haas, J. Eugene [1973] "Social Aspects of Weather Modification." *American Meteorological Society* 54 (July):647–657.

Haas, J. Eugene [1972] "Research on the Socio-Economic Impact of Geophysical Hazards in the U.S." Pp. 159–164 in *Proceedings of the Japan–United States Disaster Research Seminar: Organizational and Community Responses to Disasters.* Columbus, Ohio: Disaster Research Center, The Ohio State University.

Haas, J. Eugene [1970] "Lessons for Coping with Disaster." Pp. 39–51 in *The Great Alaska Earthquake of 1964: Human Ecology,* Committee on the Alaska Earthquake of the National Research Council (ed.). Washington, D.C.: National Academy of Sciences.

Haas, J. Eugene, Harold C. Cochrane, and Donald G. Eddy [1977] "Consequences of a Cyclone on a Small City." *Ekistics* 44 (July):45–50.

Haas, J. Eugene, Harold C. Cochrane, and Donald G. Eddy [1976] "The Consequences of Large-Scale Evacuation Following Disaster: The Darwin Australia Cyclone Disaster of December 25, 1974." Natural Hazards Research Working Paper No. 27. Boulder, Colorado: Institute of Behavioral Science, The University of Colorado.

Haas, J. Eugene, and Thomas E. Drabek [1973] *Complex Organizations: A Sociological Perspective*. New York: The Macmillan Company.

Haas, J. Eugene, and Thomas E. Drabek [1970] "Community Disaster and System Stress: A Sociological Perspective." Pp. 264–286 in *Social and Psychological Factors in Stress,* Joseph E. McGrath (ed.). New York: Holt, Rinehart and Winston, Inc.

Haas, J. Eugene, Robert W. Kates, and Martyn J. Bowden (eds.) [1977] *Reconstruction Following Disaster*. Cambridge, Massachusetts, and London: The MIT Press.

Haas, J. Eugene, Patricia B. Trainer, Martyn J. Bowden, and Robert Bolin [1977] "Reconstruction Issues in Perspective." Pp. 25–68 in *Reconstruction Following Disaster,* J. Eugene Haas, Robert W. Kates, and Martyn J. Bowden (eds.). Cambridge, Massachusetts, and London: The MIT Press.

Hall, Jerry A. [1983] "The Place of Climatic Hazards in Food Scarcity: A Case Study of Belize." Pp. 140–161 in *Interpretations of Calamity,* K. Hewitt (ed.). Boston: Allen & Unwin Inc.

Hall, Philip S., and Patrick W. Landreth [1975] "Assessing Some Long Term Consequences of a Natural Disaster." *Mass Emergencies* **1**:55-61.

Hammarstrom, Gunhild, Orjan E. Hultaker, and Jan E. Trost [1980] *Ett Forgiftat Samhalle*. (A Poisoned Community) (in Swedish with an English summary). Disaster Studies 8. Uppsala, Sweden: Uppsala University.

Hammarstrom-Tornstam, Gunhild [1977] *Varningsprocessen*. (Warning Process) (in Swedish with an English summary). Disaster Studies 5. Uppsala, Sweden: University of Uppsala.

Hannigan, John A., and Rodney M. Kueneman [1978] "Anticipating Flood Emergencies: A Case Study of a Canadian Disaster Subculture." Pp. 129–146 in *Disasters: Theory and Research,* E. L. Quarantelli (ed.). Beverly Hills, California: Sage.

Hannigan, John A., and Rodney M. Kueneman [1977] "Legitimacy and Public Organizations: A Case Study." *Canadian Journal of Sociology* **2** (Winter):125–135.

Hansen, Art [1979] "Managing Refugees: Zambia's Response to Angolan Refugees 1966–1977." *Disasters* **3** (No. 4):375–380.

Hanson, Perry O., John D. Vitek, and Susan Hanson [1979] "Awareness of Tornadoes: The Importance of an Historic Event." *Journal of Geography* (January):22–25.

Hanson, Susan, John D. Vitek, and Perry O. Hanson [1979] "Natural Disaster— Long-Range Impact on Human Response to Future Disaster Threats." *Environment and Behavior* **11** (June):268–284.

Hansson, Robert O., Rita J. Henze, Mary Abby Langenheim, and Anthony J. Filipovitch [1979] "Threat, Knowledge, and Support for a Collective Response to Urban Flooding." *Journal of Applied Social Psychology* **9** (No. 5):413–425.

Harding, Donald M., and Dennis J. Parker [1974] "Flood Hazard at Shrewsbury, United Kingdom." Pp. 43–52 in *Natural Hazards: Local, National, Global,* Gilbert F. White (ed.). New York: Oxford University Press.

Hargreaves, Anne G. [1980] "Coping With Disaster." *American Journal of Nursing* **80** (April):683.

Hargreaves, Anne G., George I. Krell, Barbara Blakeney, and Mary Ryan [1979] "Blizzard 78—Dealing with Disaster." *American Journal of Nursing* **79** (February):268-271.

Harshbarger, Dwight [1974] "Picking Up the Pieces: Disaster Intervention and Human Ecology." *Omega: Journal of Death and Dying* **5** (Spring):55–59.

Hartmann, K., and J. Allison [1981] "Expected Psychological Reactions to Disaster in Medical Rescue Teams." *Military Medicine* **146** (No. 5):323–327.

Hartsough, Don M. [1982] "Planning for Disaster: A New Community Outreach Program for Mental Health Centers." *Journal of Community Psychology* **10** (July):255–264.

Harvey, Carol D.H., and Howard M. Bahr [1980] *The Sunshine Widows: Adapting to Sudden Bereavement*. Toronto: Lexington Books.

Heathcote, R. L. [1974] "Drought in South Australia." Pp. 128–136 in *Natural Hazards: Local, National, Global*, Gilbert F. White (ed.). New York: Oxford University Press.

Heathcote, R. L. [1969] "Drought in Australia: A Problem of Perception." *Geographical Review* **59**:175-194.

Heathcote, R. L., and B. G. Thom (eds.) [1979] *Natural Hazards in Australia*. Canberra: Australian Academy of Science.

Heffron, Edward F. [1977a] "Interagency Relationships and Conflict in Disaster: The Wilkes-Barre Experience." *Mass Emergencies* **2**:111–119.

Heffron, Edward F. [1977b] "Project Outreach: Crisis Intervention Following Natural Disaster." *Journal of Community Psychology* **5** (April):103–111.

Helms, John [1981] "Threat Perceptions in Acute Chemical Disasters." *Journal of Hazardous Materials* **4**:321–329.

Henderson, Scott [1977] "The Social Network, Support and Neurosis: The Function of Attachment in Adult Life." *British Journal of Psychiatry* **131** (August):185–191.

Henderson, Scott, and Tudor Bostock [1977] "Coping Behaviour after Shipwreck." *British Journal of Psychiatry* **131** (July):15–20.

Hershiser, Marvin R., and E. L. Quarantelli [1976] "The Handling of the Dead in a Disaster." *Omega: Journal of Death and Dying* **7** (No. 3):195–208.

Hewitt, K. (ed.) [1983] *Interpretations of Calamity*. Boston: Allen & Unwin Inc.

Hewitt, Kenneth, and Ian Burton [1971] *The Hazardousness of a Place*. Department of Geography Research Publication #6. Toronto: University of Toronto.

Hirose, Hirotada [1982] "Community Reconstruction and Functional Change Following a Disaster in Japan." Columbus, Ohio: Disaster Research Center, The Ohio State University.

Hirose, Hirotada [1979] "Volcanic Eruption and Local Politics in Japan: A Case Study." *Mass Emergencies* **4**:53–62.

Hirose, Hirotada (ed.) [1981] *Socio-Scientific Approach to Disasters* (in Japanese). Tokyo, Japan: Shinyosha.

Hirose, Hirotada, and Tomoichi Ishizuka [1983] "Causal Analysis of Earthquake Concern and Preparing Behavior in the North Izu Peninsula." *Japanese Psychological Research* **25**:103–111.

Hirschon, R., and S. Thakurdesai [1979] "Housing and Cultural Priorities: The Asia Minor Greek Refugees of 1922." *Disasters* **2** (No. 4):247–250.

Hocking, Frederick [1965] "Human Reactions to Extreme Environmental Stress." *The Medical Journal of Australia* **2** (September 18):477–483.

Hodge, David, Virginia Sharp, and Marion Marts [1979] "Contemporary Responses to Volcanism: Case Studies from the Cascades and Hawaii." Pp. 221–248 in *Volcanic Activity and Human Ecology*, Payson D. Sheets and Donald K. Grayson (eds.). New York: Academic Press.

Hodler, Thomas W. [1982] "Residents' Preparedness and Response to the Kalamazoo Tornado." *Disasters* **6** (No. 1):44–49.

Hoetmer, Gerard J. [1983a] "Emergency Management." *Baseline Data Reports* **15** (April): Washington, D.C.: International City Management Association.

Hoetmer, Gerard J. [1983b] "Emergency Management: Individual and County Data." *Baseline Data Reports* **15** (August): Washington, D.C.: International City Management Association.

Hogg, Richard [1980] "Pastoralism and Impoverishment: The Case of the Isiolo Boran of Northern Kenya." *Disasters* **4** (No. 3):299–310.

Hogg, Sarah Jane [1980] "Reconstruction Following Seismic Disaster in Venzone, Friuli." *Disasters* **4** (No. 2):173–185.

Hohenemser, C., R. W. Kates, and P. Slovic [1983] "The Nature of Technological Hazard." *Science* **220**:378–384.

Holdgate, Martin W., Mohamed Kassas, and Gilbert F. White [1982] "World Environmental Trends between 1972 and 1982." *Environmental Conservation* **9** (Spring):11–29.

Holloway, Ronald M. [1977] "Operations and Planning in Multiple Casualty Incidents." *Mass Emergencies* **2**:137–146.

Holmes, Roland C. [1961] "Composition and Size of Flood Losses." In *Papers on Flood Problems*, G. F. White (ed.). Department of Geography Research Paper #70. Chicago: University of Chicago.

Holy, Ladislav [1980] "Drought and Change in a Tribal Economy: The Berti of Northern Darfur." *Disasters* **4** (No. 1):65–71.

Horige, Kazuya, and Hiroshi Oura [1979] "The Cognition of the Damages, Caused By the 1978 Miyagiken Oki Earthquake, and Its Corresponding Behaviors (Jishin Higai no Ninchi to Taio Kodo)." *The Study of Sociology (Shakaigaku Kenkyu)* **38**:9–67.*

Houts, Peter S., Michael K. Lindell, Teh Wei Hu, Paul D. Cleary, George Tokuhata, and Cynthia B. Flynn [1984] "The Protective Action Decision Model Applied to Evacuation during the Three Mile Island Crisis." *International Journal of Mass Emergencies and Disasters* **2** (March):27–39.

Houts, Peter S., Robert W. Miller, Kum Shik Ham, and George K. Tokuhata [1980] "Extent and Duration of Psychological Distress of Persons in the Vicinity of Three Mile Island." *Proceedings of the Pennsylvania Academy of Science* **54** (1980):22–28.

Howard, J. A., E. C. Barrett, and J. U. Heilkema [1979] "The Application of Satellite Remote Sensing to Monitoring of Agricultural Disasters." *Disasters* **4** (No. 4):231–240.

Howard, Stephen J. [1980] "Children and the San Fernando Earthquake." *Earthquake Information Bulletin* **12** (September–October):190–192.

Hoyt, Michael F., and Bertram H. Raven [1973] "Birth Order and the 1971 Los Angeles Earthquake." *Journal of Personality and Social Psychology* **28** (October):123–128.

Huerta, Faye, and Robert Horton [1978] "Coping Behavior of Elderly Flood Victims." *The Gerontologist* **18** (December):541–546.

Huffman, James L. [1984] "Government Liability for the External Costs of Earthquake Prediction." Pp. 857–867 in *Earthquake Prediction: Proceedings of the International Symposium on Earthquake Prediction*. Paris: Terra Scientific Publishing Company (TERRAPUB).

Huffman, James L. [1983] "Government Liability and Natural Hazard Mitigation in Japan, the Soviet Union, China, New Zealand and the United States." *International Journal of Mass Emergencies and Disasters* 1 (November):379–398.

Huffman, James L. [1982] "Government Liability for Harm Resulting from Earthquake Prediction and Hazard Mitigation: A Preliminary Report on a Comparative Study." A paper presented at the Tenth World Congress of Sociology, Mexico City, Mexico, August.

Hultaker, Orjan E. [1977a] *Bortfallsproblem vid Katastrofstudier: Ett Exempel fran Andra Varldskriget.* (Problems of Nonresponse in Disaster Surveys: An Example from World War II) (in Swedish with an English summary). Disaster Studies 4. Uppsala, Sweden: University of Uppsala.

Hultaker, Orjan E. [1977b] *Evakueringar i Stobritannien under Andra Varldskriget.* (Evacuations in Great Britain during World War II) (in Swedish with an English summary). Disaster Studies 3. Uppsala, Sweden: University of Uppsala.

Hultaker, Orjan E. [1976] *Evakuera.* (Evacuate) (in Swedish with an English summary). Disaster Studies 2. Uppsala, Sweden: University of Uppsala.

Hultaker, Orjan E., and Jan E. Trost [1978] *Katastrofforskning en Lagesbeskrivning* (Disaster Research: A Description of Its Present State) (in Swedish with an English summary). Disaster Studies 6. Uppsala, Sweden: Uppsala University.

Hultaker, Orjan E., and Jan E. Trost [1976] *The Family and the Shelters.* Disaster Studies No. 1. Uppsala, Sweden: Uppsala University.

Hutton, Janice R. [1976] "The Differential Distribution of Death in Disaster: A Test of Theoretical Propositions." *Mass Emergencies* 1:261–266.

Hutton, Janice R., Dennis S. Mileti, with William B. Lord, John H. Sorensen, and Marvin Waterstone [1979] "Analysis of Adoption and Implementation of Community Land Use Regulations for Floodplains." San Francisco: Woodward-Clyde Consultants.

Ikeda, Ken'ichi [1982] "Warning of Disaster and Evacuation Behavior in a Japanese Chemical Fire." *Journal of Hazardous Materials* 7:51–62.

Illinois Department of Transportation, Division of Water Resources [1980] "Notifying Floodplain Residents: An Assessment of the Literature." Chicago: Illinois Department of Transportation, Division of Water Resources.

Instituut Voor Sociaal Onderzoek Van Het Nederlandse Volk Amsterdam [1955] *Studies in Holland Flood Disaster 1953.* Committee on Disaster Studies of the National Academy of Sciences/ National Research Council, Volumes I–IV. Washington, D.C.: National Academy of Sciences.

Irish, J. L., and B. Falconer [1979] "Reaction to Flood Warning." Pp. 313–329 in *Natural Hazards in Australia*, R. L. Heathcote and B. G. Thom (eds.). Canberra: Australian Academy of Science.

Islam, M. Aminul [1974] "Tropical Cyclones: Coastal Bangladesh." Pp. 19–25 in *Natural Hazards: Local, National, Global*, Gilbert F. White (ed.). New York: Oxford University Press.

Jackson, Edgar L. [1981] "Response to Earthquake Hazard: The West Coast of North America." *Environment and Behavior* 13 (July):387–416.

Jackson, Edgar L. [1977] "Public Response to Earthquake Hazard." *California Geology* 30 (December):278–280.

Jackson, Edgar L., and Tapan Mukerjee [1974] "Human Adjustment to the Earthquake Hazard of San Francisco, California." Pp. 160–166 in *Natural Hazards:*

Local, National, Global, Gilbert F. White (ed.). New York: Oxford University Press.

Jackson, Richard H. [1974] "Frost Hazard to Tree Crops in the Wasatch Front: Perception and Adjustments." Pp. 146–151 in *Natural Hazards: Local, National, Global,* Gilbert F. White (ed.). New York: Oxford University Press.

James, L. Douglas [1975] "Formulation of Nonstructural Flood Control Programs." *Water Resources Bulletin* 11 (August):688–705.

James, L. Douglas [1973] "Surveys Required to Design Nonstructural Measures." *Journal of the Hydraulics Division ASCE,* (October):1823–1836.

James, L. Douglas [1968] "The Economic Value of Real Estate Acquired for Right-of-Way." *Land Economics* 44 (August):363–370.

James, Thomas F., and Dennis E. Wenger [1978] "The American National Red Cross and Image Maintenance: A Research Note." *Mass Emergencies* 3:55–59.

Janerich, Dwight T., Alice D. Stark, Peter Greenwald, William S. Burnett, Herbert I. Jacobson, and Jane McCusker [1981] "Increased Leukemia, Lymphoma, and Spontaneous Abortion in Western New York Following a Flood Disaster." *Public Health Reports* 96 (July–August):350–356.

Janis, Irving L. [1951] *Air War and Emotional Stress: Psychological Studies of Bombings and Civilian Defense.* New York: McGraw-Hill.

Janis, Irving L., and Leon Mann [1977] "Emergency Decision Making: A Theoretical Analysis of Responses to Disaster Warnings." *Journal of Human Stress* 3 (June):35–48.

Janney, James G., Minoru Masuda, and Thomas H. Holmes [1977] "Impact of a Natural Catastrophe on Life Events." *Journal of Human Stress* 3 (June):22–34.

Jefferson, Jim, and T. Joseph Scanlon [1974] "The Sydney/Big Storm Report." EPC Field Report 74/7. Ottawa, Ontario, Canada: Emergency Planning Canada.

Jeffery, Susan E. [1982] "The Creation of Vulnerability to Natural Disaster: Case Studies from the Dominican Republic." *Disasters* 6 (No. 1):38–43.

Johnson, Branden B. [1979] "A Propositional Inventory of Technological Hazard Management." Worcester, Massachusetts: Center for Technology, Environment, and Development, Clark University.

Johnson, Brian [1968] "Risk Taking by Vacation Cottage Owners on the Flood Plain." *The Pennsylvania Geographer* 16 (December):6–11.

Jones, David R., and Joseph R. Fischer [1982] "Emotional Effects on USAF Personnel of Recovering and Identifying Victims from Jonestown, Guyana." Brooks Air Force Base, Texas: USAF School of Aerospace Medicine.

Kartez, Jack D. [1984] "Crisis Response Planning: Toward a Contingent Analysis." *Journal of the American Planning Association* 50 (Winter):9–21.

Kasl, Stanislav V., Rupert F. Chisholm, and Brenda Eskenazi [1981] "The Impact of the Accident at the Three Mile Island on the Behavior and Well-Being of Nuclear Workers." *American Journal of Public Health* 71 (May):472–495.

Kastenbaum, Robert [1974] "Disaster, Death, and Human Ecology." *Omega: Journal of Death and Dying* 5 (Spring):65–72.

Kates, Robert W. [1983] "The Human Environment: Penultimate Problems of Survival." Special Publication #6. Boulder, Colorado: Natural Hazards Research and Applications Information Center, The University of Colorado.

Kates, Robert W. [1977] "Major Insights: A Summary and Recommendations." Pp. 261–293 in *Reconstruction Following Disaster,* J. Eugene Haas, Robert W.

Kates, and Martyn J. Bowden (eds.). Cambridge, Massachusetts, and London: The MIT Press.

Kates, Robert W. [1971] "Natural Hazard in Human Ecological Perspective: Hypotheses and Models." *Economic Geography* **47** (July):438–451.

Kates, Robert W. [1970] "Human Adjustment to Earthquake Hazard." Pp. 7–31 in *The Great Alaska Earthquake of 1964: Human Ecology*, Committee on the Alaska Earthquake of the National Research Council (ed.). Washington, D.C.: National Academy of Sciences.

Kates, Robert W. [1962] *Hazard and Choice Perception in Flood Plain Management*. Department of Geography Research Paper #78. Chicago: University of Chicago.

Kates, Robert W., J. Eugene Haas, Daniel J. Amaral, Robert A. Olson, Reyes Ramos, and Richard Olson [1973] "Human Impact of the Managua Earthquake: Transitional Societies Are Peculiarly Vulnerable to Natural Disasters." *Science* **182**:981–990.

Kennedy, Will A. [1970] "Police Departments: Organization and Tasks in Disaster." *American Behavioral Scientist* **13** (January–February):354–361.

Kentsmith, David K. [1980] "Minimizing the Psychological Effects of a Wartime Disaster on an Individual." *Aviation, Space, and Environmental Medicine* **51** (April):409–413.

Kilijanek, Thomas S., and Thomas E. Drabek [1979] "Assessing Long-Term Impacts of a Natural Disaster—Focus on the Elderly." *The Gerontologist* **19** (December):555–566.

Killian, Charles D., Walter G. Peacock, and Frederick L. Bates [1982] "The Impact of the 1976 Guatemalan Earthquake on Inequality of Household Domestic Assets." A paper presented at the Annual Meeting of the Midwestern Sociological Society, Kansas City, Missouri, April.

Killian, Lewis M. [1956] "A Study of Response to the Houston, Texas Fireworks Explosion." National Academy of Sciences/National Research Council Disaster Study 2. Washington, D.C.: National Academy of Sciences.

Killian, Lewis M. [1954] "Some Accomplishments and Some Needs in Disaster Study." *The Journal of Social Issues* **10** (No. 3):66–72.

Killian, Lewis M. [1952] "The Significance of Multi-Group Membership in Disaster." *American Journal of Sociology* **57** (January):309–314.

Kilpatrick, F. P. [1957] "Problems of Perception in Extreme Situations." *Human Organization* **16** (Summer):20–22.

Kinston, Warren, and Rachel Rosser [1974] "Disaster: Effects on Mental and Physical State." *Journal of Psychosomatic Research* **18** (December):437–456.

Kirkby, Anne V. [1974] "Individual and Community Response to Rainfall Variability in Oaxaca, Mexico." Pp. 119–128 in *Natural Hazards: Local, National, Global*, Gilbert F. White (ed.). New York: Oxford University Press.

Kliman, Ann S. [1973] "The Corning Flood Project: Psychological First Aid Following A Natural Disaster." Pp. 325–335 in *Emergency and Disaster Management: A Mental Health Sourcebook*, Howard J. Parad, H. L. P. Resnik, and Libbie Parad (eds.). Bowie, Maryland: The Charles Press.

Klingman, Avigdor, and Zion Ben-Eli [1981] "A School Community in Disaster: Primary and Secondary Prevention in Situational Crisis." *Professional Psychology* **12** (August):523–533.

Klinteberg, Robert af [1979] "Management of Disaster Victims and Rehabilitation of Uprooted Communities." *Disasters* **3** (No. 1):61–70.

Klonglan, Gerald E., Charles L. Mulford, and Caroline S. Faisal [1973] "Problem Solution and Effectiveness: A Systems Analysis of Local Coordinators." Ames, Iowa: Department of Sociology and Anthropology, Iowa State University.

Klonglan, Gerald E., Charles L. Mulford, and David A. Hay [1973] "Impact of Career Development Program upon Local Coordinators: Final Report." Ames, Iowa: Department of Sociology and Anthropology, Iowa State University.

Knaus, Ronald L. [1975] "Crisis Intervention in a Disaster Area: The Pennsylvania Flood in Wilkes-Barre." *Journal of the American Osteopathic Association* **75** (November):297–301.

Kreimer, Alcira [1979] "Emergency, Temporary and Permanent Housing After Disasters in Developing Countries." *Ekistics* **46** (December):361–365.

Kreimer, Alcira [1978] "Post-Disaster Reconstruction Planning: The Cases of Nicaragua and Guatemala." *Mass Emergencies* **3**:23–40.

Krell, George I. [1978] "Managing the Psychosocial Factor in Disaster Programs." *Health & Social Work* **3** (August):139–154.

Kreps, Gary A. [in press] "Classical Themes, Structural Sociology, and Disaster Research." Chapter to appear in *Sociology of Disasters: Contribution of Sociology to Disaster Research,* Russell R. Dynes and Carlo Pelanda (eds.) Gorizia, Italy: Franco Angeli.

Kreps, Gary A. [1985] "Structural Sociology, Disaster, and Organization." Williamsburg, Virginia: Department of Sociology, College of William and Mary.

Kreps, Gary A. [1984a] "Review and Comment." *International Journal of Mass Emergencies and Disasters* **2** (August):304–308.

Kreps, Gary A. [1984b] "Sociological Inquiry and Disaster Research." *Annual Review of Sociology* **10**:309–330.

Kreps, Gary A. [1983] "The Organization of Disaster Response: Core Concepts and Processes." *International Journal of Mass Emergencies and Disasters* **1** (November):439–465.

Kreps, Gary A. [1982] "A Sociological Theory of Organized Disaster Response." A paper presented at the Tenth World Congress of Sociology, Mexico City, Mexico, August.

Kreps, Gary A. [1981] "The Worth of the NAS–NRC (1952–1963) and DRC (1963–Present) Studies of Individual and Social Responses to Disasters." Pp. 91–121 in *Social Science and Natural Hazards,* James D. Wright and Peter H. Rossi (eds.). Cambridge, Massachusetts: Abt Books.

Kreps, Gary A. [1980] "Research Needs and Policy Issues on Mass Media." Pp. 35–74 in *Disasters and the Mass Media: Proceedings of the Committee on Disasters and the Mass Media Workshop, February, 1979,* Committee on Disasters and the Mass Media. Washington, D.C.: National Academy of Sciences.

Kreps, Gary A. [1978] "The Organization of Disaster Response: Some Fundamental Theoretical Issues." Pp. 65–85 in *Disasters: Theory and Research,* E. L. Quarantelli (ed.). Beverly Hills, California: Sage.

Kueneman, Rodney M. [1973] "St. John River Flood Response Study." *EMO National Digest* (October–November):9–14.

Kueneman, Rodney M., and J. E. Wright [1975] "New Policies of Broadcast Stations for Civil-Disturbances and Disasters." *Journalism Quarterly* **52** (No. 4):670–677.

Kunreuther, Howard [1974a] "Disaster Insurance: A Tool for Hazard Mitigation." *Journal of Risk and Insurance* **41** June:287–303.

Kunreuther, Howard [1974b] "Economic Analysis of Natural Hazards: An Ordered Choice Approach." Pp. 206–214 in *Natural Hazards: Local, National, Global*, Gilbert F. White (ed.). New York: Oxford University Press.

Kunreuther, Howard, Ralph Ginsberg, Louis Miller, Philip Sagi, Paul Slovic, Bradley Borkan, and Norman Katz [1978] *Disaster Insurance Protection: Public Policy Lessons*. New York: John Wiley and Sons.

Kunreuther, Howard, and Eryl Ley (eds.) [1982] *The Risk Analysis Controversy: An Institutional Perspective*. Berlin, Heidelberg, New York: Springer–Verlag.

Kunreuther, Howard, Joanne Linnerooth, and others. [1983] *Risk Analysis and Decision Processes: The Siting of Liquefied Energy Gas Facilities in Four Countries*. New York: Springer-Verlag.

Kutak, Robert I. [1938] "The Sociology of Crises: The Louisville Flood of 1937." *Social Forces* **17**:66–72.

Lachman, Roy, Maurice Tatsuoka, and William Bonk [1961] "Human Behavior during the Tsunami of May, 1960." *Science* **133**:1405–1409.

Lamson, Cynthia [1983] " 'I Think They're All Caught Up': An Inquiry of Hazard Perception among Newfoundland and Inshore Fishermen." *Environment and Behavior* **15** (July):458–486.

Larson, James F. [1980] "A Review of the State of the Art in Mass Media." Pp. 75–126 in *Disasters and the Mass Media: Proceedings of the Committee on Disasters and the Mass Media Workshop, February, 1979*, Committee on Disasters and the Mass Media. Washington, D.C.: National Academy of Sciences.

Laube, Jerri [1973] "Psychological Reactions of Nurses in Disaster." *Nursing Research* **22**:343–347.

Lechat, Michel F. [1976] "The Epidemiology of Disasters." *Proceedings of the Royal Society of Medicine* **69** (June):421–426.

Leik, Robert K., T. Michael Carter, John P. Clark, and others. [1981] "Community Response to Natural Hazard Warnings: Final Report." Minneapolis: University of Minnesota.

Leik, Robert K., Sheila A. Leik, Knut Ekker, and Gregory A. Gifford [1982] "Under the Threat of Mount St. Helens: A Study of Chronic Family Stress." Minneapolis: Family Study Center, University of Minnesota.

Leitko, Thomas A., David R. Rudy, and Steven A. Peterson [1980] "Loss Not Need: The Ethics of Relief Giving in Natural Disasters." *Journal of Sociology and Social Welfare* **7** (September):730–741.

Leivesley, Sally [1977a] "Toowoomba: The Role of An Australian Disaster Unit." *Disasters* **1** (No. 4): 315–322.

Leivesley, Sally [1977b] "Toowoomba: Victims and Helpers in an Australian Hailstorm Disaster." *Disasters* **1** (No. 3):205–216.

Lessa, William A. [1964] "The Social Effects of Typhoon Ophelia (1960) on Ulithi." *Micronesia* **1** (Nos. 1–2):1–47.

Levine, Adeline Gordon [1982] *Love Canal: Science, Politics, and People*. Toronto: Lexington Books.

Levy, Charlene C., and Janet K. Smith [n.d.] "Apathy and Inexperience: A Study of Hurricane Hazard Perception in Sarasota County." Tampa, Florida: Environmental Studies Program, New College of the University of South Florida.

Lewis, James [1975] "Awareness and Response." Pp. 29–32 in *A Study in Predisaster Planning*. Occasional Paper #10. Bradford, Yorkshire, England: University of Bradford, Disaster Research Unit.

Lewis, James, Philip O'Keefe, and Kenneth N. Westgate [1977] "A Philosophy of Precautionary Planning." *Mass Emergencies* **2**:95–104.

Lifton, Robert Jay, and Eric Olson [1976] "The Human Meaning of Total Disaster: The Buffalo Creek Experience." *Psychiatry* **39** (February):1–18.

Lindell, Michael K., Ronald W. Perry, and Marjorie R. Greene [1980] "Race and Disaster Warning Response." Seattle: Battelle Human Affairs Research Centers.

Lindy, Jacob D., Mary C. Grace, and Bonnie L. Green [1981] "Survivors: Outreach to a Reluctant Population." *American Journal of Orthopsychiatry* **5** (July):468–478.

Lindy, Jacob D., and Joanne G. Lindy [1981] "Planning and Delivery of Mental-Health Services in Disaster—The Cincinnati Experience." *Urban and Social Change Review* **14** (Summer):16–21.

Logue, James N., and Holger Hansen [1980] "A Case-Control Study of Hypertensive Women in a Post-Disaster Community: Wyoming Valley, Pennsylvania." *Journal of Human Stress* **6** (June):28–34.

Logue, James N., Holger Hansen, and Elmer Struening [1981] "Some Indications of the Long-Term Health-Effects of a Natural Disaster." *Public Health Reports* **96** (January–February):67–79.

Logue, James N., Holger Hansen, and Elmer Struening [1979] "Emotional and Physical Distress Following Hurricane Agnes in Wyoming Valley of Pennsylvania." *Public Health Reports* **94** (November–December):495–502.

Logue, James N., Mary Evans Melick, and Elmer L. Struening [1981] "A Study of Health and Mental Health Status Following a Major Natural Disaster." Pp. 217–274 in *Research in Community and Mental Health*, Roberta G. Simmons (ed.). Greenwich, Connecticut: JAI Press, Inc.

Loizos, Peter [1977] "A Struggle for Meaning: Reactions to Disaster amongst Cypriot Refugees." *Disasters* **1** (No. 3):231–239.

Lomnitz, Cinna [1970] "Casualties and Behavior of Populations during Earthquakes." *Bulletin of the Seismological Society of America* **60** (August):1309–1313.

Long, Frank [1978] "The Impact of Natural Disasters on Third World Agriculture: An Exploratory Survey of the Need for Some New Dimensions in Development Planning." *American Journal of Economics and Sociology* **37** (April):149–163.

Lorelli, James T. [1968] "Coping With the Flood Threat: Public Acceptance of Flood Insurance." *The Pennsylvania Geographer* **16** (December):1–5.

Lowrance, William W. [1976] *Of Acceptable Risk: Science and the Determination of Safety*. Los Altos, California: William Kaufmann.

Lucas, Rex A. [1969] *Men in Crisis: A Study of a Mine Disaster*. New York: Basic Books.

Ludwig, Harvey F. [1954] "Sanitary Engineering in 'Operation Tulip.' " *Public Health Reports* **69** (June):553–537.

Luloff, A.E., and Kenneth P. Wilkinson [1979] "Participation in the National Flood Insurance Program: A Study of Community Activeness." *Rural Sociology* **44** (Spring):137–152.

Mack, Raymond W., and George W. Baker [1961] "The Occasion Instant." National Academy of Sciences/National Research Council Disaster Study #15. Washington, D.C.: National Academy of Sciences.

Mader, George G., William E. Spangle, Martha L. Blair, Richard L. Meehan, Sally W. Bilodeau, Henry J. Degen Kolb, George S. Duggar, and Norman Williams, Jr. [1980] "Land Use Planning After Earthquakes." Portola Valley, California: William Spangle and Associates, Inc.

Maderthaner, Rainer, Giselher Guttman, Elisabeth Swaton, and Harry Otway [1978] "Effect of Distance upon Risk Perception." *Journal of Applied Psychology* 63 (June):380–382.

Maley, Roger F. [1974] "Comments on Conceptual Disasters About Disasters." *Omega: Journal of Death and Dying* 5 (Spring):73–75.

Margolis, Maxine [1980] "Natural Disaster and Socioeconomic Change: Post-Frost Adjustments in Parana, Brazil." *Disasters* 4 (No. 2):231–235.

Margolis, Maxine [1979] "Green Gold and Ice: The Impact of Frosts on the Coffee Growing Region of Northern Parana, Brazil." *Mass Emergencies* 4:135–144.

Marshall, Mac [1979] "Natural and Unnatural Disaster in the Mortlock Islands of Micronesia." *Human Organization* 38 (Fall):265–272.

Martin, Morgan [1964] "The True Face of Disaster." *Medical Times* (February):163–166.

Martin, Russell D. [1980] "Disaster Planning for Psychiatric Casualties for General Hospitals with Psychiatric-Services." *Military Medicine* 145 (No. 2):111–113.

Maxwell, Christopher [1982] "Hospital Organizational Response to the Nuclear Accident at Three-Mile-Island—Implications for Future-Oriented Disaster Planning." *American Journal of Public Health* 72 (March):275–279.

May, Peter J. [1985] *Recovering from Catastrophes: Federal Disaster Relief Policy and Politics.* Westport, Connecticut: Greenwood Press.

McBride, Danny [1979] "Psychosocial Stress and Natural Disaster." Pp. 124–127 in *Planning for People in Natural Disasters,* Joan Innes Reid (ed.). Townsville, Queensland, Australia: James Cook University of North Queensland.

McComb, David [1980] *Big Thompson: Profile of a Natural Disaster.* Boulder, Colorado: Pruett Publishing Company.

McCubbin, Hamilton, David H. Olson, and Joan M. Patterson [1983] "Beyond Family Crisis: Family Adaptation." *International Journal of Mass Emergencies and Disasters* 1 (March):73–94.

McDonald, N. S. [1979] "Hazard Perception in Northern New South Wales." Pp. 260–269 in *Natural Hazards in Australia,* R. L. Heathcote and B. G. Thom (eds.). Canberra: Australian Academy of Science.

McDonald, Peter [1979] "A Training Model for Disaster Counsellors." Pp. 128–132 in *Planning for People in Natural Disasters,* Joan Innes Reid (ed.). Townsville, Queensland, Australia: James Cook University of North Queensland.

McGrath, Joseph E. (ed.) [1970] *Social and Psychological Factors in Stress.* New York: Holt, Rinehart and Winston, Inc.

McIntire, Matilda S., and Esmaeel Sadeghi [1977] "The Pediatrician and Mental-Health in a Community-Wide Disaster—Lessons From Aftermath of a Tornado." *Clinical Pediatrics* 16 (No. 8):702–705.

McLoughlin, David [1985] "A Framework for Integrated Emergency Management." *Public Administration Review* 45 (January):165–172.

McLuckie, Benajmin F. [1977] "Italy, Japan, and the United States: Effects of Centralization on Disaster Responses 1964–1969." The Disaster Research Center Historical and Comparative Disasters Series, No. 1. Columbus, Ohio: Disaster Research Center, The Ohio State University.

McLuckie, Benajmin F. [1975] "Centralization and Natural Disaster Response: A Preliminary Hypothesis and Interpretations." *Mass Emergencies* 1:1–9.

McLuckie, Benajmin F. [1970] "A Study of Functional Response to Stress in Three Societies." Dissertation. Columbus, Ohio: The Ohio State University.

McPherson, H. J., and T. F. Saarinen [1977] "Flood Plain Dwellers' Perception of the Flood Hazard in Tucson, Arizona." *The Annals of Regional Science* **11** (July):25–40.

Melick, Mary Evans [1978a] "Life Change and Illness: Illness Behavior of Males in the Recovery Period of a Natural Disaster." *Journal of Health and Social Behavior* **19** (September):335–342.

Melick, Mary Evans [1978b] "Self-Reported Effects of a Natural Disaster on the Health and Well-Being of Working Class Males." *Crisis Intervention* **9** (No. 1):12–31.

Meltsner, Arnold J. [1978] "Public Support for Seismic Safety: Where Is It in California?" *Mass Emergencies* **3**:167–184.

Menninger, W. C. [1952] "Psychological Reactions in an Emergency (Flood)." *American Journal of Psychiatry* **109** (August):128–130.

Merton, Robert K. [1969] "Foreword." Pp. vii–xxxvii in *Communities in Disaster: A Sociological Analysis of Collective Stress Situations*, Allen H. Barton. Garden City, New York: Doubleday and Company, Inc.

Merton, Robert K. [1957] *Social Theory and Social Structure*. Rev. Ed. New York: The Free Press.

Mileti, Dennis S. [1983] "Societal Comparisons of Organizational Response to Earthquake Predictions: Japan vs. the United States." *International Journal of Mass Emergencies and Disasters* **1** (November):399–413.

Mileti, Dennis S. [1982] "Earthquake Prediction Response: Cultural Comparisons Between Japan and the United States." A paper presented at the Tenth World Congress of Sociology, Mexico City, Mexico, August.

Mileti, Dennis S. [1980] "Human Adjustment to the Risk of Environmental Extremes." *Sociology and Social Research* **64** (April):327–347.

Mileti, Dennis S. [1975a] *Disaster Relief and Rehabilitation in the United States: A Research Assessment*. Boulder, Colorado: Institute of Behavioral Science, The University of Colorado.

Mileti, Dennis S. [1975b] *Natural Hazard Warning Systems in the United States: A Research Assessment*. Boulder, Colorado: Institute of Behavioral Science, The University of Colorado.

Mileti, Dennis S. and E. M. Beck [1975] "Communication in Crisis: Explaining Evacuation Symbolically." *Communication Research* **2** (January):24–49.

Mileti, Dennis S., Thomas E. Drabek, and J. Eugene Haas [1975] *Human Systems in Extreme Environments*. Boulder, Colorado: Institute of Behavioral Science, The University of Colorado.

Mileti, Dennis S., Donald M. Hartsough, Patti Madson, and Rick Hufnagel [1984] "The Three Mile Island Incident: A Study of Behavioral Indicators of Human Stress." *International Journal of Mass Emergencies and Disasters* **2** (March):89–113.

Mileti, Dennis S., Janice R. Hutton, and John H. Sorensen [1981] *Earthquake Prediction Response and Options for Public Policy*. Boulder, Colorado: Institute of Behavioral Science, The University of Colorado.

Miller, D. J., W. A. R. Brinkmann, and R. G. Barry [1974] "Windstorms: A Case Study of Wind Hazard for Boulder, Colorado." Pp. 80–86 in *Natural Hazards: Local, National, Global*, Gilbert F. White (ed.). New York: Oxford University Press.

Miller, Joan [1973] "Community Development in a Disaster Community." *Community Development Journal* **8** (October):161–166.

Miller, Judith A., Joseph G. Turner and Edith Kimball [1981] "Big Thompson Flood Victims: One Year Later." *Family Relations* **30** (January):111–116.

Milne, Gordon [1979] "Cyclone Tracy: Psychological and Social Consequences." Pp. 116–123 in *Planning for People in Natural Disasters,* Joan Innes Reid (ed.). Townsville, Queensland, Australia: James Cook University of North Queensland.

Mitchell, Glenn, and Stuart Piggin [1977] "The Mount Kembla Mine Explosion of 1902: Towards the Study of the Impact of a Disaster on a Community." *The Journal of Australian Studies* **1** (July):52–69.

Mitchell, Jeffrey T. [1982] "The Psychological Impact of the Air Florida 90 Disaster on Fire-Rescue, Paramedic and Police Officer Personnel." *Proceedings of the First International Assembly on Emergency Medical Services* (Baltimore, Maryland, June 13–17, 1982). Washington, D.C.: U.S. Department of Transportation.

Mitchell, William A. [1977] "Partial Recovery and Reconstruction after Disaster: The Lice Case." *Mass Emergencies* **2**:233–247.

Mitchell, William A. [1976a] "Reconstruction after Disaster—Gediz Earthquake of 1970." *Geographical Review* **66**:296–313.

Mitchell, William A. [1976b] "The Lice Earthquake in Southeastern Turkey: A Geography of the Disaster." Final Report. USAF Academy, Colorado: Department of Economics, Geography and Management, USAF Academy.

Mitchell, William A., and Timothy H. Miner [1978] "Environment, Disaster, and Recovery: A Longitudinal Study of the 1970 Gediz Earthquake in Western Turkey." USAF Academy, Colorado:Department of Economics, Geography and Management, USAF Academy.

Moline, Norman T. [1974] "Perception Research and Local Planning: Floods on the Rock River, Illinois." Pp. 52–59 in *Natural Hazards: Local, National, Global,* Gilbert F. White (ed.). New York: Oxford University Press.

Moore, Gwendolyn B., and Robert K. Yin [1983a] "Innovations in Earthquake and Natural Hazards Research: Local Government Liability." (Case Study No. 1). Washington, D.C.: Cosmos Corporation.

Moore, Gwendolyn B., and Robert K. Yin [1983b] "Innovations in Earthquake and Natural Hazards Research: Unreinforced Masonry Buildings." (Case Study No. 2). Washington, D.C.: Cosmos Corporation.

Moore, Gwendolyn B., and Robert K. Yin [1983c] "Innovations in Earthquake and Natural Hazards Research: The Social Consequences of Earthquake Predictions." (Case Study No. 3). Washington, D.C.: Cosmos Corporation.

Moore, Harry Estill [1958] *Tornadoes Over Texas.* Austin: University of Texas Press.

Moore, Harry Estill [1956] "Toward a Theory of Disaster." *American Sociological Review* **21** (December):734–737.

Moore, Harry Estill with the collaboration of Frederick L. Bates, Jon P. Alston, Marie M. Fuller, Marvin V. Layman, Donald L. Mischer, and Meda Miller White [1964] *And the Winds Blew.* Austin, Texas: The Hogg Foundation for Mental Health, University of Texas.

Moore, Harry Estill, Frederick L. Bates, Marvin V. Layman, and Vernon J. Parenton [1963] "Before the Wind: A Study of Response to Hurricane Carla." National Academy of Sciences/ National Research Council Disaster Study #19. Washington, D.C.: National Academy of Sciences.

Moore, Harry Estill, and H. J. Friedsam [1959] "Reported Emotional Stress Following a Disaster." *Social Forces* 38 (December):135–139.

Morentz, James W. [1980] "Communication in the Sahel Drought: Comparing the Mass Media with Other Channels of International Communication." Pp. 158–183 in *Disasters and the Mass Media: Proceedings of the Committee on Disasters and the Mass Media Workshop, February, 1979,* Committee on Disasters and the Mass Media. Washington, D.C.: National Academy of Sciences.

Moric-Petrovic, Slavka, Milica Jojic-Milenkovic, and Milica Marinkov [1972] "Mentalno-Higijenski Problemi Dece Evakuisane Posle Katastrofalnog Zemljotresa U Skoplju" (Mental Hygiene Problems of Children Evacuated after Catastrophic Earthquake in Skopje) (in Serbo-Croatian). *Anali Zavoda Za Mentalno Zdravlje* 4 (No. 1):53–64.

Morren, George E.B., Jr. [1983a] "The Bushmen and the British: Problems of the Identification of Drought and Responses to Drought." Pp. 44–66 in *Interpretations of Calamity,* K. Hewitt (ed.). Boston: Allen & Unwin Inc.

Morren, George E.B., Jr. [1983b] "A General Approach to the Identification of Hazards and Responses." Pp. 284–297 in *Interpretations of Calamity,* K. Hewitt (ed.). Boston: Allen & Unwin Inc.

Muckleston, Keith W., Michael F. Turner, and Richard T. Brainerd [1981] "Floodplain Regulations and Residential Land Values in Oregon." Completion Report. Corvallis, Oregon: Oregon State University.

Mulford, Charles L., Gerald E. Klonglan, and Joseph P. Kopachevsky [1973] "Securing Community Resources for Social Action." Ames, Iowa: Department of Sociology and Anthropology, Iowa State University.

Mulford, Charles L., Gerald E. Klonglan, and Dan L. Tweed [1973] "Profiles on Effectiveness: A Systems Analysis." Ames, Iowa: Department of Sociology and Anthropology, Iowa State University.

Mulford, Charles L., Gerald E. Klonglan, Richard D. Warren, and Janet B. Padgitt [1976/77] "A Multidimensional Evaluation of Effectiveness in a Non-Economic Organization." *Organization and Administrative Sciences* 7 (Winter):125–143.

Mulford, Charles L., Gerald E. Klonglan, Richard D. Warren, and Paul F. Schmitz [1972] "A Causal Model of Effectiveness in Organizations." *Social Science Research* 1 (April):61–77.

Murton, Brian J., and Shinzo Shimabukuro [1974] "Human Adjustment to Volcanic Hazard in Puna District, Hawaii." Pp. 151–159 in *Natural Hazards: Local, National, Global,* Gilbert F. White (ed.). New York: Oxford University Press.

Mushkatel, Alvin H., and Louis F. Weschler [1985] "Emergency Management and the Intergovernmental System." *Public Administration Review* 45 (January):49–56.

Nakamura, Y. [1981] "Helping Behavior in a Disaster" (in Japanese). Pp. 165–194 in *Socio-Scientific Approach to Disasters,* Hirotada Hirose (ed.). Tokyo, Japan: Shinyosha.

National Governors' Association [1979] *Comprehensive Emergency Management: A Governor's Guide.* Washington, D.C.: U.S. Government Printing Office.

National Science Foundation [1980] *A Report on Flood Hazard Mitigation.* Washington, D.C.: National Science Foundation.

Neal, David M. [1984] "Blame Assignment in a Diffuse Disaster Situation: A Case Example of the Role of an Emergent Citizen Group." *International Journal of Mass Emergencies and Disasters* 2 (August):251–266.

Neal, David M., Joseph B. Perry, and Randolph Hawkins [1982] "Getting Ready for Blizzards—Preparation Levels in the Winter of 1977–1978." *Sociological Focus* **15** (January):67–76.

Needham, R. D., and J. G. Nelson [1977] "Newspaper Response to Flood and Erosion Hazards on the North Lake Erie Shore." *Environmental Management* **1** (November):521–540.

Neff, Joan L. [1977] "Responsibility for the Delivery of Emergency Medical Services in a Mass Casualty Situation: The Problem of Overlapping Jurisdictions." *Mass Emergencies* **2**:179–188.

Nehnevajsa, Jiri, and Henry Wong [1977] "Flood Preparedness 1977: A Pittsburgh Area Study." Pittsburgh: University of Pittsburgh, University Center for Urban Research.

Neldner, Brian W. [1979] "Settlement of Rural Refugees in Africa." *Disasters* **3** (No. 4):393–402.

Nelson, L. D. [1977] "Continuity in Helping Roles: A Comparison of Everyday and Emergency Role Performance." *Pacific Sociological Review* **20** (April):263–278.

Nelson, L. D. [1973] "Proximity to Emergency and Helping Behavior—Data From Lubbock-Tornado-Disaster." *Journal of Voluntary Action Research* **2** (No. 4):194–199.

Nelson, L. D., and Russell R. Dynes [1976] "The Impact of Devotionalism and Attendance on Ordinary and Emergency Helping Behavior." *Journal for the Scientific Study of Religion* **15** (March):47–59.

Neville, Robert G. [1978] "The Courrières Colliery Disaster, 1906." *Journal of Contemporary History* **13** (No. 1):33-52.

Newman, C. Janet [1977] "Children of Disaster: Clinical Observations at Buffalo Creek." Pp. 149–161 in *Annual Progress in Child Psychiatry and Child Development*, Stella Chess and Alexander Thomas (eds.). New York: Brunner/Mazel, Publishers.

Newman, C. Janet [1976] "Children of Disaster: Clinical Observations at Buffalo Creek." *American Journal of Psychiatry* **133** (March):306–312.

Nichols, Thomas C., Jr. [1974] "Global Summary of Human Response to Natural Hazards: Earthquakes." Pp. 274–284 in *Natural Hazards: Local, National, Global*, Gilbert F. White (ed.). New York: Oxford University Press.

Nielsen, Joyce McCarl [1976] "Crowding Models, Stress, and Wilderness." *Mass Emergencies* **1**:249–260.

Nigg, Joanne [1982] "Awareness and Behavior: Public Response to Prediction Awareness." Pp. 71–96 in *Perspectives on Increasing Hazard Awareness*, Thomas F. Saarinen (ed.). Boulder, Colorado: Institute of Behavioral Science, The University of Colorado.

Nilson, Linda Burzotta, and Douglas C. Nilson [1981] "Resolving the 'Sooner vs. Later' Controversy Surrounding the Public Announcement of Earthquake Predictions." *Disasters* **5** (No. 4):391–397.

Nimmo, Dan [1984] "TV Network News Coverage of Three Mile Island: Reporting Disasters as Technological Fables." *International Journal of Mass Emergencies and Disasters* **2** (March):115–145.

Nolan, Mary Lee [1979] "Impact of Parícutin on Five Communities." Pp. 293–338 in *Volcanic Activity and Human Ecology*, Payson D. Sheets and Donald K. Grayson (eds.). New York: Academic Press.

Ohta, Hideaki [1972] "Evacuating Characteristics of Tokyo Citizens." Pp. 175–183 in *Proceedings of the Japan–United States Disaster Research Seminar: Organizational and Community Responses to Disasters*. Columbus, Ohio: Disaster Research Center, The Ohio State University.

Ohta, Hideaki, and Kitao Abe [1977] "Responses to Earthquake Prediction in Kawasaki City, Japan in 1974." Pp. 273–282 in *Earthquake Precursors: Proceedings of the U.S.–Japan Seminar on Theoretical and Experimental Investigations of Earthquake Precursors*, C. Kisslinger and Z. Suzuki (eds.). Tokyo: Center for Academic Publications Japan, Japan Scientific Societies Press.

Okabe, Keizo, and Shunji Mikami [1982] "A Study on the Socio-Psychological Effect of a False Warning of the Tokai Earthquake in Japan." A Paper presented at the Tenth World Congress of Sociology, Mexico City, Mexico, August.

Okabe, Keizo *et al.* [1981a] *A Disaster Warning and Responses of Residents: A Study of Evacuation Behavior after a Warehouse Fire in Ohbu City (Saigai Keiho to Jumin no Taio)*. Tokyo: Institute of Journalism and Communication, University of Tokyo, (Shimbun Kenkyusho).*

Okabe, Keizo *et al.* [1981b] "Experimental Study on Insurance Purchasing Behaviors." Chapter 4 in *The Earthquake Prediction Warning and the Social Responses, Part II (Zoku Jishin Yochi to Shakaiteki Hanno)*. Tokyo: University of Tokyo Press.*

Okabe, Keizo *et al.* [1979a] *A Survey Research on People's Responses to an Earthquake Prediction Warning (Jishin Yochi Joho eno Taio)*. Tokyo: Institute of Journalism and Communication, University of Tokyo (Shimbun Kenkyusho).*

Okabe, Keizo *et al.* [1979b] "Survey Research on the Attitude of Tokyo Residents toward the Prospective Earthquake and the Prediction Warning (Saigai ni kansuru Tomin no Ishiki Chosa)." Pp. 137–303 in *The Earthquake Prediction Warning and the Social Responses (Jishin Yochi to Shakaiteki Hanno)*, Institute of Journalism and Communication (ed.). Tokyo: University of Tokyo. (Shimbun Kenkyusho).*

Okura, K. Patrick [1975] "Mobilizing in Response to a Major Disaster." *Community Mental Health Journal* 11 (Summer):136–144.

Okura, K. Patrick [1974] "Mobilizing in Response to a Major Disaster." Pp. 15–33 in *Beyond Clinic Walls*, A.B. Tulipan, C.L. Attneave, and E. Kingstone, (eds.). University, Alabama: University of Alabama Press.

O'Leary, Michael [1980] "Responses to Drought in Kitui District, Kenya." *Disasters* 4 (No. 3):315–327.

Oliver, John [1980] "A Review of Flood Problems in Tropical Queensland." *Disasters* 4 (No. 4):459–468.

Oliver, John [1979] "Human Response to Natural Disaster." Pp. 24–30 in *Planning for People in Natural Disasters*, Joan Innes Reid (ed.). Townsville, Queensland, Australia: James Cook University of North Queensland.

Oliver, John [1975] "The Significance of Natural Hazards in a Developing Area: A Case Study from North Queensland." *Geography* 60:99–110.

Oliver, John (ed.) [1983] *Insurance and Natural Disaster Management*. Townsville, Queensland, Australia: Centre for Disaster Studies, James Cook University of North Queensland.

Oliver, John, and G. F. Reardon [1982] *Tropical Cyclone 'Isaac': Cyclonic Impact in the Context of the Society and Economy of the Kingdom of Tonga*. Townsville, Queensland, Australia: Centre for Disaster Studies, James Cook University of North Queensland.

Oliver, John, and D. H. Trollope [1981] *Hurricane Allen: A Post-Impact Survey of a Major Tropical Storm.* Disaster Investigation Report No. 3. Townsville, Queensland, Australia: Centre for Disaster Studies, James Cook University of North Queensland.

Oliver-Smith, Anthony [1979a] "Post Disaster Consensus and Conflict in a Traditional Society: The 1970 Avalanche of Yungay, Peru." *Mass Emergencies* **4:**39–52.

Oliver-Smith, Anthony [1979b] "The Yungay Avalanche of 1970: Anthropological Perspectives on Disaster and Social Change." *Disasters* **3** (No. 1):95–101.

Oliver-Smith, Anthony [1978] "Guatemala—Aid Disaster Relief Program and Reports on Post-Earthquake Distribution of Building-Materials." *Mass Emergencies* **3:**268–269.

Oliver-Smith, Anthony [1977a] "Disaster Rehabilitation and Social Change in Yungay, Peru." *Human Organization* **36** (Spring): 5–13.

Oliver-Smith, Anthony [1977b] "Traditional Agriculture, Central Places, and Postdisaster Urban Relocation in Peru." *American Ethnologist* **4** (No. 1):102–116.

Ollendick, Duane G., and Sister Margeen Hoffmann [1982] "Assessment of Psychological Reactions in Disaster Victims." *Journal of Community Psychology* **10** (April):157–167.

Olson, Richard Stuart, and Douglas C. Nilson [1982] "Public Policy Analysis and Hazards Research: Natural Complements." *The Social Science Journal* **19** (January):89–103.

Olson, Robert A., and Richard Stuart Olson [1977] "The Guatemala Earthquake of 4 February 1976: Social Science Observations and Research Suggestions." *Mass Emergencies* **2:**69–81.

O'Riordan, Timothy [1974] "The New Zealand Natural Hazard Insurance Scheme: Application to North America." Pp. 217–219 in *Natural Hazards: Local, National, Global,* Gilbert F. White (ed.). New York: Oxford University Press.

Orr, David W. [1979] "Catastrophe and Social Order." *Human Ecology* **7** (March):41–52.

Osterling, Jorge P. [1979] "The 1970 Peruvian Disaster and the Spontaneous Relocation of Some of Its Victims: Ancashino Peasant Migrants in Huayopampa." *Mass Emergencies* **4:**117–120.

Page, Gillian A. [1980] "The Canadian Flood Damage Reduction Program." *Disasters* **4** (No. 4):411–421.

Palm, Risa [1981] *Real Estate Agents and Special Studies Zones Disclosure: The Response of California Home Buyers to Earthquake Hazards Information.* Boulder, Colorado: Institute of Behavioral Science, The University of Colorado.

Palmer, Ellen L. [1980] "Student Reactions to Disaster." *American Journal of Nursing* **80** (April):680–682.

Palmer, George J., and S. B. Sells [1965] "Behavioral Factors in Disaster Situations." *Journal of Social Psychology* **66:**65–71.

Panel on the Public Policy Implications of Earthquake Prediction [1975] *Earthquake Prediction and Public Policy.* Washington, D.C.: National Academy of Sciences.

Parad, Howard J., H. L. P. Resnik, and Libbie Parad (eds.) [1976] *Emergency and Disaster Management: A Mental Health Sourcebook.* Bowie, Maryland: The Charles Press.

Parker, Dennis J., and Donald M. Harding [1978] "Planning for Urban Floods." *Disasters* **2** (No. 1):47–57.

Parker, Gordon [1977] "Cyclone Tracy and Darwin Evacuees: On the Restoration of the Species." *British Journal of Psychiatry* **130** (June):548–555.

Parker, Gordon [1975] "Psychological Disturbance in Darwin Evacuees Following Cyclone Tracy." *The Medical Journal of Australia* **1** (May 24):650–652.

Parker, Stanley D., Marilynn B. Brewer, and Janie R. Spencer [1980] "Natural Disaster, Perceived Control, and Attributions to Fate." *Personality and Social Psychology Bulletin* **6** (September):454–459.

Parr, Arnold Richard [1970] "Organizational Response to Community Crises and Group Emergence." *American Behavioral Scientist* **13** (January–February):423–429.

Parr, Arnold Richard [1969a] "A Brief on Disaster Plans." *EMO National Digest* **9** (August–September):8.

Parr, Arnold Richard [1969b] "Flood Preparation—1969: Observations Concerning the Southern Manitoba Spring Flood Preparations." *EMO National Digest* **9** (June–July):25–27.

Patrick, V., and W. K. Patrick [1981] "Cyclone '78 in Sri Lanka: The Mental Health Trail." *British Journal of Psychiatry* **138** (March):210–216.

Paul, R. L. [1981] "Recovery From Disaster." *Journal of System Management* **32** (No. 2):18–20.

Paulozzi, Leonard J. [1980] "Great Myths in Disaster Relief—Epidemics." *Journal of Environmental Health* **43** (No. 3):140–143.

Paulsen, R. L. [1981] *Human Behavior and Fire Emergencies: An Annotated Bibliography*. Washington, D.C.: National Bureau of Standards, U.S. Department of Commerce.

Peacock, Walter G., and Frederick L. Bates [1982] "Ethnic Differences in Earthquake Impact and Recovery." Pp. 792–892 in "Recovery, Change and Development: A Longitudinal Study of the 1976 Guatemalan Earthquake," Frederick L. Bates (ed.). Athens, Georgia: Guatemalan Earthquake Study, University of Georgia.

Pelanda, Carlo [1982a] "Disaster and Order: Theoretical Problems in Disaster Research." A paper presented at the Tenth World Congress of Sociology, Mexico City, Mexico, August.

Pelanda, Carlo [1982b] "Disastro e Vulnerabilità 'Sociosistemica" (Disaster and Social Vulnerability) (in Italian). *Rassegna Italiana di Sociologia* **22**:507–532.

Pelanda, Carlo [1979] "Behavioral and Social Tendencies after the Friuli Earthquake: State of the System." A paper presented at the International Symposium for Disaster and Accident Research, Kiel, September.

Penick, Elizabeth C., B.J. Powell, and W.A. Sieck [1976] "Mental Health Problems and Natural Disaster: Tornado Victims." *Journal of Community Psychology* **4** (January):64–68.

Perez, Robert [1982] "Provision of Mental-Health Services During a Disaster—The Cuban Immigration of 1980." *Journal of Community Psychology* **10** (January):40–47.

Perlberg, Mark [1979] "Trauma at Tenerife: The Psychic Aftershocks of a Jet Disaster." *Human Behavior* **8** (No. 4):49–50.

Perrow, Charles [1984] *Normal Accidents: Living with High Risk Technologies*. New York: Basic Books.

Perry, Helen Swick, and Stewart E. Perry [1959] "The Schoolhouse Disasters." National Academy of Sciences/National Research Council Disaster Study #11. Washington, D.C.: National Academy of Sciences.

Perry, Joseph B., Jr., Randolph Hawkins, and David M. Neal [1983] "Giving and Receiving Aid." *International Journal of Mass Emergencies and Disasters* **1** (March):171–188.

Perry, Ronald W. [1985] *Comprehensive Emergency Management: Evacuating Threatened Populations*. Greenwich, Connecticut, and London: JAI Press, Inc.

Perry, Ronald W. [1984] "Evaluating Emergency Response Plans." *Emergency Management Review* **1** (Winter):20–23.

Perry, Ronald W. [1983] "Population Evacuation in Volcanic Eruptions, Floods and Nuclear Power Plant Accidents: Some Elementary Comparisons." *Journal of Community Psychology* **11** (January):36–47.

Perry, Ronald W. [1982] *The Social Psychology of Civil Defense*. Lexington, Mass.: Lexington Books.

Perry, Ronald W. [1979a] "Detecting Psychopathological Reactions to Natural Disaster—A Methodological Note." *Social Behavior and Personality* **7** (No. 2):173–177.

Perry, Ronald W. [1979b] "Evacuation Decision-Making in Natural Disasters." *Mass Emergencies* **4**:25–38.

Perry, Ronald W. [1979c] "Incentives for Evacuation in Natural Disaster—Research Based Community Emergency Planning." *Journal of the American Planning Association* **45** (October):440-447.

Perry, Ronald W., David F. Gillespie, and Dennis S. Mileti [1974] "System Stress and the Persistence of Emergent Organizations." *Sociological Inquiry* **44** (No. 2):111–119.

Perry, Ronald W., and Marjorie R. Greene [1983] *Citizen Response to Volcanic Eruptions: The Case of Mount St. Helens*. New York: Irvington Publishers.

Perry, Ronald W., and Marjorie R. Greene [1982a] "Emergency Management in Volcano Hazards: The May 18, 1980 Eruption of Mt. St. Helens." *The Environmental Professional* **4** (Fall):340–350.

Perry, Ronald W., and Marjorie R. Greene [1982b] "The Role of Ethnicity in the Emergency Decision-Making Process." *Sociological Inquiry* **52** (Fall):306–334.

Perry, Ronald W., Marjorie R. Greene, and Michael K. Lindell [1980a] "Enhancing Evacuation Warning Compliance: Suggestions for Emergency Planning." *Disasters* **4** (No. 4):433–449.

Perry, Ronald W., Marjorie R. Greene, and Michael K. Lindell [1980b] "Human Response to Volcanic Eruption: Mount St. Helens, May 18, 1980." Seattle: Battelle Human Affairs Research Centers.

Perry, Ronald W., Marjorie Greene, and Alvin Mushkatel [1983] "American Minority Citizens in Disaster." Seattle: Battelle Human Affairs Research Centers.

Perry, Ronald W., and Hirotada Hirose [1983] "Volcanic Eruptions and Functional Change: Parallels in Japan and the United States." *International Journal of Mass Emergencies and Disasters* **1** (August):231–253.

Perry, Ronald W., and Hirotada Hirose [1982] "Volcanic Eruptions and Functional Change: Parallels in Japan and the United States." A paper presented at the meetings of the International Sociological Association, Mexico City, Mexico, August.

Perry, Ronald W., and Michael K. Lindell [1978] "The Psychological Consequences of Natural Disaster: A Review of Research on American Communities." *Mass Emergencies* **3**:105–115.

Perry, Ronald W., Michael K. Lindell, and Marjorie R. Greene [1982a] "Crisis Communications: Ethnic Differentials in Interpreting and Acting on Disaster Warnings." *Social Behavior and Personality* **10** (No. 1):97–104.

Perry, Ronald W., Michael K. Lindell, and Marjorie R. Greene [1982b] "Threat Perception and Public Response to Volcano Hazard." *Journal of Social Psychology* **116**:199–204.

Perry, Ronald W., Michael K. Lindell, and Marjorie R. Greene [1981] *Evacuation Planning in Emergency Management*. Lexington, Massachusetts, and Toronto: Lexington Books.

Perry, Ronald W., Michael K. Lindell, and Marjorie R. Greene [1980] "The Implications of Natural Hazard Evacuation Warning Studies for Crisis Relocation Planning." Seattle: Battelle Human Affairs Research Centers.

Perry, Ronald W., and Alvin H. Mushkatel [1984] *Disaster Management: Warning Response and Community Relocation*. Westport, Connecticut, and London: Quorum Books.

Perry, Stewart E., Earle Silber, and Donald A. Black [1956] "The Child and His Family in Disaster: A Study of the 1953 Vicksburg Tornado." National Academy of Sciences/ National Research Council Disaster Study #5. Washington, D.C.: National Academy of Sciences.

Petak, William J. [1984] "Natural Hazard Mitigation: Professionalization of the Policy Making Process." *International Journal of Mass Emergencies and Disasters* **2** (August):285–302.

Petak, William J., and Arthur A. Atkisson [1982] *Natural Hazard Risk Assessment and Public Policy: Anticipating the Unexpected*. New York, Heidelberg, Berlin: Springer-Verlag.

Platt, Rutherford H. [1984] "Review and Comment." *International Journal of Mass Emergencies and Disasters* **2** (August):308–315.

Platt, Rutherford H. [1982] "The Jackson Flood of 1979—A Public-Policy Disaster." *Journal of the American Planning Association* **48** (Spring):219–231.

Platt, Rutherford H. with the assistance of George M. McMullen, Richard Paton, Ann Patton, Michael Grahek, Mary Read English, and Jon A. Kusler [1980] *Intergovernmental Management of Floodplains*. Boulder, Colorado: Institute of Behavioral Science, The University of Colorado.

Ploeger, Andreas [1974] "Lengede—Zehn Jahre danach: Medizinisch-psychologische Katamnese einer extremen Belastungssituation." (Lengede—Ten Years Later: Ten-Year Follow-Up of Miners Trapped for Two Weeks in 1963) (in German with an English summary). *Psychotherapie und Medizinische Psychologie* **24** (July):137–143.

Ponting, J. Rick [1976] "Human Behavioural Reactions to an Accidental Explosion: A Test of a Sociological Theory of Panic." Calgary, Alberta, Canada: Department of Sociology, The University of Calgary.

Ponting, J. Rick [1974] " 'It Can't Happen Here': A Pedagogical Look at Community Co-ordination in Response to a Toxic Gas Leak." *Emergency Planning Digest* **1** (May):8–13.

Popkin, Roy S. [1978] "The American Red Cross Response to Disasters." *Mass Emergencies* **3**:49–53.

Poulshock, S. W., and E. S. Cohen [1975] "Elderly in Aftermath of a Disaster." *The Gerontologist* **15** (August):357–361.

Predescu, V., and St. Nica-Udangiu [1979] "Postseismic Reactions, Observations on a Group of Patients Displaying Psychic Disorders Determined by March 4, 1977 Earthquake in Romania." *Revue Roumaine de Médecine—Neurologie et Psychiatrie* **17** (No. 3):179–188.

President's Commission on the Accident at Three Mile Island [1979] *Report of the President's Commission on the Accident at Three Mile Island.* (The Need For Change: The Legacy of TMI). Washington, D.C.: U.S. Government Printing Office.

Prince, Samuel Henry [1920] "Catastrophe and Social Change, Based Upon a Sociological Study of the Halifax Disaster." Ph.D. thesis. New York: Columbia University Department of Political Science.

Py, Y. [1978] "Comptements Dans un Cas de Secours D'urgence" (Behavior in Emergency Situations) (in French). *Le Travail Humain* **41** (No. 1):67–80.

Quarantelli, E. L. [1984] *Organizational Behavior in Disasters and Implications for Disaster Planning.* Emmitsburg, Maryland: National Emergency Training Center, Federal Emergency Management Agency.

Quarantelli, E. L. [1983a] *Delivery of Emergency Medical Services in Disasters: Assumptions and Realities.* New York: Irvington Publishers.

Quarantelli, E. L. [1983b] "Evacuation Behavior: Case Study of the Taft, Louisiana Chemical Tank Explosion Incident." Columbus, Ohio: Disaster Research Center, The Ohio State University.

Quarantelli, E. L. [1982a] "Sheltering and Housing after Major Community Disasters: Case Studies and General Conclusions." Columbus, Ohio: Disaster Research Center, The Ohio State University.

Quarantelli, E. L. [1982b] "Social and Organizational Problems in a Major Community Emergency." *Emergency Planning Digest* **9** (January):7–10, 21.

Quarantelli, E. L. [1982c] *Inventory of Disaster Field Studies in the Social and Behavioral Sciences: 1919–1979.* Columbus, Ohio: Disaster Research Center, The Ohio State University.

Quarantelli, E. L. [1981a] "Disaster Planning: Small and Large—Past, Present, and Future." Pp. 1–26 in *Proceedings: American Red Cross EFO Division Disaster Conference.* Alexandria, Virginia: Eastern Field Office, American Red Cross.

Quarantelli, E. L. [1981b] "Panic Behavior in Fire Situations: Findings and a Model from the English Language Research Literature." Pp. 405–428 in *Proceedings of the 4th Joint Panel Meeting, The U.J.N.R. Panel on Fire Research and Safety.* Tokyo: Building Research Institute.

Quarantelli, E. L. [1981c] "Psycho-Sociology in Emergency Planning." *International Civil Defense Bulletin* **28** (November/December):1–6.

Quarantelli, E. L. [1981d] "Sociology and Social Psychology of Disaster." Pp. 1–8 in *Complete Record of the Proceedings 9th World Civil Defense Conference,* Part 2. Geneva, Switzerland: International Civil Defense Organization. (Disaster Research Center Reprint Article 147).

Quarantelli, E. L. [1980a] "Community Impact of Airport Disasters: Similarities and Differences When Compared with Other Kinds of Disasters." *Managing the Problems of Aircraft Disaster Conference.* Minneapolis: Department of Conferences, University of Minnesota.

Quarantelli, E. L. [1980b] "Evacuation Behavior and Problems: Findings and Implications from the Research Literature." Columbus, Ohio: Disaster Research Center, The Ohio State University.

Quarantelli, E. L. [1979] "The Vaiont Dam Overflow: A Case Study of Extra-Community Responses in Massive Disasters." *Disasters* 3 (No. 2):199–212.

Quarantelli, E. L. [1977] "Panic Behavior: Some Empirical Observations." Pp. 336–350 in *Human Response to Tall Buildings*. Stroudsburg, Pennsylvania: Dowden, Hutchinson and Ross, Inc.

Quarantelli, E. L. [1976] "Human Response in Stress Situations." Pp. 99–112 in *Proceedings of the First Conference and Workshop on Fire Casualties*, B. M. Halpin (ed.). Laurel, Maryland: Applied Physics Laboratory, Johns Hopkins University.

Quarantelli, E. L. [1970a] "The Community General Hospital: Its Immediate Problems in Disaster." *American Behavioral Scientist* 13 (January–February):380–391.

Quarantelli, E. L. [1970b] "Emergent Accommodation Groups: Beyond Current Collective Behavior Typologies." Pp. 111–123 in *Human Nature and Collective Behavior: Papers in Honor of Herbert Blumer*, Tamatsu Shibutani (ed.). Englewood Cliffs, New Jersey: Prentice Hall.

Quarantelli, E. L. [1966] "Organizations Under Stress." Pp. 3–19 in *Symposium on Emergency Operations*, Robert Brictson (ed.). Santa Monica, California: Systems Development Corporation.

Quarantelli, E. L. [1965] "Mass Behavioral and Governmental Breakdown in Major Disasters: Viewpoint of a Researcher." *The Police Yearbook:*105–112.

Quarantelli, E. L. [1964] "The Behavior of Panic Participants." Pp. 69–81 in *Panic Behavior*, D. P. Schultz (ed.). New York: Random House.

Quarantelli, E. L. [1960a] "A Note on the Protective Function of the Family in Disasters." *Marriage and Family Living* 22 (August):263–264.

Quarantelli, E. L. [1960b] "Images of Withdrawal Behavior in Disasters: Some Basic Misconceptions." *Social Problems* 8 (Summer):68–79.

Quarantelli, E. L. [1957] "The Behavior of Panic Participants." *Sociology and Social Research* 41 (January–February):187–194.

Quarantelli, E. L. [1954] "The Nature and Conditions of Panic." *American Journal of Sociology* 60 (November):267–275.

Quarantelli, E. L. (eds.) [1978] *Disasters: Theory and Research*. Beverly Hills, California: Sage.

Quarantelli, E. L., and Russell R. Dynes [1977] "Response to Social Crisis and Disaster." *Annual Review of Sociology* 3:23–49.

Quarantelli, E. L., and Russell R. Dynes [1976] "Community Conflict: Its Absence and Its Presence in Natural Disasters." *Mass Emergencies* 1:139–152.

Quarantelli, E. L., and Russell R. Dynes [1972] "When Disaster Strikes (It Isn't Much Like What You've Heard and Read About)." *Psychology Today* 5 (No. 9):66–70.

Quarantelli, E. L., and Russell R. Dynes [1970] "Property Norms and Looting: Their Patterns in Community Crisis." *Phylon* 31 (Summer):168–182.

Quarantelli, E. L., and Russell R. Dynes [1969] "Dissensus and Consensus in Community Emergencies: Patterns of Looting and Property Norms." *Il Politico* 34:276–291.

Quarantelli, E. L., and Russell R. Dynes [1967] "Operational Problems of Organizations in Disasters." Pp. 151–175 in *1967 Emergency Operations Symposium*, Robert Brictson (ed.). Santa Monica, California: Systems Development Corporation.

Quarantelli, E. L., Clark Lawrence, Kathleen Tierney, and Ted Johnson [1979] "Initial Findings from a Study of Socio-Behavioral Preparations and Planning for Acute Chemical Hazard Disasters." *Journal of Hazardous Materials* 3:79–90. (Disaster Research Center Reprint Article No. 119 pp. 1–22).

Quarantelli, E. L., J. Rick Ponting, and John Fitzpatrick [1974] "Police Department Perceptions of the Occurrence of Civil Disturbances." *Sociology and Social Research* 59 (October):30–38.

Quarantelli, E. L., and Kathleen Tierney [1981] "A Model for Studying Community Preparedness for Acute Chemical Disasters." Pp. 336–353 in *Unfall-und Katastrophen-Forschung,* H. Graf-Baumann and Stephen Metreveli (eds.). Erlangen, West Germany: Fachbuch.

Quarantelli, E. L., and Kathleen Tierney [1979a] "Disaster Preparation Planning." Pp. 263–313 in *Fire Safety and Disaster Preparedness.* Washington, D.C.: Office of Public Sector Programs, American Association for the Advancement of Science.

Quarantelli, E. L., and Kathleen Tierney [1979b] "Social Climate and Preparations for Sudden Chemical Disasters." Pp. 457–460 in *Sociological Research Symposium IX,* E. P. Lewis, L. D. Nelson, D. H. Scully, and J. S. Williams (eds.). Richmond, Virginia: Department of Sociology, Virginia Commonwealth University.

Rabin, Robert L. [1978] "Dealing with Disasters: Some Thoughts on the Adequacy of the Legal System." *Stanford Law Review* 30 (January):281–298.

Raker, John W., and Hiram J. Friedsam [1960] "Disaster-Scale Medical Care Problems." *Journal of the American Medical Association* 173:1239–1244.

Rangell, Leo [1976] "Discussion of the Buffalo Creek Disaster: The Course of Psychic Trauma." *American Journal of Psychiatry* 133 (March):313–316.

Raphael, Beverley [1979–80] "A Primary Prevention Action Programme: Psychiatric Involvement Following a Major Rail Disaster." *Omega: Journal of Death and Dying* 10 (No. 3):211–226.

Raphael, Beverley [1979] "The Preventive Psychiatry of Natural Hazard." Pp. 330–339 in *Natural Hazards in Australia,* R. L. Heathcote and B. G. Thom (eds.). Canberra: Australian Academy of Science.

Raphael, Beverley [1977] "The Granville Train Disaster–Psychological Needs and Their Management." *The Medical Journal of Australia* 1 (February 26):303–305.

Regulska, Joanna [1982] "Public Awareness Programs for Natural Hazards." Pp. 36–70 in *Perspectives on Increasing Hazard Awareness,* Thomas F. Saarinen (ed.). Boulder, Colorado: Institute of Behavioral Science, The University of Colorado.

Reid, Joan Innes (ed.) [1979] *Planning for People in Natural Disasters.* Townsville, Queensland, Australia: James Cook University Press.

Research Committee of the Miyagiken Oki Earthquake, 1978 (Nihon Kenchiku Gakkai, Tohoku Shibu) [1979] *Report on the Investigations into the Actual Condition Caused by the 1978 Miyagiken Oki Earthquake ('78 Miyagiken Oki Jishin Saigai no Jittai).* Japan: Architectural Institute of Japan, Tohoku Branch.*

Richard, Wayne C. [1974] "Crisis Intervention Services Following Natural Disaster: The Pennsylvania Recovery Project." *Journal of Community Psychology* 2 (July):211–219.

Ridington, Robin [1982] "When Poison Gas Come Down Like A Fog—A Native Community's Response to Cultural Disaster." *Human Organization* 41 (No. 1) (Spring):36–42.

Roder, Wolf [1961] "Attitudes and Knowledge on the Topeka Flood Plain." In *Papers on Flood Problems*, G. F. White (ed.). Department of Geography Research Paper #70. Chicago: University of Chicago.

Rogers, Everett M., and Rahul S. Sood [1980] "Mass Media Communication and Disasters: A Content Analysis of Media Coverage of the Andhra Pradesh Cyclone and the Sahel Drought." Pp. 139–157 in *Disasters and the Mass Media: Proceedings of the Committee on Disasters and the Mass Media Workshop, February, 1979*, Committee on Disasters and the Mass Media. Washington, D.C.: National Academy of Sciences.

Rogers, George Oliver, and Jiri Nehnevajsa with contributions by Thomas M. Landry, Virginia Kissel, Janet E. Chump, Richard Andersen and Patricia Lomando White [1984] "Behavior and Attitudes under Crisis Conditions: Selected Issues and Findings." Pittsburgh: University Center for Social and Urban Research, University of Pittsburgh.

Rogers, George W. [1970] "Economic Effects of the Earthquake." Pp. 58–76 in *The Great Alaska Earthquake of 1964: Human Ecology* Committee on the Alaska Earthquake of the National Research Council (ed.). Washington, D.C.: National Academy of Sciences.

Rooney, John F. [1967] "The Urban Snow Hazard in the United States." *Geographical Review* **57**:538–559.

Rose, Adam [1980] "Mandating Local Government Emergency Services." *The Urban Interest* **2** (No. 1):65–73.

Rosenberg, Steven A., Paul M. Fine, and Gay L. Robinson [1980] "Emotional Effects of the Omaha Tornado." *Nebraska Medical Journal* **65** (February):24–26.

Rosengren, Karl Erik, Peter Arvidson, and Dahn Sturesson [1975] "The Barseback 'Panic': A Radio Programme as a Negative Summary Event." *Acta Sociologica* **18** (No. 4):303–321.

Rosow, Irving L. [1977] "Authority in Emergencies: Four Tornado Communities in 1953." The Disaster Research Center Historical and Comparative Disasters Series, No. 2. Columbus, Ohio: Disaster Research Center, The Ohio State University.

Rosow, Irving L. [1955] "Conflict of Authority in Natural Disasters." Dissertation. Cambridge, Massachusetts: Harvard University.

Ross, G. Alexander [1980] "The Emergence of Organization Sets in Three Ecumenical Disaster Recovery Organizations—An Empirical and Theoretical Exploration." *Human Relations* **33** (January):23–39.

Ross, G. Alexander [1978] "Organizational Innovation in Disaster Settings." Pp. 215–232 in *Disasters: Theory and Research*, E. L. Quarantelli (ed.). Beverly Hills, California: Sage.

Ross, James L. [1970] "The Salvation Army: Emergency Operations." *American Behavioral Scientist* **13** (January–February):404–414.

Rossi, Peter H., James D. Wright, and Eleanor Weber-Burdin with the assistance of Marianne Pietras and William F. Diggins [1982] *Natural Hazards and Public Choice: The State and Local Politics of Hazard Mitigation*. New York: Academic Press.

Rossi, Peter H., James D. Wright, Eleanor Weber-Burdin, and Joseph Pereira [1983a] "Victimization By Natural Hazards in the United States, 1970–1980: Survey Estimates." *International Journal of Mass Emergencies and Disasters* **1** (November):467–482.

Rossi, Peter H., James D. Wright, Eleanor Weber-Burdin, and Joseph Pereira [1983b] *Victims of the Environment: Loss from Natural Hazards in the United States, 1970–1980.* New York: Plenum Press.

Rossi, Peter H., James D. Wright, Sonia R. Wright, and Eleanor Weber-Burdin [1978] "Are There Long Term Effects of American Natural Disasters?" *Mass Emergencies* 3:117–132.

Roth, Robert [1970] "Cross-Cultural Perspectives on Disaster Response." *American Behavioral Scientist* 13 (January–February):440–451.

Rowe, William D. [1977] *An Anatomy of Risk.* New York: Wiley Interscience.

Rubin, Claire [1981] "Long-Term Recovery from Natural Disasters: A Comparative Analysis of Six Local Experiences." Washington, D.C.: The Academy for Contemporary Problems, The Resource Referral Service.

Rubin, Claire B., and Daniel G. Barbee [1985] "Disaster Recovery and Hazard Mitigation: Bridging the Intergovernmental Gap." *Public Administration Review* 45 (January):57–63.

Rubin, Claire B. with Martin D. Saperstein and Daniel G. Barbee [1985] *Community Recovery from a Major Natural Disaster.* Boulder, Colorado: Institute of Behavioral Science, The University of Colorado.

Ruch, Carlton [1984] "Human Response to Vertical Shelters: 'An Experimental Note.' " *International Journal of Mass Emergencies and Disasters* 2 (November):389–401.

Saarinen, Thomas F. (ed.) [1982a] *Perspectives on Increasing Hazard Awareness.*Boulder, Colorado: Institute of Behavioral Science, The University of Colorado.

Saarinen, Thomas F. [1982b] "The Relation of Hazard Awareness to Adoption of Mitigation Measures." Pp. 1–35 in *Perspectives on Increasing Hazard Awareness,* Thomas F. Saarinen (ed.). Boulder, Colorado: Institute of Behavioral Science, The University of Colorado.

Saarinen, Thomas F. [1966] *Perception of Drought Hazard on the Great Plains.* Department of Geography Research Paper #106. Chicago: University of Chicago.

Sandman, Peter M., and Mary Paden [1979] "At Three Mile Island." *Columbia Journalism Review* (July/August):43–58.

Sank, Lawrence I. [1979] "Psychology in Action: Community Disasters, Primary Prevention and Treatment in a Health Maintenance Organization." *American Psychologist* 34 (April):334–338.

Scanlon, T. Joseph [1982] "The Roller Coaster Story of Civil Defence Planning in Canada." *Emergency Planning Digest* 9 (April–June):2–14.

Scanlon, T. Joseph [1981] "Coping With the Media: Police-Media Problems and Tactics in Hostage Takings and Terrorist Incidents." *Canadian Police College Journal* 5 (No. 3):129–148.

Scanlon, T. Joseph [1980] "The Media and the 1978 Terrace Floods: An Initial Test of a Hypothesis." Pp. 254–266 in *Disasters and the Mass Media: Proceedings of the Committee on Disasters and the Mass Media Workshop, February, 1979,* Committee on Disasters and the Mass Media. Washington, D.C.: National Academy of Sciences.

Scanlon, T. Joseph [1979] "Day One in Darwin: Once Again the Vital Role of Communications." Pp. 133–155 in *Planning for People in Natural Disasters,* Joan Innes Reid (ed.). Townsville, Queensland, Australia: James Cook University of North Queensland.

Scanlon, T. Joseph [1977] "Post-Disaster Rumor Chains: A Case Study." *Mass Emergencies* **2**:121–126.

Scanlon, T. Joseph [1976] "The Not So Mass Media: The Role of Individuals In Mass Communication." Pp. 104–119 in *Journalism, Communication and the Law*, G. Stuart Adam (ed.). Scarborough, Ontario: Prentice Hall of Canada.

Scanlon, T. Joseph [n.d.] "The Terrace Floods." Ottawa, Ontario, Canada: Emergency Communications Research Unit, Carleton University.

Scanlon, T. Joseph [n.d.] "The Woodstock Tornado." Ottawa, Ontario, Canada: Emergency Communications Research Unit, Carleton University.

Scanlon, T. Joseph, and Suzanne Alldred [1982] "Media Coverage of Disasters: The Same Old Story." *Emergency Planning Digest* **9** (October–December):13–19.

Scanlon, T. Joseph with Kim Dixon and Scott McClellan [1982] "The Miramichi Earthquakes: The Media Respond to an Invisible Emergency." Ottawa, Ontario, Canada: Emergency Communications Research Unit, School of Journalism, Carleton University.

Scanlon, T. Joseph, and Alan Frizzell [1979] "Old Theories Don't Apply: Implications of Communications in Crises." *Disasters* **3** (No. 3):315–319.

Scanlon, T. Joseph with Darlene Harapiak and Mary Lou Tario [1977] "The Goulds Fire: Emergency Communications in Newfoundland." (EPC Field Report 77/1). Ottawa, Ontario, Canada: Emergency Planning Canada.

Scanlon, T. Joseph, Jim Jefferson, and Debbie Sproat [1976] "The Port Alice Slide." (EPC Field Report 76/1). Ottawa, Ontario, Canada: Emergency Planning Canada.

Scanlon, T. Joseph with Rudy Luukko and Gerald Morton [1978] "Media Coverage of Crisis: Better Than Reported, Worse Than Necessary." *Journalism Quarterly* **55** (Spring):68–72.

Scanlon, T. Joseph, and Brian Taylor [1977] "Two Tales of a Snowstorm: How the Blizzard of January, 1977 Affected the Niagara Region of Ontario." (ECRU Field Report 77/3). Ottawa, Ontario, Canada: Emergency Communications Research Unit, School of Journalism, Carleton University.

Scanlon, T. Joseph, and Brian Taylor [1975] "The Warning Smell of Gas." (EPC Field Report 75/2). Ottawa, Ontario, Canada: Emergency Planning Canada.

Scanlon, T. Joseph, and Massey Padgham [1980] *The Peel Regional Police Force and the Mississauga Evacuation*. Ottawa, Ontario: Canadian Police College.

Schatzman, Leonard [1960] "A Sequence of Pattern Disaster and Its Consequences for Community." Dissertation. Bloomington, Indiana: Indiana University.

Schiff, Myra [1977] "Hazard Adjustment, Locus of Control, and Sensation Seeking:Some Null Findings." *Environment and Behavior* **9** (June):233–254.

Schneider, David M. [1957] "Typhoons on Yap." *Human Organization* **16** (Summer):10–15.

Schorr, John K., Raymond Goldsteen, and Cynthia H. Cortes [1982] "The Long-Term Impact of a Man-Made Disaster: A Sociological Examination of a Small Town in the Aftermath of the Three Mile Island Nuclear Reactor Accident." A paper presented at the Tenth World Congress of Sociology, Mexico City, Mexico, August.

Schulberg, Herbert C. [1974] "Disaster, Crisis Theory, and Intervention Strategies." *Omega: Journal of Death and Dying* **5** (Spring):77–87.

Schware, Robert [1982] "Official and Folk Flood Warning Systems: An Assessment." *Environmental Management* **6** (May):209–216.

Seaman, John, and Julius Holt [1980] "Markets and Famines in the Third World." *Disasters* 4 (No. 3):283–297.

Seitz, Steven Thomas, and Morris Davis [1984] "The Political Matrix of Natural Disasters: Africa and Latin America." *International Journal of Mass Emergencies and Disasters* 2 (August):231–250.

Sendai Research Committee of Urban Sciences (Sendai Toshi Kagaku Kenkyukai) [1979] *The Comprehensive Summary and Assessment of Several Empirical Studies on the Miyagiken Oki Earthquake (Miyagiken Oki Jishin Saizai ni Kansuru Sho-Chosa no Sogoteki Bunseki to Kyoka).* As cited in Yasumasa Yamamoto and E. L. Quarantelli. *Inventory of the Japanese Disaster Research Literature in the Social and Behavioral Sciences.* Columbus, Ohio: Disaster Research Center, The Ohio State University, 1982, p. A-184.

Senior Executive Policy Center [1984] *Issues in Emergency Management.* Emmitsburg, Maryland: Senior Executive Policy Center, National Emergency Training Center, Federal Emergency Management Agency.

Shamgar-Handelman, Lea [1983] "The Social Status of War Widows." *International Journal of Mass Emergencies and Disasters* 1 (March):153–170.

Shaw, Robert [1979] "Health-Services in a Disaster—Lessons From the 1975 Vietnamese Evacuation." *Military Medicine* 144 (No. 5):307–311.

Shear, David, and Bob Clark [1976] "International Long-Term Planning for the Sahel." *International Development Review* 18 (No. 4):15–20.

Sheets, Payson D. [1979] "Environmental and Cultural Effects of the Ilopango Eruption in Central America." Pp. 525–564 in *Volcanic Activity and Human Ecology,* Payson D. Sheets and Donald K. Grayson (eds.). New York: Academic Press.

Sheets, Payson D., and Donald K. Grayson (eds.) [1979] *Volcanic Activity and Human Ecology.* New York: Academic Press.

Shimada, Kazuo [1972] "Attitudes toward Disaster Defense Organizations and Volunteer Activities in Emergencies." Pp. 208–217 in *Proceedings of the Japan–United States Disaster Research Seminar: Organizational and Community Responses to Disasters.* Columbus, Ohio: Disaster Research Center, The Ohio State University.

Shippee, Glenn E., Richard Bradford, and W. Larry Gregory [1982] "Community Perceptions of Natural Disasters and Post-Disaster Mental-Health Services." *Journal of Community Psychology* 10 (January):23–28.

Short, James F., Jr. [1984] "Toward the Social Transformation of Risk Analysis." *American Sociological Review* 49 (December):711–725.

Short, Patricia [1979] " 'Victims' and 'Helpers'." Pp. 448–459 in *Natural Hazards in Australia,* R. L. Heathcote and B. G. Thom (eds.). Canberra: Australian Academy of Science.

Simpson, Robert H., and Herbert Riehl [1981] *The Hurricane and Its Impact.* Baton Rouge, Louisiana, and London: Louisiana State University Press.

Simpson-Housley, Paul, and Peter Bradshaw [1978] "Personality and the Perception of Earthquake Hazard." *Australian Geographical Studies* 16 (April):65–72.

Sims, John H., and Duane D. Baumann [1972] "The Tornado Threat: Coping Styles of the North and South." *Science* 176:1386–1392.

Singer, Benjamin D., and Lyndsay Green [1972] *The Social Functions of Radio in a Community Emergency.* Toronto: Copp Clark.

Singer, Timothy J. [1982] "An Introduction to Disaster: Some Considerations of a Psychological Nature." *Aviation, Space, and Environmental Medicine* 53 (March):245–250.

Singh, Bruce, and Beverley Raphael [1981] "Post-Disaster Morbidity of the Bereaved—A Possible Role for Preventive Psychiatry." *Journal of Nervous and Mental Disease* **169** (April):203–212.

Sjoberg, Gideon [1962] "Disasters and Social Change." Pp. 356–384 in *Man and Society in Disaster*, George W. Baker and Dwight W. Chapman (eds.). New York: Basic Books.

Slovic, Paul, Baruch Fischhoff, Sarah Lichtenstein, Bernard Korrigan, and Barbara Combs [1977] "Preference for Insurance against Probable Small Loss: Implications for Theory and Practice of Insurance." *Journal of Risk and Insurance* **44** (June):237–258.

Slovic, Paul, Howard Kunreuther, and Gilbert F. White [1974] "Decision Processes, Rationality, and Adjustment to Natural Hazards." Pp. 187–206 in *Natural Hazards: Local, National, Global,* Gilbert F. White (ed.). New York: Oxford University Press.

Smith, D. I., P. Den Exter, M. A. Dowling, P. A. Jelliffe, R. G. Munro, and W. C. Martin [1979] *Flood Damage in the Richmond River Valley, New South Wales.* Canberra,: Australian National University.

Smith, D. I., J. W. Handmer, and W. C. Martin [1980] *The Effects of Floods on Health: Hospital Admissions for Lismore.* Canberra: Australian National University.

Smith, Keith, and Graham Tobin [1979] *Human Adjustment to the Flood Hazard.* London and New York: Longman.

Smith, Martin H. [1978] "American Religious Organizations in Disaster: A Study of Congregational Response to Disaster." *Mass Emergencies* **3**:133–142.

Smith, Robert A., Clarence C. Traum, and Lorna H. Poole [1977] "The Provision of Primary Care During a Period of Natural Disaster or Large Scale Emergency." *Mass Emergencies* **2**:19–23.

Snarr, D. Neil, and E. Leonard Brown [1980] "User Satisfaction with Permanent Post-Disaster Housing: Two Years After Hurricane Fifi in Honduras." *Disasters* **4** (No. 1):83–91.

Snarr, D. Neil, and E. Leonard Brown [1979] "Permanent Post-Disaster Housing in Honduras: Aspects of Vulnerability to Future Disasters." *Disasters* **3** (No. 3):287–292.

Snarr, D. Neil, and E. Leonard Brown [1978] "Post-Disaster Housing in Honduras after Hurricane Fifi: An Assessment of Some Objectives." *Mass Emergencies* **3**:239–250.

Society for the Behavioral Science of Disaster (Saigai Kodo Kagaku Kenkyukai) [1978] *A Psychological Analysis of Evacuation Behavior in the Case of the Great Sakata Fire (Sakata Taika ni okeru Hinan Kodo no Shinrigakuteki Bunseki).* As cited in Yasumasa Yamamoto and E. L. Quarantelli, *Inventory of the Japanese Disaster Research Literature in the Social and Behavioral Sciences.* Columbus, Ohio: Disaster Research Center, The Ohio State University, 1982, p. A-179.

Soderstrom, E. Jonathan, John H. Sorensen, Emily D. Copenhaver, and Sam A. Carnes [1984] "Risk Perception in an Interest Group Context: An Examination of the TMI Restart Issue." *Risk Analysis* **4** (No. 3):231–244.

Sofue, Takao [1972] "A Japanese Perspective: Japanese Reactions to Disasters as One Aspect of National Character." Pp. 257–263 in *Proceedings of the Japan–United States Disaster Research Seminar: Organizational and Community Re-*

sponses to Disasters. Columbus, Ohio: Disaster Research Center, The Ohio State University.

Sood, Rahul [1982] "Communicating for Improved Hazard Awareness." Pp. 97–129 in *Perspectives on Increasing Hazard Awareness,* Thomas F. Saarinen (ed.). Boulder, Colorado: Institute of Behavioral Science, The University of Colorado.

Sorensen, John H., Neil J. Ericksen, and Dennis S. Mileti [1975] *Landslide Hazard in the United States: A Research Assessment.* Boulder, Colorado: Institute of Behavioral Science, The University of Colorado.

Sorensen, John H., and Philip J. Gersmehl [1980] "Volcanic Hazard Warning System: Persistence and Transferability." *Environmental Management* **4** (March):125–136.

Southern, R. L. [n.d.] "Effectiveness of Tropical Cyclone Warning Terminology (A Study at Port Hedland, Western Australia), Appendix B." Pp. B-1–B-16 in *Human Response to Tropical Cyclone Warnings and Their Content, Project No. 12,* World Meteorological Organization, Tropical Cyclone Programme. Geneva, Switzerland: World Meteorological Organization.

Spencer, Harrison C., Arturo Romero, Roger A. Feldman, Carlos C. Campbell, Otto Zeissig, Eugene R. Boostrom, and E. Croft Long [1977] "Disease Surveillance and Decision-Making after the 1976 Guatemala Earthquake." *The Lancet* (July 23):181-184.

Spiegal, John P. [1957] "The English Flood of 1953." *Human Organization* **16** (Summer):3–5.

Spring, Anita [1979] "Women and Men as Refugees: Differential Assimilation of Angolan Refugees in Zambia." *Disasters* **3** (No. 4):423–428.

Stallings, Robert A. [1984] "Evacuation Behavior at Three Mile Island." *International Journal of Mass Emergencies and Disasters* **2** (March):11–26.

Stallings, Robert A. [1978] "The Structural Patterns of Four Types of Organizations in Disaster." Pp. 87–103 in *Disasters: Theory and Research,* E. L. Quarantelli (ed.). Beverly Hills, California: Sage.

Stallings, Robert A. [1975] "Differential Response of Hospital Personnel to a Disaster." *Mass Emergencies* **1**:47–54.

Stallings, Robert A. [1971] "A Comparative Study of Community as Crisis Management System." Dissertation. Columbus, Ohio: The Ohio State University.

Stallings, Robert A., and E.L. Quarantelli [1985] "Emergent Citizen Groups and Emergency Management." *Public Administration Review* **45** (January):93–100.

Star, Leon D., Louis C. Abelson, Louis R. M. Delguercio, and Campbell Pritchett [1980] "Mobilization of Trauma Teams for Aircraft Disasters." *Aviation, Space, and Environmental Medicine* **51** (November):1261–1266.

Stein, Sherry [1974] "An Earthquake Shakes up a Mental Health System." Pp. 34–45 in *Beyond Clinic Walls,* A.B. Tulipan, C.L. Attneave, and E. Kingstone, (eds.). University, Alabama: University of Alabama Press.

Stoddard, Ellwyn R. [1961] "Catastrophe and Crisis in a Flooded Border Community: An Analytical Approach to Disaster Emergency." Dissertation. East Lansing, Michigan: Michigan State University.

Strassoldo, Raimondo, and Carlo Pelanda [1980-81] "Quattro Anni Dopo la Catastrofe: Le Conseguenze Psico-sociologiche—Alcune Risultanze di Una Ricerca sul Friuli Terremotato" (Four Years after the Friuli Disaster: The Sociopsychological Consequences—Some Results of a Research Study on the Friuli Earthquake) (in Italian). *Quaderni di Sociologia* (No. 3):447–480.

Strope, Walmer E., John F. Devaney, and Jiri Nehnevajsa [1977] "Importance of Preparatory Measures in Disaster Evacuations." *Mass Emergencies* **2**:1–17.

Strumpfer, D. J. W. [1970] "Fear and Affiliation during a Disaster." *Journal of Social Psychology* **82**:263–268.

Susman, Paul, Phil O'Keefe, and Ben Wisner [1983] "Global Disasters, A Radical Interpretation." Pp. 263–283 in *Interpretations of Calamity*, K. Hewitt (ed.). Boston: Allen & Unwin Inc.

Symons, Leslie, and Allen Perry [1979] "The Blizzards of Early 1978 and the Use of Helicopters to Alleviate the Resulting Economic and Social Disruption." *Disasters* **3** (No. 1):8–12.

Syren, Sverker [1981] *Organiserad Aktivitet efter Tuveskredet* (The Tuve Landslide—Organized Activities) (in Swedish with an English summary). *Disaster Studies* 10. Uppsala, Sweden: Uppsala University.

Takuma, Taketoshi [1978] "Human Behavior in the Event of Earthquakes." Pp. 159–172 in *Disasters: Theory and Research*, E. L. Quarantelli (ed.). Beverly Hills, California: Sage.

Takuma, Taketoshi [1972] "Immediate Responses at at Disaster Sites." Pp. 184–195 in *Proceedings of the Japan–United States Disaster Research Seminar: Organizational and Community Responses to Disasters*. Columbus, Ohio: Disaster Research Center, The Ohio State University.

Taylor, A. J. W. [1983] "Hidden Victims and the Human Side of Disasters." *UNDRO News* (March/April):6–9, 12.

Taylor, A. J. W., and A. G. Frazer [1982] "The Stress of Post-Disaster Body Handling and Victim Identification Work." *Journal of Human Stress* **8** (December):4–12.

Taylor, A. J. W., and A. G. Frazer [1980] "Interim Report of the Stress Effects on the Recovery Teams after the Mt. Erebus Disaster, November, 1979." *New Zealand Medical Journal* **91** (April 23):311–312.

Taylor, Alan J. [1979] "Assessment of Victim Needs." *Disasters* **3** (No. 1):24–31.

Taylor, James B. [1972] "An Approach to the Analysis of Emergent Phenomena." Pp. 110–129 in *Proceedings of the Japan–United States Disaster Research Seminar: Organizational and Community Responses to Disasters*. Columbus, Ohio: Disaster Research Center, The Ohio State University.

Taylor, James B., Louis A. Zurcher, and William H. Key [1970] *Tornado: A Community Responds to Disaster*. Seattle: University of Washington Press.

Taylor, Verta A. [1977] "Good News about Disaster." *Psychology Today* **11** (No. 5):93–94, 124, 126.

Taylor, Verta with G. Alexander Ross and E. L. Quarantelli [1976] *Delivery of Mental Health Services in Disasters: The Xenia Tornado and Some Implications*. Disaster Research Center Book and Monograph Series No. 11. Columbus, Ohio: Disaster Research Center, The Ohio State University.

Theoret, John J. [1979] "Erfahrungen mit einer Katastrophen-Einsatzübung in einer Kanadischen Grosstadt" (Lessons with a Disaster Exercise in a Major Canadian City) (in German). *Langenbecks Archiv für Chirurgie* (No. 349):213–216.

Thompson, James D., and Robert W. Hawkes [1962] "Disaster, Community Organization and Administrative Process." Pp. 268–300 in *Man and Society in Disaster*, George W. Baker and Dwight W. Chapman (eds.). New York: Basic Books.

Thompson, Michael, and Aaron Wildavsky [1982] "A Proposal to Create a Cultural Theory of Risk." Pp. 145–161 in *The Risk Analysis Controversy: An Institutional Perspective*. Howard C. Kunreuther and Eryl V. Ley (eds.). Berlin, Heidelberg, New York: Springer-Verlag.

Thompson, Stephen A. [1982] "Trends and Developments in Global Natural Disasters, 1947 to 1981." Working Paper #45. Boulder, Colorado: Natural Hazards Research and Applications Information Center, The University of Colorado.

Thurber, Steven [1977] "Natural Disaster and the Dimensionality of the I-E Scale." *Journal of Social Psychology* **103**:159–160.

Tierney, Kathleen J. [1985] "Emergency Medical Preparedness and Response in Disasters: The Need for Interorganizational Coordination." *Public Administration Review* **45** (January):77–84.

Tierney, Kathleen J. [1981] "Community and Organizational Awareness of and Preparedness for Acute Chemical Emergencies." *Journal of Hazardous Materials* **4**:331–342.

Tierney, Kathleen J. [1980] *A Primer for Preparedness for Acute Chemical Emergencies*. Columbus, Ohio: Disaster Research Center, The Ohio State University.

Tierney, Kathleen J., and Barbara Baisden [1979] *Crises Intervention Programs for Disaster Victims: A Sourcebook and Manual for Smaller Communities*. Rockville, Maryland: National Institute of Mental Health.

Tierney, Kathleen J., and Verta A. Taylor [1977] "EMS Delivery in Mass Emergencies—Preliminary Research Findings." *Mass Emergencies* **2**:151–157.

Titchener, James L., and Frederick T. Kapp [1976] "Family and Character Change at Buffalo Creek." *American Journal of Psychiatry* **133** (March):295–299.

Tobin, Graham A. [1979] "Flood Losses: The Significance of the Commercial Sector." *Disasters* **3** (No. 2):217–223.

Tokyo Fire Department (Tokyo Shobo-Cho) [1980] *Research on Obstructive Factors to the Fire Fighting Activities in Underground Shopping Malls (Jishinji Chikagai no Shobo Katsudo Sogai Yoin ni kansuru Kenkyu Hokokusho)*. Tokyo, Japan: Tokyo Fire Department (Tokyo Shobo-Cho).*

Tonkinson, Robert [1979] "The Paradox of Permanency in a Resettled New Hebridean Community." *Mass Emergencies* **4**:105–116.

Torry, William I. [1980] "Urban Earthquake Hazard in Developing Countries: Squatter Settlements and the Outlook for Turkey." *Urban Ecology* **4**:317–327.

Torry, William I. [1979a] "Anthropology and Disaster Research." *Disasters* **3** (No. 1):43–52.

Torry, William I. [1979b] "Intelligence, Resilience and Change in Complex Social Systems: Famine Administration in India." *Mass Emergencies* **2**:71–85.

Torry, William I. [1978a] "Bureaucracy, Community, and Natural Disasters." *Human Organization* **37** (Fall):302–308.

Torry, William I. [1978b] "Natural Disasters, Social Structure and Change in Traditional Societies." *Journal of Asian and African Studies* **13** (July–October):167–183.

Trainer, Patricia, and Robert Bolin [1977] "Persistent Effects of Disasters on Daily Activities." *Ekistics* **260** (July):52–55.

Trainer, Patricia, and Robert Bolin [1976] "Persistent Effects of Disasters on Family Activities: A Cross-Cultural Perspective." *Mass Emergencies* **1** (October):279–290.

Trost, Jan [1983] *Manniskans Reaktioner I Kris och Vid Katastrof* (Man's Reaction in Crises and Disaster) (in Swedish with an English summary). Disaster Studies 15. Uppsala, Sweden: Uppsala University.

Tubbesing, Susan K. (ed). [1979] *Natural Hazards Data Resources: Uses and Needs*. Boulder, Colorado: Institute of Behavioral Science, The University of Colorado.

Tuckman, Alan J. [1973] "Disaster and Mental Health Intervention." *Community Mental Health Journal* **9** (Summer):151–157.

Turner, Barry A. [1979] "The Social Aetiology of Disasters." *Disasters* **3** (No. 1):53–59.

Turner, Barry A. [1976a] "The Development of Disasters—A Sequence Model for the Analysis of the Origins of Disasters." *The Sociological Review* **24** (November):753–774.

Turner, Barry A. [1976b] "The Organizational and Interorganizational Development of Disasters." *Administrative Science Quarterly* **21** (September):378–397.

Turner, Ralph H. [1983] "Waiting for Disasters: Changing Reactions to Earthquake Forecasts in Southern California." *International Journal of Mass Emergencies and Disasters* **1** (August):307–334.

Turner, Ralph H. [1980] "The Mass Media and Preparation for Natural Disaster." Pp. 281–292 in *Disasters and the Mass Media: Proceedings of the Committee on Disasters and the Mass Media Workshop, February, 1979*, Committee on Disasters and the Mass Media. Washington, D.C.: National Academy of Sciences.

Turner, Ralph H. [1978] "Earthquake Prediction Volunteers: What Can the United States Learn from China?" *Mass Emergencies* **3**:143–160.

Turner, Ralph H. [1976] "Earthquake Prediction and Public Policy: Distillations from a National Academy of Sciences Report." *Mass Emergencies* **1**:179–202.

Turner, Ralph H., Joanne M. Nigg, Denise Heller Paz, and Barbara Shaw Young [1981] "Community Response to Earthquake Threat in Southern California." Part Ten, Summary and Recommendations. Los Angeles: Institute for Social Science Research, University of California, Los Angeles.

Turner, Ralph H., Joanne M. Nigg, Denise Heller Paz, and Barbara Shaw Young [1979] "Earthquake Threat: The Human Response in Southern California." Los Angeles: Institute for Social Science Research, University of California, Los Angeles.

Turton, David [1977] "Response to Drought: The Mursi of Southwestern Ethiopia." *Disasters* **1** (No. 4):275–287.

University of Oklahoma Research Institute [1953] *The Kansas City Flood and Fire of 1951*. Baltimore: Operations Research Office, The Johns Hopkins University.

Vinso, Joseph D. [1977] "Financial Implications of Natural Disasters: Some Preliminary Indications." *Mass Emergencies* **2**:205–217.

Visvader, Hazel, and Ian Burton [1974] "Natural Hazards and Hazard Policy in Canada and the United States." Pp. 219–231 in *Natural Hazards: Local, National, Global*, Gilbert F. White (ed.). New York: Oxford University Press.

Waddell, Eric [1983] "Coping With Frosts, Governments and Disaster Experts: Some Reflections Based on a New Guinea Experience and a Perusal of the Relevant Literature." Pp. 33–43 in *Interpretations of Calamity*, K. Hewitt (ed.). Boston: Allen & Unwin Inc.

Wall, G., and J. Webster [1980] "Consequences of and Adjustments to Tornadoes: A Case Study." *International Journal of Environmental Studies* **16**:7–15.

Wallace, Anthony F. C. [1957] "Mazeway Disintegration: The Individual's Perception of Socio-Cultural Disorganization." *Human Organization* **16** (Summer):23–27.

Wallace, Anthony F. C. [1956] "Tornado in Worcester." National Academy of Sciences/ National Research Council Disaster Study #3. Washington D.C.: National Academy of Sciences.

Wallace, William A., and Frank De Balogh [1985] "Decision Support for Disaster Management." *Public Administration Review* **45** (January):134–146.

Walsh, Edward J. [1984] "Local Community vs. National Industry: The TMI and Santa Barbara Protests Compared." *International Journal of Mass Emergencies and Disasters* **2** (March):147–163.

Walsh, Edward J. [1981] "Resource Mobilization and Citizen Protest in Communities around Three Mile Island." *Social Problems* **29** (October):1–21.

Walsh, Edward J., and Rex H. Warland [1983] "Social Movement Involvement in the Wake of a Nuclear Accident: Activists and Free Riders in the TMI Area." *American Sociological Review* **48** (December):764–780.

Walters, K. J. [1978] "The Reconstruction of Darwin after Cyclone Tracy." *Disasters* **2** (No. 1):59–68.

Ward, Robert M. [1974] "Decisions by Florida Citrus Growers and Adjustments to Freeze Hazards." Pp. 137–146 in *Natural Hazards: Local, National, Global*, Gilbert F. White (ed.). New York: Oxford University Press.

Warheit, George J. [1976] "A Note on Natural Disasters and Civil Disturbances: Similarities and Differences." *Mass Emergencies* **1**:131–137.

Warheit, George J. [1972] "Organizational Differences and Similarities in Disasters and Civil Disturbances." Pp. 130–141 in *Proceedings of the Japan–United States Disaster Research Seminar: Organizational and Community Responses to Disasters*. Columbus, Ohio: Disaster Research Center, The Ohio State University.

Warheit, George J. [1970] "Fire Departments: Operations During Major Community Emergencies." *American Behavioral Scientist* **13** (January–February):362–368.

Warheit, George J. [1968] "The Impact of Four Major Emergencies on the Functional Integration of Four American Communities." Dissertation. Columbus, Ohio: The Ohio State University.

Warrick, Richard A. [1983] "Drought in the US Great Plains: Shifting Social Consequences?" Pp. 67–82 in *Interpretations of Calamity*, K. Hewitt (ed.). Boston: Allen & Unwin Inc.

Warrick, Richard A. [1975a] *Drought Hazard in the United States: A Research Assessment*. Boulder, Colorado: Institute of Behavioral Science, The University of Colorado.

Warrick, Richard A. [1975b] *Volcano Hazard in the United States: A Research Assessment*. Boulder, Colorado: Institute of Behavioral Science, The University of Colorado.

Warrick, Richard A., with Jeremy Anderson, Thomas Downing, James Lyons, John Ressler, Mary Warrick, and Theodore Warrick [1981] *Four Communities under Ash after Mount St. Helens*. Boulder, Colorado: Institute of Behavioral Science, The University of Colorado.

Watts, Michael J. [1979] "The Etiology of Hunger: The Evolution of Famine in a Sudano-Sahelian Region." *Mass Emergencies* **4**:95–104.

Wauty, E., C. de Ville de Goyet, and S. Chaze [1977] "Social Integration among Disaster Relief Volunteers: A Survey." *Mass Emergencies* **2**:105–109.

Waxman, Jerry J. [1973] "Local Broadcast Gatekeeping during Natural Disasters." *Journalism Quarterly* **50** (Winter):751–758.

Waxman, Jerry J. [1972] "Changes in Response Patterns of Fire Departments in Civil Disturbances." Disaster Research Center Report Series No. 12. Columbus, Ohio: Disaster Research Center, The Ohio State University.

Weinberg, Sanford B. [1978] "A Predictive Model of Group Panic Behavior." *Journal of Applied Communications Research* **6** (April):1–9.

Weller, Jack M. [1974] "Organizational Innovation in Anticipation of Crisis." Disaster Research Center Report Series No. 14. Columbus, Ohio: Disaster Research Center, The Ohio State University.

Weller, Jack M. [1972] "Innovations in Anticipation of Crisis: Organizational Preparations for Natural Disasters and Civil Disturbances." Dissertation. Columbus, Ohio: The Ohio State University.

Wenger, Dennis E. [1980] "A Few Empirical Observations Concerning the Relationship between the Mass Media and Disaster Knowledge: A Research Report." Pp. 241–253 in *Disasters and the Mass Media: Proceedings of the Committee on Disasters and the Mass Media Workshop, February, 1979*, Committee on Disasters and the Mass Media. Washington, D.C.: National Academy of Sciences.

Wenger, Dennis E. [1978] "Community Response to Disaster: Functional and Structural Alterations." Pp. 17–47 in *Disasters: Theory and Research*, E. L. Quarantelli (ed.). Beverly Hills, California: Sage.

Wenger, Dennis E. [1972] "DRC Studies of Community Functioning." Pp. 29–73 in *Proceedings of the Japan–United States Disaster Research Seminar: Organizational and Community Responses to Disasters*. Columbus, Ohio: Disaster Research Center, The Ohio State University.

Wenger, Dennis E., James D. Dykes, Thomas D. Sebok, and Joan L. Neff [1975] "It's a Matter of Myths: An Empirical Examination of Individual Insight into Disaster Response." *Mass Emergencies* **1**:33–46.

Wenger, Dennis E., Thomas F. James, and Charles F. Faupel [1980] *Disaster Beliefs and Emergency Planning*. Newark, Delaware: Disaster Research Project, University of Delaware.

Western, John S., and Gordon Milne [1979] "Some Social Effects of a Natural Hazard: Darwin Residents and Cyclone Tracy." Pp. 488–502 in *Natural Hazards in Australia*, R. L. Heathcote and B. G. Thom (eds.). Canberra: Australian Academy of Science.

Westgate, Kenneth N. [1978] "Hurricane Response and Hurricane Perception in the Commonwealth of the Bahamas (1)." *Mass Emergencies* **3**:251–265.

Westgate, Kenneth N. [1977] "A Philosophy of Precautionary Planning." *Mass Emergencies* **2**:95–104.

Westgate, Kenneth N. [1975] "Flixborough—The Human Response." Occasional paper No. 7. Bradford, Yorkshire, England: Disaster Research Unit, University of Bradford.

Wettenhall, R. L. [1979a] "Disaster and Social Science in Australia." *Disasters* **2** (No. 4):241–245.

Wettenhall, R. L. [1979b] "Organisation and Disaster: The 1967 Bushfires in Southern Tasmania." Pp. 431–435 in *Natural Hazards in Australia.* R. L. Heathcote and B. G. Thom (eds.). Canberra: Australian Academy of Science.

White, Anne U. [1974] "Global Summary of Human Response to Natural Hazards: Tropical Cyclones." Pp. 255–265 in *Natural Hazards: Local, National, Global,* Gilbert F. White (ed.). New York: Oxford University Press.

White, Gilbert F. [1945] *Human Adjustment to Floods.* Department of Geography Research Paper #29. Chicago: University of Chicago.

White, Gilbert F. (ed.) [1974a] *Natural Hazards: Local, National, Global.* New York: Oxford University Press.

White, Gilbert F. (ed.) [1974b] "Natural Hazards Research: Concepts, Methods, and Policy Implications." Pp. 3–16 in *Natural Hazards: Local, National, Global,* Gilbert F. White (ed.). New York: Oxford University Press.

White, Gilbert F. with the collaboration of Waltraud A. R. Brinkmann, Harold C. Cochrane, and Neil J. Ericksen [1975] *Flood Hazard in the United States: A Research Assessment.* Boulder, Colorado: Institute of Behavioral Science, The University of Colorado.

White, Gilbert F., and J. Eugene Haas [1975] *Assessment of Research on Natural Hazards.* Cambridge, Massachusetts, and London: The MIT Press.

White, Gilbert F., Wesley C. Calef, James W. Hudson, Harold M. Mayer, John R. Shaeffer, and Donald J. Volk [1958] *Changes in Urban Occupance of Flood Plains in the United States.* Department of Geography Research Paper #57. Chicago: University of Chicago.

Whitehead, George I., and Stephanie H. Smith [1976] "The Effect of Expectancy on the Assignment of Responsibility for a Misfortune." *Journal of Personality* **44** (March):69–83.

Whyte, Anne [1980] *Survey of Households Evacuated during the Mississauga Chlorine Gas Emergency November 10–16, 1979.* Toronto: Emergency Planning Project, Institute for Environmental Studies, University of Toronto.

Whyte, Anne V., and Ian Burton (eds.) [1980] *Environmental Risk Assessment.* New York: John Wiley and Sons.

Williams, Harry B. [1964] "Human Factors in Warning-and-Response Systems." Pp. 79–104 in *The Threat of Impending Disaster,* George H. Grosser, Henry Wechsler, and Milton Greenblatt (eds.). Cambridge, Massachusetts: The MIT Press.

Williams, Harry B. [1957] "Some Functions of Communication in Crisis Behavior." *Human Organization* **16** (Summer):15–19.

Williams, Harry B. [1956] "Communications in Community Disasters." Dissertation. Chapel Hill, North Carolina: University of North Carolina.

Williams, R. M., and C. M. Parkes [1975] "Psychosocial Effects of Disaster— Birth Rate in Aberfan." *British Medical Journal* **2** (No. 5966):303–304.

Wilson, Robert N. [1962] "Disaster and Mental Health." Pp. 124–150 in *Man and Society in Disaster,* George W. Baker and Dwight W. Chapman (eds.). New York: Basic Books.

Wiseberg, Laurie [1976] "An International Perspective on the African Families." Pp. 101–127 in *The Politics of Natural Disaster: The Case of the Sahel Drought,* Michael H. Glantz (ed.). New York: Praeger Publishers.

Wisner, Ben [1979] "Flood Prevention and Mitigation in the People's Republic of Mozambique." *Disasters* **3** (No. 3):293–306.

Wisner, Ben, Phil O'Keefe, and Ken Westgate [1977] "Global Systems and Local Disasters: The Untapped Power of Peoples' Science." *Disasters* **1** (No. 1):47–57.

Withey, Stephen B. [1976] "Accommodation to Threat." *Mass Emergencies* **1**:125–130.

Withey, Stephen B. [1962] "Reaction to Uncertain Threat." Pp. 93–123 in *Man and Society in Disaster*, George W. Baker and Dwight W. Chapman (eds.). New York: Basic Books.

Wolensky, Robert P. [1984] "Power, Policy, and Disaster: The Political-Organizational Impact of a Major Flood." Stevens Point, Wisconsin: Center for the Small City, University of Wisconsin-Stevens Point.

Wolensky, Robert P. [1979] "Toward a Broader Conceptualization of Volunteerism in Disaster." *Journal of Voluntary Action Research* **8** (Nos. 3–4):33–42.

Wolensky, Robert P. [1977] "Comment: How Do Community Officals Respond to Major Catastrophes?" *Disasters* **1** (No. 4):272–274.

Wolensky, Robert P., and Edward J. Miller [1981] "The Everyday versus the Disaster Role of Local Officials—Citizen and Official Definitions." *Urban Affairs Quarterly* **16** (No. 4):483–504.

Wolf, Charlotte [1975] "Group Perspective Formation and Strategies of Identity in a Post-threat Situation." *The Sociological Quarterly* **16** (Summer):401–414.

World Meteorological Organization, Tropical Cyclone Programme [n.d.] *Human Response to Tropical Cyclone Warnings and Their Content, Project No. 12*. Geneva, Switzerland: World Meteorological Organization.

Worth, Marti F., and Benjamin F. McLuckie [1977] "Get to High Ground! The Warning Process in the Colorado Floods June 1965." Disaster Research Center Historical and Comparative Disasters Series. Columbus, Ohio: Disaster Research Center, The Ohio State University.

Worth, Marti F., and Janet Stroup [1977] "Some Observations on the Effect of the EMS Law on Disaster Related Delivery Systems." *Mass Emergencies* **2**:159–168.

Wright, James D., and Peter H. Rossi [1981] "The Politics of Natural Disaster: State and Local Elites." Pp. 45–67 in *Social Science and Natural Hazards*, James D. Wright and Peter H. Rossi (eds.). Cambridge, Massachusetts: Abt Books.

Wright, James D., Peter H. Rossi, Sonia R. Wright, and Eleanor Weber-Burdin [1979] *After the Clean-Up: Long-Range Effects of Natural Disasters*. Beverly Hills, California: Sage.

Wright, Joseph E. [1978] "Organizational Prestige and Task Saliency in Disaster." Pp. 199–213 in *Disasters: Theory and Research*, E. L. Quarantelli (ed.). Beverly Hills, California: Sage.

Wright, Joseph E. [1977] "The Prevalence and Effectiveness of Centralized Medical Responses to Mass Casualty Disasters." *Mass Emergencies* **2**:189–194.

Wyner, Alan J. [1984] "Earthquakes and Public Policy Implementation in California." *International Journal of Mass Emergencies and Disasters* **2** (August):267–284.

Wyner, Alan J., and Dean E. Mann [1983] "Seismic Safety Policy in California: Local Governments and Earthquakes." Santa Barbara, California: Department of Political Science, University of California, Santa Barbara.

Yamamoto, Yasumasa [1981a] "An Inductive Theory of Interorganizational Coordination in Crises." Preliminary Paper No. 71. Columbus, Ohio: Disaster Research Center, The Ohio State University.

Yamamoto, Yasumasa [1981b] "Disasters and Organizations" (in Japanese). Pp. 49–81 in *Socio-Scientific Approach to Disasters,* Hirotada Hirose (ed.). Tokyo, Japan: Shinyosha.

Yamamoto, Yasumasa, and E. L. Quarantelli [1982] *Inventory of the Japanese Disaster Research Literature in the Social and Behavioral Sciences.* Columbus, Ohio: Disaster Research Center, The Ohio State University.

Yancey, Thomas N., Jr., L. Douglas James, D. Earl Jones, Jr., and Jeanne Goedert [1976] "Disaster-Caused Increases in Unit Repair Cost." *Journal of the Water Resources Planning and Management Division,* ASCE, **102** (November):265–282.

Yasuda, Takashi, and Yasuyuki Sato [1979] "Some Problems of the Damages of Residential Lans-Houses, and in Its Repairing Process—After-Research on Disasters Caused by the 1978 Miyagiken Oki Earthquake." (Takuchi Kaoku Higai to Sono Fukkyu Katei ni okeru Shomondai). *The Study of Sociology (Shakaigaku Kenkyu)* **38**:121–174.*

Yin, Robert K., and Gwendolyn B. Moore [1985] "The Utilization of Research: Lessons from the Natural Hazards Field." Washington, D.C.: Cosmos Corporation.

Young, Michael [1954] "The Role of the Extended Family in a Disaster." *Human Relations* 7 (August):383–391.

Yutzy, Daniel [1970] "Priorities in Community Responses." *American Behavioral Scientist* **13** (January–February):344–353.

Zarle, Thomas H., Don M. Hartsough, and Donald R. Ottinger [1974] "Tornado Recovery: The Development of a Professional–Paraprofessional Response to a Disaster." *Journal of Community Psychology* 2 (October):311–320.

Zeigler, Donald J., Stanley D. Brunn, and James H. Johnson, Jr. [1981] "Evacuation from a Nuclear Technological Disaster." *Geographical Review* **71** (January):1–16.

Zurcher, Louis A. [1968] "Social-Psychological Functions of Ephemeral Roles: A Disaster Work Crew." *Human Organization* **27** (Winter):281–297.

Author Index

Subject Index